Contemporary Risk Assessment in Safeguarding Children

Edited by
Martin C. Calder

RHP

Russell House Publishing

First published in 2008 by:
Russell House Publishing Ltd.
4 St. George's House
Uplyme Road
Lyme Regis
Dorset DT7 3LS

Tel: 01297-443948
Fax: 01297-442722
e-mail: help@russellhouse.co.uk
www.russellhouse.co.uk

British Library Cataloguing-in-publication Data:
A catalogue record for this book is available from the British Library.

ISBN: 978-1-905541-20-1

Typeset by TW Typesetting, Plymouth, Devon

Front cover artwork by Abbie Leyland

Printed by the MPG Books Group in the UK

Russell House Publishing

Russell House Publishing aims to publish innovative and valuable materials to help managers, practitioners, trainers, educators and students.

Our full catalogue covers: social policy, working with young people, helping children and families, care of older people, social care, combating social exclusion, revitalising communities and working with offenders.

Full details can be found at www.russellhouse.co.uk/ and we are pleased to send out information to you by post. Our contact details are on this page.

We are always keen to receive feedback on publications and new ideas for future projects.

Contents

Dedications

To Janet, Stacey and Emma

Thanks for making me smile and reminding me every day of the things that really matter

Martin C. Calder

*Congratulations to Abbie Leyland from Lowton Junior and Infant School for winning the drawing competition.
Her winning picture is on the front cover.
Every Child does matter.*

Dedicated to the children of Lowton Junior and Infant School to keep them safe and healthy and to my Mum and Dad for keeping me safe and healthy

Abbie Leyland

Preface

Risk is a key concern and preoccupation for both staff and managers in the safeguarding and assessment of children and young people, especially given the level of public and subsequent media scrutiny and blame in the event of negative outcomes and loss of credibility. However, life without risk would be sterile and would limit positive outcomes being achieved for and by some children.

We are all risk managers

All of us who work in the protection and safeguarding of children and young people are all risk managers already. We all take decisions every day, often without thinking about it. Without realising it, we might be taking unnecessary or excessive risks or we might be too timid about taking reasonable risks that offer better outcomes or rewards. Risk taking and management has to be balanced against exposing oneself and others to unnecessary harms and dangers. The right to protection and the right to risk have to be carefully considered and many risk assessments will produce professional dilemmas as they attempt to reconcile the two positions. Risk management can and should be seen as seizing opportunities, not just to avoid danger, but to increase the odds of good outcomes, and reduce the odds against bad ones.

The context of risk management

Risk and risk assessment are complex issues, aggravated by an inadequate knowledge base to inform practice and by the removal of the terms from professional social care vocabulary and official guidance relating to safeguarding children (*Safeguarding Children*; DfES et al., 2006) (see earlier note). There are no standardised definitions of risk or risk assessment, particularly about whether risk means only the possibility of harmful outcomes, whether it involves a balancing of possible good and possible harm, and whether it even includes the idea of positive events.

The chapters in this book reflect that different professionals working in different organisations have very different understandings of evidence based practice as well as the focus of their risk assessments. The chapters are designed to help the reader to think through the meanings of words and phrases and in so doing increase the possibility of developing a common language, essential for safe decision making.

Risk is clearly related to dangerousness, resulting in harm. This is not restricted to service users but is also a feature of professional and organisational practice that has to be acknowledged and redressed. Risk is not a value free activity and risk assessment represents a significant intrusion into family privacy and we need to consider how we engage service users in the task of risk assessment.

The aspiration of this book

The chapters in this book have been brought together since the editor became aware that there was precious little material relating to the many areas of risk assessment subsumed under the safeguarding umbrella. This book thus attempts to:

- Provide a readily understood explanation of the concept of risk and risk assessment.
- Provide an accessible discussion of the key areas where risks need to be assessed.
- Provide an overview of the state of research and practice wisdom in this field.
- Examine some of the dilemmas which staff and managers take in their daily decision-making.
- Consider how managers and staff are isolated when trying to redress the local and national guidance void in the area of risk assessment and safeguarding children, with the ensuing inconsistent and un-standardised approaches and decision making.
- Examine the place of actuarial risk tools compared to clinical judgement in the risk assessment process, and the tensions and confusions that can arise between professionals talking at cross purposes with each other.
- Explore the arguments and means of assessment in an accessible manner with a practice-based emphasis.
- Identify and examine the origins and contemporary features of professional and organisation dangerousness with some antidotes.
- Examine the links between strengths (needs)-led and risk assessment practice.
- Consider ways of engaging service users in the risk assessment and management processes.
- Consider the emerging dilemmas in the areas of rights, protection and responsibilities.
- Provide some suggested contemporary risk assessment frameworks for consideration.

In so doing, there is a link made between theory, research and practice; the past, the present and the future; between academics, researchers and practitioners. The book cannot offer a magic formula that will always provide us with the right answers, but it can offer a way of thinking that will give us better answers to better questions that leads to better outcomes. The reader should be able to see the house being built as they read the chapters and through this they will be more able to understand their own approach to risk and thus manage their professional practice better. Staff need to learn how to conduct risk assessments that are evidence-based, comprehensive and equitable, and which produces risk management strategies where levels of intrusion are commensurate with levels of risk.

Staff will always have to live with uncertainty. But we can refine the exercise of professional judgement in estimating and managing uncertainties prospectively, rather than being judged retrospectively with the benefit of hindsight.

The importance of inter-agency approaches in policy, practice and training

The material is drawn from a number of different professional groups and disciplines, and as such should make the text a broadly appealing one. The emergence and ongoing development of safeguarding, which unifies prevention and protective structures and systems, will benefit from considering the messages within the book when all those with levels of responsibility are constructing their policies, procedures and practice guidance in relation to risk assessment across all the agencies serving children.

Who this book is for

This will be an essential text for staff in the social care and criminal fields, psychologists, counsellors, as well as students on many courses -especially social work training at degree and PQ levels – and Safeguarding Board trainers. It should also appeal to government staff with a responsibility for policy development or review.

It can be read end-to-end, or be dipped into, chapter by chapter. It is strongly recommended that any chapter that is being looked into be read in its entirety. Pulling out sections can result in missing part of the message. But numerous and descriptive subheads have been added to help anyone seeking specific topics as their starting point. This is felt to be more appropriate than an index.

About the Contributors

Chris Beckett is a Senior Lecturer at Anglia Ruskin University. His main interests are the care proceedings process, the discrepancies between the rhetoric of policy makers and day-to-day practice experience. He has written or co-written five books including (with Stephen Walker) *Assessment and Intervention in Social Work* (Russell House Publishing, 2003) and *Child Protection: An introduction* 2nd edn. (Sage, 2007).

Martin C. Calder established Calder Training and Consultancy in 2005 after 20 years in frontline child protection practice. His aim has been to generate and collate the available and necessary assessment tools for frontline staff, especially in times of massive change. He also critiques central government guidance and attempts to provide remedial materials to help fill the gap left between aspiration and reality. He is contactable through his website at www.caldertrainingandconsultancy.co.uk

Jo Clarke PhD, is a chartered forensic psychologist and Associate Fellow of the British Psychological Society. She is also an honorary teaching fellow in the Department of Psychology, University of York and an Associate Trainer with the Work Skills Centre and Centre for Supervision Training. Jo has extensive experience working in a diverse public sector organisation, as well as a range of private and charitable companies, as a clinician, trainer, consultant and researcher. In recognition of the multiple and complex challenges facing staff in critical occupations, Jo's work focuses on working with both individuals and organisations to achieve and maintain good psychological health.

Shelley Cohen Konrad PhD, LCSW is Assistant Professor of Social Work at the University of New England in Portland, Maine, USA. Prior to teaching at UNE Shelley worked as a clinical social worker with children and families in residential, school, and outpatient settings. Her work has centred on relational practice that emphasises the quality of the alliance between clients and practitioners as well as the collaborative and interactive nature of change. Shelley recently ventured into filmmaking with her production of the *Art of Hope*, which chronicles the lives of three families dealing with the death of a child.

Liz Davies is a senior lecturer in Social Work at London Metropolitan University. Liz provides consultancy to the media and writes widely on child protection issues. Whilst a team manager in Islington she exposed extensive abuse of children within the care system and later, as child protection manager in Harrow, developed her specialism in child interview skills and the investigation of organised abuse networks. In 2005 she was the expert witness at the Care Standards Tribunal for Lisa Arthurworrey, social worker to Victoria Climbié. More recently, with the publisher Akamas, she designed online child protection training and is the author of a practice based resource book entitled *Protecting Children*.

Dr John Devaney is a lecturer in social work at Queen's University Belfast, where he delivers teaching at undergraduate and postgraduate levels, and is involved in research in the area of child protection and violence against the person. Prior to joining Queen's University in 2006 he was a Principal Social Worker at the Eastern Health and Social Services Board and policy advisor to the Eastern Area Child Protection Committee. He has advised central government on the development of strategies in relation to domestic violence and sexual violence.

Clay T. Graybeal PhD is Professor of Social Work at the University of New England in Portland, Maine, USA. His work has focused on strengths-based assessment, solution-focused practice, and the creative arts in social work. He is also a playwright, and the videotape of his play, *The Calling*, has been screened at multiple national conferences in the US. His most recent article, *Evidence for the Art of Social Work*, traces the history of the evidence-based practice movement and challenges its conclusions. His first book, *Transformative Social Work Practice*, will be published in the near future.

Phil Heasman qualified and practised as a generic social worker, senior practitioner (child protection) and practice teacher before becoming involved in social work and inter-professional education, professional development and research as a senior and then principal lecturer at Canterbury Christ Church University College, as a trainer for Kent and Medway Social Services Departments and PQ Child Care Award programme director.

Philip is currently a principal staff development officer (Safeguarding Children) and training co-ordinator for the Derbyshire Safeguarding Children Board and has long-standing interests in children and young people's rights; service user, patient and carer participation; multi-agency and inter-professional practice; effectiveness and impact evaluation; and international social development.

Anne Hollows, PhD, BA (Hons), Grad Dip in Social Work, CQSW is Principal Lecturer in Social Work at Sheffield Hallam University, where she combines teaching on child and family work and research methods with her research work. She directs the MA in Collaborative and Therapeutic Work with Children and Young People and the MA in Social Research methods for Social Work. She has undertaken evaluations of Sure Start programmes and has undertaken several studies relating to inter-professional practice. Recent work includes a study of thresholds of concern regarding parenting, a study of evaluation of user participation for SCIE (The Social Care Institute for Excellence) and supervision of a study of recruitment and retention in child and family social work. She is currently writing a book on analysis, judgement and decision making in work with children and families.

Hazel Kemshall is currently Professor of Community and Criminal Justice at De Montfort University. She has research interests in risk assessment and management of offenders, effective work in multi-agency public protection, and implementing effective practice with offenders. She has completed research for the Economic and Social Research Council, the Home Office, and the Scottish Executive, and both teaches and consults extensively on public protection and high risk offenders. She has written numerous publications on risk, including *Understanding Risk in Criminal Justice* (Open University Press, 2003). She recently completed an evaluation of multi-agency public protection panels for the Home Office (with Wood, Mackenzie, Bailey and Yates) and is currently investigating pathways into and out of crime for young people under a European Social Research Council network (with Boeck and Fleming) and has recently completed an evaluation of *Stop it now! UK and Ireland* (with Mackenzie and Wood). She has developed training and guidance materials on high risk offenders for the National Offender Management Service (with Mackenzie and Wilkinson).

Roger Kennington has specialised in work with sex offenders since 1991. He was a member of the Northumbria Probation Service Specialist Sex Offender Team and now coordinates the Sexual Behaviour Unit in Newcastle upon Tyne. He developed and co-authored *The Accredited Sex Offender Treatment Programme from Northumbria* and the treatment programme for it. He has co-authored books on the assessment and management of men who sexually abuse.

Robert E. Longo, MRC, LPC is Corporate Director of Special Programming and Clinical Training for New Hope Treatment Centers, Charleston, South Carolina. He also serves as a consultant, educator, trainer, and author dedicated to sexual abuse prevention and treatment. Robert was previously Director of the Safer Society Foundation, Inc. and the Safer Society Press from 1993 until 1998. He has published four books, five workbooks, more than forty chapters and articles in the field of sexual abuse treatment, and pioneered the adult sexual offender workbook series formerly published by the Safer Society Press and now published by NEARI Press.

Roger Smith is currently Professor of Social Work Research at De Montfort University, Leicester. He previously held posts as Head of Policy with the Children's Society, Project Director (Corby Juvenile Liaison Bureau) and Probation Officer (Northamptonshire Probation Service). He is currently Chair of the East Midlands

Regional Social Work Network and a member of the Editorial Board for the British Journal of Social Work. His research interests span youth justice, social work theory, childhood, learning difficulties and inter-professional learning.

Jo Thakker received her PhD from Canterbury University in New Zealand. She currently holds a senior lecturer position at the University of Waikato, where she teaches in the clinical psychology training programme. Her research interests include sexual offending, substance use and abuse, diagnosis and classification of mental disorders, and environmental psychology. She is also a contracted clinical psychologist for the Department of Corrections, and specialises in the assessment of sexual offenders.

James Vess received his PhD in clinical psychology from Ohio State University. He spent 15 years at Atascadero State Hospital, California's 1,250 bed maximum security forensic state hospital, where he served in a variety of clinical and supervisory positions. He is currently a senior lecturer at Victoria University of Wellington, and Deputy Director of the clinical training programme. His research is in psychometric assessment, personality disorders and psychopathy, especially as they relate to risk assessment in forensic populations. He also maintains a forensic clinical practice, conducting risk assessments and serving as an expert witness in violent and sexual offender cases.

Tony Ward PhD, MA (Hons), DipClinPsyc is Professor of Clinical Psychology and Clinical Director at Victoria University of Wellington, New Zealand. His research interests include the offence process in offenders, cognitive distortions and models of rehabilitation. He has published over 200 research articles, chapters and books. His most recent books are *Theories of Sexual Offending*, with Devon Polaschek and Anthony Beech (Wiley, 2006) and *Rehabilitation: Beyond the Risk Paradigm*, with Shadd Maruna (Routledge, 2007).

Nicki Weld lives in Wellington, New Zealand, and has had experience in a variety of social service roles including senior social worker, supervisor, acting team leader, senior trainer, and national social work advisor. She has had involvement in key capacity building initiatives particularly within the New Zealand Statutory Child Protection Agency, and delivers workshops both nationally and internationally. Nicki is a registered social worker who believes in the application of creativity and innovation in social service work to inspire people to reach their true potential.

Acknowledgements

To Janet, Stacey and Emma for giving me the space and the encouragement to finish the task

To Debbie Hulme for her creative wizardry

To each of the contributors for producing materials of such a high quality

Introduction

This book was conceived when managing the transition from child protection to safeguarding service in Salford, when the reality of the extent of the changes was realised. The first indication of the demise of risk in government vocabulary and thinking had appeared in the assessment framework (DoH, 2000) and has never resurfaced since. This is worrying since the core population of families for social care professionals is child protection and this requires enhanced risk assessment skills and frameworks. Moreover, those minded to correct this unsatisfactory state of affairs could find little in the field that was up-to-date and contemporary. Ironically, the health and criminal justice fields have moved in the opposite direction, developing more refined frameworks for measuring risk, although there are inherent dangers of importing these as a natural corrective to the social care void as they measure risk of re-offending for the index offence rather than the risk of harm which is significantly broader. I decided to assemble a group of professionals and practitioners to try and produce a text that would:

- Attempt to provide a link between historical and contemporary thinking and materials.
- Examine the place of actuarial risk tools compared to clinical judgement.
- Examine the links between strengths (needs-led) and risk assessment practice.
- Consider a re-conceptualisation of risk assessment.
- Provide a contemporary vision of child protection structures, thinking and assessment tools.

The book is divided into two parts: contextual considerations and operational considerations. There is clearly a significant amount of overlap but I wanted to allow for an examination of issues within the structures and systems that impact significantly on practice before moving on to look at issues facing frontline practitioners and trying to furnish them with some operational considerations and frameworks for practice. The book is not designed to produce assessment frameworks designed to assess different kinds of presenting risk as these have been adequately covered elsewhere (Calder, 2000; Calder and Hackett, 2003; Calder, in press; Hackett and Calder, forthcoming). Risk and involuntary clients seem to be opposite sides of the coin and whilst a chapter is dedicated to this subject here it is examined in significantly more detail in Calder (in press b). This book is not designed to be the answer to all the issues and problems in the field currently but it is designed to stimulate discussion and clarification of the available tools in the field and to assess whether they are fit for purpose and in what context.

In Chapter 1, Roger Smith locates risk in the ever changing social care landscape, summarises the current position and reflects on potential future trajectories as the safeguarding revolution continues to unfold. He lays down some important foundations for the book and identifies areas requiring further and more detailed consideration in other chapters. In Chapter 2, John Devaney takes us sideways to examine the issue of performance management which has been introduced centrally and prioritised locally because of the status and financial incentives/restrictions associated with good or bad performance. What he seeks to do is to challenge such output based measures as being in any way connected with good outcomes for children and in fact produce diversionary practice with huge consequences. He maps the evolution of the performance management systems and focus and then offers a critique of these as a mechanism of governance for the child protection system. This is an important area as frontline practitioners are often confused about processes and priorities that seem to be divorced from their work, yet are grounded in the performance management framework. In Chapter 3 Liz Davies encourages us to reclaim the language of child protection. She argues that since the mid 1990s the refocusing of children's services away from child protection work has represented a backlash following the success of child protection investigations across the country and that this trend has accelerated since the publication of the Green Paper, *Every Child Matters*, with an increased emphasis on prevention as the prime solution to child abuse. She argues that such a focus on prevention is a pretence camouflaging the reality of wide spread destruction of child protection services known to protect vulnerable children. Family support has been framed as diametrically opposed to proactive child protection investigation and prevention is presented as the opposite of interventionist strategies. She suggests that the government has reinforced these policy divides in order to segregate service provision between the two extremes of prevention/family support and child protection. This has allowed for the restructuring of service delivery to 'child in need' teams, has increased centralised control of child protection work and has facilitated privatisation of family support services. A service focus on the needs of children and their families has diverted attention from the proactive investigation of perpetrators outside of the family network. She advocates a dual strategy of protection and prevention as the way forward. In Chapter 4, Chris Beckett examines the thorny issue of thresholds and the increased pressure for certainty within the system that has the potential to paralyse professionals who fear blame when anything goes wrong. He does accept that thresholds are important. For resource reasons, for reasons to do with the right to privacy and self-determination and for reasons to do with the negative consequences of intervention itself, it is both inevitable and appropriate that the most extreme interventions should be focussed only on those situations where the risks of adverse events are high. For all the same reasons it makes sense that there should be progressively lower thresholds for less intrusive interventions and for various levels of assessment. But child protection professionals should be absolutely clear, both with themselves and with their political masters, that a threshold is – and only ever can be – a line drawn across a pyramid of probability, not a line that neatly divides families that will definitely seriously harm their children from families that definitely will not. In Chapter 5 Anne Hollows examines professional judgement within the child protection process – a critically essential ingredient in evidence-based defensible risk assessment practice.

In Chapter 6, I examine professional dangerousness in the current context and examine the definition, the impact of child protection work on the workers, the circumstances when professionally dangerous practice may emerge and the wider context of professional practice. The hope is that early recognition and identification of the concept can promote safe professional practice. In Chapter 7 Phil Heasman introduces the professional dimension as an integral part of the system surrounding a child or young person – playing a part through complementary and/or substitute services in tipping the balance towards the safeguarding and promoting of health and development immediately and in relation to longer term optimal outcomes. However, it is suggested that in some circumstances the professional dimension through omission, and less commonly through commission, may contribute to tipping the balance towards risk and danger. He presents a three point model to assist reflection and analysis of the potentially complex professional domains, dimensions and dynamics operating at an individual, agency and inter-agency level. In Chapter 8, I move outwards in line with Heasman's proposed model to examine the broader concept of organisational dangerousness that represents the cultivating and facilitating environment in which professional dangerousness can be found. Some element of crossover exists between the two and indeed the seeds of individually dangerous practice are frequently traceable to the organisational context and the origins of their problems are further traceable to the political and policy context. What is clear is that there continues to be displacement of responsibility for poor outcomes from the top down, showing that politicians and managers are potentially part of the problem rather than part of the solution. Finally in this section, Jo Clarke introduces us to some groundbreaking work in the HM Prison service that examines the concept of resilience in high risk jobs. This is a critical component of promoting safe and sustainable risk assessment and which is a potential ingredient and antidote to organisational and professionally dangerous practice.

In Chapter 10, Clay Graybeal examines the opportunities as well as limitations of incorporating a strengths perspective within the conceptual framework of risk assessment. In Chapter 11 Kemshall examines actuarial and clinical risk assessment processes and tools and examines their potential working relationship. The development of formal risk assessment tools to enhance the reliability of decisions and improve their defensibility is a key feature of the criminal justice system. The most robust of these tools combine actuarial and clinical factors into structured assessment tools and their use is now commonplace. Social care professionals need to have some grasp of the tools and rules for use of the actuarial tools if they are not to just uncritically import them into their operational assessments. In Chapter 12, I attempt to provide workers with an operational framework for conducting risk assessments by exploring the definition, components and parameters of the concept. By using the concept of risk in its fullest sense, e.g. assessing for strengths and protective mechanisms as well as weaknesses, then it remains an important and central consideration in our work designed to safeguard the child. This chapter moves on to consider the forgotten stages of the risk process: risk analysis and risk management. In Chapter 13, Weld introduces us to the three houses approach to assessment with teenagers. It is an information-gathering tool that supports risk assessment by providing a thorough exploration of a person's situation. It was developed from the concepts of Te Whare Tapa Wha – a Maori model of health, resiliency theory, solution-focused theory, and Signs of Safety. It was created in New Zealand in 2003 and tested within the statutory child protection setting, as part of a wider strengths based practice initiative. The chapter provides an overview of the tool's principles, a practical description of its application with young people, parents and carers, and children within the context of child protection, and discuss its use as a reflective tool for workers, and in a family group conferencing setting.

The next few chapters move on to consider risk in the field of sexual abuse since it is the birthplace of many of the recent significant conceptual and practice developments in risk assessment. In Chapter 14, Roger Kennington examines the developments in the field of adult male sexual offenders. In Chapter 15, I examine the further refinement and development of risk materials in the young people who sexually abuse field and examine the potential to export the structural ideas to other areas of work. One of the proud achievements has been the progress made in relation to developing better frameworks for assessing risk with young people who sexually abuse and how this has now reached a level where it is informing developments needed in the adult sex offender field (Calder, 2005). As historically the case, the starting point, was importing the developments from the adult sex offender field. These took the form of actuarial risk tools and the emergence of stable and dynamic risk factors so we did not concentrate exclusively on previous behaviour. Robert Longo in Chapter 16 considers the broad approach to risk assessment but then shifts the focus onto treatment. Longo has developed a holistic treatment model that shifts the emphasis from relapse prevention to wellness planning (Longo, 2001, 2002). In his current chapter he outlines the current thinking about assessing youth with sexual behaviour problems and youth who are sexually aggressive from both a sexual risk perspective as well as risk in other life areas, and recommendations for treatment.

In Chapter 17, Thakker, Vess and Ward consider cross-cultural issues in general assessment. These include language and communication, acculturation, and the use of explanatory models. The middle section of the chapter then focuses on the cross-ethnic use of the Psychopathy Checklist Revised (PCL-R) which is one of the psychometric tools commonly used in the assessment of risk. The final section of the chapter presents a model that may be used as a guide for the implementation of culture-sensitive risk assessments.

In Chapter 18, I consider the issue of involuntary clients within the risk assessment process. The aim of this chapter is to map the contextual considerations in relation to partnership and paternalism and relate these to how they affect client-worker interactions in the child protection sphere, dominated by the need for risk assessments and the presence of involuntary clients. The mapping of the terrain should provide us with some understanding of the contributory problems and also provide us with a pathway toward solutions when attempting remedial strategies in practice. The reader is signposted to a more substantial text in relation to working with involuntary clients in a range of contexts (Calder, 2007). The reader should also make links with Chapter 6 (this volume) that attempts to provide a contemporary framework for understanding professional dangerousness as such considerations clearly impact directly on the worker-client relationship.

References

Calder, M.C. (2000) *A Complete Guide to Sexual Abuse Assessments.* Lyme Regis: Russell House Publishing.

Calder, M.C. (2005) Looking Towards the Future of Treating Sexually Abusive Youth. In Longo, R. and Prescott, D. (Eds.) *Current Perspectives: Working With Aggressive Youth and Youth With Sexual Behaviour Problems.* Holyoke, MA: NEARI Press.

Calder, M.C. (Ed.) (2007) *The Carrot or the Stick? Engaging Involuntary Clients in Child Protection Work.* Lyme Regis: Russell House Publishing.

Calder, M.C. (Ed.) (in press) *The Complete Guide to Sexual Abuse Assessments.* 2nd edn. Lyme Regis: Russell House Publishing.

Calder, M.C. and Hackett, S. (Eds.) (2003) *Assessment in Childcare: Using and Developing Frameworks for Practice.* Lyme Regis: Russell House Publishing.

Hackett, S. and Calder, M.C. (Eds.) (forthcoming) *Assessment in Child Care (Volume 2): Theory, Research and Practice Applications.* Lyme Regis: Russell House Publishing.

Longo, R.E. (2001) *Paths to Wellness: A Holistic Approach and Guide for Personal Recovery.* Holyoke, MA: NEARI Press.

Longo, R.E. (2002) A Holistic Approach to Treating Young People Who Sexually Abuse. In Calder, M.C. (Ed.) *Young People Who Sexually Abuse: Building the Evidence Base for Your Practice.* Lyme Regis: Russell House Publishing.

Contextual Considerations

From Child Protection to Child Safety: Locating Risk Assessment in the Changing Landscape

Roger Smith

The influence of 'risk'

The mechanisms and processes by which 'risk' has emerged as a defining preoccupation of the contemporary era have been well documented by key social theorists such as Giddens (1991) and Beck (1992). These concerns have also been applied to the specific contexts of social work and child protection by a number of authoritative commentators (for example, Parton et al., 1997; Ferguson, 2004; Garrett, 2003; Stalker, 2003; Sharland, 2005; Parton, 2006; Webb, 2006). At the same time, there has been a parallel expansion in the range of texts and materials available which seek to offer practical guidance on the identification, measurement, management and control of risk, whether through official sources (such as, DoH, 1999, 2000; DfES, 2006) or practical guidance (see Kemshall and Pritchard, 1996, 1997; Holland, 2004; Corby, 2005).

This is an area of practice which has been thoroughly researched and theorised, and in light of this the purpose of this brief review can only be to summarise the present position and to reflect on the possible trajectory of current developments in the specific context of *Safeguarding Children* (see Munro and Calder, 2005).

The agenda set out by government in its *Every Child Matters* reform programme crystallises some of the key issues and ambiguities which have been highlighted in previous discussions of risk and child protection, and it is important to be as clear as we can be about the reasons for the persistence of these concerns, and the impossibility of attaining the kind of certainty to which we sometimes aspire. 'Ambivalence' is an inevitable feature of the practice setting, it appears (Webb, 2006). The aim of the present discussion is to establish the reasons for the emerging emphasis on risk in broad terms, the problematic aspects of this development, the implications for processes designed to promote children's safety, and the consequences in terms of the challenges faced by those whose responsibility it is to implement these processes.

Parallel lines: the risk society and the Children Act 1989

Although the concept of 'risk' has featured in social consciousness for a very long time (Stalker, 2003) it has only recently become a key (perhaps dominant?) feature of theoretical debate and practice interventions. The work of Giddens (1990, 1991) and Beck (1992) has been particularly influential in exploring and explicating the relationship between changing social structures and relationships, on the one hand, and perceptions, attitudes and beliefs, on the other. They suggest that the emergence of 'risk' as a distinguishing characteristic of this particular period of time is a consequence of the specific changes occurring in the late 20th century, in the 'developed' world, at least. Modern society has become complex and diffuse, leading to an increasing sense of uncertainty and insecurity. For Beck, processes of globalisation and wealth creation are 'systematically' associated with the generation of new and different forms of risk over time. These risks permeate both productive processes and our forms of social organisation, permeating even long-established institutions such as the family. These processes may be both 'liberating' and simultaneously destabilising, for individuals, groups and communities. Even one's sense of identity becomes problematic (Giddens, 1991) resulting in a greater fear of personal and social breakdown. These theoretical reflections helped to articulate a set of emerging doubts about the inevitability of progress. Instead, the modern era 'is portrayed as a period of change, dislocation and uncertainty ... As a result we are constantly re-evaluating our actions and our place in the world in order to understand what is going on around us and thus gain a greater sense of control' (Stalker, 2003: 214). Our doubts and fears have thus provided an increased impetus towards finding scientific and technical solutions that will enable us to understand what is going on, measure the level of threat and take planned action to deal with it. We thus turn to the certainties and regularities of predictive scientific methods to generate that renewed sense of certainty in our knowledge base and the methods we apply to solve potential problems. There appears to be a powerful need to find systems of investigation, assessment and control which enable us to regain a sense of normality and regularity in our daily existence. Hence we note the emergence of the 'expert' and the faith that is placed in this particular source of wisdom. Indeed, it is the very nature of increasing complexity that leads to a proliferation of specialised expertise:

Modern expertise . . . is generally oriented towards contin-
ual internal improvement or effectiveness. Expert problem-
solving endeavours tend very often to be measured by their
capacity to define issues with increasing clarity or preci-
sion (qualities that in turn have the effect of producing
further specialisation).

(Giddens, 1991: 31)

The role of experts is, therefore, to break complex problems down into manageable components and to rationalise them so that they are controllable, and interventions can be applied which will lead to predictable and positive outcomes.

However, this aspiration in turn encounters a number of further problems, according to Giddens and Beck. For the former, the process of specialisation itself generates difficulties, as the certainty achieved in one narrowly focused area of practice may lead to 'unintended and unforeseen' outcomes in other fields, leading, ironically, to calls for the 'development of further expertise' to address the new problems which arise. For Beck, too, the concern of the sciences to achieve authoritative solutions and objective judgements of phenomena such as 'risk' and 'need' leads to a failure to acknowledge their own limitations, in a context where constant change requires a continual process of reflection and re-evaluation of prior assumptions. At the same time, it is possible that scientific techniques themselves (say, video interviews with children who have experienced abuse) may generate unwanted and unacceptable 'side effects' (Beck, 1992: 170) in the search for certainty.

Social work and child protection can also be seen to have been influenced by the tendencies mapped out by risk theorists, leading to a number of specific developments such as the approach to safeguarding children taken by the

Children Act 1989. Parton (1996) associates the emerging concern with 'risk' in social work with the collapse of 'welfarism' in the late 1970s and early 1980s, with a decline in the belief in social and collective citizenship and an increasing focus on individual risks and needs. Clearly, changing family structures and community transformations were also likely to contribute to the pressure to re-evaluate conventional approaches to welfare interventions. In relation to child protection, and probably not coincidentally, the sense of failure was intensified by the publication of a series of highly critical reports into child protection practice during the 1980s.

The consistent message from the inquiries into the deaths of Jasmine Beckford, Tyra Henry and Kimberley Carlisle was that social workers had not behaved with sufficient professionalism, relying instead on 'naïve and sentimental' beliefs in the positive intention of parents and carers, even in light of evidence to the contrary (Parton, 2006: 33). The inquiry reports thus made consistent recommendations to the effect that practitioners should adopt a more 'rational' approach and that their skills in identifying the 'signs and symptoms of child abuse' should be enhanced. By contrast, social workers were accused of intervening over-enthusiastically in the Cleveland 'affair', when 121 children were removed from their homes on suspicion that they were being sexually abused. In this case, too, the subsequent inquiry found that professionals (in health as well as social work) had not demonstrated appropriate standards of competence in taking such precipitate action.

It was partly as a consequence of these inquiries that the Children Act 1989 took the shape that it did. It combined an emphasis on protecting the rights of individuals and families with a reframing of the responsibilities of professionals, notably, to *anticipate* the possibility of harm to a child, based on the evidence available. Social workers should neither wait uncertainly until it was too late (as in the cases of those whose deaths were found to be preventable), but nor should they dive in precipitately on the basis of supposition and guesswork. Judging when to intervene thus became a matter of systematic evidence gathering and risk assessment, and the 1989 Act for the first time incorporated a forward-looking element in this context. Social workers were now expected to carry out investigations in cases of possible child abuse in order to identify the likelihood of 'significant harm' in the future (Section 47(1)). It would thus become possible to initiate protective action through the courts where this threshold condition was demonstrably met.

This future orientation of the new legislation has been identified as an important departure by Parton (2006: 39) and it does appear to provide further evidence of the emerging centrality of risk identification and risk management as a feature of modern child welfare practice. At the same time, however, it was made clear that intervention could only be justified once the potential for a substantial degree of harm to the child had been demonstrated. Thus, evidence must be clear and unequivocal, and the threshold must be set at a high level:

> For the first time the criteria for state intervention includes a prediction of what may or is likely to occur in the future. The necessity to identify 'high risk' is thus embedded at the core of the legislation.
>
> (Parton et al., 1997: 35)

In order to be able to achieve this kind of classification, based on what *might* happen, there must be grounds to believe in the practicability of making explicit assessments of what constitutes risk and at what level. As Munro and Calder (2005) have observed, the possibility of mistakes being made and resulting in highly adverse outcomes is particularly telling in relation to child protection. The consequence, in this instance, was an intensification of the emphasis on 'getting it right'. Detailed guidance emerged to support the implementation of the Children Act 1989 (DoH, 1991) and this has been subject to repeated augmentation and revision since (DoH, 1999, 2006) suggesting a continuing preoccupation with achieving precision:

> With the clear message that errors of any type were unacceptable, the only rational avenue for professionals was to try and increase their accuracy by having more thorough investigations of suspicions of abuse . . . This led to the current dominance in practice of child protection.
>
> (Munro and Calder, 2005: 441)

This observation points to one of the abiding ironies of the Children Act 1989. That is to say, the act was put in place largely to reduce a perceived imbalance whereby child protection had taken priority in terms of resource allocation and practice orientation. It was believed that a more sophisticated definition of the levels and grounds of intervention could enable more

resources to be devoted to earlier (and thus preventative) interventions.

The 1989 act itself explicitly linked the objectives of 'safeguarding and promoting' children's welfare in support of this aspiration (both in Section 17 which provided for meeting their needs, and Section 47 which supported protective intervention). However, as we shall see, both the prevailing ethos of risk control, and the sheer practical challenges of developing comprehensive and robust investigative mechanisms, continued to distort the statutory arrangements for meeting children's welfare needs. To move away from an excessive preoccupation with 'safe' practice, not only for children, but also to protect the interests of practitioners and agencies (Munro and Calder, 2005: 441) would require not just a rebalancing of resources, but a fundamental change in the ethos and ideology of children's services, it seemed (Parton et al., 1997: 217).

Implementation failure: the proliferation of risk

As the previous section indicates, the persistent preoccupation with identifying and responding to concerns about 'significant harm' provided a difficult backdrop for the implementation of the more inclusive and preventive aims of the Children Act 1989. The ensuing years, indeed, saw a broadening and intensification of the emphasis on protecting children, if anything, and in line with the arguments of Beck and Giddens, an increased sensitivity to new and previously unacknowledged threats to children's safety and well-being.

Worries about the trends in child welfare practice were crystallised with the publication of the DoH's (1995) research overview *Child Protection: Messages from Research*. The research on which this summary was based revealed a number of worrying features of contemporary practice in child protection. Notably, it seemed that there was little evidence of the adoption of the kind of systematic approach on which practice decisions were predicated. For instance, it was observed that a considerable number of children were referred to social services departments each year because of concerns about their safety and well-being, but of these cases, very few actually met the criteria for formal statutory intervention. Around 160,000 children were being referred 'to the child protection process' annually (DoH, 1995: 28). Of these, 25 per cent were filtered out immediately, with no further action taken; 120,000 (75 per cent) received a 'family visit', at which point a further 80,000 were deemed to need no further investigation; and 40,000 became the subject of a 'child protection conference'. However, even at this point, the filtering process meant that 11,000 of this group were deemed to require no further action. Following child protection conferences, the names of 24,500 children were added to the child protection register each year, and in 6,000 cases, children were either voluntarily accommodated or taken into care.

Not only was there very limited evidence of substantive action being taken on the basis of this very substantial number of referrals, but the research also revealed a fairly inconsistent approach to information gathering and recording, suggesting that investigative practices were some way removed from the organised and rigorous approach intended. Indeed, practice appeared to equate rather more to the pragmatic approach personified in Lipsky's (1980) notion of the 'street level bureaucrat', who actively interprets and extends official rules and guidance to make them 'fit' with the exigencies of real life.

Whilst it could be argued that the process of 'weeding out' non-urgent cases was in one sense successful, in that excessive intervention into the lives of families was avoided, except where the evidence demanded action, nonetheless, the achievement of this end appeared to involve the expenditure of a considerable amount of time, resources and expertise. Equally, questions could be asked about the basis on which initial decisions were based, given that in many cases nothing further happened. Did this mean that needs were identified which were not addressed because children were not 'at risk'? This was certainly the conclusion of the research overview, which argued 'that too much of the work undertaken comes under the banner of child protection'; a more rounded approach to helping children 'in need' would 'help rebut the criticism that many investigations are undertaken, many families are visited and case conferences called but that, in the end, little support is offered to the family' (DoH, 1995: 55).

Not only was there evidence of inefficiency and over-reaction in the investigative process, but other findings captured by the same research programme also raised questions about the

legitimacy of the judgements being exercised. It was noted, for example, that many of the 'indicators' of abuse were imprecise and broadly based, to the extent that many of them could be observed in the general population. Thus, a number of apparently problematic sexualised behaviours could be found in many families selected at random from the population at large (DoH, 1995: 13). 'Signs' which might be indicative of abuse thus appeared to rely on context and interpretation, as much as factual evidence. As a result, of course, this evidence might also be contestable.

Clearly, a number of significant concerns arose from this detailed programme of research into child protection processes. Firstly, as Giddens (1991) predicts, many of the supposedly 'scientific' methods of inquiry and analysis brought to bear on the problem were not found to be precise or effective even in their own terms. As a result, problems such as the continuing possibility of substantial numbers of 'false positives' and 'false negatives' (Munro and Calder, 2005) were likely to persist. Secondly, the emphasis on identifying and assessing the incidence and impact of significant harm to children led to the emergence of a child welfare system which was heavily concentrated at the 'front end' of the intervention process, with much investment of time and money in determining whether or not a child was being harmed, and relatively little attention being paid to the development of preventive services beyond this point. In fact, it seemed that it was still the occurrence of harm that triggered intervention in a relatively small number of cases, rather than the *possibility* of future mistreatment. There was evidence of a persisting imbalance between 'protection' and 'need', distorting both the form of intervention and the nature of the relationship between statutory agencies and service users.

Finally, it became increasingly clear that the approach taken, with its emphasis on protecting children within the family, was offering little in terms of addressing the broader range of threats to their safety and well-being which were increasingly being recognised. The narrow focus on what was actually happening in families, that is, a concentration on 'events' (DoH, 1995: 48) did not offer the range of vision necessary to predict the possibility of harm, in the sense of considering a child's 'protection career'. The evidence that children might equally be harmed as a consequence of action taken to protect them, such as experiencing bullying in care, suggested the need for an 'approach that encourages a perspective on cases as *children in need in circumstances where there may be a protection problem* is more likely to lead to a wider range of services being used to ensure the child's safety and recovery' (DoH, 1995: 48). This conclusion sought to reassert the forward-looking approach to risk identification and management implicit in the Children Act 1989.

Other developments also contributed to the process of 'refocusing' approaches to the prevention of harm to children. The search for a broader anticipatory strategy, which sought to prevent a range of adverse consequences, suggested that attention should be focused on a series of connected problems encountered by particular sectors of the population. The process of reconceptualising 'risk' in this context was given further impetus by a number of parallel developments, as Parton (2006) observes. The connections being made between a range of factors associated with social exclusion indicated that a more 'holistic' approach should be taken towards dealing with these which would be beneficial in their own right, whilst also reducing the likelihood of child abuse. At the same time, a number of inquiries and research studies were also beginning to make new links between different contexts of 'abuse' (Smith, 2002). Children were found to be experiencing bullying in schools, exploitation 'on the streets', criminal victimisation, and abuse *within* the child care system itself (Utting, 1997). Not only was it becoming clear that children were experiencing harm in a much wider range of settings than previously recognised, but it also seemed that it was often the same children who were subject to a multiple pattern of abuse. Parton (2006) suggests that a further component of this refocusing of concern can be attributed to the emergence of a more explicit threat to children from another source, the paedophile. Fears about the abuse of children within the family gradually merged with and were overtaken by the preoccupation with this external threat, mediated by rising fears of 'organised abuse' (Parton, 2006: 118).

Thus, it is argued, the 'risk' of harm faced by children was progressively reframed, with less weight being placed on substantiated evidence of past mistreatment within the family, and greater attention directed towards developing the capacity to predict the substance and severity of a range of future dangers. Despite this change of focus, there were also continuities with earlier approaches to child protection. The threat represented by paedophiles seemed to bridge the gap between child abuse within the family; sexual exploitation within childcare settings; and attacks by strangers. Thus, 'risk' and the potential for children to come to harm, although redefined, remained very much at the forefront of thinking when it came to formulating policy.

The change of emphasis reflected broader social changes encapsulated in the appearance and continuing transformation of the 'risk society' (Parton, 2006: 84). The processes by which the family had become more fragmented and diverse, the diminution of community ties, and the loss of historical certainties can all be associated with a diffusion of 'threat', which as a result appears to require new and radically different policy responses.

The accession to power of New Labour provided a specific twist to this agenda, through the incorporation of a number of wider concerns about social exclusion, community disintegration, the lack of family support and parenting problems, alongside what had previously been a fairly narrowly defined 'refocusing' initiative, which had been concerned merely to shift the balance between meeting needs and preventing harm under the umbrella of existing children's services. The consequences of these developments would include a significant rethinking of the structures put in place to 'safeguard' children (Parton, 2006: 100).

Not fit for purpose? The safeguarding agenda and the end of the Area Child Protection Committees

At the same time as the conceptualisation of 'risk and harm' was changing, the structures and systems for protecting children were also found to be failing. For example, concerns over the purposes, functions and capability of bodies such as Area Child Protection Committees were widely aired (Hallett, 1995; Sanders and Thomas, 1997; Barton, 2002; Parton, 2002; Smith, 2002). The scope of their responsibilities and their role in promoting the safeguarding of children remained unclear, despite copious guidance over the years (for example, DoH, 1991). Criticisms of the arrangements in place at this point could broadly be grouped under three headings:

1. Their scope was too narrow with many areas of potential harm to children being overlooked.
2. The focus on individual 'case management' prevented connections being made with broader questions of strategy and service development.
3. The reactive nature of the mechanisms in place limited the possibility of innovation, or preventive action.

Thus, for example, organisations such as NSPCC (2000, 2001) began to raise concerns about the extent of 'child maltreatment' that extended well beyond conventional concerns with abuse within the family. It was noted, too, that some sense of being constrained was experienced by those responsible for making arrangements to protect children. Some members of Area Child Protection Committees 'expressed . . . frustration at being compelled to focus so much of their energy on one narrow aspect of service provision . . . Many of them want to widen the scope of their collaborative activity . . .' (Sanders and Thomas, 1997: 134).

The limited scope of activity indicated by these views could partly be explained by the emphasis of existing guidance on managing individual cases where child protection concerns were identified. In other words, documentation such as *Working Together* (DoH, 1991, 1999) appeared somewhat out of step with the emerging forward-looking approach identified earlier. There was no doubt that this guidance was overwhelmingly concerned with dealing with the consequences of prior events, rather than creating a strategic and anticipatory framework for preventing future harm. Parton (2006: 104) suggests that the revision of *Working Together* (DoH, 1999) may have begun to shift the emphasis, but the advice offered, for instance to extend the range of bodies involved in coordinating networks, was outweighed by the continuing pre-occupation with individual cases of harm to children.

The rather limited role and objectives set for ACPCs contributed to the impression that there was a lack of strategic vision and leadership in the area of safeguarding children. Parton's (2002) view was that the arrangements in place were: 'narrow, restrictive and reactive'. Further research commissioned by the DoH appeared to suggest that the 'preventive' aspirations of the Children Act 1989 were not being achieved, and

that responses to children's needs were characterised by a 'sticking plaster' approach, based on the services available in the 'medicine box' (Aldgate and Statham, 2001: 119). In effect, there had been no real movement since the earlier round of government-sponsored research (DoH, 1995) with the machinery of child protection being 'geared to sifting cases according to set criteria, only triggering intervention of any kind when certain thresholds are judged to have been met' (Smith, 2002: 254).

According to one source, at least, this state of affairs could be attributed to 'bad faith' on the part of those with overall responsibility:

Area Child Protection Committees have never been allowed to develop the more strategic roles that official guidance implies that they should have. Essentially, they have no budget and are really only concerned with case management issues.

(Parton, 2002: 25)

As a result, the ACPCs as then constituted could not exercise a wider function in terms of identifying potential threats to children's well-being, and acting to forestall these: 'In the work of Area Child Protection Committees, prevention is . . . a neglected area when compared with the emphasis put on investigation . . .' (Sanders, 1999: 139). The work of ACPCs was restricted to troubleshooting, rather than focusing on the 'greater body of child welfare policy' (Sanders and Thomas, 1997: 137). This translated into a limited form of 'managerialism' (Barton, 2002) whereby ACPCs came to focus intensively on the investigation and assessment of individual cases, paying little attention to prevention or to direct interventions and their effects. This imbalance appeared to be wasteful in resource terms and likely to be unproductive in terms of achieving improved outcomes for children and families. In addition, we can see how this led to a restricted perception of the child protection agenda, excluding wider issues of child safety and a secure environment from consideration.

It therefore appeared that the policies and machinery put in place to develop effective approaches to child protection were somewhat anachronistic, being concerned with manifest harm, rather than with the broader range of threats to children's well-being, and the means by which these could be anticipated and averted. At another level, too, it seemed that the changing perceptions of 'risk' emerging from the broader social realm, and the consequent reappraisal of relevant management strategies, also necessitated a change of approach to safeguarding children.

The impetus for change was hastened with the deaths of Victoria Climbié and other children, such as Lauren Wright and Ainlee Labonte, which reawakened fears that social workers and other professionals were failing significantly in their task of preventing harm to children. It is clear that such cases may be unrepresentative, but that they do generate an acute level of public concern and media attention (Munro and Calder, 2005: 442), and therefore they do tend to act as defining moments in terms of changes to policy and practice. As Parton (2006: 47) points out, the inquiry into the death of Victoria Climbié was explicitly welcomed by government as a critical opportunity to, once and for all, learn the lessons which had so frequently emerged from previous inquiries of a similar nature. He notes that the urgency to achieve radical change was further heightened by the recognition that many of the factors associated with Victoria Climbié's death could also be found present in the case of Maria Colwell, who had similarly died of abuse and neglect in 1973. In both cases, the inquiry reports 'argued that these failures resulted not only because of individual incompetence but also because of major inadequacies in the responses of the "systems" in place at their respective times' (Parton, 2006: 48). He pinpoints a number of specific shortcomings identified on both occasions:

- communication failures
- poor recording of basic information
- non-use of existing case files
- lack of direct communication with the children themselves
- over-readiness by professionals to believe what was said to them by carers
- absence of appropriate supervision

These appear to have been more than technical failings, but because they were repeated in both these and other cases, they are symptomatic of deeper and persistent problems. At the same time, argues Parton, the changes associated with wider processes of globalisation and individualisation have generated new dynamics in the search for coherent and credible contemporary solutions. He notes ironically that Victoria Climbié's case provides concrete evidence of the impact of these dynamics, in that

her very mobility contributed to the isolated and dangerous circumstances in which she suffered and died. The rapid pace of change and its increasing diffusion and intensity lead to a series of consequences that define 'late modern society':

- 'heightened choice ...
- a questioning of established beliefs and certainties
- an increased sense of reflexivity
- a lack of embedded biography and life trajectory
- an increased confrontation with the plurality of social worlds and beliefs'

(Parton, 2006: 57)

It is the shifting nature of the social context and the dynamic nature of 'late modern society' that leads to a rather different approach to solving the persistent problem of child abuse in the present. Parton argues that we have witnessed a progressive loss of certainty and stability, associated with a 'growing relativism of values' (2006: 57). The impact of these changes is felt at two levels relevant to child protection; firstly, the character of family and adult-child relationships has changed, and secondly, partly as a consequence, our conception of childhood has also been transformed. As we become more uncertain about the permanence of social relationships and structures around us, it seems that we are likely to invest more emotional commitment and more concern into our children, both individually, and as the embodiment of our collective future. This process results in a heightening of fears at the same time as we become increasingly unsure of our abilities to safeguard children effectively. Thus:

Increased social anxiety about risk to children has been superimposed on the earlier 'protective discourse', where children are seen as vulnerable innocents who need to be shielded from the dangers of the wider adult social world as well as their own, on occasions, unsocialised natures. Such a development engenders a growing preoccupation with prevention, where it is argued there is a need for constant vigilance in order to anticipate and guard against potential threats to children's 'well-being'.

(Parton, 2006: 60)

Of course, it must be acknowledged that the form of 'prevention' alluded to in this context does not take the same form as the kind of early child-centred services advocated consistently by a number of other champions of better provision for 'children in need' (Tunstill and Aldgate, 2000). Indeed, as we shall see, one of the key questions arising from recent reform initiatives is exactly what kind of preventive interventions are to be prioritised, and how these might be translated into the practice setting.

Managing risk: *Every Child Matters?*

As already indicated, the inquiry into the death of Victoria Climbié was a key focal point for the tranche of reforms encapsulated under the heading *Every Child Matters*. The inquiry provided the opportunity for a number of recurrent themes to be brought together systematically, in order to achieve a lasting solution to the problem of safeguarding children. The direct investigation into the circumstances of the case was accompanied by a lengthy consultation, drawing on a wider range of available knowledge and expertise (Laming, 2003). This broader exercise appeared to offer the opportunity to draw general conclusions, rather than concentrating excessively on one particularly tragic situation.

Significantly, this exercise led the report to conclude that:

It is unrealistic to expect that it will ever be possible to eliminate the deliberate harm or death of a child – indeed, no system can achieve this.
(Laming, 2003: 361)

This statement demonstrates a degree of consistency with the broader tendency articulated by Beck (1992) which has seen a significant shift in our beliefs in the nature of science. It is no longer possible to see our methods of investigation, detection and analysis as being perfectible, as the shortcomings of these techniques become recognised. Even as things become more and more uncertain around us, and the desire for precision and predictability is heightened, our mechanisms for achieving knowledge and understanding are shown to be 'fallible' (Beck, 1992: 166). However, as Beck points out, this does not mean that the whole edifice of systematic inquiry and objective knowledge is swept away, but it needs to be more modest in its claims. Thus, he concludes:

Science is becoming human. It is packed with errors and mistakes. Science can be conducted even without truth,

perhaps even better, more honestly, with greater versatility, more audaciously and bravely.
(Beck, 1992: 167)

Thus, by implication, we must not abandon the effort to unearth evidence and apply methods effectively, although there can be no guarantees that even this degree of rigour will produce the desired results. According to the Victoria Climbié report:

... there is great hope for services to be operated more efficiently and effectively. This will require action at all levels, ranging from agreed outcomes for children to having a well-managed, properly-resourced and adequately-trained workforce.
(Laming, 2003: 361)

The evidence of 'system failure' is thus attributed to the demonstrable inadequacies of implementation rather than the shortcomings of the investigative methods themselves. Thus, Lord Laming was able to observe in relation to Victoria Climbié's case: 'I remain amazed that nobody in any of the key agencies had the presence of mind to follow what are relatively straightforward procedures . . .' (2003: 4).

As a consequence, the inquiry's recommendations focused on finding better ways of organising the processes in place to identify and manage the risk of harm to children. Once again, the influence of wider social and ideological changes can be identified in the formulation of these proposals. Perceptions of a diffusion of sources of potential harm, the increasing complexity of children's needs and the growing diversity of agencies with responsibility for their well-being together pointed towards a series of recommendations proposing a more integrated, corporate approach to concerns about children's welfare; a 'common language', shared training and a common approach to information gathering should be adopted by the relevant agencies, for example. Detailed procedural recommendations concentrated substantially on better systems for identifying and responding to potential harm to children, ranging across social care, health and police services; whilst it was also proposed that government should 'actively explore the benefit to children of setting up and operating a national children's database on all children under the age of 16' (Laming, 2003: 373). This database would, argued the report, provide additional safeguards to avoid children 'slipping through the net' (Laming, 2003: 368) partly as a result of changes in family structure and population movement.

The inquiry report, then, helped substantially to underpin the drive towards improved machinery for identifying and pre-empting possible risks faced by children. The response of government was to publish the Green Paper *Every Child Matters*, which, as Parton points out, was promoted as being 'centrally concerned' with child protection (2006: 151). Although it was the culmination of a developing reform process, the way it was presented ensured that the predominant emphasis would be on risk, that is, the possibility that *any child* might be vulnerable to risk at some point in their life. Once again, the prevailing concern with the unpredictability and insecurity of modern life in general (Giddens, 1991; Beck, 1992) could be correlated with the tone and substance of the changing policy agenda. Thus, as Parton notes (2006: 152), the reforms proposed were not just about improving the way in which conventional child protection mechanisms operated, or even about extending preventive services to the wider group of children in need, but 'it was the *safeguarding of all children and childhood itself* which was the central concern'. Indeed, there appeared to be a common thread, in that children who experienced problems in other respects, such as educational failure, were also missing out because of a failure to identify and respond effectively and early enough.

At the level of rhetoric, *Every Child Matters* made explicit connections between the need to protect children at risk of harm with the task of averting the negative consequences of a range of other potential problems of childhood, including poor educational achievement, ill health, teenage parenthood and anti-social behaviour (Chief Secretary to the Treasury, 2003: 5). The protection of children at risk should be pursued within the framework of effective universal services for all children, and thus measures should be put in place to 'ensure children receive services at the first onset of problems' (p. 8). The means of achieving this would be improved information sharing and 'a common assessment framework'. At the same time Local Safeguarding Boards were proposed, with the objective of creating a statutory body with collective responsibility for guaranteeing children's safety within each area. Earlier failings in the collaborative arrangements for safeguarding children (Smith, 2002) led

government to propose a strengthening of the duties of local agencies in this respect.

The Children Act 2004 gave legislative substance to these proposals, and subsequent guidance provided detailed instructions as to their implementation (HM Government, 2006, for example). At this level of detail, it is clear that there has been a substantial recasting of what is meant by 'safeguarding children', with a much wider range of risks identified, including racism and bullying, and a more 'pro-active' tone to the central message. The statutory basis for this approach is provided by Section 11 of the 2004 Act which specifies that agencies working with children must make arrangements to ensure that they 'safeguard and promote the welfare of children', whilst the guidance makes it clear that this is an active requirement, under which:

> Everybody who works or has contact with children, parents and other adults in contact with children should be able to recognise, and know how to act upon, evidence that a child's health or development is or may be being impaired and especially when they are suffering, or at risk of suffering, significant harm.
>
> (HM Government, 2006: 77)

There is a clear expectation that 'early referral and information sharing' will be the norm, and this will be underpinned by the Common Assessment Framework (DfES, 2004) the Information Sharing Index and practitioner guidance (DfES, 2006).

As the bundle of *Every Child Matters* reforms gathers pace, it is clear that the message about reframing the notion of child safety has been taken up by practitioners and managers in the recently constituted children's services departments. One strategic manager is quoted as saying: 'My brief used to be to consider children at risk of abuse and neglect; now we think about road safety, environmental issues, self-harming, substance abuse, bullying and discrimination' (*The Guardian*, 11 October 2006). This, in turn, requires 'all the other childcare providers' to be equally alert to issues of safety and to be ready to take action.

The policy shift reflected in these developments seems to represent the culmination of a number of trends. In particular, there appear to have been both a broadening of the basis on which initial concerns about children's safety and well-being may be raised; and, at the same time, there appears to have been a positive measure of encouragement to practitioners to raise initial fears about possible harm to children, even where their worries may be relatively minor (Chief Secretary to the Treasury, 2003: 53). The vague and unsubstantiated nature of such 'concerns' would also appear to considerably broaden the scope for further action to be taken, albeit subject to 'professional judgement'. The inclusive nature of the Information Sharing Index, which is intended to include at least basic details for *all* children, is meant to ensure that every child will be offered the basic level of protection that this provides, in other words, no child should disappear from view:

The index will be an important tool to help improve the communication between the key professionals needed for the effective delivery of services for children and families and, when necessary, to protect children.

(DfES, 2006a)

At the same time, as soon as any cause for concern arises, this should be brought to the attention of the relevant agency, and action should follow to ensure that the child concerned is safeguarded. This, in any case, is the idealised view of the *Every Child Matters* reforms.

The new world of child safety

It is possible to trace the logical patterns of the 'risk society' through the changing shape of policies and services to safeguard children over a period of time (Lupton, 1999). A growing sense of unease appears to be associated with increasingly complex and diverse social dynamics, as family and other relationships become more transitory, fragmented and uncertain. New forms of risk are identified, as, for example, the new electronic technologies apparently create yet more opportunities for the exploitation and abuse of children (HM Government, 2006). We do not appear to know each other very well any more; and, as our lives become more atomised we do not know what others are doing, including our children.

As Parton (2006: 57) observes, the consequences are 'ontological insecurity and a growing sense of social anxiety', as a result of which the need for protective measures and reassurance only increase. At the same time, however, experience demonstrates that the measures in place, based in 'scientific' claims of

reliability and predictability, are not failsafe. The recurrent images of child deaths, at the hands of those close to them as well as strangers, fuel our desire to find sure solutions, and therefore drive attempts to rethink and reshape the protective systems and procedures in place.

One potential answer lies in a reframing of approaches to risk management and control, based on the kind of forward-looking perspective heralded by the Children Act 1989. Once we begin to think in terms of 'anticipation' (Webb, 2006: 189) certain other consequences follow. Precision is impossible to achieve, so the reconstituted methodological approach must rely on 'probabilities' and the analysis of risk factors associated with harmful outcomes to children. Thus, attention turns to the construction of suitable models of information gathering and analysis which can identify those combinations of circumstances and characteristics that suggest that danger may be present. This line of thought leads quite straightforwardly to the construction of a database of all children, and the Information Sharing Index, which is intended to provide just this kind of reliable indicator of the likelihood and level of threat faced by children. Similar population-wide strategies also inform the creation of the paedophile register, and the universal application of criminal record checks to all those who work with children. Everybody who falls within a relevant category is thus subject to active monitoring:

Intervention increasingly becomes probabilistic and antici-patory and is not just based on the diagnosis of pathology in an individual subject or set of relationships but on an actuarial analysis of risk factors which are continuously monitored and managed.

(Parton, 2006: 175)

However, the reassurance offered by this inclusive and comprehensive strategy of risk identification and control may be problematic in a number of respects. Firstly, in the need to achieve positive solutions, it is important that we avoid succumbing to the illusion of certainty. Thus, whilst the systems put in place by the *Every Child Matters* reform programme may be more sophisticated and detailed than their predecessors (*Working Together to Safeguard Children* has expanded to 239 pages, for example), the extension of the range of indicators of risk and the dispersal of responsibility amongst a wider range of practitioners are factors which might generate greater inconsistencies in practice. A recent report from the Social Care Institute for Excellence also suggests 'broadening the focus of risk management strategies in children's services from one concentrating on 'serious cases' alone' (Bostock et al., 2005).

Secondly, the expansion of the monitoring system to accommodate a wider range of concerns and *all* children leads to questions about the practicability of generating and maintaining effective infrastructure and procedures. Vastly more data will be generated, often of uncertain quality, with pressures to respond both quickly and appropriately when concerns are identified, in order to achieve harm prevention. It seems inherently implausible that the systems put in place to discriminate between urgent and non-urgent situations will be sufficiently sensitive to guarantee exactly the right level of response in individual cases. This is especially so, given the probabilistic nature of the information gathering and evaluative frameworks put in place, and the likelihood that many 'false negatives' and 'false positives' will occur (Munro and Calder, 2005). Such an approach also gives rise to a heightened possibility of 'net-widening', with more children and families (and others) being caught up in the 'safeguarding' process on spurious grounds. At the same time, it may become increasingly difficult to distinguish those situations where there is substantial cause for concern.

Thirdly, the greater emphasis on information gathering, the wider scope of the systems put in place, and the need to offer some kind of response to indicators of 'concern' suggest that already limited time and energy will be diverted into these processes. This intensification of activity will be underpinned, in Parton's view (2006: 185) by the increased levels of accountability held by professionals should anything 'go wrong'. It is pointed out, too, that this diversion of energy into identifying and managing signs of 'risk' may leave some of the core functions of child protection relatively under-resourced. That is to say, both non-targeted preventive services and interventions to help children who are harmed may actually lose resources in relative terms (Munro and Calder, 2005: 445).

Finally, the concern with 'risk' and the preoccupation with its identification and management may well have unintended consequences in terms of the relationship between practitioners and those who use services.

Increasing levels of surveillance, and a concentration on externally defined indicators of 'concern' could result in a diminished capacity to engage with the complex and ambiguous nature of children's lives and relationships. The underlying fear is that children will be 'placed at the centre of the new services', but that 'the services will not be child-centred' (Parton, 2006: 185). Whilst the emerging policy agenda is informed by a recognition that the problems children encounter are often inter-connected, and that 'holistic' and child-centred interventions are needed, an undue focus on superficial indicators of risk and actuarial calculations may fundamentally undermine these laudable aspirations.

References

Aldgate, J. and Statham, J. (2001) *The Children Act Now: Messages from Research*. London: HMSO.

Barton, A. (2002) *Managing Fragmentation: An Area Child Protection Committee in a Time of Change*. Aldershot: Ashgate.

Beck, U. (1992) *Risk Society: Towards a New Modernity*. London: Sage.

Bostock, L. et al. (2005) *Managing Risk and Minimising Mistakes in Services to Children and Families*. London: SCIE.

Chief Secretary to the Treasury (2003) *Every Child Matters*. London: The Stationery Office.

Corby, B. (2005) *Child Abuse: Towards a Knowledge Base*. 2nd edn Buckingham: Open University Press.

DfES (2004) *Common Assessment Framework*. London: DfES.

DfES (2006) *Information Sharing: Practitioners' Guide*. London: DfES.

DfES (2006a) *Information Sharing Index: Consultation on Draft Information Sharing Index (England) Regulations and Partial Regulatory Impact Assessment*. http://www.dfes.gov.uk/consultations/downloadableDocs/s12%20Regs-Consultati onDoc-26Sep06.pdf

DoH (1991) *Working Together Under the Children Act 1989*. London: HMSO.

DoH (1995) *Child Protection: Messages from Research*. London: HMSO.

DoH (1999) *Working Together to Safeguard Children*. London: The Stationery Office.

DoH (2000) *Framework for the Assessment of Children in Need and their Families*. London: HMSO.

Ferguson, H. (2004) *Protecting Children in Time: Child Abuse, Child Protection and the Consequences of Modernity*. Basingstoke: Palgrave.

Garrett, P. (2003) *Remaking Social Work with Children and Families: A Critical Discussion on the 'Modernisation' of Social Care*. London: Routledge.

Giddens, A. (1990) *The Consequences of Modernity*. Cambridge: Polity Press.

Giddens, A. (1991) *Modernity and Self-Identity*. Cambridge: Polity Press.

Hallett, C. (1995) *Inter-agency Co-ordination in Child Protection*. London: HMSO.

HM Government (2006) *Working Together to Safeguard Children*. London: The Stationery Office.

Holland, S. (2004) *Child and Family Assessment in Social Work Practice*. London: Sage.

Kemshall, H. and Pritchard, J. (Eds.) (1996) *Good Practice in Risk Assessment and Risk Management: 1*. London: Jessica Kingsley.

Kemshall, H. and Pritchard, J. (Eds.) (1997) *Good Practice in Risk Assessment and Risk Management: 2*. London: Jessica Kingsley.

Laming, H. (2003) *The Victoria Climbié Inquiry*. London: The Stationery Office.

Lipsky, M. (1980) *Street Level Bureaucracy*. New York: Russell Sage Foundation.

Lupton, D. (1999) *Risk*. London: Routledge.

Munro, E. and Calder, M. (2005) Where Has Child Protection Gone? *Political Quarterly*, 76: 3, 439–45.

NSPCC (2000) *Child Maltreatment in the UK*. London: NSPCC.

NSPCC (2001) *Child Safety in the Community*. London: NSPCC.

Parton, N. (1996) Social Work, Risk and 'The Blaming System. In Parton, N. (Ed.) *Social Theory, Social Change and Social Work*. London: Routledge.

Parton, N. (2002) Narrow, Restrictive and Reactive. *Community Care*, 21–7 Feb, 24–5.

Parton, N. (2006) *Safeguarding Childhood*. Basingstoke: Palgrave.

Parton, N., Thorpe, D. and Wattam, C. (1997) *Child Protection: Risk and the Moral Order*. Basingstoke: Macmillan.

Sanders, R. (1999) *The Management of Child Protection Services*. Aldershot: Arena.

Sanders, R. and Thomas, N. (1997) *Area Child Protection Committees*. Aldershot: Ashgate.

Sharland, E. (2005) Risk Taking and Risk Making: Some Thoughts for Social Work. *British Journal of Social Work*, doi:10.1093/bjsw/bch254

Smith, R. (2002) The Wrong End of the Telescope: Child Protection or Child Safety? *Journal of Social Welfare and Family Law*, 24: 3, 247–61.

Stalker, K. (2003) Managing Risk and Uncertainty in Social Work. *Journal of Social Work*, 3: 2, 211–33.

Tunstill, J. and Aldgate, J. (2000) *Services for Children in Need: From Policy to Practice*. London: HMSO.

Utting, W. (1997) *People Like Us: The Report of the Review of Safeguards for Children Living away from Home*. London: HMSO.

Webb, S. (2006) *Social Work in a Risk Society*. Basingstoke: Palgrave.

CHAPTER 2

Challenging Output Based Performance Management in Child Protection

Dr John Devaney

Introduction

Within the United Kingdom there has been an increasing focus over the last decade on the effectiveness of the child protection system in safeguarding children. This has been part of a wider government agenda aimed at ensuring that public sector managers and professionals deliver against the policy objectives set in Whitehall.

In this chapter the concept of governance of the child protection system by measurement will be explored and critiqued. There are signs that the government is beginning to appreciate that some families and their children are both harder to reach and to help, and this may provide a space to renegotiate the dichotomy between the autonomy of professionals and the directive approach of central government.

New Labour and the Third Way

The election of a Labour Government led by Tony Blair in May 1997 heralded a shift in the conceptualisation and out working of the relationship between the state and the individual. In reaction to four successive electoral defeats the Labour party wanted to be seen as both competent and disciplined to the swing voters of middle England. This was encapsulated in a manifesto that mixed what the party would not do (raise income tax, enter the single European currency without a referendum, diverge from the spending limits of the Major Government for the first two years of office) alongside a list of five explicit pledges with attendant targets of what they would do. Whereas the New Right agenda had become dominated by the twin concerns of financial stringency and a reduced role for the state in both private affairs and public services, the New Labour manifesto pledged a future Government 'to help build strong families and strong communities' (Labour Party, 1997).

Inspired by the economic success of the United States, the new government wanted to move away from the old style socialism that many voters associated with trade union militancy and poor public services, whilst repairing the clefts hewn in society by the individualistic economic policies of the New Right. The former leader of the Labour Party, the late John Smith, had established a Commission on Social Justice in the early nineties to reassess the understanding of the concept of social justice, and to update thinking on how best to respond to old challenges, whilst also accounting for new inequalities and divides. The commission's subsequent report in 1994, *Social Justice: Strategies for National Renewal*, offered a strong vision for a more progressive Britain grounded in a clear understanding of forces shaping the world we live in. It proposed a model of investment that was an alternative to that of 'de-regulation' and 'levelling' with '. . . the emphasis . . . on economic opportunity in the name of social justice as well as of economic prosperity and the achievement of security through investment in and the redistribution of opportunities rather than just incomes' (Lister, 2003: 429).

Upon gaining power the Labour Government subsequently went about refocusing its role into one of an entrepreneur (Perkins, Nelms and Smyth, 2004) – through using public expenditure to bolster human capital (Giddens, 1998). The Conservative governments of the previous eighteen years had downplayed the role of the state in the rearing of children, and advocated individual advancement, whereas the New Labour Government sought to equalise opportunity and reframe the welfare state as a trampoline (to support people to get back on their feet) rather than a safety net (of last resort). In October 1998 the Home Office published a discussion document, *Supporting Families*, which, as the foreword pointed out, was the first time any government had sought to consult the nation about the centre's obligations and responsibilities towards the family:

Family life is the foundation on which our communities, our society and our country are built. Families are central to this government's vision of a modern and decent country . . . But families are also under considerable stress. As ever it is a hard job to be a parent. More marriages end in divorce. More children are brought up in lone parent families. Government could not turn the clock back even if it wanted to do so. There never was a golden age of the family. Family life has continually changed – and changed for good reasons as well as bad . . . But what families – all families – have a right to expect from government is support.

(Home Office, 1998: x)

This support, though, was heavily prescribed around three core themes (Millar and Ridge, 2002):

- The importance of paid work as a route out of poverty and social exclusion, and therefore the need to encourage and support parents to work through specific measures, such as New Deal, and the promotion of family friendly employment practices.
- A commitment to the maintenance of financial support for children, such as working families tax credits and child benefit, and an end to child poverty.
- An emphasis on ensuring that families recognised and met their responsibilities and obligations towards one another, for example through Parental Responsibility Orders.

The most ambitious of these policy initiatives was the commitment to end child poverty by 2020:

Child poverty is a scar on the soul of Britain . . . When we came into government one in three children were living in low income families with a higher number of children growing up in workless households than any other European country. It is essential that we address the causes of poverty and provide support where and when it is most needed. For when some are poor our whole society is impoverished . . . By investing in our children we are investing in our future. Instead of, as in the past, investing in some of the potential of some of our children, it is time to develop all the potential of all of our children. We know that children who grow up in poor families are less likely to reach their full potential, less likely to stay on at school, or even attend school, more likely to fall into the dead end of unemployment and poverty as an adult, more likely to become unmarried teenage mothers, more likely to be in the worst jobs or no jobs at all, more likely to be trapped in a no win situation – poor when young, unemployed when older.

(Chancellor of the Exchequer, 1999)

The Chancellor set out a four point plan that would address the duality of cause and effect that was child poverty. Firstly, as mentioned, poverty was seen as being inextricably linked to employment, with a range of measures brought in to deal with the absence of work, the problem of the in-work poor and increasing financial support to families who were caught in the benefit trap of work not being worth their while financially. Secondly, a new compact was needed to tackle the cumulative effects of poverty in the poorest communities, not just between central and local government, but also involving voluntary help and community action. Next, echoing one of the major rallying calls of the 1997 general election, the standard of education across all schools needed to be brought up to the standard of the best in order to challenge the inequality whereby the education system was seen only to advance the ambitions of the few. And finally, public services would need to both adapt and improve in order to meet the needs of the poorest and most often excluded, under the banner of 'modernisation'.

The mantra of performance management

Welfare reforms were designed to promote the three key social policy drivers of tackling the root causes of inequality in society through shifting the focus of services from remedy to prevention; recasting social protection as a set of corresponding responsibilities between the state and the individual; and to set in place systems for modernising public services through the setting, implementation, monitoring and audit of explicit standards and performance targets.

When entering power the government initiated a Comprehensive Spending Review, which has been characterised as '. . . an attempt to move from an incremental to a more rational pattern of spending' (Powell, 2002: 8). The thrust of this approach was to explicitly link spending priorities to the government's policy objectives:

Clear objectives have better enabled the Government to make informed decisions about the allocation of resources. Subsequently, this has facilitated the setting of clear and quantifiable targets . . . and show what each department aims to deliver over the lifetime of the Parliament, and against which performance will be measured.

(HM Treasury, 1998a: 2)

The Comprehensive Spending Review resulted in the publication of a government White Paper (HM Treasury, 1998b) that set out the specific objectives and attendant targets for each branch of government. As the Prime Minister made clear in the preface:

> Too often in the past, governments have only made commitments for what they put into public services – money, manpower and policies – not for what the public will get out in return. That is what really matters. People rightly expect modern services that work well, meet real needs, and use public money fairly and efficiently. That is why Public Service Agreements set out each department's aims and objectives and then show how much progress we expect to make and over what timescale, through concrete targets. As far as possible, these targets are set in terms of specific improvements in services or in the results those services will achieve.
>
> (HM Treasury, 1998b: Foreword)

In November 1998 the government published the White Paper *Modernising Social Services* (DoH, 1998a) which took up these themes by arguing that social services were currently failing to deliver:

> It is a concern for everyone that social services should be providing the best possible service. That objective is not being met. Despite some excellent services in many places, and a generally high appreciation of services by users, social services are often failing to provide the support that people should expect.
>
> (DoH, 1998a: 1.3–1.4)

It went on to state:

> Our third way for social care moves the focus away from who provides the care, and places it firmly on the quality of services experienced by, and outcomes achieved for, individuals and their carers and families.
>
> (DoH, 1998a: 1.7)

In 1999 the government consulted on proposals outlining the new approach to the measurement of social services performance (DoH, 1999) formally launching the Performance Assessment Framework for Social Services in 2000.

When the Public Administration Select Committee held a review of the government's use of performance management as a tool for improving the delivery of public services, the Treasury and the Delivery Unit of the Cabinet Office, in response to the question 'Why set targets?', answered by setting out the key

aspirations of this policy (HM Treasury, 2003). Firstly, they make a clear statement about the government's aims and priorities for improving public services and the specific results the government is aiming to deliver. Secondly, they enable Departments to prioritise their work around these key objectives, which should assist in business planning and communicating a clear message to staff and the various other public bodies that contribute to delivering each department's programme. Next, the focus is clearly on delivery of results, by stating the government's desired outcome. In turn this allows greater transparency in tracking progress over time. Finally, the targets provide accountability to both the public and central government through the regular reporting of progress by departments against targets.

The rationale behind the development of the 'government by measurement' approach thus had three basic assumptions (Public Administration Select Committee, 2003):

- That the public wants and expects sustained improvements in the delivery of public services, which is also a government priority.
- That service providers in receipt of public funds ought to be publicly accountable for their performance.
- That setting targets can be one means of stimulating better performance by those who deliver services.

As noted by Hood (2006) the United Kingdom took this target based approach to public management further than any other developed westernised nation, and was ranked highly by the World Bank as a result. But did this mean that public services improved and that children have been better served?

Performance management and child protection

Upon election in 1997 the government was concerned about the number of children involved in the child welfare system for whom it could be argued that the outcomes were poor. Both audits (Audit Commission, 1994) and research (DoH, 1995) had highlighted the frailties and failings of the system for children in need, including those in need of protection and public care. In relation to child protection, a significant proportion of children had multiple periods of child protection registration or were subject to a child protection plan for lengthy periods of their childhood. Research by Farmer (1997) indicated that approximately one quarter of all children with their name on the child protection register fell into these categories.

In September 1998 the Quality Protects Programme was launched in the United Kingdom (DoH, 1998b). This five-year initiative sought to improve the management and delivery of children's social services through five key elements:

- The setting of new national objectives for children's services which for the first time set out clear outcomes for children, and in some instances gave precise targets to be achieved.
- The role of local councillors in delivering the programme and ensuring, as corporate parents of children looked after that they received services of the highest quality, was highlighted.
- There was to be an annual external evaluation of the Management Action Plans which set out how councils intended to improve their services.
- A new compact between and within central and local government and with the health service and voluntary sector was at the heart of the strategy.
- A new children's services grant of £885m was to be made available over five years to support Management Action Plans and the meeting of the objectives.

The government set two very specific targets for child protection services aimed at focusing professional and managerial attention on the factors causing concern – a reduction in the proportion of children subject to repeat registration; and a reduction in the proportion of children in need of a child protection plan beyond two years. By choosing these two particular issues it was intended that they could be used as proxies for the effectiveness of the whole system.

At a policy level the debate had at its core the twin goals of providing preventative services to support families and therefore reducing the likelihood of crisis, breakdown or abuse at a later stage, alongside offering a better standard of service to those currently in need of protection or care. Through the Quality Protects Programme central government sought to focus professional practice on the children seen as being ill-served by the child protection system:

> . . . the Government believes that there is still a place for setting clear, and in some cases very stretching, national targets, particularly where a step change in performance is sought.
>
> (Public Administration Select Committee, 2003: 6)

The target and terror regime

The introduction of performance management and attendant targets became synonymous, within the health and social care sectors, with a culture of 'terror', to the extent that the targets were often referred to in the vernacular as 'hanging targets' or 'P45 targets' (Hood, 2006: 515). The government adopted a 'carrot and stick' approach to public sector reform, for example offering financial grants in exchange for improvements, increased autonomy in spending for the 'best performing' local authorities and the threat to have social services departments placed on 'special measures' if deemed to be performing poorly. Hospitals and social services departments were awarded stars to reflect their level of performance and senior managers could expect to lose their jobs if their organisations lost stars. This process of public disclosure captured the attention of the media. But were children any better protected as a result?

Critique of government by measurement

A number of criticisms have emerged from empirical research of this conceptualisation of performance management as it relates to child protection.

Quality of data

As noted by Oliver et al. (2001) the data collected by and used to inform departmental policy making is not always accurate or uncontested. In the first instance, the government has recognised that social services data does not have a high confidence level given the level of underinvestment in data collection systems. As a consequence the roll out of the Quality Protects Programme included funding to redress this deficit, but concerns continue to remain (Commission for Social Care Inspection, 2006).

This has also led the government to question the accuracy of international comparisons between the United Kingdom and other developed nations (UNICEF, 2007) based on data which is out of date or just plain wrong.

As such, this raises a very serious issue in terms of the reliability of using statistical measures as a benchmark of performance.

Contested meaning

Oliver and colleagues (2001) also found widespread ambiguity in the meaning attached to the data collected. For example, senior managers from different local authorities in England were each able to argue that both high and low levels of the same measurement indicated that their local authority was performing well. For example, a high level of re-registration on the child protection register could be argued to indicate that families continue to receive a higher degree of monitoring and support when children's names are removed from the register, to ensure that issues of concern that re-emerge are dealt with promptly. Conversely, another local authority could argue that low levels of re-registration indicate that the initial period of child protection registration successfully dealt with both the presenting and underlying issues, and thus reduced the chances of a relapse in the situation.

As Spratt and Callan (2004: 205) note, there may be an alternative meaning behind the performance measures:

> We must leave aside the dubious practice of aggregating local authority statistics to produce performance means that become normative (what is the 'right' rate of children's names on registers?) for the purposes of such tables are primarily to pull the errant into line. In this way a measure of governance becomes an instrument of governance.

Focus on outputs rather than outcomes

Whilst the policy aims of performance management could be seen as laudable, there are problems with the construction of these policies that are echoed within a Cabinet Office report:

> ... whilst it [is] assumed that the approaches set out in the Modernising Government White Paper will bring about better policy-making processes, the link between better processes and better outcomes has been untested until recently.
> (Bullock et al., 2001: 16)

It has been argued by Devaney (2004) that the current measures of performance have been chosen because of the availability of data rather than for the usefulness of the data. If the measures are to act as a proxy for the effectiveness of the whole system then it must also be questioned as to why measures of output – length of child protection registration and number of periods of registration – are being used, as they do not bear any tangible link to the outcomes for individual children. Rather they measure the operation of the system which can be affected by a range of inter and intra organisational factors largely unrelated to the actual specifics of the safety or well-being of individual cases within the system (Glisson and Hemmelgarn, 1998).

Complexity

Haynes (2003) has argued that there is a danger that performance management sees issues in terms of simplistic cause and effect rather than complex entanglements and changing dynamics. This has been borne out by researchers such as Pugh (2007) who, in his review of variations in child protection registration in Wales on behalf of the Welsh Assembly, has highlighted the interplay between broad socio-economic and demographic factors, operational processes, professional perceptions and actions, and vulnerability factors arising in the particular situations of individual children as confounding any simplistic explanation of what is happening within the child protection system.

As Chapman (2004) notes, policy makers and managers want to believe that the outcomes of an intervention or policy are predictable and that the organisation which they are managing is controllable. In reality:

> What makes prediction especially difficult in these settings is that the forces shaping the future do not add up in a simple system-wide manner. Instead, their effects include non-linear interactions among the components of the systems. The conjunction of a few small events can produce a big effect if their effects multiply rather than add ... It is worth noting that the difficulty of predicting the detailed behaviour of these systems does not come from their having large numbers of components ... For us 'complexity' does not simply denote 'many moving parts'. Instead, complexity indicates that the system consists of parts which interact in ways that heavily influence the probabilities of later events.
> (Axelrod and Cohen, 2001: 67)

Checking rather than trusting

Davies and Mannion (1999) have argued that there exists a tension between charging managers and professionals with the responsibility for delivering efficient and effective public services, and checking that they are exercising their authority appropriately. Their analysis emphasises:

> . . . the need for a balance between techniques that seek to compel performance improvements (through externally applied measurement and management) and approaches that trust to intrinsic professional motivation to deliver high quality services.
>
> (Davies and Mannion, 1999: 2)

Le Grand (2003) building on Douglas MacGregor's motivational theory (1960) has put forward the thesis that policy makers are caught in the dilemma of whether to view public servants as knights, who are driven by altruistic motives to deliver high quality public services even at the expense of their own position, or as knaves, who seek to minimise demands on their time and efforts and advance their own agendas rather than policy makers. The construction of public servants as either knights or knaves by policy makers then results in policy makers devising systems that either encourage knightly behaviour through, for example, giving greater autonomy, or discourages knavish behaviour through, for example, increased monitoring. The evidence would indicate that this balance is swinging away from trusting towards checking (Hood, James and Scott, 2000) and towards centralisation (Prabhakar, 2006).

Perverse consequences

The introduction of new policy in one area with attendant targets and measures of performance could produce perverse effects in other parts of the system (National Audit Office, 2006). In their evidence to the Public Administration Select Committee (2003: 20) the National Audit Office '. . . tactfully described the government's reporting against targets as still "developing", noting that there is an absence of both centrally accepted standards for reporting performance and a general requirement for the validation of the results reported'. As such, evidence has emerged about the falsification of data in order to present a more favourable picture of performance against targets. For example, the National Audit

Office identified nine NHS Trusts where patient waiting lists for operations had been adjusted inappropriately, including the deliberate manipulation and misrepresentation of figures, affecting nearly six thousand patients:

> For the patients concerned this constituted a major breach of public trust and was inconsistent with the proper conduct of public business.
>
> (National Audit Office, 2001: 1)

Where to next?

The above section would seem to indicate that the use of performance management in child protection has been a failed exercise. Whilst it may not have achieved what it set out to do – to improve the outcomes for individual children – it has forced those charged with operating the child protection system to examine what they are doing and the consequences for the children in the system. It has also challenged central government to acknowledge that the children who are the most disadvantaged are also the one's least susceptible to simplistic attempts at improving their situation.

Nearly ten years after the election of Tony Blair as Prime Minister he has stated that '. . . about 2.5 per cent of every generation seem to be stuck in a life-time of disadvantage and amongst them are the excluded of the excluded, the deeply excluded. Their poverty is, not just about poverty of income, but poverty of aspiration, of opportunity, of prospects of advancement.' (Blair, 2006).

As such, there seems to be a growing recognition that the needs of at least 140,000 families in the United Kingdom who live in complicated situations and have complex needs are still proving elusive to help (Social Exclusion Task Force, 2007) with consequences for the child, their family and wider society (Figure 2.1).

An analysis of the Department of Work and Pensions longitudinal Families and Children Study (http://www.dwp.gov.uk/asd/asd5/facs/) has identified a number of key indicators of disadvantage:

- No parent in the family is in work.
- Family lives in poor-quality or overcrowded housing.
- No parent has any qualifications.
- Mother has mental health problems.

Costs to child	Costs to society
Exposure to parent-based risk factors can be devastating for children's life chances: • Children from the 5 per cent most disadvantaged households are more than 50 times more likely to have multiple problems at age 30 than those from the top 50 per cent of households • 63 per cent of boys whose fathers go to prison are eventually convicted themselves • 61 per cent of children in workless couple households live in poverty • 60 per cent of children in the lowest reading attainment group at age 10 had parents with low literacy scores • Children who experience parental conflict and domestic violence are more likely to be delinquent	The negative consequences of exclusion inflict huge costs on the economy and society: • Anti-social behaviour costs the public £3.4 billion a year • The annual cost of school exclusion is estimated at £406 million • The additional costs of being not in education, employment or training at age 16–18 have been estimated at around £8.1 billion in terms of public finance costs • We could save £300 million over three years if care leavers had the same rates of going into education, employment and training as their peers • If one in ten young offenders received effective early intervention, it would save in excess of £100 million a year

Social Exclusion Task Force, 2007: 7

Figure 2.1   Examples of the costs of children living in families that experience disadvantage

• At least one parent has a long-standing limiting illness, disability or infirmity.
• Family has low income (below 60 per cent of the median).
• Family cannot afford a number of food and clothing items.

As such, the probability of experiencing multiple problem outcomes at age 30 rises from 5 per cent for those who did not display any problems in childhood to 70 per cent for those who experienced problems at four separate stages during childhood (DfES, 2007). Similarly, research conducted in California (Anda et al., 2006) has shown that adults who were exposed to a range of adverse experiences in childhood (Figure 2.2) have a significantly higher likelihood of developing physical and mental health problems in later life. As a consequence both the prevalence and risk (adjusted odds ratio) increased for smoking, severe obesity, physical inactivity, depressed mood, and suicide attempts as the number of childhood exposures to adverse experiences increased. When persons with four categories of exposure were compared to those with none, the odds ratios ranged from 1.3 for physical inactivity to 12.2 for suicide attempts. Similarly, the prevalence and risk (adjusted odds ratio) of alcohol abuse, use of illicit drugs, injection of illicit drugs, more than 50 sexual partners, and history of a sexually transmitted disease increased as the number of childhood exposures increased. In comparing persons with

four or more adverse childhood exposures to those with none, odds ratios ranged from 2.5 for sexually transmitted diseases to 7.4 for alcohol misuse and 10.3 for injected drug use (Felitti et al., 1995).

In the context of the child protection system we know that the majority of children who come to the attention of social services and who subsequently have their name added to the child protection register are, as noted by Cleaver and Freeman (1995) children living in families with multiple problems. The challenge posed is that policy makers and practitioners must start to appreciate the complicated pathway between cause and effect for this group of children. Whilst it is right that governments seek to ensure that policies lead to the intended outcomes, the current conceptualisation of policy implementation is premised on the notion of 'delivery':

This conception sees implementation as something which turns preconceived policy into action on the ground. It happens with the minimum of noise in a timely and effective fashion … Moreover, in the rhetoric of New Labour ministers, failure in 'delivery' is associated with a very particular view about the major obstacle to effective implementation, where lack of commitment – or, willingness – among public professionals and local agencies is identified as the main culprit.

(Peck and Perri 6, 2006: 3–4)

In reality there is no 'right way' to both manage child abuse and to measure this performance. Research and practice wisdom have contributed

Growing up (prior to age 18 years) in a household with:
- recurrent physical abuse
- recurrent emotional abuse
- sexual abuse
- an adult abusing substances
- an imprisoned household member
- someone who is chronically depressed, suicidal, institutionalised or suffering from mental illness
- a mother being treated violently
- one or no parents
- emotional or physical neglect

Figure 2.2   Adverse childhood experiences

to the development of sophisticated systems for the identification of, response to and management of concerns about the safety of children. Yet in spite of this professionals and policy makers continue to be confounded by the enormity of the task and the complexity of the issues. As previously noted, policy makers and managers want to believe that the outcomes of an intervention or policy are predictable and that the organisation which they are managing is controllable (Chapman, 2004).

The Performance Assessment Framework approach to policy making seeks to effect a change in the operation of the child protection system that is mechanistic and reductionist, setting targets for the desired performance of the system that are neither rooted in any agreed definition of what are acceptable levels of registration, re-registration and length of registration, or in any clear linkage between the needs of children and the outcomes sought. Indeed, whilst the Performance Assessment Framework repeatedly mentions outcomes, the targets set are in relation to system outputs rather than outcomes such as the psycho-social adjustment of children to their situation as a consequence of professional interventions. By seeking to make improvements in the child protection system through a linear reductionist approach, the subtleties and complexities of the interplay between the many factors placing children at risk of significant harm and affecting their physical, social and emotional development can be overlooked. The focus shifts from one of attempting to better meet children's needs to one of ensuring the throughput of the workload. Indeed, having a plan in place for a lengthy period of time that both protects and supports a child to live with their birth family may be a better outcome for a child than admission to the public care system.

In conclusion, there is now considerable evidence to indicate that the children within the child protection system in the United Kingdom come from families where the standard of parenting has been compromised by the effects of substance misuse, domestic violence, parental mental illness and sexual violence (Devaney, 2007). These types of problems are the least amenable to short-term solutions, and as such, professionals must be charged with keeping the child safe whilst also attending to the underlying problems. If we really want to improve the outcomes for these children, we could start by recognising that statistical measures of the outputs of the system are only part of the picture.

References

Anda, R.F. et al. (2006) The Enduring Effects of Abuse and Related Adverse Experiences in Childhood: A Convergence of Evidence From Neurobiology and Epidemiology. *European Archives of Psychiatry and Clinical Neuroscience*, 256: 174–86.

Audit Commission (1994) *Seen But Not Heard: Co-ordinating Community Child Health and Social Services for Children in Need*. London: Audit Commission.

Axelrod, R. and Cohen, M.D. (2001) *Harnessing Complexity: Organisational Implications of a Scientific Frontier*. New York: The Free Press. (E-book version downloaded from eReader.com)

Blair, T. (2006) *Our Sovereign Value: Fairness*. Speech to the Joseph Rowntree Foundation 5 September 2006. Available at: http://www.number-10.gov.uk/output/Page10037.asp

Bullock, H., Mountford, J. and Stanley, R. (2001) *Better Policy Making*. London: Centre for Management and Policy Studies.

Chancellor of the Exchequer (1999) *Speech by the Chancellor of the Exchequer, Gordon Brown MP, at the National Sure Start Conference, 7 July.* Available at: http://www.hm-treasury.gov.uk/newsroom_and_speeches/speeches/chancellorexchequer/speech_chex_70799.cfm

Chapman, J. (2004) *Systems Failure: Why Governments Must Learn to Think Differently.* 2nd edn. London: DEMOS.

Cleaver, H. and Freeman, P. (1995) *Parental Perspectives in Cases of Suspected Child Abuse.* London: HMSO.

Commission for Social Care Inspection (2006) *Social Services Performance Assessment Framework Indicators: Children.* London: CSCI.

Commission on Social Justice (1994) *Social Justice: Strategies for National Renewal.* London: Institute for Public Policy Research.

Davies, H.T. and Mannion, R. (1999) *Clinical Governance: Striking a Balance Between Checking and Trusting.* York: Centre for Health Economics, University of York.

DfES (2007) *Policy Review of Children and Young People: A Discussion Paper.* London: DfES.

DoH (1995) *Child Protection: Messages from Research.* London: DoH.

DoH (1998a) *Modernising Social Services: Promoting Independence, Improving Protection, Raising Standards.* London: HMSO.

DoH (1998b) *The Quality Protects Programme: Transforming Children's Services.* London: DoH.

DoH (1999) *A New Approach to Social Services Performance.* London: DoH.

Devaney, J. (2004) Relating Outcomes to Objectives in Child Protection. *Child and Family Social Work,* 9: 1, 27–38.

Devaney, J. (2007) Chronic Child Abuse: Children Caught in the Child Protection System. *British Journal of Social Work.*

Farmer, E. (1997) Protection and Child Welfare. In Parton, N. (Ed.) *Child Protection and Family Support: Tensions, Contradictions and Possibilities.* London: Routledge.

Felitti, F. et al. (1998) Relationship of Childhood Abuse and Household Dysfunction to many of the Leading Causes of Death in Adults: The Adverse Childhood Experiences (ACE) Study. *American Journal of Preventive Medicine,* 14: 4, 245–58.

Giddens, A. (1998) *The Third Way: The Renewal of Social Democracy.* Cambridge: Polity Press.

Glisson, C. and Hemmelgarn, A. (1998) The Effects of Organisational Climate and Interorganisational Co-ordination on the Quality and Outcomes of Children's Services Systems. *Child Abuse and Neglect,* 22: 5, 401–21.

Haynes, P. (2003) *Managing Complexity in the Public Services.* Maidenhead: Open University Press.

HM Treasury (1998a) *Comprehensive Spending Review Aims and Objectives.* London: HMSO.

HM Treasury (1998b) *Public Services for the Future: Modernisation, Reform, Accountability.* London: HMSO.

HM Treasury and the Delivery Unit of the Cabinet Office (2003) *Memorandum by the Government in Response to the Select Committee on Public Administration Inquiry into the Measurement Culture within HM Government.* Available at: http://www.publications.parliament.uk/pa/cm200203/cmselect/cmpubadm/62-x/3032406.htm

Home Office (1998) *Supporting Families: A Consultation Document.* London: HMSO.

Hood, C., James, O. and Scott, C. (2000) Regulation of Government: Has it Increased, is it Increasing, Should it be Diminished? *Public Administration,* 78: 2, 283–304.

Hood, C. (2006) Gaming in Targetworld: The Targets Approach to Managing British Public Services. *Public Administration Review,* 66: 4, 515–21.

Labour Party (1997) *New Labour: Because Britain Deserves Better. Election Manifesto.* Available at: http://www.psr.keele.ac.uk/area/uk/man/lab97.htm

Le Grand, J. (2003) *Motivation, Agency, and Public Policy.* Oxford: Oxford University Press.

Lister, R. (2003) Investing in the Citizen-Workers of the Future: Transformations in Citizenship and the State under New Labour. *Social Policy and Administration,* 37: 5, 427–43.

MacGregor, D. (1960) *The Human Side of Enterprise.* New York: McGraw-Hill.

Millar, J. and Ridge, T. (2002) Parents, Children, Families and New Labour: Developing Family Policy? In Powell, M. (Ed.) *Evaluating New Labour's Welfare Reforms.* Bristol: Policy Press.

National Audit Office (2001) *Inappropriate Adjustments to NHS Waiting Lists.* London: HMSO.

National Audit Office (2006) *PSA Targets; Performance Information.* London: NAO.

Oliver, C. et al. (2001) *Figures and Facts: Local Authority Variance on Indicators Concerning Child Protection and Children Looked After.* London: Institute of Education, University of London.

Peck, E. and 6, P. (2006) *Beyond Delivery: Policy Implementation as Sense-Making and Settlement.* Basingstoke: Palgrave Macmillan.

Perkins, D., Nelms, L. and Smyth, P. (2004) *Beyond Neo-liberalism: The Social Investment State?* Available at: http://www.bsl.org.au/pdfs/beyond_neoliberalism_social_investment_state.pdf

Powell, M. (Ed.) (2002) *Evaluating New Labour's Welfare Reforms.* Bristol: The Policy Press.

Prabhakar, P. (2006) *Rethinking Public Services.* Basingstoke: Palgrave Macmillan.

Public Administration Select Committee (2003) *On Target? Government by Measurement.* London: House of Commons Public Administration Select Committee.

Pugh, R. (2007) Variations in Registration on Child Protection Registers. *British Journal of Social Work,* 37: 1, 5–21.

Social Exclusion Task Force (2007) *Families at Risk: Background on Families With Multiple Disadvantages.* Available at: http://www.cabinetoffice.gov.uk/social_exclusion_task_force/documents/families_at_risk/risk_data.pdf

Spratt, T. and Callan, J. (2004) Parents' Views on Social Work Interventions in Child Welfare Cases. *British Journal of Social Work,* 34: 2, 199–224.

UNICEF (2007) *Child Poverty in Perspective: An Overview of Child Well-being in Rich Countries.* Report Card No.7. Available at: http://www.unicef.org.uk/publications/pub_detail.asp?pub_id = 124

Reclaiming the Language of Child Protection: Mind the Gap Family Support Versus Child Protection: Exposing the Myth

Liz Davies

I was following the family support model of social work. That's what we were taught on my course and that is what Haringey practised. Child protection was only for emergencies.

(Lisa Arthurworrey (LA) in conversation with the author, April 2004)

Lisa Arthurworrey, social worker for Victoria Climbié, was clear that she was doing the job her employer wanted her to do. She empathised with the carer being a refugee needing services to enable her to care for the child she said was her daughter. This was the approach Arthurworrey's various managers required throughout the eight months that she was the allocated social worker. 'It was my managers and not I who instructed that this was not a child protection case which required a Section 47 inquiry but instead a family support case which is more routine general support of a family' (LA, 2004: 100). The Duty and Investigation Team procedures she was following contained 'nothing requiring the social worker to liaise with the police to make checks or hold joint strategy meetings' and a notice displayed in her office declared *'No police'* (LA, 2004: 144). Laming commented that in the case he had 'heard no evidence of what I would term a Section 47 inquiry ever being carried out by Haringey Social Services (Laming, 2003: 6, 217). Ann Bristow, Haringey Director of Social Services, considered that Lisa Arthurworrey 'was not an inexperienced social worker in the context of the position in many London Boroughs' (Bristow, 2004: 32). Yet Lisa Arthurworrey had no training in joint investigation or investigative interviewing of children. She had never worked on a case with police before and whilst she thought she was conducting a Section 47 inquiry in fact she had little idea what it would involve to do so. 'I thought that what I was doing was a S 47. No one told me otherwise' (LA, 2004: 64). Neither of the strategy meeting minutes convened by managers in the case even mentioned a Section 47 inquiry (LA, 2004: 101). Reder and Duncan reviewed the case and commented: 'A referral received by social services which indicated the likelihood of non-accidental injuries to Victoria was labelled from the outset as 'child in need'. This framed all of that departments subsequent activities on the case so that no child protection assessment was performed' (Reder and Duncan, 2004: 104).

Arthurworrey's successful appeal at the Care Standards Tribunal (CST) of the Secretary of State's decision to place her name on the Protection of Children Act List importantly challenged the use of the list for cases of poor professional practice (Jarman and Davies, 2005). Judge Pearl, chair of the Tribunal, concluded that: 'there has been another victim of the failures in Haringey in 1999 and early 2000 and we see Ms Arthurworrey as such a victim . . . Ms Arthurworrey is today suitable to work with children' (CST, 2005: 143). He said that: 'the office environment was chaotic, the reference tool totally inadequate and the mistakes made by Ms Arthurworrey in dealing with Victoria's case must be considered within that context as well as her inexperience, lack of training and lack of any effective supervision'. The General Social Care Council, however, eighteen months later refused to accept her application to the Social Care Register.

The tragedy of Victoria's murder may well have taken place whatever social work philosophy had been followed at the time. However, it is important to recognise that the London Borough of Haringey's lack of focus on protecting children reflected a national trend actively promoted by government since the mid-1990s. A warning of the policy's impact on future tragedies was given when in 1996 the Director of Social Services in Oxford wrote, following a case involving the manslaughter of two children, that: 'It is important the mistakes are seen in the context of the publication of the Department of Health's *Messages from Research* which promoted the value of family support. These messages were in the forefront of the minds of the workers involved at the time this case was investigated' (Robertson, 1996).

In this chapter it will be suggested that since the mid 1990s the refocusing of children's services away from child protection work has represented a backlash following the success of child protection investigations across the country and that this trend has now accelerated since the publication of the Green Paper, *Every Child Matters*, with an increased emphasis on prevention as the prime solution to child abuse (HMG, 2003). It will be argued that the concept of prevention in this context is a pretence camouflaging the reality of a wide scale destruction of child protection services known to protect vulnerable children. Family support has been framed as diametrically opposed to proactive child protection investigation and prevention is presented as the opposite of interventionist strategies. It will be suggested that the government has reinforced these policy divides in order to segregate service provision between the two extremes of prevention/family support and child protection. This has allowed for the restructuring of service delivery to 'child in need' teams, has increased centralised control of child protection work and has facilitated privatisation of family support services. A service focus on the needs of children and their families has diverted attention from the proactive investigation of perpetrators outside of the family network.

Child protection reduced to common sense

As a specialism, child protection social work seems to be fast disappearing and protecting children is increasingly perceived as a simple and obvious task. Media comment, at the time of the Employment Tribunal decision to uphold Haringey's dismissal of Lisa Arthurworrey, was that much of her role as Victoria's social worker was common sense. 'Common sense dictates that 19 pages of medical evidence have to flag serious reasons not to be cheerful about the outcome for a child' (Roberts, 2004). 'These mistakes seem due to a lack of common sense rather than inadequate guidance and supervision' (Batty, 2004). In her evidence to the Employment Tribunal Bristow said that it was common sense to know that a child of eight years old should be in school (Bristow, 2004). Yet, because each of the six

charges against her were far from simple when analysed in an organisational context, one question needs to be asked: 'which is not why Lisa Arthurworrey got it wrong but why anyone would have expected her to get it right' (Davies, 2004a). Parton in his submission to the Victoria Climbié Inquiry clarifies this point: 'At its crudest this was handled as a "family support case" when it could and should have been handled as a "child protection case" '. The essential question becomes "is it possible to hold both possibilities open and equally valid at the same time?" I suspect that this is a much more complex and demanding task that appears on the face of it . . . It almost certainly requires well-trained, experienced and very able staff' (Parton, 2002: 4).

There is considerable lack of understanding about the level of training needed for child protection investigation as a complex task. Monaghan, whose report formed the basis of the Haringey case against Lisa Arthurworrey, stated that: 'Lisa had been trained to attempt to get all relevant information from a child where there was suspicion of abuse' (Monaghan, 2004). This was contradicted by Laming who stated that she 'was not trained in the Memorandum of Good Practice and could not therefore see a section 47 child protection inquiry through to its conclusion' (Laming, 6: 10). Both demonstrate a lack of understanding that social workers and police must complete joint investigation training as well as training in investigative interviewing skills. Arthurworrey had completed a multi-agency 'working together' awareness course but DS Cooper-Bland who had delivered this course said in his evidence to the CST that: 'I cannot see how the Haringey course could equip a social worker to carry out an investigation. It was not the aim of the course to provide that level of instruction' (CST, 2005: 91). Judge Pearl in his concluding comments restated the author's statement that: 'Without training at an advanced level I would not expect Ms Arthurworrey to have understood how to properly investigate an allegation of child abuse. I would not expect her to have understood her role as a social worker in relation to that of the police, the detailed function and purpose of strategy meetings and conferences or how to assess and confront parent/carer responses in relation to child abuse allegations'. He concluded that the basic social work training she was given did not prepare her for the responsibilities she had in Victoria's case (Davies, L. cited in CST, 2005: 93).

The recent version of *Working Together* (DfES, 2006: 95) re-designates the levels of training required and loses the clarity of the previous document's three tier approach which specified the need for joint investigation and interview training for those engaged in the statutory investigation of child abuse (DoH, 1999). This has been replaced with a third tier now, including a wide range of professionals and stating broad, vague and ill-defined training requirements. Specialist advanced level investigative child protection training is increasingly difficult to access with variable commitment to such courses by Local Safeguarding Children's Boards and no associated performance targets. The training standards also omit to emphasise these specialist training requirements (Shardlow, 2004). In London, such training is in crisis as the numbers of police child protection trainers has been reduced to four whereas there were previously thirty-two i.e. one for each Borough. This significantly reflects a shift in police commitment to joint working in the capital.

A recognition of specialist training requirements also demands an understanding that the child protection task draws on a well documented knowledge base. Reder and Duncan, with reference to the Climbié case comment that:

> Recommendations accumulated over 30 years of fatal child abuse inquiries do not seem to have transformed the performance of child protection systems ... since the findings of any next inquiry could reasonably be predicted before it has taken place, we would like to propose that no further public inquiries are commissioned before all training and resource deficiencies identified over the last 30 years have been remedied.

A recent Community Service Volunteer project, involving volunteers working alongside social workers with children whose names are on the child protection register, illustrates one concerning implementation of the 'common sense' approach. Based on a project in California, which does not operate within a child protection service comparable to that of the UK, these volunteers have only one day training in child protection, visit families at least three times a week (including when professionals are not available) and offer their life experience and flexible approach (Leason, 2004, Child Abuse Prevention Council of Sacramento, 2001). Child victims of abuse need professional social workers, not a volunteer. The work is too complex.

The former Minister for Children has added to a simplistic perception of the social work task by speaking of a young person being taken to McDonalds every day of the week by a different worker from a range of agencies and adding that: 'at the moment the professional silos in which people operate do not impact effectively on that child's needs' (Hodge, 2004). This example actually indicates that multi-agency planning was not in place for this young person. By demeaning the social work task, professionals are undermined. Instead, recognition of the importance of each specialism, separate but working together confidently and complying with multi-agency procedures, is awarded little profile. Munro states clearly that: 'Victoria would have been saved if professionals had followed basic principles of practice' (Munro, 2003). Silos were not the problem but the lack of compliance with procedures, which would have provided the opportunity for expert analysis and professional debate.

A view that child protection work is simple feeds into the belief that social workers can mechanistically implement managerial instructions and manage large caseloads based on sets of instructions rather than quality supervision. The Haringey Director of Social Services acknowledged that although Arthurworrey's workload was higher than the accepted norm of 10–12 cases, she did: 'not accept that this was necessarily excessive at that time' (Bristow, 2004: 33). She also did not acknowledge the complexity of the 19 (including 10 child protection) cases for which Arthurworrey held sole responsibility. The Monaghan Report did not consider workloads at all but Laming agreed that there was no proper system of caseload weighting in place (Laming, 6, 577) and that no-one seemed to have given any thought as to whether Arthurworrey had: 'sufficient time to deal adequately with Victoria's case' (op. cit. 6.57).The CST panel were:

> ... unimpressed with the theory suggested by Mr Monaghan of the 'baton being with Ms Arthurworrey'. A more telling image would be of the most inexperienced member of the team attempting to retain a hold on an errant hot air balloon when everyone else had lost interest. We can think of no instance throughout the entire period when Ms Arthurworrey was given real help and support from her managers. Likewise we can think of no instance when her handling of the case had ever been criticised by a manager, and no instance of her ever attempting to conceal or dissemble any errors she may have unwittingly have been making.
> (CST, 2005)

Munro comments on the work context stating that: 'the staff responsible for Victoria Climbié were not incompetent through malice or laziness and they cannot be made competent by hectoring or bullying them' (Munro, 2003). Arthurworrey certainly referred to her experience of a top-down, conveyor belt culture: 'we were regarded as children who should be seen and not heard' (Laming, 6, 19).

Professional boundaries are becoming increasingly blurred with the development of common assessment frameworks, core training and the merging of health, education and social services within Children's Trusts.

Social work as a profession is under attack and like police are rarely mentioned within the Green Paper (HMG, 2003). Social workers do provide a buffer between the child and family and the state and represent children's views in a way that has perhaps become too uncomfortable for those who exploit children.

Proactive working together does protect children

There is little doubt that agencies working together to protect children is effective. The Safeguarding Children Joint Inspector's Report was clear that there were good working relationships between agencies and that: 'In the vast majority of individual cases examined the children were protected from risk of further harm' (DoH, 2002). Studies of serious case reviews demonstrate that very few of the children who died had been the subjects of child protection procedures (Reder et al., 1993; Reder and Duncan, 1999). Abused children are most at risk when either they are not referred to social services at all or from the point of referral they are not defined as in need of protection. They slip the protective net.

The author's experience as a team manager in the London Borough of Islington, where she exposed extensive abuse of children within the childcare system, provides a model of joint investigation of abuse at practitioner level. All agencies worked with social services to identify the abuse and to intervene to protect. Each professional felt confident within their specialism and complied with legislation and policy specific to their role and agency. Each communicated in a context of mutual trust and respect and with common goals. Judgements were made to act in

the best interests of children within a context of a vast industry of child abuse targeting and entrapping children in the community and within the local agencies and systems. There was no difficulty in sharing information within Section 47 procedures and formal analysis took place through the structures of strategy meetings and child protection conferences. Young people coming to the attention of social services were silent about the abuse but through rigorous investigation the abuse network became apparent. Detailed mapping of names, places and forms of abuse slowly made sense of the clues and innuendos the young people were providing and their behaviour spoke loudly of the impact of the abuse on their lives: family conflict, running away, drug and alcohol abuse, crime, mental health problems, self-harm and attempted suicide. Social workers made time for the young people. Their needs were prioritised.

A range of information was collated in order to identify the young people who were victims, the child sex abusers and those within the child care systems who were colluding with the abuse network. Probation Officers and police provided information about known sex offenders and about young people being exploited by abusers to commit crime. Education social workers and teachers knew of abusers targeting children and identified child victims, noting patterns of behaviour and absences. Health visitors, GPs, midwives and school nurses also noted signs of abuse and had current and historic knowledge of abusive families. Paediatricians liaised with the Genital Urinary Medicine and family planning services and collated information about sexually abused children coming to their attention. Child and adult psychiatrists treated victims of the same abuse networks. Housing and environmental health officers knew of community concerns about houses used by abusers and procurers. Lawyers and Guardians ad litem made links across cases and local journalists were an important source of archived information. Most importantly, the local community reported their concerns.

Professionals work together well when they feel confident, well supported, trained and supervised against a backdrop of legislation and procedures. In Islington, police and social work practitioners were instructed by their managers not to comply with guidance. They were told not to convene conferences or work jointly and not to interview children. In the absence of support from management the practitioners continued to progress their investigations despite some receiving direct threats and others being scapegoated. On leaving the authority the author took information to the Paedophile Unit at New Scotland Yard and with the assistance of the media the child abuse scandal was exposed leading to a number of Inquiries (White, 1995; Fairweather, 1998).

Islington was only one of hundreds of joint investigations into child abuse across the country from the mid-1980s onwards (Bennetto, 2001; Wolmer, 2000). The abuse of children was undoubtedly widespread. Phil Frampton provides a recent account of abuse within the care system. He speaks of being: 'the scum, the rotting detritus of societal inadequacy that collected itself in the silent waters where human indifference met society's net protecting itself with welfare. We were neither meant nor expected to fare well . . . In Britain they housed children for paedophiles to sodomise' (Frampton, 2004: 286).

Investigations such as that at Castle Hill School, Shropshire, provided the basis of much learning about joint investigation (Brannan, 1992) as did, among others, Operation Badger (Bird and Hennesey, 1997) and Operation Michigan (Jeffrey, 1996).

The decline of good practice in child protection – two recent examples

Given the wealth of knowledge about how to protect children from abuse, along with excellent legislation, national and local guidance, it has to be questioned how the situation arose, leading Laming to state: 'It is clear to me that the agencies with responsibility for Victoria gave a low priority to the task of protecting children' (Laming, 2003: 1, 18). This view was reiterated by the Joint Chief Inspector's Report which stated: 'councils have unusually high thresholds for responding to child protection referrals and in taking action to protect children' (CSCI, 2005). A subsequent summary of an inquiry in Haringey also raised similar issues.

In March 2004 the Haringey Area Child Protection Committee published the *Executive Summary of the Serious Case Review* on 'Adam' aged two years old who had suffered serious accidental burns to 28 per cent of his body following pulling a boiling kettle onto his head. There was a history of concern and a previous

burn. Following the incident there was no professional face-to-face contact for eight days with the parents and limited time spent with the child. The GP, who had considerable knowledge of the case, was hardly involved. However, the summary provided no reference to Section 47 investigation or child protection conference. The Director of Social Services expressed concern that, given the knowledge about the mother's mental health: 'professionals hadn't realised the trigger for child protection had been reached'' (BBC, 2004; Jayarajah-Dent, 2004; Martin, 2004).

The many referrals regarding child victims of Ian Huntley were not collated or addressed within child protection procedures and his offending escalated to the murder of two children. There is no doubt that each case of the young people Huntley sexually abused coming to the attention of police and social services should have triggered organised abuse procedures: 'Abuse involving one or more abusers and a number of related or non-related abused children and young people' (DfES, 2006: 6.7; Home Office and DoH, 2002). Sir Christopher Kelly refers to 13 cases and that: 'even these are not likely to be a complete list' (Kelly, 2004: 32). He comments that: 'Huntley's penchant for relationships with vulnerable girls below the age of consent was well known in the local community', and 'we know from media reports that he had a number of other relationships' (op. cit. 215 and 32).

There may have been more than one abuser. One woman spoke of a lot of young men in a flat that Huntley visited (op. cit. 117) while another came to know Huntley through an adult male (op. cit. 78). Patterns of targeting were evident and there were links through school, friendships, places, and being known to social services. It was possible to analyse the connections, even possibly to predict who might have been his next victim and detect the escalation of offending behaviour. Instead, Kelly acknowledges that: 'connections were not made' (op. cit. 1) that: 'in practice each case was treated in isolation' (op. cit. 209) 'there was a focus on individual cases with no attempt to consider the wider picture' and 'decisions to close cases were not informed by proactive gathering of information' (op. cit. 224).

Yet neither Bichard, whose remit was to 'urgently inquire into child protection procedures,' nor Kelly, in his analysis of social services role in the case, make mention of the organised abuse procedures or their lack of implementation (Bichard, 2004; Davies, 2004b;

Kelly, 2004). The reports focus on the importance of police intelligence systems rather than joint investigation processes.

It seemed as if the lessons from the many investigations of organised abuse of the 1990s which led to successful prosecutions had not been learnt.

This point is emphasised by the narrow remit of the Home Affairs Committee of investigation into past cases of abuse in children's homes which was to consider possible miscarriages of justice. Quite remarkably it did not include any consideration of whether or not the system achieved justice for children by the conviction of perpetrators which is key to the healing process for children. Sarah Nelson states in her research with women survivors of child sexual abuse: 'the survivors felt strongly that they should have been protected at an early age and that the perpetrators should have faced legal justice many years before' (Nelson, 2001).

Effective joint investigation was resource intensive and also led to legal claims against the authorities (Osuh, 2007). High profile people were exposed or close to being exposed. The Islington scandal, like many others across the country, included components of ritual abuse although this was denied by the Inquiry (White and Hart, 1995). A parliamentary question about ritual abuse research, which included the Islington case, conducted by the Metropolitan Police, received the response that 'It will be for the Commissioner of the Metropolitan Police to decide what information he wishes to make public' (Alton, 1994). The research was never published. Events in Belgium of large child abuse networks intimated similar issues in the UK although there had not been the equivalent of the white march where thousands of the Belgian public demonstrated for children (Pyck and Eeckels, 1998). A recent critique of the professional response to organised child sexual abuse was that of the inspection into the care and protection of children in Eilean Siar, Scotland (SWIA, 2005). Although no criminal prosecutions achieved convictions the review made a finding that three children were repeatedly sexually abused and concluded that there was an 'unhelpful imbalance in the weight given to the rights and duties of parents as against the needs and rights of the children' (2005: 17). Professionals had been over-optimistic about the capacity of the parents to protect the children, large amounts of information had been logged

and shared as part of assessment but there had not been analysis of the meaning of that information or proper debate among professionals enabling tough decisions to be made (2005: 21).

Police and social workers working together effectively, targeting abusers and protecting children, presented a threat to those in power. Abuse is abuse of power and as such it involves all echelons of society. It remains to be seen when and if child protection ever becomes a political issue influencing voting patterns and gaining a mention on political manifestos. Children do not vote and therefore have little political voice.

The backlash

Minimisation of a proactive interventionist approach to child abuse developed following the refocusing debate and interpretation of the findings of *Messages from Research* (DoH, 1995). The latter was a collection of studies commissioned prior to the Children Act 1989 but it gained the status of policy. 'While there was never an overt instruction for social services to refocus their work away from investigation, it is common knowledge that they understood that this was expected of them' (Reder and Duncan, 2004). It was argued that social work was too forensically and incident led and that too many children were being caught in the child protection net (DoH, 1995: 16). Particularly since the introduction of the *Framework of Assessment for Children in Need and their Families* (DoH, 2000) social workers were being told to change their approach to child protection – to pull away from colleagues in the police and work at a preventative level with health and education. However, 'simply re-labelling allegations as Section 17 children in need doesn't address the thorny issue of how children can be protected' (Douieb, 2004). The use of words such as *risk, protection* and *investigation* were discouraged and replaced with *need, safeguarding* and *enquiries*. Policy became focused on assessment rather than assessment of risk. One recent example is that of Kelly's report which emphasised that: 'The review team gained the impression that . . . some staff in the social services department adopted a rather mechanistic approach to the management of cases rather than one based on the assessment of risk and the application of professional knowledge (Kelly, 150: 35).

The timescales of the Initial and Core assessment took over from intervention moving swiftly from a child protection referral to action to protect (DoH, 2000). The detailed proactive collation of information about children and perpetrators, the mapping and seeking of patterns and complex multi-agency work often over months was no longer understood. Most importantly, children no longer had the time and space to trust professionals enough to share their horrific stories. The ADSS submission to the Bichard Inquiry stated that social services 'does not deal with the risks to children from outside their families unless the behaviour of the child is exposing them to risk' (Bichard, 2004). However, it is an essential aspect of the Section 47 duty for social workers to work with police in the investigation of perpetrators. The skills of a detective are relevant for social workers (Munro, 2003: 170). These skills are of analysis, forming and testing hypotheses and probing beneath the surface. Instead, Kelly reported cases brought to swift closure and Arthurworrey spoke of being under pressure from management to close the case four months prior to Victoria's death. 'I was told to close Victoria's file on 15th November and again on 23rd December and again on 18th January. In my mind there were still issues which needed to be resolved' (Kelly, 2004: 14; LA, 2004: 169). Judge Pearl confirmed that 'the managers should have been driving the case forward' (CST, 2005: 139).

Current methods over-rely on children providing evidence. The Kelly Review demonstrated that cases were closed because the child withdrew or retracted allegations or didn't want to proceed to prosecution (Kelly, 2004). But why is it expected that a child who has suffered so much should provide information? Information must also be sought from other sources such as forensic evidence or adult witnesses, to take pressure off the child. A child may have a positive view of the relationship and not define it as abusive. Four of Huntley's victims defined him as a boyfriend. Children may be directly threatened or convinced that the sexual activity is acceptable. It is important to match the complexity of the interventions with the complexity of the abuse.

Such a clear shift away from proactive investigation made it apparent that 'refocusing' spelt a backlash. Islington child victims of abuse would have gained no protection without multi-agency strategies and the extent of the child abuse industry was obviously vast and clearly indicated that the protective net was actually nowhere near large enough. But the government was emphasising a message that some practitioners had struggled against in Islington – to pull back from joint investigation with the police and those who continued to struggle to protect children were at risk of being labelled 'over-zealous'.

Many children requiring protection do not access protective systems. In 2006 there were 25,400 children's names on the Child Protection Register, which represented a decrease of 26 per cent since 1995. The categories of physical and sexual abuse were half that of 2001 (DfES, 2006). Comparisons with statistics of known child sex offenders and sexual crimes against children illustrate that the number subject to protection planning is very small indeed (Breslin and Evans, 2004). Statistics of the number of child victims of abusive images indicate how few enter the protective systems. Operation Ore involved 7,200 men in the UK accessing a gateway to abusive images of children but few of these led to Section 47 investigations in relation to the children placed at possible risk. Max Taylor, Director of Combating Paedophile Information Networks in Europe: 'found pictures of 13,000 individual children in 2002. Of these, 25 have been identified in the UK, 50 in Europe and 100 in the US and the rest of the world' (Sunday Herald, 2003). Carr stated that: 'the victims of these horrendous crimes – the children themselves – are so often not being found and helped' (Carr quoted in Police Oracle 2004).

Similarly, children trafficked for domestic or sexual slavery are unrepresented on the Child Protection Register. Operation Paladin Child analysed the cases of 1,738 unaccompanied minors entering the country at Heathrow airport in a three month period and found 28 were untraceable. Of these, 29 per cent were under the age of 11 years (Reflex, 2004). Of course, the majority of trafficked children will be entering the UK accompanied and are even less likely to be identified than those unaccompanied. Of the many children who go missing in the UK there are no police statistics of those children who are not found. In a study based in the north of England, 48 illegally trafficked children were missing from care, representing almost half the sample (Beddoe, 2007). The Children's Society research 'Still Running 2', identified two-thirds who said they had not been reported as missing to the police (Rees and Lee, 2005). They were 'throwaways' who were lost to child protection systems.

The Joint Inspector's Report *Safeguarding Children* commented that they couldn't be confident of the child protection response to young people in prison. Since 1990 there have been 29 deaths of young people in prison without serious case reviews or public inquiries being held. There is also concern about children who are held in segregation and treated as adult prisoners and the use of lengthy prison sentences for non-violent crimes. The same report was also critical of the lack of protection for asylum seeking children in detention centres (CSCI, 2005; Davies, 2007: 26). Concern can also be extended to the protection needs of UK child soldiers following the Deepcut Review where young recruits died in questionable circumstances. The review debated the application of the Children Act to young people in the armed forces (Blake, 2006).

Dr Adrian Falkov's research on the children who died from abuse who had a parent with mental illness confirmed that professional attention was primarily on the parent and not the child (Falkov, 1996) and to this list may be added the protection needs of disabled children which was also of concern to the inspectors, while children physically abused by adults in the name of 'reasonable chastisement' are denied the right of equal protection under the law of assault as adults. There is no doubt that there are numbers of children who require the protection of a very large child protection net. Between 1994 and 2004, 29 children from 13 families were killed during contact arrangements (Saunders, 2004). If rigorous child protection investigation is not conducted by social workers and police then it may be predicted that the courts will have increased difficulty in making safe decisions for children where there is parental conflict, and lack of evidence will lead to delays in risk assessment rendering children more vulnerable prior to decisions being made.

Perhaps it was awareness of the wide scale need of children for protection that has steered policy away from child protection work – a perspective influenced by Farrow, Director of the Center for the Study of Social Policy, Washington DC. He points out:

If a growing number of families are seeing their incomes shrink, are having trouble obtaining the basics of food, *clothing and shelter and are plagued by substance abuse, rates of child maltreatment will go up, not down. The reason a community's overall family support system is critical to effective child protection is that it creates the possibility of stemming the flow of vulnerable, at risk families.*

(Farrow, 1997: 48)

Little and Axford describe a recent Dartington Report as requiring 'a shift in emphasis to focus on prevention . . . ensuring resources are not sucked into a continual fire-fighting exercise to support children whose social and psychological needs have become entrenched'. The authors acknowledge that both prevention and intervention are essential elements to effective children's services but there is no mention of protection in the entire article (Dartington, 2004; Little and Axford, 2004). Children will always need fire-fighting social workers to intervene to protect them and they also may well need protection when they have entrenched needs – because the cause of such needs may indeed be adult abuse of power.

The *Framework of Assessment of Children in Need and Their Families* (DoH, 2000) was accompanied by a training programme which was swiftly implemented (DoH et al., 2000). In contrast, there were no such government initiatives to promote *Working Together* (DoH, 1999), the statutory guidance concerning inter-agency working. Recognising the dangers in this procedural split Laming recommended a merging of the *Framework of Assessment and Working Together* (DoH, 2000; DoH, 1999; Laming, 2003: 17.111). However, instead the government produced the leaflet '*What to do if you are worried a child is being abused*' with its plethora of flow charts. Charles Clarke at the launch of the Green Paper stated: 'as a single set of guidelines we intend to eliminate any need for local bodies to produce their own' (DoH, 2003; Clarke, 2003). The mass of information in this document about data protection has confused practitioners who now seem to lack confidence in sharing information within Section 47 investigations and more seriously, some practitioners might be led to think that this limited leaflet replaced *Working Together*. There is no replacement for locally agreed multi agency procedures clearly based on national guidance which cater for local need and reflect good practice owned by practitioners. All current protocols relating to child protection are now based upon the Assessment Framework model which is not an appropriate tool for investigative work.

Retaining the paramountcy of children's best interests

The splitting of assessment from protection led to a division replicated in service restructuring. New structures implemented after the *Framework of Assessment* were a move towards increased privatisation (DoH, 2000). The statutory element of child protection work was to be minimised and separated off from family support services which would then become available for privatisation. Farrow presented the case for community partnerships, not just as an assessment approach, but as a means to offer help to families through a community based delivery system (Farrow, 1997). The Children's Trust 'presents a statutory basis for partnership working' (DfES, 2004: 1). The partnership will be accountable to central rather than local government with funding streams dependant on the fulfilment of government targets. The intention is clear there will be 'proportionate intervention in localities that fall below minimum standards' (DfES, 2004: 28). Local democratic control of children's services will be increasingly undermined. Glendinning usefully analyses the role of partnerships under New Labour:

> Partnership working benefits powerful partners. Such partnerships reinforce power inequalities that are already in existence . . . They divert resources away from the core business of welfare service delivery . . . The private sector cannot be controlled within the present political climate by central dicktat and any claims that improved welfare outcomes can be achieved by public-private partnerships should be treated with scepticism
>
> (Glendinning et al., 2002: 243)

It was therefore no surprise at the launch of the Green Paper to see the Wyeth pharmaceutical company awarded prominence on the initial flyer as co-hosting the conference with the Institute of Public Policy and Research – although they later withdrew (IPPR, 2003). Wyeth markets medical supplies for children. Children's Trusts organised through partnerships with the private sector would obviously open up markets to such providers. 'Wyeth has already worked in partnership with a number of organisations to help support health education and best practice within the NHS' (Wyeth, 2004). The distinction

must be made between the concept of partnership working and partnerships with the private sector. In *Every Child Matters: Next Steps*, this philosophy is unequivocally stated:

> We will commission a study to scope the current and potential market for providing children services to inform a strategy for greater contestability. This may include incentivising excellent local authorities or other organisations to set up trading companies or other organisational models able to franchise or contract to provide a successful business model.
>
> (DfES, 2004: 28)

Checks and balances are important in child protection. *Working Together* has been effective because the multi-agency approach allows for balance and scrutiny (DfES, 2006). Increased privatisation places financial interests in the fore and therefore demands a high level of rigorous monitoring. The centralisation of children's services solely within the Department for Education and Skills, and Ofsted as a single centralised inspectorate, creates structures with a considerably reduced possibility of counteracting corruption or abusive systems. Social work is now centrally regulated by the General Social Care Council which has set the scene for removal of many child care social work positions from local authorities and repositioning within the private sector as well as in extended schools and children's centres, both of which may eventually become subject to privatisation.

Losing the language of child protection

An obvious aspect of the reprogramming of social work intervention in child protection was to alter the language used and to introduce the concept of safeguarding in the sense of minimisation of harm and promotion of wellbeing rather than protection from significant harm (Parton, 2006: 7). The *Every Child Matters* agenda has promoted prevention within safeguarding but the protection aspect has been almost lost (House of Lords, 2003; HMG, 2003). The very language of child protection needs to be reclaimed and prevention re-established within the concept of protection.

The new focus is prevention of abuse and solutions located solely within a family context. Yet abuse of children by strangers is grossly underestimated. For example, a Home Office report states that 56 per cent of all police-recorded child abductions involved a stranger (Newiss and Fairbrother, 2004). Risk is framed within the concept of disadvantage which deflects attention from abuse as an issue often unrelated to poverty and taking place in all sectors of society. Sexual abuse and other exploitation of children is not correlated with disadvantage. Even if child poverty was eliminated there would still be extensive networks of powerful adults abducting, marketing, murdering, and raping children for profit and exploitation.

Children are also defined as at risk of presenting a problem to society rather than as at risk of abuse by adult perpetrators. Universal, preventative policies to promote welfare instead: 'tackle youth offending, truancy, anti-social behaviour and improve life chances. The policy package presented by New Labour is thus primarily focused on advancing social order and a work ethic rather than averting child abuse' (Douieb, 2004). Yet research confirms that of children in custody significant numbers have suffered physical and sexual abuse (Monaghan, G., 2003: 20–1; SEU, 2002). Abuse of children by organised networks of abusers, evident on an unprecedented scale, is absent from the new agenda. *Keeping Children Safe* lists a children's safeguarding system for the 21st century but omits any reference to targeting abusers and seeking justice for abused children (DfES, 2004: 11). It is highly significant that *Every Child Matters* does not include probation, which has a key part to play in identifying and managing child abusers, in the information hub and the new training standards omit probation as a key professional group relevant to child protection work, failing even to make note of the omission. However, as the standards are said to reflect the frameworks contained in the Green Paper perhaps this omission should not surprise (HMG, 2003: 54; Shardlow, 2004: 3).

The decline of proactive child protection in two key areas of practice – the police role and the child protection register

Since Recommendation 99 of the Victoria Climbié Inquiry there has been a move towards a police

emphasis on the investigation of crime rather than of likely or actual significant harm in Section 47 inquiries. This represents a significant reduction in police involvement in child protection joint investigation work:

> *The Working Together arrangements must be amended to ensure the police carry out completely and exclusively, any criminal investigation elements in a case of suspected injury or harm to a child including the evidential interview with a child victim.*
>
> (Laming, 2003: 14.57)

This is in stark contradiction to the Achieving Best Evidence Guidance which requires a child-centred interview conducted collaboratively:

> *Provided both the police officer and social worker have been adequately trained in interviewing vulnerable and/or intimidated child witnesses there is no reason why either should not lead the interview.*
>
> (Home Office, 2002: 1: 2, 74)

This narrowing of the police role has been reiterated by Bichard who stated that social workers must report crimes to police, but did not comment on the need for joint investigation of significant harm – a threshold which may or may not include allegations of crime (Bichard, 2004: 139). The police child protection teams now screen referrals and it is the author's view that social workers are finding it increasingly difficult to engage police in any child protection matter that does not constitute a potential or actual crime.

Child protection is a grey area demanding multi-agency debate and analysis, not rigid barriers to collaborative processes. It is of concern that in *Every Child Matters: Next Steps*, the police role is defined only as within the Youth Offending Team with no mention at all of the police child protection or community safety teams. The Multi Agency Public Protection Panels gain a small mention in this document in relation to safeguarding children within public protection arrangements, but there is no reference at all of joint working to bring abusers to justice (DfES, 2003: 4.19 and 4.24).

Most concerning is the abolition of the child protection register by April 2008. The register was completely airbrushed out of the revised *Working Together* (DfES, 2006), thus implementing the intentions stated in *Keeping Children Safe*: 'The child protection register will become redundant and can be phased out gradually across the country alongside the introduction of the Integrated Children's System' (DfES, 2003: 77). Department of Health research is quoted as identifying some 'worrying practices', but the source of the research is not stated. It is said that professionals fear the use of the register as a passport to services or consider that there is a lack of attention paid to a child whose name is not on the register – but surely such concerns signify the need for training rather than a total annihilation of the system? (DfES, 2003: 75). Although Thomas states that: 'they know they will have access to better services if their child is on the register so they threaten their children so they get put on it' (Valios, 2003), this pathologisation of parents and misuse of the process is not evidenced. A ministerial response to a parliamentary question has confirmed that 'no research has been commisioned by the DfES specifically on the use of the child protection register' (Dhanda, 2007).

The Child Protection Register is the most important tool professionals have in protecting children. It is tried and tested and has implemented the findings of many child abuse inquiries since the 1970s. If Victoria Climbié's name had been on the register she would have had a child protection plan to keep her safe and hospitals and police would have been alerted to the risks and professionals would have followed her care from borough to borough. She would have had a key worker with statutory responsibility to coordinate all relevant information and to implement the planning with other professionals. Most importantly, the case would have been analysed and debated in a multi-agency setting and responsibilities would have been shared across agencies.

Laming expressed his own concerns about current practice:

I was told that staff feel under pressure to reduce the number of section 47 inquiries. As a result, there is widespread practice of driving down child protection case conferences and the number of children whose names are placed on the child protection register.

(Laming, 17.110)

However, he unfortunately proceeded to condemn these important procedures:

There is the danger that other agencies may make unwarranted assumptions of the level of help and support being given to a child whose name is on the register. It is for this reason that I now have considerable doubt about the usefulness of these registers in the safeguarding of children.

(Laming, 17.110)

In conversation with the author and Lisa Arthurworrey at the Victoria Climbié Memorial Lecture (26th February 2007) he said he had thought the Register was a 'comfort blanket' for professionals but acknowledged that he was 'not an expert in child protection'.

Performance targets became more achievable if registration was kept to a minimum. Because of this some children have been excluded from the protection of the register such as older children and children Looked After. There may be: 'a conscious decision to remove those children's names from the child protection register on the basis they are already significantly protected by statute' (Dobson, 2004: 24). Care planning is distinct from child protection planning and there may be risks posed through contact or other situations that expose the child to abuse. Registration must be agreed between professionals making considered judgements, not by managerial imposition.

Some authorities have already disposed of the register prior to the deadline of April 2008. Children will now be defined as 'subject to a Child Protection Plan'. The Custodian of the Register, which is currently a highly specialist senior social work post, is to be replaced with an essentially IT role 'designated manager for managing and providing information about a child'. ContactPoint, a database for every child in the country, the Common Assessment Framework, which targets one in three families and the Integrated Children's Systems for recipients of social work services, each form part of a massive web of information which is being streamlined into place about children and their lives in the UK (ARCH, 2007; Anderson, 2007). What is actually needed is a National Child Protection Register for children identified as at high risk of harm which should include a register of missing children. This would represent a justifiable level of state intervention into family life. Instead, the new systems based on assessment represent an unprecedented form of population surveillance. The information available online to a wide range of agencies will make children vulnerable to child abusers. Non-professionals will have access to the information who will have no accountability to professional bodies. Emergency services will have to trawl the databases for every child instead of being instantly alerted to a child whose name is on the register. The question has seriously to be asked why an excellent protective system has been destroyed?

The current government shift to prevention aims to reduce referrals overall, not just reduce those on the register. In North Lincolnshire, where the single assessment process is now in place, there has been a reduction by 64 per cent of referrals to social services (HMG, 2003: 58). Early intervention to prevent the downward spiral of abuse is very important. If the young people in Islington hadn't been poor and homeless it is clear abusers would not have had such an easy time in accessing them. However, a key aspect of real prevention is to remove abusers from the child's world – which has little mention in recent policy.

An alternative approach to community involvement is to create protective networks of adults within the community in order to inform investigation of abuse and to increase, rather than decrease, appropriate reporting. Such a model is unapologetic in striving to protect children from abuse and to seek justice for them by prosecution of the abusers.

A redefining of prevention

A focus on prevention is essential in order to gather intelligence from the local community which can lead to the arrest of child abusers. Most members of the public are not aware of how to report child abuse. Community awareness strategies involving positive local media coverage, posters, public meetings and exhibitions can engage those members of the public who may form a network of protective adults for children. Neighbourhood mapping to identify child support networks enables close working with professionals to inform the investigation of crimes against children (Nelson, 2004). Laming suggested that 'the general view was that the 'eyes and ears' of the community are not used enough in the identification of children potentially in need' (Laming, 2003: 17.30). Such community involvement should increase appropriate reporting to social services and police.

An Area Child Protection Committee prevention project in North London, between 1995 and 2000, included members from social services, police, probation, education, health and local survivors organisations. The objectives were to raise public awareness of child protection work, encourage reporting and to promote a positive view of child protection work. Posters were widely distributed in the community stating: 'Children may need you to see. Children may need you to hear. Children may need you to speak out about physical, sexual, emotional abuse and neglect. The difference between child abuse and child protection could be you'. Public meetings covered topics such as 'Listening to Children,' 'Child Abuse Everyone's Business and Domestic Violence-Change is Possible.' An extensive database of identified protective adults was established through mapping local groups and specific individuals working with or having contact with young people. A 'Knowing the Basics' awareness programme addressed the 'What, How and When' of child abuse (*What is Abuse? How to refer abuse? When to refer?*). Key members of the network attended a two day introductory child protection course alongside professionals. All the training included survivors as contributors. Organisations were then assisted in establishing internal child protection procedures and safer care protocols and with these in place they could be affiliated to the ACPC. It was the view of ACPC members that an increase in referrals, particularly those of physical abuse and neglect, had demonstrated that the community awareness strategy had resulted in abusive situations being appropriately reported at an early stage.

The network of protective adults also played a key role in the safe implementation of community notification strategies. When a child sex abuser was released into the community some of this network were able to inform professionals of any noted contact with young people. They also reassured the community that there were professional systems in place to protect local children. Some worked closely with police and social services in the investigation of complex abuse networks and this led to the police child protection team allocating time for proactive investigation work. In this way concerns about individual adults were collated and analysed and led to joint investigation. It was clear that effective protection of children depended on professional liaison with the local community (Davies, 2004c).

Conclusion

Society pays for its neglect.
Children become adults.

(Frampton, 2004: 290)

Safeguarding children requires a dual strategy of protection and prevention. The concepts are not mutually exclusive. Prevention is in itself protective by increasing appropriate reporting of child abuse and engaging the community in the targeting of abusers. Proactive protection should result in the prevention of further abuse by removing abusers from the child's world. The current splitting of prevention from protection, and of family support from investigation, diverts scarce professional resources from rigorous protective processes addressing all forms of abuse within all sectors of society. Effective child protection requires a professional response. If a community network is in place to inform that response, through both appropriate referral and involvement in investigation strategies, children will have an increased chance of protection from all child abusers, not solely those within the family. Current government policies and proposed legislation are propelling professionals swiftly into the abandonment of proven effective methods of protecting children in favour of universal and unrealisable solutions to narrowly defined concepts of child abuse.

References

Alton, D. (1994) *Written Parliamentary Question No 178* 10.02.

Anderson, R. et al. (2007) *Children's Databases. Safety and Privacy. A Report for the Information Commissioner*. London. Foundation for Information Policy and Research (FIPR).

ARCH (2007) http://www.arch-ed.org/issues/databases/IS%20Index.htm

Arthurworrey, L. (2004) *Witness Statement in the Case 'Lisa Arthurworrey and The Mayor and Burgesses of the London Borough of Haringey'.* Employment Tribunal (London Central) Case No: 220586B.2002 (available from the author: e.davies@londonmet.ac.uk)

Batty, D. (2004) *The Blame Game*. The Guardian 03.09.04. http://society.guardian.co.uk/print/0,3858,5007721-108813,00.html

Beddoe, C. (2007) *Missing Out. A Study of Children Trafficked in the North West, North East and West Midlands*. London ECPAT.

Bennetto, J. (2001) *Child Sex Abuse Inquiries 'will top 100.'* The Independent 08.01.2001

Bichard, M. Lord (2004) *The Bichard Inquiry Report*. HMSO Norwich www.thebichardinquiry.org

Bird, K. and Hennessy, J. (1997) *Operation Badger*. Essex Child Protection Committee.

Blake, N. (2006) *The Deepcut Review. A Review of the Circumstances Surrounding the Deaths of Four Soldiers at Princess Royal Barracks, Deepcut between 1995 and 2002*. London TSO.

Brannan, C. et al. (1992) *Castle Hill Report, Practice Guide*. Shropshire County Council.

Breslin, R. and Evans, H. (2004) *Key Child Protection Statistics. Sex Offenders and Sex Offences against Children*. www.nspcc.org.uk/inform/Statistics/KeyCPstats/12.asp

Bristow, A. (2004) *Verbal evidence presented on cross-examination at the Employment Tribunal* (London Central) Case No: 220586B.2002.

Bristow, A. (2004) *Witness statement in the case 'Lisa Arthurworrey and The Mayor and Burgesses of the London Borough of Haringey'*. Employment Tribunal (London Central) case No: 220586B.2002

Bristow, A. (2004) *speaking on Today programme*. www.bbc.co.uk/radio4/today/listenagain 25.06.04

Care Standards Tribunal (2005) Lisa Arthurworrey v The Secretary of State for Education and Skills (2004) 355.PC. available from www.carestandardstribunal.gov.uk/documents/digest6.doc

CSCI (2005) *Safeguarding Children: The Second Joint Chief Inspector's Report*. Newcastle CSCI.

Child Abuse Prevention Council of Sacramento Inc. (2001) *California Alliance for Prevention Executive Summary. First Year Evaluation Report*. Available from: Child Abuse Prevention Council of Sacramento Inc. 8795 Folsom Boulevard, Suite 103, Sacramento, CA 95826. USA.

Clarke, C. (2003) *Vulnerable Children*. Hansard 16.07.03 p. 364.

Dartington Social Research Unit (2004) *Refocusing Children's Services Towards Prevention: Lessons from the Literature*. Research Report 510. London. DfES.

Davies, L. (1997) The Investigation of Organised Abuse. In Westcott, H. and Jones, J. (Chapter 9) *Perspectives on the Memorandum*. London. Arena.

Davies, L. (2004a) *Why I believe in Lisa*. Evening Standard, 06.09.2004.

Davies, L. (2004b) Viewpoint: Limited Resources to Snare Abusers, p. 21. *Community Care*, 5–11th August.

Davies, L. (2004c) The Difference between Child Abuse and Child Protection could be You. Creating a Network of Protective Adults. Short Report. *Child Abuse Review*, 13.

Davies, L. (2007) *Protecting Children. A Resource Book and Course Reader*. Gloucester. Akamas

DfES (2003) *Every Child Matters: Next Steps*. Nottingham, DfES.

DfES (2004) *Statistics of Education: Referrals, Assessments and Children and Young People on Child Protection Registers: Year ending 31 March 2006*. London. DfES. http://www.dfes.gov.uk/rsgateway/DB/SFR/s000692/SFR45-2006V1.pdf

DfES, DoH and Home Office (2003) *Keeping Children Safe*. Norwich: HMSO.

DfES et al. (2006) *Working Together to Safeguard Children: A Guide for Inter-agency Working to Safeguard and Promote the Welfare of Children*. London: HMSO.

Dhanda, P. (2007) Written parliamentary question no. 117707. May.

DoH (2000) *Framework for the Assessment of Children in Need and their Families*. London: HMSO.

DoH (2002) *Safeguarding Children. A Joint Chief Inspector's Report on Arrangements to Safeguard Children*. London: HMSO.

DoH (1995) *Child Protection: Messages from Research*. London: HMSO.

DoH, Home Office, DoEE (1999) *Working Together to Safeguard Children*. London: HMSO.

DoH (2003) *What to Do if you're Worried a Child is being Abused*. London: HMSO.

Dobson, A. (2004) A Brighter Future. *Care and Health*, October 26–November 1.

Douieb, B. (2004) *Do Abused Children Matter? An Investigation of New Labour's Policies in England* Unpublished MA dissertation.

Fairweather, E. (1998) Exposing the Islington Children's Home Scandal: A Journalist's View. Chapter 1 In Hunt, G. (Ed.) *Whistleblowing in the Social Services: Public Accountability and Professional Practice*. London: Arnold.

Falkov, A. Dr (1996) *A Study of Working Together Part 8 reports. Fatal Child Abuse and Parental Psychiatric Disorder*. London: DoH Publications.

Farrow, F. (1997) *Child Protection: Building Community Partnerships. Getting from Here to There*. Cambridge. MA: John F Kennedy School of Government. Harvard University.

Frampton, P. (2004) *Golly in the Cupboard*. Manchester: Tamic.

Glendinning, C., Powell, M. and Rummery, K. (2002) *Partnerships, New Labour and the Governance of Welfare*. Bristol: The Policy Press.

Her Majesty's Government (2003) *Every Child Matters*. Cmnd 5860. London: The Stationery Office.

Hodge, M. (2004) *House of Commons Select Committee on Education and Skills*. Minutes of Evidence 09.06.2004. www.publications.parliament.uk/pa/cm200304/cmselect/cmeduski/658/4060902.htm p. 5

Home Office. (2002) *Achieving Best Evidence in Criminal Proceedings for Vulnerable and/or Intimidated Witnesses including Children*. London: HMSO.

Home Office and DoH (2002) *Complex Abuse Investigation: Inter-agency Issues*. London: Home Office.

House of Commons Home Affairs Committee (2002) *The Conduct of Investigations into Past Cases of Abuse in Children's Homes. Fourth Report of Session 2001–2 Vol 1*. Norwich: HMSO.

House of Lords (2004) *The Children Bill. HL Bill 82*. London: The Stationery Office.

IPPR (2003) *All Together Now: The Future of Children's Services. One day conference*. www.ipr.org. 16.09.03.

Jarman, M. and Davies, L. (2005) Social Workers' Professional Practice after Climbié. *Family Law* October, 35: 814–19.

Jayarajah-Dent, R. (2004) *Executive Summary of the Overview Report from the Serious Case Review on Adam*. London. NCH-The Bridge http://www.haringey.gov.uk/search.htm?col=cmhar&qt=adam

Jeffrey, J. (1996) *Learning from Michigan*. Buckinghamshire County Child Protection Committee.

Kelly, Sir C. (2004) *Serious Case Review 'Ian Huntley' for North Lincolnshire Area Child Protection Committee*. 21.07.04.

Laming, Lord. 2003. *The Victoria Climbié Inquiry. Report of an Inquiry by Lord Laming*. London: HMSO.

Leason, K. (2004). Benefit or Burden. *Community Care*, 20–26 May, 30–1.

Little, M. and Axford, N. (2004) Focus on Prevention. *Community Care*, 42, 29 July – 4 August.

Martin, D. (2004) Haringey takes Action after Criticism. *Children Now*, 30 June–6 July 8.

Monaghan, B. (2004) *Witness statement in the case Lisa Arthurworrey and The Mayor and Burgesses of the London Borough of Haringey.* Employment tribunal (London Central) case No: 220586B.2002.

Monaghan, G., Hibbert, P. and Moore, S. (2003) *Children in Trouble. Time for Change.* Essex: Barnardo's.

Munro, E. (2003) This would not have saved Victoria. *The Guardian.* 10.09.2003. www.society.guardian.co.uk/print/0,3858,4749959-108861,00.html

Munro, E. (2002) *Effective Child Protection.* London: Sage.

Nelson, S. (2001) *Beyond Trauma: Mental Health Care Needs of Women who Survived Childhood Sexual Abuse.* Edinburgh: Health in Mind (EAMH).

Nelson, S. (2004) *Neighbourhood Mapping for Children's Safety: A Feasibility Study in Craigmillar.* Edinburgh: Womanzone.

Newiss, G. and Fairbrother, L. (2004) *Findings 225. Child Abduction: Understanding Police Recorded Crime Statistics.* London: Home Office.

Osuh, C. (2007) Anger over care home victim's payouts. *Manchester Evening News,* 08.03.2007.

Parton, N. (2002) *Submission to Phase 2 of the Victoria Climbié Inquiry.* http://www.victoria-Climbié-inquiry.org.uk/Evidence/p2subs/15march.htm

Parton, N. (2006) *Safeguarding Childhood.* Basingstoke: Palgrave Macmillan.

Police Oracle (2004) *No Funds to Tackle Child Porn.* www.policeoracle.com/news/print_detail.h"f?id=5634 02.11.2004

Pyck, K. and Eeckels, R. (1998) *Polarisation and Backlash in Belgium: The Dutroux case, 1996–8.* Lecture presented at the Twelfth International Congress on Child Abuse and Neglect, Auckland, New Zealand, Sept 6–9, 1998.

Reder, P., Duncan, S. and Gray, M. (1993) *Beyond Blame.* London: Routledge.

Reder, P. and Duncan, S. (1999) *Lost Innocents.* London: Routledge.

Reder, P. and Duncan, S. (2004) Making the Most of the Victoria Inquiry Report. *Child Abuse Review,* 13: 95–114. Wiley.

Rees, G. and Lee, J. (2005) *Still Running 2. Findings from the Second National Survey of Young Runaways.* London: Children's Society.

Reflex, Metropolitan Police, UK Immigration Service, ADSS, NSPCC and London Borough of Hillingdon (2004) *Operation Paladin Child. A Partnership Study of Child Migration to the UK via London Heathrow.*

Roberts, Y. (2004) But is no excuse for not getting it right. *Community Care,* 23, 9–15 September.

Robertson, M. (1996) Open about mistakes. *Community Care,* Letters. 21.01.1996.

Safe on the Streets Research Team (1999) *Still Running: Children on the Streets in the UK.* London: The Children's Society.

Saunders, H. (2004) *29 Child Homicides.* London: Women's Aid.

Shardlow, S. et al. (2004) *Education and Training for Inter-Agency Working: New Standards.* Salford Centre for Social Work Research: Manchester University of Salford.

Sheerman, B. (2003) *Oral Evidence of Margaret Hodge.* House of Commons Minutes of Evidence taken before Education and Skills Committee 15.12.03 www.parliament.the-stationery-ffice.co.uk/pa/cm200304/cmselect/cmeduski/u

Smith, C. (2004) Softly Softly. *Care and Health,* 21, April 6–12.

Social Exclusion Unit (2002) *Reducing Re-offending by Ex-prisoners, Annex D – Juveniles.* www.cabinet-office.gov.uk/seu/publications/reports

Social Work Inspection Agency SWIA (2005) *An Inspection into the Care and Protection of Children in Eilean Siar.* Edinburgh: Scottish Executive.

Sunday Herald. 2003 *Slipping the Net.* 19.01.2003 www.sundayherald.com/print30756

Valios, N. (2003) Up in the Air. *Community Care,* 26–7, 4–10 September 2003.

White, I. and Hart, K. (1995) *Report of the Inquiry into the Management of Child Care in the London Borough of Islington. A Report Commissioned by Islington Council following Serious Allegations about Child Care in the Borough.*

Wolmer, C. (2000) *Forgotten Children: The Secret Abuse Scandal in Children's Homes.* London: Vision.

Wyeth. (2004) www.wyeth.uk

CHAPTER 4

Risk, Uncertainty and Thresholds

Chris Beckett

In this chapter I will discuss the issues involved in working with thresholds for intervention. My discussion will focus entirely on the child protection field, which I know from personal experience, although most of the points I make are general ones to do with the difficulties and challenges involved in working with uncertainty and are therefore relevant to other areas too.

Probability and the hindsight fallacy

A major difficulty for anyone trying to develop a rational approach to risk assessment is that it involves thinking clearly about the idea of probability. Most of us struggle with probability. What our intuitions tell us about it are often simply not consistent with the facts, as can be seen by the many varieties of magical thinking that attend on buying lottery tickets, betting on horses and playing fruit machines. For example, if I throw a dice three times and each time it comes up six, my rational head knows (a) that this is a random event which will happen on average once out of every 216 triple throws of a dice and (b) that if I throw the dice a fourth time, the chance of a six coming up again is one in six, no higher and no lower than it would be on any other throw of the dice. But my *instinct* says one of two quite different things: *either* 'I'm on a roll, I'm on a lucky streak, I bet I get another six' *or* 'I've already had three sixes in a row, no way will a six come up again'.

A difficult consequence of this kind of muddled thinking for workers in the child protection field is the prevalence of the 'hindsight fallacy' among professionals, policy-makers and the general public, the belief that if a risk assessment concludes that the probability of an undesirable event is low, and if that event does in fact happen, then the risk assessment must have been incompetent. In fact, while risk assessments can of course be incompetent, the fact that an event assessed as unlikely does in fact occur does not in itself prove the assessment was wrong at all, any more than my throwing three sixes in a row proves that I was wrong in saying that there is only a one in 216 chance of this happening.

Kenneth and Geraldine Macdonald (1999: 23–4) describe the hindsight fallacy in action in the Kimberly Carlisle inquiry in an account which would actually be rather funny if the case itself were not so tragic and if such muddled thinking did not unfortunately have the capacity to wreck careers, deform policy-making and dangerously distort decision-making in individual cases. They quote first a social worker's evidence to the inquiry (in italics) and the commentary on it in the inquiry report:

> [After an interview with the family] *I walked with the family to the door of the building, and watched as they walked across the road to where their old car was parked. I still have a clear mental picture of the way in which they all walked across the road and got into the car, parents holding children by the hand, children leaping around in the car as they got in, laughing, shouting and playing happily with each other. It was almost an archetype for a happy family time.*

> Far from being reassured [the social worker] should have been alive to the risk of being manipulated. Plainly he had been deceived . . .
> (London Borough of Greenwich, 1987)

Finally, they illustrate the absurdity of this comment by imagining the following alternative statement from a hypothetical social worker 'alive to the risk of being manipulated':

> *It was almost an archetype for a happy family scene. So I realised I was being manipulated and forthwith arranged for the child to be taken into care.*
> (Macdonald and Macdonald, 1999: 24)

Choosing between risks

Talk of taking children 'into care' leads me to another difficulty in assessing risk in child protection situations. Child protection professionals are not simply assessing the risk of harm to a child in a given situation. They are also – or, if not, they certainly should be – in the business of weighing that risk against the risks posed by various alternative situations that they might be able to bring about through their own interventions. I will come back to this later. For the present I will just note that the hindsight fallacy makes it hard for us to accurately appraise this weighing-up process after the event. We see the *actual* consequences of the particular choice made, and it is difficult not to allow this to dominate our thinking.

To make things more complicated still, child protection professionals are not just weighing up the various courses of action available in an individual case. They are also attempting to reach a judgement as to how much of their limited resources to invest in a given case as opposed to the many other cases for which they are also responsible. Even the activity of risk assessment itself creates new dangers. The more time workers spend in assessing the risks in one case, the less time they have available for assessing the risks in another. The more time they spend on risk assessment and information-gathering in general, the less time they will have available for providing services that might actually improve things.

These judgements too tend to be obscured by the hindsight fallacy. It is easy to see that if more time had been spent on Victoria Climbié's case, she might quite easily have been saved. But, looking at this tragic story after the event, it is quite hard for us to hold in our minds the fact that until people knew what we *now* know, her case would only have been one of many potentially worrying cases, all jostling for the limited time and attention of child protection professionals. It is difficult to hold in mind that if more time had been given to her case – more time doing the things like making the phone calls and checking the records that we now know led to the failure of the system to recognise the severity of her situation – less time would have been available to other children whose names we don't even know. Without the benefit of hindsight these other children might well have appeared, even to a highly skilled observer, as every bit in need of attention as she was, given that there was limited information about all of them and given that gathering more information about any of them would in itself have required diversion of resources from elsewhere. Inquiries seldom look at those other unnamed children, as Eileen Munro notes in relation to the Climbié case:

The inquiry comments on several things that [the social worker] failed to do but tells us nothing about what she was doing instead. Presumably, they seemed more important to the worker at the time and, without further detail, how can we judge whether she was wrong or not?

(Munro, 2005: 537)

Inevitable uncertainty

Child protection inquiries typically trace problems back to missing pieces of information, connections not made. As I've just discussed, competing claims on resources do severely limit the amount that can be known about a given situation and this means that risk assessments – and particularly decisions about how detailed a risk assessment should be carried out – must be made on the basis of limited data.

But actually uncertainty is not *just* caused by limited resources. In fact, regardless of resources, there are always severe limits in principle to our ability to predict the future behaviour of any highly complex system. This is true even in the physical sciences, which non-scientists like myself tend to imagine to be very precise and exact:

At the moment scientists cannot even use the fundamental laws of physics to predict when the drips will fall from a leaking tap, or what the weather will be like in two weeks time. In fact it is difficult to predict very far ahead the motion of any object that feels the effect of more than two forces, let alone complicated systems involving interactions between many objects. Recently researchers in many disciplines have begun to realise that there seems to be inbuilt limits to predicting the future at all levels of complexity . . .

(Hall, 1991: 8)

If it is impossible to precisely predict drips from a tap, or the weather, then it is *certainly* impossible to precisely predict human behaviour, where there so many more variables, few of them amenable to precise measurement and many of them not even available for direct observation. Uncertainty is an inevitable part of life in an area like child protection. This is why we have to think in terms of probability. Indeed, this is what the idea of probability is *for*. When we can't say for certain what may happen at some point in the future, we are reduced to considering the *likelihood* of it.

We find this hard to accept, though. As I've already noted, human beings in general have difficulty thinking about uncertainty and probability. Gerd Gigerenzer notes: 'The creation of certainty seems to be a fundamental tendency of human minds' and he draws a parallel with the way 'our perceptual system automatically transforms uncertainty into certainty' (Gigerenzer, 2002: 9). He suggests that, just as this tendency allows our brains to be misled in a predictable way by certain optical illusions, so it also leads us, in an equally predictable way, to misinterpret certain types of information about probability. There are 'cognitive illusions' as well as optical ones, in other words, the hindsight fallacy being one obvious example.

But I suggest there is an additional reason why we have so much difficulty with accepting the inevitability of uncertainty in a field like that of child protection which is that there are powerful emotional factors at play here as well as purely cognitive ones. Uncertainty is *particularly* hard to bear when there is so very much at stake. Jon Elster discusses the difficulty experienced by those professionals involved in arbitrating custody disputes between parents and speaks of a 'psychological tension in decision makers that many will be unable to tolerate' resulting from the gravity of the decision taken together with the lack of a precise, incontrovertible way of making it. He suggests some may resolve this tension 'by an irrational belief in the possibility of rational preference' (Elster, 1989: 124), a belief that, given enough information and expertise, an incontrovertibly 'right' answer will emerge. Similar irrational beliefs, I would suggest, can come into play in care proceedings and can contribute either (a) to participants placing a naïve and excessive faith in the ability of experts or (b) to a tendency to prolong proceedings and introduce yet more assessments in search of a degree of certainty which may in fact be simply unattainable (Beckett and McKeigue, 2003). The same sorts of psychological tension surely also exist for decision-makers in the child protection field and various 'irrational beliefs' can and do emerge if we are not very careful. Even if we are able to resist these various forms of magical thinking ourselves, which in itself is quite a tall order, we will certainly still be up against the irrational beliefs of others. The hindsight fallacy is a typical manifestation of them.

Present and future harm

I should note here that while for simplicity I tend to talk about predicting events in the future,

exactly the same difficulties arise in relation to identifying harmful events that are *already happening*. Unless we are actually present when the event in question occurs, we are in the position (like a jury in a court of law) of having to form a judgement as to the *likelihood* of a given event having occurred, on the basis of limited information which may not offer conclusive proof one way or the other.

For example: a seven-year-old girl has become rather subdued in class, she has had a number of urinary infections, she appears uneasy when her stepfather comes to pick her up from school, she is evasive when asked about how things are at home . . . How likely is it that she is being sexually abused? Would it be appropriate to carry out a formal investigation on the basis that she is at risk of abuse?

So the reader should bear in mind that when I talk about predicting events in the future, I might equally well be talking about coming to a judgement, on limited information, about events occurring in the present or the past.

Pyramids of risk

It is a huge simplification, but I find it helpful to conceptualise the kinds of judgement we make about risk in the following diagrammatic way. Suppose that we are looking at a number of different families and are assessing the risk of some adverse event occurring in each case. Having weighed up the information that is in practice available to us (within the limitations (a) of our resources, and (b) of what it is possible in principle to know), we come to a judgement about the likelihood of this event occurring which allows us to arrange the different families in a hierarchy of risk (see Figure 4.1).

In this illustration, the pyramid represents all families. Those where there is deemed to be a high risk of the given event happening are at the top, those where there is deemed to be a low risk are at the bottom. The top is narrower than the bottom because – assuming we are talking about a seriously adverse event – high-risk families will be comparatively rare. According to our assessment, the Smith family are high-risk, the Tate family low-risk and the Desai and Jones families in between.

For the purposes of the following discussion, it does not matter what adverse advent is being discussed. It could be the risk of a child being

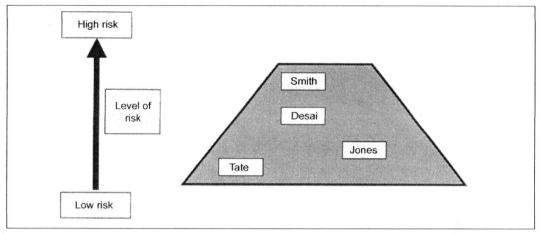

Figure 4.1 A pyramid of risk

seriously injured or sexually abused. It could be something more complex such as 'long-term emotional harm exceeding the harm that would be done by placement in a substitute family' (something which the professionals involved in care proceedings are often trying to come to a judgement about). In the following discussion, I am not going to look at the process by which professionals *arrive* at a judgement about the likelihood of a particular event occurring. This has been explored elsewhere in this book. I will simply assume that professionals, by drawing on experience and research and by using appropriate assessment tools, are able to come to judgements of this kind. My purpose is to explore what these judgements actually mean and how we utilise them.

Probability not certainty

'Likelihood' is the key word in the previous paragraph. However thorough and skilled the risk assessment, it is rarely, if ever, possible to know with *absolute certainty* that a particular adverse event will occur in a given situation (though there are certainly events and situations where the likelihood of a given event occurring is very high: the likelihood of a child being abused in a household controlled by a predatory paedophile, for example, or the likelihood of long-term emotional harm to a child in a family where there is chronic severe neglect and domestic violence). It is *never* possible to know for certain that an event will *not* occur in a given

situation. The fact that the Smith family in Figure 4.1 are deemed to be high risk does not mean that the adverse event will necessarily happen if no one intervenes. The fact that the Tate family are deemed to be low risk does not mean that we can be quite sure that the adverse event will not happen even in their case.

We know from studies such as Greenland (1987) that (say) a premature baby in a single parent household with a mother under 20 on a low income who uses drugs and has committed violent offences is more likely to die as a result of child abuse or neglect than a baby born at full term living in a comfortably-off two-parent family where both parents are in their thirties and there is no history of drug abuse or violence. This is not to say that the children of all young, poor, drug-abusing single-parent mothers will die from abuse or neglect. Far from it, the vast majority will not. Nor is it to say that no children of well-to-do, mature, married couples die from abuse or neglect. Some do. All we can say is that fatal abuse is more likely in the former situation, though in the case of this particular kind of adverse event, still very unlikely indeed.

So my pyramid could be viewed as an ascending series of bands, each one representing an increasing probability of the adverse event occurring (see Figure 4.2).

Of course, in practice, professionals seldom feel able to assign anything like a precise numerical value on the probability of an adverse event occurring, but if an assessment of risk is to mean anything, they should be able to say whether they think the event is more likely than not to happen,

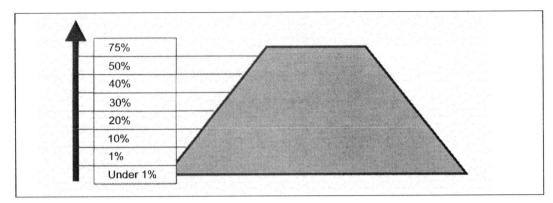

Figure 4.2   Likelihood of adverse event

whether they think there is about a fifty-fifty chance and so on. For the purposes of the discussion I will therefore make the assumption that they are able to give some sort of numerical value to the risk of given events occurring.

Having assigned families to different bands of risk, the next difficulty for the professionals is determining what is an *acceptable* level of risk. This is a value judgement, not fully reducible to rational analysis. In different cultures, social classes, historical epochs and even in different parts of the country, very different views exist or have existed about what constitutes an acceptable level of risk to a child and what level of risk warrants professional intervention. However, in practice, child protection agencies, individually and collectively operate various thresholds. For example, in the English and Welsh system at the time of writing, the following are some key thresholds:

- The threshold at which a family is accepted as being in need of services.
- The threshold at which the names of children are placed on the Child Protection Register (DoH, 1999: 55).
- The threshold at which care proceedings are initiated (*Children Act 1989*, Section 31).
- The threshold at which use of an Emergency Protection Order (*Children Act 1989*, Sections 44–6) is considered to be warranted to remove children immediately from home.

Those who make these judgements would understandably be hard pushed to state the precise likelihood of risk at which these thresholds are drawn, not least because these judgements are rarely made on the basis of the

risk of a single adverse event, but rather on the basis of a constellation of adverse events occurring which in English and Welsh law are collectively referred to as 'significant harm' (see, for example, *Children Act 1989*, Section 47 (1) (b)). However, in principle, a threshold is a line drawn across a pyramid of risk. If a family falls above the line one course of action is taken. If a family falls below the line another course of action is taken (see Figure 4.3).

Here, the Smith family are above the threshold. The Desai family, though also some way up the risk pyramid, are below it. What is at stake here could be a decision to place the children on the child protection register, or a decision to initiate court proceedings. The risk of a particular adverse event occurring in the Smith family (or more likely, the risk of a number of different adverse events) is considered sufficient for the professional decision-makers to treat them in a different way to the Desais, even though the risk is not considered negligible in the case of the Desais themselves. A line has to be drawn somewhere.

False negatives and false positives

Now let us pretend for a moment that we can look forward into the future and see how things would actually turn out for the families in this pyramid if no action was taken. Let us also assume (ambitiously) that the numerical estimations of risk arrived at by the risk assessment are accurate. It follows if we consider those families assigned to the top band in Figure 4.2, where the likelihood of the event happening was estimated at 75 per cent, in due course the event would indeed occur in 75 per cent of cases,

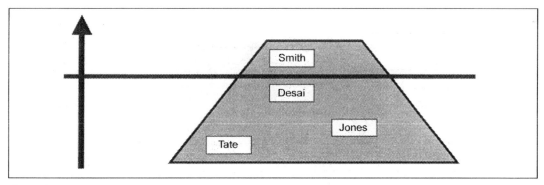

Figure 4.3   A threshold

but in 25 per cent of cases it would not occur. (This is what a 75 per cent probability means: the event will occur in 75 out of every hundred situations of the specified type.) In the bottom band, where it was estimated that the likelihood of the event happening was less than 1 per cent, it would not have occurred in over 99 per cent of cases. The imaginary position in the future can be represented by Figure 4.4 where the dark band represents those families where the adverse event has actually occurred. The dark band gets wider as we move up the pyramid because the likelihood of the event occurring – and therefore the proportion of families within a band where it does in fact occur – increases.

Now let us put the threshold back into the picture (Figure 4.5) and let us assume for the purposes of discussion that it is the threshold at which some action would be taken which really would have prevented the adverse event from occurring. Let us assume, for instance, that it is the threshold at which a child is actually physically removed from a family.

What we see here is, above the threshold, a darkly shaded area that represents those cases where protective action has been taken to prevent an adverse event that would otherwise have occurred and a lightly shaded area where protective action has been taken even though, in fact, the adverse event would never have occurred if action had not been taken. The former are labelled TP for True Positives, the latter FP for False Positives. Below the line is a large lightly shaded area, where the protective action was not taken and the adverse event never happened, and a smaller darkly shaded area where the protective action was also not taken but where the adverse event did in fact happen. These are, respectively, True Negatives and False Negatives. When the adverse event in question is the fatal injury of a child, False Negatives are the nightmare scenario for British child protection professionals. These are the children of whom it will be said that the professional agencies failed in their job and allowed the child to die. Sometimes such a charge is valid, sometimes it is based (as we have

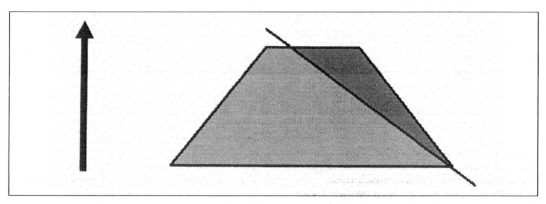

Figure 4.4   Looking into the future

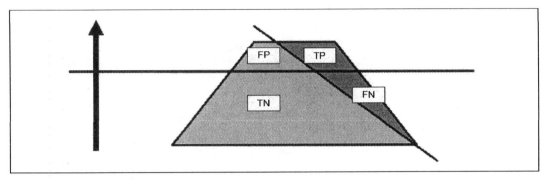

Figure 4.5   True and false negatives, true and false positives

already discussed) on a fundamental misunderstanding of what is entailed in risk assessment, and what can feasibly be asked of child protection professionals.

False negatives are extremely easy to spot with the benefit of hindsight. False positives on the other hand often can't be spotted even after the event because we can never be sure what *would* have happened. One fear that I have about this is that the relative invisibility of false positives as compared to the very high visibility of false negatives is likely to result in a dynamic that leads towards more and more interventionist practice (this might go some way, for example, towards explaining the steady increase in the use of statutory powers in the UK over the last decade, see Figure 4.6).

But the fact is that False Positives can also be a disaster for a child. A false positive might mean a family broken up, a child separated from parents in order to avoid a perceived danger, which in fact would never actually have come to pass.

Even though individual cases are harder to spot, child protection professionals and the general public are very aware of this. As a former child protection professional I have often been haunted by cases where I was involved in removing children from their parents. Was this draconian action justified? Would the adverse events that we were trying to avoid actually have happened? (The worry is even greater of course when the child's experience in substitute care has not been a good one, something I will return to presently.)

The problem is that 'if we try to reduce one type of error then, given the same level of professional skill, we shall increase the other type' (Munro and Calder, 2005: 441). In a given context of skills and resources, you can only reduce the number of false positives by increasing the number of false negatives. This can easily be seen by moving the threshold up and down my pyramid diagram. Figure 4.7 shows that a high threshold means fewer false positives (lightly shaded areas above the line) but more

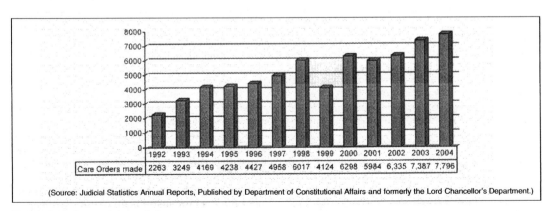

| Care Orders made | 2263 | 3249 | 4169 | 4238 | 4427 | 4958 | 6017 | 4124 | 6298 | 5984 | 6,335 | 7,387 | 7,796 |

(Source: Judicial Statistics Annual Reports, Published by Department of Constitutional Affairs and formerly the Lord Chancellor's Department.)

Figure 4.6   Care orders made by year

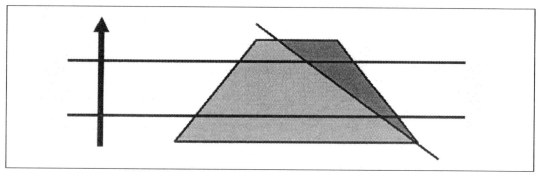

Figure 4.7 High and low thresholds

false negatives (dark areas below the line) while a lower threshold means more false positives and less false negatives, though it is important to note that the picture is further complicated in practice by the different resource implications of setting thresholds in different places. (Setting a lower threshold for access to any service means that this service will either need to take more resources from elsewhere, or it will have to be provided in a watered-down form.)

What seems to happen in actual fact is an oscillation, a swinging pendulum. When public concern is centred on false negatives, thresholds move down. When public concern rises about children separated needlessly from their parents, or about excessive state intervention in families, thresholds move up. (The dip in care orders in 1999 which you can see if you look back at Figure 4.6, is perhaps an instance of this.) Either way, the shift can be presented – or 'spun' – in the political arena as progress, as a step which will avoid the making of mistakes in the future, because in a sense this is always true: a move in either direction really *will* reduce mistakes of one kind or the other. But the downsides of such threshold shifts, the inevitable trade-offs, are seldom openly acknowledged and are sometimes ingeniously obscured by rhetoric ('spin') which seems to imply that thresholds can move in two opposite directions at the same time. Thus, discussing the political agenda set out in the Green Paper *Every Child Matters* (DfES, 2003) Eileen Munro and Martin Calder observe:

[The government] want to shift practitioners' focus to-wards preventative services; this has the logical implica-tion of shifting the focus away from its current emphasis on child protection. The consequences of this have not been explicitly addressed, leaving it to agencies and individual

practitioners to grapple with the inconsistency of being told to focus on family support without taking attention away from child protection.
(Munro and Calder, 2003: 444. Their emphasis)

Stripped of political 'spin' and magical thinking, the problem of where to draw thresholds for interventions of various kinds – or even thresholds at which a more thorough assessment should be carried out – is a very complex matter, involving painful choices between different combinations of desirable and undesirable outcomes. As Munro and Calder (2005: 441) point out, given that both false negative errors and false positive errors are politically unacceptable, the recourse that child protection agencies seem to take is to invest more and more resources in the investigative function in the hope that – to use my terminology rather than theirs – more accurate placement of families on the pyramid of risk will result, in the hope that this will reduce the likelihood of families falling on the wrong side of thresholds.

However, this course of action *itself* carries costs and creates new dangers because it involves diversion of resources into child protection investigation and away from other activities such as prevention or intervention. Neil Guterman speaks of 'an increasingly narrowed focus on screening, decision-making and monitoring activities, driving out any remaining capacity to provide direct services to families' (Guterman, 2001: 4), and while he is speaking of the situation in the USA, his words ring true in a UK context also. Incidentally, this narrowed focus may also fail to achieve *even its desired objective* if the emphasis on information-gathering results in no more than 'an unwieldy heap of uninterpreted data' (Munro, 2005: 540).

Risk thresholds applied to intervention

In some contexts a false positive is a relatively benign phenomenon. We do not resent all the checks and double-checks that are carried out by the crew of an airliner before it takes off – for example the fact that the doors are locked by one air hostess and then immediately checked by another – even though in most cases the plane would arrive safely at its destination even if these checks had not been carried out. The checks and double-checks may perhaps result in some delay, but this seems a trivial cost to us in the context of our whole lives. We don't mind a 'belts and braces' approach to reducing the risk of a plane crash because the belts and braces themselves are fairly innocuous.

Child protection, however, is not like this. The belts and the braces can in themselves cause harm. Actions taken to reduce the probability of one kind of adverse event will typically increase the probability of other kinds. Indeed, any intrusion by the child protection system into a family runs the risk of making things worse, as Neil Guterman points out:

> The adversarial and stigmatising nature of protective services intervention, although aimed at promoting children's safety, can rather jeopardise parents' feelings of support and confidence during a highly vulnerable time. To the extent that such intervention thus engenders in parents deeper feelings of powerlessness and adds additional ecological challenges, it may even heighten the risk of child maltreatment – precisely the opposite of the stated purpose of the intervention.
>
> (Guterman, 2001: 49)

Child protection professionals should therefore not see intervention as being analogous to an air hostess double-checking a door – something that may be unnecessary but is always benign – though I think some child protection professionals *do* mistakenly see it in this way. A better comparison would be with a surgeon considering an operation that might bring benefits but could create new problems or even result in death. The air hostess can say 'better safe than sorry' but the surgeon cannot honestly do so, because neither option – to operate or not to operate – represents safety.

The closest child protection equivalent to radical surgery is perhaps permanent removal of a child from their own family for placement in a substitute family. This obviously eliminates the specific risks that the child faced in their family of origin, but it exposes the child to new risks. Actual abuse in foster and adoptive homes is far from unknown, for one thing, but placement in public care can often be harmful in other ways. Placement breakdowns and multiple placement moves – potentially devastating in their effects on a child's self-esteem and capacity to trust – are really quite common experiences for children in public care (see Beckett and McKeigue, 2003, for some examples).

I suggested earlier that a full risk assessment in respect of a child should look not only at the risks entailed in the current situation but also at the risks entailed in the various courses of action that might be taken. I am not sure that this is always done by child protection professionals, who can be overly reassured by their own good intentions. For example, as June Thoburn has pointed out, there was a time when 'the reader of the statement "the plan is permanence" at the end of a court report was led to believe that to plan for permanence was to achieve it' (Thoburn, 2002: 514). But in fact, if the best interests of the child are to be served, exactly the same test should be applied to a plan for permanent placement as to a plan for a child to return home. What are we realistically going to be able to offer? What are the risks this would pose to the child? What constitutes an acceptable threshold of risk? On the basis of what we know about this child and the circumstances – including our own skills and resources – does our plan fall above or below this threshold?

Outcome studies reveal that the risks involved in 'permanent placement' are actually quite high. Borland et al. (1991), looking at permanent placements between three and five years on, found that 20 per cent of the placements had in fact broken down. Age at placement was the most important of a number of different variables associated with increased risk of breakdown: the likelihood of a placement breaking down for a child in the 11–14 age group was almost 37 per cent. Thoburn et al. studied another cohort of permanent placements and found a breakdown rate that was 24 per cent overall, 29 per cent in the 5–8 age group and nearly 50 per cent in the 10–12 age group (Thoburn et al., 2000: 173). Studies such as these make it perfectly feasible to arrange children in a pyramid of risk based on the likelihood of a permanent placement failing. The question then is where we should draw the threshold above which permanent placement is no longer an appropriate route to go down? (At what risk of placement breakdown is it no longer appropriate to present a new family to a child as her 'forever family'? 5 per cent? 20 per cent? 50 per cent?) This type of question should be no less important, and no less to the forefront of our minds, than questions about what levels of risk are tolerable *within* natural families.

Writing not about child protection but about medical practice, Gerd Gigerenzer comments:

> *Many a physician confronts the patient with an apparent choice between certainty and risk rather than a choice between risks. Each alternative carries its own uncertain consequences, which need to be compared for an informed decision to be made.*
>
> (Gigerenzer, 2002: 99)

In just the same way, decisions about intervention in a child protection context need to be conceptualised as a choice between risks.

The base-rate fallacy

Figure 4.5 was intended to illustrate a particular point about thresholds, but in one important way it was misleading, for in respect of many kinds of risk the ratio of false and true positives is vastly different from the one suggested by this illustration. This is particularly so in respect of very rare events such as death caused by child abuse or neglect. The problem can be illustrated as follows.

Suppose that we possessed a formula into which we could convert information about families into numerical values and then combine these to arrive at a total score. Suppose that this score would be positive for parents who would kill their children through abuse or neglect, and negative for those who would not. Let us suppose that this formula had been thoroughly tested and shown to work with *100 per cent* of families who would otherwise go on to kill a baby, correctly giving them a positive score. (In other words there would be no false negatives at all). And let us suppose that it had also been proven to work with 99 per cent of those who would not go on to kill their child, correctly giving them a negative score, leaving a mere one per cent false positive rate. This would be an extraordinarily reliable tool, *far* more precise than any that actually exist or could exist. If you used this formula to place families above or below a fatal abuse threshold, it would accurately place above the threshold *every single one* of the five or so babies per million who would die without protective intervention.

I am guessing that, unless you have encountered this kind of example before or are well versed in the theory of probability, you will be thinking that this formula (if it existed) would solve the problem of predicting fatal child abuse. But in fact it wouldn't. The fact is that the five children correctly identified would be hidden among almost *ten thousand* others. This is because, with something as rare as child murder, the apparently tiny one per cent false positive rate would still be big enough to swamp the accurate predictions. It may be only one per cent, but it is one per cent of a million (or, at any rate, of a million minus five). Figure 4.8 tries to represent this. You can see how all the positives (shaded dark) are indeed true positives, correctly placed above the threshold, but how they are nevertheless swamped by the false positives (shaded light) – which our formula also places above the threshold.

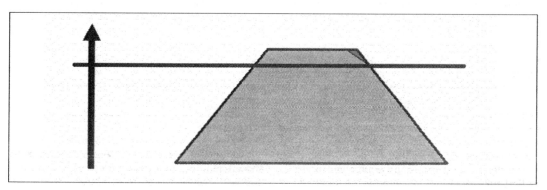

Figure 4.8   True positives swamped by false ones

Actually even this diagram drastically over-estimates the ratio of true positives to false ones. The narrow wedge of true positives above the threshold, if truly drawn to scale, would be no wider than the line on the edge of the pyramid. The threshold should really also be drawn much higher, since those in the positive-scoring group above the threshold would constitute only one per cent of the total population.

If you were misled by the absence of false negatives and the very low percentage of false positives in my example into thinking that the formula would more or less exactly sort out the children who would be killed from the others, then you were victim to another common cognitive illusion known as the base-rate fallacy (Gigerenzer, 2002: 213–14). Like the hindsight fallacy, this illusion can result in child protection failures seeming much more crassly incompetent that they actually are. The business of identifying situations where a child might die without protective intervention is often wrongly imagined to be simply a matter of placing children accurately above or below a risk threshold. 'How could this child have failed to stand out?' is a typical question that is asked when the long sad catalogue of known family problems and worrying incidents emerges into the public domain after some tragic event, and indeed if you pick any well-known case where a child has died and compare the case with an average family, the differences do seem very obvious indeed.

But child protection agencies don't deal with average families. They are not as a rule failing to identify families where there are lots of problems and risk factors. What they are failing to do is to pick out which of those obviously risky families to focus on, given that they can't simultaneously focus on them all. You can quite correctly identify the small minority of families where there are many risk factors, but yet still fail to identify the far, far tinier minority *within* that high risk category where a catastrophic event will occur without immediate intervention.

In the past, when I was the manager of a social work team, I was often faced with precisely this type of dilemma when going through a batch of new referrals and deciding which ones needed allocating quickly. It was easy to eliminate those where there seemed to be no imminent risks. The difficulty lay in determining which of the cases still remaining should be immediately followed up, given that we could not immediately follow up them all. *Whichever* ones I chose, I could not be certain that one of the others would not, in fact, turn out to have a catastrophic outcome which, with hindsight, would look predictable. But without hindsight it simply was not possible to know. I am clear in my own mind that the fact that no child died 'on my watch' is as much a matter of luck as of judgement. (Incidentally, while the rather primitive system whereby a manager sorts through a pile of referrals may now have been supplanted by a more complex one involving several levels of assessment, exactly the same principles apply to each stage in that process. At the end of every stage someone, based on necessarily limited information, must choose which cases to progress to the next stage.)

Conclusion

I have offered what some might feel to be a rather gloomy picture of risk assessment and its limitations. It is not my intention to be negative, however, but rather, within the limits of my own understanding, to be *realistic*. I think that the child protection system in the UK has been damaged and distorted as a result of essentially irrational decision-making resulting from cognitive illusions, 'spin' and magical thinking. We have got ourselves into a position where the criterion of success by which the system is judged is that it should, at the minimum, achieve the impossible. And by striving for the impossible – by aiming for an impossibly high level of certainty about the dangers faced by individual children – we have created a system that serves families and children less well than would a system based on a more realistic understanding of what is possible and what is not.

Thresholds are important. For resource reasons, for reasons to do with the right to privacy and self-determination and for reasons to do with the negative consequences of intervention itself, it is both inevitable and appropriate that the most extreme interventions should be focused only on those situations where the risks of adverse events are high. For all the same reasons it makes sense that there should be progressively lower thresholds for less intrusive interventions and for various levels of assessment. But child protection professionals should be absolutely clear, both with themselves and with their political masters, that a threshold is – and only ever can be – a line drawn across a pyramid of probability, not a line that neatly divides families that will definitely seriously harm their children from families that definitely will not.

References

Beckett, C. and McKeigue, B. (2003) 'Children in Limbo: Case where Care Proceedings have taken Two Years or More'. *Adoption and Fostering*, 27: 3, 31–40.

Borland, M., O'Hara, G. and Tresiliotis, J. (1991) 'Placement Outcomes for Children with Special Needs'. *Adoption and Fostering*, 15: 2, 1991.

DoH (1999) *Working Together: A Guide to Interagency Working to Safeguard and Promote the Welfare of Children*. London: Stationery Office.

Elster, J. (1989) *Solomonic Judgements*. Cambridge: Cambridge University Press.

Gigerenzer, G. (2002) *Reckoning with Risk*. London: Penguin.

Greenland, C. (1987) *Preventing CAN Deaths: An International Study of Deaths due to Child Abuse and Neglect*. London: Tavistock.

Guterman, N. (2001) *Stopping Child Maltreatment before it Starts: Emerging Horizons in Home Visitation Services*. Thousand Oaks, CA: Sage.

Hall, N. (1991) *The New Scientist Guide to Chaos*. Harmondsworth: Penguin.

London Borough of Greenwich (1987) *A Child in Mind: The Report of the Commission of Inquiry into the Circumstances Surrounding the Death of Kimberley Carlisle*. London: London Borough of Greenwich.

Macdonald, K. and Macdonald, G. (1999) 'Perceptions of Risk', pp. 17–52. In Parsloe, P. (Ed.) (1999) *Risk Assessment in Social Work and Social Care*, London: Jessica Kingsley.

Munro, E. (2005) 'A Systems Approach to Investigating Child Abuse Deaths', *British Journal of Social Work*, 35: 4, 531–46.

Munro, E. and Calder, M. (2005) Where has Child Protection Gone? *The Political Quarterly*, 76: 3, 439–45.

Thoburn, J. (2002) 'Out-of-home Care for the Abused or Neglected Child: Research, Policy and Practice'. In Wilson, K. and James, A. (Eds.) *The Child Protection Handbook*, 2nd Edn. Edinburgh: Baillière Tindall, pp. 514–37.

Thoburn, J., Norford, L. and Parvez Rashid, S. (2000) *Permanent Family Placement for Children of Minority Ethnic Origin*. London: Jessica Kingsley.

CHAPTER 5

Professional Judgement and the Risk Assessment Process

Anne Hollows

The purpose of this chapter is to explore the contribution of theory and research about professional judgement making to the analysis and assessment of risk in social work with children and families. It begins with an overview of professional judgement making in social work and outlines the principles of judgement making, before examining some of the weaknesses of current practice in risk assessment and concluding with a discussion of how we may harness and apply knowledge about judgement making to promote better practice in identifying and managing 'risks' and 'concerns' in professional practice. The chapter has been written in the recognition that, although social work practice is, and is likely to remain, central to decision making about the assessment and management of risk, it is taking place in a changing world of professional practice. The development of Children and Young People's services as an integrated, multi-professional endeavour means that a wide range of professionals may be more actively involved in the assessment and management of risk. This chapter therefore also acknowledges critical issues in inter-professional practice, in particular highlighting areas of communication difficulties and inter-professional misunderstanding, which require attention within the new service environment.

What is professional judgement?

The centrality of professional judgement to the process of assessment and case management within social work is far from innovatory, having first been recognised by one of the early social work academics, Mary Richmond (Nurius and Gibson, 1917). Its significance in the social work professional task has always been challenged by both professional epistemologies and political ideologies. During the 90s there were claims among UK writers that judgement making had been effectively – and possibly deliberately – ruled out of the social work task (Henkel, 1994:

302; Pietroni, 1995: 305) by contemporary government distrust of professional mystique and its associated power. By the end of that decade however, a change of government led to new guidance in the *Framework for the Assessment of Children in Need and their Families* that placed a high priority on professional judgement, grounded in the knowledge base for practice (DoH, 2000). Neither the Framework, nor the accompanying Practice Guidance (DoH, 2000), nor any of the subsequent publications from government have provided a clear view of what professional judgement is and how it should be exercised, nor has there been any clear guidance on how it might link with evidence based practice (Webb, 2002).

The literature on professional judgements is closely entwined with that on decision making. Indeed, many of the contested issues about the one apply equally to the other. Nonetheless, there is a clear message from writers about judgement and decision making that professional judgements are made *before* decisions are taken. Goldstein's description of judgement making as the ways in which people 'integrate multiple, probabilistic, potentially conflicting cues to arrive at an understanding of the situation' as opposed to *decision making* in which people 'choose what to do next in the face of uncertain consequences and conflicting goals' (Goldstein, 1997). Judgement, then, is about understanding a situation. It must therefore involve analysis and synthesis of a range of cues and facts. While judgement making is less likely to be concerned with some of the characteristics of decision making – particularly decision making in groups – many of the difficulties in decision making are also experienced in judgment making.

These difficulties surround the possibility of accuracy and error. In short, there is considerable evidence from research that clinical judgement is inherently unsafe when compared with the results of actuarially based assessment tools (see for example Kahneman, Slovic et al., 1982; Nurius and Gibson, 1990). There is, however, another perspective. Plous, an advocate of actuarial judgement, questions whether the research on the outcomes of clinical judgement is subject to the same errors as the judgements that are the subject of criticism (Plous, 1993). When Hammond, who has devised a 'third way' of judgement making, asks whether anyone would choose intuitive analysis of a problem compared with a systematic, research driven model (Hammond, 1996) his irony is immediately apparent. His view is that there are, quite simply, horses for courses in the judgement making stakes. Different approaches to judgement making will be more – or less – effective in different circumstances. To make effective actuarial judgements requires good and accurate information, a strong evidence base of research on outcomes and time to undertake the work. In reality, the evidence base for the sort of multi-problem situations that make up the caseload of child and family practitioners is limited, while many judgements are made where information is uncertain and where there is what Hammond describes as multiple, fallible indicators. In his 'third way' approach Hammond does not, however, throw actuarial judgement out of the window. He recognises that it has a place for some circumstances and he produces a continuum 'The cognitive continuum' (Hammond, 1987) of judgement making that enables a match between situations and circumstances and mode of judgement making. Where time is of the essence, intuitive judgement making is often all that is available. Moving along the continuum, there is peer aided judgement including supervision, system or protocol aided judgement, quasi experiment (trying things out) and finally actuarial judgement (Hollows, 2003). The expertise in social work – or indeed any other field – is, according to Hammond, the ability to match the judgement with the optimal approach and, in a complex case, to combine different forms of judgement making across the continuum he provides.

Hammond has provided a route map for judgement making that validates clinical judgement as incorporating a range of approaches. This leaves, however, a fundamental criticism of the judgement making *practice* of social workers, namely the biases and distortions plainly evident in professional judgements. Indeed, Nurius and Gibson (1990) have provided a detailed and daunting typology of the errors arising from inferential short cuts (known as heuristics in the judgement literature). Munro, in her extensive writing (Munro, 1999, 2002, 2005)

has critiqued these issues, but has drawn the conclusion that the greatest potential for error lies in the combination of confirmatory bias, coupled with a strong reluctance to change a view. In practice, this means that social workers get a 'frame' on a case too quickly, and seek out information that will confirm that view. New information is ruled out unless it conforms to the previous view. It may be that teaching *Bayes Theorem* to social workers could assist in their recognition of the need to change judgements in the light of new information (Macdonald, 2001) . On the other hand a clear awareness of the inherent weaknesses in both practice and the systems of the organisations in which social workers operate could go a long way to reducing the problems. There is an important distinction between intuitive reasoning and confirmatory bias. The one depends on extensive knowledge and experience – indeed Schon would suggest that it is the apotheosis of professional expertise (Schon, 1983). But it must be tested and challenged through enquiry. The other is a starting point based on a mental short cut or heuristic that defines and frames further enquiry, thus pre-determining the outcome of enquiry. Hammond (1996) cites a range of eminent scientific sources who suggest that intuition is the starting point for many mathematical developments and he provides a series of measures within his continuum that are designed to provide constant challenges to initial thinking as new information becomes available. Hammond's concept of peer-aided judgement is usually known in social work as supervision. That does not mean the managerial supervision that so many practitioners experience, but the careful and mutual testing of ideas against evidence, seeking out potential threats and biases.

The problem of changing one's mind is more complex. Systems, structures and workplace cultures mean that many practitioners feel that changing their mind could be seen as a sign of weakness (Hollows, 2001).

The value of professional judgement in risk assessment is to assist in establishing the nature of the problem and the appropriate response in the short, medium and longer term, relating this to decision thresholds, determining interventions and assessing progress and consequent actions.

The key to effective use of judgement in social work practice is the importance of seeing professional or clinical judgement as a sequence of judgements, rather than a single process, in a way that mirrors the 'Assess, Plan, Intervene, Review 'framework of contemporary practice (Hollows, 2001, 2003; Hollows and Nelson, 2006). The sequence involves:

- critical appraisal/hypothesising
- holding judgements
- issues judgements
- strategic judgements
- evaluation judgements

In summary, the sequence starts with *critical appraisal*: a sceptical examination of the available information to identify fact, opinion and what may sometimes be classed as little more than gossip – though not necessarily discounted. The initial stages of assessment may require a *holding judgement* designed to enable the worker to gain time, stability and information while stabilising the situation for the children in the family. At this stage the overall goal is to progress to a full assessment while keeping the children safe and avoiding any reduction of options for the future. The next stage requires a detailed judgement about the issues in the case, acute and long standing. This enables a strategy to be developed including a careful assessment of management of the issues as well as change and reparative interventions. Following on from this there must always be an evaluation to establish what has changed or helped, what more may need to be done, or indeed where earlier judgements should be revised. In a complex case this would take place cyclically. Before turning to the potential of such a model to support risk assessment we will now address some of the current challenges to risk assessment.

Challenges to risk assessment in contemporary practice

Goldstein's description of judgement making outlined above (Goldstein, 1997) resonates with much of the daily activity of social workers, particularly those working in contemporary local authority settings. The emphasis of local authority social work has migrated away from early interventions and preventive work to support families, to the relentless safeguarding task. With a caseload of what are known as 'high risk' situations, social workers are called upon to try to make sense of information that is often ambiguous and where every latest piece of

information seems to conflict with previous understanding – Hammond's 'multiple fallible indicators'. Social workers in local authority settings now carry caseloads in which the majority of cases threaten the sort of undesirable outcomes that are synonymous with contemporary meanings of 'risk' (Beck, 1992; Munro, 2002). But as has been noted throughout this book, there has been a continuing silence from government as to the process of assessment of the complex and entrenched difficulties found in these cases. Into this vacuum, with a natural inevitability, have stepped approaches to assessing risks that carry varying levels of authenticity.

If evidence based practice is to mean anything at all, it should imply that a procedure or protocol or intervention has been developed on the basis of comprehensive research evidence, including service user and practitioner perspectives, and is then subjected to rigorous evaluation and review. As has been discussed elsewhere in this book, there are at best mixed reviews of the virtue and value of such tools. There is also a continuing thread of anecdotal evidence which confirms Doueck's findings (Doueck, English, et al., 1993) that child protection workers are able to 'fix' the outcome of a risk assessment tool to match their professional judgement.

But without a way of doing risk assessment there is some evidence from discussion with practitioners (Dalgleish and Hollows, forthcoming) that there is considerable variation in the understanding of the concept of risk. There has also emerged also a way of referring to cases, which I call 'risk talk'.

Risk talk

Listening to social workers and other practitioners with children discussing risk is a central component of understanding the weaknesses and the strengths of current practice (Dalgleish and Hollows, forthcoming). Risk, as we have seen throughout this book, is a complex concept and one which few professionals grasp in an abstract sense, notwithstanding the many journal articles, books and training courses that focus on it. In practice, the word 'risk' is used in conversation as if the word had a precise meaning. Practitioners, whether discussing a case within or between occupational groups working with children use the terms 'low', 'medium' and 'high' (sometimes even 'very high') to categorise and define the level of their concerns about a family and in particular about the safety of the children. The phrase 'careless talk costs lives' is somewhat apt here: Dalgleish's work has shown us that these terms rarely reflect a consistent, quantifiable, or mutually recognised level of concern (Dalgleish, 2003). But the level of risk is not the only concern here. The often heard expression 'there's a lot of risk' applied to a case suggests that risk itself is a unitary concept; that there is a shared, if tacit, understanding of what the speaker refers to.

In reality, what is happening when a professional describes a case as having 'a lot of risk' is that they are signalling considerable concern about a situation involving children. The implications are that they need support, guidance, help or even respite. In this way, 'risk' has become a synonym for individual professional anxiety and the unbearable nature of the social work task. Within the turbulence, stress and tension of the professional experience of social work (Hughes and Pengelly, 1997) this may signal the need for peer or manager support, but in terms of the immediate professional task, the concept of risk needs to be carefully unpacked before the required support and guidance can be given. The concern expressed in the word 'risk' may be about the nature and extent of a parent or carer's behaviour, about a child's behaviour or response, or about environmental situations. It may reflect concerns about immediate or longer-term consequential outcomes for children. It may be about the agglomeration of a range of different 'risk factors' in a case. It may be about the difficulty in securing effective risk management strategies and resources. Indeed, it may be more than one of these possibilities. Whatever the meanings there is little doubt that, presented in these terms, the professional is expressing an undigested assessment of risk in terms of specific issues, or of cause and likely or possible effect. As such, these concerns cannot effectively be shared within or between professional groups, except to signify that 'something must be done'. The impact of this is to encourage a rush to action, and may not be based on an analysis of the issues or needs in the case.

At its heart, the 'lot of risk' concept is closer to the findings of Farmer and Owen's study than to some of the more recent research findings discussed below (Farmer and Owen, 1995). It fits closely with the approach they identified to

analysis within assessment in which problems were merely listed as if the weight of problems on its own would guarantee registration as a child protection case or define the risks in the case. As a short cut approach, or judgement heuristic, there is some degree of relationship between the number of difficulties and the severity of the outcome for children. There are, however, at least two provisos and a caveat to this relationship. The first proviso is the recognition that it is not simply the presence of a problem but its nature that can cause difficulties. A parent may have mental health problems, or substance using problems, but may still be able to provide satisfactory parenting. This is, in a nutshell, the difficulty of the checklist approach to risk assessment, for example the widely used (in North America and Australia) Structured Decision Making approach. It is the qualification of the so-called 'risk factors' by detailed supplementary information that enables us to distinguish between the successfully methadone managed parent and the one who is out-of-control in their substance dependence (Adams, 1999).

The second proviso is the need to recognise that some of the 'difficulties' or 'risk factors' inevitably march together. To be a young single mother, for example, is very often to be poor, socially isolated, living in a less desirable neighbourhood, have no job and often have little contact with friends and family (Browne and Herbert, 1997). While all of these factors signify *needs* they do not necessarily ratchet up the level of *risk* in a case. It is the likelihood that the factors will lead to adverse outcomes, rather than simply their presence, that is the issue. That requires consideration of the processes by which a factor will activate harmful behaviours or situations for a child.

The caveat is that a simple weighing of the number of factors, rather than their nature and the mechanisms that might convert them to negative actions represents a failure to recognise the nature of the problem for families and children who are negotiating a number of difficulties simultaneously. The compound incidence of challenges is in itself a cause of yet another difficulty, namely family stress (Kelley, 1992; Rodriguez and Green, 1997; Ghate and Hazel, 2002) that rarely features within risk assessments. It is possibly within this aspect of compound factors that the greatest threat to children's well being arises.

The intrinsic problems of the 'a lot of risk' concept, then, are the misuse and inter-professional misunderstanding of the word 'risk' and the absence of any sense of the scale, nature, agency or timing of the risk. Leaving aside the fascinating semantic detours regarding the derivation of the word 'risk' and its contemporary usage in the vernacular of practice, the concept of risk is, in contemporary social work terms inextricably linked with harmful consequences, brought about through actions or prevailing circumstances. It has to be considered in terms of the possibility that something (adverse) will happen and that harm to someone will ensue. There is an implicit assumption that the person harmed is in some way vulnerable or unable to defend themselves against the harm. 'Risk factors', then, means factors of both an acute and a long standing nature that may contribute to the likelihood of adverse consequences. Within the UK jurisdictions, the terminology for such adversity is 'significant harm' (*Children Act 1989*, s 31). Significant harm has implications for parents and carers as well as for society (Bentovim, 1998). The presence of particular features in a case that are linked with significant harm would in turn suggest which interventions are most likely to deliver a pay-off in terms of reduction of the level of risk of adversity for the children in the case.

Another element of this undifferentiated risk talk is that it omits any recognition of the need to identify strengths. Risk balancing requires the careful and measured identification of strengths, if it is to be more than superficial. It offers the potential to incorporate an empowerment approach into safeguarding practice.

The contribution of professional judgement

Important obstacles to effective assessment of risk can be identified from the judgement literature (Dalgleish and Hollows, forthcoming) which also provides frameworks to improve practice:

- The unknown – inadequate knowledge of signs and symptoms or law policy and procedure.
- The 'busy screen' – the need to identify what is important from a 'flood of data'.
- Interpretation – being able to correctly interpret information in the context of assessing risk.

- Status of information – failure to distinguish fact from opinion, being too trusting and uncritical.
- Unappreciated data – information may not be appreciated if it has come from a source that is distrusted.
- The decoy of dual pathology – information may be missed if the receiver is decoyed by a different problem.

Fundamental to the assessment of risk is the detailed collection of information and analysis of the issues in the case. Who? What? When? Where? Why? and How? are key questions that require answers. At the start of an assessment, referral information may heighten concerns and anxieties – not least because some referrers know what is required to gain access to services. Children's professionals will often form a picture in their minds of the worst case scenario at this stage in the case (Dalgleish and Hollows, forthcoming). Goldstein's notion of choosing what to do next in the face of uncertain consequences and conflicting goals (Goldstein, 1997) is central to the task of judgement making and the concept of critical appraisal (Sheppard, Newstead et al., 2000) enables early information to be disaggregated into fact, opinion and gossip. At the same time this process guards against the confirmatory bias that can be engendered by early, graphic descriptions of injuries or home conditions. Hammond (1996) notes that pictorial images encourage intuitive judgements, which will require testing through peer supervision at the very least. Judgements in the early stages of a case are based on limited information, and the social worker's task is to keep the children safe while trying to gain time so that information can be gained and the situation can be stabilised. Here the holding judgement can be a real asset in risk assessments. One of the key elements of a holding judgement is that as far as possible it should not prejudice future decisions or bind future actions. A holding judgement is essentially an assessment strategy. At this stage in a risk assessment it is essential to try to keep options open wherever possible. While continually ensuring the child's safety, the central feature of practice at this stage is the gathering of necessary information. The ability to gather this information can often obstruct assessment (Munro, 2005). The nature of information that would contribute to an effective assessment of risk is not always recognised by social workers (Corby, 2003;

Warner, 2003). At this critical stage of the risk assessment, then, the first two elements of the model of judgement making can provide support to the crucial stage of gathering information, through a critical appraisal of the initial case information and a holding judgement to stabilise the case and produce a strategy for collecting the information.

The next stage of risk assessment is to analyse the information. This is an area where practice often needs support. In research on judgement making (Hollows, 2001), it was found that there could be errors of judgement in some cases and an absence of judgement in some others. One of the most notable of these difficulties surrounds perceptions of certainty: investigators may have a false sense of security about a particular approach to eliciting information and the subsequent interpretation (e.g. medical assessments of sexual abuse in Cleveland). A further problem stems from information that is known and not assembled, where individuals may hold information that they can withhold or which is not pieced together with the rest. Sometimes this is because information does not fit the current mode of understanding. Together with the influence of assumptions made at an early stage of the assessment this demonstrates how confirmatory bias can create errors in assessment. The stage of analysing the information collected and the method of analysis adopted is critical. Here, Hammond's (1996) guidance that the expert will be able to move up and down the judgement continuum using appropriate methods to analyse different elements of the assessment is the key. It may be helpful to remind ourselves of the purpose of a risk assessment here. It is the systematic collection of information to identify if risks are involved, and if so, what these are; identifying the likelihood of their future occurrence (prediction); whether there is a need for further work; and what form this should take. It can also be used to predict the escalation of the presenting behaviour as well as the client's motivation for change (Calder, 2003). This brings us back to the issues of Who? What? When? Where? Why? and How? These are the central features of an issues judgement. What is required at this stage is considerably greater clarity than simply what might happen. It is essential to address the mechanisms by which harms can arise and here the *Framework for Assessment of Children in Need and their Families* (DoH, 2000) provides a potential model for mapping issues of

concern. What is critical here, however, is making the links between the aspects of parenting or environment that are likely to have an adverse impact on a child. It is also important to remember that judgements about issues are not intended to be an end in themselves, but to inform strategies for managing and reducing risk. The 'Why?' question has some significance here. It is simply not sufficient to say that 'mother is often binge drinking, therefore the children are neglected'. If mother is to stop drinking it is essential to know what her drinking patterns involve and what triggers them. Only then will it be possible to identify the appropriate strategies and resources to support mother in this process.

Perhaps the most difficult area of analysis is the prediction of severity of harm. This needs to incorporate both an understanding of the causation of present harm and its potential for management, as well as predictions about the likelihood of escalation. As noted above this is not just a case of describing, for example, mother's tendency to binge drink in certain situations. It needs also to be clear what the triggers for such drinking are, how often they are likely to occur and what then happens to the children. At this stage, it will in some cases be necessary to draw on assessments made by other practitioners, for example in the situation of the binge drinking mother, mental health and alcohol treatment assessments. Each of these kinds of assessments uses frameworks that owe more to actuarial models than clinical judgement. They are not, on their own, a complete risk assessment of a situation but add essential information in terms of detailed predictions about an individual in relation to a specific area of their life. It is important also to remember that actuarial assessments cannot cover all permutations of situations or undertake compound predictions in complex situations. It is therefore essential to be able to incorporate evidence from such assessments into a broader clinical judgement about risks.

The next stage of the assessment is to determine what interventions may reduce or manage the risks identified in the report. Logically, this step requires a full statement of the issues before it can be undertaken, although in some cases, actions to safeguard children may have pre-empted some considerations. This is the area of risk assessment that concerns change. Recent work (Corden and Somerton, 2004) has cast doubt on the applicability of the

Trans-Theoretical Model of Change to parenting problems. This stems from the concern that motivational approaches are appropriate for addictive behaviours, for example substance use, but will be less effective with other problematic behaviours. That means that risk assessments need to have a clear understanding of what needs to change and how that change might be accomplished. If identification of the issues in a case sometimes appears to resemble peeling off layers of an onion, it should be assumed that the interventions required will also be multilayered. The complexity of the cases that are now managed by local authority social workers is such that there is usually no single magic bullet to resolve them. This requires social workers who undertake risk assessments to be well-versed in the 'What Works' literature and to be conversant with not just the services that provide therapeutic services, but in their processes and outcomes. They need, also, to recognise that simply laying on a service or intervention may not be sufficient to make it happen. A single parent with several children who has to travel to a regular therapy session will need to consider transport and childcare. These are not simply frivolous considerations in the process of risk assessment but aspects of holistic thinking which careful professional judgement about strategies should be able to incorporate.

The final phase of the judgement model is evaluative judgements. Here, there is a clear correlation with effective risk assessment. In social work, risk assessment is not a static process designed simply to label a situation or an individual. A risk assessment that has identified all the issues and the strategy will be a tool for evaluation and review of risk as time passes and situations change. It provides the opportunity to focus on outcomes, rather than outputs, of practice and can equally provide a measure of encouragement to service users as and when they see their progress reducing the tally of risks and concerns for their family (Turnell and Essex, 2006). Within the model of professional judgement making, regular evaluative judgements also enable previous judgements to be amended if progress is not being made. Where a case is not improving it should be possible to go back to the original judgements and examine whether the issues were incorrectly identified, the strategy was in some ways inappropriate or whether other, new circumstances have intervened.

The benefits of applying the judgement framework to risk assessment, then, is not to provide a prescriptive approach to risk assessment but to harness the social worker's natural process and to fine tune the ways in which they collect, analyse and apply information in practice. All of this leads to a further dimension that has always been central to child protection but is now more critical because of the organisation of children's services. That is the process and content of inter-professional communication. Whatever the nature of inter-professional practice in children's services, social workers retain a distinct brief and need to be taken seriously by other professionals (Clifford and Burke, 2004). Being taken seriously involves articulating concerns in ways that are transparent to other professionals – as well as to service users themselves. The centrality of communication between professionals in the assessment process is well established (Reder and Duncan, 2003) but requires both mutual respect and the detailed information that is needed to make the communication effective. Risk assessment practice that relies on inaccurate and unshared meanings is never likely to enhance communications and understanding. On the other hand, a model of risk assessment that enables social workers and other professionals to clearly articulate concerns, fears, hopes and strategies and to review those in practice, will empower social workers to undertake their unique role in child protection and to win respect from other professionals. In summary, it will enable the social worker to say:

- *This was my starting point. I am aware of other potential starting points and I have borne these in mind as the assessment has proceeded.*
- *These were the actions I took to ensure that the child was safe while I gathered all the relevant information. I endeavoured to avoid actions that would prejudice future decisions.*
- *I formed the judgement that the issues causing concern in the case included these elements, and my view on the available evidence was that in these circumstances there could be harm to this degree.*
- *I therefore developed the following strategy to intervene, manage and reduce the risks in the case. These were the outcomes of the strategies.*
- *I can therefore now say that concerns identified have changed in the following ways and the level of risk to the child is now as follows.*

Interspersed with appropriate evidence from the case, this would be a model of how professional judgement could influence risk assessment practice. There is a world of difference from 'a lot of risk' – for professional self-confidence and self-esteem, for inter-professional respect and understanding and above all for children and their families.

References

Adams, P. (1999) Towards a Family Support Approach with Drug Using Parents: The Importance of Social Worker Attitudes and Knowledge. *Child Abuse Review*, 8: 15–28.

Beck, U. (1992) *Risk Society: Towards a New Modernity*. London: Sage.

Bentovim, A. (1998) Significant Harm in Context. In Adcock, M. and White, R. *Significant Harm*. 2nd edn. Croydon: Significant Publications.

Browne, K. and Herbert, M. (1997) *Preventing Family Violence*. Chichester: John Wiley.

Calder, M. (2003) The Assessment Framework. In Calder, M. and Hackett, S. *Assessment in Child Care*. Lyme Regis: Russell House Publishing.

Clifford, D. and Burke, B. (2004) Morals and Professional Dilemmas in Long Term Assessment of Children and Families. *Journal of Social Work*, 4: 3, 305–21.

Corby, B. (2003) Supporting Families and Protecting Children: Assisting Child Care Professionals in Initial Decision Making and Review of Cases. *Journal of Social Work*, 3: 2, 195–210.

Corden, J. and Somerton, J. (2004) The Trans-Theoretical Model of Change: A Reliable Blueprint for Assessment in Work with Children and Families. *British Journal of Social Work*, 34: 7, 1025–44.

Dalgleish, L. (2003) Risk, Needs and Consequences. In Calder, M. and Hackett, S. *Assessment in Child Care*. Lyme Regis: Russell House Publishing.

Dalgleish, L. and Hollows, A. (2008) *Risk Assessment and Decision Making in Child Protection*. Lyme Regis: Russell House Publishing.

DoH (2000) *Assessing Children in Need and their Families: Practice Guidance*. London: HMSO.

DoH (2000) *Framework for the Assessment of Children in Need and their Families*. London: HMSO.

Doueck, H.J., English, D.J. et al. (1993) Decision-making in Child Protective Services: A Comparison of Selected Risk-Assessment Systems. *Child Welfare*, 72: 5, 441–52.

Farmer, E. and Owen, M. (1995) *Child Protection Practice: Private Risks and Public Remedies*. London: HMSO.

Ghate, D. and Hazel, M. (2002) Parenting in Poor Environments: Stress, Support and Coping. London: Jessica Kingsley.

Goldstein, W.M. and Hogarth, R.M. (1997) Judgement and Decision Research: Some Historical Context. In Goldstein, W.M. and Hogarth, R.M. *Research on Judgement and Decision Making: Currents, Connections and Controversies*. Cambridge: Cambridge University Press.

Hammond, K.R. (1996) *Human Judgement and Social Policy: Irreducible Uncertainty, Inevitable Error, Unavoidable Injustice*. New York: Oxford University Press.

Hammond, K.R. et al. (1987) Direct Comparison of the Efficacy of Intuitive and Analytical Cognition in Expert Judgement: IEEE Transactions on Systems, Man, and Cybernetics. *SMC*, 17: 5, 753–70.

Henkel, M. (1994) The Challenge of Social Work. *British Journal of Social Work*, 28, 839–62.

Hollows, A. (2001) Good Enough Judgements: A Study of Judgement Making in Social Work With Children and Families. Reading: Department of Health and Social Care, University of Reading.

Hollows, A. (2003) The Problem of Judgements In Child Welfare. In Calder, M. and Hackett, S. *The Child Care Assessment Manual*. Lyme Regis: Russell House Publishing.

Hollows, A. and Nelson, P. (2006) Equity and Pragmatism in Judgement-Making about the Placement of Sibling Groups. *Child and Family Social Work*, 11: 4, 307–15.

Hughes, L. and Pengelly, P. (1997) *Staff Supervision in a Turbulent Environment*. London: Jessica Kingsley.

Kahneman, D., Slovic, P. et al. (Eds.) (1982) *Judgement Under Uncertainty: Heuristics and Biases*. Cambridge: Cambridge University Press.

Kelley, S. (1992) Parenting Stress and Child Maltreatment in Drug Exposed Children. *Child Abuse and Neglect*, 16: 317–28.

Macdonald, G. (2001) *Effective Interventions for Child Abuse and Neglect*. Chichester: Wiley.

Munro, E. (1999) Common Errors of Reasoning in Child Protection Work. *Child Abuse and Neglect*, 23: 8, 745–58.

Munro, E. (2002) *Effective Child Protection.* London: Sage.

Munro, E. (2005) Improving Practice: Child Protection as a Systems Problem. *Children and Youth Services Review,* 27: 375–91.

Munro, E. (2005) What Tools Do We Need to Improve Identification of Child Abuse? *Child Abuse Review,* 14: 374–88.

Nurius, P.S. and Gibson, J.W. (1990) Clinical Observation, Inference, Reasoning and Judgement in Social Work: An Update. *Social Work Research and Abstracts,* June: 18–25.

Pietroni M. (1995) The Nature and Aims of Professional Education for Social Workers: A Postmodern Perspective. In Jelloly, M. and Henkel, M. *Learning and Teaching in Social Work: Toward Reflective Practice.* London: Jessica Kingsley.

Plous, S. (1993) *The Psychology of Judgement and Decision Making.* New York: McGraw Hill.

Reder, P. and Duncan, S. (2003) Understanding Communication in Child Protection Networks. *Child Abuse Review,* 12: 82–100.

Richmond, M. (1917) *Social Diagnosis.* Philadelphia, Russell Sage Foundation.

Rodriguez, C. and Green, A. (1997) Parenting Stress and Anger Expression as Predictors of Child Abuse Potential. *Child Abuse and Neglect,* 21: 4, 367–77.

Schon, D. (1983) *The Reflective Practitioner.* Aldershot: Arena.

Sheppard, M., Newstead, S. et al. (2000) Reflexivity and the Development of Process Knowledge in Social Work: A Classification and Empirical Study. *British Journal of Social Work,* 30: 465–88.

Turnell, A. and Essex, S. (2006) *Working With Situations of Denied Child Abuse: The 'Resolutions' Approach.* Buckingham: Open University Press.

Warner, J. (2003) An Initial Assessment of the Extent to Which Risk Factors, Frequently Identified in Research, Are Taken into Account When Assessing Risk in Child Protection Cases. *Journal of Social Work,* 3: 3, 339–63.

Webb, S. (2002) Evidence Based Practice and Decision Analysis in Social Work. *Journal of Social Work,* 2: 1, 45–63.

CHAPTER 6

Professional Dangerousness: Causes and Contemporary Features

Martin C. Calder

Introduction

It is important that we understand professional dangerousness as it helps workers from all disciplines to be more aware that our protective intentions and actions can inadvertently be contributing to extending dangerous behaviour in some families. This concept is not a new one and writers such as Tony Morrison have articulated this well in the past but there is a very clear need to offer a contemporary framework to embrace the emerging diversity and evidence base. This chapter will examine the definition, the impact of child protection work on the workers, the circumstances when professionally dangerous practice may emerge and the wider context of professional practice. The hope is that early recognition and identification of the concept can promote safe professional practice.

This chapter cannot and should not be read alone. Chapter 8 addresses the organisational dangerousness that represents the cultivating and facilitating environment in which professional dangerousness can be found. Some element of crossover exists between the two and indeed the seeds of individually dangerous practice are frequently traceable to the organisational context and the origins of their problems are further traceable to the political and policy context. What is clear is that there continues to be displacement of responsibility for poor outcomes from the top down, showing that politicians and managers are potentially part of the problem rather than part of the solution. Chapter 8 will conclude by examining some potential antidotes and solutions to this perverse state of affairs.

Dangerousness: current considerations

When considering dangerousness, there is an expectation that professionals offer their expert judgement of a client's potential risk to themselves and to others. It can be defined as the potential to cause serious physical and psychological harm to others, including fear-inducing, impulsive and destructive behaviours. Predictions of dangerousness are made using actuarial or clinical judgements (see Chapter 11 for a detailed examination of these concepts). The agencies that use these approaches use them for very different reasons and they use very different processes. A failure to understand this within the system can lead to very dangerous practice. Table 6.1 highlights the differences between the two approaches.

Prediction

Prediction, regardless of the method or tool used, remains an imperfect science. Figure 6.1 (overleaf) illustrates nicely the four risk prediction quadrants and each has their own strengths.

Table 6.1 Differences between actuarial and clinical approaches

Actuarial	Clinical
• Statistically derived.	• Utilises a range of research not restricted to statistics.
• Systematic, standardised, rule governed, number-bound.	• Promotes use of professional judgement.
• Deny professional judgement.	• Required across convicted and un-convicted populations.
• Used to predict risk of re-offending over a lifetime.	• Allows workers to generate their own evidence-based drawing on theory, research and practice wisdom.
• Dependent on conviction as baseline.	• Denied the term 'risk' in government and professional vocabulary.
• Used by police, probation and prisons.	
• Risk is a central tenet of professional vocabulary.	

A	B
True positive prediction e.g. harmful behaviour will occur.	False negative prediction e.g. risk of harm not identified but does occur; the consequences are acute.
C	D
False positive prediction e.g. risk of harm predicted but does not occur. Over-intervention?	True negative prediction e.g. harmful behaviour will not occur.

Figure 6.1   A framework for predictive outcomes (Kemshall, 2001)

When we choose to (A and C) do something or (B and D) not do something we can (A and D) get it right or (B and C) get it wrong. Professionals often worry most about (B) – failing to recognise the risk and then harm occurs. Although this may be the one we find out about (physical/sexual abuse) but rarely (emotional abuse/neglect) (C) over-intervention may be just as harmful an error to make but we may never know we were wrong (e.g. thinks child needs removing but they shouldn't be).

Many believe that in many situations the prediction of harm is no better than chance. This is certainly most evident in circumstances where the threshold for professional action is crisis not process driven (Calder, 2005). Since many forms of harm are accumulative (especially neglect but also sexual abuse and domestic violence) (see Calder, 2006), this requires a careful consideration of when to communicate small pieces of information to try and assemble a jigsaw over time to act as a predictive tool (see Srivastava et al., 2003). This would challenge the practice of awaiting a crisis to trigger professional responses.

Prediction, risk assessment and thresholds

Munro (1999b) astutely pointed out that having identified the probability of certain outcomes their undesirability has then to be considered. For example, the risk of repeat physical abuse may be high in a parent who thinks they have the right to chastise the child as they see fit and experienced themselves as a child, but the consequences of removing the child may be worse. There is no objectively right evaluation of risk: values differ between people and the consensus changes over time. Since risk assessment is, by definition, making judgements under conditions of uncertainty, there is an unavoidable chance of

error. We cannot infallibly identify which children are in serious danger of abuse, but only reach a judgement with a degree of probability. There are, however, two types of error that can be made: false positives and false negatives. With a false positive, innocent parents are mistakenly classified as abusive. Angela Cannings, who was wrongfully convicted of killing three children, is an extreme and tragic example of this type of mistake. With a false negative, children are left in a dangerous setting and come to harm. Victoria Climbié is the most prominent recent example of this type of error (Munro and Calder, 2005).

Neither type of error is wholly acceptable but neither type is wholly avoidable. Moreover, if we try to reduce one type of error then, given the same level of professional skill, we shall increase the other type. At any one time and place, children's services will operate within a culture that prioritises the avoidance of one type of error over the other. If we look at the history in England, we can see that throughout the 1970s and 80s, a series of high profile inquiries into children's deaths from abuse led to professionals striving to avoid false negatives. This had the logical consequence of increasing false positives, leading to a public backlash against this apparent over-intrusion in family life. The outcry in Cleveland in 1988 over the rise in diagnosed cases of sexual abuse was the most vivid expression of this disquiet. With the clear message that errors of any type were unacceptable, the only rational avenue for professionals was to try and increase their accuracy by having more thorough investigations of suspicions of abuse, which obviously took more time and money. This led to the current dominance in practice of child protection. Managing risk, not only for the child but also for oneself and the agency, has become a major preoccupation in front line work (Munro and Calder, 2005).

Munro (1999b) argues that within the governmental focusing initiative there is no explicit recognition of the increased risk of inaccurate risk assessment. Yet it seems inevitable that more errors will occur. If social workers are trying to divert families at an early stage from the child protection route into a more welfare-orientated service, to protect them from the trauma (and the expense) of a full scale investigation, then their judgements about which referrals are serious will be based on less evidence and therefore more prone to error. The child abuse inquiries amply illustrated the dangers of interpreting information in a narrow context (Munro, 1996). The information known to one professional may look benign or only slightly worrying until collated with evidence known to others. Another factor that will affect accuracy is the move toward greater partnership with parents. Efforts to establish good relations with parents are liable to flounder if the professionals keep showing scepticism of their honesty. Yet inquiries have shown how pleasant and convincing abusive parents can be and criticised practitioners for taking information on trust. If professionals are trying to carry out less intrusive and upsetting investigations, then it will affect their ability to collect and check essential data that a family may not want them to have.

Munro cuts to the chase when she points out that the government proposals 'seem to be putting the onus on professionals to eliminate the undesirable elements of the current system without acknowledging that they have been created as a well-intentioned effort to respond to the unreal expectations of the general public' (p. 125). She then goes on to ask 'when errors occur, as they will, who will bear the brunt of the public reaction? Will it continue to be individual social workers scapegoated as being responsible or will government and local authorities step in, accepting responsibility for the policies they have introduced?'

Avoidable and unavoidable mistakes in child protection (Munro, 1996, 1999)

Ideally, social workers should protect all children who are at risk of abuse while not disrupting any family providing adequate care. Abused children should return only to families who have changed and no longer pose a threat to their offspring. These ideals, however, are impossible to achieve. Predicting which children will be safe and which will be at risk is an uncertain business. We can only aim to reach the decision that is 'best'

according to our current general knowledge and understanding of the particular case.

The inevitability of some mistakes in this type of work has been overshadowed by cases where the errors seemed avoidable. Society's horror and outrage at some well-publicised cases where children endured terrible abuse before being killed has fuelled a public expectation that social workers should be able to protect children and, if a child dies from abuse, social workers have done something wrong. The problem for social workers is how to distinguish between good and bad mistakes. Which errors of judgement are due to our limited knowledge and which to inadequate investigation and woolly thinking? Analysis of the many public inquiries into child abuse tragedies reveals that inquiries understand the distinction between reasonable misjudgements and errors that deserve to be censured. However, closer study of these reports shows how resistant social workers are to changing their minds and how powerful an influence this has on the conduct of a case. This reluctance to abandon beliefs should not be seen as a particular fault of social workers but as a general weakness of intuitive reasoning.

Some mistakes involve a judgement or decision that is later shown to be wrong but that was reasonable given the information available at the time it was made. Social workers were criticised in the inquiry reports for avoidable mistakes when they failed to make reasonable efforts to collect information – like the social worker who failed to read the file and so did not notice that the children were on the child protection register – or to interpret the evidence they had, as in the case where known abuse to an elder sibling was ignored when assessing current risk.

A more critical approach to child protection work requires time: time to check information, not just when you are highly suspicious of it, time to read files and phone other agencies to get more information, time for detailed supervision, but most of all time to think. In a management culture increasingly concerned with financial accountability, the accountant may be suspicious of the social worker sitting at her desk gazing into space but she may be doing the most valuable thing to help a family, by thinking long and hard about the case and reappraising the evidence for her judgements and decisions. Senior management needs to ensure that time for thinking and supervision is valued and protected from competing demands.

Munro argues paradoxically, that, in child protection work, making mistakes can be a sign of good practice insofar as recognition of one's fallibility is part of a general approach involving a willingness to be self-critical and to change one's mind. All social workers make many misjudgements because of the complexity of the work but skilled social workers recognise their fallibility and are open to rethinking their assessment and decisions. Therefore they will more often decide their previous view was misguided. Both the general public and social workers need a clear understanding of the distinction between avoidable and unavoidable errors.

Although the death of a child is proof that the services failed to protect him or her, it is not proof that anyone acted improperly. Many inquiries have understood this. Many have indeed been highly critical of social workers and other professionals but a substantial minority (42 per cent) concluded that social workers' judgements, though clearly wrong with hindsight, were reasonable given the evidence they had at the time. The main purpose of inquiries is not to allocate blame but to see if any valuable lessons can be drawn from the tragedy to improve services in the future. The lessons drawn have been that social workers are slow to be critical of their own assessments and judgements. Therefore inaccurate judgements that were unavoidable (in that they were reasonable on the evidence available at the time they were made) become avoidable errors when they are not critically reviewed and revised as more information becomes available. The reports demonstrate the common human failing of tending to notice evidence that supports one's beliefs while overlooking or dismissing evidence that challenges them.

To reduce errors in child protection work, social workers need to regard their opinion of a family as tentative and open to revision. They can feel confident that they are making 'the best' decision insofar as they have made reasonable efforts to collect and check the evidence on which it is based but they should not base their confidence on an inner conviction that they are 'right'. Although some errors are unavoidable in relation to our knowledge at that time, the knowledge base alters. As new information is found or reflection produces new ways of looking at the case, previous conclusions should be re-examined and sometimes revised. The old view is seen to be mistaken, but recognising this type of error should be encouraged-a sign of good practice, not something to be defensive about.

Professional dangerousness

Defining professional dangerousness

There have been a number of key definitions that have a different focus and emphasis:

> *The risk of being caught in a system where the professional is psychologically and emotionally battered by clients, by colleagues, by the system and defensively may make inappropriate and sometimes destructive responses.*

Professional dangerousness can arise from embarking upon forms of intervention which fail to consider the assumptions and emotional responses of the people involved. Whilst this is covered in a later section around impact of the work on the worker, it is worth noting here several of the key effects of limited emotional qualities that include:

- Blunted emotional responsiveness.
- Reduced sensitivity.
- Inadequate reflection.
- High levels of stress.
- Dangerous decision-making.
- Defensiveness, depersonalisation.
- Detachment and denial.
- Reframing and minimising the true nature of concern.
- Ritualised task performance that is procedural compliance.
- Redistribution of responsibility, blaming of other individuals or agencies.
- Clinging to the familiar even when it has ceased to be functional.

It is also important to note that it is not a static concept and as such there is going to be evidence of the changing effects of professional dangerousness over time, influenced by deep emotional defensiveness, leading to cognitive distortions, whereby the painful realities are warded off via denial of dissonant information and attitudes. Whilst this offers a temporary but false sense of security, if this process worsens with more wilful and sustained ignorance it may eventually lead to total disengagement.

The circumstances when professionally dangerous practice will emerge

There are a large number of potential examples of issues that can arise and which could include:

- Collusion with the family to avoid the 'real' issues, and to avoid having to raise concerns with the parents.
- Over-identification with the needs and difficulties of the adults in a family whilst giving scant regard to the needs of the children.
- Over-involvement and over-identification with a family so that professional boundaries become unclear and practical needs are addressed whilst potentially dangerous risky patterns of behaviour may be missed or ignored.
- Avoiding contact with the family because of unacknowledged fears about violence and personal safety.
- Avoidance of discussion of workers feelings and values, especially in relation to race, culture, class, religion and gender.
- Working with a family in an unsystematic, incoherent way without clear objectives so that real concerns are not addressed.
- Unresolved and undisclosed inter-agency differences of approach or assessment.
- Over-reassuring a child or parent about unlikelihood of removal from home may subsequently lead to overlooking or ignoring evidence of abuse and neglect.

These patterns of behaviour have been observed in many different agencies at different times, and we need to take account of the possibility that they also apply to us, unless we are aware of the dangers. It is important that we understand the reasons behind these patterns as a stepping-stone to remedial measured safe practice and they could include:

- The cornerstone of help in this field is the worker-client relationship (empathic engagement).
- The interdependence of family, agency and organisational systems.
- Defensive responses to violence and helplessness.
- 'No win' situation.
- Abusing families are part of the multi-disciplinary system rather than separate

from it i.e. in systemic terms the family and professional system are inter-related and affect each other. The impact of abusing families within the agency/family system has been vastly under-rated (Reder et al., 1993). This can be reflected in the following levels of dangerousness framework:

Professional dangerousness is also a process whereby individual practitioners and agencies can be drawn into maintaining situations of risk:

> . . . the process by which individual workers or multi-disciplinary networks can, most unwittingly, act in such a way as to collude with, maintain or increase the dangerous dynamics of the family in which the abuse takes place.
> (Reder et al., 1993)

Where professionals reframe their social control role into a care and support function, there are immense dangers of watching, but not intervening in, a dynamic that may put a child at risk. It can present as focusing on the mother in our interventions rather than holding men accountable (see Calder and Regan, 2007) or unintentionally, for example, by being overtly optimistic about a child's safety despite evidence to the contrary.

We also have to be clear that professional dangerousness can exist at an individual, agency or societal level. These are interlocking rather than discrete systems even though each may have their own specific characteristics (see Figure 6.2 overleaf).

The cycle of dangerousness

Drawing on this literature review it is possible to develop a cycle of dangerousness (see Figure 6.3 overleaf) that professionals get sucked into in some circumstances and which requires effective reflective time, supervision or consultation time and organisational support to prevent and effectively control or cure.

Evidence-based messages for consideration

What are the key messages emanating from child abuse enquiries, inspection reports and consumer feedback? Do they identify that professional practice is dangerous? Does it suggest that they are located within individual, organisational and inter-organisational contexts?

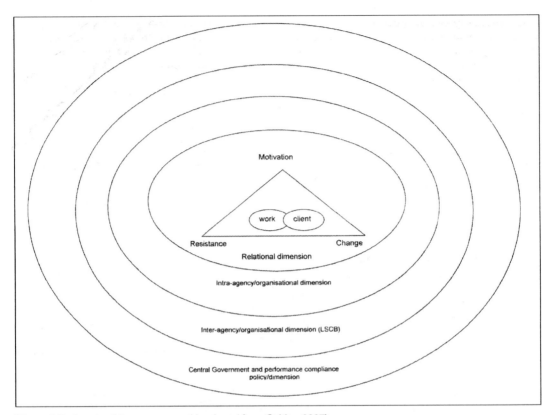

Figure 6.2   Levels of dangerousness (developed from Calder, 2007)

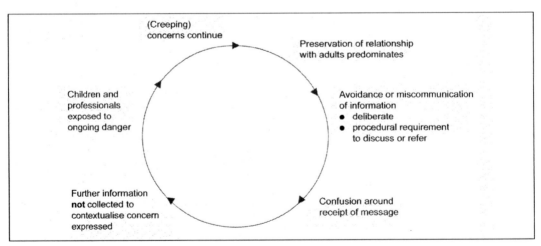

Figure 6.3   Cycle of dangerousness

A compulsory starting point around professionally dangerous practice has to be the growing literature arising from numerous child abuse enquiries that have identified a number of pervasive themes that include:

'The rule of optimism'

- Finding the most positive explanation for an injury.
- Over-estimating the level of progress made.
- Too readily accepting explanations without exploring other possibilities.
- Taking a situation at face-value.
- Putting off taking action until a later date.
- Failing to follow procedures and informally talking to parents directly about concerns that should have been addressed through a strategy meeting or formal investigation.
- Failure to consider the significance of past agency experiences of dealing with the family, for example, poor co-operation.
- Making decisions based upon opinion rather than fact.

Neglect of child protection investigation role

- Blurring of care and control functions.
- Over-sympathising with their client's life experiences.
- The worker meeting their own needs by being a nurturer to the parent rather than focusing on the child.
- Becoming over-supportive of carers need.
- Not sharing concerns because workers feel uncomfortable.
- Workers not wanting to damage their relationship with the family.
- Workers being too trusting of carers.

Responses to stress

- Child protection work is demanding of time and energy.
- Operating under extreme pressure can lead to workers acting dangerously.
- Many inquiries have specifically referred to the effects of stress upon professional actions and decision-making.

Several key themes arise from this include over-involvement leading to loss of objectivity – failure to notice situations deteriorating or only focusing upon current events; under-involvement

avoidance of family – failure to visit or the use of gatekeeping to exclude the need to make contact with the family; and a failure to act at all because of fear, stress or burn out.

Failure to focus on the child

- Focusing on the needs of the adults rather than those of the child.
- Becoming caught up in solving the family's problems and the child becomes lost.
- Not aware of how many children there were in the family.

Working to different professional standards

- Child abuse is socially constructed.
- This leads to different interpretations being placed on the same behaviour at different moments in time.
- Operating floating thresholds.
- Operating with different assumptions.
- Operating different standards for different areas.
- Allowing the use of personal (subjective) value systems.

Failure to communicate or share concerns

- Poor communication has been highlighted as a significant factor leading to professional dangerousness.
- Failure to seek the advice or perspective of others or share crucial information can give an incomplete picture and leave other children vulnerable.

Common themes include professionalism – workers feeling they know the family best and feel it unnecessary to discuss the case with others; an unwillingness to break confidentiality; working alone – deciding not to share crucial information; rivalry between agencies who do not see themselves as part of the wider agency network; staff being unaware or unclear about the inter-agency procedures; and workers accepting behaviours because it is assumed that they are cultural and therefore permissible.

Failure to recognise indicators of child abuse

- Ignoring clinical evidence – not noticing physical signs of child abuse during visits.

- Failing to consider the impact on children, parents and carers the negative responses to other adults (such as domestic violence or aggression).
- Failure to gain entry or asking to see the children.
- Natural love – assuming a carer is incapable of harming a child.
- Dual pathology – focusing on one type of abuse and not considering whether the carer may be capable of other types of abuse.
- Not taking referrals seriously because the source is not valued or the source is distrusted.
- Workers being too certain about their assessment of a situation and failing to consider other possibilities.
- Failing to appreciate a 'cry for help' from carers.
- Failing to link together information or identify clusters of signs.

Assessment paralysis

Assessment paralysis has also been identified in several inquiries. Sometimes professionals feel helpless and incapacitated. It may be that change is hard to achieve because the family have always lived in an abusive way and it is just their way of life. Chronic neglect is often ignored because of this attitude. There has also been great emphasis on this issue relating to adult mental health problems in the adults who were parents. There is often a different focus from different professionals – with adult services seeing the adult as their patient who is the focus of their intervention; whilst children are often the focus of the intervention for children's services. There is also an issue of focus: if we get hung up on a diagnosis as a preface to intervention then we are taking our eye of the focus about the experience of the child living with a parent whose behaviour may be problematic and erratic and who needs protection regardless of diagnosis. When workers pursue their own task a-contextually or when they hesitate until a diagnosis is made then the danger to the child is forgotten or lost. Similar issues also arise in working relationships between substance misuse workers and childcare professionals.

False compliance

False compliance is also relevant here. Parents may be able to convince professionals that they are cooperating to protect the child but in fact a skilled practitioner who can analyse parental behaviour will be open to considering the possibility of them abusing the child. Professionals may become enmeshed with the family – so collusive with the carers that they do not see the needs of the child (for a more detailed discussion refer to Calder, 2007).

Blocks to identifying risk

Cleaver et al. (1998) identified the following professional blocks to identifying risk:

- The unknown – that is knowledge of signs and symptoms and knowledge of the law that was not adequate.
- The known but not fully appreciated – the need to identify what is important from a 'flood of relevant data'.
- Interpretation – being able to correctly interpret information in the context of assessing risk.
- Objective and subjective information – failure to distinguish fact from opinion, being too trusting and uncritical.
- Unappreciated data – information may not be appreciated if it has come from a source that is distrusted.
- The decoy of dual pathology – information may be missed if the receiver is decoyed by a different problem.
- Certainty – investigators may have a false sense of security about a particular interpretation (e.g. medical assessments of sexual abuse in Cleveland).
- Competing tasks within the same visiting schedule, e.g. fostering and child protection.
- The known and not assembled – individuals may hold information, which they can either withhold or which is not pieced together with the rest.
- Not fitting the current mode of understanding – this has also been described as a loss of objectivity, and the importance of supervision is highlighted.
- Long-standing blocks – assumptions made at an early stage that influenced later interpretation of information.

Casting the net too wide? (Hetherington, 1998)

Several recent researchers have concluded that statutory child protection services have become over-intrusive by investigating families where 'the harmful intent of parents towards their children was not much in evidence; abuse was more a question of failings, negligence or over-zealous and inappropriate controls' (Cleaver and Freeman, 1995: 138).

The conclusion drawn from the UK research is that child protection systems should refocus on the issue of children's needs and the cumulative harm to children caused by destructive family environments (for example, high criticism, low warmth) rather than on the investigation of individual incidents of reported abuse (DoH, 1995).

As Tomison (1996) points out, much of the current thinking on child protection advocates a 'family support' framework and aims at 'addressing family problems holistically'. This benign reframing of the task focuses squarely on needs and underplays the other roles of statutory child protection that may conflict with the partnership endeavour. Statutory child protection departments must ensure the safety of children in imminent danger and reduce the risk of future abuse to children, as well as addressing children's and families' needs.

In particular, there are two aspects of the proposed needs-based approach to child protection that require clarification. First, how should the system distinguish between reports requiring investigation and those requiring support? Second, how can the system ensure consistency (inter-rater reliability) between the assessments of workers making such distinctions?

'Seeing Double'

Workers can sometimes find it difficult to identify in these situations the focus of their work: whether it is the child, the family or both. Ann Fleck-Henderson (2000) used the term 'seeing double' to describe what child protection workers (in the broadest sense) need to be able to do. They need to be able to hold and see, simultaneously, the needs of the parent and the child. In particular, she explores the challenges in doing this when the mother is also a victim of domestic violence. This involves being able to have empathy and concern for the parent, but also to be able to recognise the effects on the child and advocate for them as the most vulnerable member of the family. The question has to be asked whether it is possible to 'see double'? Even noticing and recognising the risk and harm to the child becomes difficult when you are focused on

what can be the all-consuming needs of the adult client. Killen (1996) points out that whilst it is painful to witness a child's harm and abuse, it is equally painful to understand and accept the parent's losses and their grief for the life that never materialised, the help to grow up that they never had when they needed it and the experience of inadequacy, pain and hopelessness they are left with.

The inherent challenges in trying to 'see double' can also lead to significant inter-agency conflict. Morrison (1999) says that changes in thresholds for intervention need to be debated at an inter-agency level. The meaning of key terms such as 'need', 'prevention', 'family support' and even 'child protection' varies with agency, discipline and community, and requires open debate and clarification. It is these sorts of discussions that allow workers to explore the tensions they experience that will result in better identification of children at risk. Workers need to be assisted to see the need to look out for the most vulnerable family member. This often involves reconnecting them with the child's powerlessness to protect themselves.

Seeing children

Children, too, are overlooked (Munro, 1996). The case of Victoria Climbié (Lord Laming, 2003) provides a classic example. Despite being known to numerous agencies over several months, no professional engaged her in any significant conversation.

History as well as the 'here and now' focus

Another recurrent omission in collecting information is a failure to look at past history for details that will inform the assessment of current functioning and the prediction of future behaviour. A study of 45 inquiry reports found that 16 (36 per cent) criticised social workers' failure to make use of past history in their assessments (Munro, 1999). In eight reports, social workers were criticised for not reading their own agency reports and so overlooking significant information. In one memorable case, this was a failure to notice the child was on the child protection register. The picture is given of professionals absorbed in present-day issues and failing to stand back and place them in the longer-term history of the family.

The advent of IT systems do not deal with the more intractable problems such as helping professionals to know what information they need to collect and to have the skills required to collect it.

Missing the effects on children

Because adults are usually more experienced at getting their needs met, the experiences of children in these situations can be minimised or lost. It can be hard for workers to actually witness and hear the effects of abuse and neglect on children. Killen (1996) states it is also painful to face the anxiety, the emptiness, the grief, and the aggression that the child expresses in various ways. She proposes that workers find ways to protect themselves from really confronting this, stating: 'Our ability to close our eyes to the suffering of children seems at times to be unlimited and I am not speaking first and foremost of society, but of us as professionals.'

Killen goes on to describe a projective identification that can occur where we project onto parents our own feelings about what we believe parents would or should feel and be toward their children, instead of empathising with, and facing, the parents and children's realities. This can lead to plans and goals that have little to do with either the parents' potentials or the child's needs. As a result, we can base our work on hope and optimism where there is no basis for this. Killen also states that children learn at a very early age what is expected of them, and these children learn that they are to look after adults, even protect them. This is often referred to as 'parentification' where children have to be the adult in the relationship. She suggests they then sometimes look after professionals by telling us what we want to hear. Children learn what the adult world does not want to know and what even we as professionals cannot cope with. It is crucial that we try harder to see and hear children's real experiences.

Workers reluctance to give up

When we have invested a lot of time working with parents, seeing some progress, hoping for more, it can be very hard to acknowledge that things are either not changing, or not progressing fast enough for the child. There can be a sense, conscious or unconscious, that we have failed as workers, that it was our job to solve the family's dilemmas, rather than recognising that some parents cannot, or do not wish to change, to meet the child's needs. We can run around trying so hard that we fail to see that change is not occurring and that the workers are more invested in 'success' than the client. We can overlook the needs of the child and this can lead to years of postponing the inevitable, sometimes resulting in removal after it is almost too late for a successful outcome for the child.

When is progress not quick enough? When is it too harmful?

The question of timeframes is something that arises primarily in situations of neglect. Often the neglect a child is experiencing is no worse today than it was yesterday, or last week, or six months ago – so why act now? Chronic neglect is hard to reconcile with the incident based approach to child protection that has dominated over the past two decades (see Calder and Ayre (2007) and Calder (2007) for further discussion of this point).

Assessing change and change capability

It is suggested that alongside any intervention or therapeutic work, there needs to be an assessment of willingness and/or capacity to effect change. In families where children are being harmed, things do need to change, and those things must be factors that increase the safety and outcomes for the child. The author advocates the use of early assessment as to the capacity of the parent to take on board new information and effect change. This can be measured in small, open and transparent tasks with the client, and needs to continue throughout involvement. The other question that needs to be considered consciously and regularly, alongside capacity to change, is whether it is occurring fast enough for the child's needs. These are questions that can get lost in the complexities of involvement, or minimised in terms of their importance. This is where a supervisor has a responsibility to assist a worker to maintain this focus.

The illusion of change (Cousins, 2005)

We also need to be careful that workers are not being confused by the illusion of change. Sometimes, in our own hope to see things improve we can read more improvement into a situation, focusing on improvements that are not actually about change for the child. We can focus on things that are more easily achievable, but are only one aspect of the problem. Assisting a child reach their milestones, or assisting a family to budget will have a good flow on effects but it does not stop abuse and neglect. There are also consequences for parents if we fail to acknowledge they are having difficulty meeting the required goals. It can result in expectations and demands that are beyond them, and leads to new disappointments. This can also be a form of collusion where the worker and the parent know deep down they can't do it, but as no one is prepared to shatter the dream this actually sets parents up to fail in the long term. It is also irresponsible in terms of our obligation to the child.

Communication issues

Communicating information effectively

It is in the psychological complexities of communicating effectively that the major problems are found. Effective communication is not akin to moving a datum from one computer to another; it is 'the process by which information is transferred from one person to another *and is understood by them*' (Reder and Duncan, 2003: 85). Technical issues are relevant to the practical form in which the message is sent and received but not to the way the message is understood. Reder and Duncan (1999, 2003, 2004) have made extensive studies of professional communication in public inquiry reports and Part Eight reviews and have concluded that problems arise mainly from psychological factors, that is: 'how professionals thought about the case, processed information available to them and interacted with other informants' (Reder and Duncan, 2003: 83). Communication needs to be seen as an interaction: it is not enough for the speaker to send the message; the recipient has to receive it and understand it as intended.

Communication in a professional network is influenced by the relationships between agencies and professional groups. Research in child protection has found that these are affected by territorialism, status and power, competition for resources, differing priorities, differing value systems and disrespect for each other's expertise (Stevenson, 1989). Brandon et al. (1999) in an analysis of Part Eight reviews, judged that major

failures in communication arose from a lack of respect or mistrust of other professionals' perspectives. White and Featherstone's (2005) ethnographic study of multi-agency work highlighted the importance of 'professional narratives that maintain ritualised ways of working and reinforce professional boundaries' and that can operate as an obstacle to clear communication between different professional groups.

Reder and Duncan (2003) produced an excellent paper around understanding communication networks in child protection. The following section identifies some of the key issues and themes from this seminal paper. They note that inter-agency communication is not a new idea although it remains woefully deficient in some areas. Whilst most workers understand the practicalities of this there are constraints highlighted when you consider how many attempts are made before the busy GP responds to enquiries from other professionals? Or how can a fellow professional reach a teacher in the only free slot she has available in the working week?

Common errors in sharing information in practice

Problems in collecting information

Munro (2005) identified that one significant area of complexity is that much of the relevant (and more sensitive) information has to be collected from the family being investigated and this requires interviewing skills of a distinctive nature and a high calibre. Alleged abusers, whether innocent or guilty, tend to react with strong emotions – anger, fear, distress, anxiety. Their emotional state influences both their willingness and their ability to answer questions. Physical violence is a common hazard of the job.

The case of Maria Colwell (1973) identified the need for professionals to share information in order to get an accurate picture of what was happening to a child. Maria was known to a wide range of agencies and personnel. Each had concerns about Maria's wellbeing but interpreting that information within their limited picture of the family, mistakenly underestimated its significance. The inquiry established the current child protection system: procedures for professional communication and collaboration; case conferences; and the child protection register. After the inquiry little mention was made about the failure to share information, rather the emphasis was on . . .

Problems in understanding what it means

In the Leanne White case, 'although agencies are talking to each other, it is though the message is being lost somewhere in the process'. The type of information rarely consists of simple, verifiable factors but more often of descriptions of human actions. This involves interpreting the meaning of the observed behaviour to the actor. Against a background of ambiguous, open-to-interpretation information, this is rarely straightforward. This may be compounded when the family comes from another culture. Experience is the main source of increasing expertise in this task. Interpreting information becomes particularly problematic when it is being used to determine whether it has reached a particular threshold that determines child abuse and neglect. Increasing the volume of information is not helpful. Workers have 'bounded rationality' – a limited ability to process data – so that increasing the quantity they are expected to process can lead to deterioration and not improvement in their reasoning skills. Workers may also be resistant to any revision of their judgements until a crisis requires that they do so.

Problems in communicating it effectively to other professionals

Communication is an interaction: it is not enough for the speaker to send the message; the recipient has to receive it and understand it as intended. Errors in communication occur where the recipient heard the message inaccurately or recorded it wrongly – they are not a trivial problem. Munro (1999) found that such mistakes had a significant impact on the subsequent conduct of the case in 40 per cent of inquiry cases.

Communication involves a complex interplay between information-processing, interpersonal

relating and inter-agency collaboration. The need to communicate purposefully and with meaning to relevant others must be borne in mind by all practitioners at all times. Effective communication is the responsibility of both the message initiator and the receiver. As such it is a mindset and a skill that can be learned, rehearsed and refined. Only then will policies and technological aids have their optimal benefit.

Examples given of communication failures in child abuse work include delays in sending and receiving messages or letters, delays in transferring files, lost messages, inaccuracies in written material and notes being handwritten and difficult to read.

Other key inquiry findings included changes of emphasis between written and verbal communications; a lack of understanding about issues of confidentiality, consent and referral processes, and an uncertain knowledge base.

Other communication variables identified by Reder and Duncan (2003) appear in Table 6.2.

Episodes of communication

Meta-communication is communication about the communication and may involve tone of voice, facial expression, body language, sentence structure. These inflections may reinforce the message and provide further details about the feelings behind them e.g. anxious tone of voice stating 'I am very worried'.

Attributed meaning

> I cannot account for the way people interpreted what I said. It was not the way I would have liked it to have been interpreted.
> (Paediatrician to the Victoria Climbié inquiry)

A paediatrician and social worker had entirely different recollections about whether they had agreed over the telephone that Victoria's burns

Table 6.2 Communication and coordination

Communication	Coordination
• Communication is person to person. • Individuals write, speak or gesture to each other. • Communication is a behavioural enactment of the intention to coordinate.	• Coordination is a strategy or policy agreed between whole organisations to work toward some mutually identified aim. • Occurs in an inter-agency context within which inter-professional communication can occur.

were accidental and that no further action was needed.

The purpose of the communication

A message given thoughtlessly and without purpose is likely to get lost in the transmission. For the communication to be received and to be useful, there must be an identifiable reason as to why that person has decided to convey that information and at that time and in that way. If people are simply complying with procedures this may be reflected in an absence of thought in the communication and less emphasis on ensuring the recipient understands all aspects to the message.

The people communicating

Intellectual capacity is relevant: it determines the individuals understanding of abstract concepts or contextual cues and their ability to differentiate between important and incidental aspects. The recipients' concentration may be reduced by fatigue, boredom, concurrent demands or personal emotional issues. Memory for detail is sensitive to similar factors.

Communicating people and their contexts

These include each individual's immediate prevailing circumstances (e.g. workload), their position within the agency (e.g. their job description), their confidence in their own abilities, the adequacy of supervision, the overt and covert rules within the organisation about behaviour (all telephone calls must be taken by a senior member of staff), the overall working atmosphere and prevalent belief systems.

Communication and assessment

Communication is a way of thinking. As such these skills need to be rehearsed until they become automatic. Successful communication requires some degree of reflection.

Structural changes and professional dangerousness

Compliance based approaches to risk management, where performance targets and protocols dominate the scene, along with automated approaches for identification, tracking and referral systems, will never be sufficient. Too much emphasis placed on these systems can

eclipse individual responsibility and may lead to a sense of deskilling and more risk aversive practice. Such practice increases risks or fuels 'professional dangerousness'.

Discourse and decision-making in child protection (Firkins, 2003)

Decision-making in child protection depends on cooperation and the communication of information. Information is exchanged, and in the process co-constructed, between community members, professionals and agencies in a multi-stage process. Protection information is framed in particular ways to achieve particular outcomes. In the context of limited resources the effects of framing becomes a critical dimension in decision-making. The longer and more intricately structured the chain of decision making, the more a final decision is influenced by communication. These decision-making chains, typical of statutory agencies such as child protection, often have multiple links and sub-links. Information is subjected to change or re-contextualisation at each stage in the chain. Re-contextualisation is the word used to describe the process of reframing which occurs as information is transferred from one context to another or from one modality to another i.e. spoken to written form. Through a decision-making chain, information can attain the status of unquestioned fact (see Figure 6.4).

Different participants form their own judgements about the case. Judgements are based on the urgency or severity of danger in the situation, what information is taken to be relevant to the case, what counts as evidence, who is listened to and what is recorded in reports. The final decision to intervene in a case may come at the end of a long chain of communication and negotiation between a range of people and groups. The further the decision is removed from the original source of concern, the more the process depends on communication. This means that errors in communication can have serious repercussions on the case (Munro, 1996, 1999).

Errors can be traced to a number of causes. Munro finds a range of errors in natural reasoning in child protection decisions. These underline the importance of cooperation and communication:

- Failure to revise risk assessments and persistence of first impressions.

Stage	Case description
Report	His relatives went to the police to report their concerns that this little boy might be at risk of physical injury from his mother's boyfriend and they were unable to find either the child or his mother.
Risk assessment	The senior social worker, after a long chain of communication, heard that a little girl, living with her mother at a specified address was in danger of neglect. He visited, and like the relatives, found no one at home.
Decision	. . . but since the case did not sound urgent, he took no further action.

Figure 6.4   Case example from Munro (1999) illustrates a typical chain of decision making

- Basing of decisions on insufficient information or evidence.
- Access to information known to others but not collated.
- Reliance on evidence gathered in only one context.
- Failure to use past case history.
- Admission of differing levels of scepticism about new evidence.
- Reliance on people's oral testimony rather than on written records.

Caseworkers are called up to make a judgement on the risk of harm to the child. The process of risk assessment is influenced by the caseworkers individual opinion, professional training and the policies of the child protection agency, generally expressed in the form of a risk assessment/decision-making framework. The way risk is assessed is heavily influenced by issues of identity i.e. who or what does the decision-maker identify with.

The influences on how risk is assessed include the professional background of the decision maker; the life history background of the decision maker; and the institutional influences placed on the decision-maker. The influences on individual judgements include the urgency or severity of danger in the situation; what facts are held to be relevant to the case, what counts as evidence, what facts are recorded and how they are summarised, when and how information is passed on to other professionals; who is spoken to while investigating the case; the relative power of the individuals involved; and the resources and support made available to the decision maker.

Child protection agencies attempt to categorise risk within risk assessment models and frameworks. Such categorisation directs the vision of the practitioner towards particular indicators the agency determines are important. Through formalised risk assessment frameworks an agency attempts to direct and control judgement. Each indicator of risk encodes a particular assumption about the nature of harm and safety in the context of care. Categorisation mediates between cause and effect. However, most categories are ad hoc. The categorisation of risk is problematic to the practice, as there is still not enough empirical evidence to support the categorisations used (English and Pecora, 1994; Wald and Woolverton, 1990). In the last resort, risk is what risk a assessment framework defines it to be.

Discourse plays a significant role in the categorisation and communication of risk. Written risk assessment tools and frameworks categorise risk. Department policies, guidelines and legislation provide a written framework within which judgements can be made. The practitioner's professional training provides mental categories through which they assess risk. The practitioner's own personal opinions about child abuse/neglect also categorises how they communicate and assess risk.

How people see and interpret the facts of a case is influenced by their professional background. Practitioners are influenced by explicit policies and frameworks designed to guide and support their judgement; implicit practices and norms within the institution and their own personal opinions based on experience (see Figure 6.5).

Individual judgements, including judgements by expert professionals, are often subjective and unpredictable. Practitioners display a number of problems in exercising their judgement, especially in stressful situations:

- They take mental short cuts.
- They are prone to retaining initial impressions.
- They are swayed by attitudes and beliefs of powerful participants, particularly other professionals.
- They jump to conclusions.

Factor	Example
Personal	• Involvement in the situation • Personal values and ideologies • Attitudes about the case, especially first impressions • Influence of involved people
Professional	• Professional affiliation • Level and kind of training • Role and responsibilities • Experience
Institutional	• Agency policies and protocols • Risk assessment framework • Resources • Outside pressure and influences

Figure 6.5 Personal, professional and institutional factors

- They fail to revise their judgements in light of new evidence.
- They have difficulty explaining how a judgement was formed.

Differing judgements about the facts and urgency of case can lead to miscommunication and misinterpretation of information as it passes through the decision making chain.

Serious injuries to infants and babies (Cousins, 2005; Dale et al., 2002a, b)

Certain cases can be used to highlight a range of concerns that impact on attempts to protect children from harm, particularly in the long term, and to work effectively with families. For example, some cases are clearly complex, involving complex personalities and family dynamics that can culminate in serious injuries to babies and infants (Dale et al., 2002b). They challenge professionals to: 'distinguish parents who present risks born principally of contextual pressures [the majority] from a smaller group where high-risk stems from more inherent, concealed and ominously explosive violent personalities' (Dale et al., 2002b: 56). Paradoxically, the former group often score higher on traditional risk indicators than the latter, involving serious injuries to infants cases.

Inter-agency collaboration

Such cases have implications for inter-agency collaboration. For example, with a number of the

case studies it appeared that DoCS and the police service were unable to persist with statutory child protection intervention or prosecution, either through a lack of resources or options for action. Similarly, Dale and colleagues (2002b) found that sometimes incomprehensible case management decisions appeared to be made because of the inability to act effectively. More specifically, where the case concerned a middle-class family, it often appeared that the child protection and legal systems became paralysed.

Semi-voluntary clients and leverage

As Goddard and Carew (1993) argue, the exercise of authority reaches right to the heart of a longstanding area of contention in social work (especially child protection work), and that is the balance between care and control (authority). From a service perspective, it can be a struggle to provide appropriate therapeutic interventions for families with children at risk of abuse. It is possible for counsellors, if not the service, to fall dangerously to either side of the care/control distinction by either colluding with parents or failing to invoke adequate controls. This fine line requires constant vigilance. While too much control can alienate parents, insufficient control can place children in a situation of further risk.

A focus on responsibility

Some theorists focus strongly on the need for acceptance of responsibility for abuse. Proponents such as Jenkins (1990) and Morrison (1995) allude to the tension between making clients accept responsibility for their actions while trying to engage with them positively. From a service perspective, it is the adults who are responsible for change and, therefore, those upon whom the primary therapy must be focused. In the process of engaging with parents, there is often an invitation to accept their view of the world and their child. It is sometimes easy to empathise with the parents' life experience or history of victimisation, to accept their explanation for what may have occurred and to avoid further confrontation. Furlong (2001) aptly calls this 'colluding or colliding'.

In his article on professional 'dangerousness', Morrison (1995) explores the way in which practitioners sometimes collude with parents and the system through reframing the social control role into a care and support function. He notes the danger of watching, but not intervening in, a dynamic which may put a child at risk, citing numerous child deaths in which social workers failed to be sufficiently 'suspicious of the manipulative acts of abusing parents' (1995: 11). He also questions the notion of the client being the whole family, when the child is the most vulnerable member, arguing that this is, at best, conflict avoidance behaviour, and at worst a minimisation of the child's experience and needs (1995: 11). He writes '. . . the shared fantasy is the illusion of change, when in reality, a dangerous equilibrium is being maintained that satisfies the covert needs of both the professionals and the family' (Morrison, 1995: 25).

One further dilemma is the failure to hold all possible parties accountable when engaging with families. There has been a history of the mother or female caregiver (generally the primary caregiver) being held responsible for the abuse, and being the target of any interventions – perceived as a form of 'mother blaming' by some (Magen, 1999) – while the person not held responsible is usually the male father-figure. In these cases, the child protection system focuses on the mother, in what Burke (1999) refers to as the 'invisible man syndrome', leaving a caregiver who may have either contributed to, or perpetrated the physical abuse outright, never assessed, never questioned, and not incorporated in any case plan to prevent the recurrence of abuse.

A focus on strengths

In contrast to the use of authority to ensure change, the increasing popularity and appeal of a strengths-based approach is hard to resist when working with vulnerable families. The approach offers much by respecting clients as authorities within their own lives, and capable of finding their own solutions. The approach is client-owned and client-directed. Fundamental principles include empowerment, hope, resilience and self-determination. Elliot, Mulroney and O'Neil (2000) promote the strengths-based approach and an optimistic therapeutic approach, arguing that change *is* possible, and lies in the strengths and capacities of family members. However, they do acknowledge that misplaced optimism is dangerous and can end in tragedy where vulnerable children are involved.

Dingwall, Eekelaar and Murray (1983) highlighted the role of individual workers' attitudes, experiences, and biases in decision-making. They developed the *'rule of optimism'* to explain how health and social workers reduced, minimised, or removed concerns for a child's welfare or safety, achieved through taking an overly positive interpretation of the family. A major component of the *rule of optimism* was labelled as *'natural love'*. Dingwall et al. suggested that there was a general assumption in society that parents love their children. Faced with this norm, workers were seen to interpret all evidence of child abuse under the assumption of *natural love*, a positive assumption about the nature of the parent–child relationship of such power that the worker's task of finding incontrovertible proof of child maltreatment becomes extremely difficult. These researchers suggested that the *rule of optimism* was only discounted when parents refused to cooperate with workers and rejected help, or when there was a 'failure of containment' where a number of workers became involved with the case and the pressure for statutory action became too great.

The operation of such biases was supported by Munro's (1999) assessment of errors of reasoning in child protection work. Munro reported that professionals were slow to revise their judgements of families, even in the face of contradictory evidence. They also tended to rely too much on the family's outward appearance and circumstances to determine risk of harm to the child. Thus, outwardly 'respectable' parents appeared able to resist statutory intervention, despite the risk to the child of significant harm, because they didn't seem like 'abusers'. Thus, in adopting a strengths-based approach there is some potential to create a therapeutic environment where a desire to engage with clients over-rides evidence that a child is at risk of harm. The danger is in focusing too much on ensuring that parents remain cooperative, looking for strengths too early (and failing to work on family 'risks'), or in over-emphasising strengths that may have little to do with parenting capacity at the expense of addressing the underlying causes or deficits that led to child abuse. Furlong (1989) states that there are good reasons for being positive, and while this is preferable most of the time, such an approach can become an obstacle: '[Our] preferred language can encourage habits that de-emphasise or even disqualify gritty and often unpleasant practicalities . . . thus making it impossible to be explicit about the breach of major social norms'. As noted above, the idea of individual responsibility for actions is one that child protection workers have generally subscribed to for some time. Put simply, the premise is that in order for change to occur, responsibility must be taken for abusive behaviour (see, for example, Jenkins, 1990). In contrast, other commentators state that the strengths-based approach is not necessarily about owning responsibility for past actions, but owning responsibility for solutions. This presents a dilemma for those wanting to adopt a primarily strengths-based approach. An invitation to accept responsibility involves looking at what has led to the abusive incident, and holds that one cannot move forward until it would appear that there is a potential danger of 'therapising' or even ignoring what could be criminal acts when using a strengths-based approach, if an exploration of past behaviours is not incorporated. Overall, it is contended that for SIDE-type cases, while some of the strengths-based tools may be of use, the approach could be dangerous if used in isolation, too early in intervention, and without ensuring the protection of the child remains paramount.

Strengths-based or strengths-focused practice in child protection work?

Some writers have examined the misplaced emphasis on strengths-based practice by social workers operating in their statutory child protection roles. Strengths-based practice is a term that has gained momentum in social work literature and teaching in the past decade. In essence, strengths-based practice is defined by

the idea that social work is principally about enabling people to function autonomously within society, by collaborating with individuals (through social casework) to identify the resources they have available to them to make the changes they would like to make (McMillen et al., 2004). In practice it gives emphasis to overcoming the systemic problems of entrapment and welfare dependency in socially disadvantaged people, and perhaps challenges the notion that social problems are directly proportional to the number of social workers available to deal with them. This is significant in itself, given that at times it seems that the sector discusses the need to improve child protection as much as it discusses the need to prevent child abuse and neglect. Importantly, strengths-based practice is not a discrete theory – but a framework for directing social work interventions such as casework (Saleebey, 2002). Strengths-based practice begins with the worker engaging with, and assisting the client in a process of 'client-led' identification of needs and solutions. Strengths-based practice presumes that clients are in effect the principal resource for change and that the motivation for change is at some level related to the clients being able to identify the usefulness of such change (Saleebey, 1997).

The virtue of strengths-based approaches in casework practice is that they reinforce the benevolent helping and supportive elements of social work theory that grounds the profession's identity and character. It is the worker who responds to the clients' resources and abilities. The worker collaborates with the client to achieve the changes that the client has identified as required in a process that the client understands and leads within their own means and abilities (Blundo, 2001). The focus on identifying client strengths poses a challenge for statutory child protection workers whose role is primarily defined by the statutory powers and responsibilities they are mandated to exercise on behalf of the child protection agency and the broader society. Such mandates require statutory child protection workers to remedy the protective concerns that impact upon the safety and wellbeing of children. Consequently, the worker engages with the family on issues that are externally perceived and labelled (if not externally identified) as problematic.

The process of engaging clients and collaborating to identify the client's strengths and needs is also challenging for the statutory child protection worker. One of the more consistent messages from the many child protection inquiries that have occurred is that workers can form 'allegiances' with parents in child protection practice that are not helpful and are potentially quite dangerous for the child in need of protection. 'Allegiances' in this context refers to the concept of 'professional dangerousness', where the worker's emphasis upon preservation of the working relationship with the parent, interferes with the professional's ability to respond protectively to harmful situations (Dale, Davies, Morrison and Waters, 1986). Cousins (2005) illustrated the concept of 'professional dangerousness' in her discussion of the difficulty for adult-focused drug and alcohol workers to identify the needs of the child due to their close working relationship with the parent. The emphasis upon collaboration with parents in strength-based practice is often a challenge for child protection workers to address in the context of avoiding being seen to be professionally dangerous. This is not to say that workers (and their agencies) are not acutely aware of the environmental contexts that contribute to and sustain the risks and threats to a child's safety and wellbeing (Trotter, 2004). Interestingly, many students taking the child protection subject define their professional identity in terms of their role and duties – that is, that their profession is child protection work, not social work or welfare work. In doing so, the students' rationale for strengths-based practice appears to be as much about the adoption of the latest agency training and policy directions, rather than integrated practice from both a reflective and evidentiary knowledge base. This is most concerning as it suggests that workers may engage with clients on a premise of focusing upon their strengths, because that is 'the way to do it' (child protection work) rather than engaging with clients on the basis of how they (the worker) can collaborate effectively with the client to utilise the client's strengths in their practice (helping to protect children).

Strengths-based practice invites workers to make some effort to listen to the client's 'story' as a vehicle for identifying with the client's capacities and strengths, particularly in response to their client's adverse experiences. Yet students' unwillingness to hypothesise suggests that there is little refinement on the client's story. This would seem to support a distinction between strengths-*focused* practice (identifying the client's existing strengths) over strengths-*based* practice (collaborating with the client to identify the resources they have to work with to create *change*). Driving much of this appears to be a case-management imperative to minimise the direct ongoing involvement of protective services (that is, by taking an optimistic approach to client's existing strengths it may be possible to rationalise minimal statutory involvement). This seems to inform the emphasis upon client strengths as much as the capacity for change.

The rule of optimism

It is at this point that the significance of Dingwall, Eekelaar and Murray's (1983) *Rule of Optimism* becomes apparent in the consideration of strengths-based practice. The Rule of Optimism is predicated upon the notions of 'cultural relativism' and 'natural love' informing a casework approach that is *under-responsive* to critical needs and events in child abuse cases. The worker is allowed to rationalise inaction in respect of child protection needs on the basis of arguments around the capacities and aspirations of the parents or carers (*natural love*) and the contextual environment of the child within the family and community (*cultural relativism*). The worker focused upon clients' strengths (and relying on other services to support change based upon those strengths), may find this challenging if they also consciously apply their statutory obligations to respond to the child's needs for safety and security.

Natural love

For many students, the strengths identified for clients were often the basis for an attempt to establish a relationship that is less conflicted and threatening between the worker and the parent or carer in the interests of both the clients and themselves (the worker). While it is not desirable that children be exposed to conflict between worker and parent, they may also not be well served by avoidance of conflict on significant points of contention. Students tended to identify strengths that were usually derived from parental emotional reactions to children. They often used these reactions to inform an expectation that the parent will want to do 'right by their children'. This is more coercive than collaborative, as it creates an expectation on parents that may prevent them from being open about the issues that have previously prevented them from providing adequate care to their child. Parental affection (natural love) may be a legitimate strength that should derive a desirable protective outcome for the children, yet there appears to be a substantial burden of expectation upon the parent to make this occur without constructive input on how to do so. It appears that students are not comfortable in trying to evaluate parental affection or to critique it, and so cannot help the parent to use this latent resource to effectively protect the child – but still they rely upon its presence to motivate parents to effect such change.

Competing approaches to case management

Crucially, the potential arises for 'track jumping' between the two approaches to case management: the 'strength' and 'risk' approaches. When confronted by critical safety events or non-agreement from other participants, students frequently make a sudden and dramatic 'switch' in their approach to the case, adopting an often highly directive and forensic response to issues of risk and safety, which is seemingly at odds with the established strengths-based practice approach that they endorse. Furthermore, this dilemma creates for child

protection workers a parallel process between strengths-focused assessment of needs, and risk-focused assessment of safety being followed by students as illustrated in Figure 6.6. These two diverse approaches appear to have little structural integration for students in their overall case management. Students find themselves engaged positively with clients in a strengths-based approach, but also keeping a wary eye for the elements of threat or risk toward the child's safety or wellbeing, that would require them to intervene directly. The competing 'strength' and 'risk' approaches to case management are characteristic of any planned intervention strategy being implemented cooperatively by other services and the client, at the orchestration of the statutory protection worker. Many students felt that giving such direction was justifiable to prevent collusion between those services and families so as to minimise the imminent threat or risk of harm to the safety and wellbeing of the child (such direction may also have been a pre-emptive defence of the worker and agencies practice in the event of external scrutiny). The adoption of strengths-based casework practices that support organisational needs, such as workload management, or placement availability and support, underpin much of the value students place in such approaches.

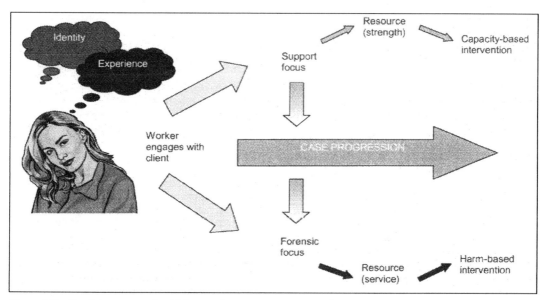

Figure 6.6   Parallel processes in child protection case management (Barber, 2005: 14)

Expertise, common language and child protection

Brandon et al. (2005) attempted to draw on their analysis of 20 serious case reviews for the Welsh Assembly Government to highlight the need for more skilled expertise.

Expertise is crucial to the safeguarding process but is often overlooked, discounted or used haphazardly. From their studies of child abuse inquiries and reviews, Reder and Duncan argue that no single professional appreciated the whole picture because either they lacked information, or failed to seek information from wider sources, or had a narrowly defined perception of their involvement in the case (Reder and Duncan, 2003). Expertise is not the exclusive domain of professionals. There is agreement from government policy and professional bodies as diverse as the General Medical Council (2001) and the General Social Care Council (2002) that the notion of 'expertise' should encompass children and their families as experts on their own lives. Children and their parents and carers have valuable contributions to offer both as a family unit and as separate individuals, possibly with conflicting interests, but clearly with an expertise on their lived experience. For the contribution of children and families to be properly heard and understood by professionals, it is essential to develop a greater sense of clarity about what is meant or intended by the words used. Communicating effectively and developing a common understanding of terms across agencies is advocated in *Every Child Matters* (DfES, 2003a). This is notoriously difficult to achieve between professionals and arguably harder between policy-makers, professionals, and the children they aim to hear. Although the aim is the creation of child-centred services, we know that misunderstandings between agencies are also mirrored in the communication difficulties between policy-makers and the children for whom the policies are devised. Sinclair established that although the Government uses the terms 'protection' and 'being safe' almost interchangeably, these concepts are not universally regarded as the same. Most children, when asked, interpreted 'protection' as over-protection, while 'being safe' had benign and positive associations (Sinclair, 2004).

Brandon and her colleagues developed a framework for understanding expertise in safeguarding (see Figure 6.7). The top axis represents a continuum of familiarity with child protection and the safeguarding process and the degree of participation, the side axis shows the expertise of the various actors involved. Rarely, however, is the knowledge and experience from these interconnecting groups brought together in a systematic fashion to construct rigorous analytical assessments or to act to protect the children.

The impact of child protection work on the workers

The effects of working in the area of child protection include being stressed, rewarded, upset, enriched, pained, educated and being necessary. Contributing factors to worker trauma include multiple/historical nature of trauma, the horror of presentation, the vulnerability and powerlessness of the child, pain, suffering, sadness and love, the level of abuse by others, the crisis of the experience and difficulty in relating to others, often a response to past abusive experiences.

We need to consider the impact of client communications and behaviours as vital feedback which can affect ourselves, our work and the quality of decision making e.g. dynamics of abuse, involuntary client. Workers frequently report certain issues more difficult to deal with than others, such as a demanding, aggressive, intimidating, threatening, obstructive, uncooperative family; a lack of a family's concern or empathy for child and their prognosis, as well as communications between teams/parents.

It is important that we locate where in the system the risks may lie and to this end we must consider whether they occur in the intrapersonal, relational or organisational domains. For instance, practitioners may mirror the dynamics of abuse. Individuals, teams, professional networks and entire communities can become trapped in conflict and defensive re-enactments of abuse. The paradox of helping people who have been traumatised being itself tragic or even dangerous to workers.

Personal reactions to the work and its effects

The emotional challenge of working with parents who have the desire to change, but where this is not in a quick enough time frame, is a very real

	Familiarity with child protection High participation	Lack of experience in child protection Low participation
Expertise about child	Social workers Health visitors Midwives	Consultant paediatricians Health visitors Midwives Teachers School health nurses Educational Welfare Educational psychologists Children and parents Child disability specialists
Expertise about parent	Police	Adult psychiatry/substance use Learning disability Probation Housing Children and parents
Expertise about child and parent	Social workers Health visitors	GPs A + E Staff Voluntary agencies Children and parents

Figure 6.7   Expertise and safeguarding

matter for workers. It is understandable we sometimes shy away from making tough decisions. As Kari Killen notes: 'we work in a highly emotionally charged field, and as professionals we have to find ways to both function and survive' (1996: 791). Identified were a range of feelings which seemed to interfere with effective service delivery from workers (in Killen, 1996) including:

- Anxieties about being physically harmed by angry parents.
- The serious nature of the effects of a decision.
- A need for emotional gratification from clients.
- Feelings of incompetence.
- Denial or projection of responsibility.
- Feeling totally responsible for what happens to assigned families.
- Ambivalent feelings towards clients.

Other studies found that it was more important for workers to protect themselves than to protect children and the parents. Studies since then have shown that even seeing neglectful and abusive processes is a continual struggle for workers. These findings are backed up by research which proposed that workers experience a form of hostage adaptation that results in them minimising or not seeing the seriousness of situations in order to be able to continue working in them.

The effective and appropriate use of authority also presents a real challenge for those entering this field. It highlights the inadequate preparation of social workers, in particular for the use of power in practice and the dilemmas this raises for those who find themselves working in child protection. Many struggle with the use of power over a group who are often some of the most disadvantaged in society on so many levels. This again raises the difficult issues surrounding 'seeing double'.

Appreciating the consequences

Vicarious traumatisation

This is a relatively new term coined in 1990 by McCann and Pearlman who defined it as 'a transformation in the helper's inner experience, resulting from empathic exposure to client's trauma material'. They argued that it was an inevitable result of trauma work and may result in disruptions to the trauma helper's sense of identity, world view, ability to tolerate strong affect, spirituality and central cognitive schemas (i.e. core beliefs about safety, trust, esteem, control and intimacy). The effects of vicarious traumatisation will be unique to each helper depending on his personality, defensive style and resources. It differs from burnout and counter-transference. Burnout may be defined as the result of unrealistic expectations in a difficult and unrewarding job, and is not limited to therapeutic relationships. However, it may be a precursor to burnout. Counter-transference focuses on the individual and refers to the activation of the trauma helper's unconscious or unresolved conflicts and its effects are specific to the therapy relationship. Vicarious traumatisation focuses on the interaction between the situation and the trauma helper and relates specifically to trauma work. It is a normal response to the work and does not reflect the trauma helper's competence. It is cumulative and those who work alone are especially susceptible to it. Conversely, those who share their concerns and reactions with others who do not allow themselves to be alone with the traumatic material and who engage in 'gallows humour' tend to be less vicariously traumatised. Other mitigating factors could include self-care, personal therapy and supervision.

Vicarious trauma is defined as disruptive and psychological effects experienced by professionals working with victims of trauma. These experiences include intrusive imagery related to the client's disclosure of trauma, feelings of helplessness, disassociation, isolation from family and social support, and even sleep disturbance (Dane, 2000; Figley, 1995; Figley and Kleber, 1995; McCann and Pearlman, 1990).

Corovic (2006) in her research highlighted that the meaning of these experiences was shaped within an organisational and social context. Participants acknowledged that it was in the work environment that they revealed their experiences and it was within the work environment that meanings such as 'being a strong, resilient worker' or being 'a weak worker' took place. Working conditions identified as contributing factors to unresolved vicarious trauma were: high case workload, increased recording requirements, lack of supervisory and peer support in the area of vicarious trauma, and high staff turnover. Participants made helpful suggestions for future child protection practice in the areas of *worker-supervisor relationship* and *peer relationship*. In terms of the *supervisory support*, participants advised that supervisors need to have the capacity to provide a warm and friendly environment where workers can speak about all aspects of their work, including their emotional and cognitive experiences. Regarding *peer support*, participants suggested that senior workers should be encouraged to provide meaningful support to new workers, and team networks within the agency need to be brought closer together.

Secondary traumatic stress (STS)

STS is an inevitable consequence of the work and it leaves staff at risk of making poorer judgements. It is correlated with shortened careers, large caseloads, increased contact with clients and long working hours and it can lead to psychological distress or dysfunction; cognitive shift; or relational disturbances.

Cognitive shifts in the beliefs, expectations and assumptions that workers hold include:

- Dependence/trust to chronic suspicion.
- Safety to heightened sense of vulnerability.
- Power to an extreme sense of helplessness.
- Independence to a loss of personal control and freedom.
- 'Witness guilt' for either not being traumatised, as well as for enjoying life while dealing with other people's trauma.
- Victim blaming from a growing sense of the client victimising, threatening, manipulating or exploiting the worker (victim-persecutor-rescuer).

Relational disturbances create: difficulties in trust and intimacy; over-identification, detachment or emotional distancing; feeling overwhelmed or vulnerable; numb reactions or a form of 'paralysis'; excessive responsibility; compassion fatigue; traumatic counter-transference and helplessness.

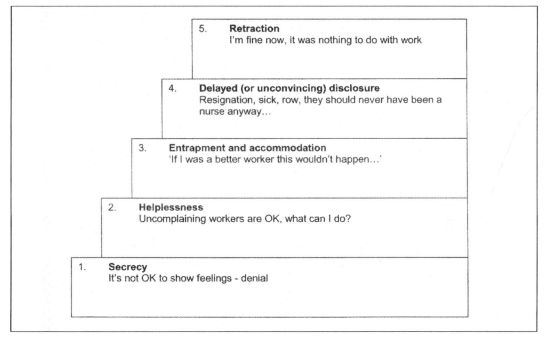

Figure 6.8　Professional accommodation syndrome (Morrison, 1997)

Burnout

Burnout is a syndrome of emotional exhaustion, depersonalisation and reduced personal accomplishment that occurs among individuals who work with people in some capacity (Maslach, 1982). It is '. . . a state of physical, emotional and mental exhaustion caused by long-term involvement in emotionally demanding situations' (Pines and Aronson, 1988), or a gradual process that progresses in intensity over time, e.g. job strain, erosion of idealism and a void in achievement and feeling incapable of facilitating positive change (Figley, 1995). 'It is hard to build a caring society out of the remains of people in whom the capacity to care has been systematically exhausted' (Morton, 2002).

Horizontal violence

Horizontal violence refers to all acts of unkindness, discourtesy, sabotage, infighting, lack of cohesiveness, scapegoating, bullying and criticism. It is a form of bullying and acts to force conformity from people who are different from the status quo (Hastie, 2002).

Professional accommodation syndrome (PAS) (Morrison, 1997)

PAS (see Figure 6.8) offers a theoretical framework to understand the damaging effects of this process on staff. It is an adaptation of Summit's child sexual abuse accommodation syndrome. It is transferable to staff because it helps to explain the experience of staff in terms of what is known about the processes of victimisation and discrimination.

The process is best described as sequential and each step is described below:

Secrecy

Many staff don't want to talk about the impact on them. They may feel the agency or colleagues covertly or subtly denies them permission to do so.

Helplessness

Helpless staff feel a sense of shame as they perceive the agency as despising helplessness in adult professionals who should 'cope'. Men who cannot cope are 'wimps'; women are 'hysterical'.

Entrapment and accommodation

Telling the truth about their feelings is seen as unprofessional, yet maintaining the 'pretence' is seen as 'coping'. Accommodation occurs when the worker decides the fault lies with themselves for feeling as they do and things would not happen if they were a better professional. The solution lies in suppressing their feelings and working harder.

Delayed (or unconvincing) disclosure

Disclosure of the distress may be triggered by conflict, illness, deterioration of performance, training or talking to a colleague. It may present with unpredictable behaviour such as aggression, mood swings, resignation or sickness. If the origins of the behaviour are not understood then the underlying distress will remain undetected (the iceberg principle).

Regan and Butterworth (2004) identified a useful framework for children who have negative experiences that I have converted to the professional (see Figure 6.9).

Retraction

Delayed or unconvincing disclosure is greeted by agency disbelief, insensitivity or avoidance. This leaves the worker psychologically and professionally abandoned. They fear they will be written off as incompetent and this has enormous implications in terms of career opportunities. The solution is seen as a return to coping and secrecy resumes.

Professionals' negative experiences

The sheer scale of resistance and hostility that professionals have to bear in child protection and its implications demands further recognition (see Calder, 2007). The disturbing degree to which violence to workers occurs in child protection is also apparent from Stanley and Goddard's (2002) recent study of 50 cases of child abuse where children had been the subjects of a legal protection order, although all were living at home at the time of their study. They interviewed the workers from the 50 cases and recorded the amount of violence to which they had been subjected during the six months prior to the interview:

- 23 workers had received at least one death threat.
- 9 workers had been assaulted by a person.
- 4 workers had been assaulted by a person using an object.
- 7 workers had been subject to attempted assault.
- 3 workers had been threatened with a knife or other sharp object.
- 5 workers had been threatened with a gun.
- 22 workers had been threatened with assault.
- 13 workers had been threatened with an implement.
- 32 workers had received intimidating phone calls.
- 28 workers reported that complaints had been made about them to supervisors, the media or politicians.
- 18 workers had received threats to their families, friends or colleagues.
- 5 workers had been threatened with sexual assault.
- 14 workers described other major intimidation, including blocking exits, grabbing car keys, etc.
- 28 workers reported that complaints had been made about them to supervisors, the media or politicians.
- 18 workers had received threats to their families, friends or colleagues.

(Stanley and Goddard, 2002)

Serious incidents were common and psychological violence appeared to be all-pervasive in everyday practice. The assaults included pushing and shoving, punching, hair pulling, hitting with a chair, coffee table and ashtray, and an attempted strangulation. And this only covered the previous six months. Many workers were keen to relate previous episodes of serious violence and threat. More worrying still was the fact that workers were not entirely open about their experience: 85 per cent censored information they told their families about their own safety, most in order to prevent families worrying about them (Stanley and Goddard, 2002).

Stanley and Goddard argue that we need to think about social workers' exposure to this kind of violence and threat in terms of trauma. They use what they call 'hostage theory' to explain key aspects of why children are re-harmed and some die. Feelings of fear and helplessness in the face of indiscriminate violence and death define the hostage experience. Hostages – classically in the

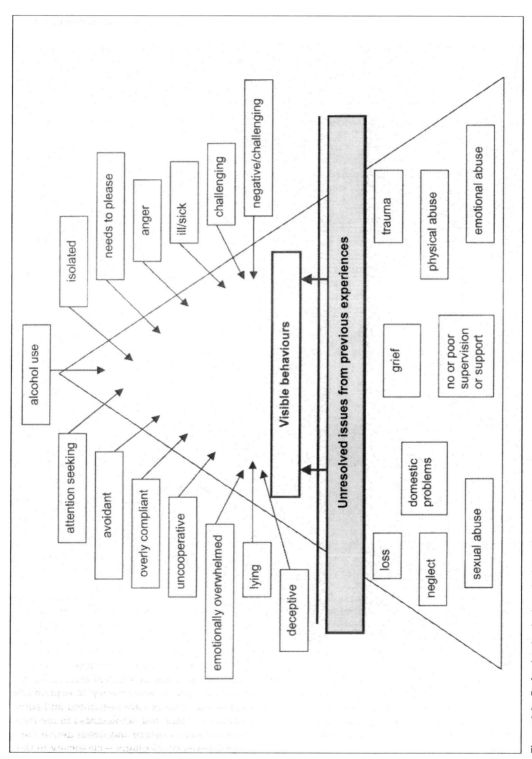

Figure 6.9   Professionals who have had negative experiences

Stockholm syndrome – adjust to their helplessness by attempting to please and meet the needs of their captors. Even in situations where their captors randomly attack or kill some hostages, hostages sense the vulnerability of their captors, and empathise with them. Studies of hostages show that the most compliant are the least likely to get hurt. Submission to your violent captor works, it enhances your chances of survival. The key implication for child protection concerns the ever-present danger that social workers and other child care professionals are not only at risk of real harm and trauma from being assaulted, but that psychologically they become 'captives' to their violent clients. This should not be taken literally, as obviously workers are not often held captive as such and are free to leave home visits and specific encounters in the sense of walking away from the client. But they are not necessarily free to leave the relationship, at least until the safety of children has been established and some attempt made to get the client to change their behaviour. The notion of the 'professional as captive' refers to the psychological impact of such violent and threatening encounters and the psycho-dynamics of having to endure such relationships. Workers' capacities to protect children are seriously diminished as they do not have relationships with children in any meaningful sense because abusers are controlling and orchestrating what happens.

What this points to is the deep emotional impact of child protection work on workers and their capacities to protect children. Everyone involved in this kind of work knows these feelings. That sense in which you are so preoccupied with your own safety and survival that the safety and survival of the child becomes an afterthought, where just getting out of the house alive or relatively unscathed becomes the defining criteria of a good intervention – but of course this is never made explicit. Or when not getting to see the child becomes not a source of concern, but a relief – in fact, you have written to the family to pre-announce your visit not as a strategy to ensure they are there, but (un)consciously to sabotage the visit by giving them a chance to be out, or hiding in the house when you call. And when you knock at the door and there's no reply, you skip back up the path and suddenly the world seems like a better place again, all because you don't have to struggle through yet another torturous session with angry parents or carers. Yet through it all, you keep going back as you feel drawn into a profoundly ambivalent relationship with the aggressive carer.

Simon Hackett has developed a useful interactive framework for understanding the impact of working with young people who sexually abuse that has some export potential. He set out the areas that influence impact and a series of considerations for personal or supervisory analysis (see Figure 6.10).

He then went on to examine the areas of the work that could influence the affective, cognitive or behavioural domains as in Figure 6.11.

Pre-existing influences (both worker and offender)	Thoughts/values/prior life experiences/gender and race status What are my previous experiences of practice in this field? How do they influence my approaches and responses?
The environment	What is happening in my external life/personal life currently? How does the environment I work in contribute to, or influence, the impact of my experience?
The interpersonal dynamics	What are the minute details of the interpersonal exchange I have with my clients? What are the particular themes and struggles associated with my direct contact with sex offenders?
Impact – cognitive – affective – behavioural	 In what ways are my thoughts, beliefs and attitudes being changed, eroded or strengthened through the work? What feelings are promoted in me as a consequence of the work about me, my work and my world view? What is different now about my behaviour than when I first engaged in this work? To what degree are my behaviours appropriate and effective wasy of coping?

Figure 6.10   Impact factors: an interactive framework (Hackett, 1999)

Impact area

	Dynamics	Affective domain	Cognitive domain	Behavioural domain
Sex and sexuality	Worker is bombarded by sexual stimuli in the work Worker listens to accounts of abusive sexuality Worker subject to sexually deviant fantasies Young person's sexual behaviours force the worker to make an association between sex, children and abuse	Repulsion by sexual issues Worker feels victimised sexually Worker feels like an abuser Fear of being perceived an abuser Own sexual development and experiences highlighted Unresolved feelings about own victimisation experiences resurface Feeling that all sex is dirty and sordid	Re-evaluation of sexual values Distorted views of sexual normality (abuse = the norm, or all sex = abuse) 'Reading sex into everything' – over-salience of sex in cognitive schema Sexual imagery intrudes into sexual experiences – affective flashbacks to the work/an account of abuse, esp. during sex Development of deviant fantasies	Sexual abstinence Questioning of sexual identity (positive and negative connotations) Over-emphasis on sex Sexual fixation and increased sexual drive Arousal problems Consensual sex becomes a behavioural fix – a way of 'cleansing' self from influence of work Relationship strain and break-up
Gender and personal identification	Worker subject to overwhelming accounts of male sexual and non-sexual violence Abuser attempts to recruit workers into exaggerated gender stereotype; e.g. men into collusion to distortions about women, women into submissive roles, etc	Feelings of gender confusion Feelings of loss; of innocence, of self, of elements of gender socialisation Anger at abusers for damaging own gendered identity and gender assumptions Fear of being associated as an abuser through commonality of gender or other personal aspect Self-guilt and gender shame (men) Pride in new gender awareness Personal isolation	Distorted sense of responsibility for actions of all men Distorted view of masculine and feminine roles Review of self and own socialisation, leading to negative or positive new self awareness Make worker experiences a 'gender crisis' Sense of distance from members of same gender (esp. men)	Career revision to cope with gender role strain Exaggerated behavioural attempts to distance self from identification as 'abuser' Reluctance to engage in certain professional or personal life activities/roles; e.g. bathing children Review of external life activities, e.g. protection of own children

Power and powerlessness	Abuser engages worker in power struggle	Worker feels overwhelmed by extent of young person's unmet need	Distorted sense of own power	Punitive behaviours towards others
	Worker is required to exercise an uncomfortable level of power and control over young person	Feelings of exaggerated power – euphoria	Increased self confidence and increased level of self esteem	Increased respectful behaviours within own relationships
	Young person projects overwhelming level of need upon worker	Feelings of exaggerated powerlessness – depression	Non abusive relationships given added value	New found assertiveness
		Deep cynicism about society and the denial of sexual abuse issues		
		Desire for revenge – wish to right wrongs of victim		

Figure 6.11 The interactional dynamics of impact in work with young people who abuse (Hackett, 2002). Reproduced by permission of the author

The Stockholm syndrome

The phrase 'Stockholm syndrome' derives from events during and after a bank robbery in the Swedish capital in 1973, when bank employees held hostage showed loyalty and affection to the robbers and used their own bodies to protect them from police fire when the robbers surrendered. It can be used to describe the way in which individuals can form an attachment to their persecutor, with them trying to protect their perpetrator. They show gratitude and loyalty towards them, turning hostility away from their oppressor and onto potential rescuers. Some eventually adopt the perpetrator's values and beliefs and emulate the abusive behaviour. This process can be applied to sexually abused children.

Compliance and denial

The inability to escape leads to frozen fright, which is not just a suspension of emotional response and activity, but a total focusing of energy and attention on the source of threat. In this state, the victim will become quiet and compliant. This is often safer than trying to resist when the odds are overwhelming and the perpetrator is determined to exert power. Another early response to threat is denial – often of the reality or the severity of the situation. This is a useful temporary state, which helps people from being overwhelmed, but it becomes counterproductive if entrenched. They may dismiss the severity, pain and distress of their abuse and this can lead to a view that there is no harm in treating others in the same way.

Coping with fear and anger

Frozen fright, shock, numbness and denial are all passive emotions. This state of passivity does not always continue. These responses can be replaced by more active and possibly more painful emotions, namely fear and anger. The uncomfortable feeling of powerlessness is all the greater if the victims fear the perpetrator. In order for the level of fear to be tolerated, it is usually repressed. It can lead to anger against society or the helping professionals rather than their perpetrator, leading to a rejection of all adults and authority figures. It can also be projected against vulnerable others, especially other children who remind them of their own frailty and powerlessness.

Hope and gratitude

In order to preserve hope, victims will convince themselves that the perpetrator is basically good and suppress a reminder of their malevolence. This can lead to them believing that not only is the perpetrator good but the behaviour and beliefs are equally good.

Deserving, deprecation and depression

Many victims come to a logical conclusion that, if their tormentor is good and yet they are suffering, it must be because they are bad or have in some way deserved the abuse. They can turn their anger and self-deprecation inwards and become depressed.

Accepting and adapting

The final stage for many victims is one of acceptance, and this has attached dangers. The child may not complain about the abuse and they may be poorly motivated to seek help to escape from the situation. They may also accept the beliefs, values and behaviour of their perpetrator, and do not see that their behaviour is in any way wrong.

This theory is based on hostage situations where the people taken hostage begin to identify with the terrorists. It is thus a survival mechanism common in child abuse cases. Sometimes a parent or abuser is intimidating and powerful, perhaps critical of professionals and the worker will begin to see the adult's point of view rather than the child's. It is one way that the worker feels safe at the expense of the vulnerable child.

Contemporary context of professional dangerousness

In a time of massive change it is important to examine the context and political drivers which are arguably attempting to redress professional dangerousness. To begin to document the pace and volume of change exceeds the parameters of this chapter although three key areas have been selected to provide the reader with a flavour of the general tone and direction of change coupled with the actual effect it has on practice and most probably outcomes for children. The three areas are the changes to the systems and structures

governing children; the demise of risk from the social care vocabulary; and the changing emphasis from child protection to safeguarding.

Changes to the systems and structures governing children

Improving the way key people and bodies safeguard and promote the welfare of children is crucial to improving outcomes for children. In his report into the death of Victoria Climbié, Lord Laming concluded that: '. . . the suffering and death of Victoria was a gross failure of the system'. One of the key reasons why the system failed Victoria so badly, and why it has failed other children over the years, is because key people and bodies which come into contact with children on a regular basis often fail to give sufficient priority to safeguarding and promoting the welfare of children. This means that:

- The system does not always focus on the child's needs. For example in Victoria Climbié's case, the focus was on the needs of the adults responsible for her, rather than the child herself.
- Senior managers, including Chief Executives and others in key governance roles, have insufficient knowledge of safeguarding and welfare issues and fail to take sufficient responsibility for the actions of their employees in relation to safeguarding and promoting the welfare of children.
- It is difficult for key people and bodies to share information and work together effectively to safeguard and promote the welfare of children.
- Many employees are not adequately trained in safeguarding and promoting the welfare of children. This is a particular problem for employees who often come into contact with children and families but are not considered to be 'child protection specialists'.

In the wake of the Victoria Climbié inquiry the government in England embarked on a structural overhaul of the system to try and promote earlier intervention, promote prevention and encourage closer intra and inter-agency and inter-professional cooperation. The end product has achieved the opposite of what it set out to achieve but rather than evaluate the process and outcomes they have adopted a 'big brother' stance and forced compliance through a renewed and heightened emphasis on performance targets that prioritise outputs from systems rather than good outcomes for children (see Calder, 2007b; Devaney, 2007).

A couple of examples can highlight the confusing state of affairs. The problem in the Victoria Climbié inquiry case was not that the child protection system failed Victoria, but the failure in maintaining her within a child in need system. Whether it was right to initiate a major overhaul as a result is a redundant question now, but it is clear that the raft of structural reforms were designed to create a platform for safe practice and in reality we have diverted too much time and resources to the development of structural solutions to non-structural problems (Munro, 2006). The fact that these structural solutions have evolved in an uncoordinated way from many different departments with different remits and projected outcomes has simply modelled the confusion that has followed.

The Assessment Framework emerged to provide a contemporary replacement to the 'orange book' (DoH, 1988). It has been singularly unsuccessful in standardising assessment practice (it has many other frameworks to compete with), in addressing risk (which is deleted from the package and the social care vocabulary, yet remains the spine of the criminal justice system), in nurturing professional confidence and judgements in the staff who use it, in allowing partnerships to develop in a straightjacket of performance indictor-led timescales that are alienating , and in achieving better outcomes for children as there is a deficit, or even a void, of guidance on analysis that links assessment practice with planning processes and outcome projection.

Even at the point of its formal introduction, the next step of integrating the Assessment Framework with the LAC system had begun and the notion of an Integrated Children's System emerged. Unfortunately, bolting two malfunctioning systems together is not usually the required prescription to ease the pain of using them and what has followed is a confusion of different processes, with an emphasis on business and performance as well as electronic recording systems – overriding children and their outcomes. Neither is an assessment tool, as there is a growing expectation that professionals in social care utilise their own professional judgment coupled with practice wisdom and research to generate their own. This is increasingly unlikely given the pressure of work on staff, the vast expanse of evidence they are expected to scan, select, read, in order to generate an assessment tool and then apply it to the individual cases before then realising they also have to become the sole source of analysis. The ICS has also failed to be developed as a tool for all agencies to try and coordinate services better and use a common language, and we now have the emergence of a Common Assessment Framework for agencies operating below the social work threshold. This tries to build assessment capacity without an accompanying assessment tool and attempts to introduce the concept of a lead professional to coordinate any services that arise from their assessment.

Other agencies see themselves being hijacked to do a social work job given the combination of social worker recruitment and retention problems that is also evident across other professional groups. There are also massive agenda changes for Health (HALL 4) which is significantly restructuring health services and is taking away routine health surveillance that is causing professional alarm and is likely to expose children to heightened harm. There is little value in trying to resolve the information sharing arrangements (still in disarray and massive professional confusion) if there is no capacity or requirement for children to be seen, as there will be nobody with any information to share! The continually changing notion of a cross-agency information sharing system (Information, Referral and Tracking (IRT) to Information Sharing and Assessment (ISA) to Contact Point) is the essential spinal connection if the divisive systems of Integrated Children's System (ICS) and Common Assessment Framework (CAF) are to be functionally connected. Scotland has redressed this by having the foresight to develop a unified cross-agency assessment framework that Northern Ireland looks destined to follow (Unified Needs of Children in Northern Ireland – UNOCINI). If I was to add in the structural merging of education and social services we identify issues such as mutual perceptions of takeover, senior management without the requisite and relevant background to head up the new changes; the separation of adult and children's services is problematic as it will make effective communication less likely and is likely to encourage crisis led responses; the move towards children's trusts, extended schools and children's centres. All these factors simply make the jigsaw very difficult to assemble and most professionals do not even know how many pictures there are to the jigsaw, never mind knowing what picture they are expected to create. This has resulted in massive professional confusion of role, which informs problems of communication, which results in professionally unsafe practice and which is the opposite of what was set out to be achieved. We are witnessing the single biggest recipe for the creation of a professionally dangerous environment that we have ever seen, yet workers remain concerned that they will be held personally responsible if they get anything wrong. This is what they see and experience and which drives their day-to-day decision making and practice. For a more detailed discussion of these points the reader is referred to Calder (2003, 2004a, b, 2005, 2007b; Calder and Hackett, forthcoming; Munro and Calder, 2005).

The demise of risk from the social care vocabulary

The dilution or deletion of risk terminology

The concept of risk has been abolished within government guidance involving child protection. Instead, it has been replaced with concepts of 'weaknesses' and 'strength' in order to reinforce the preferred notion of children in need (section 17) of the Children Act 1989, given that 'risk' is equated with the idea of child protection (section 47 Children Act 1989) which the government is seeking to redefine. This suggests that there has been a misunderstanding about the meaning of risk in government circles since need clearly must be balanced with risk when weighing up the options in the light of all the available information (Calder, Chapter 12 this volume). Had this more balanced view of risk been embraced, it would have been consistent with holistic assessments and provided an opportunity to debate a more contemporary view of risk located within the change agenda.

The relegation of risk from the framework also creates a huge operational problem as, since the advent of thresholds for the provision of social work services, necessary because need outstrips resources 3:1 (see Calder, 2005), the primary focus of social work intervention falls within the child protection arena. The outcome of this change of emphasis is that frontline staff undertaking

primarily child protection work cannot talk about risk and struggle to incorporate risk into their assessment practice. The child protection vocabulary has thus been diluted because those involved in the provision of children's services must now refer to broader, less specific and more ambiguous tasks such as safeguarding. For managers, this means that they have the task of furnishing frontline staff with circumstance-specific risk assessment frameworks to overcome the generic, strengths-loaded assessment framework and this is challenging, since managers will struggle to have such a range and depth of evidence-based and up-to-date knowledge.

Risk retention and differential focus

The picture of confusion is incomplete without considering that those agencies operating within the criminal justice field are required to focus on multiple risks: risk to the public, to others and to self. They are required to use actuarial risk tools with all the problems associated with the tick-box mentality and this means that they are most likely measuring the risk of re-offending only for the relevant offence (missing dual or more offence types); they do not focus on harm to particular children or and undertake other assessments of the children and their parent to add to the equation; and there is a danger that professionals in the social care domain may accept a risk assessment undertaken by criminal justice agencies, thankful that one has been done, thus importing it uncritically. This again offers fertile ground for professionally dangerous practice to flourish.

Avoiding risk (Cooper et al., 2003)

Avoiding risk lies at the other end of the continuum to professional dangerousness. It suggests workers are deterred from taking risks and so risk is avoided all together. Risk avoidance rules predominate. Shaming mechanisms are in place because they symbolise failure to avoid risk – such as serious case reviews. Risk avoidance leads to the paradox of protective intentions inadvertently creating the likelihood of more risk. The system frequently gives greater support to hierarchical accountability than to professional judgements held by those closest to the relevant information and where the potential for quality risk management is most direct.

Messages from inquiries

Inquiries reinforce the dominance of rules and procedures rather than by giving weight to sound judgements, based on the worker's knowledge, experience and authority.

Protocols solve problems of communication. One achievement of inquiries has been to help highlight how we can misunderstand the communications from families. However, they do not enhance the personal confidence and pride which workers in the child care and protection fields have in their work. Inquiries do not promote public confidence in the skills and expertise of professionals. Instead, they reinforce a 'blaming culture' where all professionals feel blame by association and feel at risk that they could be next. Inquiries reinforce the belief that the 'cure' is often worse than the 'disease' and promote the family's right to non-intervention. Inquiries do not help professionals to conquer or manage their own fear of working with dangerous families or of being professionally and personally pilloried in public if things go wrong. Inquiries do not protect children, since it is professionals, acting with shared values and purposes, who protect children when their families are overwhelmed by their own needs and which erupt in significant harm and, sometimes, fatal attack.

The changing emphasis from child protection to safeguarding

Safeguarding and promoting welfare are two sides of the same coin. Safeguarding has two elements: protecting children from maltreatment and preventing impairment of children's health or development, whereas promoting welfare is a proactive responsibility, that is, ensuring that children are growing up in circumstances consistent with the provision of safe and effective care, and creating opportunities to enable children to have optimum life chances such that they can enter adulthood successfully. The merging of prevention and protection under a safeguarding umbrella points to the need for a robust structure for the LSCB. Considerable work is required locally to ensure that there is a smooth transition from ACPC to LSCB. Morrison and Lewis (2005) developed a toolkit for just such an exercise. However, what we know is that there are territorial disputes and system differences

that need to be redressed if safeguarding is to materialise – both for professionals as well as the recipient children and families. The drive away from child protection is premised on a belief that the exclusive gateway to resources is child protection registration and as such families are pushed through the child protection system unnecessarily to access the requisite resources. The decision to abolish the child protection register but not the child protection process is testament to the government commitment to eradicate child protection as a practice, although inter-agency concerns about who will retain lead responsibility for cases will dictate which cases are framed in what terms and the unacceptable status quo will again return. There is also some contradictory movement within the Safeguarding guidance issued centrally (DfES et al., 2006) as we are expected to limit the number of section 47 enquiries ('investigation' now aborted from their vocabulary if not the legislation), yet the catchment definitions of harm continues to expand as other harmful practices to children emerge (forced marriage, internet sexual abuse, children involved in prostitution, etc). Professionals are able to interpret child protection as narrowly or broadly as they want using the selected sections of the guidance, and this again offers a recipe for division and poor communication between child care professionals. 'Every child' certainly 'matters', yet there is no evidence in the government structures of response that they know how to achieve it. Ironically, their drive to do so in unrealistic timescales (that they themselves cannot keep) means that the professional focus is on compliance and performance returns, rather than on frontline resources to achieve the much stated and applauded outcomes.

Summary

This chapter has attempted to provide a contemporary overview of the key issues in relation to professionally dangerous practice and the circumstances in which it may arise. It should be read in conjunction with Chapter 8 around organisational dangerousness.

References

Blundo, R. (2001) Learning Strengths-based Practice: Challenging our Personal and

Professional Frames. *Families in Society*, 82: 3, 296–304.

Brandon, M., Owers, M. and Black, J. (1999) *Learning How to Make Children Safer: An Analysis of Serious Child Abuse Cases in Wales*. Norwich: University of East Anglia/Welsh Office.

Buckley, H. (2003) *Child Protection Work: Beyond the Rhetoric*. London: Jessica Kingsley.

Calder, M.C. (2003) The Assessment Framework: A Critique and Reformulation. In Calder, M.C. and Hackett, S. (Eds.) *Assessment in Childcare: Using and Developing Frameworks for Practice*. Lyme Regis: Russell House Publishing.

Calder, M.C. (2003b) Child Sexual Abuse and Domestic Violence: Parallel Considerations to Inform Professional Responses. *Seen and Heard*, 12: 3, 14–24.

Calder, M.C. (2004a) The Integrated Children's System: Out of the Frying Pan and into the Fire? *Child Care in Practice*, 10: 3, 225–40.

Calder, M.C. (2004b) Child Protection: Current Context, Central Contradictions and Collective Challenges. *Representing Children*, 17: 1, 59–73.

Calder, M.C. (2005) *Eligibility Criteria and the Threshold for the Provision of a Social Work Service: Conceptual and Implementation Issues*. Care Knowledge Briefing, London: OLM.

Calder, M.C. (2006) Domestic Violence and Child Protection: Challenges for Professional Practice. *Context 84*, April: 11–4.

Calder, M.C. (Ed.) (2007a) *The Carrot or the Stick? Engaging with Involuntary Clients*. Lyme Regis: Russell House Publishing.

Calder, M.C. (2007b) Child Protection in Changing Times: A Manager's Perspective. In Wilson, K. and James, A. (Eds.) *The Child Protection Handbook*. 3rd edn. London: Bailliere Tindall.

Calder, M.C. and Ayre, P. (2007) *Neglect*. Briefing for Community Care.

Calder, M.C. and Hackett, S. (forthcoming) The Changing Context to Services for Children and Families Throughout the UK. In Hackett, S. and Calder, M.C. (Eds.) *Assessment in Child Care Vol. 2: Theory, Research and Practice Applications*. Lyme Regis: Russell House Publishing.

Calder, M.C. and Regan, L. (2007) Working with Mothers in Cases of Sexual and Domestic Abuse: Reframing Resistance as Restricted Choices. In Calder, M.C. (Ed.) *The Carrot or the Stick? Engaging with Involuntary Clients*. Lyme Regis: Russell House Publishing.

Cleaver, H., Wattam, C. and Cawson, P. (1998) *Assessing Risk in Child Protection*. London: NSPCC.

Cleaver, H. and Freeman, P. (1995) *Parental Perspectives in Cases of Suspected Child Abuse*. London: HMSO.

Cooper, A., Hetherington, R. and Katz, I. (2003) *The Risk Factor: Making Child Protection Systems Work for Children*. London: DEMOS.

Corovic, T. (2006) Child Protection Workers and Vicarious Trauma: A View from the Edge. *OACUS Journal*, 50: 1, 11–4.

Cousins, C. (2005) 'But the Parent is Trying . . .' The Dilemmas Workers Face. *Child Abuse Prevention Newsletter*, 13, 1, Summer.

Dale, P. et al. (1986) *Dangerous Families: Assessment and Treatment of Child Abuse*. London: Tavistock.

Dale, P., Green, R. and Fellows, R. (2002a) Serious and Fatal Injuries to Infants with Discrepant Parental Explanations: Some Assessment Case Management Issues. *Child Abuse Review*, 11, 296–312.

Dale, P., Green, R. and Fellows, R. (2002b) *What Really Happened? Child Protection Case Management of Infants with Serious Injuries with Discrepant Explanations*. London: NSPCC.

Dane, B. (2000) Child Welfare Workers: An Innovative Approach for Interacting with Secondary Trauma. *Journal of Social Work Education*, 36: 1, 27–41.

Davis, B. (2001) The Restorative Power of Emotions in Child Protection Services. *Child and Adolescent Social Work Journal*, 18, 437–54.

Devaney, J. (2007) *Challenging Output-based Performance Management in Child Protection*. In Calder, M.C. op. cit.

Dingwall, R., Eekelar, J. and Murray, T. (1983) *The Protection of Children: State Intervention and Family Life*. Oxford: Blackwell.

DoH (1988) *Protecting Children: A Guide For Social Workers Undertaking a Comprehensive Assessment*. London: HMSO.

DoH (1991) *Child Abuse: A Study of Inquiry Reports 1980–1989*. London: HMSO.

DoH (1995) *Child Protection: Messages from Research*. London: HMSO.

DoH (1995b) *The Challenge of Partnership*. London: HMSO.

DoH (1999) *Working Together to Safeguard Children: A Guide to Inter-Agency Working to Safeguard and Promote the Welfare of Children*. London: HMSO.

DoH (2000) *Assessing Children in Need and their Families: Practice Guidance*. London: HMSO.

DoH (2001) *Studies Informing the Framework for the Assessment of Children in Need and their Families*. London: HMSO.

DoH (2002) *Learning from Past Experience: A Review of Serious Case Reviews*. London: HMSO.

Elliot, B., Mulroney, L. and O'Neil, D. (2000) *Promoting Family Change: The Optimism Factor*. Sydney: Allen and Unwin.

English, D.J. and Pecora, P.J. (1994) Risk Assessment as a Practice in Child Protective Services. *Child Welfare*, 73, 451–73

Figley, C.R. and Kleber, R.J. (1995) Beyond the 'Victim': Secondary Traumatic Stress. In Kleber, R.J., Figley, C.R. and Gerson, B.P. (Ed.) *Beyond Trauma: Cultural and Social Dynamics*. New York: Plenum.

Figley, C.R. (1995) Compassion Fatigue: Toward a New Understanding of the Costs of Caring. In Stamm, B.H. (Ed.) *Secondary Traumatic Stress: Self-Care Issues for Clinicians, Researchers and Educators*. Lutherville, MA: Sidran Press.

Firkins, A. (2003) *Discourse and Decision Making in Child Protection Practice*. Australasian Conference on Child Abuse and Neglect Sydney Convention Centre, Darling Harbour, 24th–27th November.

Fleck-Henderson, A. (2000) Domestic Violence in the Child Protection System: Seeing Double. *Children and Youth Services Review*, 22, 333–54.

Furlong, M. (1989) Can a Family Therapist do Statutory Work? *Australian and New Zealand Journal of Family Therapy*, 10: 4, 211–18.

Furlong, M. (2001) Neither Colluding Nor Colliding: Practical Ideas for Engaging Men. In Pearse, B. and Camilleri, P. (Eds.) *Working with Men in the Human Services*. Sydney: Allen and Unwin.

General Medical Council (2001) *Good Medical Practice*. London: GMC.

General Social Care Council (2002) *Codes of Practice for Social Workers and Employers*. London: HMSO.

Goddard, C. and Carew, R. (1993) *Responding to Children: Child Welfare Practice*. Sydney: Longman.

Goddard, C. and Stanley, J. (2002) *In the Firing Line: Violence and Power in Child Protection Work*. West Sussex: John Wiley and Sons.

Hackett, S. (1999) Empowered Practice. In Erooga, M. and Masson, H. (Eds.) *Young People who Sexually Abuse Others*. London: Routledge.

Hackett, S. (2002) Negotiating Difficult Terrain: The Personal Context to Work with Young People who Sexually Abuse Others. In Calder, M.C. (Ed.) *Young People who Sexually Abuse: Building The Evidence Base for your Practice*. Lyme Regis: Russell House Publishing.

Hastie, C. (2002) Horizontal Violence in the Workplace. Retrieved from http://www.acegraphics.com.au/articles/hastie02.html

Hetherington, T. (1998) A New Approach to Child Protection. *National Child Protection Clearinghouse Newsletter*, 6: 1, 7–11 (at www.aifs.gov.au/nch/nlaut98.html)

Jenkins, A. (1990) *Invitations to Responsibility: The Therapeutic Engagement of Men who are Violent and Abusive*. Australia: Dulwich Centre Publications.

Kemshall, H. (2001) *Risk Assessment and Management of Known Sexual and Violent Offenders: A Review of Current Issues*. Police Research Series Paper 140. London: The Home Office.

Killen, K. (1996). How far have we Come in Dealing with the Emotional Challenge of Abuse and Neglect. *Child Abuse and Neglect*, 20: 9, 791–5.

Lord Laming (2003) *The Victoria Climbié Inquiry. Report of an Inquiry by Lord Laming*. London: HMSO.

Magen, R.H. (1999) In the Best Interests of Battered Women: Reconceptualising Allegations of Failure to Protect. *Child Maltreatment*, 4: 2, 127–35.

Maslach, C. (1982) *Burnout: The Cost of Caring*. Englewood Cliffs, NJ: Prentice-Hall.

McCann, I.L. and Pearlman, L.A. (1990) Vicarious Traumatisation: A Framework for Understanding the Psychological Effects of Working with Victims. *Journal of Traumatic Stress*, 9: 10, 131–49.

McMillen, J.C., Morris, L. and Sherraden, M. (2004) Ending Social Work's Grudge Match: Problems versus Strengths. *Families in Society*, 85: 3, 317–25.

Morrison, T. (1986) Professional Dangerousness. In Dale, P. and Morrison, T. (Eds.) *Dangerous Families*. London: NSPCC.

Morrison, T. (1997) Emotionally Competent Child Protection Organisations. In Bates, J. et al. (Eds.) *Protecting Children: Challenges And Change*. Aldershot: Arena.

Morrison, T. (1994) *Collaboration in a Changing World: Developing an Integrated Response to Child Sexual Abuse*. Presented at a National Conference on Child Sexual Abuse: 'Developing an Integrated Response to the Prevention and Treatment of Child Sexual Abuse', Melbourne, March.

Morrison, T. (1995) *Teaching, Training and Change in Child Protection Organisations.* Keynote presentation to the National Child Protection Trainers Conference, 15 March, 1995.

Morrison, T. (1996) Partnership and Collaboration: Rhetoric and Reality. *Child Abuse and Neglect*, 20: 2, 127–40.

Morrison, T. (1998) *Inter-agency Collaboration and Change: Effects of Inter-Agency Behaviour on Management of Risk and Prognosis for Change in Dangerous Family Situations.* Presented at International ISPCAN Congress on Child Abuse and Neglect, 'Protecting Children: Innovation and Inspiration', Auckland, New Zealand, September 6–9.

Morrison, T. (1998) Partnership, Collaboration and Change Under the Children Act. In Adcock, M. and White, R. (Eds.) *Significant Harm; Its Management and Outcome.* Croydon: Significant Publications.

Morrison, T. (2001) *Staff Supervision in Social Care.* Brighton: Pavilion.

Morrison, T. and Lewis, D. (2005) Toolkit for Assessing the Readiness of Local Safeguarding Children's Boards: Origins, Ingredients and Applications. *Child Abuse Review*, 14, 297–316.

Munro, E. (1996) Avoidable and Unavoidable Mistakes in Child Protection Work. *British Journal of Social Work*, 26, 793–808.

Munro, E. (1998) Improving Social Workers' Knowledge Base In Child Protection Work. *British Journal of Social Work*, 28, 89–105.

Munro, E. (1999) Common Errors of Reasoning in Child Protection Work. *Child Abuse and Neglect*, 23, 745–58.

Munro, E. (1999b) Protecting Children in an Anxious Society. *Health, Risk and Society*, 1: 1, 117–27.

Munro, E. (2002) *Effective Child Protection.* London: Sage.

Munro, E. (2004) The Impact of Child Abuse Inquiries Since 1990. In Stanley, N. and Manthorpe, J. (Eds.) *The Age of Inquiry: Learning and Blaming in Health and Social Care.* London: Routledge.

Munro, E. (2005) Improving Practice: Child Protection as a Systems Problem. *Children and Youth Services Review*, 27, 375–91.

Munro, E. (2006) Eileen Munro's Response to Jane Akister's Comment on Munro, E. (2005) A Systems Approach to Investigating Child Abuse Deaths. *British Journal of Social Work*, 36: 1, 63–164.

Munro, E. and Calder, M.C. (2005) Where has Child Protection Gone? *Political Quarterly*, July.

Pines, A. and Aronson, E. (1988) *Career Burnout: Causes and Cures.* New York: Free Press.

Reder, P. and Duncan, S. (1999) *Lost Innocents: A Follow-up Study of Fatal Child Abuse.* London: Routledge.

Reder, P. and Duncan, S. (2002) Predicting Fatal Child Abuse and Neglect. In Browne, K.D. et al. (Eds) *Early Prediction and Prevention of Child Abuse: A Handbook.* Wiley: Chichester.

Reder, P. and Duncan, S. (2003) Understanding Communication in Child Protection Networks. *Child Abuse Review*, 12, 82–100.

Reder, P. and Duncan, S. (2004) From Colwell to Climbié: Inquiring into Fatal Child Abuse. In Stanley, N. and Manthorpe, J. (Eds.) *The Age of Inquiries.* London: Brunner/Routledge.

Reder, P. and Duncan, S. (2004) Making the Most of the Victoria Climbié Inquiry Report. *Child Abuse Review*, 13, 95–114.

Reder, P., Duncan, S. and Gray, M. (1993) *Beyond Blame: Child Abuse Tragedies Revisited.* London: Routledge.

Regan, L. and Butterworth, J. (2004) Safe Care. In Wheal, A. (Ed.) *The RHP Companion to Foster Care.* 2nd edn. Lyme Regis: Russell House Publishing.

Saleebey, D. (1996) The Strengths Perspective in Social Work Perspective: Extensions and Cautions. *Social Work*, 41: 3, 296–305.

Saleebey, D. (2002) *The Strengths Perspective in Social Work Practice.* 3rd edn. Boston: Allyn and Bacon.

Scourfield, J. (2002) *Gender and Child Protection.* Basingstoke: Palgrave.

Sinclair, R. (2004) Participation in Practice: Making it Meaningful, Effective and Sustainable. *Children and Society*, 18, 106–18.

Srivastava, O.P. et al. (2003) The Graded Care Profile: A Measure of Care. In Calder, M.C. and Hackett, S. (Eds.) *Assessments in Child Care: Using and Developing Frameworks for Practice.* Lyme Regis: Russell House Publishing.

Stanley, J. and Goddard, C. (2002) *In the Firing Line: Power and Violence in Child Protection Work.* London: Wiley.

Stevenson, O. (1989) Multi-disciplinary Work in Child Protection. In Stevenson, O. (Ed.) *Child Abuse: Professional Practice and Public Policy.* New York: Harvester Wheatsheaf.

Summit, R. (1983) The Child Sexual Abuse Accommodation Syndrome. *Child Abuse and Neglect*, 7, 177–93.

Tomison, A. (1996) Child Protection Towards 2000. *Child Abuse Prevention*, 4, 2.

Trotter, C. (2004) *Helping Abused Children and Their Families*. Sydney: Allen and Unwin.

Wald, M.S. and Woolverton, M. (1990) Risk Assessment: The Emporors New Clothes? *Child Welfare*, 69: 6, 483–511.

White, S. and Featherstone, B. (2005) Communicating Misunderstandings. *Child and Family Social Work*, 10, 207–16.

CHAPTER 7

Dimensions of Risk: Professionals Tipping the Balance?

Phil Heasman

Introduction

Not one of the agencies empowered by Parliament to protect children in positions similar to Victoria's – funded from the public purse – emerge from this Inquiry with much credit. The suffering and death of Victoria was a gross failure of the system and was inexcusable. It is clear to me that the agencies with responsibility for Victoria gave a low priority to the task of protecting children. They were under-funded, inadequately staffed and poorly led . . . The extent of the failure to protect Victoria was lamentable. Tragically, it required nothing more than basic good practice being put into operation. This never happened.
(From *The Victoria Climbié Inquiry: Report of an Inquiry by Lord Laming*, 2003)

This chapter seeks to identify and explore the 'professional'* domains and dimensions of practice (specifically risk assessment and management) with vulnerable children and young people, suggesting that a theoretical construction of risk and safety rooted in ecological and systemic ideas must identify professionals as part of the dynamic system around a vulnerable child or young person – potentially 'tipping the balance' towards safety and a positive outcome. However, it is suggested that professional domains and dimensions may also potentially tip the balance towards risk and add dangers and hazards (after Brearley, 1982), contributing to the possibility that a child or young person may fail to attain their optimal development and that, in the worst of cases, such a failure may prove fatal.

It is argued that if we can better recognise and understand the professional domains and dimensions to both 'risk' and 'safety' then perhaps strategies may be developed to: (a) identify and 'accentuate the positive', the frequently unsung safeguarding work that occurs day in, day out, by and between professionals,

and (b), 'eliminate the negative' of, at best, ineffective and, at worst, dangerous individual, agency and inter-agency practice.

Firstly, some elements of a contemporary discourse of children and young people's welfare are identified in order to establish the professional dimension in this discussion of 'risk':

- Recognition of the role of 'the children's workforce' in the context of the relationship between the individual, the family, civil society and the state, as the breadth of formalised service provision expands within a needs-based/deficit approach, within a currently limited but emergent rights-based approach, and within an understanding of the complementary or substitutionary professional role alongside that of parents, carers, wider family, networks and communities.
- The breadth of a contemporary construct of 'risk' and 'safety' – from 'child abuse' to 'wellbeing'; from 'child protection' to 'safeguarding and promoting'; where what is at risk is the 'optimal development' of children and young people into adulthood.
- Developments in an understanding of the factors that can impact on the opportunities for a child or young person to attain her/his optimal potential, embracing a delicate 'balance' model of: strengths, promoting, resilience, mitigation, safeguards and safety – balanced with – weaknesses, demoting, inhibiting, jeopardy, compromise, dangers, hazards and risk.

Secondly, a new model of professional domains and dimensions is offered, constructed deliberately to mirror and complement the near ubiquitous 'triangle' model of assessment and intervention in relation to children in need, parenting capacity, wider family and the environment offered through the statutory guidance of *Working Together* (DoH, 1999), the accompanying *Framework for the Assessment of Children in Need and their Families* (DoH, 2000a) and related *Practice Guidance* (DoH, 2000b), and

---

* 'Professional' is taken broadly to represent members of 'the children's workforce': those who work with children and young people in the statutory sector and in formally recognised, constituted and approved agencies and organisations in the voluntary, community or independent sector.

reiterated in the *Common Assessment Framework* (DfES, 2006) and *Working Together* (HMG, 2006).

Finally, suggestions are made as to how an enhanced understanding of professional domains and dimensions may continue to 'tip the balance' in favour of vulnerable and 'at risk' children and young people.

Professional dimensions of risk – in context

The role of professionals

The first element identified as part of a contemporary discourse of children/young people and 'risk' is recognition of the role of professionals in the dynamic of mutual and reciprocal responsibilities, duties, expectations and rights of individuals, the family and the state. With the coining of the phrase 'the children's workforce' (not least with the establishment of the Children's Workforce Development Council and defined by such publications as the *Common Core of Skills and Knowledge for the Children's Workforce*, DfES, 2005), the idea of 'the state' in this relationship has perhaps been expanded formally beyond the confines of public agencies, services and staff, to embrace 'civil society'* and a wider category of people whose paid or voluntary work brings them into contact with children and young people, but also requires more formal regulation and guidance.

Whilst primary, day-to-day care of children and young people is rooted in parents, carers and families located in neighbourhoods and communities (*Children Act 1989* s. 17 (1)(b)), it is recognised that a 'professional dimension' plays a *complementary* role through, firstly, the provision of universal services, especially primary health care and education, although it is acknowledged that the qualifications of citizenship and 'official' status may exclude some children and young people in theory, whilst discrimination, questions about access and unequal geographical provision may exclude others in practice. Secondly, when needs are not met by the capacity of primary carers or family with the support of universal services, a more formal relationship is defined through legislation for some children e.g. those

'in need'. For a smaller number still the professional role can become more *substitutionary*, extending under statute to protection in the face of actual or likely to suffer 'significant harm' (e.g. *Children Act 1989* s. 44, 47), or in the provision of alternative care (*Children Act 1989* s. 31).

> . . . *a child shall be taken to be in need if: (a) he is unlikely to achieve or maintain, or to have the opportunity of achieving or maintaining, a reasonable standard of health or development without the provision for him of services by a local authority . . . (b) his health or development is likely to be significantly impaired, or further impaired, without the provision for him of such services; or (c) he is disabled.*
> (The Children Act 1989 s. 17)

The introduction of the *Common Assessment Framework* (DfES, 2006) as both a process and an assessment tool could be seen as an attempt to guide and link a broader range of agencies, including non-statutory, in to the formal recognition and management of a response to unmet need that may comprise a risk to a child or young person's health and development at a stage between 'universal' provision and 'child in need.'

Thus, civil society organisations, public sector organisations, with health, social care and education especially, and, to an extent, independent profit-making organisations ('the market' in Anheier's definition), provide complementary or substitutionary services. In *Working Together* (HMG, 2006, 1.1, 31), this is done because children are 'deserving', but the expectations of the professional role are further increased if a rights-based approach is embraced. The proclamation of rights enshrined in international convention (the United Nations Convention on the Rights of the Child, 1989) and the UK's signature in 1991, suggests recognition of the responsibilities of being a 'duty-bearer' and guarantor, especially by the accountable signatory, the 'state party'.

Whether the ideological basis for complementary or substitutionary involvement is rights-based or one focusing on children and young people's needs – professionals comprising the children's workforce have a vital role to play in a spectrum of responsible parties, including parents, carers, families, neighbourhoods and communities, responding generally to children and young people in a policy framework where 'every child matters', but especially responding to those who are vulnerable or at risk.

---

* 'Civil society . . . is the sphere of institutions, organisations and individuals located between the family, the state and the market in which people associate voluntarily to advance common interests' (Anheier, 2004: 22).

Developing constructs of risk and safety

The second element of a contemporary discourse on children, young people and risk that I would identify is the breadth of the potential construct of 'risk'. It is suggested above that the state has acknowledged its duty, responsibility and role in responding to children and young people vulnerable and at risk, but I would suggest that it has also perhaps played a part in *creating* and constructing the very definitions of risk used. An examination of the developments in statutory guidance issued through four editions of *Working Together* (1988, 1991, 1999 and 2006) serve to illustrate the point.

Whilst the exhortation to work together (again and again and again) provides the common refrain and primary title to the four editions of statutory guidance in England and Wales, the changes in the full title and stated aims of the various editions are significant and perhaps indicative of a developing perspective and narrative of what constitutes risk for children and young people.

The sub-title: 'A guide to arrangements for inter-agency co-operation for the protection of children from abuse' (DHSS, 1988) was supplemented in the second edition (1991) with the words 'under *The Children Act 1989*' to represent the passing of the legislation that still provides the foundation and primary enabling powers for statutory involvement. By 1999 the document:

> . . . sets out how all agencies and professionals should work together to promote children's welfare and protect them from abuse and neglect . . .

additionally describing:

> . . . how actions to safeguard children fit within the wider context of support to children and families
>
> (1999: vii)

From a seventy-two page A5 document in 1988, to a two hundred and fifty-six page A4 document in 2006, the expansion in both overall content and in specific sections provides a picture of increasing complexity and the accumulation of lessons from research, inspections, reviews and practice experience – and, not least, increasing regulation and procedure. Key sections have remained in every edition: roles and

responsibilities of agencies; guidance on managing individual cases (24 pages in 1988, 49 in 2006); training; and 'case reviews', for example. But the 1999 edition introduced a section (6) entitled 'child protection in specific circumstances', which by 2006 had become a major section (11) on 'safeguarding and promoting the welfare of children who may be particularly vulnerable', addressing fifteen areas of potential risk including bullying, race and racism, domestic violence, child abuse and information technology, unaccompanied asylum-seeking children etc.

Thus, the breadth of the contemporary agenda and an indication of what might be 'at risk' is revealed in the 2006 edition of *Working Together* by the *reduced* stated intention of the guidance which: 'sets out how organisations and individuals should work together to safeguard and promote the welfare of children' (p. 9). 'Protection' has become 'safeguarding and promoting'; a focus on 'abuse' has become the broader concept of the 'welfare of children'.

The Children Act 1989 s. 1: 1 sets the standard for 'welfare': that the child's welfare is paramount, specifically in relation to proceedings under the act, but more generally in practice providing a principle for every aspect of work and decision-making. In *Working Together*, 1999 (1.1) welfare is expressly linked to the idea of 'full potential' which, if denied, constitutes 'risk . . . of an impoverished childhood . . .'. Full potential is defined as:

- 'Be as physically and mentally healthy as possible.
- Gain the maximum benefit possible from good-quality educational opportunities.
- Live in a safe environment and be protected from harm.
- Experience emotional well-being.
- Feel loved and valued, and be supported by a network of reliable and affectionate relationships.
- Become competent in looking after themselves and coping with everyday living.
- Have a positive image of themselves, and a secure sense of identity including cultural and racial identity.
- Develop good inter-personal skills and confidence in social situations.'

Whilst these attributes and aspirations primarily relate in 1999 to the immediate or imminent experience of childhood, another element of the discourse around children's welfare is also hinted at in section 1.1 which asserts that if children and young people 'are denied the opportunity to achieve their potential in this way, children are at risk not only of an impoverished childhood, but that they are also more likely to experience disadvantage and social exclusion in adulthood.'

Seven years' later and the policy initiative has moved from *Quality Protects* (DoH, 1999) to *Every Child Matters* and the long-term consequences for an increased likelihood of disadvantage and social exclusion in adulthood has perhaps combined with a more recently emerging discourse on citizenship during childhood, into adulthood and across the lifespan to produce a list of 'five outcomes' that define and express contemporary aspirations for all children and young people. These outcomes:

- stay safe
- be healthy
- enjoy and achieve
- make a positive contribution
- achieve economic wellbeing

are 'key to children and young people's wellbeing' – and an additional concept has entered the narrative (DoH, 2006, 1.1: 31).

A new section in *Working Together* 2006 perhaps provides the clearest indication of the current breadth of the 'safeguarding and promoting' vision, and, consequently, the related breadth of 'risk' that some children may face:

Safeguarding and promoting the welfare of children is defined for the purposes of this guidance as:
- *protecting children from maltreatment*
- *preventing impairment of children's health or develop-ment*
- *ensuring that children are growing up in circumstances consistent with the provision of safe and effective care and undertaking that role so as to enable those children to have optimum life chances and to enter adulthood successfully.*

(DfES, 2006, 1.18: 34–5)

The notion of 'health and development', constructed around the seven dimensions of health, education, emotional and behavioural development, identity, family and social relationships, social presentation and self-care skills (originally in DoH, 1995; expanded in DoH, 2000a) has provided the basis for state sanctioned intervention in the lives of children and young people considered to be at risk. Risk that a child's 'health and development may be impaired/significantly impaired ... without the provision of services' is the test for a 'child in need' (*The Children Act 1989* s.17); risk that a child may be 'suffering or likely to suffer significant harm' (with the definition of such a relative phrase actually 'turning' on the very notion of health and development, Sn.31, 10) is the test for child protection involvement (*The Children Act 1989* s. 47 (1) (b), s. 44 (1) (a), s.46 (1) and s.31 (2) (a).

However, with the five outcomes (embedded through section 10 of the Children Act 2004 in the responsibilities and duties of local authorities and in co-operation with other specified agencies, DfES, 2006: 27) providing the organising rationale for the very structure and recording of assessments, plans and programmes of intervention and their review and evaluation through the Integrated Children's System (DoH, 2002), the horizons both of risk and responsibility seem to have expanded. The here and now of 'impairment' or 'significant impairment' or the actual or likely prospect of 'significant harm' for some children and young people has expanded to embrace the idea of an impoverished childhood and a yet more ambitious aim: successful entrance to adulthood and 'optimum life chances' for every child and young person. The breadth of a definition of what is now 'at risk' has thus expanded, constructed through statutory guidance and linked to expectations of a response from professionals across the children's workforce – safeguarding and promoting the wellbeing of children and young people now and into their future.

Optimal potential; a delicate balance

The importance of a complementary and sometimes substitutionary role for the professional dimension identified above can be highlighted further through the exploration of a (delicate) 'balance' model of children and young people's health and development, welfare and wellbeing and the factors that may impact on it.

Building on ideas propounded by both child development and systems theorists (such as Bronfenbrenner, 1979; Pincus and Minahan, 1973; Checkland, 1999) and an ecological approach (Jack, 2001), perhaps representing the influence of underlying social, economic and technological narratives about networks and real and virtual

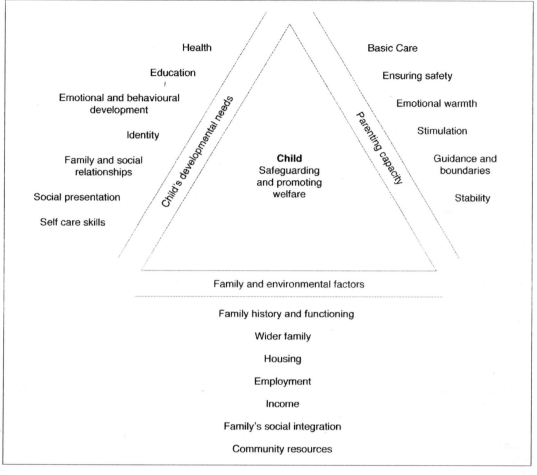

Figure 7.1 Assessment framework triangle (DoH, 2000a)

communities, has provided a way of thinking about children and young people's development in the context of the immediate care and nurturing that they receive (parenting capacity) and of the wider family and environment in which they live. *Working Together* (DoH, 1999), the *Framework for the Assessment of Children in Need and their Families* (DoH, 2000a and the *Assessing Children in Need and their Families: Practice Guidance* (DoH, 2000b) literally shaped these ideas in to à model that has dominated assessment and responses in recent years.

Whilst two dimensional models are inevitably static, it may be helpful to reconfigure the ideas into an alternative illustrative model that can hint at the potentially complex, dynamic interaction of factors that contribute to the outcomes for any

and every child and each young person. Moreover, this alternative model has at its heart the notion that such outcomes may be the product of a delicate 'balance' of influences both positive and not so positive; that the balance at stake is the 'balance of probabilities' that either an endangered or safe 'wellbeing' outcome is indicated for a particular child or young person. The step-by-step, accumulative construction of such a model may therefore provide some additional insight into risk and safeguarding factors, into both the problem locus and the solution focus when there are concerns about a child or young person's immediate or likely health and development, welfare or long-term wellbeing even into adulthood – and into the significance of the professional dimension.

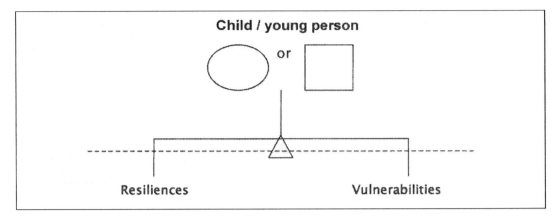

Figure 7.2   Resilience/vulnerability balance

(a) Focusing on the child or young person

Firstly, the model takes as its primary reference point the child or young person; it references the 'child' domain of the DoH assessment framework 'triangle' and introduces the idea of balance pivoting the interplay between strengths and hazards, risk factors and safeguarding factors, resiliences and vulnerabilities (Gilligan in Daniel et al., 1999).

   With this initial emphasis solely on factors inherent, intrinsic and relating directly to a child or young person her/himself, there may be a number that tip the balance either in favour of, or away from, the optimisation of outcomes, a situation where optimal life chances are supported, promoted and nurtured (safeguarded) or where they are inhibited, demoted, threatened or compromised (put at risk). Some examples of such factors can be taken from an assessment tool that has gained considerable prominence recently in social and health care work with children and young people: a 'vulnerability and resilience matrix' (see Figure 7.3) which also reflects the idea of balancing 'strengths' (resiliences) and areas of concern or 'weaknesses' (vulnerabilities) (Gordon et al., 2000; Module 3: 83). These include age, temperament, disability, IQ, 'innate' characteristics, problem solving skills, and the type of factors identified by Garmezy as contributing to 'stress-resistant children' and explored by Rutter in a consideration of psycho-social resilience in a context of protective mechanisms (both in Rutter, 1985).

   The dotted line in Figure 7.2 represents an illustrative line of intervention which may 'turn'

on the child's health and development. When vulnerabilities outweigh resiliences in a force-field style analysis, signs and symptoms (physical, emotional, verbal) of concern may be identified and trigger action, whether this is the catalyst for an assessment and co-ordination of additional needs and related services under the *'Common Assessment Framework'*, or a referral under the statutory designations of 'children in need' or 'child protection'/safeguarding processes.

(b) Focusing on parenting and caring capacity, the wider family and environment

The ecological, systemic approach adopted by the framework 'triangle' additionally recognises domains of influence on the health and development or wellbeing of children and young people that are 'extrinsic', which again may be assessed as providing a locus for both concerns and a focus for solutions. These include parenting and caring capacity, and the wider family and environment.

   Using the vulnerability and resilience matrix again, such factors might include domestic violence, minority status, serious parental difficulties such as drug abuse and alcohol misuse, and/or parental mental illness. The *Framework for Assessing Children in Need and their Families* (DoH, 2000a: 21–3) offers an exposition of the dimensions of parenting and caring capacity and the wider family and environment including: basic care, ensuring safety, emotional warmth, stimulation, guidance and boundaries, stability;

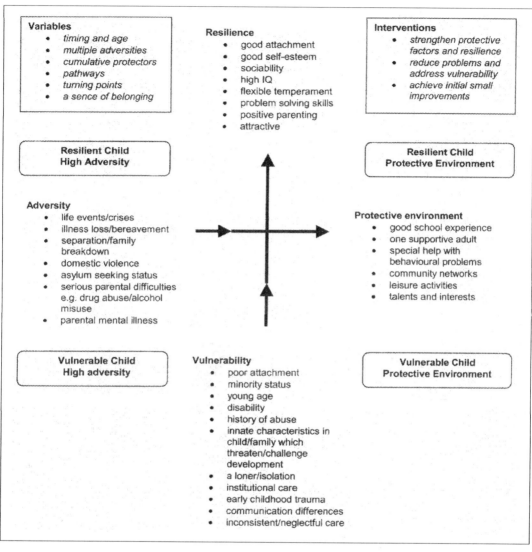

Variables
- *timing and age*
- *multiple adversities*
- *cumulative protectors*
- *pathways*
- *turning points*
- *a sence of belonging*

Resilience
- good attachment
- good self-esteem
- sociability
- high IQ
- flexible temperament
- problem solving skills
- positive parenting
- attractive

Interventions
- *strengthen protective factors and resilience*
- *reduce problems and address vulnerability*
- *achieve initial small improvements*

Resilient Child
High Adversity

Resilient Child
Protective Environment

Adversity
- life events/crises
- illness loss/bereavement
- separation/family breakdown
- domestic violence
- asylum seeking status
- serious parental difficulties e.g. drug abuse/alcohol misuse
- parental mental illness

Protective environment
- good school experience
- one supportive adult
- special help with behavioural problems
- community networks
- leisure activities
- talents and interests

Vulnerable Child
High adversity

Vulnerable Child
Protective Environment

Vulnerability
- poor attachment
- minority status
- young age
- disability
- history of abuse
- innate characteristics in child/family which threaten/challenge development
- a loner/isolation
- institutional care
- early childhood trauma
- communication differences
- inconsistent/neglectful care

Figure 7.3 Resilience/vulnerability matrix

family history and functioning, wider family, housing, employment, income, family's social integration and community resources.

The idea of balance within and between these sub-systems embraces ideas illustrated by Horowitz (in Bee 1994: 13) where 'goodness' of outcome is dependent upon 'need' being matched or surpassed by the 'capacity' of the care and the 'facilitativeness' of the environment. The vulnerability/resilience matrix (Gordon et al., 2000) also offers a dynamic equation where four quadrants are defined by the multiple

combinations of 'vulnerability' and 'resilience', 'protective' and 'adverse' environments. For example, following a risk assessment of actual or likely significant harm, the process of placing a child in foster care through the granting of an Emergency Protection Order (*The Children Act 1989* s.44) should represent a move for a 'vulnerable child in an adverse environment' to a (still) 'vulnerable child in a protective environment', but now with the prospect of change in the balance of the child's locus from vulnerability to resilience being promoted on a

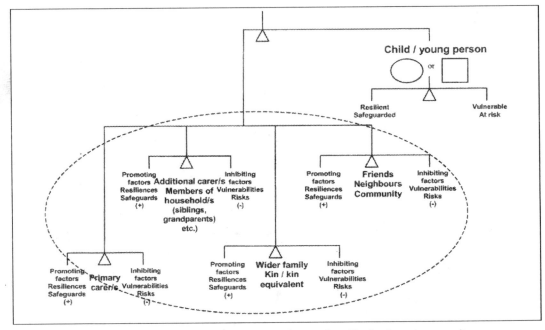

Figure 7.4   A delicate balance: child/young person, parents/carers, the wider family and community

longer term basis through a new therapeutic milieu.

Thus the 'delicate balance' model that 'turns' on a child or young person's health and development could be expanded as illustrated in Figure 7.4.

Working best as an illustrative aid to thinking, the model can be imagined (and was inspired) as a 'mobile' (hanging from a ceiling) functioning in such a way that the component parts of the various systems move round and up or down, eliding into multiple encounters and interactions (especially perhaps in the turbulence of crises). The sub-systems of 'primary carers', 'additional carers or members of the household', the 'wider family, kin or kin equivalent' and 'friends, neighbours and community' represent a complex unique and yet holistic balance of 'promoting factors, resiliences and safeguards' (Boushel, 1994) as well as potentially 'inhibiting factors, vulnerabilities and risks', where the overall effect is greater than the sum of its component parts.

An inhibiting factor within the 'primary carer' system, for example domestic abuse that may then lead to a child or young person's unmet emotional needs, may be 'balanced' by positive or 'promoting' relationships in the wider family, or indeed through supportive relationships in

school or community groups; the continuation of long-term care for a disabled child by her/his parents may be maintained by the respite afforded by a grandparent on an occasional basis; the impact of poverty may be balanced at times of crisis by support from a community-based charity or the favourable rates of a credit union when loan sharks circle!

(c) Focusing on the professional dimensions: part of the 'delicate' balance

The model as it stands thus far represents a re-conceptualisation of the domains presented in the *Framework for Assessing Children in Need and their Families* (2000a) and seeks to convey something of the potential dynamic interaction between sub-systems and the balance between safeguarding factors and risk factors.

However, in keeping fully with an ecological, systemic and network approach to understanding children and young people's development 'in an holistic context' and as an extension of the earlier argument, this chapter suggests that it is vital to incorporate into the model a consideration of professional domains and dimensions.

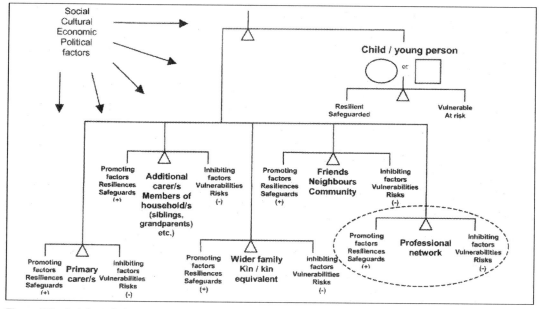

Figure 7.5 A delicate balance: adding the professional dimension

As outlined above, there is an expectation that children and young people's wellbeing is promoted, enabled and supported *positively* within a range of service provision in a partnership between parents/carers, the family, the community, civil society and the state. It is recognised that 'a wide range of services and professionals support families in bringing up children' (DfES, 2006: 31) and the presumption remains that optimal wellbeing may be risked without professional involvement. Without involvement the prospects of a child or young person failing to achieve their full potential is jeopardised: again, '. . . if they are denied the opportunity and support they need to achieve (the five outcomes), children are at increased risk not only of an impoverished childhood, but also of disadvantage and social exclusion in adulthood' (DfES, 2006: 31).

Therefore, in the final, full version of the model, illustrating all these domains and dimensions, sub-systems and balancing factors, professionals (members of the children's workforce across the relevant agencies, be they statutory, voluntary, community and independent), are recognised as an integral part of the system around a child in providing positive services, compensating, promoting resilience, filling gaps and deficits of capacity or competence in other parts of the system, helping

to off-set and minimise risk, and tipping the balance towards a favourable outcome.

However, less positively, such a model fundamentally implies that the professional sub-system within a delicate balance may also actually inhibit and compromise, undermine, jeopardise, add vulnerability and add risk – contributing to tipping the balance *away* from the prospects of a child or young person achieving their optimal wellbeing, and towards a critical pathway of risk.

The broad definition of abuse offered by the Report of the National Commission of Inquiry into the prevention of abuse entitled *Childhood Matters* (NSPCC, 1996: 2) challenges any complacency regarding the delicate balance:

> *Child abuse consists of anything which individuals, institutions, or processes do or fail to do which directly or indirectly harms children or damages their prospects of safe and healthy development into adulthood.*

The 'anything' serves to remind that children and young people, their parents and carers, the wider family, community and professionals, indeed, the whole system, is influenced by, and may perpetuate, much wider cultural, social, economic, and political factors (the 'climate' under which service users and professionals all operate – after Milner and O'Byrne, 1998: 60), which in turn may promote or inhibit, may add risk or add safety, may tip the balance positively or negatively throughout the system and for all elements of the system, especially children and young people – and that this effect may operate disproportionately and unfairly for some (perhaps the most vulnerable) in a society of personally, culturally or socially institutionalised inequality and discrimination. Furthermore, the definition is particularly challenging when it is considered that 'individuals' may be members of the children's workforce, the 'institutions' may be our agencies, and the 'processes', those ones that we seek to follow.

Acts of commission ('anything which individuals, institutions, or processes do') perpetrated by the 'professional dimension' might include the institutionalised abuse of children and young people in residential care (Levy and Kahan, 1991), and cases of abuse at the hands of those in a formal caring role or position of authority such as priests, teachers and youth leaders. Acts of omission ('anything which individuals, institutions, or processes . . . fail to do'), may be represented within the pages of many, many public inquiries, part 8 reviews and serious case reviews. A consideration of these narratives of 'risk realised' can add to an understanding of the professional dimension.

> *When a child dies, and abuse or neglect is known or suspected to be a factor in the death . . . organisations should consider whether there are any lessons to be learnt about the ways in which they work together to safeguard and promote the welfare of children.*
>
> (DfES, 2006: 8.2: 169)

In such circumstances or where 'a child sustains a potentially life-threatening injury or serious and permanent impairment of health and development through abuse and neglect'; or when 'a child has been subjected to particularly serious sexual abuse'; or when 'a child has been murdered and a homicide review is being initiated'; or, finally, when 'a child has been killed by a parent with a mental illness' – then a serious case review should be conducted or considered (ibid.).

Additionally, Local Safeguarding Children Boards should always consider whether a serious case review should be conducted where '. . . the case gives rise to concerns about inter-agency working to protect children from harm . . .' (ibid.)

– a circumstance that points to the heart of this chapter.

Indeed, an analysis of the professional dimension is the *only* formally stated purpose of all reviews, whatever the initial concern and reason for their conduct, in order to:

- *Establish whether there are lessons to be learnt from the case about the way in which local professionals and organisations work together to safeguard and promote the welfare of children.*
- *Identify clearly what those lessons are, how they will be acted on, and what is expected to change as a result.*
- *As a consequence, improve inter-agency working and better safeguard and promote the welfare of children.*

(DfES, 2006, 8.3: 169–70)

Despite the distressing cataloguing of chronologies and narratives of increasing, accumulating or catastrophic and unmitigated risk and deterioration in the health and welfare of particular and all too real children and young people that public inquiries and latterly serious case reviews inevitably provide, the limits to the value of an analysis of any specific dangerous dynamic between the child, their parents or carers and the wider family and community have been recognised. For example, the inquiry into the death of Liam Johnson (1989) suggested that:

> *It was said to us before we started hearing evidence that if we could suggest ways in which families like this, who in no way stand out from hundreds of others with whom the agencies deal, could somehow be identified before the tragedy occurs it would be an enormous help. It will be clear from the pages that follow that although we suggest ways in which practice might be improved, we have been unable to suggest any infallible method of spotting potential child killers.*
>
> (DoH, 1991: 63)

Thirteen years and many inquiries and reviews later, Sinclair and Bullock (2002: 60) concluded their review of forty randomly selected Serious Case Reviews by suggesting that:

> *Only one of the 40 cases scrutinised was seen as highly predictable and only three as highly preventable . . .*

acknowledging that:

> *. . . unfortunately the factors common to cases have limited predictive value for identifying which children will become*

victims of child abuse within the general population. The lessons to be learned ... are, therefore, more about processes for handling risk of harm than for identifying vulnerable children.

(p. 57)

Following this analysis of the professional dimension in contemporary context, and having established that professional domains and dimensions must be considered amongst a multiplicity of risk or safety factors influencing outcomes for children and young people in a complex, interactive and potentially delicately balanced dynamic – a separate and sophisticated model is required to help us to understand 'processes for handling risk of harm' (ibid.) and to enable a more detailed exploration.

(d) A complementary model; a missing triangle

Calder (2003: 55). in a reformulation of the assessment framework incorporated the 'worker' alongside the 'child' at the heart of the 'triangle', and the first draft of the professional domains and dimensions model below was deliberately constructed in 1999 to complement and mirror the 'assessment framework' triangle. It had far fewer dimensions at first but was informed partly by the public inquiry report into the death of Jasmine Beckford (Blom-Cooper, 1985) that identified certain characteristics of 'dangerous professionals'. Secondly, there was a sense that however helpful the child/parenting capacity/wider family and environment construction was, the 'assessment triangle' missed out the professional dynamic – both in relation to risk and potential intervention. Reflection and discussion with practitioners and students since the first version, and recognition of the many lessons and myriad recommendations from subsequent public inquiries, serious case reviews and inspection reports, has added a number of dimensions to each domain and has served to reinforce key elements that seem to feature in many overall analyses.

The findings and recommendations of public inquiries, 'part 8 reviews', and, indeed, the very stated purpose of serious case reviews under *Working Together* 2006 relate to the professional dimension.

Galilee contends that the recommendations of inquiries have generally remained consistent over the last sixty years:

- the need for inter-agency working
- improved communication between agencies
- better understanding of other agencies and their role
- improved information sharing between agencies
- enhanced recording
- better staff support and supervision.

Reder, Duncan and Gray (1993) reviewed thirty-five inquiries and assert that: 'If one feature ... stands out above all others, it is the panel's repeated conclusions that inter-agency communication was flawed.' They quote negative critical comments relating to inter-professional communication from sixteen reports from 1974 to 1989. The litany begins with words from the Maria Colwell inquiry report from 1974: 'Maria, despite an elaborate system of 'welfare provisions', fell through the net primarily because of communication failures.' Variations on these words continue to challenge practice to the present day (p. 60–1). The inquiry into the death of Jasmine Beckford (Blom-Cooper, 1985) seems to suggest that the attitudes and actions of some workers and agencies involved contributed to the risk that she faced: over-optimism about the prospects of rehabilitation; belief in parental co-operation; over-sensitivity to the needs and feelings of parents; a reluctance to accept a 'policing' role in child abuse cases; a lack of shared values between agencies; a lack of experience; inadequate supervision of the family; denial of risks; failure to detect significant warning signs; poor communication between workers; confusion about case responsibility or accountability; lack of skills in communicating with children; lack of awareness about the impact of adverse environmental conditions and lack of supervision from senior staff.

Sinclair and Bullock (2002: 15–6) cite the most common practice shortcomings in their review of forty serious case reviews sampled from those undertaken between 1998 and 2001. Broad themes are identified: inter-agency working; collecting and interpreting information; decision-making and relations with families with more specific difficulties relating to inadequate sharing of information; poor assessment processes; ineffective decision-making; a lack of inter-agency working and poor recording of information.

Working Together (DfES, 2006: 32) highlights the influence of the inquiry into the death of Victoria Climbié recognising that:

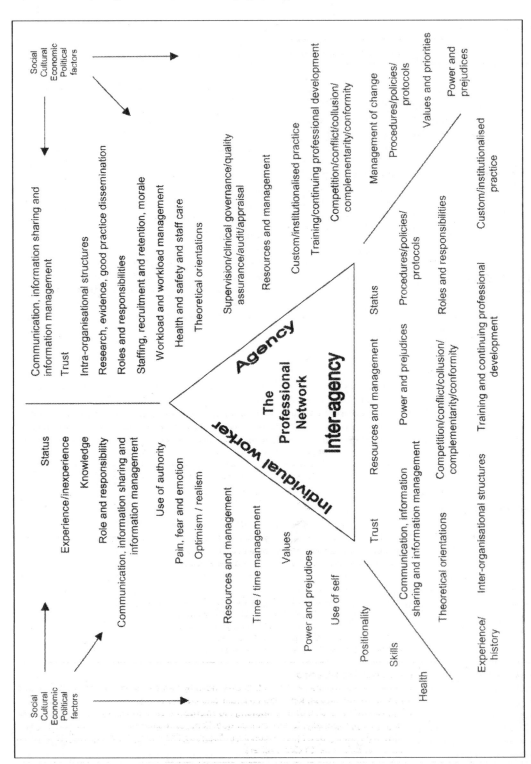

Figure 7.6 A complementary triangle: professional domains and dimensions

Table 7.1

Dimension	Characteristics and considerations
'Worker' domain	
Status	For potential consideration: • *Formal* status accorded a particular worker linked to job title and role. • *Informal* status rooted in either workers' perceptions and/or others' perceptions. • *Perceived* status resulting from social position.
Experience	For potential consideration: • Personal and professional experience. • An accumulation (and testing/validation) of 'practice wisdom'. • Levels of confidence in relation to what works. • Levels of competence – knowledge, skills and values. • A range of working knowledge that informs individual practice in the context of multi-agency work from within a specific agency and in a particular community, in partnership with parents and carers and with children and young people.

Knowledge	For potential consideration:
	• A typology of 7 areas of knowledge (e.g. Kent/Medway CCA students 2000):
	  • know what
	  • know when
	  • know why
	  • know how
	  • know who
	  • know self
	  • know others
	• Knowledge that is conscious and articulable; sub-conscious accessible with prompting; unconscious or latent knowledge.
	• 'Residual messages' (Heasman, 2006) informing how a worker: analyses, assesses, 'makes' sense', theorises in relation to the situations she or he is involved in; and how she/he 'forms a response' that leads to a plan and actual implementation/intervention to promote change, maintain or 'manage decline'.
	• Levels of commitment to evidence-based approaches – knowledge of 'what works'.
	• Consideration of relevance of *general* evidence-based findings applied to *particular* circumstances.

Role and responsibility	For potential consideration: • *Actual* role expectations and responsibility linked to post and position, self and others (both specific to a worker's agency, legislation, statutory requirements and profession e.g: compliance with professional codes of conduct). • Worker's *perception* of their role and responsibility.
Communication, information sharing and information management	For potential consideration: • Ability to communicate effectively through various appropriate media. • Understanding of the boundaries of confidentiality. • Understanding of information sharing protocols: what, when, to whom, why? • Understanding of data protection issues. • Processes of analysis and decision-making.
Use of authority	For potential consideration: • Understanding of the authority that they have by virtue of their position (personal and professional), status, legislation (Holder and Corey, 1987). • Appropriate exercise of that authority: to maintain a child focus, to communicate and engage appropriately, to ask difficult questions, to respond to threats, to challenge others (including other professionals, colleagues, line managers if required), to 'make a case', to influence, to direct others.

Table 7.1   *Continued*

Pain, fear and emotion (vulnerability and resilience)	For potential consideration: • The impact of challenging, complex and potentially distressing aspects of work with children and young people and the circumstances that they face (Simmonds, in Adcock and White, 1998). • Varying responses from different workers according to the emotional vulnerability or resilience of the worker. • Fear of violent or threatening parents/carers (Newham ACPC, 2002).
Optimism/realism	For potential consideration: • Workers' knowledge and understanding of explanations and factors contributing to an 'at risk' aetiology. • Workers' knowledge and understanding in relation to protective or safeguarding factors. • Workers' knowledge and understanding in relation to the capacity for potential for change and improvement. • Consideration of the dynamic of hope and the reality of experience.
Resources/resource management	For potential consideration: • Availability of appropriate, quality assured, effective resources (preventative, responsive). • Skills, strategies and guidance to manage finite resources effectively.
Time and workload/time and workload management	For potential consideration: • Appropriate balance between workload and time to manage it effectively. • Realistic identification and recognition of all aspects of work: direct practice, administration, continuing professional and personal development/training, supervision, networking. • Skills, strategies and guidance to manage finite (including personal) resources effectively.
Values	For potential consideration: • Recognition of the social, cultural, political, professional and personal construction of values. • Adherence to professional codes and statements of values (e.g. Nursing Midwifery Council/General Teaching Council/GSCC 2006). • Anti-discriminatory, anti-oppressive practice, promoting equality of opportunity and access, valuing diversity. • A key element of competence.
Power and prejudice	For potential consideration: • Recognition, understanding and response to power differentials, prejudice and discrimination: personal, organisational, institutionalised, structural, social, political.
Emotional intelligence/ Reflexivity/Use of self/ Confidence/Sensitivity/ de-sensitivity	For potential consideration: • Empathy, compassion, self awareness. • 'Relational' (Folgheraiter, 2004), reflective and reflexive practice. • Communicate, engage, work 'in partnership', promote participative approaches, recognise expertise rooted in experience. • Ability to respond and adapt in the here and now, in 'dialogue', in congruence. • Ability to make a case and persuade. • Workers' relative perceptions, feelings ('gut instinct') of 'risk' and 'safety'/'safeguarding' factors. • Keeping a focus on 'this' child/young person when characteristics of a situation are shared amongst a number of 'similar' children/young people (*The Children Act 1989* s.31: 10). • The importance of a maintaining a 'fresh pair of eyes' (Ayre, 1998). • An ability to recognise changing circumstances.

Table 7.1   *Continued*

'Positionality'	For potential consideration:
	• Workers' awareness of their own position (gender, class, orientation, ethnicity, culture, disability status etc.) and the potential impact on their understanding and responses (Takacs, 2003).
	• Workers' ability/willingness to consider others' positions and the potential impact on their understanding and responses.
Skills and agency	For potential consideration:
	• Appropriate and corroborated/endorsed *sense* of competence, confidence and agency – further key element required for effective practice.
	• Workers' *actual capacity* to act, to influence, to respond (proactively, preventatively, reactively) using a range/repertoire of evidence/practice wisdom informed tools and strategies; recognising and making the most of opportunities.
	• Workers' *perceptions* of their capacity to act, influence and respond (proactively, preventatively, reactively).
Health	For potential consideration:
	• Workers' own health (physical and emotional – see below) and implications for optimal effectiveness.
	• Levels of stress and the effects.

'Agency/organisation' domain

Communication, information sharing and information management	For potential consideration:
	• Ability to communicate effectively through various appropriate media.
	• Understanding of the boundaries of confidentiality.
	• Understanding of information sharing protocols: what, when, to whom, why . . .
	• Understanding of data protection issues.
	• Processes of analysis and decision-making.
Trust	For potential consideration
	• Respect and confidence between staff and in relation to competence, respective roles and responsibilities, processes and procedures, etc.
Intra-organisational structure	For potential consideration:
	• Comprehensive, complementary, coherent, transparent and accountable (checks and balances) levels and layers of service provision and management within the agency.
Research, evidence, good practice dissemination for effective policy and practice	For potential consideration:
	• Effective strategies for dissemination of research findings/good practice initiatives to critique and challenge current policy and practice and to inform, develop and promote effective future policy and practice.
Roles and responsibilities	For potential consideration:
	• Clear, transparent, agreed, negotiated and accepted shared understanding of respective complementary roles and responsibilities between agencies.
Staffing, recruitment, retention and morale	For potential consideration:
	• Realistic appraisal of required capacity.
	• Retention strategy including opportunities for continuing professional development, progression, flexible working arrangements and appropriate benefits.
	• Commitment to agreed staffing levels at appropriate differentiated levels.
	• Effective recruitment strategy to minimise vacancies.
	• Recognition that public and voluntary services are probably effectively maintained by goodwill and unpaid overtime.
Workload and workload management	For potential consideration:
	• Appropriate workloads – volume, range of work, using complementary strengths.
	• Sophisticated and responsive workload weighting systems to recognise all aspects of workers' (changing) roles and responsibilities.
	• Effective management, advice and guidance.

Table 7.1   *Continued*

Health and safety and staff care	For potential consideration: • Recognition that the workforce is perhaps the most valuable asset that an agency has. • Strategies to protect staff, to fulfil 'duty of care', to promote and protect health and welfare (physical and psychological), to prevent health and safety being compromised, to protect and provide support as appropriate.
Theoretical orientations	For potential consideration: • Adoption and promotion of appropriate theoretical approaches underpinning practice and policy – complementary and shared following critical appraisal of effectiveness/what works. • Promoting key priorities such as participation, partnership working, anti-discriminatory/anti-oppressive strategies, equal opportunities etc.
Supervision, clinical governance, quality assurance, audit, appraisal	For potential consideration: • Comprehensive (multi-function), regular, child-centred/focussed supervision including appropriate practice critical analysis, reflection, guidance and direction, decision-making and SMART goals linked to anticipated outcomes and signs of success defined in relation to child/young person's health and development (optimal outcomes), rooted in awareness of 'what works'. • Critical, independent (where appropriate) structures and processes for clinical governance, quality assurance, audit and appraisal. • Meeting internal and external/local and national standards, benchmarks, priorities and performance indicators.
Resources and management	For potential consideration: • Realistic, planned and monitored allocation of resources to achieve goals linked to anticipated outcomes and sign of success defined in relation to child/young person's health and development (optimal outcomes), rooted in awareness of 'what works'. • Effective management of resources – with both fixed and responsive capacity.
Custom and institutionalised practices	For potential consideration: • Critical recognition of the strengths and especially the limitations of practice (personal and organisational) and policies that may be pursued and perpetuated as a matter of custom or may be institutionalised (including 'hidden', structurally embedded discriminatory practice). • The danger of 'organisational malaise' (Laming, 2003).
Training and continuing professional development	For potential consideration: • Opportunities for training and continuing professional development: • A range of courses, activities and events (individual, team, agency, multi-agency). • Differentiated and targeted (linked to roles and responsibilities). • Clear aims, objectives and well-defined learning outcomes. • Referenced to contemporary key benchmarks and documents e.g. ECM 'Change for Children Outcomes Framework'; National Occupational Standards and related Statement of Expectations of Service Users and Carers; Codes of professional conduct; 'W.T.' learning outcomes; UNCRC; Post-Qualifying/Post-Registration frameworks; legislation; policies and procedures etc. • Promoting ADP, diversity, equal opportunities. • Promoting children and young people's/parents' and carers' participation. • Promoting multi-agency practice and integrated working. • Research-informed (including findings from serious case reviews) and promoting research-informed practice. • Resulting in realistic (SMART/goal-based) action-plans linked to learning outcomes. • Evaluated (baseline, added-value, impact on participants, impact on service users). • Accredited where possible and appropriate.

Table 7.1 *Continued*

Competition/conflict/ collusion 'complementarity'/ conformity	For potential consideration: • Recognition that intra- and inter-personal and group dynamics may operate within an agency overtly and/or covertly to impede effectiveness.
Management of change	For potential consideration: • Recognition and management of continuing processes of change and development: participatory, transparent, clearly communicated, emotionally intelligent.
Procedures, policies and protocols	For potential consideration: • Up to date, clear, accessible, agreed, complied with, embedded and supported by people, structures and processes across an agency. • Reviewed and developed.
Values and priorities	For potential consideration: • Recognition of the social, cultural, political, professional and personal construction of values. • Adherence to professional codes and statements of values (e.g: NMC/GTC/GSCC 2006). • Anti-discriminatory, anti-oppressive practice, promoting equality of opportunity and access, valuing diversity.
Power and prejudice	For potential consideration: • Recognition, understanding and response to power differentials, prejudice and discrimination within an agency or organisation: personal, organisational, institutionalised, structural, social, political, cultural, etc.

'Inter-agency' domain

Trust	For potential consideration: • Respect and confidence between staff and in relation to competence, respective roles and responsibilities, processes and procedures, etc.
Resources and management	For potential consideration: • Realistic, planned, monitored, allocation of *complementary* resources to achieve shared goals linked to anticipated outcomes and sign of success defined in relation to child/young person's health and development (optimal outcomes), rooted in awareness of 'what works'. • Effective management of resources – with both fixed and responsive capacity between and across agencies.
Status	For potential consideration: • *Formal* status accorded workers linked to job titles and roles. • *Informal* status rooted in either workers' perceptions and/or others' perceptions. • *Perceived* status resulting from social positions.
Communication, information sharing and information management	For potential consideration:: • Ability to communicate effectively through various appropriate media. • Understanding of the limits of confidentiality. • Understanding of information sharing protocols: what, when, to whom, why. • Understanding of data protection issues. • Processes of analysis and decision-making.
Power and prejudice	For potential consideration: • Recognition, understanding and response to power differentials, prejudice and discrimination between agencies and organisations: personal, organisational, institutionalised, structural, social, political.

Table 7.1   *Continued*

Procedures/policies/ protocols	For potential consideration: • Up to date, clear, accessible, agreed, complied with, embedded and supported by people, structures and processes across agencies. • Individual agency procedures and policies to be complementary and compatible. • Reviewed and developed.
Theoretical orientations	For potential consideration: • Adoption and promotion of appropriate theoretical approaches underpinning practice and policy – complementary and shared following critical appraisal of effectiveness/what works. • Promoting key shared priorities such as participation, partnership working, anti-discriminatory/anti-oppressive strategies, equal opportunities etc.
Competition/conflict/ collusion/complementarity/ conformity	For potential consideration: • Recognition that intra- and inter-personal, group, agency and organisational dynamics may operate between agencies overtly and/or covertly to impede effectiveness.
Roles and responsibilities	For potential consideration: • Clear, transparent, agreed, negotiated and accepted shared understanding of respective complementary roles and responsibilities between agencies.
Experience/history	For potential consideration: • The sum of individual experience that may be pooled, shared and accumulated such that the whole is greater than the parts, or may be fragmented and unshared, such that the whole is less than the individual parts. • The accumulated experience of working together.
Inter-agency/organisational structure	For potential consideration: • Comprehensive, complementary, coherent, transparent and accountable (checks and balances) levels and layers of service provision and management between agencies.
Training and continuing professional development	For potential consideration: • Opportunities for training and continuing professional development: • A range of courses, activities and events (individual, team, agency, multi-agency). • Differentiated and targeted (linked to roles and responsibilities). • Clear aims, objectives and well-defined learning outcomes. • Referenced to contemporary key benchmarks and documents e.g: ECM 'Change for Children Outcomes Framework'; National Occupational Standards and related Statement of Expectations of Service Users and Carers; Codes of professional conduct; 'W.T.' learning outcomes; UNCRC; Post-Qualifying/Post-Registration frameworks; legislation; policies and procedures etc. • Promoting ADP, diversity, equal opportunities. • Promoting children and young people's/parents' and carers' participation. • Promoting multi-agency practice and integrated working. • Research-informed (including findings from serious case reviews) and promoting research-informed practice. • Resulting in realistic (SMART/goal-based) action-plans linked to learning outcomes. • Evaluated (baseline, added-value, impact on participants, impact on service users). • Accredited where possible and appropriate.
Custom and institutionalised practice	For potential consideration: • Critical recognition of the strengths and especially the limitations of practice (personal and inter-organisational) and policies that may be perpetuated as a matter of custom or may be institutionalised (including 'hidden' discriminatory practice). • The danger of inter-'organisational malaise' (Laming, 2003).

Shortcomings when working to safeguard and promote children's welfare were brought into the spotlight once again ... and the inquiry revealed themes identified by past inquiries that resulted in a failure to intervene early enough. These included: poor co-ordination; a failure to share information; the absence of anyone with a strong sense of accountability; and frontline workers trying to cope with staff vacancies, poor management and a lack of effective training.

As with the previous model, this further model is offered illustratively rather than definitively. Three domains are included: a worker domain; an agency domain; and an inter-agency domain. Again, these need to be encircled both with a ring of recognition that wider cultural, social, economic and political factors will be influential throughout and that inequality and discrimination (prejudice empowered) are likely to be at work. Each domain is divided into a number of dimensions and some commentary is included in the table following – a format parallel to that offered in relation to the 'dimensions of child's developmental needs', 'dimensions of parenting capacity' and 'family and environmental factors' in the *Framework for the Assessment of Children in Need and their Families* (DoH, 2000a: 19 onwards).

As noted many of these dimensions have been included as a result of their occurrence and re-occurrence in many public inquiries and serious case reviews where the details are all too tragically illustrated and analysed.

Other dimensions in the model are included because their relevance has emerged from discussions with practitioners and service users, through training and development activities and through research projects. Many perhaps serve to highlight the complexity of the dynamics involved within and between elements of the various systems surrounding a child or young person, including the professional. The place of knowledge includes research awareness, theoretical considerations and an understanding of 'what works'; a focus on values, 'positionality', power and prejudice, custom and institutionalised practice; a consideration of competition, conflict, collusion, complementarity and conformity; the place of emotions from over-optimism to fear, and the capacity for reflective and reflexive practice. Finally, the emerging literature, research and growth in practice wisdom associated with effectiveness, 'what works' (e.g. Hill, 1999; Macdonald, 2001;

McAuley et al., 2006) has been influential in recognising positive features across the model, whilst a rapidly developing experience and understanding of effective inter- and multi-agency work has informed thinking about that particular domain. All these dimensions, that may play out in a more or less covert way in the delicate balance of dynamic influences around a child or young person, would seem to merit further consideration in research, in reports, and by members of the children's workforce in and across agencies, perhaps helping to reduce the unpredictable and increase the preventable.

(e) Implications and applications

From a basic framework of three domains designed to complement the Department of Health emphases on the child, parenting capacity and the wider family and environment, the model offered here has evolved and developed in discussion with health and social care practitioners and managers, in the light of further inquiry reports and serious case reviews, and alongside an interest in research regarding effectiveness and inter-professional work.

It is important to remember that such a model is itself a construct, an attempt to capture and articulate ideas about the elements of a professional network that can promote or inhibit optimal outcomes, which can add safety or risk to vulnerable children and young people. As such, it is neither necessarily an accurate representation of reality nor a final statement. Perhaps the greatest potential value is to provide a conceptual framework to help individuals, teams or groups of practitioners, and those with operational responsibility or with strategic responsibility, to reflect, discuss and analyse critically their own practice and the structures, procedures, processes and systems that support and direct it. Only some of the dimensions offered within each domain may be relevant for particular individuals or groups, whilst the discussion and generation of individual, agency and inter-agency network-specific elements could be a valuable exercise in its own right.

The dimensions could be used as an assessment checklist. Self-assessment and/or independently gathered evidence (including service user feedback) relating to each one could be sought; strengths of practice could be identified, celebrated, promoted and shared; weaknesses, gaps in the professional 'safety net' or downright dangerous elements of practice, process, procedures or systems might also be identified and challenged. The model could serve as a rich tool for supervision, performance review, training and development. Following reflection and analysis, an individual, team, agency and inter-agency plan might be developed to identify and implement strategies to improve practice and work towards achieving smart, measurable, achievable, realistic and targeted goals relating to increased worker, agency and inter-agency competence, confidence and capacity and aimed at ensuring that the professional dimensions of balance are tipped towards optimal outcomes for children and young people; towards safety not risk.

Unfortunately, these dimensions might also serve to focus and structure aspects of analysis in the management or Serious Case Review of the lives and possibly deaths of children where the whole system or network of parents/carers, additional carers, members of households, wide family, friends, neighbours, the community *and* the professional network has failed to protect. The domains could be used to provide a common structure and conceptual framework for the various professional groups' contributory reports to a case review, the full analysis or, indeed, a meta-analysis addressing several inquiries, reports or reviews over a period of time such that any generalised list of potential 'risk factors' (e.g. Greenland, 1987 cited in Kemshall and Pritchard, 1996) might include the possibly pivotal issue of professional involvement.

(f) Conclusion

This chapter has argued that the professional dimension is an integral part of the system surrounding a child or young person – playing a part through complementary or substitutionary services in tipping the balance towards the safeguarding and promoting of health and development immediately and in relation to longer term optimal outcomes.

However, it is suggested also that in some circumstances the professional dimension through omission, and less commonly through commission, may contribute to tipping the balance towards risk and danger.

A three point model has been constructed and presented to assist reflection and analysis of the potentially complex professional domains, dimensions and dynamics operating at an individual, agency and inter-agency level.

Finally, whilst the focus of this analysis has been rooted in the discourses and narratives of children's and young people's lives, particularly those who may be vulnerable and at risk, the model could have a wider relevance for and application to all and any health and social care service users, any situation where professionals may play a part in safeguarding and promoting and tipping the balance towards wellbeing.

References

Anheier, H.K. (2004) *Civil Society: Measurement, Evaluation, Policy.* London: Earthscan.

Ayre, P. (1998) Significant Harm: Making Professional Judgements. *Child Abuse Review* 7: 5, 330–42.

Bee, H. (1994) *Lifespan Development.* New York: Harper Collins.

Blom-Cooper, L. (1985) *A Child in Trust: The Report of the Panel of Inquiry into the Circumstance Surrounding the Death of Jasmine Beckford.* London: HMSO.

Boushel, M. (1994) The Protective Environment of Children: Towards a Framework for Anti-oppressive, Cross-cultural and Cross-national Understanding. *British Journal of Social Work,* 24, 173–90.

Brearley, C.P. (1982) *Risk and Social Work (Hazards and Helping).* Law Book Co of Australasia.

Bronfenbrenner, U. (1979) *The Ecology of Human Development.* Cambridge, MA: Harvard University Press.

Calder, M.C. and Hackett, S. (Eds.) (2003) *Assessment in Child Care – Using and Developing Frameworks for Practice.* Lyme Regis: Russell House Publishing.

Checkland, P. (1999) *Soft Systems Methodology: A 30-Year Retrospective.* London: J. Wiley.

Cleaver, H., Unell, I. and Aldgate, J. (1999) *Children's Needs: Parenting Capacity.* London: HMSO.

Corby, B., Doig, A. and Roberts, V. (2001) *Public Inquiries into Abuse of Children in Residential Care.* London: Jessica Kingsley.

Daniel, B., Wassell, S. and Gilligan, R. (1999) *Child Development for Child Care and Protection Workers.* London: Jessica Kingsley.

DfES (2006) *Common Assessment Framework: Practitioners' and Managers' Guides* (April 2006).

DHSS, Welsh Office (1988) *Working Together: A Guide to Arrangements for Inter-agency Co-operation for the Protection of Children from Abuse.* London: HMSO.

DoH, Home Office, DfES, Welsh Office (1991) *Working Together Under the Children Act 1989: A Guide to Arrangements for Inter-agency Co-operation for the Protection of Children from Abuse.* London: HMSO.

DoH (1991) *Child Abuse: A Study of Inquiry Reports 1980–1989.* London: HMSO.

DoH (1999) *The Children Act Report 1995–1999.* London: HMSO.

DoH, Home Office, DfEE (1999) *Working Together to Safeguard Children: A Guide to Inter-agency Working to Safeguard and Promote the Welfare of Children.* London: HMSO.

DoH (2000a) *Framework for the Assessment of Children in Need and their Families.* London: HMSO.

DoH (2000b) *Assessing Children in Need and their Families: Practice Guidance.* London: HMSO.

DoH (2000c) *Lost in Care: Report of the Tribunal of Inquiry into the Abuse of Children in Care in the Former Council areas of Gwynedd and Clwyd since 1974.* London: HMSO.

DoH (2000) *Integrated Children's System: Working with Children in Need and their Families.* Consultation document. London: HMSO.

Folgheraiter, F. (2004) *Relational Social Work – Toward Networking and Societal Practices.* London: Jessica Kingsley.

Fowler, J. (2003) *A Practitioner's Tool for Child Protection and the Assessment of Parents.* London: Jessica Kingsley.

Galilee, J. (2005) *Learning from Failure: A Review of Major Social Care/Health Inquiry Recommendations.* The Scottish Office.

Gordon, R. et al. (2000) *The Child's World – Training and Development Pack.* NSPCC/University of Sheffield.

Grotberg, E. (1996) The International Resilience Project. In John, M. (Ed.) *A Charge against Society: The Child's Right to Protection.* London: Jessica Kingsley.

HM Government (2006) *Working Together to Safeguard Children – A Guide to Inter-agency Working to Safeguard and Promote the Welfare of Children.* London: HMSO.

Heasman, P.E. (2006) *'Praxis Makes Perfect? An Exploratory Study of the Fate of Research in SW Education and Practice'.* MPhil. Thesis: University of Kent.

Hendry, E. and Lewis, P. (1990) Risk and Child Abuse. *Practice,* 4, 3.

Hill, M. (Ed.) (1999) *Effective Ways of Working with Children and their Families.* London: Jessica Kingsley.

Holder, W. and Corey, M.K. (1987 revised 1991) *The Child at Risk Field System – A Family Preservation Approach to Decision Making in Child Protective Service.* North Carolina: Action for Child Protection.

Horowitz, F.D. (1987) *Exploring Developmental Theories: Toward a Structural Behavioural Model of Development.* London/New York: Lawrence Erlbaum Associates.

Jack, G. (2001) Ecological Perspectives in Assessing Children and Families. In Horwath, J. (Ed.) *The Child's World: Assessing Children in Need.* DoH, NSPCC, University of Sheffield.

Kemshall, H. and Pritchard, J. (Ed.) (1996) *Good Practice in Risk Assessment and Risk Management* London: Jessica Kingsley.

Levy, A. and Kahan, B. (1991) *The Pindown Experience and the Protection of Children: The Report of the Staffordshire Child Care Inquiry.* Staffordshire County Council.

London Borough of Newham ACPC (2002) *Newham Report into the Death of Ainlee Labonte/Walker.* London Borough of Newham.

Madonald, G. (2001) *Effective Interventions for Child Abuse and Neglect – An Evidence-based Approach to Planning and Evaluating Interventions.* Chichester: J. Wiley and Sons.

McAuley, C., Pecora, P.J. and Rose, W. (2006) *Enhancing the Well-being of Children and Families Through Effective Interventions – International Evidence for Practice.* London: Jessica Kingsley.

Milner, J. and O'Byrne, P. (1998) *Assessment in Social Work.* London: Macmillan.

Morrison, T. (1990) The Emotional Effects of Child Protection Work on the Worker. *Practice,* 4, 4.

NSPCC (1996) *Childhood Matters: Report of the Commission of Inquiry into the Prevention of Child Abuse.* Volume 1. London: The Stationery Office.

Pincus, A. and Minahan, A. (1973) *Social Work Practice: Model and Method.* Itasca, ILL: F.E. Peacock.

Reder, P., Duncan, S. and Gray, M. (1993) *Beyond Blame: Child Abuse Tragedies Revisited.* London: Routledge.

Reder, P. and Lucey, C. (1995) *Assessment of Parenting: Psychiatric and Psychological Contributions.* London: Routledge.

Reder, P. and Duncan, S. (1999) *Lost Innocents: A Follow-up Study of Fatal Child Abuse.* London: Routledge.

Rutter, M. (1985) Resilience in the Face of Adversities. *British Journal of Psychiatry*, 147: 598–611.

Shaw, T. *Holistic Abuse – Systematic Review of Young People in Residential Settings 1950–1995.* (unpublished report) http://fbga.redguitars.co.uk

Simmonds, J. (1998) Making Decisions in Social Work: Persecuting, Rescuing or Being a Victim. In Adcock, M. and White, R. (Eds.) *Significant Harm: Its Management and Outcome.* Croydon: Significant Publications.

Sinclair, R. and Bullock, R. (2002) *Learning from Past Experience – A Review of Serious Case Reviews.* London: DoH.

The UK's First Report to the UN Committee on the Rights of the Child (1994). London: HMSO.

Takacs, D. (2003) How Does Your Positionality Bias Your Epistemology. *Thought and Action*, Summer 2004.

White, R., Carr, P. and Lowe, N. (1990) *A Guide to the Children Act 1989.* London: Butterworths.

CHAPTER 8

Organisational Dangerousness: Causes, Consequences and Correctives

Martin C. Calder

Introduction

Too often the apex of the organisation doesn't have a clue of what child protection work is like and are much more preoccupied with value for money and performance indicators than they are with their most valuable asset – the workers. Also, I often see performance indicators being collected just for the sake of it. Findings are seldom fed back in an analysed format that might inform practice. It leaves workers persecuted for statistical information but none the wiser when it comes to its interpretation.

(Paul Harrison, 2007, personal communication)

In Chapter 6 I examined professional dangerousness and clearly indicated that the environment in which it flourishes and is sustained is within the organisational environment. This chapter moves on to examine the organisational context and attempts to map the causes, consequences and considers some correctives. In the child protection field, this requires us to consider an inter-agency context as well as the intra-agency context.

Coordination issues in child protection

Coordination in child protection networks has been generally adopted in the western world as a desirable work practice (Morrison, 1994). There is a belief that a coordinated response to the problem of child abuse results in more effective interventions. Specifically, good coordination can lead to greater efficiency in the use of resources, improved service delivery by the avoidance of duplication and overlap between existing services; the minimisation of gaps or discontinuities in services; clarification of agency or professional roles and responsibilities in 'frontier problems' and demarcation disputes; and the delivery of comprehensive services (Hallett and Birchall, 1992). They contended that the desire for a coordinated response to child protection was often '. . . asserted, rather than demonstrated, and was taken to be self-evident'.

While there would appear to be overall agreement that coordination in child protection is a necessary and valuable practice, it has been commonly reported as being difficult to achieve (Dale et al., 1986).

The literature is full of studies and inquiry reports indicating the problems that may arise in case management when communication between workers breaks down. The problems of poor inter-professional communication in research studies differ appreciably to the problems that may arise for children when worker communication breaks down.

If services are not properly coordinated, workers are not aware of the roles of other agencies or professions involved with cases, or are simply not fully apprised of the 'facts' of a case, the probability of problems arising in case management appears to be far more likely. In extremes, this can potentially lead to the network's failure to protect the child, and perhaps leave the child open to the risk of serious injury or death.

Challis et al. (1988) noted the important role that informal professional relationships and communication paths can play in combination with formal child protection structures. Morrison (1994, 1998) also emphasised the benefits of informal contacts or relationships in strengthening the formal child protection system. It should be noted that in both cases it is acknowledged that informal linkages need to operate in *conjunction* with more formal communication structures.

Taken to extremes, the tendency to rely on informal communication methods may lead to the variety of inter-agency communication problems. That is, running a child protection network on an ad hoc basis may result in poor information sharing and at times, the loss of cases through inter-professional 'gaps' in the system. The probability of 'losing' cases is amplified in child protection networks, given the vast number of inter-professional links commonly occurring.

Organisational climate and coordination

While inter-organisational services coordination appears to be a logical and obvious way of addressing the multiple needs of those individuals most at risk, evaluations of services coordination efforts have been unsuccessful in documenting any major benefits (Hoagwood, 1997). Although the poor findings have been frustrating to those interested in developing mechanisms for improving service effectiveness, this lack of success actually supports some prior theoretical work on inter-organisational relationships. While the initial theories of inter-organisational relationships assumed coordination was always beneficial, especially for human services (Aiken et al., 1975) these benefits were questioned in subsequent work. Scott (1985) specifically questioned the benefits of coordination for the mental health sector. This scepticism was based on the potentially positive features associated with both loosely-coupled systems and redundancy (Bendor, 1985). Scott (1985) suggested that an emphasis on coordination ignores the important roles played by the variety, responsiveness, and redundancy that are found in uncoordinated service systems. Bendor (1985) in particular, pointed out the benefits of having several uncoordinated but parallel systems provide services to the same population. His notion was that such parallel systems create a healthy competitiveness and provide backup systems for any systems that fail. In spite of the conceptual critiques of services coordination and the limited empirical evidence to date supporting the value of coordination, most of the recent literature continues to argue for the benefits of inter-organisational services coordination in the human service sector generally and in the mental health service sector in particular (Glisson, 1994).

Glisson's (1994) study found that improvements in psychosocial functioning are significantly greater for children served by offices with more positive climates. The success that caseworkers have in improving children's psychosocial functioning depends heavily on their consideration of each child's unique needs, the caseworkers' responses to unexpected problems, and their tenacity in navigating bureaucratic and judicial hurdles to achieve the best placement and the most needed services for each child. This requires non-routinised and individualised casework, personal relationships between the caseworker and child, and a results rather than process oriented approach (Glisson, 1992). These findings suggest that agencies with higher levels of job satisfaction, fairness, role clarity, cooperation, and personalisation, and lower levels of role overload, conflict, and emotional exhaustion are more likely to support caseworkers' efforts to accomplish these objectives. In short, positive climates reflect work environments that complement and encourage the type of service provider activities that lead to success. A second important finding is that improved service quality does not translate into significantly more positive outcomes. This suggests that caseworkers can meet service quality objectives without contributing to improvements in the psychosocial well-being of the children who are served. Although perplexing, a close examination of this finding explains why the process-related requirements for quality service are not necessarily related to outcome criteria. As shown in recent examples from government agencies, process-oriented job requirements are not sufficient for desired service outcomes (Osborne and Gaebler, 1992). This occurs because process-oriented approaches emphasise pre-programmed activities that limit employee discretion and responsiveness to unexpected problems and opportunities. In comparison, results-oriented approaches focus employee attention on the desired outcomes and require employee flexibility and discretion in the development of individualised approaches to reaching those outcomes (see Chapter 2 for a fuller discussion on this point).

At the same time, most researchers would agree that high quality children's service systems are characterised by the process-oriented indicators (i.e. availability, responsiveness, comprehensiveness, and continuity). But consensus about the desirability of these service system characteristics must be distinguished from the conclusion that related process-oriented activities can ensure positive service results. That is to say that these characteristics of quality service are not sufficient for positive service outcomes. This is because effective children's services require non-routinised, individualised, service decisions that are tailored to each child (Glisson, 1992, 1996). Therefore, decisions that are in the best interests of a particular child may not fit predetermined criteria for service system quality. In summary, findings presented here suggest that service effectiveness is related more to organisational climate, the service provider attitudes that characterise a given service system, than to service system configurations.

Johnson and Petrie (2004) highlight how organisational issues need to be given a higher profile to ensure avoidable tragedies do not occur as a result of organisational failure. Sociologists have made three relevant observations. First, physical risks are always created and affected in social systems, for example by organisations and institutions which are supposed to manage and control the risky activity. Second, the magnitude of the physical risks is therefore a direct function of the quality of social relations and processes. Third, the primary risk, even for the most technically intensive activities (indeed perhaps most especially for them) is therefore that of social dependency upon institutions and actors who may well be – and arguably are increasingly – alien, obscure and inaccessible to most people affected by the risks in question (Beck, 1992).

The inability of social services and other agencies to protect children known to them who were suffering abuse, sometimes for prolonged periods, is frequently underpinned by significant systemic as well as practice failures. Indeed, in some instances, where additional harm was caused to children by institutional action during child protection investigations, systemic failures appear to be the most significant factors. Most major child abuse inquiries of the 1980s identified organisational issues as significant contributory factors (Dingwall, 1986; DoH, 1991). Problems identified included staff shortages due to recruitment failure, high levels of staff turnover and sickness, lack of cover for leave and sickness, inadequate levels of skill and specialist knowledge, inadequate resources, such as administrative and clerical assistance, and inadequate premises for workers and public (DoH, 1991). Yet the recent study of Serious Case Reviews (DoH, 2002) discounts organisational factors as significant. Since the reviews themselves concentrate on practice issues and policy compliance and do not undertake a systematic examination of organisational and managerial effectiveness this is not surprising.

Laming and others note that the factors that predispose to the likelihood of tragedies occurring include the repeated failure of individual workers to perform their roles adequately, allied to an organisational framework that lacks the managerial rigour and the will or robustness to ensure that responsibilities are discharged and effective multi-agency working happens. When these factors occur in tandem, conditions are created that increase the probability of system failure. The Social Services Inspectorate (SSI) concurs, recently noting that, '67 social services departments (45 per cent) could not be judged to be serving most or all children well'.

Organisational issues raised by inquiries

Parton (2004) compared the Marie Colwell and the Victoria Climbié cases and identified a worrying number of similarities, even though they were a generation apart: considerable confusion and a failure to communicate key information, so that as a consequence both children fell through the elaborate welfare net; very poor and often confusing recording of very basic information relating to visits, phone calls, conversations and messages passed between different professionals, and a general failure to use the case file in a productive and professional way; considerable failure to engage and communicate directly with the children themselves about their feelings and circumstances; considerable deceit on behalf of the key primary carers and insufficient critical analysis and scepticism on behalf of the professionals as to what was being told and being presented to them; and a severe lack of consistent and rigorous supervision. Both cases attracted considerable media attention and can be seen not just as politically sensitive but as posing fundamental questions about the health and welfare systems available to children and families. He also noted a number of key differences. While both reports talk about the failures of the respective systems, the nature of these systems is very different. There were major systematic failures in relation to Maria Colwell, but primarily concerning the sharing of information and the failure of professionals in different agencies to liaise. More specifically, the report identified the failure to communicate and liaise between two workers, one from the NSPCC and one from social services, as absolutely crucial in the final eight months of Maria's life. It was the failure of these two workers to liaise with each other and to involve others, preferably via a case conference, which was seen as key to the final outcome.

The failures of communication and inter-agency collaboration seem much more complex in the Climbié Inquiry. These problems appear to be located: between workers; between frontline workers and first-line managers; between different professionals and workers in different organisations and agencies, whether these be social services, health or police, and to a lesser extent the NSPCC; between senior managers and their employees; and between senior managers themselves.

Similarly, we are not talking only of verbal communication and written records but of the whole system of exchanging information and the way information is collated and gathered on a variety of sophisticated yet inadequate information systems. The examples of failures with information data systems are many and varied in the report. Rather than aiding communication, such systems seem to both complicate and make things worse.

What we see here is an important and significant shift. Whereas in the case of Maria Colwell the problems derived primarily from failure to communicate between case workers, in the case of Victoria Climbié, they related much more to wide-ranging and complex system failures, of which communication between individual workers was simply a part. This is a consequence not only of the growth of a variety of new procedures which has taken place over the intervening 30 years but also the growth in the use of information technology. The failures were not so much in sharing, but *managing* information, and it is in this respect that the notion of 'systematic care' is seen as so important for ensuring that information and knowledge are managed rigorously, with clear lines of accountability and responsibility.

There are large sections of the report which talk about the organisational and managerial contexts of the work. However, we are presented with something of a conundrum. There is no doubt that the last 30 years have witnessed a tremendous sea change in the way health and welfare services are organised, with an increasing emphasis on the need for clear and strong leadership, and more specifically the growth of managerialisation (Clarke et al., 2000; Newman, 2001). The increased emphasis on managerialism has been seen as a key way in which the failures of the old welfare systems could be overcome during the 1980s and 1990s. What the Climbié

report seems to indicate, however, is that rather than resolving the problems, managerialism has simply changed their nature. The report argues that senior managers and others spent far too much time not taking responsibility and not appreciating the nature of the work that was going on in 'the front office'. A major focus of the report is to try to ensure that, in the future, issues concerning responsibility and accountability are addressed, and thus what are the most appropriate forms of governance.

Reder and Duncan (2004) examined ways in which we could make the most of the Victoria Climbié Inquiry report. They noted that previous inquiry reports have indicated the need for significant training, practice and resourcing improvements which have never been adequately implemented and that the very same themes can be inferred from the Victoria Climbié Inquiry. There is a risk that this inquiry, like many others, will promote bureaucratic changes (i.e. at the level of organisational structures, written protocols and monitoring procedures) that are distant from frontline staff's need to improve their understanding of complex cases and to acquire and apply appropriate skills.

Organisational issues raised outside of inquiry reports

In addition to inquiry findings, significant attention has been drawn to the way 'systems' operate in child protection work with families, and how these 'systems' can also impede effective intervention (Howe, 1992; Morrison, 1996). As Johnson and Petrie (2005: 195) have pointed out:

> *In the public sector, child protection services have been plunged into a series of organisational changes and major policy initiatives driven by political objectives. Communication pathways have been disrupted and expert knowledge dissipated. For example, in the recent study of 40 Serious Case Reviews, a sample taken from those undertaken between 1998 and 2001, three of the six concerns most often expressed in the reports involved organisational practices. These were inadequate sharing of information (25 reports), ineffective decision-making (21 reports) and a lack of inter-agency working (17 reports) (DoH, 2002: 40). These are major 'risk' factors in services for vulnerable children and without a period of organisational stability, effective lines of communication will be impossible to establish. It is to be hoped that the Laming proposals do not further disrupt communication pathways.*

There is a distinct lack of consistency in the messages emerging from government in relation to child protection services. The emphasis placed upon 'evidence-based' practice, effective communication and wide consultation at local authority level is not reflected at the national level. The major policy and structural changes imposed on welfare organisations by government are not 'evidence-based' but are politically driven. The failure of the local authority to listen to those relatives who warned of Victoria Climbié's plight, the failure of the health trust to act upon the concern expressed by her childminder and abuse diagnosed by their paediatrician, the failure of the police to ensure Victoria was seen by their WPC, the failure of all organisations to share essential information was due, not to ignorance, but to a degree of organisational breakdown clearly evident to all those working in the child protection network (Petrie, 2003). Responses by government to authorities who fail to meet their performance criteria come in a number of ways such as punitive financial restrictions, and the imposition of 'special measures' involving further costly, demoralising, time-consuming inspections and public vilification. The devastating impact on local staff morale and the national image of social care, of Milburn's name and shame game last October is still very fresh in directors, councillors and their workforce's minds (Clode, 2002: 2). This 'naming and shaming' of individuals or agencies in the aftermath of an incident, followed by an increase in rules and regulations in an attempt to prevent future crises mirrors the developments seen within industry as efforts have been made to reduce accident rates.

The debate around evidence-based practice (Barton and Welbourne, 2005)

The technical, output-focused nature of evaluation research, coupled with a political obsession with evidence-based practice (Rawnsley, 2001) overlooks the varying organisational contexts in which service provision occurs. There are many dimensions to making 'good practice' work. The practice of omitting the organisational context from the evaluation of practice provides only a partial view of the situation being studied.

Tilley and Pawson's (1997) central argument is that by failing to examine the context in which interventions take place, most evaluation research fails to take account of the social and organisational factors that impact on the mechanisms which trigger and shape action, making replication elsewhere problematic.

Evaluation research generally works by looking at the operation ('output') of an agency before a change in work practice (or 'input') and output after new practices are introduced. Realist research challenges this notion and is based on the position that mechanism and context are two sides of the same coin; a suitable context is always necessary for the desired mechanism to fire into action, with the reverse being true – desired outcomes cannot be achieved where the context is not conducive to firing the mechanism. The implication is that any approach to replication of effective practice that fails to take agency context into consideration is overly simplistic and risks advocating modifications that may fail to improve or even exacerbate a problematic situation.

For example, child protection work is the responsibility of numerous agencies, which have greater or lesser roles in the protection of children yet which are integral parts of the overall system. Given this, multi-agency working is an essential part of the process of safeguarding and protecting vulnerable children. The mechanism for achieving this is the development of shared agreements about working practices and protocols for cooperative working, for example relating to information sharing. These in turn rest on a shared ideological commitment to multi-agency working. The ACPC/LSCB is the key agency for creating and promoting this shared commitment, as well as being a forum for 'in-house' evaluation of the effectiveness of existing arrangements for the protection of children and promotion of best practice and coordination of training.

Network awareness is vital to good working: if partners are unaware of the boundaries and abilities of their colleagues, then it follows that unawareness by agencies and workers of their partner's roles, domains of expertise and organisational and personal role boundaries will impact directly and negatively on multi-agency working. Adopting the technical fix approach implies that this can be remedied by adopting the 'good practice' of areas that have good awareness. This is an approach that is implicitly encouraged by the publication of 'league tables' by central government inspection agencies.

However, this excludes the context in which organisations operate and simplifies often complex situations. A major weakness in the 'what works' culture, with its reliance on 'objective' performance indicators and lack of attention to agency context, is that explicit consideration of the impact of the context for joint working is not built into the evaluation of performance. Gomm (2000: 175) sets out two questions that should be considered in thinking about generalising from research and dissemination of practice:

- Are the circumstances of our practice sufficiently similar to those of the research context to make it a good bet that what worked in the research will work for us?
- Insofar as there are differences, how feasible and how desirable would it be to change the context of our practice to bring it into line with that described in the research?

Organisational context should also include the geographical area covered and its population characteristics and the history of the agencies and the personalities involved in making inter-agency working 'work'. Failure to take these factors into account undermines the validity of 'technical fix' approaches to evaluation of practice and the replication and dissemination of 'what works'. The omission of contextual information means that pressure may be placed unproductively on some agencies whose organisational context is not conducive to firing the mechanisms that underpin recognised good practice derived from studies of agencies with a different context for service delivery. This is still not being fully recognised by central government.

Examining decisions in child protection

Rzepnicki and Johnson (2005) conducted research to uncover decision errors in child protection. In doing so they drew upon organisational theories. Theories of organisation describe the relationships between the organisation's goals, core activities, and the context in which activities are conducted. A basic tenet is that organisations construct their internal environment to accommodate the social mandate they serve, while simultaneously minimising threats to their survival coming from the external environment

(Manning, 1982). For example, public sympathy for abused and neglected children increases after the fatality or serious injury of a child. Media attention directed at the tragic circumstances and possible negligence of the state typically results in public outrage. This is accompanied by increased scrutiny of families investigated for child maltreatment, resulting in more substantiated reports and more children placed in substitute care. The organisation's response reduces the risk of future catastrophic events and minimises challenges to the organisation's core activities.

Systemic goals, rules and procedures, values, and outcomes define an organisation's boundaries and protect its core activities. Faced with complex problems and an indeterminate technology, child protection agencies adopt rules and procedures that limit worker discretion, with dual objectives of minimising uncertainty and preventing deleterious outcomes to ensure both child safety and agency survival (Hasenfeld, 1987). The daily operation of the organisation, however, depends on the discretion of its members in negotiating conflicting goals, interpreting rules that do not address specific problems, managing tension between organisational and individual values, and effecting desired outcomes. Over time, routine practices become established and part of the culture of the organisation. Organisational culture is shaped by management style, the level of autonomy and expectations of the employees, and institutional function. Given the stressful nature of social work, particularly work in child protection, human service organisations may exhibit a culture of stress (Thompson, Stradling, and O'Neill, 1996). Individuals respond to stress by avoiding anxiety through behaviour that is risk averse; agencies respond to stress by attempting to reduce uncertainty through the application of rules and procedures that regulate behaviour. The results of attempting to limit individual worker style, creativity, and decision-making autonomy has also been described as a culture of compliance (as compared to a culture of commitment) (Thompson et al., 1996). A practice environment regulated by rules and procedures perpetuates practices designed to minimise error by limiting worker discretion. Strict compliance to practice policies tends to reduce worker judgment and anxiety but may compromise performance (Sandfort, 1999; Smith and Donovan, 2003). For example, a culture of compliance in child welfare may place some children at greater risk when workers are required to conform to rules and procedures rather than attend to the families' unique characteristics and needs. In order to understand the culture of an organisation, it is necessary to be knowledgeable about the policies and procedures, supports, constraints and incentive structure that drive implementation at the street-level (Gambrill and Shlonsky, 2001). It also requires an intimate understanding of routine accommodation to these factors by management and staff.

Scholars investigating these events concluded that human error is rarely sufficient explanation for negative outcomes. Jones (1993) in articulating a general theory of unifying dynamic organisational self-regulation, presents one of the earliest frameworks for understanding the relationship among multilevel factors and system processes, including principles of organisational survival and failure. It is elements of the systems in which individuals are embedded that make significant contributions to organisational accidents (see Jones, 1993). In child welfare, practice is adapted to conform to worker training and experience, staff shortages, caseload size, imperfect software programmes that do not provide staff with timely information, and other factors that impinge upon job performance.

A systems perspective on organisational failure (errors and accidents) has been further developed by Reason (1990, 1997, 2003) who introduced the related concepts of active failure and latent failure to express the multi-level nature of incident causation. He maintained that active failure is usually associated with the errors and rule violations of front-line operators. In child welfare, this translates to child protection investigators or direct service staff, and has an immediate impact upon the system. Latent failure is most often generated by individuals more distant from the incident, at the upper levels of the system, such as policy makers, programme designers, managers, and may lie dormant indefinitely. Examples of latent failure in child welfare might include pressure to complete child protection investigations within 30 days and chronic staff shortages. Active failures are neither necessary nor sufficient in and of themselves to cause an accident. Reason created the Swiss cheese model to describe how organisations are built with layers of defence against error (active failures) but with holes at each level representing weaknesses and gaps (latent failures). The holes

are in constant flux, but occasionally line up perfectly, allowing an accident to occur (i.e., a child is severely injured while an abuse investigation is underway).

Anxiety and organisational issues

Morrison (1997) noted that anxiety runs like a vein throughout the child protection process. It is present in the anxious or unrewarding attachment that forms the family context in which abuse may occur. It is present in the highly charged atmosphere of the parents' first encounter with professionals concerned about their child. It is present too within the professional system, as child abuse represents a crisis not only for the family, but also for the professional network. Finally, anxiety exists not just at the level of the individual, but also, as Menzies (1970) has pointed out, as an organisational phenomenon. In the current climate of rapid change, the organisational anxiety generated by the management of risk is compounded in many organisations by the struggle for their own survival.

Failures at an organisational level to contain anxiety appropriately can permeate all aspects of the agency's work as well as affecting its relations with the outside world and other agencies. This is demonstrated in the Dysfunctional Learning Cycle described by Vince and Martin (1993) (see Figure 8.1 overleaf).

In this environment anxiety is seen as *unprofessional*, a sign of weakness or not coping. As a result, uncertainty is suppressed through fight and flight mechanisms. The exclusive 'task' focus of supervision, and absence of fora where feelings and doubts can be safely expressed, lead to defensiveness, and a resistance to share and reflect on practice. In this context the scarcity of peer group support fora, particularly for black staff or women, is significant. The environment also undermines confidence to experiment with new practice. (This may go some way to explain why it has proved so difficult to enable agencies to relinquish paternalistic practices in favour of more innovatory and participatory approaches.) Emotional defensiveness then deepens into cognitive distortion whereby the painful reality is warded off via denial of dissonant information and attitudes, offering a temporary but false sense of security. Power relations are exploited, individuals are scapegoated and attitudes

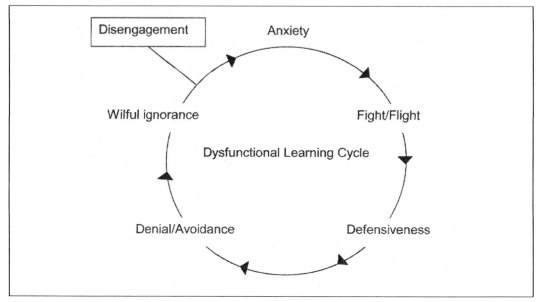

Figure 8.1   Dysfunctional learning cycle (Vince and Martin, 1993)

become polarised in a struggle for dominance and control. Oppressive processes go unchallenged. If this process worsens with more wilful and sustained ignorance, it may lead eventually to total disengagement.

Trust in decision making

Edelenbos and Klijn (2007) explored some theoretical notions of trust in complex inter-organisational networks. In public administration, there is a trend from government to governance in which public actors increasingly (have to) use more horizontal, instead of vertical, forms of steering and work together with other public actors and private actors in networks to achieve policy outcomes. It is, however, difficult to achieve joint decision making among actors, given the fact that complex inter-organisational networks are ambiguous and unpredictable. But it is precisely this joint decision making that is crucial in a modern network society. The innovative solutions that are required for today's complex world can only be achieved when different organisations combine their knowledge and resources. But because actors attempt to realise their own interests, joint decision making can be difficult. Decision making is also hampered by institutional complexity or by the

unwillingness of actors to share information, because they fear opportunistic behaviour from other actors.

The absence of trust from public administration literature may be a reflection that an alternative to trust as a mechanism is regulation. So a bureaucracy is quite likely to under use trust, even underestimate it. But with the growing attention to horizontal forms of governance, the issue of trust becomes more important. If horizontal, voluntary relations in modern societies are increasing in importance, trust seems to be an important coordination mechanism because we cannot organise all uncertainties in life through hierarchical power, direct surveillance, or detailed contracts. This is reflected by the growing attention for trust in literature on inter-organisational cooperation.

If we look at the literature on trust, some general characteristics can be traced. The first dominant characteristic of trust is vulnerability. When an actor trusts another actor, they are willing to assume an open and vulnerable position. They expect the other actor to refrain from opportunistic behaviour even if there is the possibility to show this behaviour. The actor trusts that the partner will take their interests into account in the interaction. The second dominant characteristic is risk. Trust plays an important role in ambiguous, unpredictable, and risky situations. In risky situations, trust is a precondition for undertaking any action. A conscious choice is made to take a risk because of the belief that the other party can be trusted. The assumption in most of the literature on trust is that actors will refrain from action (and cooperation) if trust is absent. The third dominant characteristic is expectations. The concept of trust presumes a stable positive expectation (or prediction) of the intentions and motives of other actors. Trust reduces unpredictability, complexity, and ambiguity in interaction because one can anticipate (some of) the behaviour of the other actor.

A further elaboration on why trust can be so important brings us to three main categories when we survey the literature on trust:

Facilitating cooperation

Substantial uncertainty and complexity exists in decision making due to differing perceptions and the variety of (sometimes conflicting) strategies. This uncertainty and complexity will drive actors to pursue 'go it alone strategies' and not cooperation, which is necessary to achieve interesting results. In general, authors argue that trust enhances the chances for cooperation between actors, and this holds true for both the public and the private spheres. Trust reduces the uncertainty of the actions of other actors. Because parties already know what they can expect from each other, the relationship will begin more smoothly. Trust will also lead more quickly to mutual commitment. Actors are willing to be vulnerable to the actions of another party. One is prepared to be dependent on other parties' actions; one is not afraid of handing business to another without installing control mechanisms. This results in a greater inclination to cooperate. In other words, the conditions for cooperation are more favourable. Another important advantage of trust is that it reduces the transaction costs involved in decision making and organising. Trust enhances the predictability of the strategies of other actors and reduces the possibility of opportunism. If we summarise the literature, trust is an important precondition for inter-organisational cooperation. It reduces the cost of cooperation and enhances the chances of cooperation.

Solidifying cooperation

Trust enlarges the robustness of inter-organisational cooperation; it promotes ongoing interaction among organisations and the continuation of cooperation. Partners in the cooperation can handle difficult times more easily and conflicts will not soon lead to a rift in the relationship. The partner is willing to believe that the reason for the breach of confidence is not the other partner's fault, but the fault of others, or can be attributed to situations beyond the control of the business partner. He or she is willing to believe that the partner has tried as much as possible to comply with the rules of the cooperation. Trust also encourages actors to invest in the cooperation both in terms of manpower and in terms of financial investments to create new and innovative products and outputs. This will encourage partners to stress long-term benefits of cooperation. This encouragement to invest will also solidify cooperation.

Enhancing performance of cooperation

In situations where trust is present, confidence in other actors will be greater and the flow of information and willingness to exchange information is likely to be greater. As a result, the problem-solving capacity is enlarged. The same reasoning can be applied to stimulating innovation. From an economic point of view, involvement in innovation is a risky and uncertain activity. No one knows what the outcome will be or if efforts to create innovative products or solutions for problems will be successful. It is also next to impossible to create adequate control mechanisms against opportunistic behaviour of other actors because nobody can know beforehand what kind of opportunistic behaviour one has to protect against. Trust can facilitate innovation because uncertainty about opportunistic behaviour is reduced and the feeling that other actors will exercise their goodwill in the search for innovative solutions is increased.

Child protection rationality

Ferguson (2005) noted that a striking feature of contemporary child protection discourse is its rationality. The overwhelming response by welfare states to child deaths and other system failures has been to seek bureaucratic solutions by introducing more and more laws, procedures and guidelines. The more risk and uncertainty has been exposed, the greater the attempts to close up the gaps through administrative changes. While these are valid concerns, the problem surrounds the one-dimensionality of the approach and the relentless focus on new forms of organising child welfare work as the key to solving problems. Here, practice is regarded as little more than rule following. But child protection is not only constituted by administrative power and the law, but by an aesthetic sensibility and an expressive dimension. The 'aesthetic' sensibility arises from how it is fundamentally a social practice based on mobility, movement and creativity, involving engagements with time and space (classically, alternating between the office and the client's home). It is only in making this move from the office into the homes of children and families that the full multi-dimensional nature of child protection comes into being, and through theorising child protection in terms of movement and its mobilities (Urry, 2000) that we can reach a fuller understanding of it. The 'expressive' dimension here concerns the psycho-social dynamics which are always present in child protection practices because they are deeply embedded in relationships. Encounters between workers and users of services are mediated through the emotions, senses and the body in ways which give rise to complex feelings and forms of reciprocity and resistance. From a psycho-analytical perspective, for instance, such practices can be interpreted in terms of processes such as transference and counter-transference and the need for workers as well as service users to contain anxiety. The conflict and ambivalence that arise from this lead to struggles that are invariably quite literally fought out on clients' doorsteps or inside their homes and are central to the contingent, unpredictable, 'psycho-social' nature of interventions. Ultimately, a full understanding of child protection depends upon considering its three-fold character in terms of its administrative powers, aesthetic, and psychosocial dimensions.

Incompetent practices identified by Lord Laming

The Laming report undoubtedly explains a lot as the source of the failures to protect Victoria are put down to a combination of events and 'woefully incompetent practices'. There was

evidence of profound organisational malaise and an absence of leadership as exemplified by senior managers' apparent indifference to children's services, which were under-funded and neglected. Local child protection procedures were way out of date and this was compounded by major staffing problems and low morale among staff who were invariably over worked and 'burning out'. Front-line workers got little support or quality supervision and were uncertain about their role in child protection. Extremely poor administrative systems existed for tracking referrals and case information. There was poor or non-existent inter-agency communication and a consistent failure to engage with the child in any meaningful shape or form as a service user or to assess the child's needs, coupled with a focus throughout on Kouao, Victoria's carer, as the client in the case (Laming, 2003). Perhaps the most significant overall contribution of this report, especially when seen in the context of all the previous inquiries, is how it connects up the experiences of front-line workers with poor management and a lack of accountability right up to the highest levels. We are left in no doubt that the workers involved in Victoria's case were over-worked and under-supported.

Lack of attention to these processes in Victoria's case was compounded by various aspects of organisational culture. The social workers did not just have to deal with menacing and manipulative clients, but similar kinds of colleagues, including managers, and acted out distorted and abusive patterns with one another. The report's descriptions of the internal politics of the social work teams demonstrate that there was little comfort or release for the workers. One social worker recalled that the 'team was very divided, and there were a lot of deep conflicts. At times the working environment felt hostile, and it was not a comfortable place to work comfortably in.' There were allegedly 'two camps', with 'insiders and outsiders within the office'. Similar distorted relationships and communications extended to relationships between agencies: social workers were afraid to challenge doctors' opinions, while at least one team of social workers had it in for the police. The very dynamics that professionals had to routinely confront in families were embedded in the workplace also. This is no mere coincidence. As systems theory and psycho-dynamic theory have helped us to appreciate, professional systems and family systems have a tendency to become enmeshed and reflect one another. Professional relationships come to mirror distorted and abusive relationships within families (Reder et al., 1993). Lisa Arthurworrey, the social worker who had most contact with Victoria, actually referred to her Team Manager as 'the headmistress. I was a child who was seen but not heard, and had seen what had happened to those who challenged [the manager]' (Laming, 2003: 192). This was compounded by a one-dimensional performance management culture. One social worker referred to the culture of 'Conveyer belt social work' and how the 'ethos seemed to be particularly about getting the cases through the system and meeting the targets, meeting the statistics, getting them through the system' rather than doing the work that needed to be done (Laming, 2003: 112). Others spoke of the 'bombardment factor' of the relentless work that came into the office. Cases were just 'plonked on social workers' desks', with no attention to the workers' needs, feelings, worries, or the degree to which the level of difficulty in the case reflected their experience or competence. As Lisa Arthurworrey, Victoria's social worker from the north Tottenham office told the inquiry: 'we always worked at a fairly cracking pace in north Tottenham' (Laming, 2003: 184).

The dominance of performance management cultures creates a reflex flow to the work, which demands that it needs to be done more and more quickly within the terms of what it is possible to make visible and measurable at an organisational level. One of the real tragedies of this case for the workers was that they worked so hard. Lisa Arthurwoorey had actually accumulated 52 days off in lieu! As is so often the case, it is not the effort or motivation to do good work that is at issue, but the (mis-) direction of it and absence of a clear conceptual understanding of what is needed to perform effective child protection. In total, there was a complete lack of attention to process and feelings, no space for reflection, for slowing things down, as the social work office itself was not a safe or nurturing space. Pressure to get cases 'through the system' also creates a situation where attention, time and resources are diverted from doing in-depth, needs-driven work with children and families in ways that can promote child safety, welfare and healing. The soul is being squeezed out of the work, pulling workers and entire systems' attention away from understanding and developing the kinds of deep relationships with the self, children and carers that are required to do meaningful child protection and welfare work.

Change in children's services

Horwath and Morrison (2007) explored the complexities and ambiguities inherent in collaborative working in children's services. They noted that collaboration in relation to safeguarding children takes place within a variety of contexts and involves different levels of integration:

- Communication: individuals from different disciplines talking together.
- Cooperation: low key joint working on a case-by-case basis.
- Coordination: more formalised joint working, but no sanctions for non-compliance.
- Coalition: joint structures sacrificing some autonomy.
- Integration: organisations merge to create new joint identity.

Increasingly, governments are advocating the highest level of collaboration as a response – integration of localised services. Integrated services are characterised by a unified management system, pooled funds, common governance, whole systems approach to training, information and finance, single assessment and shared targets. Partners have a shared responsibility for achieving the service goals through joint commissioning, shared prioritisation, service planning and auditing. Joint commissioning can be one of the major levers for integration, service change and improving the delivery of children's services. Ultimately, joint commissioning may lead to the merger of one or more agencies, who give up their individual identities for a shared new identity. While the literature places an emphasis on the potential gains from higher levels of collaboration, there are also tensions, conflicts, and dilemmas for partnership members. For example, individual agency independence and identity can be challenged with internal working practices being affected (Barton, 2002). The emphasis in higher-level collaborations can become systems, structure and funding, with little consideration given to working relationships and outcomes (Hogan and Murphy, 2002). When lack of attention to process occurs partner agencies can become preoccupied by the factors that divide them rather than those that unite them (Hallett and Birchall, 1992; Hudson, 2000; Loxley, 1997; Morrison, 1996). The implications of this are that each collaborative venture needs to resolve a range of issues if members are to be clear, committed and possess the capacity to participate effectively.

Organisational changes and confusions

Morrison (1997) also pointed to the potential created by the tremendous organisational and cultural change that we are currently experiencing. In a climate of rapid and imposed change, organisations and individuals may be forced to relinquish previous certainties, assumptions and practices, in accepting the inevitability of continuous change. For some this may provide exciting new and creative opportunities. Organisational change and fragmentation also mean that many organisational structures are embryonic and immature, and therefore potentially more available to influence, and in need of development. At an individual level too, all of the above can act as a powerful motivator for learning and development, as staff seek opportunities for reflection about changes, affirmation of existing skills and the acquisition of new ones. Training has a key role to play in the management of change. In a world of fragmenting structures and relationships, training, especially when conducted over a period, can offer staff a constructive group experience directed at meeting their needs, in which participants can feel a sense of belonging, identity, self-esteem and self-efficacy.

Since welfare organisations are now required to operate within the 'market' framework, it may be useful to compare and contrast theoretical understanding of such important events across public and commercial sectors. Although the organisational context of child protection services is now very different from that of the 1980s, organisational dysfunction highlighted in many of the public inquiries of that decade remains, as revealed by the Victoria Climbié Inquiry.

The management of local authority social services is undergoing substantial continuing

change. A key feature of this is the development of performance indicators. Since the arrival of New Labour into office in 1997 the organisation of welfare has been the subject of a continuous stream of policy initiatives from government affecting many services for vulnerable children and their families including child protection.

The 'refocusing' policy carries dangers: 'if the move towards supporting families rather than assessing risks goes too far, and if warning signs are consequently missed or ignored, the result for the child will be devastating' (Fitzgerald, 2001). The implementation of this strategy and associated policies by local authorities is monitored by government through a highly complex array of performance indicators such as a reduction in the number of children on the child protection register. The late 1990s has seen the emergence of the performance culture . . . which has developed a framework for monitoring the public sector through national performance indicators. The problematic nature of the child abuse debate makes the identification of indicators more difficult, a factor that might well sit uncomfortably with the emerging culture (Dyson, 2002). Performance criteria are given to each local authority based on macro characteristics, such as size of the target population, indices of deprivation and so on. Meeting these criteria becomes the basis for judgements about performance and further resource allocation by government. Whilst these initiatives are presented as mechanisms for ensuring the effectiveness and accountability of local authorities, fears have been expressed that form is becoming more important than content. In other words: 'Accountability, the assurance that something is managed well . . . becomes transformed into audit' (Townley, 2001). Audit does not always accurately reflect the performance of an organisation and there are indications that the requirement to meet performance indicators has become the over-riding goal of managers in some public sector organisations. Their attention becomes fixed on meeting the expectations of government departments, however inappropriate, rather than maintaining an accurate analysis of their organisations capacity to handle 'risk' and develop responses to minimise adverse outcomes through organisational failure.

The 'market economy' is an inappropriate vehicle for welfare distribution because the service-user rarely has purchasing power.

However, since health and welfare 'markets' are likely to remain in the foreseeable future it is imperative that the identification of 'best practice' in the understanding and management of 'risk' in the commercial sector should at the very least be understood by organisations operating in welfare 'markets'. This understanding may enable the transfer of learning across sectors, especially if similar problems are identified, for example the breakdown of communication within and between organisations. However, the plethora of policy and practice guidance emerging from government in relation to the assessment of vulnerable children and their families (DoH, 1999; DoH, DfEE, HO, 2000; DoH, 2000), primarily address practice and administrative issues and are aimed at practitioners and first line managers. Policy and guidance hardly address organisational practice, such as the correlation between resources and outcomes, although some public sector health and welfare organisations are now in systemic failure. There have been no public complaints of management overstretch, but it is abundantly clear that in many authorities the 'joined up' overload at middle and senior management levels is causing just as much concern as staffing shortages and recruitment blights are causing at the frontline (Clode, 2002).

Regan (2007, personal communication) pointed out that accountability is a critical issue. Organisations are now accountable and this has become more explicit since Victoria Climbié – however, what does this really mean in practice? There is more clarity about the expectation of the social work role and task; there is training provided to ensure they are better able to communicate with children, however, they are unable to put this into practice because of time constraints and caseloads. Managers 'collude' with the organisation in that they know there is a problem but this isn't addressed – the qualitative part of the work is not covered in supervision – it is still task focused. EG managers may ask or expect workers to have seen the child but do not then ask about this work – so how do they know what quality of interview was done. Worryingly, the system then makes the worker more accountable because they have structure, guidance, expectation and training – however, the fact that we know the work with children isn't happening as it should leaves them vulnerable if or when something goes wrong.

Reforming the child protection system: competing paradigms of change

Cohen (2005) noted that efforts to reform the child welfare system have been hampered by the tendency of would-be reformers to operate out of different perspectives, or paradigms, each of which is relatively closed to the others. This paper identifies four traditions of social planning and social change and relates them to different approaches to reforming child welfare. Each perspective has its own core assumptions, its own approach to knowledge building, and its own flaws or weaknesses. Due to the magnitude and complexity of the child welfare crisis, it is important to find ways to bring together the various perspectives into a more unified and systemic approach to reform.

John Friedmann (1987), in a sweeping account of planned change efforts, developed a framework that identified four major traditions for the linking of knowledge and action. According to this framework, knowledge can be derived in one of two ways. In the first, it flows from the top down through the central authority of the state, a process that Friedmann refers to as societal guidance. In the second, it flows from the bottom up, emerging from the community and its members, which Friedmann calls social transformation. Action also can take two fundamentally different forms. In its conservative form, action and change are viewed as incremental and as originating within the existing system. In its radical form, action and change are viewed as comprehensive activities or events that originate from outside of the existing system and challenge the status quo. By combining these two dimensions, Friedmann proposes a classification of our major traditions of planned change as shown in Figure 8.2 overleaf. Each of the four is briefly described.

Social reform

According to Friedmann, social reform is the central tradition in planning and social change theory. It focuses on the role of the state in guiding societal progress through the application of scientific knowledge to public affairs. Social reformers tend to believe in grand reforms at the macro-levels of society as the best way of bringing about social change. They also tend to

Action Knowledge	Conservative (Incremental)	Radical (Comprehensive)
Societal guidance (Top down)	Policy analysis	Social reform
Social transformation (Bottom up)	Social learning	Social mobilisation

Figure 8.2   Four approaches to planned change by integrating knowledge and action (Friedman, 1987)

believe that change comes from the top and so address their interventions to those at high levels of power. In the case of child welfare reform, those who are adherents of the social reform tradition tend to favour large-scale changes in macro-governmental policies, usually accompanied by massive infusions of new resources.

Social mobilisation

In contrast to the social reform tradition, the social mobilisation tradition begins with those who are oppressed or at the lower rungs of society. While fundamental and structural changes are sought, the proposed changes are based on the knowledge and experiences of those at the bottom, rather than the authority of the state. Reform is sought through confrontation and struggle with those in positions of power and it encompasses a process of self-liberation of people in their own communities.

Policy analysis

Policy analysis adherents believe that models of social problems or situations can be constructed, and scientific analysis of data can lead to best solutions. Policy analysis is based on a rational problem solving approach addressed to those in positions of power and authority. However, unlike the social reform tradition, its proposed solutions are more instrumental or programme-focused and less concerned with restructuring or macro-social objectives. The primary vehicle for change is through identifying and promoting the best policies or programmes. In the child welfare field, this tradition is illustrated by those who seek to identify and evaluate programmes that work in specific locations and that could then be replicated throughout the whole system.

Social learning

As in the policy analysis tradition, change is viewed more incrementally although from a more developmental perspective. Unlike policy analysis, change is seen as emerging from the field rather than coming down through those in positions of central authority. Knowledge is believed to be derived from experience and validated in practice, and therefore it is integrally a part of action (Friedmann, 1987). The vehicles for change in the social learning tradition are the organisations and multi-organisational systems that are engaged in the world of practice. In the child welfare field, this approach is illustrated by efforts to redesign or transform how services are organised and delivered and how participation is managed among multiple stakeholders. An essential aspect of the social learning approach is that these efforts evolve through local experimentation rather than top-down mandates and blueprints.

In summary, the four traditions of planned change can all be illustrated in recent efforts to reform the child welfare system. Each tradition leads to a different strategy for reform as shown in Figure 8.3. Each has its proponents who believe that their preferred strategy is the best way to introduce and implement change in the child welfare system.

The four approaches to reforming child welfare systems have largely been pursued in isolation from one another. This phenomena can partly be explained by what Kaplan (1964: 28) called The Law of the Instrument which states that if you give a young boy a hammer, he will soon discover that everything needs hammering. In other words, people favour different approaches depending on the tools they have at hand as determined by their training, core discipline, or ideology.

In addition, each tradition is built on its own set of underlying assumptions, as shown in

Action Knowledge	Conservative (Incremental)	Radical (Comprehensive)
Societal guidance (Top down)	Programme driven change (Policy analysis)	Legislative structural change (Social reform)
Social transformation (Bottom up)	Organisational transformation (Social learning)	Litigation court mandated reform (Social mobilisation)

Figure 8.3   Strategies for reforming child welfare derived from four traditions of planned social change

Policy analysis	Social reform
• There is one best policy/ programme and we can find it through scientific analysis. • Knowledge about what works can be diffused throughout the system through conventional communication channels flowing from the top. • Implementation issues are not a major concern, compared with finding out 'what works'.	• Macro-systems and structures have to change first before we can see changes in operational systems. • Government and the arms of the state play a crucial role in reforming social systems. • Implementation can be managed through legislation and administrative directives.
Social learning	**Social mobilisation**
• Real innovations emerge from the world of practice and 'doing'. • Champions for change inside the system can help to transform it. • Implementation and organisation are critical; key stakeholders can learn to engage with one another and create a 'negotiated order'.	• System reform is not possible without pressure brought from outside the system. • System change requires a relocation of power and resources. • Victims wouldn't suffer if everyone simply followed the rules and did what they're supposed to do.

Figure 8.4   Underlying assumptions of the four traditions

Figure 8.4. The social reformers believe that macro-economic and political systems have to change first before we can expect to reform operational systems like the child welfare system. The policy analysts, on the other hand, believe that within the existing structure and context, it is possible to determine the best possible course of action through rational analysis and problem solving. Once the best approaches have been identified, they can be codified, disseminated and adopted by decision makers who will be convinced by the scientific merit of the analyses. In the field of child welfare, they believe that we can determine which programmes work and therefore should be expanded or replicated. The adherents of the social mobilisation tradition assume that social systems cannot reform themselves, and that fundamental change can only come about through outside pressure and confrontation. Reform is seen as occurring in the arena of politics more than in the arena of rational analysis and scientific debate. They believe that reform should be driven by the experiences of those who have been dispossessed or oppressed, and that their experiences can shape the image of a reformed system.

Finally, devotees of the social learning tradition believe that knowledge, including the knowledge of how to reform social systems, is derived from experience and is an integral part of action. They believe that systems can learn how to change themselves through leadership, social experimentation, reflection and redesign. In the child welfare field, they believe that the process of reform is as important as the product, and that new patterns of organisation and relationships are critical to the implementation of change. The differences in these underlying assumptions help to explain why proponents of child welfare reform often appear to be acting in isolation from one another and even find it difficult to have a conversation about their different approaches and strategies. Each of the approaches to social change has its own weaknesses or fatal flaws that can seriously impede the success of its efforts at reform. However, another contributing factor to the plethora of failures is the observation that reformers typically operate out of only one of the four traditions described in this paper. They tend to become trapped by their own worldview and narrow assumptions about how to bring about social change, and fail to see the pitfalls of their approach or the potential advantages of others. Like the blind men and the elephant, they believe that they understand the situation at hand when none of them has actually seen the whole situation in all of its complexity. The child welfare situation is not a single problem that can be solved or resolved through analysis or simple cause and effect approaches. It is what Ackoff (1981) calls a mess: a complex system of strongly interacting problems. In order to deal effectively with a mess, he says that the system of problems should be viewed from as many different perspectives as possible before a way of treating them is selected. The best way often involves collaboration of multiple points of view (p. 18). In order to deal with the child welfare mess, we need to find ways to bring the four different traditions together in a unified reform effort.

Adding IT to the equation

Munro (2005) has applied these communication problems to the incoming ICT culture. She noted that consideration of where professionals need help to improve their practice reveals only a limited role for a computerised database. Moreover, introduction of such a database carries many risks so that, overall, it may do more harm than good.

In deciding what tools to develop or apply in a particular context, designers have tended to select those that are technically easy to operate. It seems to have been taken for granted that tools or formalisation of a work procedure are intrinsically good and so, the more the better. The trouble with this approach has been twofold. First, the tools have *not* been selected because they address the parts of the task where the operators most urgently need help. Secondly, the introduction of tools alters the nature of the tasks that are left for the operators to carry out.

A growing literature is questioning whether tools are being designed with a realistic picture of the practice world in which they will be used (Schlonsky and Wagner, 2005; Schwalbe, 2004). In contrast to the tool-centred attitude, a user-centred approach starts by asking, 'What parts of the task do humans find difficult? Given the cognitive and emotional abilities that practitioners have, where would they most appreciate help? How would the introduction of this tool alter the nature of the tasks the practitioners face?'

The advent of IT systems do not deal with the more intractable problems such as helping professionals to know what information they need to collect and to have the skills required to collect it.

Training impacts of organisational change

Morrison (1997) identified some of the opportunities and barriers for learning and training that are presented in the current climate of rapid organisational change, uncertainty about the future direction of child protection and harsh fiscal constraints. He articulated three areas affected by this context for training:

Agency perceptions and approaches to training

Significant conflicts exist over definitions of training between employers, trainers and staff. A number of consequences flow from this, which relate to wider misunderstandings over the purpose and mandate of training. These include perceptions that training should deal with poor performance; resolve staff stress; act as a substitute for a lack of policy, or as a conduit for difficult messages. Underlying these tensions are deeper conflicts as to who training is for – the organisation, the participants, the trainers, service users or the profession. The current managerial emphasis on quantitative/fiscal as opposed to qualitative outcomes, places an ever higher premium on conformity and compliance in the workforce. If training takes place in such a climate the whole process may be undermined from start to finish. Management support for learning is ambivalent; participants fail to engage; there are more frequent organisational intrusions into the learning environment; organisational issues arising are minimised or denied; issues about discrimination are marginalised; training is not evaluated or followed up; and the overall credibility of training is damaged.

The attitude and behaviour of learners

For those participating in training, whether these are on 'courses' or in work-based learning, the impact of current organisational experiences on their capacity and freedom to learn is profound. This may manifest itself in a range of ways: ambivalence or hostility to training; increase of dependency behaviours, including negative projections about authority directed to the trainers; difficulty in 'joining' training and putting down psychological/organisational baggage; lack of personal safety or containment; unwillingness to raise issues of difference and inequality; heightened sensitivity and reluctance to any exposure or risk; a felt sense of de-skilling; reduced optimism about being able to apply learning back in the work place; and more frequent withdrawal from courses, especially where a commitment over time is required. Under these circumstances the learner may never become engaged, and may be less willing to pursue subsequent development opportunities.

The demands on the trainer

In a climate of cutbacks, training may present an easy target, a worry which is compounded by the sometimes low status of training and trainers within the organisation. The effects of all these processes combine to create a number of very significant and disempowering pressures on trainers, who may also feel the need to conform for their own self-preservation, and avoid challenge, even if this involves unreasonable compromises. More specifically, trainers are experiencing far greater negative displacement of unresolved organisational issues onto training from their agencies as a whole, as well as from individuals. Training and trainers can be perceived as the only place left in an agency in which feeling and thinking can be safely expressed. The depth of emotional and philosophical strain mean that trainers are having to contain increasingly stressful experiences and primitive emotions that are brought into training from the workplace.

Staff retention and turnover

Child protective staff often must operate with excessive workloads, inadequate training and resources, poor supervision, and a lack of organisational support. These conditions have been responsible for high rates of burnout, job stress, and staff turnover.

Typically, it takes about two years for new child welfare employees to learn what needs to be done in their jobs and to develop the knowledge, skills, abilities and dispositions to work independently (Ellett et al., 2007). This professional development period represents a significant lag time for child welfare agencies to develop new professional level staff. High turnover rates among child welfare staff are also quite costly in terms of recruitment costs, differential productivity between former and new employees, and lost resources invested in months of on-the-job training required for new employees. The majority of staff turnover occurs within the first one to three years of employment.

Many people believe that frontline child welfare staff stay in their relatively low-paid, high-demand jobs because they find intrinsic value in their work. At the same time, the work is routinely criticised in newspaper accounts of tragedies or scandals, such that it may acquire a stigma, reducing intrinsic rewards and influencing staff to leave. Such factors raise questions about the applicability of extant turnover and retention research to child welfare. Also highlighting some unique aspects of child welfare work, Jayaratne and Chess (1984) found that, compared with other human services staff, child welfare staff described their work environments as more stressful, more demanding, and less challenging.

Silver et al. (1997) examining predictors of job satisfaction in supervisors in a public child welfare agency, noted that participants were 'relatively more job satisfied than might be expected given their level of emotional exhaustion'. Job satisfaction is also predicted by organisational factors, such as workload, intellectual challenge, satisfaction with promotional opportunities and factors related to agency change (Jayaratne and Chess, 1984). Age and job tenure may also play a role in job satisfaction.

A literature review by Stalker et al. (2007) found that while personal characteristics may contribute to emotional exhaustion (EE) in some child welfare workers (e.g. value conflict; Jayaratne and Chess, 1984), this state can be predicted best by organisational variables, including workload, role conflict, role ambiguity, variables related to agency change and lack of job challenge (Jayaratne et al., 1991; Bhana and Haffejee, 1996). The only client related variable that appears to affect emotional exhaustion is behaviour that leads the worker to fear physical harm (Jayaratne et al., 1991).

To find satisfaction in child welfare, one must believe that one is truly helping vulnerable children and making a positive difference in their lives. Other factors may also contribute to an individual's ability and willingness to continue in a job that takes a significant toll on personal resources. The research suggests that access to social support (both co-worker and supervisor support) may be especially important. Other personal attributes, such as the ability to find satisfaction in doing one's best and in mastering skills, even in the face of less than ideal outcomes, may be helpful. Active coping strategies, such as problem solving, cognitive restructuring, seeking social support and expressing emotions, may help workers to avoid depersonalising clients and may contribute to a stronger sense of accomplishment. For some, having control over decisions or other aspects of the work (job autonomy) seems to contribute to job satisfaction in spite of high demands. Organisational variables, such as work overload, lack of promotional opportunities, perception of problematic changes in agency policy and procedures, an unsupportive supervisor and perceptions that the job is physically unsafe, have all been found to negatively affect emotional exhaustion and job satisfaction in child welfare samples.

A few studies have looked at the relationship between job satisfaction, work environment, and staff retention in public child welfare agencies. Cohen (1992) studied the quality of working life in the Philadelphia Department of Human Services. A written survey was completed by 388 child welfare staff, or 62 per cent of the eligible population. The survey explored four major areas: the job itself, work relationships, organisational structure, and organisational effectiveness. Only 18 per cent of the respondents rated the overall quality of working life as excellent or good, while 82 per cent rated it as either fair or poor. While most staff were satisfied with specific characteristics of their jobs (e.g. meaningfulness, challenge, variety, autonomy), they were dissatisfied with many aspects of the work environment, including the high workload, inability to influence how the work was performed, poor communications among work units, and little knowledge of the actual results of their work activities. Barton, Foleron, and Busch (2003), reporting on child protective service workers in Indiana, relate job satisfaction to caseload size, working conditions, supervision, organisational supports, and role identity issues.

Smith (2005) found that factors positively associated with job retention included the perceptions that an employer promoted life–work balance, that a supervisor was supportive and competent, and that few other job alternatives were available. Factors associated with staying or the intent to stay in a child welfare job include the following: planning a long-term child welfare career (Fryer, Miyoshi and Thomas, 1989), lower ratings of emotional exhaustion (Drake and Yadama, 1996) and spending less time in court-related activities (Dickinson and Perry, 2002).

While some studies have looked at the problem of retention of human services workers and its relation to job satisfaction (Vinokur-Kaplan, 1994) little attention has been paid to the broader issue of the quality of work life (QWL) in human services and child welfare organisations (Cohen, 1992). The QWL movement has been concerned with creating work organisations that 'more effectively deliver services and products valued by society, while simultaneously being rewarding, stimulating places for employees to work' (Camman, 1984). Pioneering efforts to improve QWL in industrial settings identified six intrinsic requirements for satisfying work regardless of the level of employment:

1. For the content of the job to provide variety and challenge.
2. To be able to learn on the job and go on learning.
3. For an area of decision making that the workers can call their own.
4. For a certain degree of social support and recognition from colleagues in the workplace.
5. To be able to see a task from start to finish and how one's job contributes to a larger and meaningful whole.
6. Believing that one's job will continue to allow for personal growth and some sort of desirable future.

These requirements would appear to be as applicable to the job of the child protective worker as they are to workers in business and industry. One of the challenges facing public child welfare agencies today is how to measure the quality of work life and how to design strategies and interventions that will improve QWL for child protective staff as well as other child welfare staff.

Smith (2005) developed a conceptual model (see Figure 8.5 below) that attempts to identify the relative importance of organisational, job, and individual characteristics associated with job retention in child welfare. It embraces the role of organisational support as expressed through extrinsic rewards, supervisor support, and intrinsic job value in explaining job retention. Staff who perceive their organisations and/or supervisors to be supportive and those who find intrinsic value in the work are more committed to their jobs and less likely to leave. They found the following when applying it in research: even in a work climate where intrinsic job value is ostensibly an important motivator, extrinsic rewards such as the facilitation of life–work balance and supervisor support are associated with job retention, but reports of intrinsic job value are not. Consistent with the suggestion of other studies, reports of supervisor support are associated with job retention. Finally, findings indicate that organisation-level characteristics substantially affect the likelihood of child welfare job retention.

Ellett et al. (2007) offers us a broader ecologically based conceptual framework (see Figure 8.6).

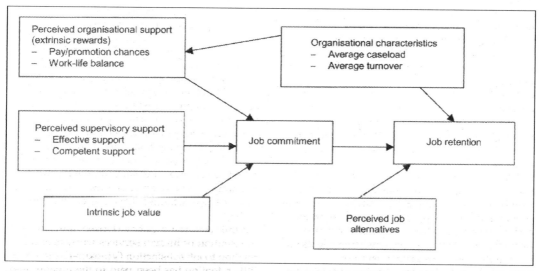

Figure 8.5   A conceptual model (Smith, 2005)

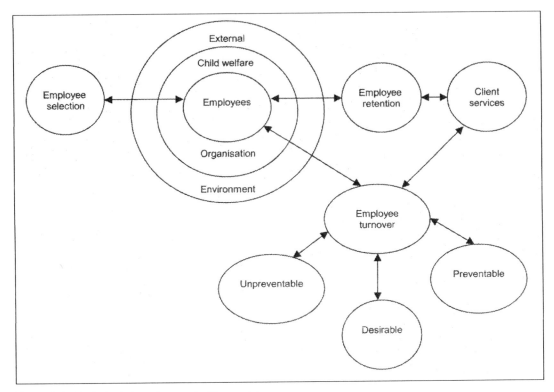

Figure 8.6   Ecologically based conceptual framework

The figure shows hypothesised linkages between the initial selection of child welfare employees, the work context in which employees are imbedded, and organisational outcomes (client services). Figure 8.6 illustrates the important consideration that must be given to careful selection when hiring employees who can successfully function in this complex and difficult work context. The work context is imbedded within the complexities of the child welfare work environment and a variety of external environments as well (e.g., the policymaking context, judicial system). As shown in the figure, the ultimate outcome of the child welfare organisation is the quality of services to children and families. Employee retention and turnover are also included as outcomes important to the child welfare organisation. Employee turnover is partitioned into three types:

(a)   Unpreventable turnover (e.g. illness, family move, retirement).

(b)   Desirable turnover (e.g. incompetents, malcontents).

(c)   Preventable turnover (competent employees who leave due to organisational factors such as low pay, lack of promotional opportunities, poor supervision, etc.).

The figure is dynamic and reciprocal in that employee retention and turnover affect organisational outcomes (client services), and the quality of client services can in turn affect employee retention and turnover. One key goal of the healthy child welfare organisation is to minimise preventable turnover and to maintain the holding power of the organisation for employees (retention). Figure 8.7 depicts the complexities of the child welfare context in which employees are imbedded. Personal characteristics (e.g. human caring, self-efficacy beliefs about work tasks) are at the core of the child welfare organisation and these interact dynamically with many organisational features and ongoing demands represented by the middle circle. The outer circle in the figure shows examples of many of the other organisations, audiences and presses

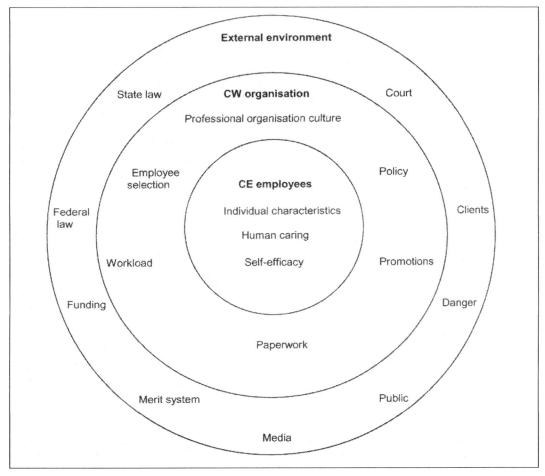

Figure 8.7   Child welfare work context

of the external environment in which the child welfare organisation is imbedded. The outer circle implies that both child welfare employees and the larger child welfare organisation are highly visible to the external environment, and demands from the external environment can ultimately affect (either positively or negatively) the quality of services to clients.

Corrective considerations

The judgement of individual professionals is influenced by explicit policies and protocols provided by their agency and implicit practices and norms within their profession. There is a need for explicit policies as no agency involved in

child protection leaves judgement totally to the practitioner's individual opinion. Agencies need consistency in decision-making across cases and standards of accountability for practitioners. Agencies need to guide and support individual judgement through explicit risk assessment frameworks for decision-making. These tools guide individual professionals in the following ways: the kind of evidence that they collect, the kinds of questions that they ask; how they classify and evaluate evidence, and the possible actions they can take.

Practitioners in different professions tend to see situations differently because they have different responsibilities, tasks and priorities. They also tend to talk about the situation in different ways. This applies to the kinds of words and terminology they choose; the classifications, criteria and concepts they use; the kinds of texts that they read and write; how the interactions are conducted and managed; and how interactions are captured in a written report are framed.

Moving from blame to quality

Lachman and Bernard (2006) identified that the result of so many inquiries into fatal child abuse is to foster a blame culture in child protection work (Munro, 2004; Reder and Duncan, 2004). This is often the approach of politicians and the media. In this regard, Stanley and Manthorpe (2004) contend that it is difficult to see how the benefits from inquiries positively inform policy, practice, and learning. What is clear is that policy changes as a result of recommendations made by child death inquiries alone do not ensure improved practice and better outcomes for children. Although the findings from inquiries provide insight and can be a tool for developing evidence-based practice, in a blame driven environment they divert attention from the day-to-day dilemmas with which child protection practitioners work. In environments where blame is individualised and society seeks scapegoats when errors and wrong decisions are made, practitioners are likely to develop defensive attitudes, which do not lead to ongoing improvement in the service provided. Given the complexity surrounding child protection work and the failures within child protection services, a fresh look at the response to these failures is required. One can adapt approaches taken in the health literature, which have attempted to understand the failures in health care. The groundbreaking report on medical error, by the Institute of Medicine, opened health care to a new way of thinking with regard to patient safety. The need to anticipate system error became evident as systems are perfectly designed to produce the results they achieve (Senge, 2006). Reason (2000) introduced the two types of failures that can exist – that at the person level and that at the system level. Too often, the focus is on person failures without recognising the inherent holes in the system that allows failures to occur. Reason's concept of a Swiss cheese model of accidents suggests that unless there are built-in defences in systems to close these holes, system failures will continue to occur. Allied to this is the need for a child protection service based on continual

improvement, and one in which quality is the central feature. The issues for professionals include the fear of blame, increased scrutiny, the lack of strong leadership and support, and the lack of a robust evidence base. An alternative blame-free approach is required to avoid apportioning of culpability, lower morale, undermined confidence, and professionals retreating from service provision. A move from a blame culture requires an attitudinal, as well as an organisational shift to promote the change process required for learning. Senior managers have a key role to play in contributing to a learning process by building an organisational culture that creates a learning organisation that cultivates the reflective practitioner. An organisational culture that learns and encourages learning provides an important context in which practitioners can confidently practice, if they are to be enabled to deliver positive outcomes for children. To achieve better outcomes for vulnerable children, a service requires flexible thinkers who are able to adopt the analytical approach that is so vital for effective child protection work. Ultimately, to facilitate this process, practitioners need to be functioning in environments where there is a constant emphasis on quality improvement as the focus of development.

One can adapt the quality paradigm in health care and other industries to the child protection field. The aim is to develop a service based on continual improvement in specific areas such as safety, access, timeliness, efficiency, equity, and child-centeredness (Berwick, 2002). Although the concepts are derived from a health paradigm, they can be applied to all areas of work with children in social care. These concepts provide a framework for professionals to improve continually the quality of the service provision. Continual development implies the adoption of a quality improvement approach to all aspects of one's work.

Child protection as a systems problem

Munro (2005) argues for treating the task of improving the child protection services as a systems problem and for adopting the system-focused approach to investigating errors that has been developed in areas of medicine and engineering where safety is a high priority. It outlines how this approach differs from the traditional way of examining errors and how it leads to different types of solutions. Traditional inquiries tend to stop once human error has been found, whereas a systems approach treats human error as the starting point and examines the whole context in which the operator was working to see how this impacted on their ability to perform well.

The systems approach was developed in engineering because traditional solutions were not working as well as expected. Mistakes still kept being made, sometimes with disastrous consequences. Power plants got close to meltdown, and planes crashed into mountains. The standard solutions of providing more tools, more detailed manuals, and closer management scrutiny were not eradicating human error. Indeed, in some cases, it seemed that they were increasing the scope for error. To deal with this puzzling outcome, engineers radically reframed the way they were looking at the problem. Instead of regarding human error as a satisfactory explanation of an accident and therefore concluding the investigation at that point, they treated it as the start of inquiry: why did the front line worker misread the dial, omit crucial steps in the procedures, or overlook signs of trouble? This led them to investigate the total system within which the person was operating so that they could better understand why the faulty action had looked the sensible thing to do at the time or why it might have been difficult for humans to perform well. The systems approach led to new types of solution. Basically, they take the form of redesigning the tasks expected of workers so that they are better tailored to the skills of human beings.

In a systems investigation, the operator is seen as only one factor; the final outcome is a product of the interaction of organisational culture, technical support, and human performance factors. The ideal image of human rationality – captured in classical decision theory – is of an individual rapt in thought, contemplating all the evidence before reaching a conclusion. Research of rationality in the wild reveals a different picture (Hutchins, 1995). Judgement and decision-making in child protection are best seen not as discrete acts performed by individuals in isolation but as part of a constant stream of activity, often spread across groups, and located within an organisational culture that limits their activities, sets up rewards and punishments, provides resources, and defines goals that are sometimes inconsistent (Woods et al., 1994). Human errors are, in general, not random and individual but follow predictable patterns that can be understood by seeing them in their context. Systems investigations have highlighted how the traditional solutions to human error can, themselves, be the source of further errors.

Acting on inquiry recommendations: a broader framework

Reder and Duncan (2004) identified that there is a growing body of opinion that the more important lessons from inquiries lie elsewhere other than policy modifications or exhortations to practitioners to change their behaviour. Stevenson (1989) considered that social workers were in need of suitable theoretical frameworks to guide their assessments and decision-making and better training in observing and talking with children. We have discussed (Reder et al., 1993; Reder and Duncan, 1999, 2003) that practitioners must become conversant with the psychology of communication and need a theoretical framework and a mindset to help them process information as part of their assessments. Similarly, Munro (1996, 1999, 2002) and Dale et al. (2002) pointed to the need for assessment improvements, with Munro describing errors of reasoning that lay behind many tragic outcomes which have significant training and supervision implications. Brandon et al. (1999) emphasised the importance of professional training and supervision in generating professional confidence. All these could be considered to refer to the more 'thinking' aspects of professional practice. They depend on the personal characteristics of the staff, the quality of their training and skills acquisition, and the nature of their working environment. They become manifest in various psychological and interpersonal processes that unfold during work on a case and are a crucial determinant of whether policies and procedures will succeed. We are strongly of the view that attention to these dimensions of professional endeavours is most likely to improve child protection practice in the future (Reder and Duncan, 2004).

The key aims of training are to arm practitioners with knowledge, skills and the capacity to think. The ability to think clearly may partially be an inherent characteristic of the individual, but it can also be taught as a fundamental approach to professional practice. Munro (2002) described different frames of thinking apparent in child protection practice which have traditionally been seen as distinct and opposite. They can be caricatured as 'qualitative', or responding 'with the heart', versus 'quantitative', or responding 'with the head'. The first approach values interpersonal skills (such as empathy), intuitive reasoning, subjective knowledge, wisdom and judgement. The second focuses on formal reasoning, objective and scientific knowledge, factual information, practical procedures and checklists. Social work has often been criticised for erring towards the former and medicine for overemphasising the latter. Munro argued that these styles should not be seen as mutually exclusive but along a continuum and complementary to each other. Different permutations of reasoning and different types of information are required, depending on the context, so that an integration is needed. Integration is also necessary because both styles are fallible, as exemplified by the limitations of either risk protocols or professional judgement in accurately predicting risk of child abuse. Munro went on to propose that training should promote both approaches, but with a shift along the continuum towards a more analytic approach at certain points. In this way, professionals would learn to consider what information to gather and observations to make (using what methods), while also pondering what sense to make of them. She also advocated the use of decision trees in decision-making, because they help organise reasoning, make use of formal and intuitive knowledge, pose possible alternative options and ensure that significant details are not overlooked. However, the more naturalistic style based on accumulating experience is also valuable, depending on the circumstances. Importantly, if a tragedy were to occur with one of their cases, the professional who could explain the thinking behind their decisions would be better placed to defend them and demonstrate that, although hindsight showed them to have been wrong, they were reasonable judgements at the time.

The management of risk – lessons from the commercial sector (Johnson and Petrie, 2005)

Commercial organisations typically view 'risk' as an inherent part of their business and indeed most businesses probably could not exist without some form of risk-taking. As already mentioned, since health and welfare organisations must now operate in similar ways to commercial organisations, it makes sense to assess the 'best practice' ways in which risks are understood and managed in the commercial sector and, where appropriate, transfer learning between the two sectors. Commercial organisations typically place more emphasis on organisational issues surrounding 'risk' and risk events than is evident in recent literature examining health and welfare organisations (DoH, DfEE, HO, 2000; DoH, 2000). 'Risk' is defined in many ways depending on the organisation in question, a broad definition being the likelihood that a decision or course of action will result in a negative or adverse outcome. The higher the risk the more likely a negative impact will occur. 'Risk' is further defined and categorised in organisations where it is an intrinsic part of their business. For example, within the financial industry 'risk' is divided into credit, market and operational elements, with the latter focused on the 'risk' involved with managing people, decision making and so on. The Bank for International Settlements (BIS) describes operational 'risk' as: 'The risk of loss resulting from inadequate or failed internal processes, people and systems or from external events' (BIS, 2001: 2).

In other words, if the behaviour of people and functioning of operational systems and their interactions are inadequate, operational risk will increase and subsequent loss may result. This type of operational risk affects all businesses including high-risk industry, financial institutions and, it can be argued, public sector agencies such as health (Smith, 2002). In many organisations the term 'risk-management' is used to describe the process of determining the risks a business faces to enable this knowledge to be used in decision-making processes. The ultimate aim for all organisations is to achieve a desired outcome with minimal adverse consequences. The severity of potential adverse outcomes and the likelihood of this occurring will obviously influence the degree of risk-taking that is felt to be appropriate in any given situation. However, 'playing safe' by making no decision does not eliminate 'risk' and in some circumstances can increase the probability of adverse outcomes. The emphasis now placed upon the management of 'risk' in the commercial sector is evident through the growth of risk-management departments, whose function is to monitor the risks facing the business, determine whether or not these are being controlled appropriately, and develop and maintain a strong 'safety culture'. The concept of safety culture is not embraced by all commercial organisations. However, where risks are high, organisations typically use safety culture as a way to understand and manage safety issues and to establish a strong, positive safety culture is seen as 'best practice' (British Safety Council, 2002).

Risk management: developing a safety culture

Many organisations recognise the need to look at their safety culture in order to determine the risks they are facing. This is especially true in industries with a high potential of risk to employees and/or the environment, such as nuclear fuel and oil companies where analysis of safety culture is recognised as an important element of accident prevention (Donald and Cantor, 1993; Mearns, Flin, Gordon and Fleming, 1998). Increasingly, similar issues are being recognised in health and welfare provision (Smith, 2002). Analysing an organisation's safety culture means looking beyond rules and regulations in order to determine what actually happens in the workplace. Critical issues include whether or not employees feel the 'risk' controls they work within are adequate. For example, do people ever take short cuts in order to get the job done? This is especially important if staff shortages are a problem, which, as discussed later, has been a major factor in the breakdown of child protection systems. Another issue is whether employees feel that management place a high value on safety, not only in policy but also through action on safe working and the reduction of 'risk' in the organisation. For example, Vinten (2000) outlines instances where, although staff were requested in organisational policy documents to voice any concerns they had about unsafe working practices, they were still victimised as a result of their 'whistle-blowing'. This is a clear demonstration of the gap that can arise between policy objectives and practice realities and unfortunately they are not isolated instances. Identifying such issues reveals everyday working practices that may not be apparent by auditing policies and procedures. Identifying everyday practices means that 'risk'

can be identified and analysed as a first step towards developing a strong safety culture.

'Safety culture' has been defined in many ways, with the most succinct simply being 'the way we do things around here', a definition that is used by many researchers and is generally attributed to the Confederation of British Industry (CBI, 1990). A weak safety culture can increase the risk of an incident and the identification of an organisation's safety culture can serve to identify risk areas and enable the organisation to take steps to avoid an adverse incident. Although definitions of an organisational safety culture vary they generally include the following factors:

- *Psychological factors* that include employees' shared attitudes, perceptions, beliefs, norms, values and behaviours.
- *Organisational factors* such as rules, regulations, equipment, structures and policies in relation to 'risk' and 'safety' (Clarke, 1999; Reason, 1990a).

It is the combination of these elements that will determine how risk is evaluated within an organisation, what steps are felt to be appropriate to reduce or eliminate risk and whether people feel empowered to take these steps once a risk is identified. A strong safety culture should express paramount concern for the safety of staff and consumers, and studies have shown that a weak safety culture is a predictor of accident rates (Donald and Canter, 1993; Zohar, 2000). A positive safety culture in industry, and in particular high-risk industry, is recognised as an important facet of accident prevention (HSE, 2002). Many inquiries following major incidents have revealed the significance of cultural aspects of an organisation in the run up to a disaster. For example, the inquiry into the Piper Alpha oil rig disaster highlighted this issue. It is essential to create a corporate atmosphere or culture in which safety is understood to be, and accepted as, the number one priority (Cullen, 1990). The regulators of financial industry, in the wake of catastrophes such as the collapse of Barings Bank (Bank of England, 1996) are also beginning to place increasing emphasis on cultural aspects of organisations as critical factors in limiting potential losses. It is recognised that risk management and the development of a safety culture needs to be a priority for all staff at all levels, including the most senior. Both the board and senior management are responsible for creating an organisational culture that places a high priority on effective operational risk management and adherence to sound operating controls. (BIS, 2002: 6)

During the last two decades strides have been made in the commercial sector in understanding the management of risk, driven in part by a number of high-profile accidents and financial fraud that had disastrous consequences with far-reaching ramifications beyond the companies involved. Several theorists, notably Reason (1990a) and Stead and Smallman (1999) have analysed such disasters and incidents and developed paradigms for identifying failure points so that similar occurrences may be avoided in the future. These influential theories acknowledge that dysfunctional interrelationships between organisational actors at all levels, including the most senior, are often the primary precursors to the unexpected disaster, even when human error was the final trigger. Both Turner (1978) and Reason (1990a) highlight the importance of organisational factors in generating adverse outcomes, rather than focusing simply upon the decision-making abilities of individual people. Although it is recognised that individual decision-making may be the final act before an incident occurs, it is the events and decisions made within an organisation prior to the onset of an incident that are critical.

Reason describes five stages of accident causation:

- *Fallible decisions made by high-level decision makers.* These are described as an almost inevitable part of the decision-making process since all organisations have to allocate resources to two distinct goals – production and safety. In the long term these goals are compatible but in the short term conflicts of interest may appear. For example, striving to attain production targets may make the choice to implement new safety measures that will slow production down a difficult decision. In relation to welfare services pressure to attain performance indicators, such as the completion of initial assessments of children in need and their families within the prescribed seven working days, may lead to staff taking 'short-cuts' in order to meet targets.
- *Line management deficiencies* can mean poor quality decisions made at the previous stage are compounded, although of course line

management competence can serve to mitigate any negative effects. Examples of line management deficiency include poor scheduling, poor procedures and deficiencies in rules or knowledge.
- *Preconditions for unsafe acts.* These are preconditions already in place for an error or a violation of rules to occur. This can result from people rather than systems, for example if people are under severe stress, fail to perceive a hazard or are simply unaware of a situation. Of course, all these issues are also the responsibility of management.
- *Unsafe acts* are violations or errors committed in the presence of a hazard by individuals or groups.
- *Weak defences.* These are the failure or absence of defences that can prevent an incident occurring (Reason, 1990b).

Reason also makes the distinction between active errors, typically made by people working on the front line, and latent errors, usually originating from decision makers higher up in the organisation. Latent errors can lie within an organisation for many years before another act occurs, which triggers an event. An example of a latent error could be inadequate or incompatible information technology within or between organisations, a theme that runs consistently through the report into the Climbié Inquiry (Laming, 2003).

Johnson and Petrie (2005) name two other potential areas of importation: empowering staff and active learning.

Empowering staff

Best practice in the commercial sector recognises that a strong safety culture also depends on empowering front-line staff, who are dealing with situations as they arise, so they feel able to make decisions judged appropriate at the time without fear of management reprisals. Staff must be clear about the options and actions available to them and be able to use their initiative to reduce or eliminate a perceived risk. If an employee knows that a certain course of action may lead to a negative event then they should be able to do something about it. An analogy can be made with the crews of aircraft carriers, where even the lowest ranking person on the ship can suspend a flight if they feel there is a need (Roberts, Stout and Halpern, 1994). The power and status of social work and social care practitioners, especially for vulnerable children and their families, has been eroded through public opinion and increasingly prescriptive legislation and policies during the last two decades. This has been fuelled in part by the consequences of media and government focus on practice failure findings emerging from public inquiries into child death.

Active learning

A strong safety culture in the commercial sector is partly built upon the continuous updating and training of staff in order to resolve some of the conflicting demands placed on organisations dealing with high-risk situations. However, such training is limited because, as highlighted above, high-risk situations require staff to be able to think for themselves and use their own initiative at critical points. Since 'failing' is not an effective learning tool in high-risk situations a more active approach to learning is required. It is recognised that there should be a high emphasis placed upon vicarious experiences and stories of 'near-misses' so as to enable expertise and knowledge to be passed between operational staff (Weick, 1987). Learning made by front-line workers has greatest impact if it is shared without editing or comment by management anxious to ensure such experiences are congruent with policies. A strong emphasis on active learning means that employees are not just expected to accept the way things are but to challenge them and continuously look for better ways of doing things. As far as child protection is concerned the voice of the practitioner in relation to the sort of failures in organisational and management practices outlined earlier is remarkably silent. For social workers and social care practitioners this implies a stronger and more effective contribution to national organisational policy and resource debates.

Managing risk and minimising mistakes (Bostock et al., 2005)

Organisational learning from mistakes

There is a drive to shift the focus from mistakes in individual cases (active failure) to a debate about the management of risk at an organisational level

(latent failures). There are ways to learn from potentially adverse events before harm is caused to children and their families.

Risk management programmes

These promote learning from adverse events and near misses. They have proved to be a powerful means of improving safety, having been pioneered in aviation and the health care sector. They are thus exportable to LSCBS who will set up child death review groups (CDRGs).

Safety management

CDRGs will review information on the deaths of all children in the local authority area, not just those in contact with organisations charged with safeguarding their welfare. They are charged with drawing conclusions on what can be learned to prevent or reduce the numbers of deaths from whatever causes in the future.

Safeguarding incidents

These cover everything that could have or did cause harm to children and families. They will review 'no harm' incidents or 'near misses' as well as serious cases and child deaths. Near misses consist of something which could have gone wrong, but has been prevented, as well as when something did go wrong but no serious harm was caused.

Cluster of near misses cases

The everyday nature of near misses makes them hard to identify. The risk of harm to children can be missed during referral and assessment as the prioritisation of cases of immediate harm occurs at the expense of early intervention (sexual and physical override neglect and emotional abuse), or professionals not having an accurate or full picture of what is happening. There is also concern relating to decisions made by other teams and agencies, difficulties at the interface between agencies, the volume of paperwork and IT expectations. Complacency on long-term cases can allow a risk of harm to go unnoticed.

Near misses

Near misses are routine: they happen all the time. Recent high profile issues have focused on a failure to identify children as needing protection

Table 8.1   Grading of safeguarding incidents (SI)

Grade	Definition
No harm	Any SI that had the potential to cause harm but was prevented, resulting in no harm to children
Harm	SI that are harmful include false negatives and false positives
Life-threatening injury or death	Any SI that leads to a child dying, suffering a life-threatening injury or being seriously sexually abused, where local agencies have known that abuse or neglect is a factor and the case gives rise to concern about inter-agency working to protect children

– over and above children having a child in need status.

Grading of safeguarding incidents (SI)

Learning from safeguarding incidents is dependent on five fundamental features of a learning organisation: structure, organisational culture, information systems, human resources practices and leadership.

Involving service users and carers

LSCBs represent a good opportunity for organisational learning to take place across agencies. Harnessing the knowledge and expertise of service users and carers presents a key means of learning about safeguarding incidents and improving systems to protect and promote the welfare of children. Young people and parents welcome an open discussion about mistakes.

Messages from users

Users have complained about partial information, social workers not listening, failing to get the full picture, misinterpreting what was said or taking down inaccurate information. They felt marginalised in the assessment process and had little opportunity to comment on, let alone challenge, social workers' judgements, yet they questioned the accuracy and interpretation of information. As a result of these factors, mistakes were made. They also acknowledged a lack of time and resources that workers faced contributing to heightened chances of safeguarding incidents.

Messages from workers

The location of some files prevented access to information e.g. in rat-infested cellars, in different buildings etc. There were ICT systems that would not allow access to inaccurate information in order to correct it, and they complained about the Eurocentric nature of ICT systems (spellings). They lacked time to analyse, interpret and reflect on information as well as collecting and inputting it.

Near misses and the role of allied professionals

Child protection is a shared responsibility. The diversity of agency functions makes child protection an issue of greater or lesser familiarity and priority to each of them. Personal hostilities, lack of respect for childcare social workers' professional specialisation and expertise, and unexplained breakdowns in communication as well as problems caused by passing the concerns about a child's welfare over to social services at the last minute. Teachers and GPs remain unclear about their role in safeguarding children and about the appropriate procedures. There is uncertainty about what constitutes risk to children yet many have low tolerance levels. Some agencies miss risk and sometimes they are unable to impress their concerns on social workers in a way in which they are received and acted upon.

Near misses and long term cases

Complacency can lead to a greater likelihood that risks to children are overlooked. Alternatively, we may give people we know more leeway than we might to those with whom we have had no previous involvement. It can occur within the process of transferring a case from one team to another (especially to or from EDT). Identification of risk needs to be accompanied by actions to address it.

Supervision

Whilst the need for supervision is generally acknowledged in the field, it is actually quite rare to find someone who is happy with their supervision and feels it is meeting their needs. Yet supervision needs to be safe enough for workers to recognise that it hurts to see children's pain. It also needs to be ok to be angry with parents and work this through, and that we will feel grief, ambivalence and aggression towards clients at times as a result of this work. We need to be able to first acknowledge, and then work through these feelings to improve our practice. One of the key points made by Munro (1999) is the extent to which assessments in child protection practice stem from intuitive and unstructured thinking processes. There is a need in both practice and supervision to enhance methods of systematic enquiry, hypothesis generation and testing in assessments, and more analytical (less intuitive) evidence-based perspective, whilst also considering research. This can be assisted by a supervisor making a worker argue the opposite view. Ask them to examine reasons why their judgment might be wrong. Changing your mind should be seen as a sign of good practice, and of strength, not weakness (Munro, 1999: 755).

Jones and Gallop (2003) considered the erosion of reflective space in supervision as line managers struggle to cope with the ever-increasing expectations. They uncovered evidence to suggest that traditional notions of supervision are becoming very vulnerable to the increasing pressures on first-line managers as they grapple with New Labour initiative overload, 'hitting' performance targets and pressing the next set of 'funding buttons'. These pressures now result in a form of supervision that is at considerable variance with the well-respected texts on the subject (Morrison, 1993) which argues that good quality supervision needs to embrace several purposes, namely accountability, support and development. In the current climate the capacity of supervision to help social workers reflect on and learn from their practice becomes compromised. The mounting pressure on managers' time comes at a time when the Assessment Framework is being implemented (DoH et al., 1999, 2000; Horwath, 2002) and professional demands to update and articulate empirical, theoretical and process knowledge in decision-making could not be greater.

Taught (and accepted) as a vehicle for accountability, support and development, supervision becomes mainly concerned with a narrow version of performance management, focusing on ensuring that procedures have been followed and that social workers are practising within agency expectations. It emphasises reaction and compliance, not critical reflection and an opportunity to question. Our concern is that this sense of too much to do and too little time will not go away; and that therefore the reliance on individual supervision as the main (or only) vehicle for work-based learning is misplaced. If this analysis is correct, we will continue to risk the safety and wellbeing of children and the reputations of social workers. As many reports highlight (Reder and Duncan, 1999) learning through reflection on practice is a basic requirement for all professionals, not a luxury for those who happen to be in well-resourced teams with no vacancies and manageable workloads. Reflection helps professionals to generate competing hypotheses about the nature of the problem and what to do about it; and to define their evidence base from relevant theory and research, the foundation of good practice which underpins the Assessment Framework.

Davis (2001) argued that one of the most significant liaisons that needs to be strengthened in acknowledging, supporting and responding to the inherent emotional currents of the work is the supervisory relationship. As the ongoing and most intimate relationship designed to monitor and foster effective practice, the supervisory relationship is the appropriate formal vehicle for conveying values and norms about the role of feelings in any discussion of practice strategies. It is here that 'the talk' is about the families, and about what happens between them and the child protection service worker. Therefore, it is here that the worker's emotional reactions, and how they hinder or foster the work, are pertinent to the expected conversation. According to researchers, there are four key components of effective supervision (Himle, Jayaratne, and Thyness, 1989):

- The capacity to provide a warm and friendly environment.
- The ability to provide useful and positive feedback.
- The capacity to be knowledgeable about how to do the job.
- The ability to help buffer the emotional stressors of the job.

To the extent that the supervisor is competent in providing these resources, they help to decrease the worker's feelings of burnout (Himle, Jayaratne, and Thyness, 1989). In a climate of positive regard and availability, a worker can speak truthfully about all aspects of their work, including their emotional, cognitive and behavioural experiences. The literature demonstrates that the ability to communicate openly and clearly about one's work significantly affects a person's perceptions about the helpfulness of the supervisory relationship (Lawton and Magarelli, 1980). Mutual problem solving in a climate of trust, respect and openness becomes a powerful source of sustenance for the worker and supervisor (Powell, 1994). In addition, it reinforces a model for behaving with families. The experience of being nurtured,

respected and accepted – even when we have negative feelings about a family – becomes a powerful template in assisting the staff's capacity to understand experientially what they must offer to families. We learn this both through our feelings and our intellect.

Regan (2007, personal communication) has developed a supervision proforma – in order to try to encourage managers to take responsibility for the parts of the job that aren't feasible and to give workers a way of reflecting this without feeling de-skilled (see Figure 8.8).

Pro-forma could be used in 1–2 cases during supervision as a way of critically analysing practice.

The shape of the 'diamond' is not of relevance in itself, but could provide a way of exploring a case from a number of aspects:

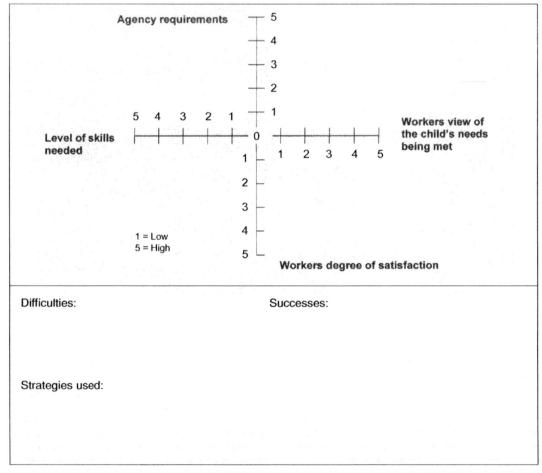

Figure 8.8   Cornerstone Project 2007: practice analysis proforma

- It would identify if a worker has met agency standards by completing tasks set and agreed.
- It would provide opportunity for staff to acknowledge how they felt about the piece of work undertaken. Consistently low satisfaction levels over a range of cases and time could help to indicate workers moving towards 'burn-out'.
- It could identify learning and development areas for workers and also identify strengths, which might be useful for co-working or mentoring on teams.

The value of using the pro-forma would be in the discussions it generates.

Managers and their needs

Morrison (1997) points out that many managers, especially middle managers and those responsible for the supervision of practitioners feel a sense of abandonment by the organisation, as spans of control increase, access to their own supervision decreases, and the quality and availability of training for them is often patchy. They are not going to feel confident to carry out their role in the development of staff unless they are equipped to do so. If managers are to play their key part as developers, then organisations must see investment in effective supervision, one that pays attention to values, beliefs and feelings as well as task, as a central strategy. This means training and supporting supervisors. And whilst supervision has been a social work tradition, all professions should recognise the need for a structured reflective process in which judgements, feelings, attitudes, practice and development can be examined, especially in a risk management field. Few child protection managers come to their roles with the management knowledge, skills and training to prepare them for the challenge of frontline child protection management. Without ongoing developmental support, it is likely that many will struggle, a number will leave their organisations, and critical child protection outcomes, such as increased child safety and wellbeing, will not be achieved. Statutory child protection managers undertake their roles in a complex and contested organisational environment. In such a context, it can be extremely difficult for them to adopt a proactive, outcome-focused approach that can enable the delivery of quality outcomes to children, their families, carers and broader communities. These difficulties are compounded by inadequate attention to the training and support needs of managers.

Goodman and Rousseau (2004) argue that effective management involves both proactive and reactive problem solving. Reactive problem solving deals with existing problems. Proactive management focuses on service system improvements to minimise the problems that would otherwise necessitate reactive problem solving. However, the statutory child protection sector is largely portrayed as a reactive service sector, led by managers who are overwhelmed by the challenges they face. It has been described as barely surviving, in crisis with untenable workloads and high levels of staff turnover resulting from worker experience of stress and burnout (Stanley and Goddard, 1998). Morrison (1996) argues that this difficult setting can create an anxious working environment, highly focused on the struggle for survival.

A central issue is the complexity of the child protection management context, which provides significant challenges for adopting a proactive management approach. These challenges arise from the demanding nature of the core business; the vulnerability of the children and families who receive services; the competing needs and expectations of the client and stakeholder base; the involuntary nature of the service delivery; pressure to be accountable for client outcomes and complex and onerous mechanisms to support this accountability; increasing complexity and ambiguity in defining the statutory role; and the impact of resource limitations (Parton, 1997). These difficulties are compounded by the fact that many managers in this area come to their position from practice with limited, if any, management training (Wilson, 2005). This occurs in a context where there have been calls for research to focus on frontline child protection management (Gustafson and Allen, 1994), though this has rarely happened.

Nevertheless, the leadership role of child protection managers, in acting as a conduit between outcomes and direct practice, is well established. Throughout many of the studies there is a permeating and consistent message that the role of management at every level is influential on service delivery. Good managers are germane to good outcomes for children and families. Managers are considered critical to client outcomes in child protection, when they use various management skills and strategies

(Schorr, 1997). Child protection managers need an appropriate balance of reactive and proactive problem solving to meet this leadership and management challenge and move beyond the struggle for survival into proactive management for quality client outcomes.

Training issues post inquiries (King, 2003)

King (2003) pointed out that the learning from inquiries very much focuses on policies, procedures and practice. However, in order to implement the learning effectively, attention must be paid to the emotional needs of staff and to the recovery of inter-agency relationships, which have frequently been affected following a serious incident. She describes the development of an ACPC training course designed to manage the aftermath of the child abuse inquiry process. In doing so, she drew heavily from Horwath's identification of lessons for trainers and managers resulting from the impact of fatal child abuse cases (Horwath, 1995). Horwath based her findings on a series of interviews with staff in one particular area and examined the responses to cases of fatal child abuse from individual workers and organisations. A number of professionals in different settings described feeling guilty, useless and worthless immediately after the death. The situation could be exacerbated by colleagues avoiding them 'as if they were contaminated', and staff who were not involved feeling, as Lawson et al. (1995: 344) put it, 'there but for the grace . . .'

Horwath (1995: 351–5) identified the following lessons from her interviews:

- All staff are affected, including the typist, receptionist, etc.
- The incident can become a taboo subject – an atmosphere of mistrust and vulnerability develops when support is needed.
- Staff could be better prepared for the process of serious case reviews by training beforehand.
- One in three social workers report abuse or neglect as a child, so the incident may awake a range of emotions for them.
- Debriefing should be offered – maybe for teams, possibly for the inter-agency network.
- Debriefing should be undertaken by someone with no link with the agencies involved.
- Debriefing should be normalised.

- Opportunities should be provided for staff to reflect on their experiences or training will occur against a backcloth of guilt, blame and mistrust.
- Training needs to acknowledge individuals' feelings and not just focus on learning the lessons.
- Impact on learning may be long term and needs to be taken into account in planning training.
- Trainers and managers must work in partnership so as not to reinforce workers' feelings of disconnectedness and uselessness – supervisors need to be involved in the preparation and debriefing of training.

The ability to recognise the likely range of reactions of staff to a serious incident involving a child is clearly important in developing effective strategies to support staff at different stages of the process, which culminate in managing the aftermath of a serious case review. Thompson et al. (1994) identify the fact that, following short periods of stress, the question of recovery hardly arises, as 'we are able to slip in and out of periods of stress without making any major adjustments'. However, after a prolonged and intense period of stress, returning to a state of equilibrium is often a difficult and lengthy process. It is important at these times that steps are taken to facilitate recovery so that the trauma does not leave a permanent scar. Trauma is here defined as occurring 'when an individual is exposed to an overwhelming event that renders him or her helpless in the face of intolerable danger, anxiety and instinctual arousal' (Pynoos and Eth, 1984). Trauma can also refer to situations which arise from extended periods of stress, and the aftermath of a serious case review clearly has elements of both definitions in the context discussed here. It is important at this stage to distinguish between posttraumatic reactions and the much more serious condition of post-traumatic stress disorder (PTSD).

Bourne and Brown (1996) identify a series of reactions commonly experienced following trauma:

- Shock – immediately following the incident, the worker might be in a state of shock, numbness and disbelief. They may have adrenalin still pumping through their body and may not be in a condition to make important decisions. Sometimes a state of psychological shock can persist for years before the worker is able to begin to assimilate and process the experience.

- Reaction – usually either rage or anguish is experienced, often with unpredictable fluctuations between the two. Disturbed sleep and violent flashbacks can be experienced. Workers might try to hide their suffering, adopting a deadpan expression.
- Blunting – as a way of reducing the pain, workers may change what they believe happened, avoid emotional contact with others, eat or drink heavily.
- Self-doubt – as time goes on, the worker might begin to feel that they are not the person they thought they were. This can lead to withdrawal and to isolation.

A crisis stage is then reached, which is very much a turning point. At this stage, it is no longer possible to continue as if nothing had happened and it may be the first point at which the worker is prepared to entertain professional help. From this crisis point, Bourne and Brown identify three routes which an individual could follow.

The first they call 'adaptation and integration'. The likelihood of the worker following this route is greatly enhanced if:

- A thorough debriefing has already been undertaken.
- The worker has an accurate impression of their colleagues' reactions to them and the incident.
- They have worked through similar traumas before.
- They have an awareness that their experience is natural and transitional.
- They were psychologically stable prior to the incident–often trauma can happen on the back of another trauma, making resolution even harder.
- The worker stops looking to the past and recognises that they have to learn anew about themselves and their world. New core beliefs begin to emerge; these are tested out and eventually incorporated into a new sense of self (Bourne and Brown, 1996: 235–43). To some extent, this process resembles that of bereavement. In this case, the loss might be thought of as the person they were or the world they believed in.

The second route which can be followed is what Bourne and Brown call 'internalisation of

depressive beliefs'. For a worker who follows this route, self-doubt, rather than being a transitional adaptation, becomes an end-point. The 'new self' becomes that of a depressed person and the worker begins to organise their life accordingly – avoiding risk and change and settling for minimal expectations of life. Suicidal feelings might be provoked.

A worker who follows the third route, 'externalisation and collapse', becomes increasingly prickly, blaming others for everything that is wrong, not only at work but in wider life also. Their physical health is likely to deteriorate and there is a tendency to greater isolation from friends and colleagues. They may not find it easy, however, to accept the need for help.

Herman (1992) notes that the most powerful determinant of psychological harm is the character of the traumatic event itself. Individual personality characteristics count for little in the face of overwhelming events. There is a simple, direct relationship between the severity of the trauma and its psychological impact, whether that impact is measured in terms of people affected or the intensity and duration of harm. She points out that research has demonstrated that the impact of traumatic events also depends to some degree on the resilience of the affected person:

> Studies of diverse populations have reached similar con-clusions: stress resistant individuals appear to be those with high sociability, a thoughtful and active coping style and a strong perception of their ability to control their destiny.
>
> (p. 60)

Herman further identifies the fact that 'those who are already disempowered or disconnected from others' (p. 61) are most at risk of the malignant psychological effects of trauma. Herman ascribes three stages to the recovery process. The central task of the first stage is 'the establishment of safety'. The central task of the second stage is 'remembrance and mourning' and of the third, 'reconnection with ordinary life'. She highlights the fact that, like any abstract concept, these stages of recovery are a convenient fiction and not to be taken too literally. No single course of recovery follows these stages through a straightforward linear sequence. Indeed, different interventions will be needed at different times for different staff.

In a survey of social workers who had been affected by distressing experiences at work, Smith and Nursten (1998) found that what workers found most unhelpful were others underestimating the experience of the impact on them. Horowitz (1998) noted, for example, that when workers become safe the expectation may be that their functioning will improve. In fact, the need for support may be greater after safety has been established than before, as 'safety' can provide the opportunity to experience and reflect on a traumatising event that had previously been pushed aside and can result in an increase in psychological turmoil and pain. The publication of a serious case review may coincide with a sense of relief and safety, thereby precipitating other buried responses.

Learning organisations

What are the key characteristics of successful companies in both the public and private sectors?

- structure
- organisational culture
- information systems
- human resources practices
- leadership

Cultures of blame, climates of fear and issues of leadership

Learning organisations ideally have an organisational culture that:

- Promotes openness, creativity and experimentation among members.
- Encourages members to acquire, share and process information.
- Provides the freedom to try new things, risk failure and learn from mistakes.
- Celebrates and shares good practice.
- Systematically gathers views from service users and carers and uses them to influence service planning.
- Creates opportunities for members to think and reflect and to learn from new evidence and research.

Organisations with this kind of culture described in such terms are likely to capture and disseminate all learning – including in principle at least, learning from near misses. Many workers express their concerns that an organisational culture of blame prevails: one that fosters a fear of talking about incidents that could have, or actually did, go wrong.

Latent failures ('Yes Minister')

This creates cultures that foster blame and create defensiveness; an unwillingness to admit to mistakes or to ever deviate from procedures even when the individual case circumstances justify it; and supervision that is blame apportioning rather than reflective.

The costs of latent mistakes include defensive attitudes from staff, a climate of fear, isolated practice to avoid exposure to others. Back covering practice predominates at an organisational level, within the management structure, across agencies and across workers.

Forums for discussion, time for reflection and a reporting system

People learn from one another and a variety of other sources to their line manager. It should be formalised into professional development meetings. These have the potential to allow for close calls and near misses to be routinely discussed and reflected upon. Importance is formalisation and permission organisationally.

Safe care system factors

Safe care system factors include a clear legislative and organisational policy, clear professional frameworks, a good stock of professional experience and knowledge as well as support to staff when they face emotional issues in cases.

From risk avoidance to risk taking

Such a transition needs to be developed with care. It must be built on the foundation of front-line children and family practitioners being able to make sound judgements. Very little in the current system encourages this. Professional judgement can only be exercised when there is clarity of task and clarity of context.

Building capacity and resilience

What is it that protects humans as they steer the path between helping people heal following a traumatic event and developing prolonged psychological difficulties themselves? Awareness, balance and connection in three realms: individual contributions, service strategies and organisational recognition.

Building an emotionally competent organisation (Morrison, 1997)

- Need to integrate feeling and thinking aspects of agency life with the doing/task focus.
- Moving from secrecy to openness.
- Moving from helplessness to empowerment.
- Moving from accommodation to clarity.
- Undertake an organisational cultural audit.

Individual

Reconciliation, working through own life histories of traumatic events may lead to workers being less naïve and have more positive coping strategies. Compassion satisfaction e.g. a positive utilisation of deep empathy and sorrow for those suffering. Hardiness (functional) (feeling in control, commitment, change as a challenge) and social support (structural) such as positive collegiate support systems.

Service strategies

Managers and employers must design strategies to protect staff from developing a stress-related illness; supervision; self-awareness programmes and a culture that values staff and promotes their care; and personal, professional and organisational support may provide protective favours to mediate against some of the risks relating to the development of secondary traumatic stress.

Organisational strategies

Organisational strategies have to include support, respect and understanding of the issues, resources, a learning organisation and forums to address issues. They have to be clear about rebuilding after problems have surfaced and this may include some or all of the following:

- Preparation.
- Debriefing.
- Establish a framework for change.
- Re-appraisal.
- Re-orientation.
- Rebuilding and moving on.

- Name the problem e.g. professionally dangerous practice.
- Break the silence about the issues.
- Ask about a process for dealing with the issue in your workplace.
- Engage in reflective practice. Acknowledge we are sometimes part of the problem, then part of the solution.
- Ensure self-caring behaviours e.g. counselling, peer support, time out, social activities, good diet and lifestyle.
- Speak up when you witness it.

Strategies for management to create a safe, happy workforce

- Gain knowledge of the issue and its causes.
- Conduct regular meetings to address the issue; supervise its operation and success.
- Undertake a formal analysis of your culture.
- Have a policy about support and encouragement of staff.
- Foster an environment of open collaboration.
- Support workers' autonomy and initiative and promote a learning culture.
- Provide education about processes to promptly report incidences of professionally dangerous practice.
- Monitor staff morale and address issues which impact negatively upon morale.
- Ensure that staffing is adequate and caseload management is in place.
- Engage in self-awareness activities and in reflective practice.
- Institute open, honest and supportive dialogue through peer review.
- Engage in self-care activities.
- Ensure access to appropriate supports and services for those affected e.g. counselling and display such information prominently.

Learning from past experiences

- Better identification of children vulnerable to abuse.
- Understanding the process of change in public services.
- The development of practice tools.

Culture

This involves knowing how to ensure that staff are engaged with and motivated to lead on, the implementation in practice. Once again, a number of relevant lessons and frameworks can be used, most noticeably from the implementation of the Assessment Framework. Research and experience tells us that:

- Change provokes anxiety, defence and unconscious behaviour.
- People issues un-addressed.
- It takes more time than anticipated.
- Major problems arise during change.
- Ineffective co-ordination of activities.
- Crises de-rail change strategy.
- Capabilities of staff insufficient.
- Inadequate training provided.

Fertile conditions for change

Charles and Glennie (2002) reported on the fertile conditions within which the assessment framework was best implemented which should be recognised and then used as a building block for similar future developments. Their conditions included:

- The Inter-agency Practice and Policy Context is known and appreciated: Identify through consultation, the ways in which, and at what level, key partners are to be involved. Make explicit the practice context for all parties and help all to see the links between competing and complementary initiatives across all agencies. Maintain attention to these issues, and their impact, throughout the implementation process.
- Vision and Ownership: The early establishment of a shared vision that is universally owned and widely communicated is crucial. Recognising the power this has to model and mirror inter-agency practice is important. Best outcomes flow from an established, shared consensus prior to action.
- Nature of Change: Understanding the nature of the change that is required, from central government down to local level is crucial in determining implementation activity. The distinction between guidance that is following, challenging, confirming or leading practice locally must be made in order to ensure that practitioners across all agencies appreciate the nature of change required in their own practice.
- Commitment: Be clear about the level of priority with each agency and identify consequences of differences.
- Driver: Identify or build a responsible or responsive driving individual or group. The

Driving Force must be multi-agency and this can be achieved in a number of different ways.
- Service Users: Consider the ways in which service users can be involved throughout the process.
- Planning and Strategy: Build a clear and flexible strategic plan. Know that you will need to change it in light of events and circumstances as the complexity of the task emerges over time. Work to timescales that take into account the local context as well as those that are externally imposed. Develop practice indicators.
- Training: The many/varied training functions of educating, consulting, informing and inquiring need to be fully understood and used in their widest sense. Training forms an integral part of the implementation process, playing a crucial role in the early stages of visioning, and subsequently in providing feedback and planning next stages. Be clear about the responsibility of single and multi-agency training. Single agency training is best used to inform and engage all partners with the primary question: 'what has this got to do with me?' before moving on to inter-agency training. This is most powerful in helping practitioners address the subsequent question of 'How best can we work with this together?'
- Process: Use processes that invite critical feedback and that have the qualities of an open system. Implementation is an iterative not a linear process. Build evaluation in from the outset.

Organisational preparation for and readiness to implement change:

- Morrison and Horwath (2000) provided us with a very useful framework for helping organisations prepare for the management and implementation of change.
- Acknowledge the need for change: It is important that the ownership of the change process is located at the right level. Assuming that the external mandate for change is established, step one is to ensure that the agenda for change becomes located at a strategic level within the relevant agencies. For instance, the need for change in practice is often identified by specialists within the agency but their capacity to manage organisational or inter-agency change is limited. A second early task is for the lead agency, usually social

services in the context of child welfare work, to identify the other key agency stakeholders, including elected members, who need to be brought on board. Depending on the scope of the task, a project coordinator might be required to undertake much of the detailed work that the next stages of the process will necessitate. One point to consider is timing for the inclusion of other agencies in the change process. Too early exposure to inter-agency debate can result in intra-agency confusion widening to inter-agency confusion. Conversely, failure to engage the other agencies early on in the process can leave them feeling excluded and consequently unwilling to engage in the change process.

- Establish agency and inter-agency ownership of the change agenda: Change cannot be properly managed if different agencies hold divergent opinions as to the rationale and desired outcomes of any change. In order to increase agency understanding and to provide a wider professional context for the changes, a research and policy briefing or seminar for a small 'driver' group can be helpful to ensure that the rationale, research and underpinning professional issues are understood. A communication strategy is important to alert and signpost staff about the changes that are coming, identify who are the lead officers, and how agencies will communicate with staff as things progress. A staff conference, newsletter or project bulletin might be vehicles for this.

- Assessing current strengths and weaknesses: Before one can begin to implement a major change within an organisation it is necessary to lay the foundations for change by undertaking an organisational audit of the readiness for change. This can be done by identifying existing strengths, good practice, the nature of the changes and the impact they are intended to have on practice.

- Audit of readiness for change: An organisational audit in many ways mirrors an assessment of a child and family. In both cases the purpose is to identify what is currently going on: what needs to change; current drivers that will promote and support change and barriers that need to be addressed. In order to assess the readiness of an organisation for change there are a number of organisational factors that need to be considered, which mirror the three domains referred to above:

- Practitioners' needs: these are the professional and organisational needs of the front-line staff who will be responsible for the assessment process.

- Agency capacity: this describes the capacity of the organisation to meet the needs of the practitioners.

- Collaborative arrangements: this domain describes external relationships with other agencies and community networks which are required by the practitioners.

- Such an audit can assist with a baseline assessment of current strengths and weaknesses. It should include direct discussion and consultation with staff, both within and across agencies. Direct consultation often refines the picture gained from paper-based analysis and provides essential insights not only to the degree of congruence between policy and practice, but also about underlying professional attitudes and responses to change. In addition, consultation engages staff at an early stage in the process of shaping the road ahead. Skipping this element carries with it the danger that subsequent prescriptions about change may be based on a partial or inaccurate view of how the current state of practice might increase staff resistance to change.

- Identify what changes are needed: The emphasis at this point is on 'what' rather than 'how', with the focus on identifying from the previous stage what changes to policy, resources, services, structures, attitudes, skills and practice are required. Often having identified good local practice the challenge is how to bring all practice up to the standards of the best. Pilot projects may have shown the way and the task is how to integrate their achievements in a range of different work and practice contexts throughout the agency (or agencies). However, creating attitudinal changes to practice is complex, not least because what workers believe in the sanctity of a training course is not necessarily how they may think under pressure at the coal-face. Intellectual and emotional belief systems can be very different. This points to the critical importance of policy, resource and practice changes being framed within an explicit rationale and value base, and the specification of key success criteria against which changes will be measured.

- Identify how best to make changes: The task here is to work out how staff can be engaged in a meaningful manner in the change process, without which changes may be either partial or superficial. The engagement strategy is therefore dependent on the quality of analysis undertaken in steps 3 and 4. It is also useful to consider how changes have been managed in the past. As with service users, previous experiences and history can be a significant indicator of future capacity for change, as can the number of other competing demands currently facing an individual or organisation. One important message is that the prospects for the successful implementation of change need to take account of the way in which other related organisational and professional changes have been handled. The better these changes have been handled, the more prepared and willing staff will be to adapt to further change. Conversely it can be seen that the prospects for change in a 'quick-fix' environment are much more problematic.
- Formulate a critical pathway for change: This involves mapping out a sequence of individual steps over a time period that together achieve the goals. The pathway provides a strategic plan for change based on steps 4 and 5. However, the pathway also needs to incorporate other changes and imperatives facing the key agencies in order to anticipate what demands are likely to be placed on which staff, or resources, at what points. The pathway enables progress to be monitored against key delivery points (for example, a new policy). This will enable momentum to be maintained and plans to be modified if necessary. Disseminating the plan is necessary too. It may well be from the practitioner' perspective that a considerable period of time has elapsed since they first heard that changes were in the wind. They may feel disconnected with the agenda, or have concluded that nothing is going to happen.
- Establish organisational infrastructure for improved practice: This step focuses on creating the changes identified in step 6 through work on values, policies, structures, resources, services, priorities, standards, skills and practice. It is likely that parallel work will be required on inter-agency policies, structures and in particular eligibility criteria and threshold levels for intervention and services. Training has a vital supportive role to play.
- Consolidate, maintain and integrate changes: The task now is to embed and integrate work undertaken on policy, etc. throughout the agency (or agencies). Successful pilot programmes need to be translated into application throughout the agency.
- Monitor and review changes: Maintaining the kinds of complex change that have been described is perhaps one of the most difficult tasks of all. The continual bombardment of change, budgetary constraints, unforeseen crises, and the very nature of large organisations combine to make the task of staying on track with change very tricky indeed. However, it is often said that what gets monitored is what gets done. The monitoring process may identify unintended effects of the changes or unforeseen gaps (for instance in training) and may highlight areas where the new policies or practices are not working or are at risk of failing or lapsing. This allows remedial or relapse prevention action to be taken rather than waiting for a more serious failure which might threaten the rest of the changes.
- Evaluate organisational and inter-agency learning from the changes for further use: First-order change refers to managing change at the level of tasks, systems and outputs. Second-order change involves change at the level of underlying attitudes, paradigm and culture. Both can occur at the same time. Second-order change occurs when the organisation is able to learn how it learns and applies that knowledge to future changes.

References

Ackoff, R. (1981) *Creating the Corporate Future*. New York: John Wiley and Sons.

ACSNI (1993) ACSNI Study Group on Human Factors. Third Report: Organising for Safety, United Kingdom: HSE. In Sorenson, J.N. (2002) Safety Culture: A Survey of the State-of-the-art. *Reliability Engineering and System Safety*, 76, 189–204.

Aiken, A. et al. (1975) *Coordinating Human Services*. San Francisco, CA: Jossey-Bass.

Anderson, D.G. (2000). Coping Strategies and Burnout among Veteran Child Protection Workers. *Child Abuse and Neglect*, 24, 839–48.

Bank of England (1996) *Bank of England Report of the Board of Banking Supervision Inquiry into the Circumstances of the Collapse of Barings.* London: HMSO.

Barner, N. (2005) Risking Optimism: Practitioner Adaptations of Strengths-based Practice in Statutory Child Protection Work. *NCPC Newsletter*, 13: 2, 10–15.

Barton, A. and Welbourne, P. (2005) Context and its Significance in Identifying 'What Works' in Child Protection. *Child Abuse Review*, 14, 177–94.

Barton, A. (2002) *Managing Fragmentation. An Area Child Protection Committee in a Time of Change.* Aldershot: Ashgate.

Barton, W.H., Foleron, G. and Busch, M. (2003) *Final Report to the Indiana Division of Families and Children: Customer Satisfaction Survey.* Indiana University School of Social Work.

Beck, U. (1992) *Risk Society: Towards a New Modernity.* London: Sage.

Behan, D. (2003) *ADSS Position Statement in Response to the Victoria Climbié Report.* http:// www.adss.org.uk/publications/policy/ Climbié100203.shtml

Bendor, J.B. (1985) *Parallel Systems: Redundancy in Government.* Berkeley, CA: University of California Press.

Berwick, D.M. (2002) A User's Manual for the IOM's 'Quality Chasm' Report. *Health Affairs*, 21: 3, 80–90.

Besharov, D. (1987) Contending with Overblown Expectations. *Public Welfare*, Winter: 45, 1.

Bhana, A. and Haffejee, N. (1996) Relation among Measures of Burnout, Job satisfaction, and Role Dynamics for a Sample of South African Child-care Social Workers. *Psychological Reports*, 79, 431–34.

BIS (2001) *Basel Committee on Banking Supervision: Sound Practices for the Management and Supervision of Operational Risk*, December. www.bis.org/publ.bcbs86.pdf

BIS (2002) *Basel Committee on Banking Supervision: Sound Practices for the Management and Supervision of Operational Risk*, July. http://www.bis.org/publ/bcbs91.pdf

Blundo, R. (2001) Learning Strengths-based Practice: Challenging our Personal and Professional Frames. *Families in Society*, 82: 3, 296–304.

Bourne, I. and Brown, A. (1996). *The Social Work Supervisor.* Buckingham: Open University Press.

Bostock, L., Barstow, S., Fish, S. and Macleod, F. (2005) *Managing Risk and Minimising Mistakes in Services to Children and Families.* London: SCIE.

Brandon, M., Dodsworth, J. and Rumball, D. (2005) Serious Case Reviews: Learning to Use Expertise. *Child Abuse Review*, 14, 160–76.

Brandon, M., Owers, M. and Black, J. (1999) *Learning How to Make Children Safer: An Analysis of Serious Child Abuse Cases in Wales.* Norwich: University of East Anglia/Welsh Office.

British Safety Council (2002) British Safety Council: Safety Culture. www.britishsafetycouncil.co.uk

Brown, K. and Rutter, L. (2006) *Critical Thinking for Social Work.* Exeter: Learning Matters.

Buckley, H. (2003) *Child Protection Work: Beyond the Rhetoric.* London: Jessica Kingsley.

Bullock, R. et al. (1995) *Messages from Research.* London: HMSO.

Burden, T., Cooper, C. and S. Petrie, S. (2000) 'Modernising' Social Policy: Unravelling New Labour's Welfare Reforms. Aldershot: Ashgate.

Butcher, T. (2002) *Delivering Welfare.* 2nd edn. Buckingham: Open University Press.

Butler, I. (2002) Abuse in Institutional Settings. In Wilson, K. and James, A. (Eds.) *The Child Protection Handbook*, 172–85. 2nd edn. London: Bailliere Tindall.

Camman, C. (1984) *Management-Labour Co-operation.* Ann Arbour: University of Michigan.

Campbell, B. (1988) *Unofficial Secrets: Child Sexual Abuse. The Cleveland Case.* London: Virago.

careandhealth.com (2001) How to Combat the Recruitment Crisis in Social Work http://www.careandhealth.com/arch/article 79.asp

Carnochan, S. et al. (2002) Child Welfare and the Courts: An Exploratory Study of the Relationship Between Two Complex Systems. Unpublished manuscript, Berkeley, CA.

CBI (1990) *Developing a Safety Culture: Business for Safety.* London: Confederation of British Industry. In Glendon, A.I. and Stanton, N.A. (2000) Perspectives on Safety Culture. *Safety Science*, 34: 1–3, 193–214.

Challis, L. et al. (1988) *Joint Approaches to Social Policy: Rationality and Practice.* Cambridge: Cambridge University Press.

Changes, Keynote address at Australasian Conference on Child Abuse and Neglect, Perth,

WA. *Children and Youth Services Review*, 21: 1, 79–107.

Charles, M. and Glennie, S. (2002) *The Implementation of Working Together to Safeguard Children and the Framework for Assessment*. PIAT.

Cichinelli, L. (1990) Risk Assessment; Expectations, Benefits and Realities. In Tatara, T. (Ed.) *4th National Roundtable on CPS Risk Assessment (US) Summary of Highlights*. Colorado: American Humane Association.

Clarke, J., Gewirtz, S. and McLaughlin, E. (Eds.) (2000). *New Managerialism, New Welfare*. London: Sage.

Clarke, S. (1999) Perceptions of Organisational Safety: Implications for the Development of Safety Culture. *Journal of Organisational Behavior*, 20, 185–98.

Cleaver, H. and Freeman, P. (1995) *Parental Perspectives in Cases of Suspected Child Abuse*. London: HMSO.

Clode, D. (2002) The 'S-word' is Banned. http://www.careandhealth.com/arch/article276.asp

Cohen, B.J. (2005) Reforming the Child Protection System: Competing Paradigms of Change. *Children and Youth Services Review*, 27: 653–66.

Cohen, B.J., Kinnevy, S.C. and Dichter, M.E. (2007) The Quality of Work Life of Child Protective Investigators: A Comparison of Two Work Environments. *Children and Youth Services Review*, 29: 474–89.

Cohen, B. (1992) Quality of Working Life in a Public Child Welfare Agency. *Journal of Health and Human Resource Administration*, 15: 2, 129–52.

Cohen, S. (2001) *States of Denial: Knowing about Atrocities and Suffering*. Cambridge: Polity Press.

Cooper, A. (2002) Keeping our Heads: Preserving Therapeutic Values in a Time of Change. *Journal of Social Work Practice*, 16, 1.

Corby, B. (2000) *Child Abuse: Towards a Knowledge Base*. 2nd edn. Buckingham: Open University Press.

Corby, B., Doig, A. and Roberts, V. (1998) Inquiries into Child Abuse. *The Journal of Social Welfare and Family Law*, 20: 4, 377–95.

Corovic, T. (2006) Child Protection Workers and Vicarious Trauma: A View from the Edge. *OACUS Journal*, 50: 1, 11–14.

Cousins, C. (2003) Where the Explanation Doesn't Fit the Injury: Child Protection and Infant Harm. *NCPC Newsletter*, 11: 2, 4–13.

Cousins, C. (2005) 'But the Parent is Trying . . .': The Dilemmas Workers Face. *Child Abuse Prevention Newsletter*, 13, 1, Summer.

Cullen, W.D. (1990) *The Public Inquiry into the Piper Alpha Disaster, Vols. I and II*. London: HMSO.

Dale, P. et al. (1986) *Dangerous Families: Assessment and Treatment of Child Abuse*. London: Tavistock.

Dale, P., Green, R. and Fellows, R. (2002a) Serious and Fatal Injuries to Infants with Discrepant Parental Explanations: Some Assessment and Case Management Issues. *Child Abuse Review*, 11, 296–312.

Dale, P., Green, R. and Fellows, R. (2002b) *What Really Happened? Child Protection Case Management of Infants with Serious Injuries with Discrepant Explanations*. London: NSPCC.

Dane, B. (2000) Child Welfare Workers: An Innovative Approach for Interacting with Secondary Trauma. *Journal of Social Work Education*, 36: 1, 27–41.

Davis, B. (2001) The Restorative Power of Emotions in Child Protection Services. *Child and Adolescent Social Work Journal*, 18, 437–54.

Dickinson, N.S. and Perry, R.E. (2002) Factors Influencing the Retention of Specially Educated Public Child Welfare Workers. *Journal of Health and Social Policy*, 15: 3–4, 89–103.

Dingwall, R. (1986) The Jasmine Beckford Affair. *The Modern Law Review*, 49, 489–507.

Dingwall, R., Eekelar, J. and Murray, T. (1983) *The Protection of Children: State Intervention and Family Life*. Oxford: Blackwell.

DoH (1991) *Child Abuse: A Study of Inquiry Reports 1980–1989*. London: HMSO.

DoH (1998) *Modernising Social Services: Promoting Independence, Improving Protection, Raising Standards*. London: HMSO.

DoH (1999) *Modern Social Services: A Commitment to Improve: The 8th Annual Report of the Chief Inspector of Social Services*. London: HMSO.

DoH (1999) *Working Together to Safeguard Children*. London: HMSO.

DoH (2000) *Assessing Children in Need and their Families: Practice Guidance*. London: HMSO.

DoH (2001) *Studies Informing the Framework for the Assessment of Children in Need and their Families*, London: HMSO.

DoH (2002) *Integrated Childrens System*. (Consultation Document) London: HMSO.

DoH, DfEE, Home Office (1999) *Working Together to Safeguard Children: A Guide to Inter-Agency Working to Safeguard and Promote the Welfare of Children*. London: HMSO.

DoH, DfEE, Home Office (2000) *Framework for the Assessment of Children in Need and their Families*. London. HMSO.

Donald, I. and Canter, D. (1993) Employee Attitudes and Safety in the Chemical Industry. *Journal of Loss Prevention in Process Industries*, 7: 3, 203–8.

Drake, B. and Yadama, G.N. (1996) A Structural Equation Model of Burnout and Job Exit among Child Protective Services Workers. *Social Work Research*, 20: 3, 179–88.

Dyson, P. (2002) Child Protection: The Manager's Perspective. In Wilson, K. and James, A. (Eds.) *The Child Protection Handbook*, 538–52, 2nd edn. London: Bailliere Tindall.

Edelenbos, J. and Klijn, E.H. (2007) Trust in Complex Decision-making Networks: A Theoretical and Empirical Exploration. *Administration and Society*, 39: 11, 25–50.

EducationGuardian.co.uk 'Six weeks to re-think A-level marking', http://education.

Ellett, A.J., Ellis, J.I., Westbrook, T.M. and Dews, D. (2007) A Qualitative Study of 369 Child Welfare Professionals' Perspectives about Factors Contributing to Employee Retention and Turnover. *Children and Youth Services Review*, 29, 264–281.

Elliot, B., Mulroney, L. and O'Neil, D. (2000) *Promoting Family Change: The Optimism Factor.* Sydney: Allen and Unwin.

Fennell, D. (1988) *Investigation into the King's Cross Underground Fire.* London: HMSO.

Ferguson, H. (2005) Working with Violence, the Emotions and the Psycho-social Dynamics in Child Protection. *Social Work Education*, 24: 7, 781–95.

Figley, C.R. and Kleber, R.J. (1995) Beyond the 'Victim': Secondary Traumatic Stress. In Kleber, R.J., Figley, C.R. and Gerson, B.P.R. (Eds.) *Beyond Trauma: Cultural and Social Dynamics.* New York: Plenum.

Figley, C.R. (1995) Compassion Fatigue: Toward a New Understanding of the Costs of Caring. In Stamm, B.H. (Ed.) *Secondary Traumatic Stress: Self-Care Issues for Clinicians, Researchers and Educators*, 2nd edn. Lutherville, MD: Sidran Press.

Firkins, A. (2003) *Discourse and Decision Making in Child Protection Practice.* 9th Australasian Conference on Child Abuse and Neglect, Sydney Convention Centre, Darling Harbour, 24th–27th November.

Fitzgerald, J. (2001) Lessons from the Past: Experiences of Inquiries and Reviews. In *Out of Sight. Report on Child Deaths from Abuse 1973 to 2000.* London: NSPCC.

Fleck-Henderson, A. (2000) Domestic Violence in the Child Protection System: Seeing Double. *Children and Youth Services Review*, 22, 333–54.

Friedmann, J. (1987) *Planning in the Public Domain: From Knowledge to Action.* Princeton, NJ: Princeton University Press.

Fryer, G.E., Miyoshi, T.J. and Thomas, P.J. (1989) The Relationship of Child Protection Worker Attitudes to Attrition from the Field. *Child Abuse and Neglect*, 13, 345–50.

Furlong, M. (1989) Can a Family Therapist do Statutory Work? *Australian and New Zealand Journal of Family Therapy*, 10: 4, 211–18.

Furlong, M. (2001) Neither Colluding nor Colliding: Practical Ideas for Engaging Men. In Pearse, B. and Camilleri, P. (Eds.) *Working with Men in the Human Services.* Sydney: Allen and Unwin.

Gambrill, E. and Shlonsky, A. (2001) The Need for Comprehensive Risk Management Systems in Child Welfare. *Child and Youth Services Review*, 23: 1, 79–107.

Gehman, H., Turcotte, S., Barry, S., Hess, K.W., Hallock, J.N., Wallace, S.B., Deal, D., Hubbard, S., Tetrault, R.E., Widnall, S., Osheroff, D.D., Ride, S. and Logsdon, J. (2003) *Columbia Accident Investigation Board Report: Volume 1.* www.caib.us/news/report/default.html accessed 27 August 2003.

General Medical Council (2001) *Good Medical Practice.* London: GMC.

General Social Care Council (2002) *Codes of Practice for Social Workers and Employers.* London: Stationery Office.

Gibbons, J., Conroy, S. and Bell, C. (1995) *Operating the Child Protection System: A Study of Child Protection Practices in English Local Authorities.* HMSO: London.

Glisson, C. and Hemmelgarn, A. (1998) The Effects of Organisational Climate and Inter-organisational Co-ordination on the Quality and Outcomes of Children's Services Systems. *Child Abuse and Neglect*, 22: 5, 401–21.

Glisson, C. (1992) Technology and Structure in Human Service Organisations. In Hasenfeld, Y. (Ed.) *Human Services as Complex Organisations*, 184–202. Beverly Hills, CA: Sage.

Glisson, C. (1994) The Effect of Services Coordination Teams on Outcomes for Children in State Custody. *Administration in Social Work*, 18, 1–23.

Glisson, C. (1996) Judicial and Service Decisions for Children entering State Custody: The Limited Role of Mental Health. *Social Service Review*, 70, 257–281.

Goddard, C. and Carew, R. (1993) *Responding to Children: Child Welfare Practice.* Sydney: Longman Cheshire.

Goddard, C. and Stanley, J. (2002) *In the Firing Line: Violence and Power in Child Protection Work.* West Sussex: John Wiley and Sons.

Gomm, R. (2000) *Case Study Method.* London: Sage Publications.

Goodman, P.S. and Rousseau, D.M. (2004) Organisational Change that Produces Results: The Linkage Approach. *Academy of Management Executive,* 18: 3, 7–20.

guardian.co.uk/alevels2002/story/o,12321,811651,00.html accessed 30 October 2002.

Gustafson, L. and Allen, D. (1994) A New Management Model for Child Welfare: True Reform means doing things Differently. *Public Welfare,* 52: 1, 31–41.

Hallett, C. and Birchall, E. (1992) *Coordination and Child Protection: A Review of the Literature.* Edinburgh: HMSO.

Hallett, C. and Birchall, E. (1992) *Coordination in Child Protection.* London: HMSO.

Hasenfeld, Y. (1987) Power in Social Work Practice. *Social Service Review,* 61, 469–83.

Health and Safety Executive (2002) *Measuring Health and Safety Performance.* www.hse.gov.uk accessed 30 October 2002.

Healy, K. (2005) *Social Work Theories in Context: Creating Frameworks for Practice.* Basingstoke: Palgrave Macmillan.

Herman, J.L. (1992) *Trauma and Recovery.* Basic Books: New York.

Hetherington, T. (1998) A New Approach to Child Protection. *National Child Protection Clearinghouse Newsletter,* 6: 1, 7–11. (retrievable at www.aifs.gov.au/nch/nlaut98.html)

Himle, D., Jayaratne, S. and Thyness, P. (1989) The Buffering Effects of Four Types of Supervising Support on Work Stress. *Administration in Social Work,* 13, 19–34.

Hoagwood, K. (1997) Interpreting Nullity: The Fort Bragg Experiment – A Comparative Success or Failure? *American Psychologist,* 52, 546–50.

Hogan, C. and Murphy, D. (2002) *Reframing Responsibilities for Well-being Outcomes.* Baltimore, MD: The Annie E. Casey Foundation.

Hogg, M., and Terry, D. (2001) Social Identity Theory and Organisational Processes. In Hogg, M. and Terry, D. (Eds.) *Social Identity Processes in Organisational Contexts.* Philadelphia 7: Psychology Press.

Horner, N. (2004) *What is Social Work? Context and Perspectives.* Exeter: Learning Matters.

Horowitz, M. (1998) Social Worker Trauma: Building Resilience in Child Protection Social Workers. *Smith College Studies in Social Work,* 68, 363–77.

Horwath, J. and Morrison, T. (2007) Collaboration, Integration and Change in Children's Services: Critical Issues and Key Ingredients. *Child Abuse and Neglect,* 31: 55–69.

Horwath, J. and Morrison, T. (1999). *Effective Staff Training in Social Care: From Theory to Practice.* London: Routledge.

Horwath, J. (1995) The Impact of Fatal Child Abuse Cases on Staff: Lessons for Trainers and Managers. *Child Abuse Review,* 4, 351–5.

Horwath, J. (2002) Maintaining a Focus on the Child? First Impressions of the *Framework for Children in Need and their Families* in Cases of Child Neglect. *Child Abuse Review,* 11, 195–213.

Howarth, J. (2001) (Ed.) *The Child's World: Assessing Children In Need.* London: Jessica Kingsley Publishers.

Howe, D. and Hinings, D. (1995) Reason and Emotion in Social Work Practice: Managing Relationships with Difficult Clients. *Journal of Social Work Practice,* 9, 5–14.

Howe, D. (1992) Theories of Helping, Empowerment and Participation. In Thoburn, J. (Ed.) *Practice – Involving Families in Child Protection,* 39. Norwich: University of East Anglia. http://www.doh.gov.uk/childrenstrusts/index.htm accessed 11 April 2003. http://www.info.doh.gov.uk/doh/intpress.nsf/page/2002–0432 accessed 23 October 2002. http://www.victoria-Climbiéinquiry.org.uk/finreport/finreport.htm accessed 10 April

Hudson, B. (1987) Collaboration in Social Welfare: A Framework for Analysis. *Policy and Politics,* 15, 175–82.

Hudson, B. (2000) Interagency Collaboration: A Sceptical View. In Brechin, A., Brown, H. and Eby, M.A. (Eds.) *Critical Practice in Health and Social Care,* 255–74. London: Sage and Open University.

Hutchins, E. (1995) *Cognition in the Wild.* London: The MIT Press.

Jayaratne, S. and Chess, W.A. (1984) Job Satisfaction, Burnout, and Turnover: A National Study. *Social Work,* 29, 448–53.

Jayaratne, S., Himle, D.P. and Chess, W.A. (1991) Job Satisfaction and Burnout: Is there a Difference? *Journal of Applied Social Sciences,* 15, 245–62.

Jenkins, A. (1990) *Invitations to Responsibility: The Therapeutic Engagement of Men who are Violent and Abusive.* Adelaide: Dulwich Centre Publications.

Johnson, S. and Petrie, S. (2004) Child Protection and Risk Management: The Death of Victoria Climbié. *Journal of Social Policy*, 33, 179–202.

Jones, J. and Gallop, L. (2003) No Time to Think: Protecting the Reflective Space in Children's Services. *Child Abuse Review*, 12, 101–6.

Jones, C.W. (1993) *The 4X4 Concept: The General Theory of Unifying Dynamic Organisational Self-regulation.* Longview, TX7: Decision Systems.

Kaplan, A. (1964) *The Conduct of Inquiry: Methodology for Behavioral Science.* Scranton, PA7: Chandler Publishing.

Killen, K. (1994) *Neglect of Neglect: Research and Practice.* NSW Child Protection Council.

Killen, K. (1996) How Far have we come in Dealing with the Emotional Challenge of Abuse and Neglect. *Child Abuse and Neglect*, 20: 9, 791–95.

King, S. (2003) Managing the Aftermath of Serious Case Reviews. *Child Abuse Review*, 12, 261–69.

Knott, C. (2007) *Reflective Practice in Social Work.* Exeter: Learning Matters.

Lachman, P. and Bernard, C. (2006) Moving from Blame to Quality: How to Respond to Failures in Child Protective Services. *Children and Youth Services Review*, 30, 963–8.

Laming, Lord (2003) *The Victoria Climbié Inquiry. Report of an Inquiry by Lord Laming* (Chairman). Cmnd 5730, January 2003. The Stationery Office: London.

Lawson, B., Masson, H. and Milner, J. (1995) 'There but for the Grace . . .': Developing Multi-disciplinary Training following a Local Child Death Enquiry. *Child Abuse Review*, 4, 340–50.

Lawton, H. and Magarelli, A. (1980) Stress among Public Child Welfare Workers. *Catalyst*, 7, 57–65.

Le Grand, J. and Bartlett, W. (1993) *Quasi-Markets and Social Policy.* Basingstoke: Macmillan.

Lee, T. (1998) Assessment of Safety Culture at a Nuclear Reprocessing Plant. *Work and Stress*, 12: 3, 217–37.

Loxley, A. (1997) *Collaboration in Health and Welfare. Working with Difference.* London: Jessica Kingsley.

Magen, R.H. (1999) In the Best Interests of Battered Women: Reconceptualising Allegations of Failure to Protect. *Child Maltreatment*, 4: 2, 127–35.

Manning, P.K. (1982) Organisational Work: Structuration of Environments. *The British Journal of Sociology*, 33: 1, 118–34.

Marsh, M. (2003) *Victoria Climbié Inquiry Report – Statement by NSPCC Director and Chief Executive, Mary Marsh.* http://www.nspcc.org.uk/home/informationresources/vcstatementmarsh.htm accessed 11 April 2003.

Mason, B. (1989) *Handing Over.* London: Karnac.

Mason, B. (1993) Towards Positions of Safe Uncertainty. *Human Systems*, 4, 189–200.

McCann, I.L. and Pearlman, L.A. (1990) Vicarious Traumatisation: A Framework for Understanding the Psychological Effects of Working with Victims. *Journal of Traumatic Stress*, 9: 10, 131–49.

McMillen, J.C., Morris, L. and Sherraden, M. (2004) Ending Social Work's Grudge Match: Problems versus Strengths. *Families in Society*, 85: 3, 317–25.

Mearns, K., Flin, R., Gordon, R. and Fleming, M. (1998) Measuring Safety Climate on Offshore Installations. *Work and Stress*, 12: 3, 238–54.

Menzies, J. (1970) *The Functioning of a Social System as a Defence against Anxiety.* London: Free Press.

Milburn, A. (2002) *Time to Break up old, Monolithic Social Services.* press release.

Moon, J. (2004) *A Handbook of Reflective and Experiential Learning: Theory and Practice.* London: Routledge Falmer

Morrison, T. (1993). *Staff Supervision in Social Care: An Action Learning Approach.* Harlow: Longmans.

Morrison, T. (1994) *Collaboration in a Changing World: Developing an Integrated Response to Child Sexual Abuse.* Paper presented at the First National Conference on Child Sexual Abuse: 'Developing an Integrated Response to the Prevention and Treatment of Child Sexual Abuse', Melbourne, March, 1994.

Morrison, T. (1995) Professional Dangerousness. In Dale, P. and Morrison, T. (eds.) *Dangerous Families.* London; Rochdale: NSPCC.

Morrison, T. (1996) Partnership and Collaboration: Rhetoric and Reality. In *Child Abuse and Neglect*, 20: 2, 127–40.

Morrison, T. (1998) Inter-agency Collaboration and Change: Effects of Inter-agency Behaviour on Management of Risk and Prognosis for Change in Dangerous Family Situations. Paper presented at the Twelfth International ISPCAN Congress on Child Abuse and Neglect, 'Protecting Children: Innovation and Inspiration', Auckland, New Zealand, September 6–9, 1998.

Morrison, T. (1998). Partnership, Collaboration and Change under the Children Act. In Adcock, M. and White, R. (Eds.) *Significant Harm; Its Management and Outcome.* Croydon: Significant Publications.

Morrison, T. (1999) Working Together to Safeguard Children: Challenges and Changes for Inter-agency Coordination in Child Protection. *Journal of Interprofessional Care,* 14: 4, 363–73.

Morrison, T. (2001) *Staff Supervision in Social Care.* Brighton: Pavilion.

Morrison, T. and Howarth, J. (2000) Identifying and Implementing Pathways for Organisational Change. *Child and Family Social Work,* 5: 3, 245–53.

Morrison, T. and Lewis, D. (2005) Toolkit for Assessing the Readiness of Local Safeguarding Children's Boards: Origins, Ingredients and Applications. *Child Abuse Review,* 14: 5, 297–316.

Munro, E. (1999b) Protecting Children in an Anxious Society. *Health, Risk and Society,* 1: 1, 117–27.

Munro, E. (2005) Improving Practice: Child Protection as a Systems Problem. *Children and Youth Services Review,* 27, 375–91.

Munro, E. (1996) Avoidable and Unavoidable Mistakes in Child Protection Work. *British Journal of Social Work,* 26, 793–808.

Munro, E. (1998) Improving Social Workers' Knowledge Base in Child Protection Work. *British Journal of Social Work,* 28, 89–105.

Munro, E. (1999) Common Errors of Reasoning in Child Protection Work. *Child Abuse and Neglect,* 23, 745–58.

Munro, E. (2002) *Effective Child Protection.* London: Sage.

Munro, E. (2004) The Impact of Child Abuse Inquiries since 1990. In Stanley, N. and Manthorpe, J. (Eds.) *The Age of Inquiry: Learning and Blaming in Health and Social Care,* 75–91. London: Routledge.

National Audit Office (2001) Inappropriate Adjustments to NHS Waiting Lists. Report by the Comptroller and Auditor General HC 452 Session 2001–2002, 19 December 2001. http://www.nao.gov.uk/publications/nao reports/01-02/0102452.pdf accessed 30 October 2002.

Newman, J. (2001) *Modernising Governance: New Labour, Policy and Society.* London: Sage.

Nocon, A. (1989) Forms of Ignorance and their Role in the Joint Planning Process. *Social Policy and Administration,* 23, 31–47.

NSPCC (2001) *Out of Sight. NSPCC Report on Child Deaths from Abuse 1973 to 2000,* 2nd edn. London: NSPCC.

Osborne, D. and Gaebler, T. (1992) *Reinventing Government. How the Entrepreneurial Spirit is Transforming the Public Sector.* Reading, MA: Addison-Wesley.

Parton, N. (2004) From Marie Colwell to Victoria Climbié: Reflections on Public Inquiries into Child Abuse a Generation Apart. *Child Abuse Review,* 13, 80–94.

Parton, N. (1991) *Governing the Family: Child Care, Child Protection and the State.* Basingstoke: Macmillan.

Parton, N. (Ed.) (1997) *Child Protection and Family Support: Tensions, Contradictions and Possibilities,* London: Routledge.

Petrie, S. (2003) Issues in Child Abuse. In Lyon, C. with contributions by Cobley, C., Petrie, S. and Reid, C. *Child Abuse,* 3rd edn. Bristol: Jordans/Family Law.

Petrie, S. and Corby, B. (2002) Partnership with Parents. In Wilson, K. and James, A. (eds.) *The Child Protection Handbook,* 387–402, 2nd edn. Edinburgh: Balliere-Tindall.

Petrie, S. and Wilson, K. (1999) Towards the Disintegration of Child Welfare Services. *Journal of Social Policy and Administration,* 33: 2, 181–97.

Powell, W. (1994) The Relationship between Feelings of Alienation and Burnout in Social Work. *Families in Society,* 75, 229–35.

Pynoos, R.S. and Eth, S. (1984) The Child as Witness to Homicide. *Journal of Social Issues,* 40: 2, 87–108.

Rawnsley, A. (2001) Servant of the People: The Inside Story of New Labour. *Observer/Guardian.*

Reason, J. (1990: 2003) *Human Error.* New York: Cambridge University Press.

Reason, J. (1990b) The Contribution of Latent Human Failures to the Breakdown of Complex Systems. In Broadbent, D.E., Baddeley, A. and Reason, J.T. (Eds.) *Human Factors in Hazardous Situations,* 27–36. London: Oxford University Press.

Reason, J. (1997) *Managing the Risks of Organisational Accidents.* Burlington, VT: Ashgate.

Reason, J. (2000) Human Error: Models and Management. *British Medical Journal,* 320, 768–70.

Reder, P. and Duncan, S. (2004) Making the Most of the Victoria Climbié Inquiry Report. *Child Abuse Review,* 13, 95–114.

Reder, P. and Duncan, S. (1999) *Lost Innocents: A Follow-up Study of Fatal Child Abuse.* London: Routledge.

Reder, P. and Duncan, S. (2002) Predicting Fatal Child Abuse and Neglect. In Browne, K.D. et al. (Eds.) *Early Prediction and Prevention of Child Abuse: A Handbook.* Chichester: Wiley.

Reder, P. and Duncan, S. (2003) Understanding Communication in Child Protection Networks. *Child Abuse Review*, 12, 82–100.

Reder, P. and Duncan, S. (2004) From Colwell to Climbié. In Stanley, N. and Manthorpe, J. (Eds.) *The Age of the Inquiry: Learning and Blaming in Health and Social Care.* London: Routledge.

Reder, P., Duncan, S. and Gray, M. (1993) *Beyond Blame.* London: Routledge.

Regehr, C., Hemsworth, D., Leslie, B., Howe, P. and Chau, S. (2004) Predictors of Post-traumatic Stress in Child Welfare Workers: A Linear Equation Model. *Children and Youth Services Review*, 26, 331–46.

Roberts, K.H., Stout, S.K. and Halpern, J.J. (1994) Decision Dynamics in Two High Reliability Military Organisations. *Management Science*, 40, 614–24.

Robinson, G. and Whitney, L. (1999) Working Systemically following Abuse: Exploring Safe Uncertainty. *Child Abuse Review*, 8, 264–74.

Rutter, M. (1987) Psychosocial Resilience and Protective Mechanisms. *American Journal of Orthopsychiatry*, 57, 316–31.

Rzepnicki, T.L. and Johnson, P.R. (2005) Examining Decision Errors in Child Protection. *Children and Youth Services Review*, 27, 393–407.

Saleebey, D. (2002) *The Strengths Perspective in Social Work Practice*, 3rd edn. Boston: Allyn and Bacon.

Sanders, R., Colton, M. and Roberts, S. (1999) Child Abuse Fatalities and Cases of Extreme Concern: Lessons from Reviews. *Child Abuse and Neglect*, 23, 257–68.

Sandfort, J. (1999) The Structural Impediments to Human Service Collaboration: Examining Welfare Reform at the Front Lines. *Social Service Review*, 73: 3, 314–39.

Schein, E. (1992) *Organisational Culture and Leadership.* San Francisco: Jossey-Bass.

Schlonsky, A. and Wagner, D. (2005). The Next Step: Integrating Actuarial Risk Assessment and Clinical Judgement into an Evidence-based Practice Framework in CPS Case Management. *Children and Youth Service Review*, 27, 409–27.

Schorr, L. (1997) *Common Purpose: Strengthening Families and Neighbourhoods to Rebuild America.* New York: Doubleday/Anchor Books.

Schwalbe, C. (2004) Re-visioning Risk Assessment for Human Service Decision-making. *Children and Youth Service Review*, 26, 561–76.

Scott, A. (2000) Risk Society or Angst Society? In Adam, B., Beck, U. and van Loon, J. (Eds.) *The Risk Society and Beyond.* London: Sage.

Scott, D. and O'Neill, D. (1996) *Beyond Child Rescue: Developing Family Centred Practice at St Lukes.* Sydney: Allen and Unwin.

Scott, W.R. (1985) Systems within Systems. *American Behavioral Scientist*, 28, 601–18.

Scourfield, J. (2002) *Gender and Child Protection.* Basingstoke: Palgrave.

Senge, P. (2006) *The Fifth Discipline: The Art and Practice of the Learning Organisation*, revised edition. New York: Currency Doubleday.

Sheaffer, Z., Richardson, B. and Rosenblatt, Z. (1998) Early-warning Signals Management: A Lesson from the Barings Crisis. *Journal of Contingencies and Crisis Management*, 6: 1, 1–22.

Silver, P.T., Poulin, J.E. and Manning, R.C. (1997) Surviving the Bureaucracy: The Predictors of Job Satisfaction for the Public Agency Supervisor. *Clinical Supervisor*, 15, 1–20.

Sinclair, R. and Bullock, R. (2002) *Learning from Past Experience: A Review of Serious Case Reviews.* London: Department of Health.

Sinclair, R. (2004) Participation in Practice: Making it Meaningful, Effective and Sustainable. *Children and Society*, 18, 106–18.

Smith, B.D. (2005) Job Retention in Child Welfare: Effects of Perceived Organisational Support, Supervisor Support, and Intrinsic Job Value. *Children and Youth Services Review*, 27, 153–69.

Smith, N. and Nursten, J. (1998) Social Workers' Experience of Distress: Moving Towards Change? *British Journal of Social Work*, 28, 351–68.

Smith, B. and Donovan, S.E.F. (2003) Child Welfare Practice in Organisational and Institutional Context. *Social Service Review*, 77: 4, 541–63.

Smith, D. (2002) Management and Medicine: Issues in Quality, Risk and Culture. *Clinician in Management*, 11, 1–6.

Stace, S. and Tunstill, J. (1990) *On Different Tracks: Inconsistencies between the Children Act and the Community Care Act.* London: Voluntary Organisation Personal Social Services Group.

Stalker, C.A. et al. (2007) Child Welfare Workers who are Exhausted yet Satisfied with their Jobs: How do they do it? *Child and Family Social Work*, 12, 182–91.

Stanley, J. and Goddard, C. (1997) Failures in Child Protection: A Case Study. *Child Abuse Review*, 6, 46–54.

Stanley, N. and Manthorpe, J. (2004). *The Age of the Inquiry: Learning and Blaming in Health and Social Care*. London: Routledge.

Stanley, J. and Goddard, C. (1998) *Child Protection Workers in the Firing Line: What the Hostage Theory says about Improving Protection for Severely Abused Children*. Paper presented at the 12th International Congress on Child Abuse and Neglect, Auckland.

Stanley, J. and Goddard, C. (2002) *In the Firing Line: Power and Violence in Child Protection Work*. London: Wiley.

Stead, E. and Smallman, C. (1999) Understanding Business Failure: Learning and Un-learning Lessons from Industrial Crises. *Journal of Contingencies and Crisis Management*, 7: 1.

Stevens, M. and Higgins, D.J. (2002) The Influence of Risk and Protective Factors on Burnout Experienced by those who Work with Maltreated Children. *Child Abuse Review*, 11, 313–33.

Stevenson, O. (1989) Multi-disciplinary Work in Child Protection. In Stevenson, O. (Ed.) *Child Abuse: Professional Practice and Public Policy*. New York: Harvester Wheatsheaf.

Strydom, P. (2002) *Risk, Environment and Society*. Buckingham: Open University Press.

Sudbery, J. (2002) Key Features of Therapeutic Social Work: The Use of Relationship. *Journal of Social Work Practice*, 16: 2, 149–62.

Taylor, S. (2006) Educating Future Practitioners of Social Work and Law: Exploring the Origins of Inter-professional Misunderstanding. *Children and Youth Services Review*, 28: 638–53.

The International Federation of Social Workers (2001) *Definition of Social Work*. http:// www.ifsw.org/Publications/4.6e.pub.html accessed 12 November 2001.

The Presidential Commission (1986) *Presidential Commission on the Space Shuttle Challenger Accident Report*. Washington, DC: Government Printing Agency.

The Victoria Climbié Inquiry. http:// www.victoria-Climbié-inquiry.org.uk/accessed 1 October 2002.

Thoburn, J. (1992) *Participation in Practice Involving Families in Child Protection*. Norwich: University of East Anglia.

Thoburn, J., Lewis, A. and Shemmings, D. (1995) *Paternalism or Partnership? Family Involvement in the Child Protection Process*. London: HMSO.

Thompson, N., Murphy, M. and Stradling, S. (1994) *Dealing with Stress*. Basingstoke: Macmillan.

Thompson, N., Stradling, M.M. and O'Neill, P. (1996) Stress and Organisational Culture. *British Journal of Social Work*, 26, 647–65.

Tilley, N. and Pawson, R. (1997) *Realistic Evaluation*. London: Sage.

Tomison, A.M. (1999) *Interagency Collaboration and Communication in Child Protection Cases: Some Findings from an Australian Case Tracking Study*. Paper presented at the Fifth ISPCAN Asian Conference on Child Protection, 26–28 November, 1999, Hong Kong.

Tomison, A. (1996) Child Protection towards 2000. *Child Abuse Prevention*, 4, 2. Melbourne: Australian Institute of Family Studies.

Townley, B. (2001) The Cult of Modernity. *Financial Accountability and Management*, 17: 4, 303–10.

Trotter, C. (2004) *Helping Abused Children and their Families*. Sydney: Allen and Unwin.

Turnbull, N. (1999) *Internal Control: Guidance for Directors on the Combined Control*. London: The Institute of Chartered Accountants: http:// www.iia.org.uk/knowledgecentre/ professionalguidance/businessguidan ce.cfm?Action = 1andARTICLE ID = 101 accessed 30 October 2002.

Turner, B.A. (1978) *Man Made Disaster*. London: Wykeham.

University of Leicester and the Department of Health (1990) *Children in Need and Their Families: A New Approach. A Guide to Part III of the Children Act 1989 for Local Authority Councillors*. Leicester: School of Social Work, University of Leicester.

Urry, J. (2000) *Sociology Beyond Societies: Mobilities for the Twenty-first Century*. London: Routledge.

Vince, R. and Martin, L. (1993) Inside Action Learning. *Management Education and Development*, 24, 205–15.

Vinokur-Kaplan, D. (1994) Job Satisfaction and Retention of Social Work. *Administration in Social Work*, 18: 3, 93–121.

Vinten, G. (2000) Whistle Blowing towards Disaster Prevention and Management. *Disaster Prevention and Management*, 9: 1, 18–28.

Wachtell, Lipton, Rosen, Katz and Promontory Financial Group (2002) Report to the Boards of Allied Irish Banks, plc. Allfirst Financial Inc. and Allfirst Bank Concerning Currency Trading Losses 12 March: http:// www.aibgroup.com

Weick, K.E. (1987) Organisational Culture as a Source of High Reliability. *California Management Review*, 29, 112–27.

Weinstein, J. (1997) And Never the Twain Shall Meet: The Best Interests of Children and the Adversary System. *University of Miami Law Review*, 52, 79–175.

White, S. and Featherstone, B. (2005) Communicating Misunderstandings: Multi-agency Work as Social Practice. *Child and Family Social Work*, 10, 207–16.

Wilson, S. (2005) *Proactively Managing for Outcomes: Developing and Initiating a Model for Managing Area Offices in Statutory Child Protection*. Brisbane: University of Queensland.

Woods, D. et al. (1994) *Behind Human Error: Cognitive Systems, Computers and Hindsight*. Wright-Patterson Air Force Base, Ohio: CSERIAC.

Zohar, D. (2000) A Group-level Model of Safety Climate: Testing the Effect of Group Climate on Micro-accidents in Manufacturing Jobs', *Journal of Applied Psychology*, 85, 587–96.

CHAPTER 9

Promoting Professional Resilience

Jo Clarke

Introduction

Some occupations are unique with respect to which members risk exposure to traumatic events. Paton and Violanti (1996) describe these as 'critical occupations', a term coined to encapsulate the critical role played by such individuals in protecting communities, as well as the fact that 'in the course of acting in this capacity, these professionals can encounter traumatic events which may, under certain circumstances, exert critical impact on their psychological well-being' (Paton and Violanti, 1996: vii). Emergency service personnel and disaster responders are two clear examples where front-line workers face acute risk owing to the nature of their work. Body recovery after natural disasters, removal of victims from vehicle crashes, attending scenes of terrorist activity can all be readily identified as situations likely to challenge any individual's psychological equilibrium.

However, more recently it has been recognised that some jobs involve considerably more *chronic* exposure to potential psychological risk, and although different from the demands of emergency work, should also be included under the umbrella term 'critical occupation'. Working in child protection is one such area. The potential for almost daily encounters with child victims of abuse, damaged families, hostile abusers, interrogative and blaming media, not to mention the complexities of inter-agency working can at times conspire to impact on the well-being of even the most hardy individuals.

Drawing up an inclusive list of non-emergency 'critical occupations' would be a considerable challenge, but therapists working with perpetrators of sexual abuse, and prison and probation staff managing incarcerated and community-based offenders would be other indisputable examples. Much of the work presented here is based on the author's research and experience in these two areas, and as such, regular reference is made to the associated literature.

The purpose of this chapter is to present an organisational strategy that has been designed specifically to enhance the well-being of staff working with the most difficult, disruptive and damaged prisoners held in High Security prison discrete units. The chapter starts by considering the concept of 'risk' in non-emergency critical occupations, particularly in relation to well-being, psychological harm, resilience and post-traumatic growth. The development of the strategy is explained, including the rationale for the five key domains. Case examples of different interventions in action are then provided. Although designed specifically for HM Prison Service staff, it becomes clear that the principles underpinning the strategy's construction are equally applicable to staff working in any occupation where chronic exposure to potentially traumatic events is high.

Risk in non-emergency critical occupations

The word 'risk' has become so overused in modern vocabulary as to have almost lost its significance. For example, the terms risk assessment, risk management, risk reduction and risk aversion are terms so regularly incorporated into organisational parlance, that people seldom seem to question anymore, 'risk of what?' However, it is argued that without explication, any efforts to reduce risk are at best ad hoc and at worst potentially damaging.

In the context of critical occupations there are a number of areas where the concept of risk requires specific consideration. The first, and the one on which the premise of critical occupations is based, is risk of exposure to events that are potentially traumatic. DSM IV (American Psychiatric Association, 1994) defines a traumatic event as one that is outside of the range of usual human experience and that would be markedly distressing to almost anyone. Examples given of such events include threat to life or physical integrity, sudden destruction of one's home, or seeing another person who has recently been or is being seriously injured or killed. Clearly, front line emergency responders face such events frequently. And so do social service and criminal justice professionals. Working with victims of abuse or being threatened with assault by someone already known to be capable of murder can be daily occurrences, not in the context of an emergency callout, but as part of the daily work routine. Indeed, studies comparing emergency responders with social services personnel, found the latter group reported higher levels of traumatic symptoms despite similar levels of exposure to traumatic stimuli (Paton, Cacioppe and Smith, 1992; Paton and du Preez, 1993).

However, if the event itself caused traumatic symptoms, the shelf-life of members of critical occupations would be dramatically short. So what other risks should be considered? Paton and Violanti (1996) refer to the 'potential' for an event to be traumatic, suggesting that a second area of risk is that of traumatic *responding* by an individual worker. As will be discussed later in the chapter, just because risk of exposure is high, it does not follow that distress is inevitable. The level of risk of such a response is embedded not just in events, but also in complex psychological and demographic individual differences. Age, gender, length of service, previous trauma history and family history are all examples of factors associated with risk of stressful responding (e.g. Burke, 2007; Clarke, 2004; Clarke and Roger, 2007; Ellerby, 1998; McFarlane, 1987).

Thirdly, organisational practices evidenced to affect risk also require attention. Conclusions from research undertaken with emergency professions suggest that organisational variables represent stronger predictors of post-trauma outcomes than the incidents themselves (Dunning, 2003; Gist and Woodall, 2000; Hart, Wearing and Headey, 1993: Paton et al., 2000; Paton, Violant and Smith, 2003; Paton, 2006). For example, organisations characterised by high levels of bureaucracy, internal conflicts regarding responsibility, persistent use of established procedures (even in novel situations), and a strong motivation to protect the organisation from blame or criticism, have all been found to increase the risk of poor post-trauma outcome (Alexander and Wells, 1991; Gist and Woodall, 2000; Paton, 1997). Conversely, positive organisational practices, such as adoption of autonomous response systems, consultative leadership styles, training to develop adaptive capacity, and tolerance of procedural flexibility, can all enhance the likelihood of positive outcomes (Dunning, 2003; Gist and Woodall, 2000; Hart et al., 1993).

Finally, the extent to which risk levels might be compounded by events removed from the work context, but significant to the individual, also needs to be understood if risk potential is to be comprehensively managed. For example, in a study of prison and community-based sex offender treatment providers, respondents who had experienced a non-work related adverse event in the previous six months, also reported significantly higher levels of dissatisfaction with their organisations (Clarke, 2004). Such events included illness, relationship breakdown, house moves and so on. Although similar research failed to find an impact of traumatic life events 12 to 24 months after the event (Creamer et al., 1990) recent occurrence does appear to impact negatively on well-being.

An approach to managing risk incorporating these areas can underpin the development of a comprehensive strategy to enhance well-being for staff in critical occupations.

Psychological well-being and resilience in critical occupations

Until recently, research into the psychological impact of traumatic events, whether in an occupational or personal context, has focused almost exclusively on the potential for deleterious outcome. In a review of the literature concerned with the impact on treatment providers of working therapeutically with sex offenders (Clarke, 2004) not one study prior to 2000 considered positive aspects of the work. Because of the invidious nature of sexual violence against children and adults and the consequent exposure of therapists to detailed accounts of sexual abuse, the pervasive acceptance of detrimental effects is perhaps not surprising. This has been reflected in the nature of the psychometric instruments and surveys employed to assess impact. Measures of burnout (e.g. Maslach Burnout Inventory, Maslach and Jackson, 1986), vicarious trauma (Traumatic Stress Institute Belief Scale – Revision L, Pearlman, 1996) secondary traumatic stress and compassion fatigue (Compassion Fatigue Self-Test, Figley and Stamm, 1995) prevail. Consequently, it should be expected that symptoms indicative of trauma, including intrusive imagery, avoidance, cognitive disturbance, mood changes and disruption of core beliefs, have been identified. In a similar review of the trauma literature, Stamm (in Figley, 1997: 5) concluded, 'the great controversy about helping-induced trauma is not, can it happen, but what shall we call it?'

It is somewhat surprising then that consistently across studies, from the UK to North America and Canada, prevalence of symptoms has been moderately low, ranging between 20 per cent and 25 per cent (Ellerby, 1998; Farrenkopf, 1992; Jackson, Holzman, Barnard and Paradis, 1997; Rich, 1997; Turner, 1992). Previous findings have also been brought into question by the retrospective, snapshot research methodology by which they were derived. Failure to incorporate longitudinal components into impact research means no conclusions can be drawn about why some people are affected and not others, how long symptoms persist, what the long term prognosis is or whether or not deleterious outcome is caused directly by work-related exposure to trauma.

The cost of the focus on measurement of psychological harm has also meant that another consistently occurring statistic has, until recently, been overlooked; that which reflects that anywhere between 75 per cent and 96 per cent of treatment providers experience their work as immensely satisfying and rewarding (Bird-Edmunds, 1997; Ellerby, 1998; Kadambi, 2001; Kadambi and Truscott, 2006; Myers, 1995; Rich, 1997; Turner, 1992). In the critical occupations literature generally, there is a growing body of evidence that positive outcomes are not only possible, but that they often outweigh the negatives (Gist and Woodall, 2000; North et al., 2002; Paton, Violanti and Smith, 2003;Tedeschi and Calhoun, 2003). Being able to exercise professional skills to achieve highly meaningful outcomes, a strong sense of personal and professional development, a sense of control over significant adverse events, protection of the public and connection to colleagues have all been cited as enhancing well-being (Kadambi and Truscott, 2006; Paton, 2006).

In an organisational context the term 'well-being' refers to establishing the right conditions for generating high levels of employee engagement. It emphasises the social and psychological dimensions of the workplace, workforce and the work people do, and is related to both physical and mental health. An engaged workforce is identified by high levels of resilience, characterised in turn by the ability to bounce back from negative emotional experiences despite threats to the individual, flexible adaptation to the changing demands of stressful experiences and high positive emotionality (Block and Kremen, 1996; Lazarus, 1993; Masten, 2001). This is illustrated by staff who are competent, autonomous, understand the difference they can make to their work place and have personal values and beliefs that fit the needs of the role they undertake. Consequently, an engaged and resilient workforce is one that has low rates of turnover, low levels of sick absence and high levels of performance. The development and maintenance of such should arguably then be the number one priority for both individuals and organisations in the critical occupations business.

A model of well-being

The number and complexity of factors implicated in risk to individual well-being outlined at the start of this chapter, highlights the need for a structured, systematic and integrated approach to their identification and management. The Model of Dynamic Adaptation (MDA) (Figure 9.1) generated from research into the well-being of staff working therapeutically with sex offenders (Clarke and Roger, 2002; Clarke, 2004) provides a useful framework for this process. So named in an attempt to encapsulate the fluid risk status of an individual at any given time, it is based on the principles emanating from the risk prediction field (Grove and Meehl, 1996). There is an emerging view that there are categories into which factors can be grouped that contribute to the prediction of risk (e.g. Hanson and Bussiere, 1998). Although not yet empirically tested as a predictive model, a large number of variables incorporated in the MDA have been identified as significant, either in terms of heightening vulnerability to risk or increasing resilience to it. The organisation of variables in the way described allows for future development of the MDA as a reliable and valid risk prediction tool.

Variables are categorised according to the following definitions: *Static Factors* are any variables from an individual's history that are either fixed or unchanging, or change in a highly predictable way. Age and gender are examples of these. *Stable Factors* are those that are potentially changeable but relatively stable. Under normal

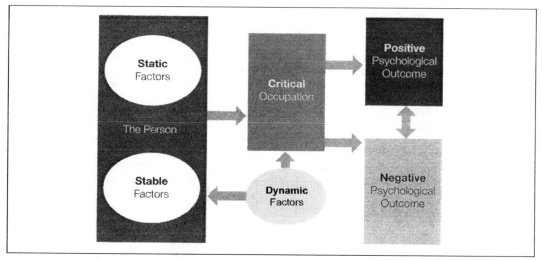

Figure 9.1   The model of dynamic adaptation

circumstances they would change only slowly, usually as a result of intervention or experience. Personality variables such as emotional sensitivity, coping styles and ability to take perspective are examples. *Dynamic factors* are those that can change rapidly, unpredictably and may well be outside the sphere of influence of the individual. Examples might include winning the lottery, a spouse losing a job, a new colleague joining the team, or having an accident.

The Critical Occupation category incorporates all those variables relevant to the workplace and the work people do. It includes risk of exposure to critical incidents, team cohesiveness, the physical environment in which the work takes place, policies and procedures, organisational support practices and so on.

The two outcome boxes refer to positive or negative psychological consequences, but are not mutually exclusive. As the figures from the sex offender treatment provider literature suggest, both rewarding and deleterious outcomes are possible simultaneously. The aim of any strategy to enhance well-being should be to tip the balance in favour of positive outcome for a majority of workers for a majority of the time.

The MDA is intended as a functional model for application to any critical occupation. However, identification of static, stable and dynamic variables, as well as rewards and costs of the work, needs to be specific to the occupation under consideration. Ideally, organisations will conduct their own longitudinal research, working

with new, experienced and former practitioners, to establish the relative importance of the multitude of potential variables. The very nature of critical occupations though, means that some variables are likely to be common to all.

For example, within the static domain, age, gender, length of time in the role, family status and previous history of trauma repeatedly emerge as significant to well-being (e.g. Clarke, 2004; Clarke and Roger, 2007; Clarke and Blythe, in preparation; Ellerby, 1998; McFarlane, 1987; Murphy, 1991). Within the stable category, dispositional optimism, emotional response style, coping strategies, perspective taking skills and empathy have all been identified as significant (e.g. Clarke, 2004; Clarke and Roger, 2007; Moran and Massam, 1997; Myers, 1995; Roger, Guarino and Olason, 2000). Dynamic factors, although little researched, include exposure to an event perceived to be traumatic within the previous six months, and quality of social support network post-event (Clarke, 2004; Pearlman and Saakvitne, 1995; Rich, 1997). Job and organisational characteristics include training, on-the-job support, preparedness and cultural issues (blame versus learning) (Alexander and Wells, 1991; Eisenberger et al., 2002; Gist and Woodall, 2000; Paton, 1997).

It is important to note that the extent to which a particular variable might influence either positive or negative outcome has not been elaborated upon here, and would need to be established in the context of other variables and the role to which it was being applied. For example, in a review of the literature on humour and coping in emergency work, Moran and Massam (1997) concluded there is scope for some but not all humour to act as a positive coping strategy. Other variables may well be double edged swords. For example, high levels of emotional inhibition have been demonstrated to be detrimental to psychological and physical health (Roger, 2002). However, emotional expressiveness needs to take account of time and place. It is unlikely to be conducive to high performance or well-being in the face managing of a critical incident.

Understanding the rewards of working in a particular critical profession is also essential if well-being is to be enhanced. In a concept mapping exercise with sex offender treatment providers, Kadambi and Truscott (2003) identified seven key areas in which providers found reward and meaning in their work. These were labelled: protection of the public, socially meaningful curiosity, enjoyment of counselling, professional benefits, connection to colleagues, offender wellness and change and offending specific change. Knowing such specifics affords organisations the opportunity to maximise workers' development in these domains.

A strategy to enhance well-being of Directorate of High Security Discrete Unit staff

HMPS Discrete Units

In 2005, HM Prison Service's Director of High Security (DHS) Prisons appointed a well-being advisor to consider the psychological support needs of staff working in DHS Discrete Units (DUs). Discrete Units comprise Close Supervision Centres (CSCs) and segregation, special secure, detainee and protected witness units. All such units are self-contained within their parent establishment, in that they are run and managed by dedicated staff teams who in most instances have been especially selected for the role. A majority of DUs accommodate the most disruptive, dangerous and often damaged individuals in the prison system. These include men who have a history of institutional violence (that may include murder) who exhibit aggressive and unpredictable behaviour and who may well have a diagnosis of personality disorder. More recently, extremist prisoners charged with, or

held on suspicion of, terrorist activity have presented a new and somewhat different psychological and emotional challenge to staff.

The types of challenges faced by staff on an almost daily basis include managing long-term prisoners with a history of serious hostage-taking (of both staff and other prisoners) and receiving constant personalised abuse from particular prisoners. The following incidents serve to illustrate other challenges: A previously quiet and reclusive prisoner mounting an unprovoked assault resulting in a member of staff being stabbed in the eye; a highly disturbed prisoner deliberately self-inflicting serious injury and excavating his own flesh to 'flick' at staff; prisoners uniting to go on 'dirty protest' whereby they urinated and defecated over their cells over a prolonged period of time.

In the late 1990s, as the development of CSCs was in progress, it was suggested that the single most difficult management issue confronting the Prison Service was creating secure and ordered conditions for long-term and difficult prisoners, while also establishing a realistic opportunity for them to progress, ultimately to less secure conditions (Morgan, 1997). Achieving such conditions without resorting to physical barriers, surveillance technology or regime deprivation was, and still is, considered to lie in the professional integrity of staff (King, 1985). The skills needed to respond to the intensely demanding nature of the work are multiple, and over the past six years, considerable effort has been put into equipping DU staff with the professional competencies to fulfil their role. However, although an integral aspect of well-being (as will be discussed later), competence is only one of a multitude of elements that requires attention if a holistic solution is to be operationalised. As Liebling (1999: 161) highlighted: 'the question of how staff cope with the fluctuating possibility of abuse and violence, while maintaining a relationship with prisoners, has never been adequately addressed'.

Wilson (2001) highlighted that one of the core principles in setting up CSCs, in recognition of the demands placed on staff, was that routines and staffing arrangements should be organised to ensure effective staff support. This is particularly pertinent given the physical environment associated with most DUs. Although far removed from the austerity described above, DUs are necessarily managed with security and control as the highest priorities. For example, electronic doors operated externally prevent free entry or exit to staff, barred windows limit natural light, furnishing and decoration is kept to a minimum to reduce the potential for weapon construction, rest rooms for staff may be difficult to access (owing to electronic doors) or, if located centrally, overlooked by prisoners. The paradox then becomes clear that the very measures designed to increase physical safety may simultaneously have a negative impact on psychological well-being.

In an attempt to support staff, operating standards evolved which included a requirement for team members to receive individual sessions with a qualified psychologist. In addition to addressing well-being issues, sessions were intended to counteract regime 'drift' and the effects of attempted conditioning by prisoners. Some units also contracted-in Employee Assistance Programmes to provided access to external counselling.

Individual support sessions, while laudable in terms of responding to potential individual need, failed to encapsulate the wider spirit of Wilson's recommendations. Consequently, they came to represent the totality of the support infrastructure, whilst neglecting a multitude of other practices, strategies and techniques evidenced to enhance well-being. Furthermore, the inflexible nature of this approach met with considerable resistance. Specifically, the mandatory requirement for attendance at individual support sessions resulted in staff perceiving that their ability to cope with high psychological demand was being undermined. This in itself resulted in distress, often exhibited as hostility, suspicion and outright anger, supporting empirical evidence that such an approach may result in greater severity and chronicity of symptoms (Bisson and Deahl, 1994; Carlier, Uchelen, van Lamberts and Gerson, 1998).

A second intuitive response designed to reduce the potential risk to staff was to limit the length of time individual officers stayed in DUs to two years. This was based on concerns surrounding capacity to cope and the potential for individuals to encounter numerous critical incidents in that time. However such a policy fails to account for individual differences in exposure, coping strategies, support networks or job satisfaction, the impact on teams of regular rotation or the financial implications of continually training new staff and inducting them to different ways of working, to name just a few. Further, there is a growing body of evidence to suggest that levels of distress may actually increase on leaving a critical occupation. For example, ex-sex offender treatment providers reported significantly higher levels of negative reactivity than practicing providers. Also noted is the depressed, bored, tired and psychologically deadened state experienced by some police officers on leaving their role. It is suggested it indicates a type of 'addiction to trauma', withdrawal from which can be extremely difficult without intervention. Therefore, any decision to impose a maximum length of service in a critical occupation should also accommodate the potential costs to the organisation of relocating staff to less demanding roles, the potential requirement for ongoing support interventions and the personal cost to the individual of a possibly unwanted transfer.

Despite these efforts to address perceived needs of DU staff, it became evident they were not combating reported distress. Evidence for this was mostly anecdotal, although on one particular unit hard evidence was available in the form of high sick absence and turnover figures.*

Clarke and Lloyd (2004) in research intended to determine support preferences of DU staff, identified 35 separate items endorsed as beneficial to well-being. Using a critical item score methodology pioneered in earlier research (Clarke, McDougall and Harris, 2003) and the principles of factor analysis, the items were broadly categorised into two key areas; Operational Support and Personal Care/ Emotional Well-Being. Items falling in the former group included 'A staff rotation plan that always leaves some experienced staff on the unit', 'Minimising the use of non-regular staff' and 'Senior managers acknowledging a job well done'. In the latter group 'Training in how to look after myself emotionally', 'Training in mental health issues' and 'Mandatory recovery time immediately after incidents and before debriefs or paperwork' were all considered supportive. Not only were many of the items far removed from previous organisational responses to minimising apparent distress, many of them were very straightforward to implement and far more in keeping with Wilson's (2001) original recommendation.

---

*Sick absence among DU staff is generally lower than the Service population as a whole (Clarke and Blythe, in preparation). This might well attest the earlier observations regarding high levels of job satisfaction in COs, despite potential for distress, and cautions against over-reliance on sick absence figures as a measure of well-being.

In an attempt to comprehensively address the support needs of DU staff, a long-term strategic approach has been adopted, incorporating many of the measures generated by staff in an effort to enhance well-being.

Strategy development and underpinning principles

The aim of any strategy is to help an organisation think through what it wants to achieve and how it will go about achieving it. Putting a strategy into practice and acting strategically ensures the organisation focuses on what needs to be done, is able to allocate resources accordingly and is not buffeted by events or distractions. The Strategy Survival Guide (2004) issued by the Cabinet Office, states that good public service strategies need to be: clear about objectives; informed by a rich understanding of causes, opportunities, trends, threats and possible futures; based on a realistic understanding of effectiveness; creative; adaptable; and, developed with, and communicated effectively to, all stakeholders. In developing the DU Well-Being strategy, a number of underpinning assumptions were made, including:

- Working in the Directorate of High Security DU is a critical occupation and presents unique psychological challenges to staff.
- Staff are in a constant process of adaptation to their work, influenced by a range of different factors.
- Allied to the point above, different staff have different needs at different times in relation to well-being.
- The Model of Dynamic Adaptation is an appropriate one on which to base an understanding of causes, threats and possible futures, given the points above.
- Pro-active, preventative strategies are more cost-effective than reactive, post-event strategies.
- The principles of evidence-based practice are highly relevant to interventions to enhance well-being. Intuitive interventions should only be implemented when theoretically supported and reinforced by thorough evaluation.

Fundamental to the success of the strategy is flexible, dynamic and holistic application in which the individual and employer have complementary responsibilities for sustaining well-being. Flexible in that elements of the strategy can be applied to the need of each unit and every individual at different times; dynamic in that it can accommodate change in the light of feedback or in response to new research evidence; and holistic in that it encompasses the preparation of staff from the point of expressions of interest to join a critical occupation through to comprehensive planning and support for departure and beyond.

To help achieve this, wider organisational and governmental considerations needed to be incorporated. In particular, the Health and Safety Executive (HSE) management standards for reducing workplace stress, and the Department of Health principles for primary, secondary and tertiary prevention were consulted.

The six HSE management standards cover the primary sources of stress at work, considered to be:

- Demands – such as workload, work patterns and the work environment.
- Control – such as how much say the person has in the way they do their work.
- Support – such as the encouragement, sponsorship and resources provided by the organisation, line management and colleagues.
- Relationships – such as promoting positive working to avoid conflict and dealing with unacceptable behaviour.
- Role – such as whether people understand their role within the organisation and whether the organisation ensures that they do not have conflicting roles.
- Change – such as how organisational change (large or small) is managed and communicated in the organisation.

Staff reporting positively about their working life in each of these domains is thought to reflect high levels of health, well-being and organisational performance. The DU Well-Being strategy is thus informed by these standards. However, the HSE acknowledges that while the organisation can take steps to reduce the potential for stressful responding, such emotional reactivity is largely a function of individual differences. Therefore, organisational measures for stress reduction need to be accompanied by protocols for addressing individual, psychological need.

To derive a framework for the strategy the organisation needs to first consider where it

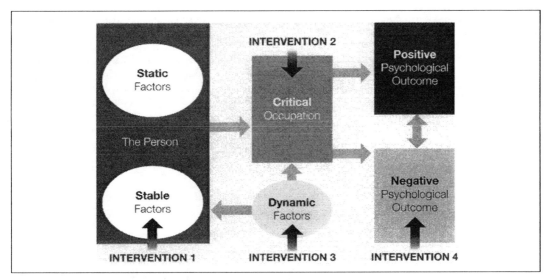

Figure 9.2   The model of dynamic adaptation with potential intervention points

wants to be (its vision), and then how it might get there, through defining aims and short, medium and long-term objectives. By considering points on the MDA where intervention is possible, a coherent framework begins to emerge.

The points of intervention may be considered primary, secondary and tertiary in nature (DoH, 2007). In the context of the well-being model, primary intervention aims to promote good psychological health and requires action on its determinants to prevent dysfunctional outcomes; secondary intervention involves the early detection of dysfunctional outcome, followed by appropriate intervention; and tertiary intervention aims to reduce the impact of the dysfunctional outcome and promote quality of life through active rehabilitation.

Intervention One is concerned with the individual. It covers issues of selection, training and preparation of the individual to undertake a critical role. In addition to skills and competencies to do the job, self-care skills also need to be considered (psychological self-maintenance). The aim here is not necessarily to deselect staff who have yet to acquire the requisite skills, competencies or values to stay psychologically well and perform highly, but to generate a profile that enables the individual and organisation to work together to achieve such a position if potential is shown to do the job. Point One is thus considered a primary intervention.

Intervention Two concerns the job itself, and relates to the workplace, the work force and the work people do. Here, consideration needs to be given to the environment, organisational policies and procedures, on-the-job support, frequency of exposure to traumatic events, recognition of distress and so on. Essentially a primary intervention, elements of secondary intervention would be applicable, if, for example, detrimental organisational practices were identified.

Opportunities to intervene at point Three are minimal. However, recognition and understanding of the impact that dynamic factors can have on well-being enables appropriate responses at both the individual and organisational level. Disclosure by a worker of difficult family circumstances, for example, can enable a manager to initiate different support options; understanding the impact on the team of a new manager can allow apposite preparation and so on. Intervention here would be an example of secondary prevention.

Intervention Four concerns action to be taken in the event of deleterious outcome, whether the result of a critical incident, other events related to organisational practices or individual circumstances. Generally tertiary in nature, responses might include referral to a mental health professional, adjustment of work demands, retraining and so on.

Table 9.1 illustrates the strategic framework for

Table 9.1 Strategic framework: enhancing the psychological well-being of staff working in DHS Discrete Units

Vision

In three years' time, the Directorate of High Security will have a comprehensive support infrastructure in place for Discrete Unit staff. It will consist of targeted selection and preparation of staff, evaluated interventions proven to enhance psychological resilience and reduce the risk of distress, and will be sufficiently flexible to accommodate the needs of a majority of staff.

Aims

1 Preparation: Selection of staff (1° prevention)	2 Preparation: Training of staff (1° prevention)	3 Practice: On-the-job support (1° and 2° prevention)	4 Post-event recovery: (3° prevention)	5 Evaluation:	6 Expert advisory panel:
Objectives					
Identify core qualities and competencies for each type of Unit	Review existing training, ensuring needs are met	Develop models of supervision	Identify a range of evidence based interventions for post event recovery e.g. Trauma disclosure	Psychological self-maintenance training	Establish a network of advisors with expertise in different elements of the strategy
Review existing selection procedures	Introduce 'top-up' training	Review the mandatory use of counselling	Review and enhance existing post-incident procedures	Trauma disclosure	
Construct a user friendly selection protocol	Develop simulation components to enhance preparation	Construct exit plan proforma	Design integrated assessments for frequent incident exposure including elements of psychological growth	Environmental Resilience	
Identify relevant psychometrics	Introduce training in Self Maintenance	Develop and implement a programme of Environmental Resilience		Use of supervision	
Construct a qualitative element to assessment	Prepare staff for integration into established teams	Identify and implement adaptive working practices		Use of counselling	
Evaluate protocol over 2 year period		Review optimum time in DUs			
		Develop early distress warning system			

enhancing the well-being of staff working in DHS Discrete Units, derived from the MDA.

In addition to the central domains of preparation, practice and post-event recovery, the strategic framework incorporates two additional strands; evaluation and expert advice. Evidence-based practice is essential if the well-being of staff in critical occupations is to be enhanced. Even though empirical evidence for the efficacy of interventions in the non-emergency critical occupations is sparse, there is considerable evidence emerging from related fields that supports the testing of specific techniques in this context. Backed up by thorough evaluation, the intention is to develop an array of evidenced-based techniques for application in non-emergency settings. To this end, the advice of a number of experts in related fields has guided and will continue to guide the development and implementation of the strategy. The fields include critical occupations, stress and emotion, statistics and experimental design, supervision, and training methodology.

Implementation of the strategy

HM Prison Service's Directorate of High Security Well-being Strategy is in the early stages of implementation. The number and range of interventions mean that it will be a number of years before all elements are in place, and even longer before empirical evidence of efficacy is available. The full version of the strategy includes justification and supporting empirical evidence for the inclusion of each element in the four central domains, and will not be elaborated upon here. However, to illustrate the strategy in action, three case examples are provided, in which two interventions from the Practice domain and one from Preparation 2: Training domain, are described.

Practice: Develop and implement a plan of Environmental Resilience

In 2005, concern was raised regarding the morale and subsequent performance of a staff team managing a small but highly disruptive group of prisoners held under conditions of close supervision. Reasons for the malaise were varied and plentiful, ranging from the implementation of new policies and procedures with little or no consultation, the long term placement of an

extremely challenging prisoner, to a difficult team member perceived to be working beyond personal competencies and at high risk of being manipulated by prisoners. Many staff reported wanting to leave the unit, sick absence was high and when staff were on duty they spent as little time as possible interacting with prisoners. The consequence was that the prisoners became more disruptive and difficult to manage, perpetuating the disquiet. The development of environmental resilience with this team was considered by the author the most appropriate way to change the prevailing conditions.

Environmental Resilience (ER) essentially refers to how an organisation can develop people's resilience to deal with adversity (for a detailed description see, for example, Paton, Violanti and Smith, 2003). Two key components are how it can facilitate a capacity for adaptability prior to exposure and how it can support individuals to sustain resilience post-incident (Johnston and Paton, 2003). Central to the ER construct is the concept of empowerment. Empowerment 'enables' people to deal with environmental demands (Conger and Konungo, 1988), with empowered people having enhanced beliefs about their ability to achieve a desired level of performance, no matter what the hoped-for outcomes. An organisation can facilitate this capacity by focusing on what are considered the four cognitive components of empowerment; Competence, Meaningfulness, Choice and Impact.

Competence describes an individual's belief that they possess the skills and abilities necessary to perform the job. Clearly related to preparation in terms of training, it also incorporates more personal skills useful for looking after oneself. The more competent staff feel, the more productive and adaptable they are and the more effort they put into their work.

Meaningfulness refers to the 'fit' between the needs of the role and the values, beliefs and behaviours of the individual. This is likely to be reflected ultimately in how much an individual cares about their work (Thomas and Velthouse, 1990). Individuals who find their work meaningful are likely to perceive problems and demands as welcome challenges (Antonovsky, 1990). In the social services and criminal justice professions, meaningfulness is likely to be high, and reflected in the large proportion of workers who report their jobs to be highly satisfying and rewarding, despite the adversity faced.

Choice, according to Spreitzer (1997) refers to the extent to which an individual perceives their behaviour as self-determined. It is likely to be evident in an individual's predisposition to act positively under adverse conditions (Dunning, 1994). Choice for staff can be difficult to facilitate in a highly structured, necessarily disciplined environment, where strict application of rules is considered to enhance equity and fairness for prisoners. However, there are opportunities for managers to exercise discretion, thus allowing staff some freedom in how units are operated.

Impact refers to the extent to which an individual perceives they can influence strategy, administration or operating outcomes at work to make a difference. Spreitzer (1997) points out that where choice concerns control over oneself, impact concerns the notion of control over organisational outcomes.

Johnston and Paton (2003) argue that identification of organisational conditions that cultivate powerlessness is the first step to developing an empowered workforce. Removal of those conditions, together with encouragement of self-reliance, leads to the experience of empowerment, resulting in behaviours characterised by initiative and perseverance.

Putting these principles into practice with the team described above required input with both the frontline staff and unit managers. With the support of the prison's senior managers (essential to the perception of meaningful intervention), a five stage process was initiated in line with Johnston and Paton's recommendations. This included:

1. Focus groups with frontline staff to identify their perceptions of barriers to well-being and high performance.
2. Examination of which of these (if any) could be removed or changed.
3. Use of training in how to manage the demands of work that cannot be adjusted.
4. Consideration of best methods to support managers.
5. Consideration of new ways of working to encourage resilience.

Focus groups with frontline staff resulted in the identification of a range of issues that concerned team members. For example, officers expressed anxiety at not feeling confident to manage prisoners' mental health issues in the absence of a specialised mental health provider. The result

was staff finishing their shift concerned they had at best, not dealt with the prisoner well, and at worst made things more problematic for their colleagues coming on duty. Clearly an issue of competence, staff had found this issue very difficult to voice outside the ER forum, partly for fear of being judged, but also simply because the question had not previously been asked. The matter was addressed through additional on-site training, and more frequently scheduled visits from the mental health nurse.

A second, less clear cut, issue was a perception that prisoners had their requests and applications expedited more efficiently than staff. One particular incident surrounded the purchase of a musical instrument for a particularly demanding prisoner that some staff felt was not deserved. They felt vexed that goods seemed to have been purchased quickly and without question. By comparison, when staff had asked for the installation of lockers for storage of their personal belongings, very little seemed to happen. The consequence was staff feeling angry, resentful and undervalued. The ER focus group not only allowed this issue to be aired, it also provided an opportunity for a number of different perspectives to be heard. It transpired that the prisoner's order had taken many months to be processed, but since it had arrived the prisoner had been far calmer and less demanding of staff. The unit manager was also able to take up the matter of the lockers and agreed to keep the team regularly updated about progress.

A third and highly emotive issue for the team concerned the working environment. As highlighted earlier in this chapter, often the very measures put in place to enhance physical security can compromise emotional well-being. A centrally located general office with 360° views of the unit and lack of rest facilities meant no privacy for staff during the core day. With a minimum of four centrally operated electronic doors, entry and egress from the unit was also problematic. It is hard to imagine the demand placed on individuals of being permanently observed. Although it took time to address, adjustments were made as a consequence of the concerns raised. The central office windows were covered with one-way reflective sheets, allowing observation of prisoners but not prisoner observation of staff, and a small office, away from the central area but within the unit, was converted into a rest room.

These examples illustrate stages one to three of the process in action. Most actions were undertaken with minimal cost implications, which in any case were likely to have been disproportionately low compared with the increased well-being of the team.

Additional focus groups were held with the first-line managers, including one Principal Officer (PO) and four Senior Officers (SOs) and two psychologists having input to both prisoner and staff well-being. First-line managers are central to the development of ER in teams for a multitude of reasons. They act as role models to their team and provide feedback to staff (Johnston and Paton, 2003). They also have the authority to introduce ER related initiatives, such as structuring team briefings (affording opportunities for impact); setting progressively more challenging targets (developing competence); increasing variety of tasks (choice) and matching skills of staff to roles within the team (meaningfulness). They also need to have their own support needs met.

The managers identified additional issues that they perceived may have been hindering the development of resilience in the team, and amongst themselves. For example, with two SOs on duty, it was not always clear who was responsible for what. SO tasks could be broadly split into either operational or administrative in nature. New practice meant the roles were clearly defined, the managers were clear about their responsibilities, and staff knew who to go to over what issue. The managers also discussed the need to enhance competence and choice by providing a supporting role to staff managing highly demanding prisoners, rather than the hands-on approach they had been adopting. It is easy for the often overwhelming operational demands on prison staff to overshadow the very solutions that can reduce or remove them. The opportunity, time and space afforded to the managers and staff by the ER process resulted in the implementation of a range of simple, straightforward and cost effective solutions that may not have otherwise been identified.

Eighteen months on from the initial intervention, the team hold ER meetings on a monthly basis. Although not yet empirically tested, morale in this well-functioning and integrated team is high. Visitors to the unit comment on the calm and ordered atmosphere and staff present as relaxed and competent in their roles.

Practice: Identify and implement adaptive working practices

Some high risk jobs involve undertaking repetitive and painstaking tasks that most of the time, do not demand high levels of emotional energy to perform well. They do, however, require vigilance and can at times become critical in nature. An example of one such job is that of monitoring the correspondence, both verbal and written, of prisoners subject to Safeguarding Children measures.

In 2006, new procedures were introduced to undertake this task, and, in one prison, a small team of ancillary grades was appointed to administer them. Despite the newness of the role, the then Director of High Security prisons raised concerns regarding the potential for the work to exert critical pressure on well-being. He asked for a review of that potential and for interventions to be considered that would reduce the risk of psychological harm to the team.

The prison concerned had 180 prisoners subject to the measures. The team was required to monitor communications and make an assessment about the nature and level of risk in relation to public protection. The gathered data may be used in a number of ways, including preventing a known sex offender gaining access to children, foiling an escape attempt, or imposing conditions on a licence prior to release. Accordingly, team members are required to remain highly vigilant in the face of potentially emotionally upsetting material, in the knowledge that their assessment is likely to have a significant impact on public safety. It is a highly responsible and high profile role.

In order to establish the nature of the risk posed to psychological well-being, a focus group comprising representatives of the team and the team leader was held. This group identified the following challenges: anticipation of the content of material they may encounter – generally found to be worse than the content itself (issues of preparation); reading security files containing graphic offence information and occasionally photographs; managing strong emotional reactions to the content of phone calls monitored (compounded by wearing headphones which give the sensation of personal involvement in the conversation); the amount of time spent monitoring conversations, which could be for eight hour stretches; and singleton working, particularly at weekends, with no opportunity to debrief.

The team identified the following areas as particularly rewarding:

- Knowing that actions taken have a far reaching effect on public safety.
- New, novel and interesting work.
- Systematic gathering of information.
- Able to use initiative.
- Able to operate independently.
- Close knit team.
- Attendance at Safeguarding Children meetings.
- Greater involvement in prison life.
- Potential to have a big impact.

The components of ER were already evident in the team (impact and meaning especially). The priority therefore was to develop healthy working practices to enhance the existing rewards of the work and reduce the risk of work content impacting negatively. To achieve this, the principles of 'Full Engagement' explicated by Loehr and Schwartz (2003) were consulted as complimentary to other practices evidenced to enhance well-being.

Loehr and Schwartz propose that 'performance, health and happiness are grounded in the skilful management of energy' (p. 5) resulting in greater empowerment and productivity. Full engagement requires an individual to be physically energised, emotionally connected, mentally focused and spiritually aligned. It involves not just the expenditure, but also the recovery of energy in these domains. In a job involving the monitoring of high risk prisoners, being disengaged in any of the domains could have disastrous consequences. Therefore practices such as monitoring phone calls continuously for eight hours for example, needed addressing.

Four interventions were proposed. To aid the management of physical energy, regular formalised breaks were introduced. Five to 10 minutes in every 90 was recommended, with team members physically leaving their work stations for that period of time. Some team members additionally opted to undertake a lunchtime exercise programme to augment their physical energy. To assist with the renewal of emotional energy, formal debriefs were recommended to provide team members with an opportunity to off-load the issues at the end of each day. Voluntary sessions with a mental health professional were also offered on an 'as needed' basis. To help staff remain mentally engaged, a rotation system was recommended, whereby team members moved between the tasks needing to be undertaken.

In addition to the above, preparedness training was also advised. Training in psychological self-maintenance skills, emotion management and the nature of psychological distress can enable staff to feel equipped and empowered to manage their emotional reactivity as it arises, rather than feel overwhelmed or baffled by it.

A recent review of the monitoring team found a psychologically and physically healthy staff group, fully engaged with their work and thriving in the face of some considerable adversity.

Preparation 2: Training

Within the Preparation 2 domain of the strategy, training, a number of initiatives have been implemented that will be summarised here by way of illustration.

An evaluation of a related but separate strategy, to reduce violence in prisons (Fylan and Clarke, 2006), identified a deficiency in the existing training for staff working with challenging prisoners. Although staff indicated they enjoyed and appreciated the training, they lacked confidence and competence to apply the new skills they had learned. Research findings from the disaster and emergency literature have identified a clear link between competence, well-being and resilience (e.g. Spreitzer et al., 1997), suggesting a priority need to address the apparent shortfall between training aims and outcome.

Two steps were taken. The first was to identify those skills based training modules considered critical, and develop them into more comprehensive packages. This aim was to provide more practice opportunities with a view to building confidence in the use of specific skills. The second step was to consider ways of making the training more engaging and relevant to the workplace. It was recognised by trainers and trainees alike that the abstract nature of the material presented in the classroom is not conducive to engagement with skills that are likely to be needed in highly emotionally charged and volatile situations. For example, applying the skills of a motivational interview to encourage a prisoner to progress is far less challenging in the training room that it is in a cell with a prisoner refusing to go to work.

To address this problem an expert in the use of dramatic techniques was bought in to advise on developing the training modules. A variety of techniques have now been incorporated that encourage far greater interactive practice of skills in much more realistic settings.

In addition to enhancing existing training, additional training was established, focusing uniquely on the development of psychological self-maintenance skills. As most practitioners in high risk jobs would probably affirm, training in the skills to do one's job is often comprehensive, but in the skills to look after oneself, non-existent. The training of choice for incorporation into the well-being strategy is that devised by Roger (2002). Based on the principles of emotional detachment, and developed from a series of experimental studies on the role of emotional inhibition and rumination in prolonging physiological recovery from stress, the programme describes the behavioural and psychological process of stressful responding and the physical correlates. Attendees generate their own risk profile, through use of established psychometric instruments and then practice methods for managing risky elements and enhancing protective ones. An empirical evaluation of the programme when used with police officers demonstrated significant increases in job satisfaction and reduced absenteeism (Roger and Hudson, 1995).

A number of research projects have been initiated in support of the strategy's development, including the construction of an early distress warning system and exit support plans. The proof of efficacy will come from long-term evaluation of projects and the ongoing feedback of frontline staff and managers.

Well-being in critical occupations

Critical occupations are unique with respect to which members risk exposure to potentially traumatic events. However, what should be evident from the review provided here is that even if risk of exposure is high, risk of deleterious outcome for individual workers need not be. Indeed, contrary to previous assumptions regarding pathological outcome in the face of trauma, an increasing body of evidence is emerging supporting what has been described as post-traumatic growth (PTG) (Tedeschi and Calhoun, 2003). PTG is defined as 'significant

beneficial changes in cognitive and emotional life beyond levels of adaptation, psychological functioning, or life awareness that occur in the aftermath of psychological traumas that challenge previously held assumptions about self, others and the future' (Paton, 2005: 226).

Understanding the processes and factors involved in both positive and negative outcomes for workers in critical occupations enables organisations and individuals to respond accordingly. Establishing and maintaining appropriate preparation, practice and post event recovery environments should ensure the risk of psychological harm is kept to a minimum and the opportunities for psychological growth substantially enhanced.

Clearly, organisations have a duty of care to their employees to generate working environments that are as safe as possible. Individuals also have a duty of care to themselves to ensure they avail themselves of all opportunities to stay psychologically well in the work context. These complimentary responsibilities are likely to be most effectively executed in environments where there is a genuine desire to enhance performance and well-being through consultation and collaboration. Organisations that impose support structures from the top down are unlikely to reap the benefits of their intentions. It should not be surprising that many of the interventions included in the DHS Well-being strategy, supported empirically in the relevant literature, were also recommended by frontline staff – testament to staff's wisdom, experience and intuition for what works in enhancing their well-being.

Acknowledgement

The author would like to thank Mr Peter Athurton, former Director of High Security Prisons, and Dr Pam Wilson, for the opportunity to undertake this work and Mr Mark Campion for his professional support and encouragement.

References

Alexander, D.A. and Wells, A. (1991) Reactions of Police Officers to Body Handling After a Major Disaster: A Before and After Comparison. *British Journal of Psychiatry*, 159, 517–55.

American Psychiatric Association (1994) *Diagnostic and Statistical Manual of Mental Disorders*, 4th edn. Washington DC; American Psychiatric Association.

Antonovsky, A. (1990) Pathways Leading to Successful Coping and Health. In Rosenbaum, M. (Ed.) *Learned Resourcefulness: on Coping Skills, Self-Control and Adaptive Behaviour*. New York: Springer.

Bird-Edmonds, S. (1997) (Ed.) *Impact: Working with Sexual Abusers*. Bradon, VT: Safer Society Press.

Bisson, J. et al. (1997) A Randomised Control Trial of Psychological Debriefing for Victims of Acute Burn Trauma. *British Journal of Psychiatry*, 171, 78–81.

Bisson, J.I. and Deahl, M.P. (1994) Psychological Debriefing and Prevention of Post Traumatic Stress: More Research is Needed. *British Journal of Psychiatry*, 165, 717–20.

Block, J.H. and Kremen, A.M. (1996) IQ and Ego-Resiliency: Conceptual and Empirical Connections and Separateness. *Journal of Personality and Social Psychology*, 70, 349–61.

Burke, K.J. (2007) *Adjusting to Life 'On The Beat': An Investigation of Adaptation to the Police Profession*. Unpublished PhD Thesis, University of Tasmania.

Carlier, I.V. et al. (1998) Disaster-Related Post-traumatic Stress in Police Officers: A Field Study of the Impact of Debriefing. *Stress Medicine*, 14, 143–8.

Clarke, J. and Blythe, C. (In Preparation) *Identifying Determinates of Well-Being in High Risk Jobs: A Review of High Security Prison Staff*.

Clarke, J. (2004) *The Psychosocial Impact on Facilitators of Working Therapeutically with Sex Offenders: an Experimental Study*. Unpublished PhD Thesis, University of York.

Clarke, J. and Lloyd, F. (2004) *Support Needs for Prison Staff Working in Discrete Units within the High Security Estate*. HMPS Directorate of High Security: Unpublished Report.

Clarke, J. and Roger, D. (2002) Working Therapeutically with Sex Offenders: The Potential Impact on the Psychological Well-Being of Treatment Providers. In Falshaw, L. (Ed.) *Issues in Forensic Psychology No. 3: The Impact of Offending*. Leicester: British Psychological Society.

Clarke, J. and Roger, D. (2007) The Construction and Validation of a Scale to Assess Psychological Risk and Well-Being in Sex Offender Treatment Providers. *Legal and Criminological Psychology*, 12, 83–100.

Clarke, J., McDougall, C. and Harris, R. (2003) *The Supporting People Survey: The Accommodation Support Needs of Offenders in North Yorkshire*. York: Centre for Criminal Justice Economics and Psychology.

Conger, J.A. and Konungo, R. (1988) The Empowerment Process: Integrating Theory and Process. *Academy of Management Review*, 13, 471–82.

Creamer, M., Burgess, P. and Pattison, P. (1990) Cognitive Processing in Post-Trauma Reactions: Some Preliminary Findings. *Psychological Medicine*, 20, 597–604.

Deahl, M.P. et al. (1994) Psychological Sequelae Following the Gulf War: Factors Associated with Subsequent Morbidity and the Effectiveness of Psychological Debriefing. *British Journal of Psychiatry*, 165, 60–5.

DoH (2007) Http://Www.Dh.Gov.Uk. *Primary, Secondary and Tertiary Prevention*.

Dunning, C. (1994) Trauma and Countertransference in the Workplace. In Wilson, J.P. and Lindy, J.D. (Eds.) *Countertransference in the Treatment of PTSD*. New York: Guilford.

Dunning, C. (2003) Sense of Coherence in Managing Trauma Workers. In Paton, D., Violanti, J.M. and Smith, L.M. (Eds.) *Promoting Capabilities to Manage Posttraumatic Stress: Perspectives on Resilience*, Springfield, IL: Charles C Thomas.

Eisenberger, R. et al. (2002) Perceived Supervisor Support: Contributions to Perceived Organisational Support and Employee Retention. *Journal of Applied Psychology*, 87, 565–73.

Ellerby, L. (1998) *Providing Clinical Services to Sex Offenders: Burnout, Compassion, Fatigue and Moderating Variables*. University of Manitoba.

Farrenkopf, T. (1992) What Happens to Facilitators who Work with Sex Offenders. *Journal of Offender Rehabilitation*, 16, 217–23.

Figley C.R. and Stamm, B.H. (1996) Psychometric Review of Compassion Fatigue Self-Test for Practitioners. In Stamm, B.H. (Ed.) *Measurement of Stress, Trauma, and Adaptation*. Lutherville, MD: Sidran.

Friedman, M. and Higson-Smith, C. (2003) Building Psychological Resilience: Learning from the South African Police Service. In Paton, D., Violanti, J.M. and Smith, L.M. (Eds.) *Promoting Capabilities to Manage Posttraumatic Stress: Perspectives on Resilience*. Springfield, IL: Charles C Thomas.

Friedman, R.J., Framer, M.B. and Shearer, D.R. (1988) Early Response to Posttraumatic Stress. *EAP Digest*, 8, 45–9.

Fylan, F. and Clarke, J. (2006) *Violence Reduction Strategy Evaluation*. HMPS Directorate of High Security, Unpublished Report.

Gist, R. and Woodall, J. (2000) There are No Simple Solutions to Complex Problems. In Paton, D., Violanti, J.M. and Dunning, C. (Eds.) *Post-traumatic Stress Intervention: Challenges, Issues and Perspectives*. Springfield, IL: Charles C Thomas.

Grove, W.M. and Meehl, P.E. (1996) Comparative Efficiency of Informal (Subjective, Impressionistic) and Formal (Mechanical, Algorithmic) Prediction Procedures: The Clinical-Statistical Controversy. *Psychology, Public Policy and Law*, 2, 293–323.

Hanson, R.K. and Bussiere, M.T. (1998) Predicting Relapse: A Meta-analysis of Sexual Offender Recidivism Studies. *Journal of Consulting and Clinical Psychology*, 66: 2, 348–62.

Hart, P.M., Wearing, A.J. and Headey, B. (1993) Assessing Police Work Experiences: Development of the Police Daily Hassles and Uplift Scales. *Journal of Criminal Justice*, 21, 553–72.

Health and Safety Executive. Www.Hse.Gov.Uk/Stress.

Jackson, K.E. et al. (1997) Working with Sex Offenders: The Impact on Practitioners. In Edmunds, B.S. (Ed.) *Impact: Working with Sexual Abusers*. Vermont: Safer Society Press.

Johnston, P. and Paton, D. (2003) Environmental Resilience: Psychological Empowerment in High Risk Professions. In Paton, D., Violanti, J.M. and Smith, L.M. (Eds.) *Promoting Capabilities to Manage Post-traumatic Stress: Perspectives on Resilience*. Springfield, IL: Charles C Thomas.

Kadambi, M. and Truscott, D. (2006) Concept Mapping Professionals' Perceptions of Reward and Motive in Providing Sex Offender Treatment. *Journal of Offender Rehabilitation*, 42, 4, 37–58.

Kavanagh, D.J. et al. (2002) Achieving Effective Supervision. *Drug and Alcohol Review*, 21, 247–52.

King, R. (1985) Control in Prisons. In Maguire, M., Vagg, J. and Morgan, R. (Eds.) *Accountability and Prisons: Opening Up a Closed World*. London: Tavistock.

Lazarus, R.S. (1993) From Psychological Stress to the Emotions: A History of Change Outlooks. *Annual Review of Psychology*, 44, 1–21.

Liebling, A. (1999) Doing Research in Prison: Breaking the Silence? *Theoretical Criminology*, 3: 2, 147–74.

Loehr, J. and Schwartz, T. (2003) *On Form*. London: Nicholas Brearley Publishing.

Maslach, C. and Jackson, S.E. (1986) *The Maslach Burnout Inventory Manual*. 2nd edn. Palo Alto, CA: Consulting Psychologists Press.

Masten, A.S. (2001) Ordinary Magic: Resilience Processes in Development. *American Psychologist*, 56, 227–38.

McFarlane, A.C. (1987) Life Events and Psychiatric Disorder: The Role of Natural Disaster. *British Journal of Psychiatry*, 151, 362–7.

Moran, C.C. and Massam, M. (1997) An Evaluation of Humour in Emergency Work. *The Australian Journal of Disaster and Trauma Studies*, 3.

Morgan, R. (1997) Imprisonment: Current Concerns and a Brief History Since 1945. In Maguire, M., Morgan, R. and Reiner, R. (Eds.) *The Oxford Handbook of Criminology*: 2nd edn. Oxford: OUP.

Murphy, S.A. (1991) Human Response to Catastrophe. *Annual Review of Nursing*, 9, 57–76.

Myers, R. (1995) *A Study to Investigate the Experiences of Staff Conducting National SOTP at HM Prison Wakefield, and to Compare the Psychological Health, Emotion Control and Coping Strategies of these Staff to Non-SOTP Group Work Facilitators*. Unpublished MSc Thesis: Middlesex University.

North, C.S. et al. (2002) Coping, Functioning, and Adjustment of Rescue Workers after the Oklahoma City Bombing. *Journal of Traumatic Stress*, 15, 171–5.

Paton, D. (1994) *Dealing with Traumatic Incidents in the Work Place*. 3rd edn. Queensland: Gull Publishing.

Paton, D. (2005) Post-traumatic Growth in Disaster and Emergency Work. In Calhoun, L. and Tedeschi, R. (Eds.) *Handbook of Posttraumatic Growth: Research and Practice*. Mahwah, NJ: Lawrence Erlbaum.

Paton, D. (2006) Critical Incident Stress Risk in Police Officers: Managing Resilience and Vulnerability. *Traumatolgy*, 12, 198–206.

Paton, D. and Du Preez, H. (1993) *Job Demands Survey: Authority for the Intellectually Handicapped*. Perth, Western Australia.

Paton, D. and Smith, L. (1996) Psychological Trauma in Critical Occupations. In Paton, D. and Violanti, J.M. (Eds.) *Traumatic Stress in Critical Occupations: Recognition, Consequences and Treatment.* Springfield, IL: Charles C. Thomas.

Paton, D. and Stephens, C. (1996) Training and Support for Emergency Responders. In Paton, D. and Violanti, J.M. (Eds). *Traumatic Stress in Critical Occupations: Recognition, Consequences and Treatment.* Springfield, IL: Charles C. Thomas.

Paton, D. and Violanti, J.M. (1996) *Traumatic Stress in Critical Occupations: Recognition, Consequences and Treatment.* Springfield, IL: Charles C. Thomas.

Paton, D., Cacioppe, R. and Smith, L.M. (1992) *Critical Incident Stress in the West Australian Fire Brigade.* Perth, Western Australia.

Paton, D., Ramsay, R. and Sinclair, D. (1992) *Occupational and Traumatic Stress in Lothian and Scottish Borders Fire Brigade.* Edinburgh, Scotland.

Paton, D., Violanti, J.M. and Smith, L.M. (2003) *Promoting Capabilities to Manage Post-traumatic Stress: Perspectives on Resilience.* Springfield, IL: Charles C Thomas.

Paton, D., Violanti, J.M. and Dunning, C. (2000) *Post-traumatic Stress Intervention: Challenges, Issues and Perspectives.* Springfield, IL: Charles C. Thomas.

Pearlman, L.A. (1996) Psychometric Review of TSI Belief Scale, Revision L. In Stamm, B.H. Ed.) *Measurement of Stress, Trauma and Adaptation.* Lutherville, MD: Sidran.

Pearlman, L. and Saakvitne, K. (1995) *Trauma and the Therapist.* New York: WW Norton.

Pennebaker, J.W. (2000) The Effects of Traumatic Disclosure on Physical and Mental Health: The Values of Writing and Talking about Upsetting Events. In Violanti, J.M., Paton, D. and Dunning, C. (Eds.) *Posttraumatic Stress Interventions: Challenges Issues and Perspectives.* Springfield, IL: Charles C Thomas.

Reeves, D., Culbreth, J.R. and Greene, A. (1997) Effects of Sex, Age and Educational Level on the Supervisory Styles of Substance Abuse Counsellor Supervisors. *Journal of Alcohol and Drug Education,* 43, 76–86.

Rich, K.D. (1997) Vicarious Traumatisation: A Preliminary Study. In Edmunds, S. (Ed.) *Impact: Working with Sexual Abusers.* Vermont: Safer Society Press.

Roger, D. (2002) *Managing Stress.* 2nd edn. Berkshire: CIM Publishing.

Roger, D. and Hudson, C. (1995) The Role of Emotion Control and Emotional Rumination in Stress Management Training. *International Journal of Stress Management,* 2: 3, 119–32.

Roger, D., Guarino, L. and Olason, D. (2000) *Emotional 'Style' and Health: A New Three Factor Model.* 14th European Health Psychology Conference, Leiden, August.

Rose, S., Bisson, J. and Wessely, S. (2003) Psychological Debriefing for Preventing Post Traumatic Stress Disorder (Cochrane Review). *The Cochrane Library,* Issue 1. Oxford: Update Software.

Schroffel, A. (1999) How Does Clinical Supervision Affect Job Satisfaction? *The Clinical Supervisor,* 18: 2, 91–105.

Spreitzer, G.M. (1997) Toward a Common Ground in Defining Empowerment. *Research in Organisational Change and Development,* 10, 31–62.

Spreitzer, G.M., Kizilos, M.A. and Nason, S.W. (1997) A Dimensional Analysis of the Relationship between Psychological Empowerment and Effectiveness, Satisfaction and Strain. *Journal of Management,* 23, 679–704.

Tedeschi, R.G. and Calhoun, L.G. (2003) Routes to Post-traumatic Growth through Cognitive Processing. In Paton, D., Violanti, J.M. and Smith, L.M. (Eds.) *Promoting Capabilities to Manage Post-traumatic Stress: Perspectives on Resilience.* Springfield, IL: Charles C Thomas.

Thomas, K.W. and Velthouse, B.A. (1990) Cognitive Elements of Empowerment: An 'Interpretive' Model of Intrinsic Motivation. *Academy of Management Review,* 15, 666–81.

Turner, C. (1992) *The Experience of Staff Conducting the Core Programme.* Unpublished MSc Thesis. University of London.

Webb, B. (1997) Auditing a Clinical Supervision Training Programme. *Nursing Standard,* 11, 34–9.

Wicks, R.J. (2006) *Overcoming Secondary Traumatic Stress in Medical and Nursing Practice: A Guide to Professional Resilience and Personal Well-Being.* New York: Oxford University Press.

Wilson, P. (2001) *The Experiences of Staff Working in Close Supervision Centres.* Unpublished MPhil Thesis, University of Cambridge, Institute of Criminology.

Operational Considerations

Strengths-based Child Assessment: Locating Possibility and Transforming the Paradigm

Clay T. Graybeal and Shelley Cohen Konrad

Introduction

The primary purpose of this chapter is to examine the opportunities as well as the limitations of incorporating a strengths perspective within the conceptual framework of risk assessment. This presented us with an interesting challenge, which is how to most accurately address the topic while not being constrained or defined by the limitations of dichotomous language. While our title begins with 'strengths-based child assessment', we felt it important to add the subtitle: 'locating possibility and transforming the paradigm'. We find it difficult to define what we do as either risk assessment, or strengths-based, as both terms carry some risk of narrowing a practitioner's field of vision. It is important to think in a more comprehensive, inclusive fashion, and this chapter will describe how we have come to identify both risks and resilience in the lives of children and families. We will do so by describing a set of core principles that underlie our practice along with how we came to these conclusions. The chapter will conclude with an extended case example designed to illustrate the contrast between a problem-based, or risk-based approach, and a transformative approach.

Our practice is guided and informed by four key principles that we have found to be essential to creating lasting change. The traditional model of problem-solving is so widely accepted that it has achieved that status of a self-evident reality, even though, we believe, it is in fact a paradigm that has over-reached its original purpose. This model consists of three purportedly discrete phases: assessment, diagnosis, and treatment. It works quite well, it turns out, when a professional is confronted with a diseased heart, a cracked sidewalk, or a car that won't start. Unfortunately, it has also been adopted and applied in the social sciences, with mixed results. Both research and practice experience suggest that it has severe limitations when applied to the thoughts, feelings, and behaviours of people, and in this case, of children.

We propose an alternative framework for practice, based on a parallel process of dialogue, discovery, and collaboration (Graybeal, 2001). This model is derived from the following principles:

1. *Assessment and intervention are two aspects of a single process which is initiated and sustained by meaningful **dialogue** between worker and client.*

   The idea that it is possible to accomplish something called an assessment, prior to intervention in a child's life, we believe, is simply not supported by the facts. From the moment a professional enters the life of a family, an intervention has begun, and it is often in the first few moments that the seeds of success, failure, or muddy ambiguity are sown. Dialogue is our shorthand description for a process that reflects conversation, mutual inquiry, and openness to the unique characteristics of the client's world.

2. *Problems and strengths are inter-related and inextricable from one another, and are **discovered** through dialogue.*

   We sometimes describe our work as strengths-based, but that is frequently misunderstood. So here we want to suggest that the point of identifying strengths is directly in relationship to the nature of the problems that individuals are struggling with. Embedded in every problem story, we believe, is a story of success waiting to be liberated. Discovery is a word that conveys our sense of the unknown, and our curiosity about clients' stories, and our commitment to sustain the dialogue until their strengths emerge.

3. *The heart of social work practice is embodied in the commitment to work together, to **collaborate** each step of the way.*

   Collaboration is a popular word, and as such, is prone to under-estimation. We see it as the heart of practice. The moment that we privilege professional knowledge and expertise over that of our clients is the moment that we begin to lose both integrity and effectiveness. 'Social workers must be willing to be influenced as much by the world of their clients as their clients are influenced by the world of professionals' (Graybeal, in development).

When professionals endeavour to truly implement these three principles, practice changes in ways that are both exciting, and at times unsettling, as they are required to let go of many cherished assumptions, and to be open to what emerges. This leads to our final principle:

4. *Relationships based on dialogue, discovery, and collaboration are* **transformative**.

Effectiveness in practice is achieved primarily through the process of applying client strengths and resources to the resolution of their problems. This has the happy consequence of helping them to see themselves as more competent, and thus prepared to handle future challenges more effectively. At the same time, as professionals learn to let go of a 'treatment' perspective, and embrace a collaborative perspective, their repertoire of skills is expanded. Both parties are transformed.

We have come to share these ideas as a consequence of our deep immersion in the traditional paradigm, and our subsequent struggles to break free its limitations. Clay's career began in a private psychiatric facility, and for a period of several years, he participated in intensive daily staffing meetings, during which patient histories and presenting problems were presented and discussed. Over time, it became evident that it was difficult for this group of learned professionals to achieve a consensus about diagnoses. This was in part due to the fact that diagnostic categories alone did a poor job of representing the unique concerns of the individual patients. But other patterns emerged as well. One of the most striking was that it was often easier to predict the diagnosis based on observing the combination of patient and doctor, than on hearing the patient's history alone. And finally, since the patients were rarely present, their voices were never included in the discussion of their lives. While this experience had primarily to do with adults, it closely parallels Shelley's early experience with children and families.

Shelley began her work with children and families in a residential treatment facility in the 1980s. Children referred to residential care were those whose behaviours could no longer be contained or tolerated within traditional school or home settings. Behaviourally, these kids were no doubt as challenging as were their parents and caregivers. In order to be placed in a residential treatment facility, children had to have made their way through other less restrictive systems of intervention. By the time they reached institutional care their intake folders were thick with reports of failures in multiple systems and their diagnostic profiles offered dire prognostic futures. Their life stories were replete with negative situational events such as early abandonment, parental substance abuse or/and psychiatric illness, sexual abuse and multiple losses. Their individual histories included failure to thrive, learning, behavioural and emotional disabilities, and medical illnesses such as asthma or attentional disorders. The care giving and supportive resources available to these children and their families were slim to none at all. These youngsters often moved from town to town in search of affordable housing; they had frequently been in a different school for each year of their school-aged lives, perhaps landing long enough in the current educational setting for a teacher to care enough to initiate the special education referral that recommended them to a residential placement.

In team meetings, often before being formally introduced to the child or family, the team would review intake reports, discuss risk factors and bookmark behaviours that would serve to fulfil the requirements of a diagnostic category. Once a diagnosis was identified it would serve from that point forward as an interventional compass. Treatment decisions, including methods for practice, medications, and estimated length of stay, were guided by pre-established criteria even when the child or family's behaviours or attitudes veered outside the expectations of the diagnostic description or defied the opinions of the experts that had determined them in the first place. Further, the purpose of diagnosis was only in part meant to determine which intervention would best serve the child's needs; it was also driven by policies that specified which diagnoses justified a child's continued funding in residential care.

Listening to and accepting these professional-centred and pathology-driven descriptions and their accompanying prescriptions for certain failure left the team feeling powerless to instigate change, and worse, seemed to cause an inevitable loss of compassion for clients and their families even before we got started. After reading intakes that referred to the child's entrenched pathologies, the 'impossible', 'noncompliant,' and 'resistant' family, the 'impoverished' life styles and the failures of multiple well-intentioned professionals, motivation and hope were hard to grasp. Furthermore, when hopefulness and positive attitudes were expressed seasoned co-workers and supervisors would caution us about our optimism. We were encouraged to keep our goals 'realistic' and to not blame ourselves if our best efforts met with failure.

Locating possibility in theory

One can easily see how this paradigm of interpreting behaviour through a diagnostic (and inherently deficit-based) framework can have a profound impact on every aspect of social work practice with children and families. Preconceived perceptions, beliefs and assumptions strongly influence how client stories are translated into professional language that is indelibly placed on record as 'a truth' about a person's life. Assessment based on language constructed from a perspective of deficits and failings is bound to produce problem-centred interventions (Blundo, 2001; Graybeal, 2001). Less obvious, but illustrated in the team members' responses cited above, is the way that deficit-focused language and problem-saturated assessment and interventions influence the assumptions and actions of the practitioner. There is a risk, for example, in the language of 'risk assessment' as it creates an overarching framework through which the world is evaluated for its threats, rather than its possibilities. The risk is that an emphasis on pathology, symptoms and failings may divert practitioners from the curiosity, compassion, and connection that are necessary for building effective and productive therapeutic alliances.

The identification of problems and pathology has a long, rich history in social work practice. 'The preoccupation with problems, human deficits, what is broken, gone wrong, or failed has dominated the attention of social work and exists today in the form of the medical/pathology/scientific paradigm that underlies the traditional social work theories, practice models and educational materials found in our texts and our social work curriculums' (Blundo, 2001: 298). The

traditional paradigm of assessment, diagnosis and treatment is the exclusive domain of professionals, and presumes that those professionals are able to accurately translate the meanings of people's lives and determine which therapeutic actions will lead to health and well being (Goldstein, 1999). Historically, this allowed professionals to blame treatment failures on client resistance, lack of motivation or intergenerational patterns of dysfunction (Blundo, 2001; Graybeal, 2001). In recent years, there has been a growing evidence-based practice movement that is based in part on the belief that treatment failures are primarily due to the failure to apply 'best practice' or evidence-based methods to specific problems, diagnoses, or populations (Reid, 1997; Gambrill, 1999; Rosen, 2003; Gellis and Reid, 2004; O'Hare, 2005).

However, this movement has failed to acknowledge or deal with the fact that the preponderance of research into the effectiveness of practice is pointing towards a different conclusion entirely. It turns out that it is not model or method that accounts for the greatest portion of client outcomes, but rather a group of factors that are common to all methods that are effective (Lambert, 1986; Lambert et al., 1986; Asay and Lambert, 1999; Maione and Chenail, 1999; Wampold, 2001; Lambert and Ogles, 2004; Lambert, 2004). This body of research suggests that it is the unique characteristics of clients and their families, combined with the unique skills and abilities of the professional, that combine to create effective alliances. In particular, it is critical that the individual or family's personal strengths and theory of change be incorporated into any planned intervention (Hubble, Duncan and Miller, 1999; Duncan, Miller and Sparks, 2004).

This research turns out to provide an empirical foundation for the strengths perspective proffered by Dennis Saleeby (1992, 1997) and Ann Weick (1989). At the heart of the strengths perspective is a shift in focus away from an exclusively pathology-based approach, and toward a practice perspective that approaches human behaviour from a holistic understanding and is inclusive of clients' capabilities, hopes and possibilities (Graybeal, 2001; Weick, 1996). Client assets, resilience, and available resources are increasingly being seen as in large part responsible for positive outcomes in psychotherapy and other forms of 'helping' (Duncan, Hubble and Miller, 1997; Lambert and Bergin, 1994). Practitioner attitude, including a belief in the client's capacity for change, the ability to convey confidence and optimism, and the capacity for empathic listening, is another key variable responsible for positive outcomes, a finding that reflects Saleebey's (1997) sentiments that collaboration with a client's strengths and hopes must be matched by the social worker's belief in them.

Even before the advent of the strengths perspective in social work practice the search for factors that promote resilience in children at risk for psychopathology, behavioural disorders and emotional problems had become a focus of psychological researchers. Since the 1970s research on children who developed well in the context of risk or adversity held the potential to inform theories and methods for practice that could guide intervention and social policy (Masten, 2001). Early ideas about resilience demarcated certain outstanding qualities and protective factors available to children that contributed to their ability to surmount risk and traumatic events (Masten, 2001; Werner and Smith, 1992). These factors include: a sense of humour, a sense of mission or direction, strong intelligence, insight, adaptive distancing, self efficacy, the possession of a talent or special skill, effective coping strategies and the presence of at least one mentoring relationship (Masten, 2001; Turner, 2001; Werner and Smith, 1992; Wolin and Wolin, 1993). In our opinion, any assessment that excludes or minimises these factors is actually likely to have the unintended but very real consequence of increasing the potency of risk factors in a child's life.

For some time, it was believed that resilient children possessed extraordinary characteristics, but this idea has been evolving to a more sophisticated understanding that suggests that resilience is endemic to human development. This shift in focus moves resilience theory from a trait-centred, static model based in the presence of intrinsic, individual qualities to a model that sees resilience as accessible to all children if they are nurtured by relational connections with competent caring adults. If major systems are impaired, or if the environment does not seed or support the development of inherent resiliency, then problems in functioning are more likely to occur (Masten, 2001). But any degree of support and protection is likely to stimulate development even in the face of adversity.

Viewing resilience in terms of expected possibility rather than extraordinary capability encourages hopefulness for those children who have suffered early negative life events and trauma or who have physical, developmental or emotional disabilities. 'Resilience does not come from rare and special qualities, but from the everyday magic of ordinary, normative human resources in the minds, brains, and bodies of children, in their families and relationships and in their communities' (Masten, 2001: 235). Hopefulness and optimism are born from the knowledge that resilience emerges from ordinary, expected developmental processes and that with individual, family, environmental and community support, positive change and healing are possible outcomes. Understanding resilience from this vantage point underscores the value of building strong professional/client alliances beginning at the point of initial contact throughout the continuum of care, because the possibility for change and growth is present within every child and every family we see.

There is another growing area of research that has added credibility to the value of the therapeutic alliance as a foundation for nurturing resilience. Research on infants' attachment patterns present strong empirical evidence that neurobiological structures are profoundly influenced by the earliest attachments between infants and caregivers (Brandell and Ringel, 2004; Schore, 1997; Tronick, 1989). Repetitive interactions between infants and their primary caregivers stimulate the development of relatively stable neuronal structures in the child that have lifelong implications including a lasting impact on physical health, affect regulation, cognition, and relational interactions (Brandell and Ringel, 2004).

For those working with young children and families this information has immediate preventive and interventive implications. Building and strengthening healthy attachments with positive and reliable adult caregivers promotes the development of stable neuronal structures that will guide future healthy internal and external functioning. The first few years of life are clearly important. But there is growing evidence that brain development occurs throughout the life course in response to new relationships and experiences (Brandell and Ringel, 2004; Siegel, 1999). This finding has significant implications for all aspects of social work practice as the skill of being open to possibilities for growth within relationship may hold the potential for both neuronal and behavioural change. In other words 'pursuing practice based on the ideas of resilience, rebound, possibility and transformation' (Saleebey, 1997: 297) may have salience not only from a perspectival posture but also from a scientific posture as well.

Transforming the paradigm

Our emphasis on transformative practice is inspired by the guiding principles of the strengths perspective, which views human behaviour from the standpoint of inherent capacities, human resilience, and the potential for individuals to create their own theories for change. From a practice perspective the framing principles of the strengths perspective invite practitioners to 'suspend disbelief' (Saleebey, 1997) and embrace and learn from the client's worldview. The social work ethic of 'beginning where the client is' (Goldstein, 1983) is taken seriously as the beginning of the assessment process. In this regard clients are viewed as having valuable resources that when identified and tapped will facilitate enduring and productive change. The role of the practitioner is to facilitate collaboration and to honour the struggles and pain of clients with hope, belief and without judgment or blame.

Blundo (2001: 299) asserts that the strengths perspective challenges social work's traditions and professional conventions and also challenges the practice models utilised in many social service and institutional settings. As a result, social workers might 'talk the talk' of strengths but don't 'walk the walk' in practice. That is, the language of strengths may merely be inserted into familiar problem-based social work paradigms:

Students and practitioners assume that because they think about strength, add strengths questions to their assessment battery, or use the words, that they have understood the significance these ideas might bring to their practice.

We view the transformation of the predominant social work practice paradigm as multi-faceted, consisting of simultaneous shifts in both attitude and action. Transforming the traditional psychosocial assessment to a strengths-based model challenges practitioners to broaden their understanding of what constitutes a meaningful assessment and to add context to their understanding of client behaviour. A meaningful assessment does not ignore the very real problems and struggles of clients. What it does do is to locate them in a context framed by the unique life circumstances of each child and each family. Understanding the biological, social, psychological, and spiritual dimensions of a client's life are key components of constructing a useful assessment. However, when we begin to replace the concept of assessment with dialogue and discovery, questions are generated that elicit information about what life is like from the client's vantage point. This serves several important functions, including giving context to the problem at hand while simultaneously conveying to the client that their worldview matters.

Assessment that truly approaches problems as only a part of a more complex life must translate that viewpoint into the language used in written and oral assessment. Contextualising client experience in strengths-based assessment considers the difference between identity, attribute, and behaviour, or being, having, and doing (Graybeal, 2001). In child assessment, how a problem is named can have broad implications for the child's self-perception, the parents' self-worth and the social worker's perception of them both. Consider, for example, these three statements: 'He's a bad boy' (identity, or being); 'He has ADHD' (attribute, or having) and 'Sometimes he loses control and acts naughty' (behaviour, or doing). Each of these statements represents a set of epistemological and ontological assumptions that impact the perceptions of the child and family being assessed. A focus on doing, rather than having or being, helps to separate facts from fiction, and reduces the sense of shame and blame.

The risks of being identified as a 'bad boy' are obvious: it is a set up for disconnections with his parents and other adults, and may have deleterious effects on his own growing sense of self. And while the attribute of ADHD may in some instances be helpful in explaining certain patterns, it also carries the risk of de-emphasising context, and thus reducing relational possibilities for change. But if the emphasis is on facts, 'Sometimes he loses control and acts naughty,' the natural next step is to ask clarifying questions that place the behaviour in context: 'He loses control sometimes when we're with a lot of people'. Thus the behaviour is even further removed from the identity of the child, and is part of a social interaction, opening up numerous additional avenues for change.

When assessments place an equal emphasis on strengths and problems, they impact the course of future therapeutic encounters, and are likely to strongly affect how clients may see themselves or their children in the world. The language we use to assess clients should be taken very seriously; language has the power to explain and clarify but it also has the power to confine and constrict, to objectify, and disrespect the complexities of human life. Linking the assessment of risk to the context of strengths assures 'that diagnosis does not become a cornerstone of identity' (Saleebey, 1996: 303).

Strength-based child assessment in practice: assessment as conversational inquiry

Most child-centred assessment models are multi-dimensional in nature and imply an ongoing, evolving process that continues throughout the life course of the therapeutic relationship (Boyd-Webb, 2003; Jordan and Franklin, 2003; Rose and Fatout, 2003). Traditional assessment practice identifies a range of multiple interrelated factors that contribute to and maintain a problematic situation for the child and his/her family (Boyd-Webb, 2003). Using a strengths-based model, factors that contribute to adaptational capacities, social assets and resources, and existential and spiritual dimensions of the child's and family's worldview are formally incorporated into an expanded assessment. There is also an emphasis on discovering the unique meanings of situations to the client and family. That is, different children and families may experience the same phenomenon in different ways. Taken as a whole, these factors are used to formulate a proposal for intervention (or as we prefer to call it, collaboration). Assessment in this regard serves to inform a series of hypotheses for action that must be constantly measured and revised, based on both observation and feedback from client (in this case the child), parent, institution (for example, the school system), and practitioner. In the best sense, assessment becomes an ongoing conversation between all concerned and involved parties, including the child.

This is inevitably a complex process requiring curiosity, patience, and impartiality. In many practice settings it is not uncommon for only one parent or caregiver to supply assessment information on a child. Hearing only part of the story inevitably leads to a partial understanding of the child's life and the problems that have brought him/her into the therapeutic setting. A common example of differential but equally valid views is seen when a child from a divorced family behaves compliantly in one home and is defiant in the other. It is quite tempting to blame the parent that has to contend with the more challenging behaviour. It becomes critical to insist on hearing the views of both parents, consider the dynamic interplay of both homes where potentially divided loyalties get played out, and seek to develop collaborative solutions that involve the child and both of their families.

In all cases it is critical to find the most effective way to elicit the individual voice of the child. But obviously, because children may not have the language skills or cognitive and emotional development to fully represent themselves, it is important to seek input from as many sources as possible, such as teachers, childcare providers, and other people engaged in the child's life who may be able to fill in the details that contribute to a fuller portrait. In addition, the assessment of children and their families typically involves a variety of professionals, who, just like the family, may offer multiple and conflicting views. Practitioners who emphasise strengths and resilience may be perceived as naïve or idealistic by practitioners who do not, just as those who focus primarily on, or emphasise diagnosis and risk, may be seen as overly rigid by those who do not. Transformative practice requires transcending such dichotomies and finding common ground and a balanced perspective, in the interest of client well-being.

Finally, and perhaps most importantly, the idea of transformative practice suggests that professional attitudes and assumptions are subject to ongoing reflection and revision. Northen (1987: 179) describes assessment as 'the worker's professional opinion about the facts and their meaning'. Professional opinion is shaped by many factors, including personal assumptions, theoretical knowledge of human development, health and well-being, evidence from research, and practice wisdom derived from experience. In many respects assessment parallels the characteristics of credible research inquiry; when conducting research the trustworthiness of findings relies to an extent on acknowledgment of and reflection upon how the researcher's analysis of the data is influenced by personal bias. Similarly, in conducting an assessment, the questions asked, the interviewing style and interpretation of the collective data is filtered through the lens of the assessor. Workers' opinions about the facts and their meaning clearly play a significant role in the conversations we call assessment, in the hypotheses we call treatment, and ultimately in what we call success in practice evaluation. Given all the dimensions of assessment considered thus far, framing assessment as an ongoing, interactive and respectful conversation, a process of dialogue, discovery, and collaboration, suggests a path to transform the dominant paradigm, and shifts our attention from deficit to capacity, from one-size-fits-all to valuing the uniqueness of human possibility.

Case example

It is always in the direct application to practice that theoretical positions either take hold or fall apart. In this section, we offer a case illustration that will be presented in two ways. The first iteration will be based on principles of good practice as derived from a diagnostic, and problem focused model. We will then offer a second version of the same case that re-interprets the information through a lens that seeks equal representation of strengths and possibilities. These are then used to create a collaborative contract, and to ultimately construct unique solutions.

Case description: 'He does bad real good'

Babette (Babs) S is a thirty-two year old mother of two who appears much older than her stated age. Babs has drawn much attention from the staff as she is dressed in tightly fitting jeans, a tank top that reads 'Born to Bruise', and biker boots. In addition, Babs has several tattoos emblazoned on her arms. Sitting on the chair next to Babs is her four-year-old son, Doug. Doug is engrossed in a book about trucks and his feet pump back and forth as he looks through the pictures. Doug is dressed similarly to his mother in jeans and a t-shirt and boots. His clothes are slightly worn but clean. His hair is short on top but he has a

skinny 'tail' of wispy blonde hair that falls to the base of his neck. What is quickly noticeable about Doug is scarring from the surgery he received for a congenital cleft palate. Also evident is Doug's constant movement and twitching as he tries to wait his turn.

Lastly, sleeping in a stroller beside Babs is her infant daughter, Elisa, four months old. Elisa sleeps soundly as her mother rocks the stroller. She is surrounded by pink blankets and is dressed in a brand new pink sleeper that says 'Daddy Loves Me'. Doug and Elise's father, Mike, is not available for the assessment as he is in prison serving time for a drug-related offence.

First version: traditional assessment

Presenting problem: Four-year-old Doug S was referred to the Child Development Clinic by his paediatrician, Dr Marble. Dr Marble felt that Doug exhibited signs of attentional difficulties and she was also concerned about his limited contact with other children his age. She also indicated concern about Mrs S's stress level and the potential it posed for possible child abuse. Mrs S stated that the only problem was that Doug 'does bad real good'. She says that Doug has always been an 'active little shit' but she believes that this will serve him well in standing up to other kids if they make fun of him. She is not concerned about his limited peer contact and insists that she has no intention of ever hurting her children.

Developmental history: Babs describes Doug as a problem from birth. Feeding problems and slow speech development occurred as a consequence of his cleft palate and related surgeries. Doug had his palate repaired for the first time when he was eight months old. He had a second surgery at 13 months for minor adjustments. Doug walked at fifteen months of age and has only recently been toilet trained. He still wets the bed, which causes Babs to be angry with him. She says she takes away privileges when he wakes up with a wet bed because she is afraid to lose her temper and hit him too hard. Doug has never attended a preschool but Babs is 'more than ready' for him to start kindergarten next fall. She thinks he's 'pretty smart' for a little kid. She attributes his intelligence to his father. Babs works nights as a bartender and her younger sister, Yvonne, sixteen, takes care of the children. Yvonne intermittently lives with Babs as their mother is an active alcoholic who can become verbally abusive towards her boyfriend and children. Despite their mother's problems, Babs says she's close with her mother and her mother's boyfriend.

Current family situation and family background: Babs and Mike were married at sixteen. Neither parent completed high school. Babs recently got a GED and plans to attend a community college to become a paralegal. Mike is a habitual offender and has been in jail off and on for most of Doug's life. The couple did not intend to have children but Babs states that she was really excited when she found out she was pregnant with Doug. Her pregnancy was uneventful except for pregnancy-related diabetes. Doug was a full term baby. Babs describes being shocked when she first saw Doug and the cleft palate. She says that the nurses and her family couldn't look at him but after a little while she told everyone that he was 'beautifully ugly'. According to Babs, 'Mike loves his son but doesn't like him because Doug doesn't listen'. Mike has yet to see Elisa.

Babs is proud that she has stayed off welfare and has always provided for her kids. She states that she is close to her family, especially Yvonne. Babs acknowledges that she smokes cigarettes and pot but does not drink alcohol because she has seen how it ruined her mother's life. Babs' father died when she was six of unknown causes. Another brother, Timmy, died in a car accident when he was thirteen years old. Babs also has a brother, Denny, twenty-five, who is in jail for armed robbery. Babs visits Denny in jail and often brings the children along to 'cheer him up'. Denny has two children who play with Doug from time to time.

Babs identifies no close friends but says she gets along with everybody unless they mess with her family.

Observation of Doug: Doug is an engaging four-year-old boy that separated with minimal distress from his mother. He acclimated quickly to the playroom but could not settle on any one toy to play with. His speech was somewhat hard to understand. Doug initiated perseverative play with a series of trucks, putting them neatly in a row and then running through them at full speed. He would laugh every time he crashed through the row of trucks. Doug got frustrated when it was time to end the truck play. He was difficult to redirect and refused to settle down to draw a picture or identify letters, numbers or shapes. Because of his non-compliance an assessment of

his cognitive development could not be completed. Doug was able to name the people in his family including his Mama, Daddy 'that's in jail', Baby Elisa, Auntie Yvonne, his Uncle Denny 'that's in jail' his Nona Linda (maternal grandmother), and his Poppy Manuel (his grandmother's boyfriend). Doug could not name any playmates. His favourite activities are trucks, motorcycles, four-wheelers and books. He doesn't like to sit in the corner, eat broccoli or 'stay at home without my Mama'. His three wishes are to go to Disney, have more toys, and see his Daddy every day.

Summary and treatment recommendations: Doug S is a four-year-old boy with a history of behavioural problems stemming from infancy. Doug's medical history is significant for cleft palate that required two surgeries. Mrs S, Doug's mother, acknowledges Doug's problems with attention and hyperactivity but has not sought any help for these behaviours. The paediatrician referred Doug because of her concerns regarding his behavioural problems, social isolation and Mrs S's capacity to appropriately and safely manage his behaviours. Family history is significant for substance abuse and antisocial behaviours on both sides of the family. Complete assessment for cognitive delays or disabilities could not be obtained due to Doug's problems with concentration.

Diagnosis: Attention deficit disorder with hyperactivity; possible cognitive delays or disabilities

Treatment recommendations: Doug needs a full scale neuropsychological evaluation to determine possible cognitive, social and emotional disorders; evaluate for stimulant medication; parent counselling; cognitive-behavioural play therapy

Second version: transforming the dominant paradigm using assessment as a conversation

Presenting problem: Four-year-old Doug S was referred to the Child Development Clinic by his paediatrician, Dr Marble. Dr Marble indicated her concern that Doug exhibited signs of attentional difficulties and limited contact with same-age peers. She also stated concern about Mrs S's stress level and the potential it posed for possible child abuse. Mrs S was asked if Dr Marble presented her with these concerns. She indicated that she had but she offered an alternative view to that presented by Dr Marble. Although she appreciated Dr Marble's concerns she felt that her only problem with Doug was that 'he does bad real good'. She says that Doug has always been an 'active little shit' but she believes that this is a strength and will serve him well in standing up to other kids if they make fun of him. When asked why 'standing up to kids' was something she thought might be a future asset, Mrs S said that kids made fun of Doug because of the scarring from his cleft palate. She stated that she would not be around to protect him forever and she hoped he would be able to defend himself well. In response to the doctor's concerns about contact with peers, Mrs S said that she works long hours and often is very tired during the day. She and Doug have some down time together and he plays with his cousins when they come to visit. In response to concern about stress and the potential for abuse, Mrs S was firm in saying that she worked hard to contain her temper and that she has no intention of ever hurting her children. Mrs S is open to assessing ways to help with Doug's attention and activity.

Developmental history: Mrs S describes Doug as a having feeding difficulties from birth as a consequence of his cleft palate. Two surgeries and accompanying recoveries affected speech development. Doug had his palate repaired for the first time when he was eight months old. He had a second surgery at 13 months for minor adjustments. Doug walked at fifteen months of age and has recently been toilet trained. Doug suffers with enuresis, which may be a temporary by-product of recent toilet training. Although Mrs S becomes angry with Doug for wetting the bed she responds by taking away his privileges rather than losing her temper or hitting him too hard. Doug hasn't attended preschool but Mrs S is 'more than ready' for him to start kindergarten next fall. She thinks he's 'pretty smart' for a little kid. She attributes his intelligence to his father.

Mrs S works nights as a bartender and her younger sister, Yvonne, sixteen, takes care of the children. Yvonne intermittently lives with Mrs S as their mother is an active alcoholic who can become verbally abusive towards her boyfriend and children. Despite their mother's problems, Babs says she's close with her mother and her mother's boyfriend. When asked about her relationship with Yvonne, Mrs S states that she appreciates her sister's support. When asked about her mother's substance abuse she states that she stays away from alcohol.

Current family situation and family background: Mr and Mrs S were married at sixteen. Neither parent completed high school. Mrs S recently got a GED and plans to attend a community college to become a paralegal. Mike is a habitual offender and has been in jail off and on for most of Doug's life. The couple did not intend to have children but Mrs S states that she was really excited when she found out she was pregnant with Doug. Her pregnancy was uneventful except for pregnancy-related diabetes. Doug was a full term baby. Mrs S describes being shocked when she first saw Doug and the cleft palate. She says that the nurses and her family couldn't look at him but after a little while she told everyone that he was 'beautifully ugly'. According to Mrs S, 'Mike loves his son but doesn't like him because Doug doesn't listen'. When asked about her comment, Mrs S stated that Mike is uncomfortable around kids and hasn't really had the opportunity to get to know either of his children. Mike has yet to see Elisa.

Mrs S is proud that she has stayed off welfare and has always provided for her kids. When asked about her job she states that she has been in her current job for three years and that it pays well and allows her to work nights while the kids are asleep. Mrs S states that she is close to her family, especially Yvonne. When asked about their relationship she comments that she feels much like a second parent and wants Yvonne to have a good life.

Mrs S acknowledges that she smokes cigarettes and pot but does not drink alcohol because she has seen how it ruined her mother's life. Mrs S's father died when she was six of unknown causes. Another brother, Timmy, died in a car accident when he was thirteen years old. Mrs S also has a brother, Denny, twenty-five, who is in jail for armed robbery. Mrs S visits Denny in jail and often brings the children along to 'cheer him up'. Denny has two children who play with Doug from time to time. When asked about her family losses and separations she notes that the reason she works nights and stays 'straight' is to make sure her kids have better options in life. She states 'family comes first'.

Mrs S identifies no close friends but says she gets along with everybody unless they mess with her family. When asked about a faith or spiritual belief she states that she doesn't go for churches but believes that there's a higher power out there to keep her kids safe.

Observation of Doug: Doug is an engaging four-year old boy. He separated with minimal distress from his mother and acclimated quickly to the playroom. Doug showed great curiosity and energy when surveying the playroom. He went from toy to toy settling for focused play with a series of trucks. Doug placed the trucks neatly in a row and then crashed through them enthusiastically. He repeated this activity many times. Doug was so involved with this activity that ending it proved challenging. He showed less interest in sitting still and participating in visual-spatial activities than he had in larger motor play. Assessing Doug's cognitive abilities will take creative planning and patience.

Although Doug's speech is somewhat hard to understand, the evaluator could determine that he was able to name the people in his family including his Mama, Daddy 'that's in jail', Baby Elisa, Auntie Yvonne, his Uncle Denny 'that's in jail', his Nona Linda (maternal grandmother), and his Poppy Manuel (his grandmother's boyfriend). Doug did not identify any playmates but named his favourite activities including trucks, motorcycles, four-wheelers and books. Conversely, Doug doesn't like to sit in the corner, eat broccoli or 'stay at home without my Mama'. His three wishes are to go to Disney, have more toys, and see his Daddy every day.

Summary and treatment recommendations: Doug S is a four-year-old boy who was referred by his paediatrician because of her concerns regarding his attentional capacities. The paediatrician also indicated her concern with his mother's capacity to manage the stresses that come with being a single parent of two small children. Doug has thus far not received any early services addressing his attention and behaviour. Mrs S, Doug's mother, shares the paediatrician's concerns about his attention and is committed to investigating the possibilities of intervention that can help Doug with his development. Doug has undergone two operations for a cleft palate that may have slowed down the pace of his development.

Mrs S is also concerned about the obstacles that face Doug as a child with a visible disability. She identifies that he has strengths and tenacity that might help him meet these future challenges. Mrs S also has strengths evidenced by her capacity to reliably financially support her young family. She is a resource for her younger sister and describes a family that despite many losses and challenges remains close. She has hopes for a positive future for her sister and for her children. Mrs S acknowledges that she gets angry with Doug but

works hard on managing her anger and consciously sets limits that do not involve physical punishment. She is also well aware that substance abuse has been an issue in her family and as a response she chooses not to use alcohol.

Further evaluation of Doug's strengths and challenges is recommended as a way to determine what early interventions would best benefit his growth and development. Since Doug is a very active youngster, any formal evaluation needs to be conducted in a way that capitalises on his attention and allows ample time for him to play and rest.

Diagnosis: Rule/out attention deficit disorder with hyperactive; possible cognitive delays or disabilities

Treatment recommendations: Request referral for a full-scale neuropsychological evaluation to determine Doug's development, cognitive, social and emotional functioning. Recommendations for child-centred interventions will be discussed with Mrs S pending the findings of the evaluation; One to three sessions of parent counselling to support Mrs S in her efforts to effectively address Doug's challenging behaviours.

Entering the conversation: some guidelines

Professionals are often the first people to usher families into the world of special education, childhood disability or other challenges of childhood and parenting. First contacts between children, families and professionals usually focus on the process and procedures of assessment, at a time that is at least stressful, if not intensely frightening and often painful. Even the characterisation of initial contacts as something called an 'assessment' invokes the memory of prior experiences of children and their families of assessments of all kinds, whether medical, psychiatric, or educational. While there may be some hope attached to the possibility of finding answers, the usual structures of assessment tend to reinforce a sense of passivity, a privileging of professional knowledge, and an expectation that something will be done to correct, repair, or heal dysfunction. The challenge for every practitioner is to transcend those expectations, and through dialogue, discovery, and collaboration, to create a different kind of alliance. It is important to remember that these initial interactions establish an emotional orientation to therapeutic alliances that have far reaching effects not only on ongoing alliances but also on future parent/professional relationships (Contro, et al., 2002, Prezant and Marshak, 2006).

The first version of 'He does bad real good' used the language and methods of traditional child-centred assessment. In this process, the goal is to compile a list of problems, implied deficits, and potential diagnoses. It is not intended to be harmful, rather its goal is to be helpful but it runs the risk of alienating an already reluctant parent by rushing to judgment and certainty and by pathologising the details of a complicated and difficult life.

The second version frames information through a different lens. It emphasises language that describes behaviour rather than interprets it. It solicits and incorporates feedback from the parent that is differentiated from professional opinion and is contained in the body of the assessment report. Including parent's responses to extended questions begins the process of contextualising the child's behaviour and the parent's response to it. As Boyd-Webb (2003) notes, the most useful way of beginning an assessment with children that are disadvantaged or present with complex lives is to consider the child's strengths. Despite the 'rough' impression that Mrs S initially makes, it is clear that she has resolved to do her best as Doug and Elisa's parent. She not only takes care of the children's basic needs, but has managed to support her young son through very difficult surgeries and recoveries. Additionally, in stating that Doug 'does bad real good' Mrs S implies that Doug has the capability to hold his own and survive adversity even in the face of disability. Taken out of context and without further questioning it would be easy to read this comment as an indictment of Doug's behaviour that could be further supported by Mrs S's comment that he's smart just like his incarcerated dad. But it is just the opposite. Mrs S has pride in her son's toughness and a belief that this 'beautifully ugly' boy will make it through future difficult circumstances.

Framing these earliest assessment conversations from a standpoint of strengths and hopefulness sets the stage for building alliances that are mutual, respectful, and effective in transforming lives. When assessments are collaboratively developed and written it is more likely that the story being told accurately reflects the child's experience, and as a consequence, interventions for practice have increased potential for success from the client's viewpoint as well as from institutionally driven practice evaluation.

Further, assessment as a conversation rather than an interview is empowering to parents because from the outset they are engaged as part of the solution. When workers acknowledge an authentic position of 'not knowing,' and emphasise discovery and collaboration, parents are invited into the solution-building dialogue. Every child's situation and every family's narrative present a vibrant, detailed, and unique story. This position of 'not knowing' cultivates a sense of curiosity that leads to different and open questions, and creates a mutual process of discovery that implies both worker and client possess essential and important knowledge. This engenders a sense of collaboration that is respectful of parent expertise in their children's lives and sees them as equal partners in the assessment process. Asking for children and parents' opinions before and after making suggestions builds the necessary bridges of authentic reciprocal dialogue. When children and parents feel listened to and heard they respond with candour and commitment. This collaborative dialogue actualises the talents, skills and resources children and their families bring with them, all factors that have been identified in the literature as contributing to the bulk of therapeutic success (Hubble, Duncan and Miller, 1999).

Transformative practice is based on three key ideas, that assessment and intervention are simultaneous, that strengths are embedded in the narrative of every problem, and that treatment is a subset of collaboration, not the other way around. Professionals have much knowledge about problems, diagnoses, and interventive methods. They also have an obligation to develop an equal competence in knowledge about strengths and resilience, unique personalities and solutions, and the skills of creating collaborative partnerships. This balance helps them to suspend disbelief by holding back on default judgments, to impart a belief in the possibilities for positive change, and to engage children and their families as collaborators in assessment, intervention and care. The consequence is the reduction of risk, and the enhancement of possibility.

References

Asay, T.P. and Lambert, M.J. (1999) The Empirical Case for the Common Factors in Therapy: Quantitative Findings. In Hubble, M.A., Duncan, B.L., and Miller, S.D. (Eds.) *The Heart and Soul of Change: What Works in Therapy.* Washington, DC: American Psychological Association.

Blundo, R. (2001) Learning Strengths-Based Practice: Challenging Our Personal and Professional Frames. *Families in Society,* 82: 3, 296–305.

Boyd-Webb, N. (2003) *Social Work Practice With Children.* 2nd edn. New York: Guilford Press.

Brandell, J.R. and Ringel, S. (2004) Psychodynamic Perspectives on Relationship: Implications of New Findings from Human Attachment and the Neurosciences for Social Work Education. *Families in Society,* 85: 4, 549–57.

Contro, N. et al. (2002) Family Perspectives on the Quality of Pediatric Palliative Care. *Archives of Pediatric and Adolescent Medicine,* 156: 1, 14–20.

Duncan, B.L., Hubble, M.A. and Miller, S.D. (1997) *Psychotherapy with 'Impossible' Cases: The Efficient Treatment of Therapy Veterans.* New York: Norton.

Duncan, B.L., Miller, S.D. and Sparks, J.A. (2004) *The Heroic Client: A Revolutionary Way to Improve Effectiveness through Client-Directed, Outcome-Informed Therapy.* San Francisco: Jossey-Bass.

Gambrill, E. (1999) Evidence-based Practice: An Alternative to Authority-Based Practice. *Families in Society,* 80: 4, 341–50.

Gellis, Z. and Reid, W.J. (2004) Strengthening Evidence-Based Practice. *Brief Treatment and Crisis Intervention;* 4: 2, 155–65.

Goldstein, H. (1999) Different Families. *Families in Society,* 80: 2, 107–9.

Goldstein, H. (1983) Starting where the Client is. *Social Casework: The Journal of Contemporary Social Work,* May, 267–75.

Graybeal, C. (2001) Strengths-Based Social Work Assessment: Transforming the Dominant Paradigm. *Families in Society,* 82: 2, 233–42.

Graybeal, C. (Under contract) *Dialogue, Discovery, and Collaboration: Transformative Social Work Practice.* Chicago: Lyceum.

Hubble, M.A., Duncan, B.L. and Miller, S.D. (eds.) (1999) *The Heart and Soul of Change: What Works in Therapy.* Washington, DC: American Psychological Association.

Jordan, C. and Franklin, C. (2003) *Clinical Assessment for Social Workers: Quantitative and Qualitative Methods,* 2nd edn. Chicago: Lyceum Books.

Lambert, M.J. (ed.) (2004) *The Handbook of Psychotherapy and Behaviour Change.* 5th edn. New York: Wiley.

Lambert, M.J. and Ogles, B.M. (2004) The Efficacy and Effectiveness of Psychotherapy. In Lambert, M.J. (Ed.) *The Handbook of Psychotherapy and Behaviour Change,* 5th edn. New York: Wiley.

Lambert, M.J. and Bergin, A. E. (1994) The Effectiveness of Psychotherapy. In Bergin, A.E. and Garfield, S.L. (Eds.) *Handbook of Psychotherapy and Behaviour Change.* New York: Wiley.

Lambert, M.J., Shapiro, D.A. and Bergin, A.E. (1986) The Effectiveness of Psychotherapy. In Garfield, S.L. and Bergin, A.E. (Eds.) *The Handbook of Psychotherapy and Behaviour Change,* 3rd edn. New York: Wiley.

Lambert, M.J. (1986) Implications of Psychotherapy Outcome Research for Eclectic Psychotherapy. In Norcross, J.C. (Ed.) *The Handbook of Eclectic Psychotherapy,* New York: Brunner/Mazel.

Maione, P.V. and Chenail, R.J. (1999) Qualitative Inquiry in Psychotherapy: Research on the Common Factor. In Hubble, M.A., Duncan, B.L. and Miller, S.D. (Eds.) *The Heart and Soul of Change: What Works in Therapy.* Washington, DC: American Psychological Association.

Masten, A. (2001) Ordinary Magic: Resilience Process in Development. *American Psychologist,* 56, 227–38.

Northen, H. (1987) Assessment in Direct Practice. In Minahan, A. (Ed.) *Encyclopedia of Social Work.* 18th edn. Silver Spring, MD: National Association of Social Workers.

O'Hare, T. (2005) *Evidence-Based Practices for Social Workers: An Interdisciplinary Approach,* Chicago: Lyceum.

Prezant, F.P. and Marshak, L. (2006) Helpful Action seen through the Eyes of Parents of Children with Disabilities. *Disability and Society,* 21: 1, 31–45.

Reid, W.J. (1997) Evaluating the Dodo's Verdict: Do all Interventions have Equivalent Outcomes? *Social Work Research,* 21, 5–18.

Rose, S.R. and Fatout, M.F. (2003) *Social Work Practice with Children and Adolescents.* Boston: Allyn and Bacon.

Rosen, A. (2003) Evidence-based Social Work Practice: Challenges and Promise. *Social Work Research,* 27, 4, Social Science Module, 197–208.

Saleebey, D. (1992, 1996) The Strengths Perspective in Social Work Practice: Extensions and Cautions. *Social Work*, 41: 3, 296–304.

Saleebey, D. (1997) The Strengths Perspective: Possibilities and Problems. In Saleebey, D. (Ed.) *The Strengths Perspective in Social Work Practice*, 2nd edn. New York: Longman.

Schore, A.N. (1997) A Century after Freud's Project: Is a Rapprochement between Psychoanalysis and Neurobiology at Hand? *Journal of the American Psychoanalytic Association*, 45, 809–40.

Siegel, D. (1999) *The Developing Mind: How Relationships and the Brain Interact to Shape who we are*. New York: Guilford Press.

Tronick, E.Z. (1989) Emotions and Emotional Communication in Infants. *American Psychologist*, 44, 112–19.

Turner, S.G. (2001) Resilience and Social Work Practice: Three Case Studies. *Families in Society*, 82: 5, 441–9.

Wampold, B.E. (2001) *The Great Psychotherapy Debate: Models, Methods, and Findings*. Mahwah, NJ: Lawrence Erlbaum Associates.

Werner, E. and Smith, R. (1992) *Overcoming the Odds, High Risk Children from Birth to Adulthood*. Ithaca, NY: Cornell University Press.

Weick, K. (1996) Drop Your Tools. *Administrative Science Quarterly*, 41, 301–13.

Weick, K. (1989) Theory Construction as Disciplined Imagination. *Academy of Management Review*, 14: 4, 516–31.

Wolin, S. and Wolin, J. (1993) *The Resilient Self*. New York: Villard Books.

CHAPTER 11

Actuarial and Clinical Risk Assessment: Contrasts, Comparisons and Collective Usages

Hazel Kemshall

Introduction

Risk has become a core concept in contemporary social policy and welfare provision (Culpitt, 1999; Kemshall, 2002), and has become a key organising principle of much social work, health and social care provision (Alaszewski et al., 1998; Kemshall et al., 1997). This is exemplified in organisational policies and procedures for service delivery, and in the identification of priorities and resource allocation. The 'risk principle' is evident in worker practices, roles and responsibilities, and in the agency framing of key tasks (Kemshall, 2002). For example, in child protection this has resulted in a decrease in preventative work and early interventions, and a greater emphasis upon child abuse (Corby, 1993). In youth policy generally, children are framed as either 'at risk' or 'risky' (Goldson, 2000, 2002), with risk framed as entirely negative.

However, it is a matter of dispute as to whether the contemporary discourse of risk in social policy and welfare is entirely negative (Titterton, 2005). In the areas of mental health provision and care of the elderly in particular there is much evidence to support a positive framing of risk, focusing on the empowerment of vulnerable people to take risks, make choices, and exercise personal autonomy (see Titterton, 2005 for a full review). In this context, risk is associated with the 'right to self-determination' and the management of risk is presented as the balance between risks and rights (Norman, 1980; Titterton, 2005). This is mirrored in significant policy documents throughout the 1990s seeking to balance the autonomy and independence of older persons with their appropriate care (particularly in residential settings) (Centre for Policy on Ageing, 1996, 1999) paralleled by similar concerns for mental health service users (Counsel and Care, 1992, 1993; Davis, 1996).

It has also been contended that the discourse of risk has replaced the discourse of need in much welfare provision, although the extent of this shift is still contested (Kemshall, 2002). Emerging work

comparing differing Anglophone countries, and also countries in Western Europe, indicate that there are different responses to the effects of globalisation and high costs of welfare (see, for example, Prince, 2005, for a review of Canadian social policy). Castles and Pierson (1996) have compared Australia, the UK and New Zealand and conclude that social policy developments remain quite diverse. It is also contended that Scandinavian countries have resisted the worst excesses of neo-liberalism and still have a strong commitment to social democracy and welfarism (Powell and Hewitt, 2002; Moses et al., 2000; Swank, 2000). Despite such contestation it is possible to conclude that universal and general entitlement need has been replaced by a language of selective entitlement and priorities (Langan, 1998); and an emphasis upon encouraging proactive, prudential citizens capable of managing their own risks (O'Malley, 2004; see Kemshall, 2002, Chapter 2 for a full review; Aharoni, 1981).

Risk assessment and risk management are now key tasks for practitioners in social care, social work and criminal justice (Kemshall and Pritchard, 1996; Parsloe, 1999).

Broadly speaking, the implications for workers have been:

- The rationing of services on the basis of risk.
- Emphasis upon regulating risky behaviours rather than upon ameliorating need.
- An increasingly compulsory element to service use.
- Risks outweigh rights.

See Kemshall, 2002.

What is risk?

Risk has had a number of meanings through the ages, ranging from value neutral definitions of 'chance' and associations with gambling; later characterisations as probability and statistical calculations for social insurance; to contemporary concerns with predictability, uncertainty and negativity (Hacking, 1990; Kemshall, 2003; Parton, 1994). Following Power (2004) the very ambiguity of risk is taken as a starting point. This enables a focus on how risk is used and framed for attention, and how risk is characterised and used by particular agencies. A broad analysis across the spectrum of health, social work, social care and criminal justice identifies two general categories:

- Those risks which people *pose to others*.
- Those risks to which people are exposed – better understood as *vulnerability to risk(s)*.

See for example Titterton, 2005 for a review.

Posing risk to others is most common within criminal justice, and to a lesser extent in forensic mental health. In common parlance it is often associated with the assessment of 'dangerousness', and more recently with public protection and the appropriate management of high-risk and high profile offenders in the community such as sex offenders (Kemshall, 2003; Kemshall et al., 2005). The assessment of vulnerability has most often preoccupied those working in mental health, care of the elderly and child protection. Such assessments are concerned with the identification and prevention of risks (often presented by others such as parents, carers and siblings), and the provision of services that will reduce such risks. Assessments often raise key ethical dilemmas, such as whether the right to independent living should override risk in care of the elderly.

However, whether the risk is posed to others or self, the key underpinning concept is harm, whether that be physical or emotional harm. It has also come to mean harm at a level that is significant, causing either extensive physical injury, death, or significant psychological trauma from which it is difficult to recover (adapted from ASSET (undated) and OASYs (Home Office, 2001)). This has resulted in an increasing preoccupation with risk avoidance, prevention and prediction (Kemshall et al., 1997).

Assessing vulnerability is more common in health, social care and social work, for example assessing the vulnerability of children, or assessing the risk of falls and strokes when the elderly are discharged from hospital. In some instances, risk assessment and subsequent protective measures may compromise rights to choice and independence, and such assessments often require a careful balance of risks to self and rights to choose (Titterton, 2005). Complex cases can arise where the person is both vulnerable and that vulnerability itself contributes to or exacerbates

their risk to others, for example mentally disordered offenders. The Boyd Committee, for example, found that mentally ill persons who do not comply with their medication regimes are more likely to commit homicides or suicides than those who do (Boyd Report, 1996), and social care failings with vulnerable mental health users have been implicated in subsequent risk management failures (Blom-Cooper et al., 1995; Sheppard, 1995). In these cases workers will have difficult decisions to make and face ethical dilemmas that are not necessarily easily resolved. However, distinguishing between the type of risk (to others or to self), and carrying out separate but inter-related assessments might assist practitioners in making such dilemmas and balances explicit, and in matching interventions to the risks posed.

To carry out a vulnerability assessment workers should focus on:

- The accurate identification of the risks to which the person is exposed and why.
- The likely impact or consequences of the risks to the person.
- Whether the risks are externally posed, or are endemic to the person and their circumstances.
- Whether the risks are acceptable – those externally posed by others (such as adult offenders to children) are usually less acceptable.
- Where the risks arise from the person and their situation a key question is whether the risk should be run. What are the costs and benefits of the risk? What are the costs and benefits of putting in place protective measures?
- Balancing the desirability of reducing the risk against the likely reduction of choice, independence and autonomy of the individual. For example the reduction of risk for older persons through the use of residential care.
- Risk management strategies are usually characterised by a desire to achieve this balance and to resolve where possible tensions between autonomy, quality of life, rights and risks.

(Kemshall, 2002)

Risk assessment

Throughout the twentieth century formalised risk assessment tools were developed and grew in sophistication. These tools ranged from formal calculations of parole recidivism (Burgess, 1928) to structured checklists in health care, social care and child protection (Alaszewski et al., 1998;

Kemshall, 2002). These formalised approaches to risk have attempted to 'tame chance' and unpredictability (Hacking, 1990) and to reduce the subjective bias of risk assessors (for example social workers and probation officers). Such formal tools have tended to utilise statistical methods to produce actuarial calculations of risk, or to develop robust risk predictors to structure professional clinical judgement. The most recent tools have combined both (Bonta, 1996; Kemshall, 2003).

Actuarial assessment

Actuarial risk assessment is based upon statistical calculations of probability and has its roots in the insurance industry (Adams, 1995). In brief, actuarial assessment predicts an individual's likely behaviour from the behaviour of others in similar circumstances. An early example of this methodology is Burgess's parole predictor (1928) and more recently the Offender Group Reconviction Score (OGRS) used in prisons and probation to predict the risk of reoffending (Copas et al., 1996). Actuarial assessment has been less developed in child protection, social care and social work where clinical judgement (often based on structured interviewing tools) tends to predominate (Kemshall, 2002). Actuarial assessment establishes a baseline prediction of likely risk, and is useful in categorising high, medium and low risks of probability (for example of prison parole release or reconviction). However, the methodology does have a number of problems. These have been summarised in the research literature as:

- The limitations of extrapolating individual risk probabilities from aggregated data about groups, better known as the 'statistical fallacy'.
- The limits of the research technique used to produce risk predictors, a technique known as 'meta-analysis'.
- The limit of low base rates, that is, predicting general risk probabilities from low frequency behaviours (such as murder, child abduction, etc.)

The statistical fallacy refers to the problem of transferring aggregated risk factors based on group data to the individual. An easy example is the transfer of parole reconviction data from white, male prisoners to women and ethnic minority offenders (Kemshall, 2003). The insurance industry recognises this issue and

offers differing premiums to different people (e.g. women drivers, young drivers), but also responds to the changing risk profiles of customers over time. Probability scores are thus refined over time, and should be applied to individuals with some caution. For example, a 60 per cent reconviction score after sentence for an offender only means that that particular offender has a 6 in 10 chance of reconvicting, not whether that individual actually will. It still remains a matter of judgement to determine whether the offender is in the 60 per cent or 40 per cent category. Dynamic or clinical factors are most often used to determine this.

Most predictive scores cluster at around the 40–60 per cent mark and where chances are almost even. Where behaviours are less frequent in the population as a whole, such as acts of extreme violence, the *base rate*, that is the known frequency of the behaviour in the population as a whole, is low. This makes prediction difficult, and transfer of such predictive data to social work and probation has been problematic because the base rates for the behaviours of concern are low (e.g. child abduction) (Corby, 1993). Pritchard (2004: 118), in discussing child abusers, points out that child murderers come from 'small, 'special' groups of population at risk' and that this 'potential pool of assailants' is very small (p. 119). For similar issues in predicting child abuse see the seminal work by Dingwall (1989).

More recently a technique called the ROC score has been developed, in effect an actuarial prediction free from base rate limitations as these are taken into account in the ROC adjusted score (Mossman, 1994). This technique has improved the predictive accuracy of risk assessment tools for grave violent and sexual offenders (see Kemshall, 2001 for a full review).

Meta-analysis refers to the research methodology used to generate actuarial risk factors. This is a statistically based technique that analyses the outcomes of a large body of primary research studies. These outcomes are then aggregated to produce the core factors that have statistical significance for risk prediction (McGuire, 1997). However, this approach has been critiqued for its inability to appropriately distinguish between factors and impacts, and a failure to appropriately examine and account for multi-variant effects (Copas, 1995; Mair, 1997; see Kemshall, 2001, 2003 for a full review).

However, despite recent and growing criticism (Kemshall, 2003), actuarial assessment can be used to establish those risk factors that have a proven track record of prediction and encourage workers to focus on the 'right stuff'. This has increased the accuracy of risk assessment (for example, in Probation by using OASys), and formalised tools do drive up consistency and reliability. To a lesser extent they have also established the base rate for less frequent behaviours (for example, serious sexual offending, see Grubin, 2004).

Clinical assessment

Traditionally based upon the subjective judgement of key professionals (such as social workers, probation officers, psychiatrists and psychologists), clinical assessment has been prone to a number of difficulties, most notably:

- Subjective bias of the assessor (for example discriminatory practice, the over-identification of vivid and unacceptable risks).
- Staff take short cuts when under pressure.
- Over identification with the subject of the assessment (for example, probation officers may prioritise the rights of offenders over those of victims, social workers may prioritise the desires of parents over the needs of children).
- Over reliance on the self-report of the subject of the risk assessment (e.g. the accounts of offending behaviour provided by offenders, parental accounts of family interactions).

See Kemshall, 2001 for a full review.

Subjective bias has been much implicated in risk management failures, not least the under-estimation of risks due to over-reliance on the self-report of the client (Milner and Campbell, 1995). Lack of investigative interviewing and partial assessments also contribute to false risk assessments (Prins, 1995), with value-judgements filtering worker perceptions of risk (for example the 'unreal optimism' of the Jasmine Beckford case (Parton, 1985; Jasmine Beckford Inquiry, 1985). The *short cuts* of intuitive reasoning are often favoured over formal risk assessment tools, with workers over-relying on case data and eschewing aggregated data. Munro (1999, 2002) has explored how these errors play a negative role in child protection risk assessment with practitioners failing to revise initial assessments in the light of new information, and where workers are slow to respond to deteriorating behaviour and escalating risks.

Combined structured risk assessment tools

More recently, structured assessment tools have been developed to encourage workers to focus on the 'right stuff', that is, the risk factors most supported by research, and to in effect follow either interviewing guides or structured information tools. The early tools, both in probation and in social work, were inventories of need and did not claim to predict risk (Kemshall, 2003). In effect, these tools were developed for targeting, intervention and change measurement. As costs of service delivery grew, and the preoccupation with effective practice increased, these tools played a greater role in identifying and prioritising service users for interventions in both the welfare and criminal justice arenas (Kemshall, 2002). Throughout the 1990s the language of need was gradually replaced by the language of risk (Kemshall et al., 1997). In probation, client need was transformed into risky offenders, and in social work need inventories were replaced by 'at risk' clients, and more latterly by risk based tools in mental health, work with the elderly and in child protection (DoH, 1999; Parsloe, 1999; Parton, Thorpe and Wattam, 1997; Titterton, 2005). These tools have a number of characteristics in common, in brief:

- Inclusion of the risk factors most supported by research.
- A simple scoring system.
- Evidence boxes for assessors to add additional information and/or to justify their scoring.
- Service delivery and resourcing decisions based on the overall score.
- Some capacity for review and evaluation of impact.
- Resource lean and user friendly (although the extent to which this is actually achieved in practice is debatable).

See OASys, Home Office, 2001; Kemshall, 2003: 70–1.

In addition, some tools explicitly combine actuarial and clinical factors, and attempt to incorporate treatment/risk management planning within their format (e.g. the OASys probation risk assessment tool, or RAMAS for mental health (Home Office, 2001; O'Rourke and Hammond, 2000; DoH, 1998). These have been dubbed 'third generation tools' and they have proved particularly useful in identifying criminogenic risks for intervention (Bonta, 1996), high risk sex offenders (Grubin, 2000, 2004), the most risky violent offenders (Cooke, 2000) and in the identification of dangerous carers (Hagell, 1998; Kemshall and McIvor, 2004).

More recent developments: decision trees

The prediction of risk for high risk offenders and high risk mental health patients is crucial to public safety and professional credibility. These areas have consequently seen some key developments to enhance predictive accuracy, but also to guide practitioners towards those interventions most likely to be effective in reducing risk. Of particular note is the development of classification trees, used predominantly for violent offenders and those suffering from psychopathy. Initial screening is carried out using the Psychopathy Checklist (PCL-R, Hart et al., 1994), followed by a pre-set list of questions which are empirically and theoretically grounded in current research on high risk violent offenders (Monahan et al., 2000). Subsequent questions are dependent upon initial answers – hence the idea of a classification tree. The method can categorise offenders into high or low risk, but a small number of offenders remain unclassified and: 'It is these individuals, whose risk level is equivocal, with whom the assessor needs most assistance' (Cooke et al., 2001: 12). Whilst such an approach does attempt to capture the 'it depends' nature of risk often encountered by practitioners, it is still a highly structured and mechanistic approach to risk.

However, the idea of differing 'risk options' depending on circumstances and the notion that practitioners may need to rehearse differing outcomes and contingencies of risk is a helpful notion. This could be particularly relevant for those practitioners dealing with high risk decisions where the differing outcomes of various actions, responses and risk management strategies may need to be considered. For example, post-release plans for prisoners, or the likely impact of various interventions in child protection cases. In effect, practitioners may need to consider: 'what will happen if I do A, and if B occurs, what is the best response?' Risks are rarely fixed, are open to change and often require a highly flexible approach to their management. One of the key flaws of recent risk assessment tools has been their tendency to engender a static response to risk, and despite good practice advice

to review assessments regularly, one-off assessments and fixed responses have become the norm (Kemshall, 2003).

Response of workers to risk assessment tools

The response of workers to risk assessment tools has been varied. Initially, workers may doubt the need for such a tool, resent its threat to discretion and judgement, and may seek to circumvent it or complete it with low integrity (Kemshall, 1998). Workers may also disagree with the prioritisation on risk, and operate from a differing value and ideological base, this has been particularly acute in probation work (Robinson, 1999). Similar ideological 'disputes' can be discerned in work with young people where they are characterised either as 'children in need' or children posing a risk (Goldson, 2000) – and workers resist tools that they believe categorise children and young people inappropriately. Poor and inaccurate completion of risk assessment tools has also been problematic, for example in Probation where recent research on high risk offenders and MAPPA found two thirds of OASys completions to be inadequate (Kemshall et al., 2005). Workers also continue to value intuitive reasoning over formalised assessment (Kemshall, 2003) but this can result in tragic failures and serious incident inquiries (HMIP, 2006a, b).

It is helpful to their acceptability if risk assessment tools have the following features:

- User friendly.
- Resource lean.
- 'Easy' to train staff to use appropriately.
- The process of use is transparent and accountable (particularly important in those cases where assessment decisions are subsequently challenged).
  (Adapted from McIvor and Kemshall, 2002: 51)

Staff also need to be convinced about the reliability, integrity, and usefulness of the tool – in essence they need to be convinced about how it was developed, what it can do, and how accurate it is. These issues are particularly important if the tool is imposed from the 'centre' with little practitioner consultation or input. In Scotland, risk assessment tools for use with offenders have been 'rated' against key and agreed criteria (RMA, 2005). This is seen as crucial to the robustness of risk assessments for courts making

Orders for Lifelong Restriction (indeterminate sentences). Both practitioners and sentencers are aware of the 'rating' of a particular tool when they use it or base decisions upon it. In terms of Human Rights challenges the basis of assessment is made clear and a collective view of the reliability of risk assessment tools is developing. Research has indicated that the following criteria are essential in judging the 'fitness for purpose' of a risk assessment tool:

- Validated for use against a relevant population.
- The risk factors used in the tool have a proven track record of reliability and predictability.
- The tool must be able to differentiate between low, medium and high risk.
- Tools must have inter-rater reliability (e.g. consistency across users).
- Assist workers to make relevant risk management plans.
  (Adapted from McIvor and Kemshall, 2002: 51)

Conclusion

Risk assessment is now a core task in health, social care, social work and probation. It takes place within a climate of intense scrutiny and harsh blame when things go wrong (Kemshall, 1998). A key response to this has been a relentless development of formal risk assessment tools to enhance the reliability of decisions and improve their defensibility. The most robust of these tools combine actuarial and clinical factors into structured assessment tools and their use is now commonplace. This has been paralleled by interest in decision trees, and attempts to structure the daily reality of risk decisions towards the most effective outcomes. A continuing difficulty is the response of staff to risk assessment tools and this requires more work by managers and policy makers to 'sell' the advantages to workers and users alike of risk assessment tools.

References

Adams, J. (1995) *Risk*. London: UCL.

Aharoni, Y. (1981) *The No-risk Society*. Chatham NJ: Chatham House.

Alaszewski, A., Harrison, J. and Manthorpe, J. (1998) *Risk, Health and Welfare*. Buckingham: Open University.

ASSET (undated) London: Youth Justice Board.

Beckford Inquiry (1985) *A Child in Trust: The Report of the Panel of Inquiry into the Circumstances Surrounding the Death of Jasmine Beckford*. Presented to the London Borough Council and to Brent Health Authority by members of the Panel of Inquiry, London Borough of Brent.

Blom-Cooper, L., Hally, H. and Murphy, E. (1995) *The Falling Shadow: One Patient's Mental Health Care 1978–1993*. London: Gerald Duckworth.

Bonta, J. (1996) Risk-needs Assessment and Treatment. In Harland, A.T. (Ed.) *Choosing Correctional Options that Work*. Thousand Oaks, CA: Sage.

Boyd Report (1996) *Report of the Confidential Inquiry into Homicides and Suicides by Mentally Ill People*. Steering Committee of the Confidential Inquiry. London: Royal College of Psychiatrists.

Burgess, E. W. (1928) Factors Making for Success or Failure on Parole. *Journal of Criminal Law and Criminology*, 19: 2, 239–306.

Castles, F. and Pierson, C. (1996) A New Convergence? Recent Policy Developments in the United Kingdom, Australia and New Zealand. *Policy and Politics*, 24: 3, 233–45.

Centre for Policy on Ageing (1996) *A Better Home Life: A Code of Good Practice for Residential and Nursing Home Care*. London: Centre for Policy on Ageing.

Centre for Policy on Ageing (1999) *National Required Standards for Residential and Nursing Home Care*. London: Centre for Policy on Ageing.

Cooke, D.J. (2000) Current Risk Assessment instruments. Annex 6 in the Maclean Report, *A Report of the Committee on Serious Violent and Sexual Offenders*. Edinburgh: Scottish Executive.

Cooke, D.J., Michie, C. and Ryan, J. (2001) *Evaluating the Risk for Violence: A Preliminary Study of the HCR–20, PCL-R and VRAG in a Scottish Prison Sample*. Occasional Paper Series 5/2001. Glasgow: Scottish Prison Service.

Copas, J. (1995) *Some Comments on Meta-analysis*. Warwick: Department of Statistics, Warwick University.

Copas, J., Marshall, P. and Tarling, R. (1996) *Predicting Offending for Discretionary Conditional Release*. Home Office Research Study 150. London: HMSO.

Corby, B. (1993) *Child Abuse: Towards a Knowledge Base*. Buckingham: Open University Press.

Counsel and Care (1992) *What if they Hurt Themselves?* London: Counsel and Care.

Counsel and Care (1993) *The Right to take Risks.* London: Counsel and Care.

Culpitt, I. (1999) *Social Policy and Risk.* London: Sage.

Davis, A. (1996) Risk Work and Mental Health. In Kemshall, H. and Pritchard, J. (Eds.) *Good Practice in Risk Assessment and Risk Management, Vol 1.* London: Jessica Kingsley.

DoH (1998) *Modernising Mental Health Services: Safe, Sound and Supportive.* London: HMSO.

DoH (1999) *Framework for the Assessment of Children-Government Guidance on Inter-agency Co-operation.* London: HMSO.

Dingwall, R. (1989) Some Problems about Predicting Child Abuse and Neglect. In Stevenson, O. (Ed.) *Child Abuse: Public Policy and Professional Practice.* Hemel Hempstead: Harvester Wheatsheaf.

Goldson, G. (2000) 'Children in need' or 'Young offenders'? Hardening Ideology, Organisational Change and New Challenges for Social Work with Children in Trouble. *Child and Family Social Work*, 5, 255–65.

Goldson, G. (2002) New Labour, Social Justice and Children: Political Calculation and the Deserving-Undeserving Schism. *British Journal of Social Work*, 32, 683–95.

Grubin, D. (2000) *Risk Matrix 2000.* Paper presented to Risk Assessment and Management Police Conference, Moat House Hotel, Cheltenham, 19–20 October.

Grubin, D. (2004) The Risk Assessment of Sex Offenders. In Kemshall, H. and McIvor, G. (Eds.) *Managing Sex Offenders.* London: Jessica Kingsley.

Hacking, I. (1990) *The Taming of Chance.* Cambridge: Cambridge University Press.

Hagell, A. (1998) *Dangerous Care: Reviewing the Risk to Children from their Carers.* London: Policy Studies Institute and the Bridge Child Care Trust.

Hart, S.D., Hare, R.D. and Forth, A.E. (1994) Psychopathy as a Risk Marker for Violence: Development and Validation of a Screening Version of the Revised Psychopathy Checklist. In Monahan, J. and Steadman, H. (Eds.) *Violence and Mental Disorder: Developments in Risk Assessment.* Chicago: University of Chicago Press.

Her Majesty's Inspectorate of Probation (2006a) *An Independent Review of a Serious Further Offence Case: Damien Hanson and Elliot White.* London: HMIP.

Her Majesty's Inspectorate of Probation (2006b) *An Independent Review of a Serious Further Offence Case: Anthony Rice.* London: HMIP.

Home Office (2001) *OASys: Manual.* London: Home Office.

Kemshall, H. (1998) *Risk in Probation Practice.* Aldershot: Ashgate.

Kemshall, H. (2001) *Risk Assessment and Management of Known Sexual and Violent Offenders: A Review of Current Issues.* Police Research Series 140. London: Home Office.

Kemshall, H. (2002) *Risk, Social Policy and Welfare.* Buckingham: Open University Press.

Kemshall, H. (2003) *Understanding Risk in Criminal Justice.* Buckingham: Open University Press.

Kemshall, H. et al. (2005) *Strengthening Multi-Agency Public Protection Arrangements (MAPPAs).* Home Office Practice Development Report, 45. London: Home Office.

Kemshall, H. and McIvor, G. (Eds.) (2004) *Managing Sex Offender Risk.* London: Jessica Kingsley.

Kemshall, H. et al. (1997) Concepts of Risk in Relation to Organisational Structure and Functioning within the Personal Social Services and Probation. *Social Policy and Administration*, 31: 3, 213–32.

Kemshall, H. and Pritchard, J. (1996) (Eds.) *Good Practice in Risk Assessment and Risk Management, Vol 1.* London: Jessica Kingsley.

Langan, J. (1998) *Welfare: Needs, Rights and Risks.* London: Open University Press and Routledge.

Mair, G. (Ed.) (1997) *Evaluating the Effectiveness of Community Penalties.* Aldershot: Avebury.

McGuire, J. (1997) A Short Introduction to Meta-analysis. *VISTA*, 3, 3 163–76.

McIvor, G. and Kemshall, H. (2002) *Serious Violent and Sexual Offenders: The Use of Risk Assessment Tools in Scotland.* Edinburgh: Scottish Executive, Social Research, Crime and Criminal Justice.

Milner, J.S. and Campbell, J.C. (1995) Prediction Issues for Practitioners. In Campbell, J. (Ed.) *Assessing Dangerousness: Violence by Sexual Offenders, Batterers, and Child Abusers.* London: Sage.

Monahan, J., Steadman, H. and Appelbaum, P. (2000) Developing a Clinically Useful Tool for Assessing Violence Risk. *British Journal of Psychiatry*, 176, 312–19.

Moses, J., Geyer, R. and Ingebritsen, C. (2000) Introduction. In Geyer, R., Ingebritsen, C. and Moses, J. (Eds.) *Globalisation, Europeanisation and the End of Scandinavian Social Democracy?* Basingstoke: Macmillan.

Mossman, D. (1994) Assessing Prediction of Violence: Being Accurate about Accuracy.

Journal of Consulting and Clinical Psychology, 62: 4 783–92.

Munro, E. (1999) Common Errors of Reasoning in Child Protection Work. *Child Abuse and Neglect*, 23: 8, 745–58.

Munro, E. (2002) *Effective Child Protection.* London: Sage.

Norman, A. (1980) *Rights and Risks.* London: Routledge.

O'Malley, P. (2004) The Uncertain Promise of Risk. *The Australian and New Zealand Journal of Criminology*, 37: 3, 323–43.

O'Rourke, M. and Hammond, S. (2000) *Risk Management: Towards Safe, Sound and Supportive Service.* Surrey Hampshire Borders NHS Trust.

Parsloe, P. (1999) *Risk Assessment in Social Care and Social Work.* London: Jessica Kingsley.

Parton, N. (1985) *The Politics of Child Abuse.* London: Macmillan.

Parton, N. (1994) Problematics of Government, (Post) Modernity and Social Work. *British Journal of Social Work*, 24: 1, 9–32.

Parton, N., Thorpe, D. and Wattam, C. (1997) *Child Protection: Risk and the Moral Order.* Basingstoke: Macmillan Press.

Powell, M. and Hewitt, M. (2002) *Welfare State and Welfare Change.* Buckingham: Open University Press.

Power, M. (2004) *The Risk Management of Everything: Rethinking the Politics of Uncertainty.* London: Demos.

Prince, M.J. (2005) From Welfare State to Social Union: Shifting Choices of Governing Instruments. Intervention Rationales and Governance Rules in Canadian Social Policy. In Eliadis, P., Hills, M.M. and Howlett, M. (Eds.) *Designing Governance: From Instruments to Governance.* Montreal and Kingston: McGill-Queen's University Press.

Prins, H. (1995) *Offenders, Deviants or Patients?* 2nd edn. London: Routledge.

Pritchard, C. (2004) *The Child Abusers: Research and Controversy.* Buckingham: Open University Press.

Risk Management Authority (2005) *Risk Assessment Tools Evaluation Directory (RATED).* Scotland: Risk Management Authority.

Robinson, G. (1999) Risk Management and Rehabilitation in the Probation Service: Collision and Collusion. *Howard Journal of Criminal Justice*, 38: 4, 421–33.

Sheppard, D. (1995) *Learning the Lessons: Mental Health Inquiry Reports Published in England and Wales between 1969–1994 and their Recommendations for Improving Practice.* London: Zito Trust.

Swank, D. (2000) *Political Institutions and Welfare State Restructuring.* In Pierson, P. (Ed.) *The New Politics of the Welfare State.* Oxford: Oxford University Press.

Titterton, M. (2005) *Risk and Risk Taking in Health and Social Welfare.* London: Jessica Kingsley.

CHAPTER 12

Risk and Child Protection*

Martin C. Calder

Introduction

The concept of risk occupies a pivotal position in current operational social work practice, yet there is surprisingly little written on the subject and the Department of Health has jettisoned the term from official guidance spanning all children and their families (DoH, 1999, 2000). This is a worrying and dangerous development since the assessment and management of risk remains the core activity of social services departments. Indeed, child protection practice is significant in signposting star ratings, curtailing professional anxieties, effectively protecting children and it is often seen as the litmus test of how safe departmental policy and practice is. Workers and agencies stand or fall by their child protection practice, and risk management is at the heart of good child protection work.

This chapter represents an attempt to try and provide workers with an operational framework for conducting risk assessments by exploring the definition, components and parameters of the concept. The author argues that by using the concept of risk in its fullest sense, e.g. assessing for strengths and protective mechanisms as well as weaknesses, then it remains an important and central consideration in our work designed to safeguard the child. Risk assessments should remain the backbone of the child care system as we know it. This chapter also moves on to

---

* An earlier version of this chapter was prepared for *Foreknowledge* as a briefing paper.

consider the forgotten stages of the risk process: risk analysis and risk management (Calder, 2003).

Definitions: identifying what we are talking about

Experience tells me clearly that you can have discussions about risk in different contexts with different people from different agencies and never actually question whether you have a shared understanding of either the term or the process. It is therefore essential to articulate what risk and risk assessment might be to ensure it is transparent and offers a platform for consensus or difference.

What is risk?

Definitions of concepts such as risk, dangerousness and significant harm are ambiguous and widely agreed to be determined by social, cultural and historical factors and we know that there are trends in public and professional recognition and responses to many different public concerns (Calder, 1999). In the 1980s there was little partnership between the professionals and families caught up in the child protection express in response to several child abuse tragedies until we hit the Cleveland barrier that re-directed us from exclusion to inclusion and with it a move towards risk management rather than risk control (Calder, 1995).

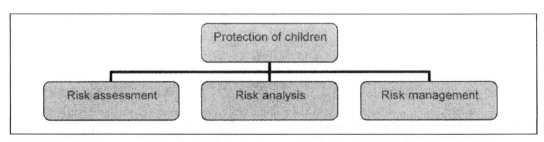

Figure 12.1 Risk assessment process in child protection

Parton (1996) persuasively argued that risk was a way of thinking rather than a set of objective realities, and that social work's preoccupation with risk at that point in time reflected changes in the way social workers viewed and undertook their practice. He saw the concerns with risk as both reflecting the anxieties and uncertainties of social workers in the 'new' welfare environment, and providing a rationale for their purpose and survival in it.

Parton and Small (1989) identified two concepts to help understand the significance attached to risk at that time. Firstly, they referred to disillusionment with the notion of rehabilitation and a growing emphasis on management and containment rather than therapy and treatment. In child protection, this meant following procedures, identifying and managing problems, rather than their treatment. The production of two different versions of the central guidance on child protection within three years (DoH, 1988, 1991) was testament to this belief. Secondly, the concept of bifurcation, that is the distinction between the responses made to a minority of 'high risk' individuals and that given to the majority of service users. There was a belief that we could screen risky people and situations by using various checklists and then target them with the most intensive of intervention approaches or filter them away if they were deemed either untreatable or where the prognosis for change was poor.

The first production of central assessment guidance for child protection work (DoH, 1988) was similarly built almost entirely on the notions of risk and dangerousness yet these concepts have been deleted from the central procedural and assessment guidance and governing child protection (DoH, 1999, 2000) a decade later. This is confusing when we know that there is on average a report each week surrounding a child death to the Department of Health and this highlights clearly a need to take the opportunity of managing risk better rather than sidelining it from our professional vocabulary.

Munro (2002) argued that risk has two significantly different meanings and the one you choose has a pervasive impact on your subsequent thinking. Historically, the 'risk' of a certain outcome referred only to the probability of it happening: the term was neutral about whether the outcome was desirable or not. Indeed, some view risk as containing positive opportunities for personal development whilst others suggest that risk must be viewed as something entirely negative to be controlled and eliminated. Therefore, in more recent times risk has been associated with unwanted outcomes only. Indeed, in discussions of 'the risk society' (Beck, 1992) the assumption is that we are talking about undesirable results. It is for this latter reason that risk appears to have been jettisoned from the government guidance as they want to promote a more inclusive, needs-led assessment process with a focus on strengths. Whilst this may engage some resistant families (Calder, forthcoming) it does not take into account that we need to assess risk alongside strengths and then conduct a risk-balancing exercise. This is a well tried and tested approach within care proceedings and suggests that the government either misunderstood the concept of risk or took a calculated gamble on a one-sided, strengths-loaded approach to steer people away from child protection (risk/control) to children in need (strength/care).

Walker and Beckett (2003) explored the implications of both the risk control and the risk management perspective that flow from the care/control or strengths/risk balancing:

Characteristics of the risk control perspective:
Definition: risk is negative – danger, threat.
Priority principles: professional responsibility and accountability.
Practice priorities: identification (assessment scales) and elimination (procedural, legalistic).

Eliminating or totally controlling risk in social work is impossible. It is undesirable to think of risk and the social work task in relation to it in this way because:

- Evidence and intuition suggests it is impossible and thus resources are wasted.
- Risk is part of social life.
- Practice which is effective in terms of promoting individual responsibility and social competence cannot be reductionist: it must recognise the person-in-context and build on strengths.
- Social work agencies have responsibilities in law in relation to certain client groups. Individual social workers must neither neglect these responsibilities nor accept unlimited liability – whether or not there are legal requirements.
- The social and individual costs of control can outweigh the social and individual benefits.

- Social work routinely brings its practitioners into contact with dangerous people and entails professional judgements which are potentially castigated by management, organisations and the media.
- Ironically the danger of such practice is that in pursuing the ultimately unattainable goal of entirely risk free practice workers may:
  - *Overlook the risks attached to intervention:* Removing a child allegedly in danger from its family opens the child up to other dangers that can be equally damaging.
  - *Neglect the rights of individuals in order to control the risks they pose to themselves or others:* Removing a child or young person from their home on the grounds that they are living in a home with poor conditions raises ethical issues about how far the state should dictate how individuals live.
  - *Lose sight of the individual-in-context, their strengths and the creative potential for development and growth this brings:* Focusing too narrowly on one aspect of the individual (e.g. dangerousness) may limit opportunities for interventions that can enable clients to build on their strengths to become less dangerous.
  - *Overlook the risk to the social worker:* Over-eagerness to control risks posed to others can expose workers to unacceptable levels of risk to themselves. This can result not only in serious harm to the worker, but add to the guilt and other problems experienced by the client involved in violence against the worker.

Characteristics of the risk management perspective:

Definition: positive – risk is part of life, balancing risks and benefits is part of individual's development, being self-determining and personally responsible.
Priority principles: self-determination, anti-oppression.
Practice priorities: solution-focused, partnership practice, empowerment.

The benefits of the risk management perspective are that they are in keeping with the values and practice of modern social work; it emphasises the process of maximising benefits as well as minimising risks, rather than the procedure of identifying and eliminating risk; and it builds on strengths. The drawbacks are that it relies heavily on

highly developed professional competence and judgement and requires commitment of the client to partnership. It also requires intellectual/cognitive competence of the client. It also involves ambiguity and uncertainty, is poorly understood by the public, and requires supportive management practice and organisational policy. Risks to social workers are virtually ignored.

(adapted from Walker and Beckett, 2003)

It is also important to differentiate between short- and long-term risks. Short-term risk relates to the immediate danger to the child and where none exists, the danger is that no services are provided. This can potentially contribute to the detrimental effects on development in the longer term through parenting deficits. It is for this reason that a more objective measure of care is required to standardise the measurement of likely or actual harm in the non-crisis orientated cases such as neglect and emotional abuse. The practice of focusing on assessing immediate harm can skew practice so that the longer-term risks are ignored or undervalued. We know from Utting (1997) that children in long-term care placements may well be the cases that become unallocated, but then the risk is that we do not pick up on changing circumstances and harm ensues.

What is a risk assessment?

It is a term which is often misused in social work because it focuses exclusively on the risk of harm, whereas in any other enterprise a risk equation also includes a chance of benefit resulting (Carson, 1994). It should thus be concerned with weighing up the pros and cons of a child's circumstances in order to inform decision-making as to what should happen with regard to intervention and protection. It involves examining the child and family situation to identify and weigh various risk factors (such as parents, family or other influences that increase the likelihood that a child will be harmed in a certain way), family strengths, family resources, and available agency services. This assessment information can then be used to determine if a child is safe, what agency resources are needed to keep the child safe, and under what circumstances a child should be removed from the family.

Calder (2002) has defined it as the systematic collection of information to identify if risks are involved and if so, what these are and the likelihood of their future occurrence (prediction), whether there is a need for further work, and what form this should take. It can also be used to predict the escalation of the presenting behaviour as well as the client's motivation for change. As such, the risk assessment aims to predict the probability of a child's suffering from abuse if the situation continues unaltered. However, given the limited knowledge base, these predictions are always couched in terms of probabilities: there is a certain degree of risk of some event happening. Risk assessment, therefore, involves computing and combining probabilities. The formal laws for doing this are expressed in probability theory. Unfortunately, humans are not good at dealing with probabilities intuitively. People's instinctive understanding of how probabilities should behave is wildly wrong, resulting in persistent and fundamental mistakes' (Munro, 2002).

Practice experience informs us that we often associate less risk with situations where we have most control, such as driving a car, as compared to travelling by airplane. We also need to guard against missing important risk cues because we are familiar with something, such as not knowing when a neglectful family situation has deteriorated to the point that child protection procedures should be invoked. Overall, knowing that we can and do over-estimate some risks and under-estimate others is essential, and good supervision should help compensate for such errors.

The term risk assessment is used to define a number of different assessment and decision-making processes in various agencies. It can often refer to both a structured form of decision-making as well as to specific instruments or frameworks that are used in the process (e.g. Calder, 1997, 1999, 2000, 2001, 2003b,c; Calder, 2004; Calder and Peake, 2003).

Cleaver et al. (1998) identified a useful list of the blocks to identifying risk within the assessment process which includes:

- The unknown – that is, knowledge of signs and symptoms and knowledge of the law that was not adequate.
- The known but not fully appreciated – the need to identify what is important from a 'flood of relevant data'.
- Interpretation – being able to correctly interpret information in the context of assessing risk.
- Objective and subjective information – failure to distinguish fact from opinion, being too trusting and uncritical.

- Unappreciated data – information may not be appreciated if it has come from a source which is distrusted.
- The decoy of dual pathology – information may be missed if the receiver is decoyed by a different problem.
- Certainty – investigators may have a false sense of security about a particular interpretation (e.g. medical assessments of sexual abuse in Cleveland).
- Competing tasks within the same visiting schedule, e.g. fostering and child protection.
- The known and not assembled – individuals may hold information which they can either withhold or which is not pieced together with the rest.
- Not fitting the current mode of understanding – this has also been described as a loss of objectivity, and the importance of supervision is highlighted.
- Long standing blocks – assumptions made at an early stage which influenced later interpretation of information.

Risk models and risk theories

The assessment of risk is guided by several underlying theories including ecological theory and theories on stress, crisis and coping and their relationship to child abuse and neglect.

Ecological theory

Ecological theory provides a framework that helps in understanding families and the complex system of which they are a part. Families live in a complex social structure and are often 'nested' within different systems at the same time and/or different times. Using this perspective allows for greater insight into what contributes to a family's crisis, the strengths and resources already present within the family, and what intervention may be most appropriate for a family.

Stress, crisis and coping

Factors contributing to the abuse or neglect of a child are often intrinsically related to theories of stress, crisis and coping. Families entering the child welfare system are often families in crisis and the abuse of a child is one possible way in which their stress is exhibited. Coping strategies and personal resources establish the foundation for a person's response to stress. A person's resources and coping strategies provide the means for which stress can be de-escalated and managed in positive, adaptive ways. Both an increase in a family's stress and/or the onset of a crisis coupled with diminished resources contributes to the likelihood of child maltreatment. Specifically related to the lack of resources is the lack of formal, pro-social networks upon whom the family can rely and utilise in times when they are experiencing significant stress. We know that formal social support mitigates the effects of stress in a person's life. Associated with this is the need for the support to be actively used as many families struggle with accepting and using the support available. A thorough risk assessment should thus take into account the strengths, support networks, and resources a family has that can be drawn upon when deciding the type of unit or service for which the case is most appropriate (Cash, 2001).

There are also a number of important models of risk assessment.

Two-stage risk assessment

A simple approach is to question the two central areas within any risk assessment: the severity of the risk and the capacity of the parent or carer to effect the necessary changes in a timeframe commensurate with the child's needs (Bridge Consultancy, 2000).

Three 'C' approach (Reder and Duncan)

The second model derives from child abuse tragedies being carefully evaluated and

countenances a three 'c' approach (Care, Control, Conflict) as follows (Reder and Duncan, 1999):

- Care and control conflicts arise when the parents' own childhood experiences of adverse parenting leaves them with unresolved tensions which spill over into their adult relationships.
- These are about being cared for and caring for others or about self-control wishing to control others and fearing control by them.
- Their children are at risk during the early months/years when they are most dependent and when they carry meanings for their parents associated with the unresolved parental conflicts.
- This is compounded for families living in stressful circumstances. Thus an escalating scenario can develop in which stresses to the parental care-control conflicts come together over days and weeks and can lead to one precipitating and serious/fatal incident.
- In addition, the particular meaning that a specific child may have for the parent may make that child more at risk than any others.
- The risk factors can be considered as either crises in the parents' relationships with their social context (e.g. being rejected by own parents or a partner or by having supportive services withdrawn) or crises in the parents' interactions with their children (e.g. increases in dependency demands – mother may be pregnant again; if a family member becomes ill; or where children are demanding attention persistently). Figure 12.3 provides some examples of the characteristics of the care and control conflict.

Generic framework

A generic framework for risk assessment practice which can take into account the two perspectives

How severe is the risk?	Can the parent change?
• If a young baby is with an alcoholic mother and basic care (safety) is not being provided then the severity of the risk is clearly high. • If the child is 14 and has a number of protective factors around him e.g. a good school, a grandmother who can spend lots of time with them, then the severity of the risk posed by the alcoholic mother may not be high.	• Does the parent have insight? • Where are they on the change continuum? • Do they want to change? • Do we have the resources to help? • How long will it take? • Can they maintain the changes? • Where should the child reside whilst these changes are being made?

Figure 12.2 Two-stage risk assessment process

Care conflicts	Control conflicts
• These arise out of actual experiences of abandonment, neglect or rejection as a child, or feeling unloved by parents. • These show themselves in later life as excessive reliance on others and fear of being left by them; or its counterpart of distancing themselves from others. • Intolerance of a partner's or child's dependency. • Unwillingness to prepare ante-natally for an infant's dependency needs, or declining to respond to the needs of a child when born.	• These are based on childhood experiences of feeling helpless in the face of sexual or physical abuse or neglect, or inappropriate limit-setting. • In adult life, these are enacted through violence; low frustration tolerance; suspiciousness; threats of violence; or other attempts to assert power over others. • Violence or control issues could become part of their relationships with partners, children, professionals or society in general.

Figure 12.3 Characteristics of care and control conflicts

on risk and the tensions between the various practice requirements has been influential since first described by Brearley (1982). His framework is based on the clear definition of danger, risk, predisposing and situational hazards, and strengths as follows:

Danger: Undesirable outcomes: these are where the child may be harmed or re-harmed or where they are unable to recover from any abuse they have experienced.

Risk: Needs to capture the two sides of the same coin: accepting that there is the potential for loss (undesirable outcome) and also the chance of gain (desirable outcome). Social work can focus too narrowly on potential losses – thereby missing the potential for gain. Competent practice involves weighing up the pro's and cons of both possibilities, which Brearley describes in terms of hazards and strengths. A hazard is an existing factor that introduces or increases the possibility of an undesirable outcome. Brearley identified two types of hazard.

Predisposing hazards: These are factors in the person's background – such as their experiences and personality – which make an undesirable outcome more likely.

Situational hazards: These are factors specific to the current situation that make an undesirable outcome more likely. This distinction between the two types of hazard is useful because it helps you to focus on those aspects of the risk situation that may be more amenable to intervention and change.

Strengths: Any factor which reduces the possibility of an undesirable outcome occurring. The dangers we have discussed of

a too narrow focus on hazards are reduced by this requirement to identify strengths. This may seem an obvious requirement of holistic assessment that fully takes account of the person-in-context, but it is one which can be easily neglected in the pressured environment of risk work.

Listing the hazards and strengths provides a way of quantifying the balance between them. You need to then identify what other information can be obtained to help analyse the whole situation, before reaching a conclusion and making a judgement about the decisions to be made.

Risk deletion: the detrimental impact of the assessment framework

Risk has become a 'hot potato' in government. Risk equates with child protection at a time in which there is a drive to re-focus on strengths. The government has thus redefined risk as need. This is not convincing when there is repeated backtracking from needs-led assessments to a reminder that the child's safety is the primary objective of professional intervention (Calder, 2000). It also represents a basic misunderstanding of what risk means. Risk is about balancing strengths and weaknesses, weighting them and then considering the type of intervention needed (Calder, 2002). Risk and need in the context of child abuse can and should be defined in terms of each other. If a child's needs are not met, there is a risk of harm. If a child is at risk of abuse, then he or she is in danger of not having some needs met (Munro, 2002). Risk is thus only one component in the assessment of a child and their family's situation.

Conceptually, there is a move towards serving more children 'in need' rather than allowing the emphasis on resources to be on inappropriate child protection investigations (DoH, 1995, 1999, 2000, 2002). Whilst this is a laudable aspiration, there remain a significant number of abused children who require, and deserve, research-grounded interventions prefaced with an accessible and credible risk assessment framework. The deletion of the term 'risk' has left many workers without an operational assessment tool, and with this, increased anxieties that disables their power of response. Many feel the baby has been thrown out with the bathwater and they have thus been scrambling round for risk assessment tools that can assist them in their task. The recording forms do not allow for child protection risk assessments and indeed the associated guidance does not direct staff to the relevant literature (Calder, 2003). It is misleading that a core assessment can provide a risk assessment when risk under section 47 has skipped the initial assessment phase.

Given the tight resource situation facing local government at present, many services are now allocated according to their perceived risk, thus requiring workers to emphasise risks rather than strengths in arguing for resources for their clients. There is also a problem for workers having only materials from the strengths-loaded assessment framework to do work at the child protection end of the spectrum. In the climate of eligibility criteria, it is a restricted range of factors that define 'high risk', notably those associated with protection rather than the safeguarding or promoting of a child's needs. Directing services only at those identified as 'high risk' also removes the potential benefit of preventative intervention. Social work becomes the last line of defence. The strategy is essentially reactive, allowing service reductions to create risk for some, with the deployment of resources only when a state of 'high risk' is reached. The danger here is that 'control' replaces 'welfare' (Calder, 1995). We end up dealing with an ambulance at the bottom of the cliff rather than investing in fences at the top of the cliff.

Risk refinement: developments in the sexual abuse field

The sexual abuse field is developing more refined tools to gauge risk at a time when the concept has been disowned by central government. We need to remember that:

- Identifying risk is a central part of our work in families where sexual abuse has taken place.
- It is an extremely difficult task for any professional, particularly given the lack of scientific evidence regarding predictions of human behaviour.
- There is a need to ensure that we construct our risk estimations based on theory and research in each sub-category of sexual abuse and not rely on a transfer of knowledge from adult male sex offenders.
- There is a need to move from general risk estimations (high, medium or low risk) to the nature of the risk and the particular situations/contexts in which they apply.
- In the absence of a quantification of risk, then it is difficult to construct a plan to manage it.

(Calder, 2000)

Hanson (1998) has argued that risk assessments consider two distinct concepts: enduring propensities, or potentials to re-offend; and factors that indicate the onset of new offences. These offence triggers are not random, but can be expected to be organised into predictable patterns (offence cycles), some unique to the individual and some common to most sexual offenders. Different evaluation questions require the consideration of different types of risk factors.

Static, historical variables (e.g. prior offences, childhood maladjustment) can indicate deviant developmental trajectories and, as such, enduring propensities to sexually offend.

Evaluating changes in risk levels (e.g. treatment outcome), however, requires the consideration of **dynamic, changeable risk factors** (e.g. co-operation with supervision, deviant sexual preferences). Dynamic factors can further be classified as stable or acute. **Stable factors** have the potential to change, but typically endure for months or years (e.g. personality disorder) and, as such, represent ongoing risk potential. In contrast, **acute factors** (e.g. negative mood) may be present for a short duration (minutes, days) and can signal the timing of offending. Most risk decisions require consideration of both static and dynamic risk factors.

Following on from this development, a series of actuarial risk tools has emerged with adult male sex offenders, the most notable of which is the Matrix 2000. This is used by the police to assess the risk posed by anyone required to comply with the Sex Offender Register. This matrix has a screening facility for violent and sexual offences.

It is important to note that these tools do not replace our more traditionally developed core assessments: they simply offer a screening facility to ensure that the most worrying cases cross the threshold for core assessment.

A framework for prediction

There have been many attempts to develop risk assessment models and guidance in order to, assist professionals in making decisions about individual children. Whilst research-derived models are better than those built on professional consensus, both struggle to embrace the diversity of practice situations, particularly in sexual abuse situations. Since many models tend to err on the side of over-prediction, professionals need to accept that they represent a tool that is not an end in itself, merely an aid to professional judgement.

Risk assessment is not an exact science; prediction involves probabilities and this means that errors can be expected. Any model must have built into it a system for anticipating and dealing with false positives as well as accepting the inevitability of false negatives (Cleaver et al., 1998).

In any risk prediction, there are four possible outcomes (Figure 12.4).

Depending on the event in question, false negatives can be tragedies, such as when a child is left in the care of a parent in a situation deemed to be low risk, but where the parent subsequently kills or abuses the child. Naturally, such events are dreaded by social workers, as they are doubtless dreaded in any profession which has responsibilities for managing risks. But we need to be clear that when such events occur, they are not necessarily mistakes and do not necessarily

reflect incompetence on the part of the social worker. Any calculated risk sometimes goes the 'wrong' way. Just because such events occur does not necessarily mean that those who assigned these cases to a low risk category were wrong.

To believe that, when something like this happens, it necessarily proves that a mistake has been made, is in itself a serious mistake. It is known as the *hindsight fallacy*:

> If a decision involves risk, then even when one can demonstrate that one has chosen the unarguably optimal course of action, some proportion of the time the outcome will be suboptimal. It follows that a bad outcome in and of itself does not constitute evidence that the decision was mistaken. The hindsight fallacy is to assume that it does.
> (Macdonald and Macdonald, 1999: 22)

This is not to say that actual mistakes cannot be made because, of course, they can. For example, important pieces of evidence can be missed, or connections can fail to be made between pieces of evidence, resulting in cases being assigned to the wrong risk category. These are actual mistakes. But we should be careful to distinguish between risk indicators that should reasonably have been noticed in advance and those whose significance could not have reasonably been seen without the benefit of hindsight.

False positives *may* be no less tragic in their consequences than false negatives, for instance, a child taken away from parents with whom they would actually have grown up quite happily. But since we cannot know what *would have* happened if we had not intervened, false positives are relatively invisible as compared to false negatives.

What *is* visible to all practitioners is that protective interventions in 'policing' mode are distressing to all concerned and should therefore be kept to a minimum.

A **True positive prediction** e.g. harmful behaviour will occur.	B **False negative prediction** e.g. risk of harm not identified but does occur; the consequences are acute.
C **False positive prediction** e.g. the risk of harm predicted but does not occur; over-intervention?	D **True negative prediction** e.g. harmful behaviour will not occur.

Figure 12.4   Categorising predictive outcomes

Actuarial and clinical prediction: relative merits

In order to assess and manage risk effectively, reliable methods are necessary. Since there are two different approaches to risk prediction, it is important to consider the relative merits of actuarial and clinical prediction. Once again, the meaning of these terms is far from clear.

Clinical methods are essentially a diagnostic assessment derived in part from the medical and mental health fields. Clinical judgement 'relies on an informal, "in the head" impressionistic, subjective conclusion reached (somehow) by a human clinical judge' (Grove and Meehl, 1996). The clinical method is useful in that it provides important information on individual risky behaviours, stresses related to environmental factors, and assists in establishing appropriate management and treatment plans. Some of the reported limitations include:

- The prediction is no better than chance.
- The prediction is too influenced by experiences: workers rely primarily on their own experience, intuition and interviewing skills.
- There is no evidence base, and factors typically have not been validated against outcome data.
- They are difficult to challenge.
- Often, they have a weak reliability.

(adapted from Kennington, 2003)

Statisticians use actuarial to refer to the mathematical techniques they use to set insurance premiums, design pension schemes and calculate liabilities. The object is to transfer and pool risk and hence to manage uncertainty. Actuarial assessment 'involves a formal, algorithmic, objective procedure (e.g. equation) to reach a decision' (Grove and Meehl, 1996). Actuarial methods utilise statistical techniques to generate risk predictors. Since no single factor is sufficient to determine whether offenders will or will not re-offend, practitioners need to consider a range of relevant risk factors. There are three plausible methods by which risk factors can be combined into overall evaluations of risk:

1. **Empirically guided clinical evaluations:** which begins with the overall recidivism base rate and then adjusts the risk level by considering factors that have been empirically associated with recidivism risk. The risk factors to be considered are explicit, but the method for weighting the importance of the risk factors is left to the judgement of the worker.

2. **Pure actuarial predictions:** in contrast, explicitly state not only the variables to be considered, but also the precise procedure through which ratings of these variables will be translated into a risk level. In the pure actuarial sense, risk levels are estimated through mechanical, arithmetic procedures requiring a minimum of judgement.

3. **Clinically adjusted actuarial predictions:** begins with a pure actuarial prediction, but then raises or lowers the risk level based on consideration of relevant factors that were not included in the actuarial method (see Quinsey et al., 1995). As research develops, actuarial methods can be expected to consistently outperform clinical predictions. With the current state of knowledge, however, both actuarial and guided clinical approaches can be expected to provide risk assessments with moderate levels of accuracy.

- They are consistent with the expectation of evidence-based social care interventions.
- They are useful in establishing those risk predictors that have a proven track record.
- They are useful in establishing the relevant base rates for clinical assessment.
- They are useful in increasing the accuracy of risk assessments.
- They increase the levels of consistency and reliability.

(adapted from Kemshall, 2001)

The consensus appears to be that the future is actuarial. However, there are some problems associated with the use of actuarial risk tools that includes using information gained from meta-analysis about a population (such as sex offenders) and then attempting to apply it to a particular individual, where it encourages the discredited tick-box approach (Hollows, 2003). It is also problematic in that it may tell us that someone is destined to re-offend, but it is not sophisticated enough to tell us when they may offend and against whom: key requirements of any prediction within the child protection field (Kennington, 2003).

Advocates of actuarial prediction argue that clinical methods are merely informal (and therefore inferior) versions of actuarial ones and describe clinical experience as a prestigious synonym for anecdotal evidence (Grove and Meehl, 1996). Advocates of clinical methods argue that information derived from groups can only be of limited value in predicting the behaviour of the individual. Both approaches face the problem that rare events will always be more difficult to predict than everyday ones because as the base-rate of the behaviour being predicted falls so the ratio of mistakes to correct prediction increases. Both approaches face the additional problem that there is no agreement as to the appropriate reaction to a given level of risk (Buchanan, 1999).

What is clear is that it is extremely difficult to develop any predictive instrument with a high degree of accuracy in child protection. Admitting that actuarial systems are inadequate is not an argument for preferring clinical judgements. In fact, there are overwhelming arguments for accepting that clinical judgements are probably far less accurate. They are certainly no more accurate.

Actuarial assessment forms a baseline. The potential pathway to accurate risk assessment lies in the integration of clinical and actuarial risk tools. One division of these instruments has thus far been on the application of actuarial risk tools for screening purposes, ensuring that precious resources are focused on the highest risk cases; and clinical assessment being utilised in the core assessment phase of the intervention process. We can reapply actuarial risk tools to evaluate and measure change. It is essential that we have space for the exercise of professional judgement in the risk process, as the deletion of the human factor in a far from mathematical equation can lead us to wrong and even dangerous conclusions (Calder and Hackett, forthcoming).

Retaining professional judgement in the risk process

Hollows (2003a, b) has provided a detailed argument for the retention of professional judgement within the risk process. The following summarises some of the points she seeks to make. Within the social work literature it is suggested that judgement is a compilation of knowledge, skills, values and experience: a mixture of professional authority, including knowledge, experience and expertise; coupled with professional autonomy, meaning a capacity for independent thought and action, is one

suggestion (Youll and Walker, 1995). A further suggestion is that judgement is the determining factor in the combination of structured sets of competencies to meet the needs of a single case, by an individual practitioner (Jones and Joss, 1995). Judgement is also inextricably linked with professional expertise.

The problem of error has come to dominate thinking and research about judgement making, with the expression 'error of judgement' offered as an explanation for most of the disasters within child welfare practice as well as in the wider world. Hammond describes the process of judgement making as one in which uncertainty is irreducible, error is inevitable and consequent injustice is unavoidable (Hammond, 1996) – not in every case but at least some of the time. While the error we tend to fear the most is that of failing to recognise a potentially dangerous situation, this is not the only concern. There is the importance of studying false positive cases of child maltreatment: 'as they can lead to great suffering. They have the potential to lead to unnecessary separation of child and parent, parental imprisonment, loss of job and reputation, quite apart from substantial distress to all concerned'. That does not mean we should avoid judgement making: to do so would be to make decisions without considering evidence. But it does mean that we should address judgement making as a serious task, and one that needs to be undertaken in full knowledge of the potential problems and pitfalls, including the possibility of error.

Hammond (1987, 1996) developed a *cognitive continuum* of judgement making (see Figure 12.5).

The *continuum* recognises that there are legitimately different approaches to judgement making from the rapid, on-the-spot processing of information and knowledge, known as intuition, to the detailed and analytical approach, sometimes using a form of experimentation. Hammond noted that clinicians would use a mode of judgement making which falls somewhere between the two points. This is based on the structural characteristics of the identified task, and the resources, particularly time, available. A less well structured task will lead to a more intuitive approach while a better structured task will lead to a more analytical or scientific approach. Less time available will lead to a more intuitive approach, while with greater time available we are more likely to apply analytical reasoning to the process. Six points are

Mode of judgement	Specific features
Intuitive judgements	Involve rapid, unconscious data processing. Combine available information by 'percentage averaging' it. Have low consistency. Have moderate accuracy.
Peer-aided judgements System aided judgement Quasi experiment Controlled trial	Involve intermediate, mixed or alternating features of analytical and intuitive judgements.
Analytical judgements	Involve slow, conscious and consistent thought. Are usually quite accurate (with occasional large errors). Apply more complex organising principles.

Figure 12.5   Modes of judgement with examples of features

identified on this continuum: intuitive judgements, peer-aided judgements, system-aided judgements, quasi experiment, controlled trial and analysis.

Practice wisdom

Practice wisdom is often viewed by workers as being equally effective in assessing risk as a risk assessment instrument. Practice wisdom can be integrated into the assessment of the risk process, specifically in the way questions are asked, the way information is gathered, and the manner in which the worker establishes rapport or a relationship with the family (see Calder, 2007). Practice wisdom can also be used in conjunction with a statistically validated instrument that assists the worker in gaining an overall picture of the family and creating a service plan that is tailored to the individual family needs (Cash, 2001). Relying solely on practice wisdom in risk assessment creates several problems:

- In relying on practice wisdom alone there is no way of establishing reliability or validity. These are of concern if we want the worker to make the same decisions concerning the same or different families in a consistent, systematic, and empirically valid way.
- A lack of objectivity is also a concern especially if someone holds a pro-family view that might lead to family interests rather than child interests being the driving force.
- Practice wisdom is a developmental process and as such a new worker's practice wisdom

will differ significantly from that of a more experienced worker.
- Workers can commit problems of human error. Statistical or measurement error can be measured or estimated a priori, whereas human error can only be measured post hoc.

Risk resurrection: the development of a framework for conducting risk assessments, analysis and management (RASSAMM) (Calder, 2003)

RASSAMM was developed to try and organise the available empirical data and combine it with our practice wisdom. The goal was twofold: to provide a guide through a complicated maze whilst also maximising best practice and hopefully outcomes for the recipient children.

Competent practice in risk work should:
- Adopt a holistic perspective.
- Appropriately employ well validated criteria of risk within a coherent framework of assessment and related intervention.
- Explicitly involve parents and children, recording their perceptions and opinions.
- Avoid gender bias (Hackett, forthcoming).
- Utilise multi-disciplinary processes of assessment and decision-making while being aware of the dangers of groupthink (see Calder, 2003d for a review).
- Be explicitly shared in supervision, recorded and endorsed at every stage by managers.

In child protection, there should be procedural guidance as to what situations require a **risk assessment**, in order to at least check for the presence of risk. Calder (2003c) identified that a risk assessment may be required in the following circumstances:

- Where previous children in the family have been removed because they have suffered harm.
- Where a schedule one offender (or someone found by an initial child protection conference to have abused) has joined a family. (Note. A schedule one offender is someone who has been convicted of an offence against a child. It is retained on their record for life.)
- Where concerns exist regarding the mother's ability to protect.
- Where there are acute professional concerns regarding parenting capacity, particularly where the parents have either severe mental health problems or learning disabilities.
- Where alcohol or substance abuse is thought to be affecting the health of the expected baby, and is one concern amongst others.
- Where the expected parent is very young and a dual assessment of their own needs as well as their ability to meet the baby's needs is required.

To this we can add:

- Where a child's name has been added to the Child Protection Register.
- Where the local authority is conducting a section 47 investigation.

The specific focus of risk assessment changes depending upon the particular step in the process, ranging from being concerned at whether and how fast to respond to the report at intake, to ensuring child safety during the investigation phase, to assessing whether the risk factors have been addressed before returning the child home or closing the case. In order for the protection process to be effective, the process must be related to the original intervention. For example, the risk may be controlled after investigation, but the risk does not go away until the sources of the risk are altered.

Calder (2002) offered the following framework for conducting risk assessments:

- **Assess all areas of identified risk** – Write them down and ensure each is considered separately, e.g. child, parent, family, surrounding environment, type and nature of maltreatment, intervention issues.
- **Then define the behaviour to be predicted** – rather than focus on the 'dangerous' individual. Assess each worrying behaviour individually as each is likely to involve different risk factors.
- **Grade the risks, and be alert for especially serious risk factors** – e.g. previous corroborated or uncorroborated concerns; unwillingness or inability to protect. While numerical weighting is hard to give, some weighting has to be given to significance. A less likely event with a serious outcome if it occurred would need to be weighted, e.g. injury, death, traumatic emotional impact. A more likely event with a high frequency, even though a not too serious outcome, would need to be weighted. Who is affected could add to the gravity, e.g. the harm to a child is often greater than if to an adult.
- **Be aware of risk factors that may interact in a dangerous manner** – e.g. a case of physical injury and the abuser is heavily drinking at present. Take into account both internal and external factors – almost all behaviour is the result of interaction between characteristics of the individual (e.g. attitudes, skills, controls) and those of the environment (demands, constraints, stressors etc).
- **Examine the nature of the risk factors** – How long have they been operating for? How severe are they? Risk factors that are long-term and relatively uncontrollable generally signal a higher level of risk.
- **Avoid focusing exclusively on the severity of the abuse** – we need to consider other factors that point to future risk, not just commissioned harm. Distinguish between the probability and the cost of the behaviour – we need to distinguish between the likelihood of the behaviour occurring from the seriousness of it if it does. Failure to do so makes any decision-making more problematic. For example, a repeat physical injury from a smack may be more likely to occur but the outcome of this may be considered to be significantly less serious than a repeat fatality.
- **Assessing family strengths and resources** – while risk assessment is essentially a negative process, workers should be examining family strengths and resources that may be used to counteract the risk factors present. For

example, good bonding; supportive networks. It is argued that the assessment process is incomplete in the absence of this dimension.

- **Use specific and descriptive terms to document the risk factors** – do not rely on terms such as 'multi-problem family'.
- **Gather real and direct evidence whenever possible** – do not relay on hunches, hearsay or circumstantial information.
- **Checking whether all necessary information has been gathered** – as in some cases, few sources of data may be needed to develop a strong understanding of the behaviour, whereas in others we may need to qualify any predictions made due to the entirely inadequate or irrelevant material.
- **Identifying if/when specialists or other outsiders need to be involved** – predictive accuracy is often improved when we utilise the combined skills across agencies and sometime beyond. Where this is lacking, workers should explicitly state how their recommendations have been affected by such omissions.
- **Awareness of probable sources of error** – which may come from the person being assessed (e.g. their poor reliability as an informant); the assessor (a difficulty in suspending personal values); or the context (such as an agency bias in favour of one or other party involved).
- **Planning key intervention** – because a sound assessment of risk will be based on the formulation of the mechanisms underlying the behaviour, it will automatically identify those processes which appear to be key elements in increasing or reducing such risk, e.g. within the individual or the couple.

Calder (2003) extended this to include:

- **Previous incidents of abuse or neglect?** Detail any previous incident of abuse or neglect (type and frequency) in this family OR any record of the current caretakers having abused or neglected other children. Is there a pattern of abuse (such as physical abuse being repeated) or is it changing (such as the concerns spanning a range of categories of child abuse)? There is widespread research evidence that children are more at risk in the care of those who have previously abused or neglected children. Do they accept any of the previous concerns? Do they have any insight into their previous

behaviour? If so, why the lapse? Do they accept or reject themselves as a continuing risk?
- **Taking a detailed social history and producing a detailed chronology.**

This section has offered a structured approach to information collection. Whilst it is important, as we know, that we should target the information we need rather than just collecting all information, we need then to do something with it. It is in this that workers often fall short, not assisted by the lack of attention to this in the government guidance on assessment or in the literature (Calder, 2003e).

From risk assessment to risk analysis

Risk analysis enables a risk assessment to be made on which decisions about action for risk management can be made and implemented. Risk analysis should thus provide information on:

- The nature of the risks and dangers these present.
- The frequency of such risks arising.
- The degree of seriousness of the dangers.
- The personal characteristics of those involved and how far these add to or minimise the risks.
- The relevant wider knowledge base on which to draw.
- The timescales for a risk decision.
- How a plan will be monitored in practice, and what feedback will indicate a change to the fallback plan to further reduce the risk if it escalates.

Calder (2002, 2003) argued that the risk analysis stage should consider the following questions:

- **What are the weaknesses in the situation being analysed?** What are the factors in the situation being analysed that make the occurrence or continuance of abuse more likely – what are the weaknesses or vulnerabilities in the arrangements for the care and protection of the child? These are usually inadequacies in the care provided by the child's family or in the protection afforded to the child. There may also be weaknesses in the services available to the family or their willingness to co-operate with them. The emphasis should be on the situation being assessed and the physical and emotional care that can be provided for the child. However, consideration should also be given to factors from the past where there is evidence that these are making current coping more difficult. For example, the fact of parents themselves having been abused or neglected in childhood would be included if it was thought to be having an effect on their capacity to care for and provide for their children. The responsibility of the parents/caretakers for previous abuse or neglect to this child or other children should be given particular consideration.

- **What are the strengths in the situation being analysed?** Understanding how to assess strengths and intervene in ways that strengthen and support family functioning is of particular importance in child protection work. It can help us work effectively with families in a way that protects the child, but does not oppress the family. A wide view should be taken of possible strengths including extended family and community supports but they should be related to the abuse or neglect under consideration. A supportive extended family will be a 'strength' where parents need to share some of their burden of child care; they will normally be of little use in protecting a child from a devious sex abuser. Here too, the emphasis is on the situation being assessed but consideration should also be given to factors from the caretaker's past where there is evidence that these are strengthening current coping capacity. For example, a parent who has 'coped' for a number of years prior to the current concerns shows the capacity under other circumstances to provide good enough care for the children. Further guidance is found in Calder (1999b).

- **Risk reducing** factors also need to be taken into account. An admission by a parent of the problem and a willingness to co-operate with a treatment and intervention programme would reduce risk. The use of interventions known to bring benefits, e.g. appropriate, regular medication for a mental illness, would also reduce risk. It is difficult to always know which questions to ask, although the following predictive questions might be of assistance:
  - Parenting skills and the capacity to learn: can methods of teaching and imparting parenting skills – matched to the parent's methods of learning – be improved?
  - Health care and safety – poor parents are as concerned as any to maintain health and

treat illness or injury. The problem is they are often slower in responding to emergencies, such as choking, thus allowing the problems to get worse.
  - Decision-making – is often high on rapidity and low on thoughtfulness, with poor quality decisions as a result.
  - Parent and child interaction – emotionally is often as warm, attached and committed as for most parents. Multiple deprivations can reinforce a tendency to a more restricted, punitive response. Research indications are that this may be due to not knowing what standards to set, what behaviour to reinforce, and non-punitive ways to ignore or reprimand undesirable behaviour. The danger of filling the gaps with middle-class family norms and patterns as goals also has to be avoided.
  - The capacity to generalise learning to adapt it to new situations.

- **What are the prospects for change in the situation and for growth?** Is there evidence of growth and positive change in the circumstances that have surrounded the abuse or given rise to the concern, or is there evidence of deterioration and negative change in the situation? A risk assessment should attempt to forecast how a situation will develop in the future, and clearly the capacity for improvement or deterioration in the current conditions is central to any such assessment.

- **What can be offered to build on strengths and combat weaknesses?** At all stages in the process it is important to see help and support as running alongside assessment, so even at an early stage it would be important to comment on the availability of help and the likelihood of it being used. There is much research evidence that the majority of child abuse investigations are trigged by poor or inadequate parenting rather than deliberate acts of abuse or neglect. Offering support services will be an outcome of many child protection investigations. Clearly, a positive response from parents to such services is helpful, but we need to be aware of the danger of discriminating against parents solely on the basis of their not co-operating with services, together with the danger of superficial co-operation hiding deeper resistance.

- **What is the risk associated with intervention?** We need to consider whether the benefits of intervention outweigh the problems of separation if we are considering removal from home; the inability to place siblings together in substitute care; the location from the placement may be some distance and can thus disrupt the child's peer networks, schooling and social life.

- **What is the family's motivation, and capacity, for change?** A key indicator of the likelihood of change is the parent's attitude to the abuse or concerns – an acknowledgement of the difficulties and a preparedness to work towards change would normally be seen as lessening the risk and the denial of the problem as increasing it. However, care needs to be taken not to discriminate against parents solely on the basis of their taking a different view of the abuse or alleged abuse from the social worker or other professionals. Co-operation also needs to be viewed in the context of the seriousness of the abuse or neglect. Some incidents are so serious that compulsory protective action may need to be taken despite evidence of co-operation from parents.
- **What is the likelihood of abuse occurring or recurring? What is the level of risk?** Determining the level of risk is a complex decision-making process where the worker considers the following conditions or criteria:
  - Number of risk factors (how pervasive are they?)
  - Severity of risk factors (how severe?)
  - Duration of risk factors (how long have they been present?)
  - Parent or child's ability to control risk factors.
  - Family strengths and resources.
  - Ability of worker or agency to provide necessary services.

In the light of the information collected a judgement of the level of risk in the current situation may be made. The level of risk is a compound of two elements:

1. How serious is the abuse or neglect that it is feared might occur or reoccur?
2. How likely is its occurrence or reoccurrence?

From risk analysis/intuition/ synthesis to risk management

Workers in child protection never face a choice between a safe and a risky option. All the possible avenues hold some dangers and they involve making complex assessments, balancing

risks and deciding on the safest path. Of equal importance is the recognition that all of the options contain some good aspects, as well as some benefits for the child, and these have to be weighed against the dangers (Munro, 2002).

Good child protection practice involves taking risks. We need to weigh the benefits of an intervention against the risk of side effects. What is often unclear is what interventions may only have positive outcomes and what the side effects of a particular intervention might be.

A risk analysis has the strength of focusing on relevant factors, organising decision-making in a way which both improves their quality, and makes them professionally defensible. It should provide a **risk strategy** which:

- Manages the risk.
- Puts the decisions into a recorded form – that enables people later to see how a decision was reached.
- Makes risk management a continuous process that links in well with other forms of sound professional (and often statutory) practice, e.g. recording methods.
- Enables the reliability of a decision reached to be assessed. The more one can move along the following scale, the higher the reliability:
  - Informed clinical judgement.
  - Personal experience of the situation and/or the client.
  - Relevant case studies.
  - Sound research which relates to the risk assessment factors involved.
  - Enables the following elements to be taken into account: the balancing of potential losses against potential gains; choices and options available; the element of responsibility, e.g. a parent who continues risky behaviour knows this means a child cannot be left dependent on them; and when professionals will move between support and intervention, i.e. balance their care and control responsibilities.

The fact that there is no single way for risk decision-making and intervention should not be a bar to sound risk analysis.

Walker and Beckett (2003) have questioned whether we should employ intuition, analysis or a synthesis of the two after completing the risk assessment, especially as there is a debate about whether intuitive or analytical thought is more suited to social work decisions. A contrast between these two distinct forms of thinking is drawn in the social work literature with the tendency to favour intuitive rather than analytical thinking, rejecting the latter as a technical, calculative approach not in harmony with social work values. As with many polarised debates the desire to simplify in order to heighten differences can obscure the valuable resources within each approach. It needs to be acknowledged that analysis is not inevitably technical, that intuition can be unreliable, but both can offer equally useful ways of thinking.

Intuition

Intuition has been variously described as the absence of analysis, the pinnacle of expertise, or the unconscious processing of data. This means that the basis for the consequent judgement is not made explicit at the time. It can be thought of as deciding in a relatively holistic way, without separating the decision situation into its various elements. This enables it to be a quick way of deciding by making use of limited information by sensing patterns and filling in gaps. To be reliable and accurate intuition needs to be based on expertise developed over time, but it has a fundamental drawback which stems from its implicit nature. This is that the reasons behind intuitive decisions are not readily available for comment and scrutiny, which is necessary for partnership practice.

Analysis

Analysis can be defined as a step by step, conscious, logically defensible process. There is deliberation over the different elements in a situation in a systematic and organised way. It can be thought of as using selected information in a precise way, whereas intuition uses all of the perceived information in an imprecise way. The strength of analysis is that it encourages openness about reasoning and so potentially holds any work open to scrutiny. The disadvantage in this approach is that it can induce misplaced faith in the ability to make predictions, particularly in the increasing social work field of risk assessment.

Synthesis

Seeing intuition and analysis as opposites can obscure the potential compatibility and complementarities of the approaches. Some social work planning decisions will require breaking down into their component parts and given careful consideration. But because this involves issues of uncertainty and values, intuition needs to be used within analysis in the making of judgements about the significance of information. Combining the explicitness of analysis with the skilled judgements of professional intuition offers the advantages of each approach. When facilitating client decision making or making decisions in partnership, some degree of analysis will be helpful as it involves being explicit about the basis of choice.

A **risk management** decision is not one for all time. It is the period until the decision is to be reviewed which provides the timescale for the **risk decision.** At the next review there will be a new risk assessment decision to be taken. Therefore the likelihood of the risk occurring needs to be assessed only for the risk period until the next review. However, good practice indicates that a contingency plan should be in place, akin to concurrent planning.

If necessary, the timescale and so the risk decision can be reduced in length to what is judged an acceptable level of risk. The very use of a sound risk analysis approach enables an agency to decrease the risk of professionally dangerous practice.

Summary

I have attempted to provide a remedial risk assessment, analysis and management framework to assist workers in conducting such a complicated and sensitive task. The framework is equally helpful for organisations when looking to develop a risk framework that will satisfy the multiple requirements within the criminal and child protection processes and compensate for the deficiencies of the Department of Health documentation (DoH, 2000, 2002).

RASSAMM is now being widely adopted in practice and consultancy settings where more complex situations are emerging. The model will continue to be extended and refined based on feedback and research developments. It is likely to find a bigger place in the market when the massive deficiencies of the incoming Integrated Children's System are recognised by frontline workers and their agencies (Calder, 2007). For copies of RASSAMM and for details of risk training courses offered by the author generically and more specifically to sexual abuse, please contact the author at martinccalder@aol.com

References

Beck, F. (1992) *Risk Society: Towards a New Modernity*. London: Sage Publications.

Bridge Consultancy (2000) *Two Stage Risk Assessment*. Manchester: Training Course handout.

Brearley, C.P. (1982) *Risk and Social Work: Hazards and Helping*. London: Routledge and Kegan Paul.

Buchanan, A. (1999) Risk and Dangerousness. *Psychological Medicine*, 29, 465–73.

Calder, M.C. (1995) Child Protection: Balancing Paternalism and Partnership. *British Journal of Social Work*, 25: 6, 749–66.

Calder, M.C. (1997) *Juveniles and Children who Sexually Abuse: A Guide to Risk Assessment*. Lyme Regis: Russell House Publishing.

Calder, M.C. (1999a) *Assessing Risk in Adult Male Sex Offenders: A Practitioner's Guide*. Lyme Regis: Russell House Publishing.

Calder, M.C. (1999b) Towards Anti-oppressive Practice with Ethnic Minority Groups. In Calder, M.C. and Horwath, J. (Eds.) *Working for Children on the Child Protection Register: An Inter-agency Practice Guide*, 177–209. Aldershot: Ashgate.

Calder, M.C. (2000) *Complete Guide to Sexual Abuse Assessments*. Lyme Regis: Russell House Publishing.

Calder, M.C. (2001) *Juveniles and Children who Sexually Abuse: Frameworks for Assessment*, 2nd edn. Lyme Regis: Russell House Publishing.

Calder, M.C. (2002) A Framework for Conducting Risk Assessment. *Child Care in Practice* 8: 1, 1–18.

Calder, M.C. (2003a) *RASSAMM*. Leigh: Calder Consultancy.

Calder, M.C. (2003b) The Internet: Problems, Potential and Pathways to Hands-on Sexual Offending. In Calder, M.C. (Ed.) (in press) *Child Sexual Abuse and the Internet: Tackling the New Frontier*. Lyme Regis: Russell House Publishing.

Calder, M.C. (2003c) Unborn Children: A Framework for Assessment and Intervention. In Calder, M.C. and Hackett, S. (Eds.) *Assessment in Childcare: Using and Developing Frameworks for Practice*. Lyme Regis: Russell House Publishing.

Calder, M.C. (2003d) Child Protection Conferences: A Framework for Chairperson Preparation. *Child Care in Practice*, 9, 1.

Calder, M.C. (2003e) The Assessment Framework: A Critique and Reformulation. In Calder, M.C. and Hackett, S. (Eds.) *Assessment in Child Care: Using and Developing Frameworks for Practice*. Lyme Regis: Russell House Publishing.

Calder, M.C. (2007) *The Carrot or the Stick? Encouraging more Effective Practice with Involuntary Clients*. Lyme Regis: Russell House Publishing.

Calder, M.C. (2004a) *Children Living with Domestic Violence: Empirically-grounded Frameworks for Intervention*. Lyme Regis: Russell House Publishing.

Calder, M.C. (2004b) *Out of the Frying Pan and into the Fire: A Critical Analysis of the Integrated Children's System*. Submitted for publication.

Calder, M.C. and Hackett, S. (forthcoming) *Actuarial Risk Tools: A Critical Analysis*.

Calder, M.C. and Peake, A. (2003) Alcohol Misusing Parents and Compromised Child Care: A Framework for Assessment and Intervention. In Calder, M.C. and Hackett, S. (Eds.) *Assessment in Childcare: Using and Developing Frameworks for Practice*. Lyme Regis: Russell House Publishing.

Carson, D. (1994) Dangerous People: Through a Broader Concept of 'Risk' and 'Danger' to Better Decisions. *Expert Evidence* 3: 2, 21–69.

Cash, S.J. (2001) Risk Assessment and Child Welfare: The Art and Science. *Children and Youth Services Review*, 23: 11, 811–30.

Cleaver, H., Wattam, C. and Cawson, P. (1998) *Assessing Risk in Child Protection*. London: NSPCC.

DoH (1988) *Protecting Children: A Guide for Social Workers undertaking a Comprehensive Assessment*. London: HMSO.

DoH (1991) *Working Together under the Children Act 1989: A Guide to Arrangements for Inter-agency Co-operation for the Protection of Children from Abuse*. London: HMSO.

DoH (1995) *Child Protection: Messages from Research*. London: HMSO.

DoH (1999) *Working Together to Safeguard Children: A Guide to Inter-agency Working Arrangements to Safeguard and Promote the Welfare of Children*. London: HMSO.

DoH (2000) *Framework for the Assessment of Children in Need and their Families*. London: HMSO.

DoH (2002) *Integrated Children's System: Working with Children in Need and their Families*. Consultation Document. London: The Stationery Office.

Grove, W. and Meehl, P. (1996) Comparative Efficiency of Informal (Subjective,

Impressionistic) and Formal (Mathematical, Algorithmic) Prediction Procedures: The Clinical-statistical Controversy. *Psychology, Public Policy and Law*, 12, 293–323.

Hackett, S. (2007) Engaging Men in Child Protection Work. In Calder, M.C. (Ed.) *Encouraging more Effective Practice with Involuntary Clients*. Lyme Regis: Russell House Publishing.

Hammond, K.R. (1996) *Human Judgement and Social Policy: Irreducible Uncertainty, Inevitable Error, Unavoidable Injustice*. New York: Oxford University Press.

Hammond, K.R. et al. (1987) Direct Comparison of the Efficacy of Intuitive and Analytical Cognition in Expert Judgement. IEEE Transactions on Systems, Man, and Cybernetics. *SMC.17*: 5, 753–70.

Hanson, R.K. (1998) *Using Research to Improve Sex Offender Risk Assessment*. Keynote presentation to the NOTA National Conference, University of Glasgow, September 17th, 1998.

Hanson, R.K. and Harris, A. (2000) *The Sex Offender Need Assessment Rating (SONAR): A Method for Measuring Change in Risk Levels*. Ontario: Department of the Solicitor General of Canada.

Hollows, A. (2003a) *Beyond Actuarial Risk Assessment: The Continuing Role of Professional Judgement*. Presentation to a one-day national conference, 'Risk Assessment: Developing and Enhancing Evidence-based Practice'. TUC Congress Centre, London, 6th February 2003.

Hollows, A. (2003b) Making Professional Judgements in the Framework for the Assessment of Children in Need and their Families. In Calder, M.C. and Hackett, S. (Eds.) *Assessment in Childcare: Using and Developing Frameworks for Practice*. Lyme Regis: Russell House Publishing.

Jones, S. and Joss, R. (1995) Models of Professionalism. In Yelloly, M. and Henkel, M. (Eds.) *Learning and Teaching in Social Work*. London: Jessica Kingsley.

Kemshall, H. (2001) Risk Assessment and Management of Known Sexual and Violent Offenders: A Review of Current Issues. *Police Research Series*, Paper 140. London: The Home Office.

Kennington, R. (2003) Assessing Men who Sexually Abuse. Presentation to a one-day national conference, 'Risk Assessment: Developing and Enhancing Evidence-based Practice', TUC Congress Centre, London, 6th February 2003.

Macdonald, K. and Macdonald, G. (1999) Perceptions of Risk. In Parsloe, P. (Ed.) *Risk Assessment in Social Work and Social Care*, 17–52. London: Jessica Kingsley.

Munro, E. (2002) *Effective Child Protection*. Thousand Oaks, CA: Sage Publications.

Parton, N. (1996) Social Work, Risk and the Blaming System. In Parton, N. (Ed.) *Social Theory, Social Change and Social Work*. London: Routledge.

Parton, N. and Small, N. (1989) Violence, Social Work and the Emergence of Dangerousness. In Langan, M. and Lee, P. (Eds.) *Radical Social Work Today*. London: Unwin Hyman.

Quinsey, V.L., Rice, M.E. and Harris, G.T. (1995) Actuarial Prediction of Sexual Recidivism. *Journal of Interpersonal Violence*, 10: 1, 85–105.

Reder, P. and Duncan, S. (1999) *Lost Innocents: A Follow-up Study of Fatal Child Abuse*. London: Routledge.

Turnell, A. and Edwards, S. (1999) *Signs of Safety: A Solution and Safety Oriented Approach to Child Protection Carework*. New York: WW Norton.

Utting, W. (1997) *People Like Us: Summary Report of the Review of Safeguards for Children Living away from Home*. London: HMSO.

Walker, S. and Beckett, C. (2003) *Social Work Assessment and Intervention*. Lyme Regis: Russell House Publishing (in press).

Youll, P. and Walker, C. (1995) Great Expectations? Personal, Professional and Institutional Agendas in Advanced Training. In Yellolly, M. and Henkel, M. (Eds.) *Learning and Teaching in Social Work: Towards Reflective Practice*. London: Jessica Kingsley.

CHAPTER 13

The Three Houses Tool: Building Safety and Positive Change

Nicki Weld

Introduction

The Three Houses model is an information gathering tool that supports risk assessment by providing a thorough exploration of a person's situation. It was developed from the concepts of Te Whare Tapa Wha – a Maori model of health (Professor Mason Durie), resilience theory and solution-focused theory (Steve De Shazer and Insoo Kim Berg), and the book *Signs of Safety* (Andrew Turnell and Steve Edwards). It was created in New Zealand in 2003 and tested within the statutory child protection setting, as part of a wider strengths-based practice initiative.

The Three Houses tool is portrayed by a graphic of three houses that individually represent vulnerabilities, strengths, or hopes and dreams. A house was chosen, as it tends to be a widely recognised symbol and is a useful metaphor when talking with people about their lives. The tool includes a pathway that outlines the intervention steps required to achieve the described goals. It can be applied with a child/young person, their parents/carers, wider family, and also the worker. The Three Houses works from a systems perspective that recognises the interdependent nature of all those involved in a person's world and aims to bring this information together to build solutions and interventions.

The Three Houses has been used successfully in a variety of situations within child care and protection, including initial investigations, court reports for children in care, Family Group Conferences, team building, and one-to-one plans for young people in residential settings. It has now been used overseas including in Sweden, where it was found to enhance information gathering and intervention planning. The following chapter will provide an overview of the tool's principles, a practical description of its application with young people, parents/carers, and children within the context of child protection, and discuss its use as a reflective tool for workers, and in a family group conferencing setting.

Principles

To use the Three Houses tool requires a philosophy or belief that people are capable of growth and change. It requires a strengths-based practice approach to people that focuses both on strengths that build toward safety and also on vulnerabilities that lead to increased danger and harm. It does not deny the existence of problems, but instead includes them in the overall picture of a person's situation. Therefore, risk is viewed on a continuum from safety through to harm (Turnell and Edwards, 2000), and explored with the added component of hopes and dreams to help bring about internally and externally supported change.

Vulnerabilities include all aspects inside and around a person and their family that make them more at risk of danger and harm. These can be psychological, social, and environmental, and are framed from the individual's and others views and perspectives. The word 'vulnerability' is used to cover factors that can cause instability and lead to an increased risk of danger or harm. Most people carry internal vulnerabilities from earlier life experiences that can then become evident at different times in their lives. Rather than trying to eliminate or deny the existence of these, we need to find ways that build safety and strength around them.

Strengths include personal attributes, values, beliefs, characteristics, attitudes, protective factors, and other factors that can be used in a positive way to contribute to change and build safety. They are not necessarily 'fixed' attributes, and discussion should be held to determine when and where they are effective and how they can be helped to become more so. They are essentially a pool of resources to help build safety and strengths against any vulnerabilities that may be present, and discussion of them helps validate the potential for change. Strengths are seen to contribute to both increased safety and protective factors, and also as building material for the realisation of hopes, dreams and goals. Viewed in this way, strengths are identified in terms of purpose, rather than a possible 'feel good' exercise that can lack meaning.

Exploring hopes, dreams, and goals provides an opportunity to help people express their aspirations for their lives and their family. It creates a sense of potential and possibility that life can be different by building a future picture of how things could be. It allows the worker and the person to see and hear beyond the presenting problems, therefore providing a possible alternative reality to the one currently being experienced. The exploration of this enables goal setting as ways are sought to achieve the hopes and dreams that have been identified. Strengths, as mentioned, are the building material toward the achievement of these goals, while vulnerabilities are recognised as possible threats to them. By enquiring about hopes and dreams, workers suggest the possibility of things being different, and a belief that this can happen. Ideally, the hopes and dreams should also contribute to increased safety and the worker is required to make connections to this if they are not obvious.

The pathway is literally just that; a pathway that connects the houses to the future picture and builds steps toward this. The pathway needs to be concrete and measurable with specific steps and tasks that each person will undertake. People's capacity, confidence and willingness should be checked out for each step or task that they undertake. (Turnell and Edwards, 1999). It is important to set goals that people can achieve, to help build their confidence in the plan. Therefore, goals should be made of small, achievable, measurable steps, so that change and progress can be noticed and reinforced.

Overall, the Three Houses is designed to help view a person's situation from a range of perspectives that recognise people as holistic beings connected to others and living within a family and community. These include internal and external factors that contribute to increasing safety or danger or harm. The tool requires the skilful use of questioning, and an appreciation of solution-focused thinking and strengths-based practice that help separate people from their problems and behaviours. The tool is designed to build independence through the recognition and strengthening of existing resources, which are then supported externally where required. Finally, the Three Houses tool is designed to encourage transparency and inclusiveness from workers when working with children, young people, and their families.

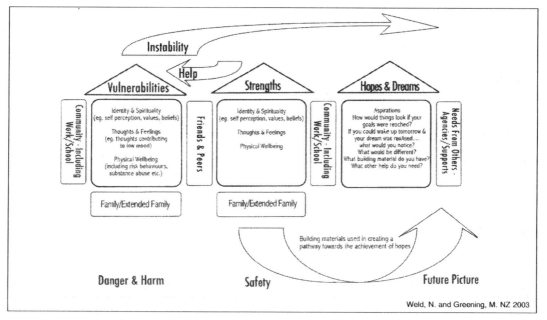

Figure 13.1   The Three Houses© Model. A tool for gathering information

Application: young people, carers/parents/children

The Three Houses tool, as illustrated above, can be completed in any order and there should be an open discussion as to why the worker has chosen to use it, and for what purposes the information will be used. It is designed to be completed with people, with the purpose of having their views heard and understood about what is happening for them, and also for workers where appropriate, to contribute their thoughts on the situation. The worker's main role is to help facilitate the completion of the tool, and this can be done with drawing, words or any other media that may be helpful.

1. Young people/parents/carers

The first house – vulnerabilities

Inside the house of vulnerabilities the first component is spirituality or identity. It looks at how a person describes their self and how they think others might see them, and is intended to highlight negative or unhelpful self-perceptions that contribute to harmful or dangerous behaviour. An example of this might be a young person who describes himself as 'useless'. This may be a label he has chosen for himself or one that has been given to him. By having an internal belief or identity such as 'useless' may cause him to partake in risk taking activities based on a 'because I am useless I don't care what happens to me' attitude. Vulnerability around identity might be specific to a key role, such as a being a parent, and how the person sees their self in relation to this.

These perceptions of identity are critical for workers to understand, as they can form the centre of a person's vulnerabilities. When a social worker completed the Three Houses with two brothers who were in long term foster care for a routine court report, they revealed that they hated being known as 'CYF (Child Youth and Family, New Zealand's Statutory Child Protection agency) kids'. The worker then took steps for their foster parents to have guardianship so they would no longer be in the custody of CYF and be required to have this label as part of their identity.

The next internal component refers to any thoughts and feelings that the person experiences that increase their risk of harm or danger. If we

take the example of the young person who believes he is useless, he may then describe thoughts or feelings such as sad, angry, dumb, or a 'waste of space'. These thoughts and/or feelings might relate to certain situations such as when they are at school or at home which affects the person's mood or behaviour. It is important that the worker makes these links and thus identifies situations when the vulnerable thoughts and feelings most often occur. Also here, learning disabilities and low self-esteem should be mentioned, as they could lead to reactionary behaviour that increases harm for the person or others.

The last component refers to physical well being, and includes sexual health, personal care, and any behaviour that affects the person's physical safety in a negative way. Information around substance abuse and at-risk behaviours such as deliberate self-harming should be included here. The worker can add their view of what has been observed should the person be unable or unwilling to name certain issues.

Moving to the outside of the first house, external vulnerabilities are examined, beginning with the family. Aspects within the person's family that increase the risk of danger and harm need to be included here. This could be the family using the person in an objectified way, responding negatively to the person, or a sanctioning of illegal or dangerous behaviour. For a young person this might be a family that has a reference group of people who frequently stay in the house and abuse alcohol. The young person may have disrupted sleep due to late night parties and exposure to family violence and substance abuse. It might be that the family may be absent, or unwilling to be involved in the person's world. Again, worker and other people's perceptions can be included after the person has first described what they perceive as vulnerabilities from their perspective.

The next area looks at friends and peers and how their behaviour might contribute to increasing the person's vulnerability to danger and harm. Again, this looks at particular behaviours and influences this group has with the person and looks at activities they are engaged in that increase danger and harm. It identifies any messages that peers give the person that do not keep them safe from danger and harm. This could include friends that encourage a young person to drink, take drugs or engage in reckless behaviour such as high speed driving.

The final component addresses community, work or school. It may highlight a lack of these elements in a person's life or community environments that are not helpful or positive due to dynamics such as bullying, learning disability, or unemployment. It is important that the person names any vulnerabilities in their own language, and that the worker suspends judgment to explore how these factors are not currently assisting the young person or adult.

The second house – strengths

Within the second house is a description of internal strengths. The same process is followed, beginning with spirituality or identity. The emphasis is on any spirituality or identity that is positive and helps the person to be safe from harm. It again draws out self-perception and focuses on core issues using key questions such as 'How would you describe yourself to someone who had never met you?' 'What are some good things people who care about you might say about you?' It is also important to draw out role identities that can be built on, such as a being a good brother, or a caring mother.

The second area gathers information about thoughts and feelings that are positive and helps the person to feel good in their everyday life. This is about self-messages and again the worker should draw out specific situations when these occur. The worker also has an opportunity here to add their perceptions and give specific examples of these to make them more real to the person. For example, instead of saying 'You are great with your little brother', they might say 'When I see the way you listen and pay attention to what your little brother says by repeating his words and acknowledging his feelings, I think you do a great job at helping him feel heard'.

The third component looks at how the person cares for themselves physically and aims to find exceptions if the person is engaged in harmful activities such as drug or alcohol abuse, identifying as well when these behaviours are not present. A discussion of basic self-care can be addressed and named if the person is achieving these, such as personal hygiene, or good sexual health practices when talking with sexually active young people.

Outside the second house the worker again begins with the family but this time about the strengths that they offer to the person. These should relate to keeping the person safe, although it is important to note that strengths may not yet offer protection (McPherson and MacNamara, 1997). An example of this might be that the mother of a 10-year-old girl phones her from work to make sure she got home safely from school, but the girl is left alone until 7 p.m. until her mother gets home. The worker also needs to reflect on the strengths they perceive in the person's family and accord these to specific individuals if need be.

The next component looks at strengths that contribute to safety from the direction of the person's friends. Again, detail needs to be drawn out and then ascertained as to what individuals specifically do to contribute to safety. Intimate relationships may be named here, and it is important that the worker be non-judgemental around these, focusing instead on what they offer in terms of safety. It is most important that the person's perception is recorded as it is their information that is being gathered.

The final area again looks at community, school and work, but this time looks at the safety that these environments bring, for example positive role models, a sense of stability, and a sense of contribution to society. It is important to get specific information about what it is these environments offer. Simple aspects such as the school giving the person a structure and context to their day can be drawn out or listed under the worker's view.

The third house – hopes, dreams, goals

For a young person or adult, this is the house or home they would wish to have or live in, actually or metaphorically, the type of person they would wish to be, and the place where their goals can occur. The emphasis is on where they would like to be, what they would like to be different in both themselves and their world. It asks simple questions beginning with the miracle question:

1. If you could wake up tomorrow and be the sort of person you would really like to be, how would you know you were different? How would you feel, what would you think? What would have changed?

Followed by:

2. How would other people know you were different? What would they see that would tell them this? Ask them to write or draw all these ideas inside the third house.

3. If you could change three things around you, what would you change? How would you know things were different around you? What would you notice had changed?
4. What would others say about your world that they would notice as different? Ask them to write or draw all these ideas around the third house.
5. Look at their picture together and then ask them to:

- Reflect on the second house (strengths) to see what building material they have available to build the third house.
- Refer to the first house (vulnerabilities) to look at what might make the third house unstable and how the second house could help with strengthening this.

Finally ask them: 'What other help do you need to build this house?' and add these ideas around the blank area of the third house. These will include agencies, programmes, therapy, behaviour strategies, people, mentors, and protective factors that will keep the house strong. The pathway to building the House of Hopes and Dreams can then begin to be detailed, using the House of Strengths as possible building blocks and keeping awareness around vulnerabilities that can threaten the achievement of goals and aspirations. The pathway is then further developed with the parent/caregiver, worker, and other agencies' information.

It is, of course, possible for people to identify goals or hopes and dreams that are harmful or counterproductive. The worker needs to explore what these goals represent and help find ways that these objectives could be achieved that would not create danger or harm to the individual or others. An example of this might be a young person whose dream is to be part of a gang that is engaged with criminal behaviour. Further exploration of this particular goal then reveals the young person wants a group to belong to and people who will stand by them and support them. By stating these as the goals, the worker can help the young person identify alternatives to joining a gang, that could meet these hopes.

2. Children

The application of the Three Houses model changes in relation to children under the age of

eight, with the concepts being simplified to be contained in one house while the emphasis remains on gathering their information and story. The concepts still remain the same but are more concrete. The worker needs to take into account developmental abilities; generally most children around six years of age and upwards can draw a simple house, and a check will ensure that the concept of a house is one they can grasp.

When using the Three Houses as a children's tool, the worker begins by asking the child to draw their house. It is important the worker be mindful of basic engagement skills such as appropriate language, positive tone, getting down on the child's level, and expressing interest and enthusiasm in the child, while continuing to remain natural and congruent.

Once the child has drawn their house, the worker invites them to say who lives in their house and to draw these people inside the house. While the child is drawing, the worker asks general questions about the people being described; are they a boy or girl, how old are they? (This may be harder for younger children to answer.) Are there any pets that live in the house?

The worker then asks the child to talk about some of the things they like doing in the house. This is about activities and interests, keeps the focus general and is easy to answer, which helps promote early confidence and gives the child a sense of being the expert. The worker can ask who they do these activities with, and also about who visits the house, including friends, in order to gain a sense of who else might be in the child's world.

Either by this natural progression or as a new question, the worker then asks the child if they could draw some of the things that they do outside of their house. These cover the child's wider world, including extended family, school, sports, clubs etc. General questions such as 'What do you like to do at school, who do you go to visit, what friends do you play with at school, or outside of school?' helps the worker understand what happens outside of the home. Open questions should be used, followed by more probing questions which builds on the child's information to develop the overall picture.

The worker and child then look over the child's house together, and the worker discusses the picture, checking with the child that they have got the correct information. This demonstrates that the worker has heard the child's information, and provides an opportunity for details to be clarified although, again, developmental aspects need to be considered when doing this.

The worker then asks the child about what things in the picture, inside the house, make them feel happy or good, and gets the child to draw yellow suns or smiley faces by these things. Another option here is to use a set of smiley face or facial expression stickers that can be placed on the picture by the child. These can be about people, pets, behaviour or activities in their lives. The worker repeats this exercise for things outside of the house.

The worker explains that sometimes things happen in and outside our houses that can make us feel sad, and asks the child if there are any things that make them feel sad at home or outside of home. If the worker is not a experienced evidential interviewer it is important that if the child discloses new abuse at this stage, that they affirm the child's feelings and explain that they will need to talk to another person about these things, someone who has a special job of helping children who have these types of sadness. Otherwise, the worker can ask the child to draw small clouds or sad faces next to the people or activities. Again, sad or frown face stickers can be used. If the child becomes sad at this point, the worker needs to affirm their feelings and be supportive.

If sadness has been named, the worker then asks the child, referring to the suns or smiley faces, if any of these things help with the sad faces or clouds. This gives the worker an idea of what strengths might be used in the future to help the child. The worker can also ask whether there is anything the child would like to be different in their house and world, and helps the child to illustrate these.

The worker then comments positively on the work the child has done in drawing their house, asking if there is anything else in the picture that the child feels is missing, as in: 'You have done such a great job of drawing your house and all the things around your house for me, I just wondered if there was anything else you felt you wanted to have in the picture?' This is an opportunity for the child to add anything extra they would like, and for the worker to ask open questions around this.

By the end of the application of the Three Houses tool in relation to a child, the worker should have a good sense of the child's home and wider world. The information has been gathered in a way that is non-threatening and is led by the child. The picture is saved as a contributing factor in the overall set of information gathered.

The worker

The Three Houses tool recognises the worker as contributing to a family situation, as it is likely they will bring their own thoughts, feelings, and experiences with them when they engage with families. In fact, it is these very things that can help the family to build safety and reduce danger and harm. The Three Houses model requires that time is taken for the worker to name these thoughts and feelings while working with a family. It is most effective for the worker to complete their part of the Three Houses tool with a supervisor, either as a case analysis or a self-reflective tool. As a case analysis tool, the Three Houses provides an ideal way to succinctly present information to a supervisor to enable both parties to reflect on what is happening. As a self-reflective tool, the worker applies the Three Houses to themselves, providing an opportunity to reflect on what qualities or insight they are bringing to the situation and what their hopes and aspirations for a child, young person and family are.

It is important that workers identify and address any beliefs and values they hold which could inadvertently contribute to a picture of increasing risk of danger and harm for this family. An example of this might be a worker who, from their own personal experiences, believes domestic violence only involves hitting, and therefore discounts emotional violence. It is critical that the worker reflects on the type of maltreatment and the parental behaviour that is present, and examines what beliefs and values they personally hold that could unwittingly increase the risk of danger and harm.

It is also essential, when trying to reduce danger and harm for a child or young person, that professional and/or inter-agency relationships are examined to ensure they are not creating difficulties or failing to increase safety. These might be due to conflict, closed professional views, or a lack of trust in others' competency. If this situation results in a lack of sharing of information or work being done in isolation of key knowledge, services can become fragmented and increased risks to the child not communicated to other professionals. Strong professional and inter-agency relationships will also provide an external support structure to an individual worker, and also identify possible resources for the family. The use of the Three Houses as a reflective tool is effective in identifying possible areas of professionally dangerousness behaviour, while recognising strengths that can help reduce worker isolation and build inter-agency communication and collaboration.

Family group conference or family meeting

On completion of the tool with each person involved, the information gathered can be collated to begin building toward an intervention plan. It is useful to do this in a family group conference or family meeting either by doing the Three Houses for the first time or bringing previously completed houses together. If Three Houses has been used previously, it is best to summarise the concerns which have led to everyone being present. It can then be useful to discuss the hopes and dreams of all those involved. From there strengths can be identified followed by vulnerabilities, as it will increase the confidence of people to share vulnerabilities if their strengths have already been named. The pathway is then built, with everyone's input, in deciding who will do what, with what type of support, this building on their strengths and managing their vulnerabilities to help get them to the new house they want to have and with increased safety in their lives.

Alternatively, the Three Houses tool can be used as a means to structure a meeting or family group conference, as it is important to gather the wider family perspective on the situation. The Three Houses tool, therefore, creates an opportunity for other family members and professionals to contribute their views, by using an approach that moves away from what can sometimes feel like question and answer sessions led by the agency. Discussing both strengths and vulnerabilities within a family can help move the situation from a place of blame to an honest discussion of both resources and impacts to building safety. The use of the pathway helps the family to identify achievable, measurable action

steps that can start an immediate progression toward the family's goals and hopes and dreams.

Using the Three Houses tool to structure family meetings or conferences also enables the professionals present to contribute their thoughts and in particular their hopes, and dreams for the family. They can clarify what they have to offer to achieving the identified goals and action steps. By the end of this process, everyone will have a clear understanding of the tasks and resources, either present or required, to support the completion of these goals. This makes it easier to review tasks and measure what progress is being made around intervention plans. It is also important to set a review date when people can come back together to share and assess changes that have occurred.

Conclusion

The Three Houses tool considers risk from a continuum perspective that identifies factors that contribute to danger and harm, and also those that contribute to building safety. The tool then takes these elements further by exploring and developing a future picture in creating a series of goals that can be worked toward and thus increase safety. The model is designed to build rapport and create a process of 'doing with' as opposed to 'doing to' or 'for'. It is holistic and systemic in nature, and reduces the need to constantly go back asking for further information. It is designed to support a sense of unity in complex situations by creating common goals, and does not dismiss any person's view, including that of professionals.

The Three Houses can be used in any order and it requires workers who are able to ask skilful questions that builds on the information received. It contributes to an intervention plan by ensuring these plans are uniquely tailored to those involved and are broken down into achievable steps that utilise existing resources and strengths while recognising potential threats or risks. As a self-reflective tool it enables workers to examine their own responses and issues around a particular individual or family. Finally, the Three Houses is designed to promote honest and free discussion that supports workers to gain understanding and insight of those they are working with.

References

Durie, M. (1998) *Whai ora, Maori Health Development.* Auckland: Oxford University Press.

De Shazer, S. (1985) *Keys to Solution in Brief Therapy.* New York: WW Norton and Co.

McPherson, L., MacNamara, N. and Hemsworth, C. (1997) A Model for Multi-disciplinary Collaboration in Child Protection. *Children Australia,* 22: 1, 21–8.

Turnell, A. and Edwards, S. (1999) *Signs of Safety: A Solution and Safety Oriented Approach to Child Protection Casework.* New York: WW Norton and Co.

Weld, N. and Greening, M. (2004) The Three Houses. *Social Work Now,* 29 Dec. New Zealand.

CHAPTER 14

Risk Assessment in Adult Sex Offenders

Roger Kennington

Introduction

It has long been argued that unstructured clinical assessment is no better than chance when clinicians are trying to predict recidivism of sex offenders (Hanson and Bussiere, 1998). There are many reasons for this. Clinicians may be influenced by their own experiences and generalise those experiences into other situations. Clinicians have been observed to dogmatically adhere to a specific theoretical perspective or value base (Butler-Schloss, 1988). The relationship between the client and clinician may influence judgement. For example, the 'rule of optimism' was observed by Blom-Cooper (1987). This may be a particular issue when the relationship has been therapeutic, and the therapist has a vested interest in observing improvements in the client (Salter, 1997). In addition, some sub-sets of clients, such as psychopaths, may be particularly adept at manipulating risk assessors or managers into making judgements which are subsequently seen to be unwise (Hare, 1994). Some practitioners have been poorly supervised, been allowed to rely on their own supposed expertise and made judgements which have been in defiance of the evidence, sometimes with tragic consequences (Aberdeen City Council, 1998).

For all these reasons, researchers and practitioners have sought for an evidence base to guide risk assessment and risk management. This chapter is a practical guide to how that evidence may be used. Readers desiring more rigorous statistical analysis of the evidence are referred to Doren (2002). Those wishing to utilise any of the measures described here in their own practice must first become qualified in their use. It is outside the scope of this chapter to describe how a particular measurement system will apply in a given case. Furthermore, judgements will always need to be applied 'in situ', particularly in relation to supposedly 'low risk' cases. The question will always remain: 'when is low risk low enough?' Indeed, the authors of one particular instrument (Risk Matrix, 2000 incorporated into Mann et al., 2002) stress that it

is not designed for use in situations where offenders who score low risk on that measure are being considered for rehabilitation into families where children live.

Different risk thresholds apply in child protection proceedings than in Multi-Agency Public Protection Panels who consider the management of convicted sex offenders, among others. In the former, the test is whether a child is 'likely to suffer significant harm', with likely being defined as 'a real risk that it is not sensible to ignore given the feared harm in a given case' (See the case of Re H in All England Law Reports, 1996). With MAPPP, the test is whether the offender presents a 'significant risk of serious harm' (National Probation Directorate, 2003). In care proceedings, the onus of proof is on Local Authorities to prove their case, against parents. However, we know the old adage that 'absence of evidence is not evidence of absence' (of risk). The precautionary principle will need to be taken into account when making recommendations with workers also needing to bear in mind that they must act within the constraints of human rights legislation.

External protective factors will also need to be taken into account when a given situation is considered. For instance, this author is commonly involved in cases where a partner's ability to protect her child from perceived risk may be considered.

In all cases the widest possible range of sources of evidence should be used including:

- Case records (contemporary and historical, including, wherever possible, victim statements).
- Interviews or other verbal self report such as in group work.
- Observations of others in as many contexts as possible.
- Psychometric testing where available.
- Psycho-physiological testing such as the penile plesythmograph, visual reaction time assessment and polygraph measures where relevant and available.

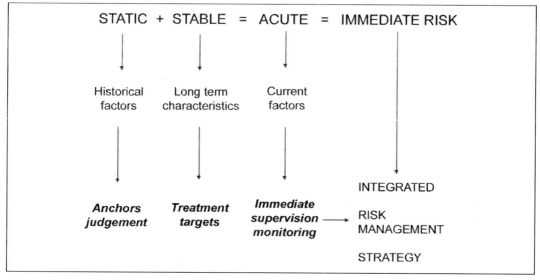

Figure 14.1 Components of risk

A framework which this author and colleagues have found helpful has involved the conceptualisation of risk factors as static, dynamic stable and acute after the work of Hanson and Harris (2000). The role of these factors has been drawn into a framework by this author and colleague Professor Don Grubin at the Sexual Behaviour Unit in Newcastle (see Figure 14.1). Each of the types of risk factors will be analysed below, but in summary they are as follows.

Static factors

These are historical factors, which cannot change. They can be subjected to statistical or 'actuarial' calculations to give a baseline risk level. Quinsey et al. (1995) argued that these factors should be used to 'anchor judgement'. They give an estimate of the probability of an occurrence **in a group of people** (in this case, recidivism in a group of sex offenders). An analogy in relation to heart disease would be that a known family history of heart disease will increase the probability of an individual suffering from the same disease.

Dynamic stable factors

As is implicit in the name, dynamic risk factors may change (for the better, which may decrease the immediate risk level, or for the worse which may increase it). Stable factors in relation to sex

offenders are those personality factors which may change, but slowly and often with the need for help from an outside source. As will be illustrated later they tend to be the factors which are targeted in sex offender treatment programmes. An analogy relating to heart disease would be obesity or high blood pressure.

Dynamic acute factors

These are factors that may change rapidly and signal an imminent return to abusive behaviour. These changes are likely to be observed by people (not necessarily professionals) who observe abusers in their everyday lives. Dynamic Acute factors should inform decisions about immediate levels of monitoring, surveillance and support. Again, an analogy with heart disease would be risk behaviours such as smoking or stressful activity.

Static factors: their role in the assessment and management of men who sexually abuse

Quinsey, Rice and Harris (1995) reported factors which they had found correlated with increased risk in known adult male sexual offenders. These factors were offence type (rapists being more risky than 'child molesters'), psychopathy (it is arguable as to whether this is a static factor), measures of general criminality and psycho-physiological measures of deviant sexual interest pre-treatment.

Thornton and Fisher (1994) published the Thornton Fisher Algorithm in which offenders were classified as low – high risk plus, based on points scored for the following factors: any sex offence conviction, four plus convictions of any kind, convictions for non-sexual violence and convictions against three or more victims.

Numerous scales have since been developed, most of which have a point scoring system with more points indicating an increased probability of recidivism within groups of offenders over a given follow-up period. It is important for assessors to know what the definition of recidivism is for the particular risk scale that is being used. For example, Hanson (1997) measures recidivism defined as further conviction or charge over five and ten year follow-up periods, whilst Thornton (2000) measures reconviction over a 20 year follow-up period. Note that actuarial assessment identifies the probability of recidivism over a given time period. Is does not predict what offence may be committed nor at what point of the follow-up period the offence may occur.

Most actuarial scales score points for combinations of the following factors:

- Sexual offence convictions or charges, with some counting the index offence and some not. Offences which do not appear as sexual convictions but which have a sexual

connotation would usually count (e.g. burglary where the intention was to commit a sexual offence).
- General offending with some scales separating out non-sexual violence.
- Non-contact offences.
- Offences against stranger or unrelated victims – definitions vary in different scales.
- Offences against a male, whether this be the only sex offence type committed or the offender has offended against males and females.
- Not having had a long-term relationship – not usually scored for younger offenders.
- Younger age.

Scales classify offenders into groups based on the number of points scored. The most commonly used system in the UK is called Risk Matrix 2000 (Thornton, 2000). Offenders are initially allocated into groups defined as low, medium, high and very high based on an initial calculation of points for sex offence convictions, general offending and age. Consideration is then given to whether the following factors are relevant in the given case: male victim; stranger victim; non-contact offence; and not having had a long term relationship. If two of these factors exist the risk level is moved up by one. If four factors exist it is moved up by two.

Risk Matrix 2000 was based on a sample of prisoners released from English prisons in 1979. In that sample the approximate number of offenders reconvicted in each group over a 20 year follow-up period was as illustrated in Figure 14.2

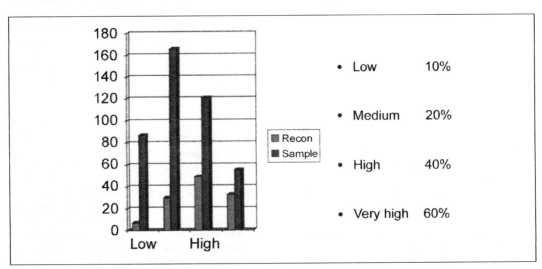

Figure 14.2 Risk Matrix 2000: approximate reconviction rates with proportions of offenders in each risk category

When such an exercise is undertaken on a subsequent sample it is not usual for correlations to be as good as in the original sample. It is therefore important for practitioners to know how accurate the predictions are for a given scale. This is most commonly assessed using a measure called the Receiver Operating Characteristics – Area Under the Curve (AUC). This is a graph of times that high risk offenders are accurately predicted to recidivate against 'false positives' (when such an offender does not recidivate). An AUC of 0.5 is no better than chance (i.e. a 50/50 chance of being right) and an AUC of 1.0 represents 100 per cent accuracy. The AUC for most actuarial scales is between 0.7 and 0.8 (Thornton, 2006).

An AUC of .75 means that when comparing a random selection of individuals from a group of recidivists and comparing these with individuals from a group of non-recidivists, the recidivists will have a higher actuarial risk score than the non-recidivists 75 per cent of the time.

In essence, then, an actuarial assessment of static factors gives the practitioner an estimate ('X' per cent, give or take a few) of the **proportion** of men, who score the same number of points as the man being assessed, who will be known to recidivate over a given follow-up period.

The *Manual for Risk Matrix 2000* warns against relying on this tool in the assessment of offenders in 'low risk' groups being (re)located in 'high risk' situations such as families or schools. Certainly 'low risk' in this context would certainly be a 'real risk that is not sensible to ignore' as described above.

Dynamic stable factors: their role in the assessment and management of men who sexually abuse

Models describing personality factors which correlate with risk in known sex offenders have been proposed since the early 1980s with researchers tending to identify similar issues. However, these are not always defined in the same way in different models, and certainly not sufficiently consistently defined to be measured. It is argued that if the offender displays a wide range of these factors, any risk will be higher. Similarly, if these factors can be changed or managed by treatment, risk will decrease or at least be better managed.

A familiar model presented by David Finkelhor (1986) describes what has been adapted by

practitioners as a 'pathway to abuse', and comprises four factors. These are: the motivation to abuse; factors which allow an offender to overcome internal inhibitors such as guilt or fear; strategies that offenders use to 'overcome external inhibitors' by manipulating the environment and; overcoming the child victim's resistance.

Finkelhor identified three motivating factors: arousal to inappropriate stimuli; emotional congruence with children and 'blockage' in legitimate relationships. Arousal to inappropriate stimuli referred to the offender either being aroused to children generally (i.e. children are what 'turns him on') or taking a sexual interest in a particular child because of various emotional and situational factors which prevailed at the time of the offences. Emotional congruence refers to the tendency of some offenders to have their emotional needs met by children in an inappropriate way. Such needs may include the need for intimacy or narcissism or to overcome a sense of powerlessness. Blockage refers to deficits that an offender may have in developing intimate relationships with adults. Such relationships may provoke anxiety or some offenders may not have the social skills or knowledge to interact appropriately.

The factors involved in overcoming internal inhibitors included attitudes and lifestyle management deficits. Attitudes which Finkelhor called 'rationalising cognitions' were prevalent in his samples of offenders. These may include familiar excuses which offenders make such as: 'She came to my bedroom so I thought she had some responsibility' or 'He didn't tell so I thought he didn't mind'. Some more entrenched beliefs might also facilitate offending. An example might be: 'Men had sex with me as a child and it didn't do me any harm'. Lifestyle management issues which Finkelhor identified as facilitating the overcoming of internal inhibitions included reactions to stress and substance misuse. This model is helpful in illustrating that these factors would not present a reason for offending without the motivation existing first.

Another approach which developed in the mid 1980s was to conceptualise these same factors as interacting in cyclical form rather than as a 'pathway' (Wolf, 1988; Ryan et al., 1987; and see Briggs et al., 1998 for a detailed description of the use of the model in practice). Practitioners guide offenders through a cycle helping them to identify the nature of their offending; the feelings which reinforced the desire to offend; 'bad feelings' and thoughts (e.g. guilt and remorse), if any, which may have inhibited offending; justifications (equating to Finkelhor's 'rationalising conditions') which might have allowed the offender to 'push away' those bad thoughts and feelings; thoughts and behaviours involved in anticipating and rehearsing offences (usually involving fantasy and sexual arousal), and then analysing how an offender targeted and groomed victims. This has been described as a 'heuristic' (Grubin in Kennington et al., 2001), rather than a validated model and tends to emphasise issues relating to 'sexual' factors and may de-emphasise 'lifestyle management' issues.

Malamuth et al. (1993) studied samples of rapists. Their findings paralleled those of Finkelhor in that those offenders who were more likely to re-offend were found to have higher degrees of arousal to rape stimuli, displayed attitudes which were supportive of rape and exhibited anti-social traits.

Beech et al. (1998) studied a sample of sex offenders in prison and found that those most likely to reoffend were differentiated on a psychometric classification that they called a measure of 'deviance'. (This is not to be confused with the concept of sexual deviance which is an indicator of how strongly aroused a person is to a deviant stimulus such as having sexual contact with a child.) They again used slightly different terminology in some cases, but found that child abusers who were most likely to offend scored lower on measures of social competence, but higher in relation to cognitive distortions; emotional congruence with children; empathy deficits (mainly measuring how much offenders understand about the effects of their behaviour rather than how they feel about it); and emotional loneliness.

Knight and Prentky (1990) studied samples of sexual offenders and developed 'typologies' of rapists and child sex offenders. In relation to rapists they identified sub-types again on the basis of social competence across five other sub-groups as follows. Opportunistic rapists exhibited a history of poor impulse control and a desire for immediate sexual gratification. One group was motivated by anger which was not generally differentiated between men and women. Their offences were characterised by extreme gratuitous rage. Sexual (non-sadistic) offenders were motivated by a desire for (normal) sex but distorted attitudes and concerns about masculinity led to them having a disregard for issues such as consent. Sadistic offenders displayed

elaborate intertwined erotic and destructive fantasies that was the prime motivator for their offending. Vindictive offenders generally displayed good impulse control but harboured a desire to humiliate women which was acted out in their offending.

More recently, two models have been developed which more rigorously define these concepts and subject them to quantitative assessment. These are the Structured Assessment of Risk and Need (Mann et al., 2002) and STABLE-2005 (Harris, 2005). These two models are configured slightly differently, but in essence cover the same content. As the former is the one currently used in the National Offender Management Service (Prisons and Probation Service) in England and Wales, it is that which is reviewed here. Access to STABLE-2005 is available via the Solicitor General of Canada's website. Again, it is stressed that these are elaborately drawn models with precise definitions and coding rules. Those wishing to use the models in their own practice should ensure that they are properly qualified.

In a precursor model to the SARN called the Structured Risk Assessment, Thornton (1999), clustered a range of factors into four 'domains'. In the SARN these are called Sexual Interest, Distorted Attitudes, Social and Emotional Functioning (i.e. managing relationships), and Self Management. Recent data (Reported by Thornton, 2006) seems to indicate that the SARN is performing with statistical significance in estimating the risk of reoffending.

The Sexual Interest Domain examines how much an offender is preoccupied with sex, and whether he has a sexual preference for rape, sexual contact with children, sexualised violence or other offence related sexual interests such as fetishes (by no means all of which are offence related).

The second domain includes a range of distorted attitudes which may be offence related. Adversarial sexual attitudes refer to the offender wishing to assert 'authority', power or dominance via sexual relationships. Sexual entitlement refers to the belief amongst some men that they are entitled to sex when they want, with whom they want, irrespective of the circumstances or needs and desires of the other person. Child abuse supportive beliefs are beliefs that excuse or promote the sexual abuse of children. A final factor in the distorted attitudes domain is a belief or 'schema' that women are deceitful. This tends to be the way that the offender 'sees the world' and is likely to be generalised to non-sexual situations.

The domain entitled Social and Emotional Functioning comprises 'social, interpersonal, emotional and intimate functioning deficits'. The first factor is inadequacy. The 'central elements of this cluster' include loneliness, self-esteem and an external locus of control (i.e. the person having a sense that they are controlled by external influences not vice versa). The second factor relates to a distorted intimacy balance. This is similar to the concept of 'emotional congruence' with children as described above. In assessments this measure only applies to those who have abused children. Grievance thinking is another feature of this domain and 'involves suspiciousness, anger, grievance, vengefulness and a reluctance or failure to see other people's point of view'. The final factor in this domain is the lack of emotionally intimate relationships with adults.

The final domain relates to Self Management and comprises lifestyle impulsiveness, and the lack of ability to deploy appropriate problem solving skills. This might include the use of substances or anger to 'solve' problems. The final factor in this domain is poor emotional control, involving uncontrolled outbursts of emotion and possibly the suppression of adaptive expressions of emotion.

The SARN is a manualised assessment tool which gives detailed instructions on how each factor is to be defined and rated. Multiple sources of evidence should be used including reference to records, self report through interview and in other settings such as groups, observed behaviour and psychometric testing. Each factor is then rated 0, 1, or 2 on the basis of how prevalent the problem was during the period of the offending and, as these are dynamic risk factors, how prevalent it is now. As noted, the performance of the SARN as a risk assessment tool in its own right is statistically significant. It is also used as a means to assess treatment need. At key stages of treatment the assessment is revisited to gauge whether factors have been appropriately addressed and risk therefore reduced.

Dynamic acute factors: their role in the assessment and management of men who sexually abuse

As noted earlier these are factors which, when they change, may indicate that a reversion to previous behaviours is imminent. These factors give a signal that case managers should act immediately to address the potentially imminent increase in the likelihood of recidivism. Hanson and Harris conducted a study in Canada which matched a sample of known offenders who recidivated with a group who had not (Harris, 2005). They found that changes on a range of factors indicated an increased risk of immediate offending to a level which was statistically significant. They entitled these factors:

- victim access
- emotional collapse
- collapse of social support
- hostility
- substance use
- sexual preoccupation
- rejection of supervision
- unique factors (e.g. specific threats to a specific victim)

Victim access may include cruising or creating opportunities for 'grooming'. Some offenders were seen to acquire 'flash' cars or bicycles which they were able to use to attract potential victims. Others took up new activities such as using computers or using the Internet. New hobbies (e.g. photography, kite flying and acquiring a boat) were sometimes precursors to recidivism.

Emotional collapse included the onset of negative moods, anger, psychiatric symptoms or an increase in life stress. Hanson (2000) has noted that 'happy sex offenders are as risky as unhappy sex offenders'. What is important here is the change of mood or symptoms. Thus those people who are not qualified psychiatrists should note if there is a possible recurrence of depressive symptoms or psychosis and make an appropriate referral to a relevant professional for assessment and intervention.

Collapse of social support refers to increased isolation or withdrawal; family conflict or rejection from family members; conflict with workers or friends or rejection by members of the community. Concerns may be raised in relation to hostility, whether this is observed to be in relation to a specific individual or generalised. The onset or return to problematic substance use was noted to be a factor associated with increased risk.

Sexual preoccupation as an acute risk factor refers to the increase in such preoccupation indicating an increase in immediate concern, in contrast to it being also a dynamic stable personality factor over time. The changes observed were not necessarily in relation to sexual behaviour that was illegal. They included the use of pornography, 'strip bars' and prostitutes. Increases in factors such as 'lusty talk', excessive masturbation, or an increase in deviant fantasies and urges were observed. Some offenders were seen to become preoccupied with sex crimes, either their own or those of others.

Rejection of supervision included disengagement from the supervisor or observing the client going through the motions or being silent or secretive. They may be manipulative, 'phony', controlling, 'buddying' or trying to 'play the system'. Being late or frequently rescheduling appointments signalled concern as did turning up for unscheduled appointments or limiting the length of meetings. Finding the clients have been lying or contradicting themselves were sources of concern. Curtness, rudeness or threatening behaviour and a sense that clients were working against their supervisor and not with them, were all areas that had been noted in some recidivists prior to their reoffending. The amount of 'out of hours' concerns that a client caused for supervisors was also a factor that was noted in some recidivists.

By definition 'unique factors' cannot be listed comprehensively, precisely because they are unique. One example might be an offender who does not raise concern in relation to any of the above measures but issues a threat against an individual (e.g. their partner or victim) as the interview terminates.

Harris (2005) illustrated how supervisors in their jurisdiction monitor each of these dynamic acute factors at each contact, forming an evidence base for their ongoing assessment.

Discussion

The above is a summary of a framework for assessing and managing risk with known sex offenders. As noted assessors should base their assessments on the widest possible range of information sources. They should work with and listen to all workers who have been involved in a given case irrespective of their status. Often staff who do not have professional qualifications are the ones who have most contact with an offender and have most information. Judgements should not be taken by one worker alone. Workers should not themselves stray outside of agreed

risk management plans and agency procedures. Working together in this regard should ensure that workers better protect the public more efficiently.

References

Aberdeen City Council. (1998) *Report on Investigation into Aberdeen City Council's Social Work Department's Handling of the Case of Mr. Steven Leisk*. Aberdeen: Aberdeen City Council.

All England Law Reports (1996) London: Butterworth.

Beech, A.R., Fisher, D. and Beckett, R.C. (1998) *STEP 3: An Evaluation of the Prison Sex Offender Treatment Programme*. London: Home Office.

Blom-Cooper, L. (1987) *A Child in Mind*. London: Borough of Greenwich.

Briggs, D. et al. (1998) *Assessing Men who Sexually Abuse*. London: Jessica Kingsley.

Butler-Schloss, Rt Hon. Lord Justice (1988) *Report of the Inquiry into Child Abuse in Cleveland, 1987*. London: HMSO.

Doren, D.M. (2002) *Evaluating Sex Offenders*. Thousand Oaks, CA: Sage.

Finkelhor, D. and Associates (1986) *A Sourcebook on Child Sexual Abuse*. Thousand Oaks, CA: Sage.

Hanson, R.K. (1997) *Rapid Risk Assessment of Sex Offence Recidivism*. Ottawa: Solicitor General of Canada.

Hanson, R.K. (2000) What is so Special about Relapse Prevention. In Laws, D.R., Hudson, S.M. and Ward, T. (Eds.) *Remaking Relapse Prevention with Sex Offenders*. London: Sage.

Hanson, R.K. and Bussiere, M.T. (1998) Predicting Relapse: A Meta-analysis of Sexual Offender Recidivism Studies. *Journal of Consulting and Clinical Psychology*, 66: 2, 348–62.

Hanson, R.K. and Harris, A. (2000) *Sex Offender Needs Assessment Rating*. Ottawa: Department of the Solicitor General of Canada.

Hare, R.D. (1994) *Without Conscience*. London: Warner.

Harris, A. (2005) Presentation at Conference of the National Organisation for the Treatment of Abusers, Dublin.

Kennington, R. et al. (2001) *Northumbria Sex Offender Programme Theory Manual*. London: National Probation Service.

Knight, R.A. and Prentky, R.A. (1990) Classifying Sexual Offenders: The Development and Corroboration of Taxonomic Models. In Marshall, W.L., Laws, R.D. and Barbaree, H.

The Handbook of Sexual Assault. New York: Plenum.

Malamuth, N.M., Heavey, C.L. and Linz, D. (1993) Predicting Men's Antisocial Behaviour against Women: The Interaction Model of Sexual Aggression. In Hall, G.C. et al. (Eds.) *Sexual Aggression: Issues in Aetiology, Assessment and Treatment*. Washington: Taylor and Francis.

Mann, R.E. et al. (2002) *Structured Assessment of Risk and Need*. London: H.M. Prison Service.

National Probation Directorate (2003) *Multi Agency Public Protection Arrangements. Guidelines for Practice*. London: Home Office.

Quinsey, V., Rice, M.E. and Harris, G.T. (1995) Actuarial Prediction of Sexual Recidivism. *Journal of Interpersonal Violence*, 10: 1, 85–105.

Ryan, G. et al. (1987) Juvenile Sex Offenders: Development and Correction. *Child Abuse and Neglect*, 2, 385–95.

Salter, A.C. (1997) *Special Issues in Risk Assessment*. Address to the Annual Conference of the National Organisation for the Treatment of Abusers, Southampton.

Thornton, D. (1999) *Structured Risk Assessment*. Presentation at the Conference of the National Organisation for the Treatment of Abusers. York.

Thornton, D. (2000) *Risk Matrix 2000*. Presentation at the Conference of the Association for the Treatment of Sexual Abusers. San Diego.

Thornton, D. (2006) *Controversial Issues in Sexual Offender Risk Assessment*. Presentation at the University of Birmingham, UK 26th July 2006.

Thornton, D. and Fisher, D. (1994) In Beckett, R.C. et al. *Community Based Treatment of Sex Offenders: An Evaluation of Seven Treatment Programmes*. London: Home Office.

Wolf, S.C. (1988) A Model of Sexual Aggression/Addiction. *Journal of Social Work and Human Sexuality*. 7.1.

CHAPTER 15

Young People Who Sexually Abuse: Risk Refinement and Conceptual Developments

Martin C. Calder

Introduction

The need to categorise risk is an essential part of the assessment process. Of concern, therefore, is the fact that workers have been forced to use for some considerable time un-validated instruments and toolkits in order to decide whether someone was high, medium or low risk – in general rather than in specific terms. There was little hope of getting very many workers to make a low risk diagnosis since if they got that wrong and the young person did re-offend, then there would be blame apportioned and further victims. High risk was the easy option: it covers backs and there are no professional consequences if you get it wrong. There are, however, immense consequences for the young person as they are labelled high risk, along with their sexually abusive behaviour. They may then act to 'the label' as they can see no way out. They have their denial entrenched and any potential for change is affected.

One of the proud achievements in the assessment field has been the progress made in relation to developing better frameworks for assessing risk with young people who sexually abuse and how this has now reached a level where it is informing developments needed in the adult sex offender field (Calder, 2005; Calder, forthcoming). This more so, as historically the case, the starting point, was importing the developments from the adult sex offender field. These took the form of actuarial risk tools and the emergence of stable and dynamic risk factors so we did not concentrate exclusively on previous behaviour.

Static, stable and dynamic risk factors

One of the breakthroughs when considering how to develop more evidence-based assessment tools with adult sex offenders was with the advent of dynamic risk factors to move the field beyond static risk factors which was maintaining a high-risk emphasis given the prior abuse history.

Not only was this inaccurate but it was incredibly de-motivating for the offenders and could potentially contribute to a relapse.

We know that future behaviour can never be predicted with certainty. Nevertheless, a growing body of research indicates that well-informed practitioners can predict sexual recidivism with at least moderate accuracy. Hanson (1998; Hanson and Thornton, 1999) argued that risk assessments consider two distinct concepts: enduring propensities, or potentials to re-offend; and factors that indicate the onset of new offences. These offence triggers are not random, but can be expected to be organised into predictable patterns (offence cycles), some unique to the individual and some common to most sexual offenders.

Different evaluation questions require the consideration of different types of risk factors. **Static, historical variables** (e.g. prior offences, childhood maladjustment) can indicate deviant developmental trajectories and, as such, enduring propensities to sexually offend. Evaluating changes in risk levels (e.g. treatment outcome), however, requires the consideration of **dynamic, changeable risk factors** (e.g. co-operation with supervision, deviant sexual preferences). The relatively low recidivism rates of sexual offenders' makes it difficult to detect dynamic risk factors. Over a four to five year period, approximately 10–15 per cent of sexual offenders will be detected committing a new sexual offence (Hanson and Bussiere, 1998). Although age is sometimes considered a dynamic factor, the most important dynamic factors are those that respond to treatment. **Dynamic factors** can further be classified as **stable or acute. Stable factors** have the potential to change, but typically endure for months or years (e.g. personality disorder) and, as such, represent ongoing risk potential. In contrast, **acute factors** (e.g. negative mood) may be present for a short duration (minutes, days) and can signal the timing of offending. Most risk decisions require consideration of both static and dynamic risk factors.

The 'trickle down' effect

Longo (2003) talks of the trickle-down effect from adult sex offender work: 'unfortunately, we continue to erroneously view these children as mini-adults, mini-perpetrators, sexual predators and the like'. There was a danger that we would simply import these developments from the adult field and apply them with some linguistic modifications to capture the developmental differences. This would have been a retrograde step given the emergence of a broader research and evidence base for young people created with recognition that their sexually abusive behaviour was not dissimilar from the behaviours exhibited by other young people with a range of different presenting problems (O'Callaghan, 2002) and that this thinking expanded the evidence base for our interventions.

At the time in the early 1990s when we were instructed to work with young people who sexually abuse, there was a paucity of theory as well as practice wisdom in the UK. We were forced to import materials to help us work with the young people that were being referred for a service. This importation took several forms and included using the materials developed in North America and from the field of working with adult male sexual perpetrators. Practice could not wait for research answers or direction. Lessons were learned en route and sometimes in a hard way.

There has been a lot of criticism about adopting materials from both these sources. For example, Myers (1998) has argued that by importing the models and findings from the US, we have constructed a philosophical and practice base that supports punitive and intensive responses, especially the notion that criminal legal mandates are necessary to enforce compliance with intervention.

There has been some recognition that because of the developmental differences between young people and adults and because of the different pathways to their sexually abusive behaviour, the transplant of expertise between the two camps is not helpful. The following differences have been highlighted:

- Most juveniles have not yet developed a relatively fixed pattern of sexual arousal and interest, which gives direction to consistent patterns of behaviour. For example, they have less fully developed cognitive distortions and the role of fantasy as a precursor to abuse is not as clearly understood in young people but appears to be less significant.
- Juveniles have greater developmental fluidity, e.g. many more juveniles have victims of both genders and engage in multiple acts of sexually abusive behaviour, and there appears to be considerable crossover between incestuous and non-incestuous offending in the juvenile population (Hunter and Becker, 1994: 536–7).

For example:

- Becker et al. (1986) found that 41 per cent of juvenile incest perpetrators had also engaged in non-incest sexual offences.
- Abel, Mittleman and Becker (1985) found that 50 per cent of juveniles admitted to multiple sexual deviations.
- Monck and New (1996) highlighted the crossover across genders in the choice of victims. They found that whilst 83 per cent of young people abused only one gender, some 17 per cent abused both genders.
- Beckett and Brown (1999) found that the younger the abusive behaviour starts, the greater the likelihood of crossover possibly because victims are likely to be those available rather than targeted children.
- James and Neil (1996) found that whilst the majority of victims are female (83.3 per cent), the more victims there are, the greater the probability that males will become the victims.
- Attention has turned recently to females who sexually abuse and there is evidence of crossover here, with 42 per cent perpetrating only against female victims, 25 per cent perpetrating exclusively against male victims and 33 per cent perpetrating against both males and females. 75 per cent perpetrated only against family members; 16 per cent against non-family members; and 9 per cent against both a family and a non-family member (Bumby and Bumby, 1997).

All these figures support a cautious approach to risk estimation.

- Perpetration and grooming strategies are less consistent and sophisticated with young people.

- The abuse process is still developing in young people, thus limiting detailed offence cycles or relapse processes that might be targeted.

- Situational and opportunity factors appear to feature more as precursors and internal cognitive factors less frequently.
- Many young people have been sexually abused (like their adult counterparts) but they are temporally closer to these abusive experiences.
- Young people have poorer sexual knowledge, yet they are learning about sex far more markedly.
- Young people live in a social world with different values, beliefs and expectations.
- The role of the family is more critical with young people.
- Young people experience and expect significant degrees of external control of their behaviour by parents or carers.
- Motivating and engaging with young people requires a different approach and different skills and is generally more difficult than with adults.
- There is far less research on young people who sexually abuse and no integrated knowledge base from which to work.
- Young people are more accustomed to education and open to learning new and acceptable skills.

(Calder, 2001)

Despite these statements, the theory and practice of that time focused on the offence and the offending behaviour and the confrontational approaches so widely used with adults. It will come as no surprise that such an approach did not engage young people in the work. If there was a mandate, it usually succeeded in getting them to the sessions, but did not facilitate their active involvement and thus change was unlikely to follow.

Theoretical developments: refining our understanding of this group

To date there is generally no accepted theory about why young people sexually abuse. A number of factors have received empirical attention, including maltreatment experiences, exposure to pornography, substance abuse, and exposure to aggressive role models. Weinrott (1996) has argued that most explanations of juvenile sexual crimes are too simplistic or are applied universally. Marshall and Eccles (1993) have suggested that a comprehensive theory of young people who sexually abuse may not be

possible, proposing that specific theories are needed for different types of sexual offence, each emphasising different processes. Clearly this cannot progress until there is some agreement reached on how to classify and group such young people. Only then will it be possible to look at which processes are associated with which type of offence.

As investigation into this population continues, its heterogeneity appears to be emerging causing the abandonment of the one-factor theory. There are a number of important developments in our understanding of this group of young people that are worthy of a brief mention:

- There is an acknowledgement that young people who sexually abuse have more similarities than differences with other young people who have significant emotional and behavioural disorders. This then allows us to draw upon a far more extensive knowledge base.
- There has been a dramatic shift from blanket approaches to more individualised packages that focus more specifically on social skills and competence than the alleged offence. This reflects a shift from seeing young people who sexually abuse not only as abusers but also as children 'in need' in their own right.
- There is growing evidence that the origins of the young person's behaviour lies within their family, especially early experiences of trauma, rejection, abuse, attachment problems, etc. The young person then seeks to meet a whole range of needs, sexual and non-sexual, through their behaviour. Hackett (2002) identified several mechanisms which may be present for male victims who then go on to sexually abuse: the re-enactment of the abuse and a replication of parallel dynamics of their own victimisation; an attempt to achieve mastery over conflicts resulting from the abuse; subsequent conditioning of sexual arousal to assaultive fantasies; and a reactive or learnt behaviour response. For an excellent review of the theory in relation to families, the reader is referred to Duane and Morrison (2004).
- Developmental issues are critical when considering their behaviour and the most appropriate materials or techniques to use when working with the young person. There is an emerging view that it is better to see young people who sexually abuse as representing a risk of repeat behaviour within their current

developmental phase rather than adults who represent a lifelong risk for re-offending. This has implications for **timely** as well as **tailored** intervention.

- One obvious difference between juveniles and adults is that juveniles have developmental needs that must be considered. Thus, workers must be concerned with the changing developmental needs of their clients while simultaneously treating their sexually abusive behaviour.

- Ryan (1998) explored the relevance of early life experiences to the behaviour of sexually abusive youth. She argued that a developmental-contextual view provides a useful framework to understand the interaction of growth and experience relevant to sexually abusive behaviours. This approach facilitates the study of both assets and risks, from birth into the future, which will moderate or exacerbate risk and prognosis. A developmental approach describes the complete phenomenology of the individual: the assimilated view of self and others which is the basis for interpersonal relationships; the acquisition of psychological coping mechanisms; and the perceptual accommodation of environment and experience which is the basis for the individual's 'view of the world'. Growth and experience are perpetually intertwined, each influencing the next, becoming the basis for future beliefs and development, and the perceptual pieces forming the contextual phenomenology, which describes the individual's world. Ryan noted that each infant is born with a unique combination of physical, neurological and temperamental characteristics, which will affect growth and experience. The infant is born into an environment that is also unique: a combination of persons and circumstances. A deviant developmental path may start in utero, with drug or alcohol exposure, inadequate nutrition etc. predisposing the infant to be born unable to distinguish or communicate needs, to be inconsolably distressed, to be difficult to care for, or to be at risk for a number of heritable traits and disorders. Simultaneously, deviance in the infant's environment may precede or be related to birth. Parents each have their own developmental history and are affected by many circumstances. They may be either chronically stressed, may lack the resources to

care for an infant or may be too preoccupied or absent. The early interactions may be empathic or un-empathic. Infants whose caregivers struggle to interpret and validate cues learn their own ability to identify their needs. The infant who is cared for abusively or on a schedule which is not responsive to cues learns about the futility of trying to communicate their needs, to ignore the internal cues of emotions and needs and rely on external sources of control. Some infants are born with, or may develop, conditions which cause them to be chronically distressed and which makes them difficult to care for, e.g. prematurity or foetal substance exposure. Any breakdown in the infant's adjustment to the world may plant the seeds of later dysfunctions. Indeed, many of the sexually abusive youth have experienced some breakdown in their earliest developmental processes. Many have a very limited understanding of what their natural cues mean (lack of empathy for self) and so are at risk for many dysfunctions, which are harmful to themselves. They have few labels for feelings and lack emotional recognition. They often have 'learning disabilities' which are very related to communication disorders and often fail to feel any sense of responsibility for the outcome of their behaviour. They are simply developmentally damaged. Their inability to develop empathic recognition severely jeopardises relationships and contributes to emotional constriction and anxious or ambivalent attachments in infancy. Overall, the individual's life experiences may overwhelm their ability to cope or alternatively, it can provide the basis for developing strong coping and problem solving skills; the child who was neglected or abused may continue to be vulnerable, or development may replace vulnerabilities with new skills, solutions and competency.

- Resilience can be considered in terms of individual psychosocial functioning, family resilience and community integration factors, such as education and social and leisure activities (Daniel, Wassell and Gilligan, 1999). Rutter (1999) suggests the available research indicates that vulnerability derives from a combination of genetic predisposition and environmental factors; the impact of adverse life experiences can be mediated by the promotion of new opportunities; and the emotional and cognitive processing of

Single-factor models	Integrated models
• Biological or medical models. • Psychodynamic theories. • Behavioural theories. • Social-cognitive theories. • Social-emotional developmental theories. • Cognitive theories. • Trauma theories. • Family theories. • Sociological theories.	• Four-factor model (Finkelhor, 1984). • Offender cycle model (Wolf, 1984). • Young abusers project integrated perspectives model. • Developmental vulnerability models (Becker and Kaplan, 1988).

Figure 15.1   A theoretical overview (from Epps, 1999)

experiences is critical to the individual mitigating the impact of adverse life experiences. In terms of the mobilisation of services to young people we need to focus on those environmental and contextual factors most associated with promoting resilience. Gilligan (2000) suggests we should aim to simultaneously reduce the accumulation of risks of risk whilst working to improve strengths i.e. to attempt and alter the balance of risks and needs. There is a very individual significance to potential resiliency experiences and whilst we can identify general themes the precise impact will vary from child to child. Gilgun et al. (2000) noted that the evidence would suggest that resilience factors are likely to have the strongest impact on children in the moderate needs/risk group.

Kevin Epps (1999) has provided a very accessible summary of the theoretical terrain in this area (see Figure 15.1). He identified influences from the adult field and went on to name the essential requirements of a theory of young people who sexually abuse that included:

• *Normal and abnormal development:* there has to be some guidance to help us differentiate between the 'normal' and the 'abusive' (see Calder, 1997). There are few characteristics of this group that distinguishes them from other young people.
• *Characteristics of young people who sexually abuse:* there must be some way of explaining the association between the characteristics (such as psychosocial problems, e.g. low self-esteem, poor social skills, peer relationship difficulties, social isolation and loneliness, educational and academic problems, gender-identity confusion, family problems, substance abuse, etc.) found

in young people who sexually abuse and their offending. At present, it remains unclear.
• *Types of offence:* any adequate theory must account for the wide variety of sexually abusive behaviours. A range of offence-related variables could be used to place the abusers into subgroups:
  – *Age of victim:* where the range may be 2 years to 23 years.
  – *Gender of victim:* some choose boys or girls only, and some choose both. The vast majority of victims are female (69–84 per cent) although as the age of the victim decreases, the victim is more likely to be male.
  – *Relationship to victim:* Most of the victims are known to the abuser. However, the more sophisticated abusers may prefer victims who are less familiar, perhaps to avoid detection.
  – *Use of force and violence:* Young men tend to use less coercion, force and violence than adult sex offenders. There is a gap in our knowledge about young people who commit serious sexual offences, such as torture and mutilation.

Epps concluded that there is no adequate theory of why young people sexually abuse. Why has this been so difficult? One answer might be that human behaviour is complex, influenced as it is by a wide range of factors ranging from the action of chemicals on the nervous system to the effect of information and ideas obtained through the media. These factors interact with one another to produce a complex myriad of variables, the effects of which are often difficult to identify and research in isolation. Complex human behaviours, such as sexual offending, are extremely difficult to explain and are seen to be the outcome of an interaction between individual and environmental factors. Trying to prove that one event (such as a particular thought) caused another (such as a particular behaviour) is difficult. Usually there are 'hidden' variables that mediate between events. The situation becomes even more complex when events are separated by a long period of time.

Hudson and Ward (1997) and Ward and Hudson (1998) have recently offered a meta-theoretical framework for the construction and development of future theory in the sexual offending area. They pointed out that there has not been any integrated approach to theory building to date, resulting in an ad hoc proliferation of theories that often overlap as well as ignoring each other's existence. Their framework takes into account a number of different theory construction principles and ideas; it differentiates between different levels of theory and stresses the importance of distinguishing between distal and proximal causal factors. They begin to locate the existing theory within the framework and argue that an integrated approach using their framework will benefit workers and researchers significantly. This is needed if we are to neutralise the offender's power base and further invite them to accept responsibility for their behaviour.

Epps and Fisher (2004) have argued that we should now aim to group offenders according to offence and offender characteristics given the evidence that different clusters of psychosocial problems are associated with different types of sexual offending which, in turn, follow different developmental pathways. Identification of these pathways will have important implications for prevention, through early intervention, and for treatment.

Developing evidence-based assessment tools

Actuarial methods utilise statistical techniques to generate risk predictors. Since no single factor is sufficient to determine whether offenders will or will not re-offend, practitioners need to consider a range of relevant risk factors. There are three plausible methods by which risk factors can be combined into overall evaluations of risk:

1. Empirically guided clinical evaluations: which begins with the overall recidivism base rate,

and then adjusts the risk level by considering factors that have been empirically associated with recidivism risk. The risk factors to be considered are explicit, but the method for weighting the importance of the risk factors is left to the judgement of the worker.
2. Pure actuarial predictions: in contrast, explicitly state not only the variables to be considered, but also the precise procedure through which ratings of these variables will be translated into a risk level. In the pure actuarial sense, risk levels are estimated through mechanical, arithmetic procedures requiring a minimum of judgement.
3. Clinically adjusted actuarial predictions: begins with a pure actuarial prediction, but then raises or lowers the risk level based on consideration of relevant factors that were not included in the actuarial method (see Quinsey et al., 1995). As research develops, actuarial methods can be expected to consistently outperform clinical predictions. With the current state of knowledge, however, both actuarial and guided clinical approaches can be expected to provide risk assessments with a moderate level of accuracy.

There are a number of strengths of adopting an actuarial approach to the work:

- They are consistent with the expectation of evidence-based social care interventions.
- They are useful in establishing those risk predictors which have a proven track record.
- They are useful in establishing the relevant base rates for clinical assessment.
- They are useful in increasing the accuracy of risk assessments.
- They increase the levels of consistency and reliability.

(adapted from Kemshall, 2001)

Equally there are a number of problems and potential pitfalls:

- Any tool has limitations if inappropriately used.
- Statistical fallacy is a problem when seeking to transfer the information about a population to an individual user under assessment.
- The use of meta-analyses (research based on the analysis of a large number of primary studies) to develop risk predictors can result in overly simple outcomes that fail to capture the

complexity of the processes involved. We often require a human dimension to explain the behaviour.

- A further problem relates to the predictions of risk where there is a low incidence of risky behaviours in the population as a whole. This is especially true in the case of child sexual abuse.
- Collect accurate information in cases – in fact it may encourage a tick box approach.
- Cover all permutations of situations.
- Undertake compound predictions in complex situations. This arises from inevitable shortage of data and base rate problems.
- Specific samples: either convicted or imprisoned people.
- Time of offending not addressed.
- Consequences not addressed (risk/ dangerousness).
- Role of other behaviours ambiguous.
- Recidivism based on official report.
- Don't apply to women, young people or un-convicted men.

There are a great many assessment tools being developed grounded on a mixture of evidence-based materials across the adult and adolescent fields that are attempting to capture the emerging evidence base and couple it with practice wisdom. The dangers of such positive developments mean that the number of emerging tools makes it difficult for practitioners to know which one to use for what purpose; they need to be clear whether they are actuarial or clinically adjusted tools and they need to know the target population they are designed for, as well as the focus e.g. re-offending or harming others. Figure 15.2 overleaf identifies some of the most advanced assessment tools in the field.

The development of a clinically adjusted actuarial risk tool

Although research is in the embryonic stages we are already identifying some primary signposts to factors associated with the persistence of re-offending and these include a general pattern of conduct disorder and other non-sexual offending, poor social functioning, discontinuity of care, trauma and neglect, high levels of family dysfunction, evidence of offence-planning or sexual pre-occupation and early drop out from treatment programmes (Bentovim, 2002; Rasmussen, 1999).

Despite such research developments in the field of young people who sexually abuse, research lags behind practice significantly. Specialist bodies such as G-MAP have analysed the cases that they have worked with over a decade and supplemented the deficit of research to produce a clinically adjusted actuarial risk tool (Print et al., 2001). This has now been extended to young people with a learning disability (O'Callaghan, 2002) and families (Morrison and Wilkinson, 2001). Similar developments have also emerged in Canada (Worling and Curwen, 2000) and in the US (Prentky et al., 2000).

The AIM model has utilised available research and literature to develop an initial assessment model that helps to provide a structured approach to the gathering and analysis of information about a young person, their problematic behaviour, their family and their environment. The model is intended as a framework that will assist practitioners in gathering and analysing relevant information in order to make initial recommendations about needs and risks. Figure 15.3 highlights four domains of AIM.

This may include recommendations about placements, supervision requirements, case management, court disposal, plans for therapeutic work with individuals and families, and an initial prognosis for outcome. The model also usefully provides practitioners with a tool to assist them in articulating a structured basis for their opinions and thereby supporting the public exercising of professional judgement.

Once gathered, the information can be used to identify which factors in the empirically/ clinically based continuums are relevant to the young person, his abusive behaviour, his family and environment (see Print et al., 2001).

The concept of wellness and holistic treatment introduced by Longo (2002) is built upon a similar premise and the extension of relapse prevention to include a focus on strengths within a broader framework is refreshing and progressive. Longo (2002) advocated a holistic approach to treatment of this group. Holistic treatment is a model that incorporates and modifies, yet moves beyond, the traditional cognitive-behavioural and relapse prevention models used by the majority of programmes. It uses both a variety of traditional and alternative treatment methods and techniques that explore and incorporate a variety of models to improve ones overall mental and physical health and

Tools	Focus of the tool
J Soap II (Prentky and Righthand 2003)	12–18-year old boys. Assesses risk of sexual offending using two static feature scales (sexual drive/ sexual preoccupation and impulsive/anti-social behaviours) whether the young person has been convicted or not. It has two further dynamic scales (intervention and community stability and adjustment) for post-treatment intervention and assessment of risk. It is not an actuarial tool but a guide to risk factors. Best use is for addressing treatment needs and their severity.
ERASOR (Worling and Curwen, 2000)	12–18 year olds. Assesses risk for sexual re-offending in those young people who have previously committed a sexual assault. Static risk factors relate to sexual aggression and dynamic risk factors relate to general delinquency. Provides extensive overview of the literature as well as difficulties inherent in risk assessments of young people who sexually abuse. Useful for evaluation, treatment planning and service delivery.
J-SORRATT (ii) (Epperson et al., 2006)	Drawn from a small sample of 636 youth convicted of a sexual offence. It is an actuarial tool with potential as an effective screening resource. It relates only to historical/static factors/items. Considered accurate in predicting recidivism in adolescence (rather than adulthood) only.
Protective Factors Scale (Bremer, 2006)	Assesses factors that might mitigate risk. Lends itself to a broad range of treatment approaches and systems – based risk management strategies. Addresses 3 factors: sexuality, personal development and environmental support. Useful in decisions re: levels of care and in developing treatment plans and interventions. It should not be used as an exclusive assessment tool.
SHARP (Richardson, 2007)	Forensic clinical guide to the risk assessment of sexually abusive behaviour by young people (males 12–19 years). Reflective of 12 risk factors, 10 risk domains and risk processes. Developmentally sensitive. Embraces static, stable and dynamic risk factors. It has potential as a core assessment tool for young people who sexually abuse.
AIM 2 (Print et al., 2007)	Clinically adjusted actuarial risk tool for males 12–18 years convicted of a sexual offence or where it is believed to have occurred or is imminent. Embraces dynamic and static elements. Not supported by up-to-date tools for learning disabled or females.
MEGA (Miccio-Fenseca, 2006; Rasmussen and Miccio-Fonseca, 2007)	Empirically guided structured inventory for all young people under 19 years – both genders and all levels of developmental ability. Derives exclusively from literature on children and young people (excludes adults). Can help treatment focus. It has 6 scales: risk, static, dynamic, principle, protectives, female and 7 aggregates (neuro-psychological, family lovemap, antisocial, sexual incident, stratagem and relationship (predatory elements). Doesn't assess recidivism but indicates a future risk for 6 months. Dynamic element used to review each 6 months.

Figure 15.2 Existing assessment frameworks for young people who sexually abuse

recovery. In addition, it uses a balance of theoretical and humanistic knowledge that embraces the concept that the therapeutic relationship is the focal point of treatment and essential if it is going to impact the client. Holistic treatment has a focus on wellness with messages of hope. It gives clients a clear message that they can heal, that they can go forward, and that they are human beings worthy of respect and dignity. Holistic treatment, in the simplest of terms, is a return to basics; looking at the four domains or aspects of self; mind, body, spirit and the

Offence specific	Developmental
• Nature of index sexual offence/abuse • Young person and family's attitude to victim • Amount and nature of offence planning • Use of threats, violence or aggression during commission of offence/abuse • Young person's offending and abusive behaviour history • Previous professional involvement with young person and family regarding offending/abusive behaviours • Motivation to engage with professionals	• Resilience factors • Health issues • Experiences of physical, sexual or emotional abuse or neglect • Witnessed domestic violence • Quality of the young person's early life experiences • History of behaviour problems • Sexual development and interests
Family/Carers • Level of functioning • Attitudes and beliefs • Sexual boundaries • Parental competence	**Environment** • Young person's access to vulnerable others • Opportunity for further offending • Community attitudes to young person and family • Wider supervisory and support network

Figure 15.3   The four domains of AIM

emotional self. In addition, a holistic model addresses the four universal needs for generosity, belonging, mastery, and independence. The need for generosity is for people to give and share of themselves. This is not a giving of materialistic goods, but rather a giving and sharing of time, of one's feelings and one's self. The need for belonging transcends all cultures and societies. Human beings are social animals with a need to belong to a family, a community, a society, and the need to feel connected to the universe. The lack of belonging leaves one feeling isolated, lonely and intimacy suffers. Our spiritual self begins to die. The need for mastery is essential for personal growth and learning. Each of us has a need to feel we have the courage and strength to master tasks from the simple to the more complex. We need to feel in control of ourselves and assured that we can master the tasks that will take us through life. Finally, the need for independence is that need to operate our lives in a fashion in which we are free from dependence upon others. This is not to say that we don't need or depend on others from time to time, we all do. However, to depend upon others consistently, especially in co-dependent ways, is unhealthy. A healthy independent self is being responsible for ourselves and being assertive in getting our needs met.

Stopping the dripping tap and creating a 'trickle up' effect

Prentky et al. (2000) and Ryan (2007) have started to consider the concept of dynamic and static risk factors with young people who sexually abuse (see Figure 15.4 overleaf). Ryan has argued that the more research that becomes available for this group shows that they are not noticeably different from other groups of young offenders, such as those who self-harm or commit violent offences. She has provided us with a useful embryonic, and at this stage hypothetical, framework for considering factors relevant to abusive functioning. The usefulness of her framework is considerable as she has extended the concept of risk factors to include assets. This is an important extension of the concepts developed in the adult field and is consistent with the view that risk assessment is about balancing risks and assets, weighting them within the presenting situation and then coming to an informed conclusion. It marks a clear stop to the trickle down effect from the adult sex offender field and is so exportable that it marks also the start of a 'trickle up' effect where the developments are ahead of other fields.

Static risk factors are historical and therefore unchangeable

Risks	Assets
• Prenatal insults	• Prenatal care
• Premature/traumatic birth	• Normative birth
• Unempathic care	• Empathic care
• Caregiver loss/disruption	• Consistent caregivers
• Trust failure	• Trustworthy relationship
• Disordered attachment	• Secure attachment
• Dysfunctional modelling	• Normal growth/development
• Witness domestic violence	• Functional modelling
• Abuse, neglect, failure to thrive, trauma.	• Nurturance and protection

Stable risk factors are those that remain somewhat constant across the life-span. They are less changeable although they may be moderated.

Risks	Assets
• Difficult temperament	• Easy/adaptive temperament
• Low functioning	• Average-high intelligence (IQ)
• Learning disability	• Positive internal working model (self and others)
• Heritable psychiatric disorders	• Normative physical and neurological functioning
• Chronic PTSD reactivity	

Dynamic risk factors are constantly changing, either purposefully or by chance. They are clearly changeable.

Global (foreseeable in life span)	**Circumstantial** (specific/fluctuating daily)
• Constant/expected stressors	• Current/unexpected stressors (conflict or emotional trigger)
• Unresolved emotional issues	• Perceived threat vulnerability
• Unsafe environment/persons	• Lowered self-esteem/efficacy
• Injury/illness	• Negative expectations
• Temporary disabilities	• Isolation/lack of support
• Lack of opportunity/support	• Mood dysregulation: anger, depression, anxiety
• Change/loss	• Projection/misattributions
• Sexual drive/arousal	• Limited options/skill deficits
• Abusive memories	• Abusive memory/fantasy
• Failed relationships	• Sexual arousal/thought
• Access to vulnerable persons	• Lowered inhibitions
	• Access to vulnerable persons

Figure 15.4   Towards a framework for assessing risk in young people who sexually abuse (Ryan, in press)

Dynamic assets

Ryan also sets out the following observable outcomes of evidence of change relevant to decreased risk:

- Consistently defines all abuse (self, others, property).
- Acknowledges risk (foresight and safety planning).

- Consistently recognises/interrupts cycle (no later than the first thought of an abusive solution).
- Demonstrates new coping skills (when stressed).
- Demonstrates empathy (sees cues of others and responds).
- Accurate attributions of responsibility (takes responsibility for own behaviour and doesn't try to control the behaviour of others).

- Rejects abusive thoughts as dissonant (incongruent with self-image).

It is important that we simultaneously consider the outcomes related to increased health:

- Pro-social relationship skills (closeness, trust and trustworthiness).
- Positive self-image (able to be separate, independent and competent).
- Able to resolve conflicts and make decisions (assertive, tolerant, forgiving, co-operative; able to negotiate and compromise).
- Celebrates good and experiences pleasure (able to relax and play).
- Able to manage frustration and unfavourable events (anger management and self-protection).
- Works/struggles to achieve delayed gratification (persistent pursuit of goals; able to concentrate).
- Able to think and communicate effectively (rational cognitive processing; adequate verbal skills).
- Adaptive sense of purpose and future.

AIM 2: embracing the theoretical developments

Print et al. (2007) have developed AIM 2 from the original AIM model for 12–18-year-olds although the level of risk (high, medium or low) has been changed to 'level of supervision required' to reflect the lack of scientific validation of risk factors and outcomes. It has also been updated to embrace and differentiate between static and dynamic risk factors. The focus is to offer an initial, brief evidence-based tool that can be used to begin to both consider the level of supervision that is required for an individual and their developmental and intervention needs. It expands the original risk factors to embrace actuarial, clinical judgement, dynamic (stable), dispositional (personality disorder/psychopathy, traits (genetic physiological or psychological) and trigger (availability of victims, conflict with parents). It is premised on an aetiological model of risk developed by Beech and Ward, 2004.

A framework of analysis (Gilgun, 1999; Gilgun et al., 2000)

The CASPARS are based on the principle that assets are significant in models of risk. Assets, too, are probabilistic concepts and can only predict to groups and not to individuals. Examples of assets are above average IQ, physical appeal, verbal ability, caring parents, resources within neighbourhoods, adequate income, and good schools (Masten et al., 1991). Some individuals with assets have poor outcomes. They are not able to use their assets to moderate risks, and sometimes their risks overwhelm the assets they have (Masten et al., 1991). Assets are protective factors when they are associated with overcoming risks (Gilgun, 1996a and b).

Some persons experience cumulative risks; that is, a series of risks that may interact and overwhelm whatever resources an individual can marshal, while in other cases persons appear to have sufficient resources to cope. This idea helps to explain why there is such a wide variation in outcomes among persons who have experienced a single known risk, such as child sexual abuse. Those who have relatively mild outcomes not only have fewer risks, but they also have turned assets into protective factors. Those who have more serious outcomes probably have many interacting risks and fewer assets on which to draw, or do not use well whatever assets their environments offer.

Gilgun went on to develop a framework that enacts this theory and which embraces assets alongside risks. She argued that it is important to have a framework that explores *assets* as well as risks (see Figure 15.5 overleaf). The ideal is that we protect children from risks. However, the power of risks can be moderated by creating an imbalance with greater assets. The child with high risks and high assets may be less dysfunctional than the child with few risks but few assets. The most dysfunctional outcome is likely to be the child with high risks and low assets.

Conclusions

We should try and move away from categorising someone as generally being high, medium, or low risk, as this is principally labelling for the purposes of worker self-protection rather than being a valuable aid to worker intervention. If we label someone high-risk then we are covered if

Low asset	High asset
Low risk	Low risk
Low asset	High asset
High risk	High risk

Figure 15.5   Balancing risks and assets (Gilgun, 1999)

they re-offend. If we label them low-risk and they re-offend then the workers may be held responsible for this. It is more helpful to try and identify broad risk bands but which split this down into a context. For example, offence characteristics, their history/background, behavioural features, and attitudes, thoughts and fantasies. The focus should then be one of risk management.

The development of more sophisticated risk tools should allow us to more effectively screen in and screen out cases according to the anticipated risk coupled with the potential for change. Decisions then have to be reached as to whether to target the high risk group where the outcomes may be average or poor or target the middle group where the risk might not be so acute but where the projected outcomes are probably significantly better.

References

Abel, G., Mittelman, M. and Becker, J. (1985) Sexual Offenders: Results of Assessment and Recommendations for Treatment. In Ben-Aron, H., Hucker, S. and Webster, C. (Eds.) *Clinical Criminology*. Toronto: M&M Graphics.

Alexander, M.A. (1999) Sexual Offender Treatment Efficacy Revisited. *Sexual Abuse: A Journal of Research and Treatment*, 11, 2.

Becker, J.V. et al. (1986) Characteristics of Adolescent Incest Sexual Perpetrators: Preliminary Findings. *Journal of Family Violence*, 1: 1, 85–97.

Beckett, R. and Brown, S. (1999) Emerging Findings of the Adolescent Sexual Abuser Project. Workshop presentation to the NOTA conference '*Effective Research, Protective Practice*', University of York, 6th Oct.

Beech, A. and Ward, T. (2004) The Integration of Etiology and Risk in Sexual Offenders: A Theoretical Framework. *Aggression and Violent Behaviour*, 10, 31–63

Bentovim, A. (2002) Research on the Development of Sexually Abusive Behaviour in Sexually Abused Males: The Implications for Clinical Practice. In Calder, M.C. (Ed.) *Young People who Sexually Abuse: Building the Evidence Base for your Practice*. Lyme Regis: Russell House Publishing.

Bremer, J. (2006) Building Resilience: An Ally in Assessment and Treatment. In Prescott, D.S. (Ed.) *Risk Assessment of Youth who have Sexually Abused*. Oklahoma City: Wood & Barnes.

Bumby, K.M. and Bumby, N.H. (1997) Adolescent Female Sexual Offenders. In Schwartz, B.K. and Cellini, H.R. (Eds.) *The Sex Offender: New Insights, Treatment Innovations and Legal Developments*, Vol 2. Kingston, NJ: Civic Research Institute.

Calder, M.C. (1997) *Juveniles and Children who Sexually Abuse: A Guide to Risk Assessment*. Lyme Regis: Russell House Publishing.

Calder, M.C. (2001) *Juveniles and Children who Sexually Abuse: Frameworks for Assessment*. 2nd edn. Lyme Regis: Russell House Publishing.

Calder, M.C. (2005) Looking Towards the Future of Treating Sexually Abusive Youth. In Longo, R. and Prescott, D. (Eds.) *Current Perspectives: Working with Aggressive Youth and Youth with Sexual Behaviour Problems*. Holyoke, MA: NEARI Press.

Calder, M.C. (forthcoming) *Juveniles and Children Who Sexually Abuse*. 3rd edn. Lyme Regis: Russell House Publishing.

Daniel, B., Wassell, S. and Gilligan, R. (1999) *Child Development for Child Care and Protection Workers*. London: Jessica Kingsley.

Duane, Y. and Morrison, T. (2004) Families of Young People who Sexually Abuse: Characteristics, Context and Considerations. In Marshall, W.L. et al. (Eds.) *Handbook of Clinical*

Intervention with Juvenile Sexual Abusers.
Chichester: John Wiley and Sons.

Duane, Y. and Morrison, T. (2004) Families of
Young People who Sexually Abuse:
Characteristics, Context and Considerations. In
O'Reilly, G. et al. (Eds.) *The Handbook of Clinical
Intervention with Young People who Sexually
Abuse.* Chichester: John Wiley and Sons.

Epperson, D.L. et al. (2006) Actuarial Risk
Assessment with Juveniles who Sexually
Offend. In Prescott, D.S. (Ed.) *Risk Assessment of
Youth who have Sexually Abused.* Oklahoma City:
Wood & Barnes.

Epps, K. and Fisher, D. (2004) A Review of the
Research Literature on Young People who
Sexually Abuse. In O'Reilly, G. et al. (Eds.) *The
Handbook of Clinical Intervention with Young
People who Sexually Abuse.* Chichester: John
Wiley and Sons.

Epps, K.J. (1999) Causal Explanations: Filling the
Theoretical Reservoir. In Calder, M.C. (Ed.)
*Working with Young People who Sexually Abuse:
New Pieces of the Jigsaw.* Lyme Regis: Russell
House Publishing.

Gilgun, J.F. (1999) CASPARS: Clinical Assessment
Instruments that Measure Strengths and Risks
in Children and Families. In Calder, M.C. (Ed.)
*Working with Young People who Sexually Abuse:
New Pieces of the Jigsaw.* Lyme Regis: Russell
House Publishing.

Gilgun, J.F., Klein, C. and Pranis, K. (2000) The
Significance of Resources in Models of Risk.
Journal of Interpersonal Violence, 15: 6, 631–50.

Gilgun, J.F. (1996a) Human Development and
Adversity in Ecological Perspective: Part 1: A
Conceptual Framework. *Families in Society,* 77,
395–402.

Gilgun, J.F. (1996b) Human Development and
Adversity in Ecological Perspective: Part 2:
Three Patterns. *Families in Society,* 77, 459–576.

Gilligan, R. (2000) Adversity, Resilience and
Young People. *Children and Society,* 14, 37–47.

Hackett, S. (2002) Abused and Abusing: Work with
Young People who have a Dual Abuse
Experience. In Calder, M.C. (Ed.) *Young People who
Sexually Abuse: Building the Evidence Base for your
Practice.* Lyme Regis: Russell House Publishing.

Hanson, R.K. and Bussiere, M.T. (1996) *Predictors
of Sexual Recidivism: A Meta-analysis.* Ontario:
Department of the Solicitor General.

Hanson, R.K. and Bussiere, M.T. (1998) Predicting
Recidivism: A Meta-analysis of Sexual
Offender Recidivism Studies. *Journal of
Consulting and Clinical Psychology,* 66: 2, 348–62.

Hanson, R.K. and Harris, A. (1998) *Dynamic
Predictors of Sexual Recidivism.* Ontario:
Department of the Solicitor General.

Hanson, R.K. and Thornton, D. (1999) *Static 99:
Improving Actuarial Risk Assessment for Sex
Offenders.* Ottawa, Ontario: Department of the
Solicitor General of Canada.

Hudson, S.M. and Ward, T. (1997) Future
Directions. In Laws, D.R. and O'Donohue, W.
(Eds.) *Sexual Deviance: Theory, Assessment and
Treatment.* NY: Guilford Press.

Hunter, J.A. and Becker, J.V. (1994) The
Relationship between Phallometrically
Measured Deviant Sexual Arousal and Clinical
Characteristics in Juvenile Sexual Offenders.
Professional Psychology: Research and Therapy, 32,
533–8.

James, A.C. and Neil, P.C. (1996) Juvenile Sexual
Offending: A One-year Prevalence Study
within Oxfordshire. *Child Abuse and Neglect,* 20:
6, 477–85.

Kemshall, H. (2001) *Risk Assessment and
Management of Known Sexual and Violent
Offenders: A Review of Current Issues.* Police
Research Series Paper 140. London: The Home
Office.

Longo, R.E. (2002) A Holistic Approach to
Treating Young People who Sexually Abuse. In
Calder. M.C. (Ed.) *Young People who Sexually
Abuse: Building the Evidence Base for your
Practice.* Lyme Regis: Russell House Publishing.

Longo, R.E. (2003) Emerging Issues, Policy
Changes, and the Future of Treating Children
with Sexual Behavior Problems. *Annals of the
New York Academy of Sciences,* 989: 1, 502–14.

Marshall, W.L. and Eccles, A. (1993) Pavlovian
Characteristics for Classifying Juvenile Sex
Offenders. In Barbaree, H.E., Marshall, W.L.
and Hudson, S.M. (Eds.) *The Juvenile Sex
Offender.* New York: Guilford Press.

Masten, A.S., Best, K.M. and Garmezy, N. (1991).
Resilience and Development: Contributions from
the Study of Children who Overcome Adversity.
Development and Psychopathology, 2, 425–44.

Miccio-Fonseca, L.C. (2006b) *Multiplex Empirically
Guided Inventory of Ecological Aggregates for
Assessing Sexually Abusive Children and
Adolescents* (Ages 19 and Under) – MEGA. San
Diego, CA: Author.

Monck, E. and New, M. (1996) *Report of a Study of
Sexually Abused Children and Adolescents and
Young Perpetrators of Sexual Abuse who were
Treated in Voluntary Agency Community
Facilities.* London: HMSO.

Morrison, T. and Wilkinson, L. (2001) Initial Assessment of Parents/carers of Young People/children with Sexually Problematic Behaviour. In Henniker, J. (Ed.) *Getting Started.* Greater Manchester: Youth Justice Trust.

Myers, S. (1998) Young People who Sexually Abuse: Is Consensus Possible or Desirable? *Social Work in Europe,* 5: 1, 53–6.

O'Callaghan, D. (2002) Providing a Research-informed Service for Young People who Sexually Harm Others. In Calder, M.C. (Ed.) *Young People who Sexually Abuse: Building the Evidence Base for your Practice.* Lyme Regis: Russell House Publishing.

Prentky, R. and Righthand, S. (2003) *Juvenile Sex Offender Assessment Protocol-II (J-SOAP-II).* Office of Juvenile Justice and Delinquency Prevention's Juvenile Justice Clearinghouse.

Prentky, R., Harris, A., Frizzell, and Righthand, S. (2000) An Actuarial Procedure for Assessing Risk with Juvenile Sex Offenders. *Sexual Abuse: A Journal of Research and Treatment,* 12: 2, 71–93.

Print, B. et al (2007) *The AIM 2 Model of Initial Assessment: Guidance Document.* Manchester: AIM Project.

Print, B., Morrison, T. and Henniker, J. (2001) An Inter-agency Assessment Framework for Young People who Sexually Abuse: Principles, Processes and Practicalities. In Calder, M.C. (Ed.) *Juveniles and Children who Sexually Abuse: Frameworks for Assessment.* Lyme Regis: Russell House Publishing.

Quinsey, V.L. et al. (1995) Predicting Sexual Offences. In Cambell, J. (Ed.) *Assessing Dangerousness: Violence by Sexual Offenders, Batterers and Child Abusers.* Thousand Oaks, CA: Sage.

Rasmussen, L. and Miccio-Fonseca, L.C. (2007) Empirically Guided Practice with Young People who Sexually Abuse: A Risk Factor Approach to Assessment and Evaluation. In Calder, M.C. (Ed.) *Working with Children and Young People who Sexually Abuse: Taking the Field Forward.* Lyme Regis: Russell House Publishing.

Rasmussen, L.A. (1999) Factors Related to Recidivism among Juvenile Sexual Offenders. *Sexual Abuse: A Journal of Research and Treatment,* 11: 1, 69–85.

Richardson, G. (2007) SHARP: The Development of a New Assessment Tool. In Calder, M.C. (Ed.) *Complete Guide to Sexual Abuse.* 2nd edn. Lyme Regis: Russell House Publishing.

Rutter, M. (1999) Resilience Concepts and Findings. *Journal of Family Therapy,* 21, 119–44.

Ryan, G. (1998) The Relevance of Early Life Experiences to the Behaviour of Sexually Abusive Youth. *The Irish Journal of Psychology,* 19: 32–48.

Ryan, G. (in press) Static, Stable and Dynamic Risks and Assets Relevant to the Prevention and Treatment of Abusive Behaviour. In Calder, M.C. (Ed.) *Complete Guide to Sexual Abuse.* 2nd edn. Lyme Regis: Russell House Publishing.

Ward, T. and Hudson, S.M. (1998) The Construction and Development of Theory in the Sexual Offending Area: A Meta-theoretical Framework. *Sexual Abuse: A Journal of Research and Treatment,* 10: 1, 47–63.

Weinrott, M.R. (1996) *Juvenile Sexual Aggression: A Critical Review.* Colorado: Institute of Behavioural Science.

Worling, J.R. and Curwen, T. (2000) *The 'ERASOR': Estimate of Risk of Adolescent Sexual Offence Recidivism.* Ontario: SAFE-T Program.

CHAPTER 16

Risk in Treatment: From Relapse Prevention to Wellness

Robert E. Longo

Today's youth present greater challenges than during any other time in recent history. The author proposes that: 'sex offending by youth is a symptom of a greater problem'. Young people with sexual behaviour problems and sexual aggression behaviours must be looked at from a holistic/ecological perspective as they may be subject to co-morbid diagnosis, traumatic histories that may have neuro-biological impact on the brain and brain development, and learning deficits and disabilities among other concerns.

This chapter will outline the current thinking about assessing youth with sexual behaviour problems and youth who are sexually aggressive from both a sexual risk perspective as well as risk in other life areas, and recommendations for treatment.

Introduction

In their recent text, Longo and Prescott (2006) describe the history and development in the field of assessing and treating young people with sexual behaviour problems and youth with sexual aggression problems. They describe a field that during the course of the past three or more decades adapted adult-based assessment and treatment models at the beginning, to one that over the course of the past six to ten years has emerged as a field that is cognisant of taking into account developmental and contextual factors, current science that addresses brain development and the impact of trauma on the brain, as well as learning styles, and the labelling of young people in harmful and counter-productive ways.

Risk assessment is no longer a simple act of determining if a young person poses a sexual risk, and if that risk can be lowered through the course of sex-offence specific treatment. Rather, risk assessment must take into account several factors that look at the young person from a developmental and contextual framework, and the youth's ability to thrive in the community. First, the findings from risk assessment of youth should be considered time-limited.

Developmental issues result in young people constantly changing and evolving into young adults. Sexual development and general development is fluid until the young person reaches maturity both physically and mentally. Risk assessments, when written into reports, should clearly indicate that such assessments only have value over a six to twelve month period before they should be considered obsolete and another assessment performed. In other words, such assessments are a snapshot in time and the factors and other points addressed in this chapter continuously influence a particular youth's risk to both sexually reoffend as well as their risk and ability to be productive and safe in a variety of arenas, i.e., family, school, community, within peer groups, and so forth (Prescott and Longo, 2006; Prescott, 2007).

A shift in paradigms

Clinical observation and preliminary research suggest that juvenile sexual abusers are a *heterogeneous population* representing a variety of developmental pathways leading to offending behaviour and various patterns of sexually abusive behaviours. Some youth appear to be at high risk for re-offending and in need of institutionalisation, while many others appear to be at lower risk and highly amenable to community-based interventions. As such, it does not appear to be clinically, legally, or fiscally prudent to formulate a 'one size fits all' approach to their management.

These young people differ in a variety of dimensions, including the extent of their sexual offending behaviour; ranging from sexual harassment, internet violation, and statutory rape, to rape of children and adults, and in some rare instances the rape and murder of a victim (Hunter, 2006). The dimensions include:

- personality characteristics
- anti-social makeup
- criminal behaviour and history

- sexual deviance
- mental health
- their own sexual victimisation

New therapies and interventions now provide us with the ability to assess and address a variety of co-morbid disorders with youth who are often diagnosed with a variety of disorders including, but not limited to, Attention Deficit Hyperactivity Disorder (ADHD), Post Traumatic Stress Syndrome (PTSD), Oppositional Defiant Disorder (ODD), Conduct Disorder (CD), depressive disorders, anxiety disorders, attachment disorders, and more (Johnson, 2006).

This is not to excuse the abusive, and in some cases horrific, sexual acts perpetrated by young people. The statistics regarding youth who commit sexual crimes vary, because uniform definitions are not applied across state or at international levels. The National Center on the Sexual Behaviour of Youth (NCSBY) defines adolescent sex offenders (ASO) as 'adolescents from 13 to 17 who commit illegal sexual behaviour as defined by the sex crime statutes of the jurisdiction in which the offence occurred' (NCSBY, 2006).

While reported statistics vary, in the United States ASO commit a substantial number of sex crimes, including approximately 17 per cent of all arrests for sex crimes, and approximately one third of all sex offences against children are committed by young persons under the age of 18. Females under the age of 18 account for one per cent of forcible rapes committed by juveniles and seven per cent of all juvenile arrests for sex offences, excluding the category of prostitution.

The NCSBY goes on to note the following (NCSBY, 2006a, 2006b):

- Adolescents do not typically commit sex offences against adults, although the risk of offending against adults increases slightly after an adolescent reaches age 16.
- Approximately one-third of sexual offences against children are committed by teenagers. Sexual offences against young children, under 12 years of age, are typically committed by boys between the ages of 12 to 15 years old.
- Adolescent sex offenders are significantly different from adult sex offenders. (They have different developmental pathways, are heterogeneous, and we should therefore never assume a 'one size fits all' approach to assessing, treating, and managing these clients):

  - Adolescent sex offenders are considered to be more responsive to treatment than adult sex offenders and do not appear to continue re-offending into adulthood, especially when provided with appropriate treatment.
  - Adolescent sex offenders have fewer numbers of victims than adult offenders and, on average, engage in less serious and aggressive behaviours.
  - Most adolescents do not have deviant sexual arousal and/or deviant sexual fantasies that many adult sex offenders have.
  - Most adolescents are not sexual predators nor do they meet the accepted criteria for paedophilia.
  - Few adolescents appear to have the same long-term tendencies to commit sexual offences as do some adult offenders.
  - Across a number of treatment research studies, the overall sexual recidivism rate for adolescent sex offenders who receive treatment is low in most US settings as compared to adults.
- ASO are different from adult sex offenders in that they have lower recidivism rates, engage in fewer abusive behaviours over shorter periods of time, and have less aggressive sexual behaviour. Adolescent sex offenders rates for sexual re-offences (5–14 per cent) are substantially less than their rates of recidivism for other delinquent behaviour (8–58 per cent).
- Adolescent sex offenders commit a wide range of illegal sexual behaviours, ranging from limited exploratory behaviours committed largely out of curiosity to repeated aggressive assaults.

The concern, however, is that despite research and knowledge over the past decade, the trickle down assessment and treatment phenomenon from adult-based treatment models to juvenile sexual abuser treatment models means the majority of these treatment programmes seldom focus on areas outside of the sexual offending behaviour (Longo, 2003). Many of these programmes and assessment centres are often forensic models designed to work with normal functioning adult male sex offenders in prison settings. Organisations such as the Association for the Treatment of Sexual Abusers (ATSA) co-founded by this author, have established practitioner guidelines that are generally for 'adult male sex offenders'. Even our labelling of youth uses adult-based terminology, despite many authors/researchers suggesting against the use of these terms, i.e., predator, perp, mini perp, paedophile, etc.

Who are juvenile sexual abusers?

Sexually abusive and aggressive youth have been described as very diverse, and:

- Are otherwise well-functioning youth with limited behavioural or psychological problems.
- Are youth with multiple non-sexual behaviour problems or prior non-sexual juvenile offences.
- Come from both well-functioning families and highly chaotic or abusive backgrounds.
    (Hunter, 2006; Hunter and Longo, 2005)

We do not have comprehensive standards of care for juvenile sexual abusers (Longo, 2002). Our current guidelines for assessment continue to develop and evolve, our current guidelines for treatment are at best tentative and based on little science, and our methods of post-treatment management (coupled with the potential damages of registration/notification laws) are of concern when they are not individualised and based upon the individual's risks, needs, and responsiveness. Mark Chaffin notes that the field of sex offender assessment and treatment has historically been ideologically driven and lacks empirical and scientifically driven evidence (ATSA, 2006). We are a field in which there is little science, and in some cases no science, to support how we assess and specifically treat young people with sexual behaviour and sexually aggressive behaviours. This makes evidence-based practice difficult at best, but supports the use of an evidence-informed model for working with these youth.

For example, the data from (McGrath et al.) The Safer Society Foundation's National Survey (2002) indicated that 9.8 per cent of community-based programmes, and 9.2 per cent of residential programmes in the Unites States use penile plethysmography, an intrusive bio-feedback technique first used with adult sex-offenders, with juvenile abusers; 25.2 per cent of community-based programmes, and 17.7 per cent of residential programmes use Abel Viewing Time; and 44 community-based programmes and 30 residential programmes routinely use polygraph with juvenile abusers despite the lack of research with this population (McGrath,

Cumming and Burchard, 2003). In some States, it is mandated that all juvenile sexual abusers must submit to initial and sometimes routine polygraph examination regardless of the frequency, severity or extent of their sexually abusive behaviours.

Typologies and risk

The first typologies for this group were 'clinical' typologies back in the early 1990s, and were not researched (Longo, 2003). In recent years, however, John Hunter and his colleagues have been researching a typology of juvenile sexual abusers (Hunter, 2006; Hunter and Longo, 2004). As this typology develops, it is hoped that it will guide our field in several positive directions. First, these data will help guide the field in risk assessment, and second, these data will hopefully guide the field in addressing the extent and types of treatment models and modalities that would be most useful and effective in working with these juveniles.

The current research by Hunter (2006) and colleagues indicates that there are two major types of JSA:

1. Adolescents who sexually abuse children.
2. Adolescents who rape peer and adult females.

Youth who perpetrate against prepubescent children differ from those who target pubescent females. Within both major groups are three sub-categories. The first category is the *life style persistent* (anti-social and aggressive) type JSA who are typically poor responders to treatment and account for approximately 5–10 per cent of all sexually abusive and aggressive youth.

The second group, which accounts for approximately 5–10 per cent of all sexually abusive and aggressive youth, are referred to as *adolescent onset paraphilic* (developing paraphilic interests) type and show an increased number of post-treatment arrests for sexual offences.

The third group, which accounts for the majority of adolescents with sexual behaviour problems and sexually aggressive behaviours, are referred to as the adolescent onset, non-paraphilic (transient interests in criminal sexual behaviours) type, and are considered to have the best response to treatment.

The general characteristics seen with sexually abusive and sexually aggressive youth do not

Table 16.1   Differences between young people who sexually perpetrate against children and those who perpetrate against peer and adult females

Youth who sexually perpetrate against children	Youth who sexually perpetrate against peer and adult females
• Less aggressive. • Victims often related or acquaintances. • Less likely to be under influence. • Less likely to use weapon. • More driven by deficits in *social competency and self-esteem* than those that target peers and adults. • Sexual offending against younger children may be more compensatory than reflective of underlying paraphilic interests. • Deficits in psychological functioning, self-esteem, and self-efficacy.	• More aggressive and violent. • Victims typically unrelated. • Substance abuse. • More likely to use weapon. • More likely to commit a non-sexual offence in conjunction with the sexual assault. • More likely to target females and strangers. • Juveniles that target peers and adults demonstrate different offending patterns and perhaps have different motives for their behaviour and appear more criminal, violent, and predatory. • It is hypothesised that upon further study these youth will show evidence of greater levels of *psychopathy* and a higher level of *delinquent peer affiliation*.

typically separate them out from other juveniles considered to be delinquent or who have non-sexual behavioural problems (Longo and Prescott, 2006; Hunter, 2006). The characteristics seen in clinical practice generally include, but are not limited to; lack of social competence, depression, anxiety, pessimism, loneliness and isolation, and immaturity. The majority reveal very high levels of exposure to; child maltreatment, abuse of females (domestic violence) and male-modelled antisocial behaviour, while having deficits in self-perception, are socially inadequate, and fear peer ridicule and rejection.

In particular, the offending of juveniles who target children may be more directly related to perceived and actual social rejection and frustrations. Highly relevant to treatment of these youth would be the identification of perceived negative self-attributes and the manner in which these cognitions give rise to feelings of depression, anxiety, and hopelessness.

Youth who sexually abuse children have characteristics that differ or in some cases are opposite of those youth who perpetrate against peers and adults as summarised in Table 16.1 above (Hunter, 2006; Hunter and Longo, 2005).

Clinical implications

Juvenile sex abusers are a heterogeneous clinical population, and have different programming needs. Treatment programmes should develop treatment protocols/clinical pathways that take into consideration the two basic typologies noted above, development considerations (i.e. grouped by developmental ages: 12–14; 14–16; 16–18) and related issues including gender, learning styles, learning deficits, co-morbid diagnosis and the mixture of patients/clientele who do not demonstrate anti-social personality traits and those who do. The author cautions against mixing youth in groups when there are gender, age, and intellectual differences, as well as mixing youth who demonstrate anti-social personality traits with those who do not.

For example, peer/adult JSA appear more influenced by delinquent attitudes and values and negative peer-group affiliations. These youth may not suffer from low self-esteem and social anxiety. Instead, cognitive distortions may centre on beliefs that they are too clever to get caught, or that legal consequences if incurred would be minimal and easily withstood. With this group of JSA, cognitive distortions regarding women and the nature of male-female relationships are likely present. These youth may be much more likely to misinterpret social cues regarding women's attraction to sexually aggressive males or feel justified in engaging in sexual aggression based on negative sexual stereotypes.

With these youth, treatment and prevention strategies would include the confrontation and correction of distorted cognitions and beliefs, the teaching of healthy masculinity and pro-social values, and careful analysis of environmental factors that contribute to the maintenance of delinquent and sexually aggressive behaviour. The latter should include altering negative peer affiliations, building-in positive socialisation experiences, and strengthening the external monitoring of the youth in the community. This may include enhanced parental monitoring, intensified probation and parole supervision, periodic polygraph assessment, and in more extreme cases, use of electronic monitoring devices.

These youth may also benefit from examining underlying cognitive distortions that exaggerate the magnitude of personal shortcomings or their ability to attenuate skill deficits. Furthermore, therapeutic attention to helping youth understand the reciprocal nature of cognitions and affect and the mutual, synergistic influence of both on behaviour would be of particular relevance. With some youth this may include explaining avoidance conditioning paradigms and the role of anxiety in triggering dangerous risk situations, such as spending time alone with children or deviant sexual fantasising. With this group of juveniles, a major thrust of relapse prevention programming would be the teaching of positive coping and social relationship skills.

Group therapy, although viewed as a staple part of most JSA programming, is not always the best modality (Hunter, 2006). There is no empirical evidence to support group over individual therapy (Longo and Prescott, 2006b); however, there is a growing literature to suggest that group therapy may have adverse effects on some youth due to iatrogenic effects (negative effects introduced through therapy). The term iatrogenic means 'caused by a doctor'.

Treatment issues

Continuum of care

Recent trends have placed an increasing number of youth in detention and residential care (Holman and Ziedenberg, 2006; Chaffin and Longo, 2004). Long-term residential care and exposure to delinquent youth may result in long-term harmful effects as younger and less disturbed youth incorporate negative anti-social values (Holman and Ziedenberg, 2006). When considering JSA for treatment one should always choose the least restrictive environment based upon risk and other factors addressed in this chapter (Chaffin and Longo, 2004).

Developmental focus

Faniff and Becker (2006) note that JSA are still maturing in many areas and specifically two major areas, (1) biological factors (neuro-psych deficits) and (2) environmental factors – i.e. parents, family, community, etc. From a biological perspective, the brain is still developing and can be impacted by:

1. Trauma to the limbic system from which emotional regulation is impaired.
2. Frontal lobe development which controls emotional, behavioural, reasoning, and problem solving and matures around age 23–25.
3. Trauma impacts frontal lobe which inhibits aggression.

Social development and social skills are a critical part of the development in young children and adolescents. Social development issues include, but are not limited to:

- self-esteem
- pro-social behaviour
- goal-directed behaviour
- self-reliance

These developmental items can be affected when there are problems with healthy attachment. Many JSA have anxious and/or resistant attachment concerns that may result in:

- increased frustration
- decreased coping abilities
- decreased social skills
- increased aggression

Abuse leads to increased risk for attachment relationships with parents, caregivers, and others. Faniff and Becker (2006) note that 95 per cent of maltreated children have insecure attachment with their abuser, and that one third of children in non-clinical settings have insecure attachment which falls into one of three styles:

1. Avoidant attachment – the child keeps distant from others.
2. Resistant attachment – the child is ambivalent towards others.
3. Disorganised attachment – the child demonstrates externalised behavioural problems and controlling of others.

As is well known, the abuse of children can lead to a variety of behavioural and psychological problems. With male JSA, Faniff and Becker (2006) caution that maternal sexual abuse tends to be associated with psychological pathology. They go on to note that moral development may be impacted by child maltreatment.

Co-morbid disorders

Brad Johnson (2006) notes that clinicians and others need to become more familiar with commonly seen diagnosis with youth. JSA are no exception. In residential care, it is not uncommon to see patients who are dual diagnosed/have co-morbid disorders that include but are not limited to: ADHD, ADD, PTSD, CD, ODD, Attachment Disorders (RAD), Bi-Polar Disorder, Dysthemia, Mood Disorders, and substance abuse.

- Johnson (2006) suggests one pay attention to youth diagnosed with ADHD, because these adolescents often:
- Engage in sexual intercourse at an earlier age.
- Are more promiscuous.
- Are more likely to have difficulty in peer relations.
- Often have other socialisation problems.

For example, Johnson (2006) notes that 73 per cent of ADHD youth:

1. Have difficulty getting along with siblings and other family members.
2. May also have conduct disorder.
3. May develop opposition defiant disorder (and then go on to have conduct disorder) and suffer from impulsivity.

He also notes that ADHD may lead to increased risk for psychopathology and conduct disorder.

Moving beyond relapse prevention

Current research shows that the sexual re-offence rate for ASO who receive treatment is low in most US settings. Studies suggest that the rates of sexual re-offence (5–14 per cent) are substantially lower than the rates for other delinquent behaviour (8–58 per cent). Additionally, the assumption that the majority of ASO will become adult sex offenders is not supported by the

current literature (NCSBY, 2006). Simply, the research is not at a point where we can categorise JSA and pick empirically supported treatment.

What we do know from clinical experience is that many JSA are successfully treated in shorter, less intensive treatment programmes; this despite the surveys that suggest that the average length of treatment in both community-based and residential sex-offence specific programmes ranges from 18–24 months (McGrath, Cumming, and Burchard, 2003). Many ASO are seen in outpatient group treatment programmes that meet once a week for 8 to 28 months (NCSBY, 2006).

With advances in our knowledge and what we know about treatment, the most pressing concern is the recognition that traditional relapse prevention for sexual offenders is no longer considered a viable model (Longo and Prescott, 2006b; Creeden, 2006, Yates, 2005, 2006). It is a medical model designed for a single pathway to re-offend, and uses avoidance and escape strategies versus positive goal setting and strength-based concepts. There are no studies that have been conducted that address the efficacy of sex-offence specific relapse prevention with youth.

Relapse prevention assumes that the client:

- Is under-regulated.
- Lacks adequate coping responses.
- Lacks self-esteem.
- Is not self-directed with recognition of strengths and positive goals (but rather sets up the self . . . based upon a negative emotional state).
- Is an inflexible model.

As we begin to look at youth from a holistic/ecological perspective it is important to address multiple problems with a broad brush of interventions designed to work with multiple diagnosis, healthy sexuality, shame issues and fairness, and take into account trauma and its impact on the brain.

Promoting healthy sexuality in youth

According to the Henry J. Kaiser Family Foundation, it is estimated that the average adolescent views 1,400 sexual references, jokes, and sexual innuendoes each year on television, yet only one in eighty-five references abstinence, contraception, or marriage (KFF, 2006). With the bombardment of society and specifically youth with incomplete, distorted, and even misinformation about human sexuality, teaching healthy sexuality while confronting unhealthy or problematic sexual behaviours is an increasingly greater challenge to professionals and families.

Brown and Schwartz (2006) note that our field tends to avoid the reality that JSA are or will be sexual people; instead we focus on containing their sexuality versus helping them become sexually healthy. The field of treating JSA does not traditionally promote sexuality, and some programmes prohibit it with youth. The focus of treatment programming is often on addressing 'deviant' and problematic sexual behaviours while seldom spending equal or greater amounts of treatment time addressing healthy sexuality and related issues. Brown and Schwartz (2006) note, we teach JSA what *'not to do'* with sexuality versus *'what to do'* in order to be sexually healthy.

As a field, we overemphasise 'abstinence' and 'grooming', and we wind up seeing normal healthy sexual behaviour in adolescents as grooming behaviours. Are we setting up our JSA patients for sexual failure? Do we inadvertently send patients the message that sex is 'dangerous'?

In order to promote healthy sexuality in adolescents, Brown and Schwartz (2006) recommend we:

1. Establish policy and mission statements related to the promotion of healthy sexuality.
2. Train staff to promote healthy sexuality (we need to be comfortable with our sexuality).

They encourage professionals to make sure assessments focus on *all* aspects of sexuality, including:

1. Establishing sensible policy on the use of touch.
2. Establishing sensible policy about what constitutes normal adolescent sexuality (i.e., masturbation).
3. Conduct formal sexuality education groups using male and female co-facilitators.
4. Support alternative sexual lifestyles.
5. Conduct psycho-educational groups for families on healthy sexuality.

Healthy sexuality should be a part of every curriculum in sex-offence specific programmes.

Comprehensive sexuality education should include:

- human sexual development
- relationships
- personal skills
- interpersonal skills
- sexual behaviour (appropriate and problematic)
- sexual health
- culture and society
- sexual attitudes and beliefs

As professionals we must remain comfortable talking about human sexuality – not judgmental!

Jargon and psychobabble

Traditional programmes for JSA often engage in practices that are not supported in the literature or science, and in some cases may result in damaging the patient instead of assisting them in their recovery. For example, some programmes still use layouts (introductions done in group therapy sessions) which contribute to the client's sexual identity . . . *'My name is xxx and I am a child molester'* or *'My name is xxx and I molest children'*.

The field-specific terminology we use in treatment programmes often does not translate to the world outside of treatment. Youth learn terms and 'parrot' treatment language or paraphrase treatment books and handouts to please therapists, without the intention of using treatment specific language outside of the treatment programme. This is often done on the part of the patient for good reason. Who, among their peers and family would understand concepts such as 'grooming', 'lapses', and 'risk factors'?

There is no recent professional literature, evidence or science to support the notion that 'once a sex offender, always a sex offender'. When applied to adult sex offenders, and there is growing literature and evidence that many adult sex-offenders do heal and do not recidivate, the message implies sexual offending is and will always be a life-long problem; in other words there is no cure. As noted above, JSA generally do not grow up to become adult sex offenders. In fact, the recidivism rates for JSA are low and many JSA will not commit future sex offences once detected and caught. Latham and Kinscherff (2006) note that the majority of JSA do not have diagnosable paraphilias, and will not go on to commit sex-offending behaviours as adults.

The therapeutic relationship

The literature is replete with information that notes that the therapeutic alliance is essential in working with *all* youth, and how we present ourselves to clients is critical (Blanchard, 1998; Castonguay and Hill, 2007; Castonguay and Beutler, 2006; Castonguay, 2006).

Geral Blanchard's book, entitled *The Difficult Connection* (1998), notes that we should keep in mind the following when working with sexual abusers:

> *The therapeutic relationship is central to any counselling process. When empathy, respect, and concern for the sex offender [client] are evident, and when the offender feels understood and empowered and has not become inappropriately dependent on the therapist, he will be less hesitant to become involved in meaningful therapy. The establishment of this type of caring relationship early in therapy will be crucial for a successful outcome. To practice this formula for success, every therapist must examine his/her prejudices, filters, dislikes, and outside influences to guarantee they will not contaminate the relationship.*

He goes on to say:

> *Referring the sex offender to a healthy therapist skilled in the use of self will fosters treatment success more predictably than the use of any specific technique. The qualities found in effective therapists almost always include the elements of congruence, authenticity, warmth, equality, vulnerability, humour, and compassion.*

Congruence is presenting what we feel, saying what we mean, and acting in accordance with the values we espouse; authenticity, simply put, is being genuine; warmth is compassionate responsiveness, and equality is acknowledging that the client is a valued partner in the change process.

Blanchard further notes:

> *A constant effort to conceal our vulnerabilities encourages the offender to respond in kind. When, however, the therapist is willing to judiciously self-disclose, his credibility – and therefore, his influence – are enhanced.*

Vulnerability, when used properly, is the natural extension of an authentic and healthy personality, and compassion is a willingness to attempt an understanding of the client's emotional condition and life situation with a concern for his growth and happiness.

Dealing with shame, fairness, and ethics

Alan Jenkins' timeless book, *Invitations to Responsibility* (1990) uses an invitational model to engage clients which combines both Narrative and Motivational Interviewing therapies and techniques. His entire approach is based on a positive growth developmental model. Current research on attachment and the impact of trauma point to the use of positive adult and peer relationship development as an essential component of treatment.

Jenkins (2006a, 2006b) notes that we want clients to:

- Declare their ethics.
- Establish goals related to their personal ethics.
- Develop personal motivation.
- Examine their personal ethics and action in relation to their personal goals.

He suggests that the principles of intervention are:

- safety
- responsibility
- accountability
- fairness
- respect

In following Jenkins' suggested principles, the therapist wants to make sure to:

- Address youth without reproducing dominant abusive practices – confrontation, the use of layouts.
- Address disadvantage of their own victimisation.
- Address the client within a developmental context.
- Avoid colonisation (the psychological invasion, benevolent bullying, protest and insurrection ['being done to'] of the client).

Many professionals acknowledge that shame is at the root of violence (Blanchard, 2006) and as reported by Jenkins (2006b) often results in:

- A challenge to the client's personal integrity.
- Avoidance of thinking about one's behaviour.
- Withdrawal.
- Negative peer relations.
- Alcohol and drug abuse.
- Self-harm, or aggression and violence.

Our field has historically shot itself in both feet with the double-barrelled shotgun phrases, 'there is no cure for sex-offenders', and 'victims are damaged for life'. Such statements may be both confusing and conflicting for JSA, and when made to patients give the message of there being no hope for getting well (from being a perpetrator or victim).

Forgiveness

All too often, JSA programmes and therapists focus on the patient taking responsibility for their actions (sexually abusive and aggressive behaviours) while de-emphasising one's personal victimisation issues. As a result, therapists give the message to patients that they should not ask for forgiveness, and seldom address the idea of forgiveness as a therapeutic theme. Forgiveness is a vehicle for addressing one's personal anger issues, especially as it pertains to forgiving one's abuser (Longo, 2001). Survivors of all forms of abuse and trauma often heal more completely when they come to forgive transgressions against them.

Forgiveness can be a significant healing process, and is a concept that must be addressed (Myss, 1997). However, forgiveness should never be a forced or public act, but rather an act done at one's own pace and time, and most generally in a private fashion (Coyhis, 1999). Caroline Myss (1997) notes: 'One of the main beliefs I want you to adopt in order to heal your life or illness is a belief in the importance of forgiveness. Forgiveness frees up the energy necessary for healing'.

Trauma and neuro-biology

It is not uncommon, especially in residential treatment settings, to see a large percentage of patients with a PTSD diagnosis. At Old Vineyard Behavioural Health Services where there are 45 beds for male JSA ranging from 11–18 years of age, over 80 per cent of the population has been diagnosed with PTSD. The literature on trauma and trauma's impact on the brain is growing at a rapid rate and professionals should not ignore the possibility of patients having this diagnosis.

Given the impact of trauma on the brain, it is important to understand how we as professionals can work with trauma in productive and healing ways. When trauma occurs, brain development is impacted (Creeden, 2006; Stein and Kendall, 2004). Helping the patient to heal and to work with trauma impact will often require the professional to go beyond 'sit-down, talk therapy'. Trauma often results in various parts of the brain not communicating and in particular the right and left hemispheres. This lack of communication between hemispheres occurs when trauma impacts the corpus callosum (see Figure 16.1).

Trauma also impacts the limbic system, the part of the brain dedicated to survival (see Figure 16.2). The thalamus senses stimuli coming into the brain. The hypothalamus maintains a sense of balance and well-being and provides communication between the brain and the body. The amygdala stores memories from fear producing experiences (trauma) and monitors incoming stimuli that may be considered as threatening. The amygdala is what activates the

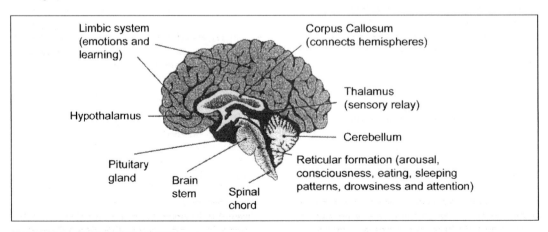

Figure 16.1   Figure Mid-line view #1

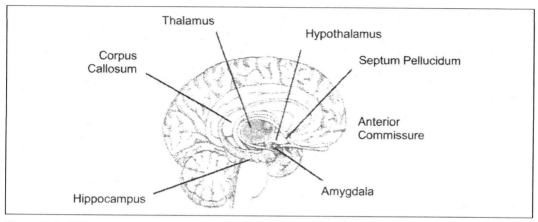

Figure 16.2   Mid-line view #2

flight-fight-freeze phenomena when we experience fear or feel a threat to our safety and well-being. The hippocampus is like a memory chip in a computer. All memory goes thought the hippocampus. The corpus callosum, which connects the two hemispheres of the brain, allows for conscious information to be exchanged between hemispheres. The anterior commissure carries unconscious, emotional information between the two hemispheres.

As we understand more about the workings of the brain, the impact of trauma to the brain, and brain development, so new treatments and technologies have begun the shape the way we work with traumatised patients. Engaging patients in experiential work, exercises, fitness programmes, yoga, and other experiences helps the brain to communicate better and re-establish healing functioning (Bergman 2006; Creeden, 2006; Stein and Kendall, 2004). Commercially available products by BrainGym® International, BrainMaster Technologies® The Wild Devine Project, The International Center for Reiki Training, among many others provide practitioners with the option to work with and teach patients a variety of self-regulation, calming, relaxation, and impulse control techniques.

Summary and conclusion

The limitations to this chapter prohibit a more detailed explanation and analysis of new trends in working with high-risk youth, and specifically youth at risk for sexual offending. What is

becoming increasingly clear, is that traditional methods and models, especially those that have trickled down from the world of adult sexual offender treatment, should be considered as inappropriate at least, and potentially harmful at worst, if applied to JSA.

Youth with sexual behaviour problems and those who are sexually aggressive pose complex problems that cannot be addressed, let alone treated, with simplistic, canned (one size fits all) programming, and/or sex-offender specific methods or models alone. Many youth come to specialised professionals with an array of problems that are directly related to their sexually abusive behaviours and problems. As professionals, we have the obligation to both understand and treat these patients with the appropriate treatment models and methods. To fully address the needs of these patients, and therefore the possible risks posed to the patient's self, others, and the greater community, we should be mindful that sexually abusive behaviour is often a symptom of a much greater problem.

References

Association for the Treatment of Sexual Abusers (2006) *Interpreting Research Evidence.* 25th Annual Research and Treatment Conference, Chicago, IL September 27.

Bengis, S.M. and Cuninggim, P. (2006) Beyond Psychology: Brain-based Approaches that Impact Behaviour, Learning and Treatment. In Longo, R.E. and Prescott, D.S. (Eds.) *Current Perspectives: Working With Sexually Aggressive*

Youth and Youth With Sexual Behaviour Problems. Holyoke, MA: NEARI Press.

Bergman, J. (2006) Personal communication, November 13.

Blanchard, G. (2006) Personal communication, April 5.

Blanchard, G. (1998) *The Difficult Connection.* (Rev.) Brandon, VT: Safer Society Press.

Brown, S.M. and Schwartz, C. (2006) Promoting Healthy Sexuality in Sexually Abusive Youth. In Longo, R.E. and Prescott, D.S. (Eds.) *Current Perspectives: Working With Sexually Aggressive Youth and Youth with Sexual Behaviour Problems.* Holyoke, MA: NEARI Press.

Castonguay, L.G. (2006) *Factors of Change in Psychotherapy: A Delineation of Empirically Based Principles of Change.* Keynote address ATSA Research and Treatment Conference. Chicago, IL. September 29.

Castonguay, L.G. and Beutler, L.E. (2006) (Eds.) *Principles of Therapeutic Change that Work.* NY: Oxford University Press.

Castonguay, L.G. and Hill, C.E. (2007) (Eds.) *Insight in Psychotherapy.* Washington, DC: American Psychological Association.

Chaffin, M. and Longo, R.E. (2004) Guidelines for Placement Within a Continuum of Care for Adolescent Sex Offenders and Children with Sexual Behaviour Problems. *Family Violence and Sexual Assault Bulletin,* 20, 3.

Coyhis, D. (1999) *Understanding Native American Culture: Insights for Recovery Professionals.* Colorado Springs, CO: Coyhis Publishing.

Creeden, K. (2006a) *A Shift in the Paradigm: Changing from a Relapse Prevention to a Development Treatment Model.* Presentation at MATSA/MASOC 8th Annual Joint Conference. Marlborough, MA. April, 4, 2006.

Creeden, K. (2006b) Neurological Impact of Trauma and Implications. In Longo, R.E. and Prescott, D.S. (Eds.) *Current Perspectives: Working with Sexually Aggressive Youth and Youth with Sexual Behaviour Problems.* Holyoke, MA: NEARI Press.

Faniff, A. and Becker, J. (2006) Developmental Considerations in Working with Juvenile Sexual Offenders. In Longo, R.E. and Prescott, D.S. (Eds.) *Current Perspectives: Working with Sexually Aggressive Youth and Youth with Sexual Behaviour Problems.* Holyoke, MA: NEARI Press.

Holman, B. and Ziedenberg, J. (2006) *The Dangers of Detention: The Impact of Incarcerating Youth in Detention and other Secure Facilities.* Washington DC: Justice Policy Institute.

Hunter, J. (2006) Understanding Diversity in Juvenile Sexual Offenders: Implications for Assessment, Treatment, and Legal Management. In Longo, R.E. and Prescott, D.S. (Eds.) *Current Perspectives: Working with Sexually Aggressive Youth and Youth with Sexual Behaviour Problems.* Holyoke, MA: NEARI Press.

Hunter, J. and Longo, R.E. (2004) Relapse Prevention with Juvenile Sexual Abusers: A Holistic and Integrated Approach. In O'Reilly, G., Marshall, W., Carr, A. and Beckett, R.C. (Eds.) *The Handbook of Clinical Intervention with Young People who Sexually Abuse.* NY: Brunner-Routledge.

Jenkins, A. (2006a) The Politics of Intervention: Fairness and Ethics. In Longo, R.E. and Prescott, D.S. (Eds.) *Current Perspectives: Working with Sexually Aggressive Youth and Youth with Sexual Behaviour Problems.* Holyoke, MA: NEARI Press.

Jenkins, A. (2006b) Discovering Integrity: Working with Shame without Shaming Young People who have Abused. In Longo, R.E. and Prescott, D.S. (Eds.) *Current Perspectives: Working with Sexually Aggressive Youth and Youth with Sexual Behaviour Problems.* Holyoke, MA: NEARI Press.

Jenkins, A. (1990) *Invitations to Responsibility: The Therapeutic Engagement of Men who are Violent and Abusive.* Adelaide, South Australia: Dulwich Centre Publications.

Johnson, B.R. (2006) Co-morbid Diagnosis of Sexually Abusive Youth. In Longo, R.E. and Prescott, D.S. (Eds.) *Current Perspectives: Working with Sexually Aggressive Youth and Youth with Sexual Behaviour Problems.* Holyoke, MA: NEARI Press.

KFF (2006) http://www.kff.org/entmedia/upload/Sex-on-TV–4-Full-Report.pdf

Latham, C. and Kinscherff, R.T. (2006) *Chasing the Dead Horse around the Bush: Misdiagnosing Children with Sexual Behaviour Problems.* Presentation at ATSA 25th Annual Research and Treatment Conference. Chicago, IL. September 27, 2006.

Longo, R.E. (2001) *Paths to Wellness: A Holistic Approach and Guide for Personal Recovery.* Holyoke, MA: NEARI Press.

Longo, R.E. (2002) Residential Standards of Care for Adolescent Sexual Abusers. In Calder, M.C. (Ed.) *Young People who Sexually Abuse: Building the Evidence Base for your Practice.* Lyme Regis: Russell House Publishing.

Longo, R.E. (2003) Emerging Issues, Policy Changes, and the Future of Treating Children with Sexual Behaviour Problems. In Prentky, R.A., Janus, E.S. and Seto, M.C. (Eds.) *Sexually Coercive Behaviour: Understanding and Management*. Annals of the New York Academy of Sciences. Vol. 989.

Longo, R.E. and Prescott, D.S. (2006b) Introduction. In Longo, R.E. and Prescott, D.S. (Eds.) *Current Perspectives: Working with Sexually Aggressive Youth and Youth with Sexual Behaviour Problems*. Holyoke, MA: NEARI Press.

Longo, R.E. and Prescott, D.S. (Eds.) (2006a) *Current Perspectives: Working with Sexually Aggressive Youth and Youth with Sexual Behaviour Problems*. Holyoke, MA: NEARI Press.

McGrath, R.J., Cumming, G.F. and Burchard, B.L. (2003) *Current Practices and Trends in Sexual Abuser Management: The Safer Society 2002 Nationwide Survey*. Brandon, VT: Safer Society Press.

Myss, C. (1997) *Why People don't Heal and How they Can*. NY: Three Rivers Press. NCSBY. http://www.ncsby.org/

NCSBY (2006a) http://www.ncsby.org/pages/publications/What%20Research%20Shows%20About%20Adolescent%20Sex%20Offenders%20060404.pdf

NCSBY (2006b) http://www.ncsby.org/pages/publications/What%20Research%20Shows%20About%20Adolescent%20Sex%20Offenders%20060404.pdf

Prescott, D.S. (2007) *Assessing Youth who have Sexually Abused: A Primer*. Holyoke, MA: NEARI Press.

Prescott, D.S. and Longo, R.E. (2006) Current Perspectives: Working with Young People who Sexually Abuse. In Longo, R.E. and Prescott, D.S. (Eds.) *Current Perspectives: Working with Sexually Aggressive Youth and Youth with Sexual Behaviour Problems*. Holyoke, MA: NEARI Press.

Schwartz, B., Cavanaugh, D., Pemental, A. and Prentky, R. (2006) Family Violence and Severe Maltreatment in Sexually Reactive Children and Adolescents. In Longo, R.E. and Prescott, D.S. (Eds.) *Current Perspectives: Working with Sexually Aggressive Youth and Youth with Sexual Behaviour Problems*. Holyoke, MA: NEARI Press.

Sisco, M.M., Sanders, M., Harvey, D. and Becker, J.V. (2006) Domestic Violence, Childhood Victimisation, and Juvenile Sexual Criminality: Research Findings and Practical Implications. In Longo, R.E. and Prescott, D.S. (Eds.) *Current Perspectives: Working with Sexually Aggressive Youth and Youth with Sexual Behaviour Problems*. Holyoke, MA: NEARI Press.

Stein, P.T. and Kendall, J. (2004) *Psychological Trauma and the Developing Brain: Neurologically Based Interventions for Troubled Children*. New York: The Hawthorne Maltreatment and Trauma Press.

Yates, P.M. (2005) *Pathways to the Treatment of Sexual Offenders: Rethinking Intervention*. ATSA Forum, Summer. Beaverton: OR.

Yates, P.M. (2006) *The Self-regulation Model of Offending: From Theory to Practice*. Presentation at ATSA 25th Annual Research and Treatment Conference. Chicago, IL. September 26, 2006.

CHAPTER 17

Cultural Considerations Within Risk Assessments

Jo Thakker, James Vess and Tony Ward

Introduction

One of the key objectives in clinical work is the development of an understanding of the client. Without an understanding of his or her unique experience and situation it would not be possible to identify the problems and issues and provide appropriate treatment. Naturally, factors pertaining to ethnicity and culture are an integral part of the person that requires understanding. When the client and clinician share a common background the process of developing a valid conceptualisation of the client is easier. Of course, there will still be differences of perspective to attend to, but these will be less significant. In the area of risk assessment an accurate understanding of the client is particularly important because there may be much at stake; in particular, the safety of others. Also, a risk assessment often has major implications for clients; it can be instrumental in decisions regarding offenders' sentencing, release, and supervision in the community.

An extensive literature search of relevant databases revealed that there is a dearth of research examining cultural considerations in risk assessment. Consequently, this chapter takes a broad perspective and attempts to extrapolate from multiple research areas. There is a vast research literature in the area of cross-cultural psychology, which it is not possible to summarise here. Rather a few selected aspects which pertain to risk assessment are included.

The chapter begins with a discussion of cross-cultural issues in general assessment. These include language and communication, acculturation, and the use of explanatory models. The middle section of the chapter then focuses on the cross-ethnic use of the Psychopathy Checklist Revised (PCL-R) which is one of the psychometric tools commonly used in the assessment of risk. Also considered briefly are current actuarial measures of risk, as these have consistently been found to have the highest levels of predictive accuracy through empirical studies with various offender populations. The purpose of this discussion is to examine whether assessment measures such as these are valid for use across ethnic groups. The final section of the chapter presents a model that may be used as a guide for the implementation of culture-sensitive risk assessments.

General cultural competence

As noted above there is little available research pertaining directly to the topic that is the focus of this chapter, hence it is necessary to examine the considerations for general cross-cultural clinical work and then determine how these may apply to risk assessment. Reddy (2006) outlines a number of key areas that require attention in order to carry out ethically appropriate psychological practice in cross-cultural contexts. First, and perhaps most obvious, are issues of language and communication. There are a number of ways in which these factors may influence the process of risk assessment. Good communication is essential for establishing rapport and for gaining informed consent (Reddy, 2006) and is fundamental to the assessment process, which requires the gathering of accurate information. While some language difficulties may be quite apparent (such as when the client and clinician do not share a common language and thus require an interpreter) others may be more subtle, and thus be more difficult to identify. For example, word meanings may be slightly dissimilar due to the clinician and client having slightly different cultural backgrounds. With regard to risk assessment it is important to be aware of potential differences in word meaning as these may impact on the validity of the information obtained from the client. This is relevant to both the clinical interview and the use of self-report psychometrics.

Spielberger (2006: 300) states: 'in the cross-cultural adaptation of psychological tests, the key words for an item in the original language may have several different translations that are equally acceptable in the target language'. Hence, psychological tests need to be translated very carefully. Spielberger points out that the words used in various languages to identify and express emotions and personality characteristics often have a number of meanings and associations and even within one language, words may have multiple meanings in different subcultures. With regard to psychometric instruments it is important to note the intensity that is transmitted by a particular term. For example, afraid and terrified suggest different levels of fear, and surprised and shocked indicate different levels of intensity of an individual's response to an unexpected event.

In the area of risk assessment, the primary psychometric or statistical concern is likely to be predictive validity, with a specific form of criminal re-offending as the criterion of interest. Therefore the most valuable form of research data will be studies that examine the predictive power of a particular measure or combination of measures when used with a cultural group similar to the offender being assessed. To the degree that the individual offender to be assessed differs from the normative groups for which a measure has been empirically validated, greater caution must be used in applying the findings of even the most widely used risk assessment measures.

According to Reddy, another factor to keep in mind is acculturation. If the client has recently emigrated it is important that the clinician develops an understanding of the client's situation. In particular, the clinician should explore the client's 'migration experience', including the experience of leaving his or her homeland and of settling into a new cultural environment. In this regard it is helpful to develop a picture of the client's strengths and his or her ability to adapt to change. This is particularly important in the context of conducting a risk assessment as acculturation can lead to a range of significant stressors and difficulties, such as social isolation, and financial hardship.

It is not only immigrants who experience acculturation stress but also indigenous populations who have been affected by colonisation and in the process become minority groups. Research has found that Native American adolescents experience significant stress in relation to their experiences of feeling alienated from the dominant culture (La Fromboise et al., 2006). La Fromboise et al. examined outcomes (problem behaviour versus pro-social behaviour)

in adolescents from three Native American reservations in the American Midwest. They found that reports of racially based discrimination were strongly associated with negative outcomes. In other words, the experience of discrimination was identified as an important risk factor for future anti-social behaviour.

Another important issue discussed by Reddy is cultural sensitivity. In order to establish rapport and develop a good therapeutic relationship the clinician must demonstrate respect for the client's culturally-embedded customs and beliefs. Reddy warns against stereotyping individuals on the basis of their appearance, and points out that there is much variation within cultures in the extent to which people adopt certain traditions. Therefore, it is important to ask about these issues at the outset rather than act on an assumption. In terms of risk assessment this is important because respect for the client's beliefs, values, and traditions will assist in the building of rapport and facilitate the acquisition of valid information. If the client feels respected then he or she is more likely to provide honest information.

Another point to consider is the potential difference across cultures in clients' willingness to discuss certain details of their lives. In order to conduct a good risk assessment it is often necessary to acquire information that may be quite difficult for clients to discuss. For example, when assessing sexual offenders it is important to inquire about their sexual functioning and sexual preferences. Such discussions may be particularly challenging for some cultural groups, especially those in which sex is less commonly discussed and is less prominently displayed in society. In the West, sexual images are routinely displayed in advertisements and sex is often quite openly discussed. Such a relaxed approach to human sexuality contrasts sharply with approaches in many other cultural settings. For example, in India, people generally have very conservative views about sexual matters (Jejeebhoy, 1998). Therefore, in conducting risk assessments, topics such as sexuality should be discussed sensitively. It may be advantageous to use self-report inventories (at least as a starting point) for some information gathering, as these may allow for the initial disclosure of sexual information with less embarrassment or distortion than direct questioning might yield. Examples of such measures include the Multiphasic Sex Inventory

(Nichols and Molinder, 1984) and the Clarke Sexual History Questionnaire (Langevin et al., 1990).

Reddy also discusses the use of explanatory models that play an important role in clinical psychology practice. These models dictate the way in which psychopathology is conceptualised and are therefore fundamental to both assessment and treatment. Individuals from non-Western backgrounds may have very different explanatory models, which they use to make sense of their experiences and their psychological difficulties. In New Zealand there is a growing recognition that the inclusion of culturally-relevant explanatory models is advantageous, and in some settings such models have been integrated into mainstream clinical practice (e.g. Nathan, Wilson and Hillman, 2003). For instance, an evaluation of an intervention programme for sex offenders in New Zealand which combines Mäori *tikanga* (customs and traditions) and cognitive behaviour therapy found the intervention to be effective in reducing the risk of re-offending in both Mäori and non-Mäori (Nathan et al., 2003).

One of the most widely used Mäori models is *Whare Tapa Wha* (four cornerstones of health) that takes a holistic approach to the understanding of health and wellbeing (refer to Rochford, 2004 for further details). This conceptualisation refers to the physical, emotional, social and spiritual dimensions of human health and proposes that each realm must be attended to, in order to restore an individual's wellbeing. Such an approach requires the clinician to gain an understanding of the client's condition or level of functioning in each of these areas, so that a satisfactory treatment programme can be developed which is suitably inclusive.

With regard to risk assessment, this has a number of implications. Once again, rapport is an issue; rapport may be compromised if the client feels that a Western view is being imposed upon them. Also, accurate assessment of risk may be more difficult to attain if the client's interpretation of their experience is not fully understood. For example, a Mäori offender may believe that a *Makutu* (curse) has been placed upon them, and propose that it played a causal role in their offending. Such an explanation has major implications for the evaluation of future risk, as it suggests that the offender has a tendency to externalise the causes of their behaviour. This may limit the likelihood that a sense of personal responsibility will develop.

Another important example of the significance of this issue is demonstrated by the culture-bound syndrome *amok* (from which the phrase 'to run amok' originated) which may involve significant violence. Apparently *amok* is frequently considered to be an acceptable form of aggressive behaviour in Malaysia, where it is most commonly reported (Aderibigbe and Pandurangi, 1995). Hence, if clients were to conceptualise their aggressive inclinations in terms of this syndrome it may influence their future behaviour and, therefore, their risk. In the practice of risk assessment, the importance of explanatory models is reflected in the development of an aetiological formulation of the individual client's risk of re-offending.

When working cross-culturally it is also important to pay attention to the client's culturally-embedded strengths (Baird, 2005). It may be easy to focus on such things as acculturation and the challenges that can arise from being part of a minority group, however aspects of an individual's cultural identity may also contribute in positive ways to their wellbeing. For instance, a person's religion or their familial roles and relationships may be an important source of personal strength and pro-social support. These factors may have a protective impact on an individual's risk level. Conversely, alienation from one's culture and isolation from one's family may present dynamic risk factors if they lead to antisocial and offence-supporting peer groups, alcohol and drug abuse, negative affect, and attitudes that facilitate the victimisation of others.

As noted by Baird (2005) one of the key steps in the acquisition of skills for working with clients from diverse cultural backgrounds is the development of self awareness. Clinicians need to be aware of their own prejudices and biases so that they can ultimately overcome them and minimise their potential impact on the assessment process. This includes learning about historical events, especially racially based injustices that may have lasting consequences for certain cultural groups. Clinicians should also develop insight with regard to the beliefs and stereotypes that they may harbour in relation to various ethnic groups.

One of the key problems with cross-cultural research is the tendency to take a Eurocentric approach and search for similarity rather than diversity (Dana, 2000) as evidenced in several major cross-cultural studies of psychopathology.

For example, in the 1970s the World Health Organisation (WHO) conducted research on schizophrenia in a number of countries (refer to Thakker and Ward, 1998 for a detailed discussion of this study) and used a standardised Western diagnostic instrument to identify so called 'core' symptoms. As noted by Kleinman (1988: 19), while the researchers were able to identify individuals with the core symptoms across cultures '. . . the similarity was an artifact of the methodology' because patients who displayed symptoms that did not fit the criteria were excluded from the study at the outset. Therefore any difference that was present in the manifestation of symptoms of psychosis would not have been documented or investigated by the research.

This issue is discussed by D'Andrea (2003) who lists the ways in which racism is evidenced in the area of mental health. These are: the disproportionate number of Caucasian individuals working in mental health, the inadequate training for working with diverse ethnic groups, the use of 'culturally biased' psychometric measures and assessment processes, and the use of Western centred theoretical approaches. While the term 'racism' may seem more extreme than is warranted by these cultural weaknesses, cultural insensitivity that disadvantages clients from other cultures may come in many forms, and it may penetrate professional practices in a variety of subtle ways.

Cross-ethnic use of actuarial risk measures and the Psychopathy Checklist Risk specific measures

Although there is continuing debate over the optimal utilisation of static and dynamic risk factors in risk assessment (see e.g. Quinsey et al., 1998; Hanson and Harris, 2001; Craig, Browne and Stringer, 2004), actuarial measures have demonstrated a statistically significant level of predictive accuracy regarding the risk of violent and sexual re-offending, and consistently outperform clinical judgements (Hanson, 1998; Hanson and Thornton, 1999, 2000). Two types of actuarial approaches have been described. One type is the use of purposefully designed actuarial risk assessment instruments. Such measures are designed to predict some future event (e.g. violent or sexual offending) based on the association of the items in the instrument with the

outcome of interest. Examples of such measures with research evidence of predictive validity include the Violence Risk Appraisal Guide (VRAG) (Harris, Rice and Quinsey, 1993) the Sex Offender Risk Appraisal Guide (SORAG) (Quinsey et al., 1998) the Rapid Risk Assessment of Sexual Offence Recidivism (RRASOR) (Hanson, 1997).

One of the actuarial measures with the most empirical support is the Static-99 (Hanson and Thornton 2000). The Static-99 combines the items from the RRASOR and items taken from the Structured Clinical Judgement Scale developed in the United Kingdom (Hanson and Thornton, 1999, 2000). Doren (2004) notes that there have been at least 22 studies of the Static-99's predictive validity beyond the Hanson and Thornton (2000) developmental study, where they originally reported a correlation with sexual recidivism of .33 and a receiver operating characteristic (ROC) area under the curve (AUC) of .71. In a review comparing six risk assessment instruments for sex offenders, Barbaree et al. (2001) reported an AUC of .70 for the Static-99 in predicting sexual re-offending in a sample of 215 sex offenders released from prison for an average of 4.5 years. Others have found similar results, with AUCs ranging from .64 (Bartosh et al., 2003) to .77 (Beech et al., 2002). In a recent development, Thornton et al. (2003, as cited in Craig, Beech and Browne, 2006) developed a risk assessment system referred to as the Risk Matrix 2000/Sexual. This new measure looks promising, but has not yet been as widely validated as previous measures.

Whereas most studies using the RRASOR or Static-99 have been conducted with North American and UK samples, Sjostedt and Langstrom (2001) cross-validated the Static-99 on a sample of 1,400 sex offenders released from prison in Sweden over a five year period. This study demonstrated the predictive validity of the Static-99 in a different cultural context, with an AUC of .76 for sexual recidivism over an average follow-up period of 3.7 years.

Another actuarial measure for sexual offender risk validated in a different cultural context is the Automated Sexual Recidivism Scale (ASRS), developed by applying a computerised set of historical variables with a sample of 1,133 male sexual offenders released from prison by the New Zealand Department of Corrections (Skelton et al., 2006). Area Under the Curve figures of .70 to .78 were obtained over periods of five to 15 years, reflecting a significant level of association with sexual recidivism. Detected rates of reoffending across risk levels were comparable to those previously reported for the STATIC-99. The validation sample for the ASRS included a substantial portion of Maori offenders, and preliminary results indicate comparable levels of predictive accuracy across ethnic groups.

This finding is consistent with those reported by Harris et al. (2003). These authors note that although most members of the original samples for the STATIC-99 were white, race has not been found to be a significant predictor of sexual offence recidivism, and that interactions between race and actuarial rates are rare. Similarly, Harris et al. (2003) cite studies indicating that the SIR Scale used in Canada works as well for Aboriginal offenders as it does for non-aboriginal offenders (Hann et al., 1993). The LSI-R scale is reported to work as well for non-white offenders as it does for white offenders (Lowenkamp et al., 2001) and as well for aboriginal offenders as for non-aboriginal offenders (Bonta, 1989). Finally, a study by Nicholaichuk (2001) is cited as providing evidence that the STATIC-99 works as well for Aboriginal sexual offenders as it does for whites. Harris et al. (2003) conclude that there is currently no indication that the STATIC-99 is culturally specific. By extension, actuarial approaches to risk assessment offer the best opportunity to empirically establish their accuracy across cultural groups.

Psychopathy measures

The second approach is the actuarial use of psychological tests or standardised measures. While they were not designed as risk assessment measures per se, research indicates that the PCL-R and PCL:SV measures of psychopathy are associated with violence risk in a meaningful way (Hart, 1998, 2001; Hare, 2003; Wilson, 2003). This approach typically uses research results to identify cut-off scores to use in risk prediction.

Psychopathy has been described as: 'the first personality disorder to be recognised in psychiatry' (Hildebrand and de Ruiter, 2004: 233) and as 'one of the most important constructs in forensic research and practice . . .' (Barbaree, 2005; Sullivan et al., 2006:, 531). Psychopathy is a severe form of personality disorder with distinctive emotional, interpersonal, and antisocial features that has a strong association with criminal behaviour (Tolman and Rotzien, 2007). Highly psychopathic offenders are characterised by emotional deficits such as a lack of empathy or remorse, a manipulative and exploitative interpersonal style, and a blatant disregard for the rights of others. Research has consistently found psychopathy to have a strong relationship to a variety of negative criminal justice outcomes. These include poor response to available treatment interventions, increased involvement in institutional misconduct while incarcerated, and higher levels of violent and sexual re-offending as compared to less psychopathic offenders.

There is wide agreement that the best standardised measure for assessing psychopathy is the Revised Psychopathy Checklist (PCL-R) developed by Robert Hare (Cooke, Kosson and Michie, 2001). It assesses 20 emotional and behavioural features that define psychopathy, based on a thorough review of file and interview information. When conducted by adequately trained individuals, the PCL-R produces highly reliable scores. Although the PCL-R was designed to measure personality, research suggests that it has an important role in risk assessments and that it is a good predictor of both general and violent re-offending (Hemphill and Hare, 2004; Looman et al., 2005). It has been noted that results from the PCL-R are often influential in a range of situations, including parole decisions and death sentence judgements (Cooke et al., 2001) and subsequently researchers warn that the PCL-R '. . . has great potential for causing harm if used improperly' (Cooke et al., 2005a: 335).

Cooke and Michie (1999) propose that due to its excellent concurrent and convergent validity, the PCL-R is an ideal measure for investigating the manifestation of psychopathy in various cultural contexts. Another reason that the PCL-R is focused on in this chapter is that it appears to have more cross-cultural research than any other psychometric tool that is used in risk assessments. Finally, it is arguably particularly appropriate for cross-cultural investigation because it has a clear conceptual basis that relates to a specific personality problem and this adds another valuable dimension to the discussion.

Research in North America

Cooke and colleagues (2001) assert that while the PCL-R is frequently used in ethnically diverse populations, most of the research supporting the validity of its use has been conducted with Caucasian offenders and some have questioned the validity of the concept (of psychopathy) in non-Caucasian populations. In exploring this issue Cooke et al. examined PCL-R ratings in two different prison-based groups: African American and Caucasian. While they found significant differences in five of the test items, these differences became inconsequential in relation to the total score. The researchers concluded that there were no significant differences in the way that the test functioned in each of these ethnic groups and subsequently proposed that the PCL-R is a valid assessment tool for use with African Americans.

McCoy and Edens (2006) conducted a meta-analysis of the three PCL measures (the Revised, the Youth and the Short Version) across Black (African descent) and White (European descent) youth. Their analysis of 16 studies found a significant yet small difference between the ratings of Blacks and Whites with the former tending to receive a slightly higher total score. McCoy and Edens point out that their study was embarked on, in part, in response to the work of Lynn (2002) who presented a rather controversial article claiming that there are major differences across ethnic groups in levels of psychopathic traits. Lynn argues that both African Americans and Native Americans are more psychopathic than those of Hispanic, Caucasian and Asian ancestry. Furthermore, Lynn proposes that these differences have a genetic (and specifically evolutionary) origin. As noted by McCoy and Edens there are numerous problems with Lynn's argument. For instance, he mistakenly equates psychopathy with general anti-social behaviour and he assumes that the ethnic differences are a result of genetic factors.

Another study (by Sullivan et al., 2006) examined the reliability and validity of the PCL-R in incarcerated Latino Americans when compared to matched African Americans and European Americans. The researchers found the PCL-R to be a valid and reliable instrument for measuring psychopathy in Latinos in comparison to the other two ethnic groups and they concluded that psychopathy – as measured by the PCL-R – is very similar across these ethnic groups. However, they found some cross-ethnic differences in the relationships between some components of psychopathy and external factors. For example, there was a significantly stronger

association between the affective component and socio-economic status (SES) in European Americans when compared to both of the other ethnic groups.

Schmidt et al. (2006) investigated the validity of the PCL:YV (Youth Version) across ethnicity and gender in community-based youth offender population. Using a three-year follow-up period, their investigation found that the youth version of the PCL predicted both general and violent offending in young Native Canadian and Caucasian Canadian males. However, the PCL:YV was found to be less valid when used with young females and they found that it did not predict non-violent recidivism in males or females. Notwithstanding the apparent utility of the PCL:YV in predicting violent recidivism in young males of both Native Canadian and Caucasian origin, the authors advised that this psychometric tool should be used with caution in adolescent populations. The mean age of participants in this study was 14.9 years, which is young in terms of applying labels of personality pathology. The researchers note that currently little is known about the development of psychopathic traits from adolescence to adulthood and they propose therefore that the label of 'psychopath' should be used very conservatively among youth given the long term connotations of being assigned this diagnostic label.

Research in the United Kingdom

In the late 1990s Cooke and Michie (1999) used the PCL-R to compare expressions of psychopathy in North American (NA) and Scottish prisoners. They determined that the PCL-R is an effective measure of psychopathy in both ethnic groups and tentatively concluded that there is a fundamental set of characteristics that comprise psychopathy that are essentially the same across cultural groups. However, they found a significantly lower prevalence of psychopathy in the Scottish sample. As noted by the researchers this was an unexpected finding given that North America incarcerates a greater proportion of its residents and therefore would be more likely to incarcerate non-psychopathic individuals. Cooke and colleague theorised that Scottish psychopaths migrate out of Scotland to major cities because they prefer the anonymity and opportunities afforded by city life, and they note that this general proposition (of psychopath migration) has been made previously by other researchers (e.g. Mealey, 1995).

Cooke and Michie also found that characteristics of psychopathy were not apparent in the Scottish inmates until relatively high levels of the traits were attained. In explaining this phenomenon the researchers suggest that there may be culture-based processes that suppress the manifestation of these characteristics in Scottish offenders. They refer to the work of Weisz et al. (1987) who argue that conduct problems in children may be greatly influenced by socio-cultural variables, so that certain types of problems may be more prevalent in one cultural setting than another, depending on specific cultural values and norms. Similarly, Cooke and Michie hypothesise that cultural variables may influence the manifestation of psychopathy. In terms of their findings they submit that in Scotland it is not considered to be socially acceptable to talk about one's abilities or accomplishments. Rather, the British way is to cultivate reserve and humility. Therefore, superficial charm and grandiosity may be less likely to emerge in Britain due to this culture of restraint.

Cooke and Michie go on to discuss what they describe as a '. . . central explanatory construct in cross-cultural psychology' (p. 65), namely the distinction between individualist and collectivist societies. They argue that individualistic cultural contexts foster the development of 'deceptive, manipulative, and parasitic behaviour', and tend to have higher crime rates than collectivistic societies. Furthermore, they note that preliminary research which has explored differences in antisocial personality traits in the West and the East has supported this view.

Of course, it is possible that these apparent cross-cultural differences may in fact be due to rater bias – the ratings that assessors ascribe to individuals may be influenced by their expectations and beliefs about specific cultural groups. An interesting study (by Cooke, Hart and Michie, 2004) explored this proposition using Scottish and Canadian raters and Scottish and Canadian prisoners. The researchers found that there was no interaction between the rater and prisoner nationalities, in other words scores were similar regardless of whether the assessor and client were the same nationality. However, results showed that ratings ascribed to Scottish prisoners were significantly lower than those given to Canadian prisoners.

A recent large-scale study (by Cooke et al., 2005a) examined the use of the PCL-R in Scottish, English, and Welsh inmates in comparison to a NA sample (comprising prisoners from the USA and Canada). The researchers determined that there was 'syndrome stability' across cultures; that is, psychopathy was found to have the same general symptom configuration. On the other hand, they also reported that scores on the PCL-R were not equivalent insofar as the UK offenders tended to receive lower scores on the PCL-R than their US counterparts, for similar levels of psychopathy. However, this finding has been questioned on the grounds that the statistical methodology was seriously flawed (Bolt, Hare and Neumann, 2007). Specifically, Bolt et al. argue that Cooke's findings were a result of bias that arose from the unsuitable choice of anchor items. However, Bolt et al. conducted their own analysis of an NA and UK sample and reported a significant difference in mean total scores, with UK offenders scoring lower. The researchers argue, though, that this is due to scoring bias across these populations, which requires further exploration.

Research in other countries

In a further study Cooke and others (Cooke et al., 2005b) broadened their research and compared PCL-R use in NA offenders with offenders and forensic psychiatric patients across Europe (which included Belgium, Denmark, Norway, Sweden, Germany and Spain). The investigators found that the factor structures were similar across nationalities; specifically, that the three factor representation of psychopathy applied equally well to all groups. However, they also found that the symptoms of psychopathy were rated differently across cultural groups, with NA individuals generally receiving higher, item, factor and total scores. They note that this difference was more pronounced for the behavioural and interpersonal symptoms and less significant for affective features and they conclude that: '. . . deficient affective experience may be the pan-cultural core of psychopathy' (p. 290).

Two studies have evaluated the use of the PCL-SV in Europe. One study (by Douglas et al., 2005), assessed the use of screening version in correctional and forensic psychiatric samples in Sweden and found that its reliability and validity in this context was comparable to that found in NA samples. Douglas et al. established that PCL-SV scores were correlated with expected phenomena, including aggression, risk of violence and personality disorder. A very recent study also examined the use of the PCL-SV in Europe. Urbaniok et al. (2007) conducted their investigation in the German language area of Switzerland. Specifically, they measured the screening version's accuracy in predicting recidivism in a group of violent and sexual offenders. They found that the test was a good predictor of recidivism in this population. For example, they reported that the 'risk of violent or sexual recidivism was increased by 18 per cent for every additional point on the PCL-SV scale' (p. 150).

Similarly, research examining the use of the PCL-R in a German prison population (by Dahle, 2006) indicated that it is appropriate for use in Germany. Specifically, Dahle reported that the PCL-R had very good inter-rater reliability and exhibited predictive accuracy that was equivalent to that reported internationally. Of the 200 offenders in a New Zealand study of psychopathy and recidivism, 48 per cent of the sample were Maori and 7 per cent were Polynesian, Indian or Asian (Wilson, 2003). This study found that the PCL:SV was an effective predictor of sexual and violent re-offending across the sample's different cultural groups.

Implications of cross-cultural research on the PCL

Taken together, these studies suggest that the various versions of the PCL allow for valid and reliable measures of psychopathy in different cultural groups. However, they also indicate that there are differences in levels of psychopathy in different cultural groups with North Americans tending to exhibit higher levels than Europeans when measured with the PCL-R. In response to their own research findings, Cooke et al. (2005) propose that a different cut-off (of 28) is applied when using the PCL-R in Europe. However, they also state that this modification may not be sufficient to allow the PCL-R to be used in a valid manner in European populations. Studies to date suggest that the affective aspects of psychopathy are the most stable across cultural groups, therefore this component should be highlighted when using the PCL-R cross-culturally. As shown

above, studies that focused specifically on the use of PCL measures in predicting risk reported positive results; the PCL was found to be a valid risk prediction tool in a non-English speaking sample.

It is possible that cultural variables shape the development and expression of psychopathic traits. Such cultural shaping of personality would not be surprising in light of general cross-cultural literature in psychology. Research has shown that major disorders, such as schizophrenia and depression differ significantly in their expression across cultures (Paniagua, 2000; Thakker and Ward, 1998). Hence, it may be argued that personality disorders may be (at least) equally variable given that they are likely to be more socially embedded.

When using the PCL-R with non-North American populations, assessors should familiarise themselves with the relevant cross-cultural literature and take such literature into consideration when interpreting the results. Also, it is recommended that assessors check to see if any local normative data is available in order to assist with appropriate interpretation. Given that there is a relatively large amount of cross-cultural research available on the PCL-R when compared with other measures used in risk assessments, these recommendations would apply even more strongly to other measures.

Advantages of using an actuarial approach include the transparency of the decision-making process and the empirical support for the utility of the variables considered. A potential disadvantage is that reliability depends on the adequacy of the training and procedural consistency of the assessor. Another concern is that a single test or measure cannot provide a comprehensive evaluation. Relatedly, such scores seldom offer information regarding intervention strategies or risk management plans.

Recommendations for culturally safe risk assessments

Optimal risk assessment and management requires the application of case formulation skills, whereby risk factors are identified within an aetiological framework (Vess, 2006). While it is important to be aware of the static and dynamic factors associated with a given type of risk, these factors are most useful for risk management when they are formulated into a coherent set of inter-related causal mechanisms. This requires examination of several categories of contributing factors, including historical (e.g. offence history, past episodes of violence, previous treatment compliance and response, performance under supervision or parole) developmental (e.g. adverse developmental events, nature of family relationships, attachment style), cognitive (e.g. level of intelligence, cognitive distortions, attitudes supportive of criminality or violence), personality (e.g. psychopathy, or traits such as impulsivity and hostility) and clinical (e.g. psychiatric diagnosis, level of functioning, substance abuse).

Whenever possible, risk assessment should be grounded in actuarial risk measures that have been empirically validated with appropriate populations. It is at the level of the individualised, aetiological case formulation of risk that the role of culture may be most thoroughly integrated. This is where the client's sense of identity, social and familial influences, and culturally specific explanatory models can be drawn upon to identify the important causal mechanisms for past offending, and to recognise the contingencies which will influence future risk. These can be drawn upon, of course, only to the degree that they have been included in the assessment process.

A model for the development of culturally safe risk assessments is provided below, Figure 17.1. This model, based on a generic risk assessment model by Towl and Crighton (1996) outlines the key considerations and components of a culturally sound risk assessment. It summarises the essential information presented thus far in this chapter.

Although the model presents a series of steps, for most aspects the order is not particularly important; it follows the logical progression that would be most likely in a standard assessment process. The model is comprehensive and represents an ideal approach. It is acknowledged that in many clinical settings some of these recommendations will not necessarily be possible, due to constraints of time and resources. For instance, it may be difficult to acquire all of the relevant literature in regard to a particular case, and relevant norms are not always accessible. The model is intended to serve as a guide to remind the clinician about the cultural issues that may arise at various points of the risk assessment process. Notwithstanding the challenges of conducting a robust cross-cultural risk assessment, it is important to be mindful of the potential consequences of falling short of current best practice. Clinicians who have been in a courtroom setting are likely to be keenly aware of how minor weaknesses become major errors when they are subjected to the scrutiny of effective cross-examination. It is essential that risk assessments have a sound empirical basis; when working cross-culturally this requires that the clinician makes a clear and defensible effort to incorporate cultural considerations into the formulation of risk.

The most important reason for utilising the most accurate available risk assessment procedures is to minimise the likelihood of future offending. Accurate risk assessment contributing to effective risk management benefits many people, not just the potential victims, but victims' families and the offenders themselves. Given the gravity of the task, the onus is clearly on clinicians to do the best possible job with the available information and resources. Velásquez et al. (2006: 109) state 'In many ways, a practitioner never reaches full competence in the assessment of culturally diverse persons because our world continues to become more and more diverse with respect to culture, language, and worldviews'. Therefore, like all areas of clinical work, conducting effective cross-cultural risk assessments involves a commitment to ongoing professional development.

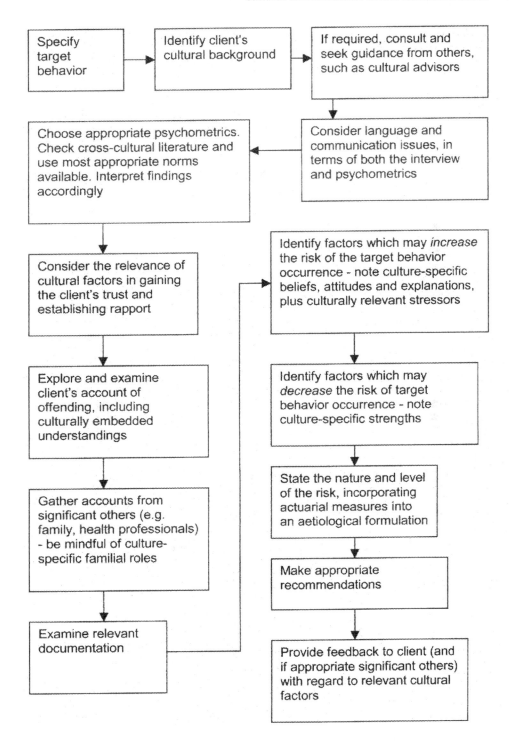

Figure 17.1 A framework for cross-cultural risk assessments (adapted from Towl and Crighton, 1996, General risk assessment framework)

References

Aderibigbe, Y.A. and Pandurangi, A.K. (1995) The Neglect of Culture in Psychiatric Nosology: The Case-bound Syndromes. *International Journal of Social Psychiatry*, 41, 235–41.

Baird, B.N. (2005) *The Internship, Practicum, and Field Placement Handbook.* Upper Saddle River, NJ: Pearson Prentice Hall.

Barbaree, H.E. (2005) Psychopathy, Treatment Behaviour, and Recidivism. *Journal of Interpersonal Violence*, 20, 1115–31.

Barbaree, H.E. et al. (2001) Evaluating the Predictive Accuracy of Six Risk Assessment Instruments for Adult Sex Offenders. *Criminal Justice and Behavior*, 28, 490–521.

Bartosh, D.L. et al. (2003) Differences in the Predictive Validity of Actuarial Risk Assessments in Relation to Sex Offender Type. *International Journal of Offender Therapy and Comparative Criminology*, 47, 422–38.

Beech, A. et al. (2002) The Relationship between Static and Dynamic Risk Factors and Reconviction in a Sample of UK Child Abusers. *Sexual Abuse: A Journal of Research and Treatment*, 14, 155–67.

Bolt, D.M., Hare, R.D. and Neumann, C.S. (2007) Score Metric Equivalence of the Psychopathy Checklist-Revised (PCL-R) across Criminal Offenders in North America and the United Kingdom: A Critique of Cooke, D.J., Michie, C. and Clark (2005) and New Analysis. *Assessment*, 14, 44–56.

Bonta, J. (1989) Native Inmates: Institutional Response, Risk and Needs. *Canadian Journal of Criminology*, 31, 49–62.

Cooke, D.J., Hart, S.D. and Michie, C. (2004) Cross-national Differences in the Assessment of Psychopathy: Do they Reflect Variations in Raters' Perceptions of Symptoms. *Psychological Assessment*, 16, 335–9.

Cooke, D.J., Kosson, D.S. and Michie, C. (2001) Psychopathy and Ethnicity: Structural, Item, and Test Generalisability of the Psychopathy Checklist-Revised (PCL-R) in Caucasian and African American Participants. *Journal of Psychological Assessment*, 13, 531–42.

Cooke, D.J. and Michie, C. (1999) Psychopathy across Cultures: North America and Scotland Compared. *Journal of Abnormal Psychology*, 108, 58–68.

Cooke, D.J. et al. (2005a) Assessing Psychopathy in the UK: Concerns about Cross-cultural Generalisability. *British Journal of Psychiatry*, 186, 335–41.

Cooke, D.J. et al. (2005b) Searching for the Pan-cultural Core of Psychopathic Personality Disorder. *Personality and Individual Differences*, 39, 283–95.

Craig, L.A., Beech, A. and Browne, K.D. (2006) Cross-validation of the Risk Matrix 2000 Sexual and Violent Scales. *Journal of Interpersonal Violence*, 21, 612–33.

Craig, L.A., Browne, K.D. and Stringer, I. (2004) Comparing Sex Offender Assessment Measures on a UK sample. *International Journal of Offender Therapy and Comparative Criminology*, 48, 7–27.

Dahle, K-P. (2006) Strengths and Limitations of Actuarial Prediction of Criminal Reoffence in a German Prison Sample: A Comparative Study of LSI-R, HCR-20 and PCL-R. *International Journal of Law and Psychiatry*, 29, 431–42.

Dana, R.H. (2000) Culture and Methodology in Personality Assessment. In Cuéllar, I. and Paniagua, F.A. (Eds.) *Handbook of Multicultural Mental Health*. San Diego: Academic Press.

D'Andrea, M. (2003) Expanding our Understanding of White Racism and Resistance to Change in the Fields of Counselling and Psychology. In Mio, J. and Iwamasa, G. (Eds.) *Culturally Diverse Mental Health: The Challenges of Research and Resistance.* New York: Brunner Routledge.

Doren, D.M. (2004) Stability of the Interpretative Risk Percentages for the RRASOR and Static-99. *Sexual Abuse: A Journal of Research and Treatment*, 16, 25–36.

Douglas, K.S. et al. (2005) Reliability and Validity Evaluation of the Psychopathy Checklist: Screening Version (PCL-SV) in Swedish Correctional and Forensic Psychiatric Samples. *Assessment*, 12, 145–61.

Hann, R.G. et al. (1993) Predicting Release Risk for Aboriginal Penitentiary Inmates. User Report 1993–12. Ottawa: Department of the Solicitor General of Canada.

Hanson, R.K. (1997) *The Development of a Brief Actuarial Risk Scale for Sexual Offense Recidivism (PRASOR).* Ottawa, Ontario: Solicitor General of Canada.

Hanson, R.K. (1998) What do we know about Sex Offender Risk Assessment? *Psychology. Public Policy and Law*, 4, 50–72.

Hanson, R.K. and Harris, G.T. (2001) A Structured Approach to Evaluating Change among Sexual Offenders. *Sexual Abuse: A Journal of Research and Treatment*, 13, 105–22.

Hanson, R.K. and Thornton, D. (1999) *Static-99: Improving Actuarial Risk Assessments for Sex Offenders*, Ottawa: Department of the Solicitor General of Canada.

Hanson R.K. and Thornton, D. (2000) Improving Risk Assessments for Sex Offenders: A Comparison of Three Actuarial Scales. *Law and Human Behavior*, 24, 119–36.

Hare, R.D. (2003) *Hare PCL-R Technical Manual*. 2nd edn. Toronto: Multi-Health Systems.

Harris, A. et al. (2003) *STATIC-99 Coding Rules Revised: 2003*. Solicitor General Canada, available at www.sgc.gc.ca.

Harris, G.T., Rice, M.E. and Quinsey, V.L. (1993) Violent Recidivism of Mentally Disordered Offenders: The Development of a Statistical Prediction Instrument. *Criminal Justice and Behavior*, 20, 315–35.

Hart, S.D. (1998) The Role of Psychopathy in Assessing Risk for Violence: Conceptual and Methodological Issues. *Legal and Criminological Psychology*, 3, 121–37.

Hart, S.D. (2001) Assessing and Managing Violence Risk. In Douglas, K.S. et al. (Eds.) *HCR-20 Violence Risk Management Companion Guide*. Burnaby, BC: Mental Health, Law, and Policy Institute, Simon Fraser University.

Hemphill, J. and Hare, R.D. (2004) Some Misconceptions about the Hare PCL-R and Risk Assessment: A reply to Gendreau, Goggin, and Smith. *Criminal Justice and Behavior*, 31, 203–43.

Hildebrand, M. and de Ruiter, C. (2004) PCL-R Psychopathy and its Relation to DSM-IV Axis I and II Disorders in a Sample of Male Forensic Psychiatric Patients in the Netherlands. *International Journal of Law and Psychiatry*, 27, 233–48.

Jejeebhoy, S.J. (1998) Adolescent Sexual and Reproductive Behaviour: A Review of the Evidence from India. *Social Science Medicine*, 46, 1275–90.

Klienman, A. (1988) *The Illness Narrative: Suffering, Healing and the Human Condition*. New York: Basic Books.

La Fromboise, T.D. et al. (2006) Family, Community, and School Influences on Resilience among American Indian Adolescents in the Upper Midwest. *Journal of Community Psychology*, 34, 193–209.

Langevin, R. et al. (1990) *Clarke Sex History Questionnaire for Males Manual*. Oakville, ON: Juniper Press.

Lowenkamp, C.T., Holsinger, A.M. and Latessa, E.J. (2001) Risk/need Assessment, Offender Classification, and the Role of Childhood Abuse. *Criminal Justice and Behaviour*, 28, 543–63.

Looman, J. et al. (2005) Psychopathy, Treatment Change, and Recidivism in High-risk, High-need Sexual Offenders. *Journal of Interpersonal Violence*, 20, 549–68.

Lykken, D.T. (1995) *The Antisocial Personalities*. Hillsdale: Lawrence Erlbaum.

Lynn, R. (2002) Racial and Ethnic Differences in Psychopathic Personality. *Personality and Individual Differences*, 32, 273–316.

McCoy, W.K. and Edens, J.F. (2006) Do Black and White Youths Differ in Levels of Psychopathic Traits? A Meta-analysis of the Psychopathy Checklist Measures. *Journal of Consulting and Clinical Psychology*, 74, 386–92.

Mealey, L. (1995) The Socio-biology of Sociopathy: An Integrated Evolutionary Model. *Behavioral and Brain Sciences*, 18, 523–99.

Nathan, L., Wilson, N.J. and Hillman, D. (2003) *Te whakakotahitanga: An Evaluation of the Te Piriti Special Treatment Programme for Child Sex Offenders in New Zealand*. Published on the New Zealand Department of Corrections website: www.corrections.govt.nz.

Nicholaichuk, T. (2001) *The Comparison of Two Standardised Risk Assessment Instruments in a Sample of Canadian Aboriginal Sexual Offenders*. Presentation at the annual conference of the Association for the Treatment of Sexual Abusers, San Antonio, Texas.

Nichols, H. and Molinder, I. (1984) *Manual for the Multiphasic Sex Inventory*: Nichols and Molinder Assessments. Tacoma, WA.

Paniagua, F.A. (2000) Culture-bound Syndromes, Cultural Variations, and Psychopathy. In Cuéllar, I. and Paniagua, F.A. (Eds.) *Handbook of Multicultural Mental Health*. San Diego: Academic Press.

Quinsey, V.L. et al. (1998) *Violent Offenders: Appraising and Managing Risk*. Washington, DC: American Psychological Association.

Reddy, P. (2006) Cultural Diversity and Professional Practice. In Morrissey, S. and Reddy, P. (Eds.) *Ethics and Professional Practice for Psychologists*. Melbourne Australia: Thomson Social Science Press.

Rochford, T. (2004) Whare Tapa Wha: A Māori Model of a Unified Theory of Health. *The Journal of Primary Prevention*, 25, 41–57.

Schmidt, F. et al. (2006) Concurrent and Predictive Validity of the Psychopathy Checklist: Youth Version across Gender a Ethnicity. *Psychological Assessment*, 18, ?

Sjostedt, G. and Langstrom, N. (2001) Actuarial Assessment of Sex Offender Recidivism Risk: A Cross-validation of the RRASOR and the Static-99 in Sweden. *Law and Human Behaviour*, 25, 629–45.

Skelton, A. et al. (2006) Assessing Risk for Sexual Offenders in New Zealand: Development and Validation of a Computer Scored Risk Measure. *Journal of Sexual Aggression*, 12, 277–86.

Spielberger, C.D. (2006) Cross-cultural Assessment of Emotional States and Personality Traits. *European Psychologist*, 11, 297–303.

Sullivan. E.A. et al. (2006) Reliability and Construct Validity of the Psychopathy Checklist-Revised for Latino, European American, and African American Male Inmates. *Journal of Psychological Assessment*, 18, 382–92.

Thakker, J. and Ward, T. (1998) Culture and Classification: The Cross-cultural Application of the DSM-IV. *Clinical Psychology Review*, 18, 501–29.

Thornton, D. et al. (2003) Distinguishing and Combining Risks for Sexual and Violent Recidivism. *Annals of the New York Academy of Sciences*, 989, 225–35.

Tolman, A.O. and Rotzien, A.L. (2007) Conducting Risk Evaluations for Future Violence: Ethical Practice is Possible. *Professional Psychology: Research and Practice*, 38, 71–9.

Towl, G.J. and Crighton, D.A. (1996) *The Handbook of Psychology for Forensic Practitioners*. London: Routledge.

Urbaniok, F. et al. (2007) Violent and Sexual Offences: A Validation of the Predictive Quality of the PCL: SV in Switzerland. *International Journal of Law and Psychiatry*, 30, 147–52.

Velásquez, R.J. et al. (2006) Interpreting Forensic Interview and Test Data of Latino Children: Recommendations for Culturally Competent Evaluations. In Sparta, S.N. and Koocher, G.P. (Eds.) *Forensic Mental Health Assessment of Children and Adolescents*. Oxford: Oxford University Press.

Vess, J. (2006) Preparing Practitioners for Assessing and Managing Risk. In Bakker, L. and McMaster, K. (Eds.) *Will they do it again: Assessing and Managing Risk*. Lyttelton, New Zealand: Hall McMaster.

Weisz, J.R. et al. (1987) Over and Undercontrolled Referral Problems among Children and Adolescents from Thailand and the United States. The Wat and the Wai of Cultural Differences. *Journal of Consulting and Clinical Psychology*, 55, 719–26.

Wilson, N.J. (2003) *The Utility of the Psychopathy Checklist-Screening Version for Predicting Serious Violent Recidivism in a New Zealand Offender Sample*. Unpublished doctoral dissertation, University of Waikato, Hamilton, New Zealand.

CHAPTER 18

Involuntary Clients and Risk Assessment: Contextual Mapping to Inform Practice Responses

Martin C. Calder

Introduction

The aim of this chapter is to map the contextual considerations in relation to partnership and paternalism and relate these to how they affect client-worker interactions in the child protection sphere, dominated by the need for risk assessments and the presence of involuntary clients. The mapping of the terrain should provide us with some understanding of the contributory problems and also provide us with a pathway toward solutions when attempting remedial strategies in practice. The reader is signposted to a more substantial text in relation to working with involuntary clients in a range of contexts (Calder, 2007) that contains a framework for working with resistance, motivation and change (Calder, 2007b). The reader should also make links with Chapter 6 (this volume) that attempts to provide a contemporary framework for understanding professional dangerousness as such considerations clearly impact directly on the worker-client relationship.

Paternalism and partnership: a portrait of a shifting pendulum

There have been a great many protracted and heated debates about the practice of state intervention and control of family life in recent years.

In the 1980s there was a catalogue of high profile child abuse inquiries that criticised social workers for taking too little action, too late, and concern was expressed not only about culturally dangerous professional practice but also poor assessment practice, culminating in the issue of the 'orange book' (DoH, 1988) providing a template for such work. The emphasis was on the identification and management of dangerous individuals that would protect children, and such an approach was intensely paternalistic and created obstacles to building effective relationships between professionals and clients.

Parton and Martin (1989) charted the emergence of legalism pre-Children Act and found that it was grounded in criticisms levelled at social workers for being overtly soft and permissive and, as a consequence, failed to protect children. They argued that many child abuse inquiries produced a catalogue of events and conclusions that suggested the tragedies had been predictable and preventable if only social workers had intervened authoritatively, using the full statutory powers invested in them.

The Children Act (1989) was introduced in an attempt to restructure the balance between protecting children and helping families. It was drafted in the wake of the Cleveland inquiry that criticised over-zealous intervention into family life, the lack of consultation with parents, and insular inter-agency consultation. Partnership was introduced as the philosophical pivot of the legislation and was seen as a natural corrective to paternalistic practice. Statutory agencies were encouraged to work in partnership with parents, with members of the extended family and with each other, first to promote the welfare of all children in need and to prevent family breakdown, and secondly, where some kind of crisis had occurred, to strive first to work on the basis of voluntary agreements before applying only as a last resort for the mandate of the court. Even where legal intervention was considered necessary, the principles of partnership should be maintained or quickly re-established wherever possible, and the level of intervention should be the minimum that is consistent with the aim of securing the child's protection. Partnership has to be worked at by both the professionals as well as the families. It is not an end in itself but it is pursued because it will enhance the protection of the child via better professional-family relationship.

In the period immediately following the implementation of the Children Act on 14 October 1991, there was a dramatic reduction in the level of court activity. Although this had been expected, the magnitude of the reduction raised concerns that we had taken too literally the Act's philosophy of minimal intervention. There were fears that the balance between family autonomy and state intervention had shifted too far and that in consequence children were now being left unprotected. Many workers were refusing to intervene legally as they saw partnership as literally 'being partners', and that we had to exhaust all options before placing the matter before the court.

In 1992, the Children Act Report (DoH, 1992: 13) explored the extent to which the new approach of minimal court intervention and working in partnership had been embedded in practice. It set out clearly that:

> In practice the decision about whether risk for the child is best managed on an entirely voluntary basis of work with families or requires the additional authority and frame-work of a court order will depend on a multiplicity of factors. These include the nature of the harm suffered or likely to be suffered, the surrounding circumstances, the parents' willingness to accept responsibility and to co-operate with the helping agencies and, where their care does not adequately meet the child's needs, an assessment of their ability to change.

The report uncovered a lower level of court activity post-Children Act implementation, which they did not view as being positive:

> ... there are genuine concerns to ensure that any shift away from the use of court would not put the child at greater risk', and 'Local authorities should not feel in-hibited by the working in partnership provisions of the Children Act from seeking appropriate court orders. Equally, the existence of court orders should not of itself impede a local authority from continuing its efforts at working in partnership ... The two processes are not mutually exclusive. Each has a role to play, often simulta-neously, in the case management of a child at risk.
>
> (p. 19)

On 17 November 1992, the first annual report of the Children Act advisory committee was published (Lord Chancellors Department, 1992) and reinforced these views. They advocated a more proactive use of court orders, where deemed necessary:

> The court should not be asked to perform in every case a strictly legalistic analysis of the statutory meanings of section 31. The words of the statute did not intend them to be unduly restrictive when the evidence clearly in-

dicated that a certain course should be taken in order to protect a child.

(p. 34)

Such comments began to reshape workers attitudes towards the application of partnership in practice, and a marked upturn in the use of court orders was subsequently noted. The number of public law applications increased steadily between 1992 and 1994, from 15,720 to 18,671 (an increase of 19 per cent) when it peaked. An 8 per cent fall in the number of public law applications was then noted in 1995 although no clear explanation for this is readily available at present (Lord Chancellors Department, 1995).

In 1992, the Social Services Inspectorate reported on a study of local authority decision-making about public law court applications. This was commissioned to explore the factors that were operating against the institution of legal proceedings, even where the grounds for statutory intervention were met. Amongst the factors found was the view that appropriate protection was being achieved through the social work plan alone, and a view that parental co-operation with the plan precluded the 'no-order' principle being satisfied, unless the partnership arrangements between parent and local authority had demonstrably broken down (p. 72).

The issuing of practice guidance around partnership (DoH, 1995) tried to offer some practical guidance for staff and there was a sharp demise in the number of high profile inquiries in the 1990s, although the arrival of New Labour into power saw a raft of structural and cultural changes in the social care field (see Calder, 2007c). There was a continued emphasis on working in partnership with families and across professionals and this was extended to a strengths-based approach to child protection work to try and facilitate partnership and reduce the likelihood of paternalistic practice and involuntary clients. This was part of the organised deconstruction of the child protection system and a renewed emphasis on children in need. The advent of the Assessment Framework (DoH, 2000) provided further emphasis on strengths and removed all reference to risk from the social care vocabulary (see Calder, 2003 for a review) and the introduction of structural changes across all agencies accompanied by performance targets shifted the emphasis from child outcomes to professional system outputs that strained partnership working significantly. In more recent times, the death of Victoria Climbié has highlighted errors in pursuing partnership to the detriment of protecting children and the social worker was professionally and publicly scapegoated for widespread failures in the system. The current and continuing changes are at a pace that are disabling to systems and professionals and this is affecting the quality of social work practice with families. The continuing dichotomy of requiring partnership and strengths-based practice on the one hand coupled with a real sense of fear about being personally accountable if something goes wrong means that the task of balancing partnership and paternalism is a very fine balance (Calder, 1995).

Paternalistic theory and practice

Paternalism has been defined as 'the interference with a person's liberty of action justified by reasons referring exclusively to the welfare, good, happiness, needs, interests, or values of the person being coerced' (Dworkin, 1971).

Fox-Harding (1991) has explored the relationship between state paternalism and child protection in some detail, and concluded that it is a school of thought favouring extensive state intervention to protect children from maltreatment. I have argued that in this context paternalism represents a precautionary political practice aimed at covering every eventuality (Calder, 1995). State paternalism assumes that the state has a primary responsibility for children and ought to exercise full control except where delegation to the family is justified. This does not embrace the reality that few families have the need for the state to perform the child protection function. Paternalism is a form of beneficence in which the helping person's concepts of benefits and harms differ from those of the client, and the helper's concepts prevail. There are two key elements in paternalism: the intent, obtaining what it is that is believed to be good for the other person, and the effect, e.g. violating the person's known wishes in the matter.

Defenders of paternalism define it in terms of assistance rather than violation, particularly when temporary interference with liberty ensures future freedom and autonomy. They argue that paternalism is justified where children are concerned as they have not attained the capacity to make an informed decision (Abramson, 1985)

although 'the very fact that paternalism does not require the consent of the subject undercuts the subject's authority to decide in his or her own interest in the future'.

The issue of gender is central to any discussion of paternalism. A patriarchal society represents a masculine society whose 'ethos embodies the masculine principle. This ethos is reflected in a philosophical 'ordering of the world' such that building blocks of social reality are assumed to be dichotomised polarised categories arranged in hierarchical order – superior to inferior, super-ordinate to subordinate' (Collins, 1986). Patriarchy remains synonymous with 'sexism' and male supremacy, which militates against any equality of status or partnership between the sexes. The term 'patriarchal mothering' is based on the assumption that the parenting role needs 'support' and that the 'family unit' has dissolved into a structure of pathology that must somehow be managed by state intervention if its protective functions are to be restored (Stark and Flitcraft, 1988).

These views of paternalism ally themselves to the notion of 'social control' (Ross, 1910), which refers to the regulation that society imposes upon individuals, and its expectation of conformity to its norms and values. Child protection represents a modern form of social control, as both concepts imply a belief that individuals require external controls. Such beliefs are synonymous with domination, discrimination (Rubin, 1972) and a decline in both family and individual autonomy (Gordon, 1986) which all reduce civil rights. Indeed, throughout the growth of child protection little attention has been paid to the possibility of abuse and loss of rights. Paternalism is synonymous with enforcement and compulsion. The means by which paternalism is practised in social work settings can be direct, informal or interpersonal. In direct intervention, the client is prevented from doing what they want. The second form of paternalism involves the manipulation of information, which includes providing false or misleading information or withholding information. The final form of paternalism is practised through the medium of the social work relationship, where the worker can use the trust invested in them to cajole, persuade, or manipulate the client into accepting the social worker's assessment of what ought to be done. Gert and Culver (1979) believe that a professional is acting paternalistically toward a person if and only if the professional's behaviour indicates that the professional believes that:

- The professional's action is for the person's good.
- The professional is qualified to act on the person's behalf.
- The professional's action involves or will involve violating a moral rule with regard to the person.
- The person's good justifies acting on the person's behalf independently of the person's past, present or immediately forthcoming future.
- The person believes, perhaps falsely, that they generally know what is for their own good.

The paternalist tradition identifies the poor, minorities and female single parents as the most likely recipients of child protection services. Most social workers in child protection utilise a paternalistic approach as a survival tactic, and through fear of committing professional suicide if they make a wrong decision. The organisation controls its staff as well as its clientele. This raises issues of gender and class. Most practitioners in child protection are white and middle-class, and have often been socialised into the oppression of class, culture and gender. If they remove children from home, they refer the matter to the courts, thus inviting decisions based upon the values of predominantly white, male, upper class judges. Paternalism arguably maintains, legitimates and perpetuates dependency as well as provoking resistance from the client.

Partnership theory and practice

When several inquiry reports highlighted the problematic state responses to child maltreatment, ranging from under- to over-reactive interventions, it became clear that a basis for responsible and accountable state intervention in child protection work was called for. It was against this background that the notion of partnership re-emerged.

'Partnership of any kind is assumed to be a good thing, like apple pie and cream, intrinsically wholesome and, almost certainly, guaranteed to satisfy' (Hughes, 1992). The dictionary defines partnership as 'state of being a partner, sharing, joint business'. Yet partnership remains a loosely defined although fashionable concept whose boundaries are fluid and permeable.

The Children Act 1989 promotes partnership as a philosophical pivot, although it did not appear in the Act itself. It is arguably only a principle (Morrison, 1991) or a philosophy, rather than a statutory requirement or a proven social work practice. Most available literature in recent times on partnership represents a repackaging of old social work ideas (e.g. autonomy and self-determination). It is arguably a cosmetic packaging for a new form of social control (Pugh and De'Ath, 1989) and thus its image of equality and openness is misleading, since the distribution of power is clearly unequal.

Partnership is a process and not an end in itself. Its current usage in different contexts denies any exact definition or meaning. It is certainly promoted as a shift towards client choice and client involvement which is universal and not restricted to child care and protection (DoH, 1991c) although few believe that partnerships are set up to fulfil these goals, particularly when they take a long time to make, are hard work, and can be painful for bureaucratic organisations. What is clear is that partnership requires a cultural shift in attitudes for worker, manager and agencies. Partnership should be but one strand of a wider framework to achieve child protection, which also needs to embrace voluntary involvement, shared accountability, and equal rights (Sayer and Heaton, 1991). At the present time, there are three clearly differentiated levels of partnership in child protection. They are:

- Partnership on a voluntary basis.
- Partnership when a child is thought to be at risk of significant harm.
- Partnership when the child is the subject of a full care order.

(DoH, 1991a)

Clearly partnerships at each level are possible. Most professionals prefer the first type of partnership, where there is a plan formulated to resolve the mutual definition of problems in a given timescale. Partnerships at this level are more likely to succeed as they are based on a greater degree of shared power. The concept of partnership does not allow workers to shy away from their duty to make assessments of risk, even when families are co-operating.

Theoretically, there are four possible models of partnership:

- *The Expert model:* where the professional takes control and makes all the decisions, giving a low priority to parents' views, wishes or feelings, the sharing of information, or the need for negotiation.
- *The Transplant (of Expertise) model:* where the professional sees the parent as a resource and hands over some skills, but retains control of the decision-making.
- *The Consumer model:* where it is assumed that parents have the right to decide and select what they believe to be appropriate and the decision making is ultimately in their control.
- *The Social Network/Systems model:* where parents, children and professionals are part of a network of formal and informal development, and social support for the family and child. They are capable of supplementing existing resources via the facilitation of the social worker, who should draw more on the extended family while complying with statutory requirements.

What is clear from this is that professionals adopting an expert model approach are operating paternalistically if it is a sustained approach. It is more understandable at the point of investigating child abuse allegations or exercising legal action but this should be a starting point, which then shifts to the lower-level models of partnership as a working relationship with the parents develops.

The concept and implementation of partnerships are more complex and varied than prevailing ideology may suggest. There is no step-by-step guide that makes it an easy option. What is clear is that parents can make a significant contribution to the protection of their children if they are provided with the right framework in which to work closely with professionals (Calder, 1991). But what constitutes the 'right framework'? One in which clients have a choice in whether or not they want to enter it, and where they have adequate information about the consequences of non-cooperation.

Partnership-based practice is not easy to define in simple terms. Marsh and Fisher (1992) developed a set of principles which outline some of the central issues in partnership and which are designed to provide a yardstick against which partnership in practice can be assessed. These are:

- Any investigation of problems must be with the explicit consent of the potential user and client, or kept to the minimum necessary by law to assess risks.

- User agreement or a clear statutory mandate is the only basis for partnership-based intervention.
- Intervention must be based on the views of all relevant family members and carers.
- Services must be based on negotiated agreement, rather than assumptions and/or prejudices concerning the behaviour and wishes of users.
- Users must have the greatest possible degree of choice in the services they are offered.

They found that attempts to change practice were most effective when they were linked directly with policy development, which needs to involve managers, workers and clients in reaching a shared understanding about what is meant by partnership. The key to partnership lies in the decision-making structures and processes, and practice needs to be developed based on the feedback of clients. Partnership therefore needs to embrace feelings and thoughts as well as decision making. Humphreys (1987) found that many parents have anticipated the move to partnership either with 'hope, enthusiasm and eager anticipation' or with 'confusion, hostility and disenchantment'.

Parent's perspectives on partnership

Many report feeling marginalised in decision making. They complain of not being listened to or understood. They value recognition of the circumstances that inhibit parental responsibility rather than simply being blamed for (the child's) problems. Respect for differing parenting styles is important. Parents have needs as adults that require recognition and appropriate responses. The power differential between parents and workers should be openly acknowledged. Parents respond well to being treated with dignity. Parents require access to high-quality legal representation and help when preparing evidence. The stigma of having children in formal professional systems (CP and LAC) remains and requires recognition and a sensitive response.

Rose and Aldgate (2000) identified several parental worries associated with their contact with child welfare professionals:

- Being vulnerable to child protection enquiries and being afraid of losing their children.
- Being perceived as failed parents.

- The impact of losing control and forfeiting their parenting responsibilities.

Parents value . . .

- Services that are targeted at the whole family not just the child.
- Inter-agency services that are well coordinated.
- Services that combine practical and emotional help.
- Services that are offered in a welcoming, non-stigmatising manner.
- Family centres that combine referred and non-referred cases and offer access to a range of services or activities.
- Transparency about the purpose and expected outcomes of services.
- Social workers who are approachable, honest, understanding, reliable, helpful and have time to listen.
- Communication, which is open, honest, timely and informative.
- Social work time with someone who listens, gives feedback, information, reassurance and advice, and is reliable.
- Services: which are practical, tailored to particular needs and accessible.
- An approach that reinforces and does not undermine their parenting capacity.

Research identifies some of the successful features of partnership as including a shared commitment to negotiation and actions about how best to safeguard and promote the child's welfare; mutual respect for the other's point of view; good communication skills by professionals; the establishment of trust between all parties; integrity and accountability on the part of both parents and professionals; shared decision-making; joint recognition of constraints on services offered; and a recognition that partnership is a process and is not an end in itself but a means to an end.

Why work in partnership with parents?

Effectiveness: A co-operative working relationship between the helping professionals and families is essential if the welfare of the child is to be ensured. This co-operative relationship is more likely to be achieved if parents are encouraged to take as large a part as possible

from the outset in decisions about the protection of the children and the appropriate services needed to ensure the child remains safe.

Families as a source of information: Family members know more about their family than any professional can possibly know. They have unique knowledge and understanding to contribute to discussions about what has and has not happened to the child and the best way to provide protection.

Citizens rights: Family members have rights as citizens to know what is said about them, and to contribute to important decisions about their lives and those of other children.

Empowering parents: Research and practice evidence demonstrates that family members experience working in partnership as beneficial. Involvement in decision-making can enhance self-esteem and encourage them to feel more in control of their lives. Professional practice which reduces a family's sense of powerlessness and helps them to feel and function more competently is likely to improve the well-being of both parents and children.

The DoH (1995) defined several approaches to partnership as follows:

Providing information
- Giving clear and accurate information is essential before effective consultation, involvement and partnership can take place.
- Such information must be readily comprehensible and useable.
- Do not assume that the information when provided has been easily understood.

Involvement and participation
- These are closely related activities.
- Involvement may be predominantly passive and amount to little more than receiving information, having a non-contributory presence at meetings, endorsing other people's decisions or making minor decisions.
- However, when involvement becomes more active and when family members are asked to contribute to discussions and decision-making on key issues, they can said to be active participants.

Partnership
- The objective of any partnership between families and professionals must be the protection and welfare of the child.
- Partnership should not be an end in itself.

- Partnership consideration should be grounded on openness, mutual trust, joint decision-making and a willingness to listen to families and capitalise on their strengths.
- It is likely that workers will have different approaches to different family members and that these will change over time.
- Words such as equality, choice and power have limited meaning at certain points in the child protection process.
- When professionals are conducting a section 47 investigation the family does not see this as a partnership and they may feel angry and refuse to co-operate.
- Partnership can vary from family to family.
- Some adults are relieved to know that the ultimate power to protect the child rests with the professionals while others chafe against the use of authority.
- It may be easier to establish partnerships with those family members who are less implicated in the abuse or those who are more consistently stable.

They also set out some useful principles for working in partnership with families:

- Treat all family members as you would wish to be treated, with dignity and respect.
- Ensure that family members know that the child's safety and welfare must be given first priority, but that each of them has a right to a courteous, caring and professionally competent service.
- Take care not to infringe privacy any more than is necessary to safeguard the welfare of the child.
- Be clear with yourself and with family members about your power to intervene, and the purpose of your professional involvement at each stage.
- Be aware of the effects on family members of the power you have as a professional, and the impact and implications of what you say and do.
- Respect confidentiality of family members and your observations about them, unless they give you permission for information to be passed to others or it is essential to do so to protect the child.
- Listen to the concerns of the children and their families, and take care to learn about their understanding, fears and wishes before arriving at your explanations and plans.

- Learn about and consider children within their family relationships and communities, including their cultural and religious contexts, and their place within their own families.
- Consider the potential and strengths of family members, as well as their weaknesses, problems and limitations.
- Ensure that children, families and other carers know their responsibilities and rights, including the right to services and their right to refuse services and any consequences of so doing.
- Use plain, jargon-free language appropriate to the age and culture of each person. Explain unavoidable technical and professional terms.
- Be open and honest about your concerns and responsibilities, plans and limitations, without being defensive.
- Allow children and families time to take in and understand concerns and processes. A balance needs to be found between appropriate speed and the needs of people who may need extra time in which to communicate.
- Take care to distinguish between personal feelings, values, prejudices and beliefs, and professional roles and responsibilities, and ensure you have good supervision to check you are so doing.
- If a mistake or misinterpretation has been made, or you are unable to keep an agreement, provide an explanation. Always acknowledge the distress experienced by adults and children and do all you can to keep it to a minimum.

Partnership pursuit: translating problems into effective solutions

There are a number of blocks to effective partnership that lie in structural and resource issues. There is a need to invest considerable time and resources; build capacities within service provider agencies; achieve changes in organisational cultures and professional attitudes to children and young people's participation; review the conventional professional styles of meetings and the use of inaccessible language and this includes timing of meetings in conventional working hours; the need to prepare children, young people and parents for participation; the need to resolve the professional resistance stemming from apprehensions about sharing power with children and young people, combined with a lack of experience in involving

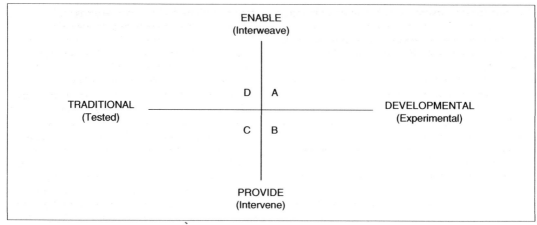

Figure 18.1   Developmental conceptualisations of partnership

them in decision-making processes. Kirby et al. (2003) offered us some useful strategies for changing cultures, a prerequisite for any meaningful change:

- *Unfreeze:* existing attitudes, procedures and styles of working
- *Catalyse:* change through the use of champions of participation, through developing a vision for children and young people's participation and through partnership working
- *Internalise:* change through communicating and developing a shared vision and understanding of participation
- *Institutionalise:* by mainstreaming practice.

Context of worker-client relationship

In pursuing any partnership a necessary prerequisite is for an anti-oppressive, anti-discriminatory, multi-cultural, multi-dimensional framework, which embraces state and individual responsibilities as well as structural inequalities. Lauerman (1990) has offered a grid for service delivery that can be used to embrace the balance between partnership and paternalism. The vertical axis locates activities along a continuum from a service, which is basically interventionist at one extreme to one where the response seeks to interweave with the arrangements already made by a service user at the other. The horizontal axis is intended to locate activities along a spectrum ranging from traditional responses to those which are developmental in nature.

In the framework shown in Figure 18.1, the developmental notion of partnership should ideally be delivered in quadrant 'A', as opposed to quadrant 'B', which advocates paternalism at odds with partnership. The emphasis is on interweaving and not intervention. Partnership may be achieved by starting in the quadrant where the recipients of the service find themselves, and by interweaving the responses rather than intervening in their lives. The dynamic of user/carer/provider is without doubt the driving force.

Drivers towards increased participation

A consumer movement which emphasises the engagement of users to give consumers more power in exercising choice and in influencing the nature and quality of the goods and services available to them.

- A broader policy move toward ensuring that the voices of service-users are heard in decision-making at all levels of the service delivery process, in order to make services more responsive and to enable a more collaborative approach to decision-making.
- The adoption and ratification of the United Nations' Convention on the Rights of the Child by the UK government in 1991 has extended the Rights agenda to include children.
- The Convention recognises children and young people's right to participate in all decisions that affect them, as individuals in their own right.

Rights to participation are, however, balanced by an acknowledgement that children and young people may be vulnerable and therefore have rights to protection and provision of services.

- The rights of children and young people are also confirmed in the Human Rights Act (1998). There is a growing understanding of the active role that children and young people can play in shaping their environments.
- An alternative approach to thinking about childhood has been advocated, which acknowledges children and young people's competencies, including those of very young children, and therefore their capacities to be involved in decision-making about their lives.

Children

We have everything to gain and nothing to lose by forging partnerships with children.

(Calder, 1995)

The Children Act 1989 sets a moral, legal and practical obligation to involve children in our work. This is by setting out a philosophy of empowerment via the extension of the duty to ascertain their wishes and feelings and to give consideration to them (in the light of age and understanding) before making any decision.

The more that children participate in decisions that affect their lives, the more they develop confidence, competencies and aspirations which have a positive effect on their health and development, relationships within their family and community. There is no standard model of participation that can be replicated everywhere. There are, however, some key principles to observe and indicators of participation are being developed to help us understand what combination of factors is most beneficial. Participation should be voluntary and not foisted on children, especially in situations where the child has experienced a traumatic event, such as harm. Children have the right to decide if they want to participate, to what degree and how. There needs to be a greater mutual understanding and sharing of power between adults and children. Attention to participation needs to be an ongoing rather than a one-off activity without a strategy for future sustainability.

There are a number of reasons for involving children: to uphold children's rights; to fulfil legal responsibilities; to improve services and decision-making; to enhance democratic processes; to promote children's protection; and to enhance children's skills and self-esteem.

Children and young people report mixed experiences in relation to being given information, allowed space to discuss anxieties and being encouraged to participate in meetings. Children's wishes and priorities may be different from those of adults and they need to be taken into account. It will be possible to work more closely with some children than others depending on the level of their development and the experiences which they have undergone. It should also include consideration as to the child's needs and abilities and each child's wish to be involved in the decision-making.

Additional factors to consider include the child's age and understanding, cognitive development, cultural and ethnic background, personality and personal preference.

Workers need to find the most appropriate balance between enabling children to be involved whilst not at the same time protecting them from exposure to stresses and conflicts inconsistent with their welfare. They will be capable of different levels of involvement and participation at different times. Age is a consideration: advice is against inclusion of children under 10 in formal processes because of the presence of strangers, language, formality and the influence of parents on what they can and cannot say etc.

How can we involve children?

Academic literature suggests there is still considerable uncertainty about how to involve children and young people in a way that is effective and brings about lasting change. Despite the expansion of participation activity there is still much left to learn – about making participation inclusive and meaningful to children and young people; about ensuring participation is simply not an end in itself but as a means to change; and about evaluating the impact of participation – on children, on professionals, on decisions and on services. The ladder concept is useful as a descriptive device to indicate different levels of participation permitted by adults, but it also has some limitations. Thomas (2002) has proposed a 'climbing wall' where the following key aspects are taken into account:

Table 18.1

Arnstein (1969)	Thoburn et al. (1995)	Hart (1997)	Sheir (2000)
Citizen control	Delegated power, involvement in service design	Child-initiated, shared decisions with adults	Children share power and responsibility for decision-making
Delegated power		Child-initiated and directed	
Partnership	Partnership participation	Adult-initiated, shared decisions with adults	Children involved in decision-making processes
Placation	Involvement consultation	Consulted and informed	Children's views are taken into account
Consultation	Keeping fully informed	Assigned but informed	Children are supported in expressing their views
		Tokenism	Children are listened to
Therapy	Placation	Decoration	
Manipulation	Manipulation	Manipulation	

Climbing wall (Thomas, 2000)

- The choice a child has over participation.
- The information they have about their situation and rights.
- The control they have over the decision-making process.
- The voice they have in the decision.
- The support they have in speaking up.
- The degree of autonomy they have in speaking up.
- The degree of autonomy they have to make decisions independently.

This suggests participation is highly complex in that a child feels able to speak up and is supported to do so but still has limited information and little control over decisions.

There are a number of key factors in individual decision-making with children and young people. McNeish and Newman (2002) identified:

- The importance of information for children and young people to make an informed decision.
- Time and explanation for children to properly understand the issues.
- Ongoing consultation: decision-making is a process not to be confined to a one-off meeting.
- The availability of support for the child or young person to talk through options in a non-judgemental environment.

- Appropriate settings for decision-making are accessible, comfortable, private and appropriate to the young person's culture. Many children find the usual style of meetings uncomfortable.
- Opportunities to prepare beforehand and talk about things afterwards are important.
- Even-handedness is needed in the handling of different points of view.
- Attention needs to be given to the child's priorities.
- Access to an advocate or supporter is helpful.
- Attention to any special needs of the child, including communication needs.
- Feedback and discussion on outcomes is important.
- It has been recognised that the children try to communicate through actions rather than words and that they cannot be relied upon to challenge explanations offered by the parents or parent figures, especially when the latter are present.
- However, the theme running throughout the enquiries in the late 1980s is that children do tell: children's telling begs the question of how to understand and to interpret what they say.

In order to create participatory processes for children and young people we need to:

- Clarify objectives – why participation? What goals are being set? What levels of participation are desired?
- Set realistic timescales – planning and preparation are needed.
- Meetings or not? – are these the most appropriate forum for children and young people? How can they be child-friendly?
- Invest resources – for participatory processes, training, support and skills development for staff and young people are needed.
- Support young people and staff – both will need information and skill development.
- Build in involvement – participation should not be an afterthought.

(McNeish and Newman, 2002)

Pathways to inclusion

Establishing a child's wishes and feelings is a first step towards enabling their participation. Building a rapport with a child cannot be hurried and there are no short cuts. Give them options about how they want to present information to meetings: attendance is only one option. As long as they feel special and know their views will be given independently many are happy. Where they want to attend they need to be prepared to maximise the chances of it becoming a positive experience for them. They need to have a clear understanding of the purpose of the meeting, how their views will be taken into account and the names and role of each person present. They are empowered by having information about how the meeting will be conducted e.g. content and agenda of the meeting, the layout of the room and where people will sit (even seeing the room).

There is no prescriptive way of securing children's participation although it is increasingly viewed as a requirement. We need to move toward meaningful participation and to avoid tokenism and misrepresentation. Representative participation, involving diverse communities of children and young people will remain challenging. Participation can require considerable local cultural change:

You are mistaken if you think we have to lower ourselves to communicate with children. On the contrary, we have to reach up to their feelings, stretch, stand on our tiptoes.
(Korczak, 1925)

Conclusions and implications for practice

Paternalistic practice is professionally safer, but more divisive and alienating for families. The culture of fear and blame for wrong decision-making remains, especially since the significant change in systems and structures across agencies – especially the advent of therapeutically grounded principles and concepts coupled with generic rather than specific assessment guidance has let individuals become responsible for self determining their own materials. Partnership is an essential building block for engagement with families and in encouraging and facilitating the necessary changes to ensure children are safeguarded. Fear remains about at what point partnership approaches become unsafe for children and they over-accommodate risk. This balancing act is key to engaging successfully with involuntary clients. For a further discussion of exactly how the reader is referred to Calder (2007).

References

Abramson, M. (1985) The Autonomy: Paternalism Dilemma in Social Work Practice. *International Journal of Law and the Family*, 3: 1, 21–39.

Arnstein, S. (1969) The Ladder of Citizen Participation. *Journal of the American Institute of Planners*, 35: 2, 216–24.

Boushel, M. and Lebacq, M. (1992) Towards Empowerment in Child Protection Work. *Child and Society*, 6: 1, 38–50.

Calder, M.C. (1991) Child Protection. *Child Abuse Review*, 5: 2, 269.

Calder, M.C. (1995) Child Protection: Balancing Paternalism and Partnership. *British Journal of Social Work*, 25: 6, 749–66.

Calder, M.C. (2003) The Assessment Framework: A Critique and Reformulation. In Calder, M.C. and Hackett, S. (Eds.) *Assessment in Childcare: Using and Developing Frameworks for Practice*. Lyme Regis: Russell House Publishing.

Calder, M.C. (Ed.) (2007) *The Carrot or the Stick? Towards Effective Practice with Involuntary Clients*. Lyme Regis: Russell House Publishing.

Calder, M.C. (2007b) A Framework for Working with Resistance, Motivation and Change. In Calder, M.C. (Ed.) *The Carrot or the Stick? Towards Effective Practice with Involuntary Clients*. Lyme Regis: Russell House Publishing.

Calder, M.C. (2007c) Child Protection in Changing Times: A Manager's Perspective. In Wilson, K. and James, A. (Eds.) *The Child Protection Handbook*. 3rd edn. London: Bailliere Tindall.

Collins, B.G. (1986) *Defining Social Work*. National Association of Social Work, USA.

DoH (1988). *Protecting Children: A Guide for Social Workers Undertaking a Comprehensive Assessment*. London: HMSO.

DoH (1991a) *Patterns and Outcomes in Child Placement: Messages from Current Research and their Implications*. London: HMSO.

DoH (1991b) *Working Together under the Children Act 1989: A Guide to Arrangements for Inter-agency Co-operation for the Protection of Children from Abuse*. London: HMSO.

DoH (1991c) *Child Abuse: A Study of Enquiry Reports 1980–1989*. London: HMSO.

DoH (1992) *Children Act Report 1992*. London: HMSO.

DoH (1995) *The Challenge of Partnership in Child Protection: Practice Guide*. London: HMSO.

DoH (1995b) *Child Protection: Messages from Research*. London: HMSO.

DoH (2000). *Framework for the Assessment of Children in Need and their Families*. London: HMSO.

Dworkin, R. (1971) 'Paternalism', in Wasserstom, R. (Ed.) *Morality and the Law*, Belmont, CA: Wadsworth.

Evans, C. (2004) Reflections on a Model of Empowered User Involvement. *Journal of Integrated Care* 12: 6, 22–27.

Fox-Harding, L. (1991) *Perspectives in Child Care Policy*. London: Longman.

Gert, B. and Culver, C.M. (1979) The Justification of Paternalism. *Ethics*, 89, 199–210.

Gordon, L. (1986) Family Violence, Feminism and Social Control. *Feminist Studies*, 12: 3, 452–78.

Hart, R. (1997) *Childrens Participation*. New York: UNICEF.

Hughes, B. (1992) Partnership in Local Government. *Community Care*, 2 July, 24–5.

Humphreys, S. (1987) Participation into Practice. *Social Policy and Administration*, 21: 1, 28–39.

Kirby, P. et al. (2003) *Building a Culture of Participation. Research Report*. London: DfES.

Korczak, J. (1925) *Als ik Weer Kleinben*. Uitgever: Bijlerald, Utrecht.

Lauerman, M. (1990) Changing our Responses. *Community Care*, 24 November.

Lord Chancellors Department (1992) *The Children Act Advisory Committee Annual Report 1991/92*. London: HMSO.

Lord Chancellors Department (1993) *The Children Act Advisory Committee Annual Report 1992/93*. London: HMSO.

Lord Chancellors Department (1995) *The Children Act Advisory Committee Annual Report 1994/95*. London: HMSO.

Marsh, P. and Fisher, M. (1992) Do We Measure Up? *Community Care*, 14.5.92, 18–19.

McNeish, D. and Newman, T. (2002) Involving Children and Young People in Decision-Making. In McNeish, D., Newman, T. and Roberts, H. (Eds.) *What Works for Children?* Buckingham: OAP.

Morrison, T. (1991) Change, Control and the Legal Framework. In Adcock, M. et al. (Eds.) *Significant Harm*. Croydon: Significant Publications.

Parton, N. and Martin, N. (1989) Public Enquiries, Legalism and Child Care in England. *International Journal of Law and Family*, 3: 6.

Pugh, G. and De'Ath, E. (1989) *Working towards Partnership in the Early Years*. London: NCB.

Rose, W. and Aldgate, J. (2000) *Framework for the Assessment of Children and Their Families*. London: DoH.

Ross, E.C. (1910) *Social Control*. London: Macmillan.

Rubin, S. (1972) Children as Victims of Institutionalisation. *Child Welfare*, 51, 1.

Sayer, J. and Heaton, K. (1991) A Discussion of some of the Implications of Integrating Community Work and Child Protection. *Applied Community Studies*, 1, 39–63.

Sheir, H. (2001) Pathways to Participation. *Children and Society*, 15, 107–17.

Stark, E. and Flitcraft, A.H. (1988) Women and Children at Risk: A Feminist Perspective on Child Abuse. *International Journal of Health Services*, 18: 1, 97–118.

Thoburn, J., Lewis, A. and Shemmings, D. (1995) *Paternalism or Partnership? Family Involvement in the Child Protection Process*. London: HMSO.

Thomas, N. (2000) *Children, Family and the State: Decision-making and Child Participation*. London: Macmillan.

Russell House Publishing Ltd

We publish a wide range of professional, reference and educational books including:

Safeguarding children and young people: A guide to integrated practice
By Steven Walker and Christina Thurston   ISBN 978-1-903855-90-4

Developing collaborative relationships in interagency child protection work
By Michael Murphy   ISBN 978-1-903855-48-5

Child exploitation and communication technologies
By Alisdair A. Gillespie   ISBN 978-1-905541-23-2

Children living with domestic violence: Towards a framework for assessment and intervention
Edited by Martin C. Calder   ISBN 978-1-903855-45-4

Secret lives: growing with substance - working with children and young people affected by familial substance misuse
Edited by Fiona Harbin and Michael Murphy   ISBN 978-1-903855-66-9

Preventing breakdown: A manual for childcare professionals working with high risk families
By Mark Hamer   ISBN 978-1-903855-61-4

The carrot or the stick? Towards effective practice with involuntary clients in safeguarding children work
Edited by Martin C. Calder   ISBN 978-1-905541-22-5

For more details, please visit our website: www.russellhouse.co.uk

Parents' anger management: The PAMP programme
By Gerry Heery   ISBN 978-1-905541-04-1

The child and family in context: Developing ecological practice in disadvantaged communities
By Owen Gill and Gordon Jack   ISBN 978-1-905541-15-7

Parental alienation: How to understand and address parental alienation resulting from acrimonious divorce or separation
By L. F. Lowenstein   ISBN 978-1-905541-10-2

Assessment in child care: Using and developing frameworks for practice
Edited by Martin C. Calder and Simon Hackett   ISBN 978-1-903855-14-0

Complete guide to sexual abuse assessments
By Martin C. Calder et al.   ISBN 978-1-898924-76-0

Juveniles and children who sexually abuse: Frameworks for assessment. Second Edition
By Martin C. Calder et al.   ISBN 978-1-898924-95-1

For more details, please visit our website: *www.russellhouse.co.uk*

Or we can send you our catalogue if you contact us at:

Russell House Publishing Ltd,
4 St George's House, Uplyme Road Business Park,
Lyme Regis DT7 3LS, England,
Tel: 01297 443948
Fax: 01297 442722
Email: help@russellhouse.co.uk